Employment Law

A. C. L. Davies

PEARSON

Harlow, England • London • New York • Boston • San Francisco • Toronto • Sydney
Auckland • Singapore • Hong Kong • Tokyo • Seoul • Taipei • New Delhi
Cape Town • São Paulo • Mexico City • Madrid • Amsterdam • Munich • Paris • Milan

Pearson Education Limited
Edinburgh Gate
Harlow CM20 2JE
United Kingdom
Tel: +44 (0)1279 623623
Web: www.pearson.com/uk

First published 2015 (print and electronic)

© Pearson Education Limited 2015 (print and electronic)

Contains public sector information licensed under the Open Government Licence (OGL) v3.0. http://www.nationalarchives.gov.uk/doc/open-government-licence/version/3/.

Contains Parliamentary information licensed under the Open Parliament Licence (OPL) v3.0. http://www.parliament.uk/site-information/copyright/open-parliament-licence/

The screenshots in this book are reprinted by permission of Microsoft Corporation.

Pearson Education is not responsible for the content of third-party internet sites.

ISBN: 978–1–4082–6360–0 (print)
      978–1–4082–6362–4 (PDF)
      978–1–292–08595–1 (eText)

British Library Cataloguing-in-Publication Data
A catalogue record for the print edition is available from the British Library

Library of Congress Cataloging-in-Publication Data
Davies, A. C. L. (Anne C. L.), author.
  Employment law / A.C.L. Davies. — First edition.
    pages cm
  ISBN 978-1-4082-6360-0
  1. Labor laws and legislation—Great Britain.   I. Title.

  KD3009.D377 2015
  344.4101—dc23

                                2015011548

ARP Impression 98

Cover image: © Corbis Images

Print edition typeset in 10/12 pt Sabon LT Pro by 71
Printed by Ashford Colour Press Ltd, Gosport

NOTE THAT ANY PAGE CROSS REFERENCES REFER TO THE PRINT EDITION

Brief contents

Contents

Acknowledgements

We are grateful to the following for permission to reproduce copyright material:

Text

Quote on page 3 from ILO Declaration of Philadelphia, Copyright © International Labour Organization 1944; Quote on page 53 from Article 8 of the ICCPR, © United Nations. Reprinted with the permission of the United Nations; Quotes on page 53, page 54 from ILO Forced Labour Convention 1930, Copyright © International Labour Organization 1930; Quote on page 54 from Article 26 ICCPR, © United Nations. Reprinted with the permission of the United Nations; Quote on page 56 from ILO Convention 143, Copyright © International Labour Organization 1978; Quote on page 74 from ILO Convention 29, Copyright © International Labour Organization 1930; Quote on page 185 from Article 2(1) ICCPR, © United Nations. Reprinted with the permission of the United Nations; Quote on page 208 from UN Convention on the Rights of Persons with Disabilities, © United Nations. Reprinted with the permission of the United Nations; Quotes on page 240, page 270 from International Covenant on Economic, Social and Cultural Rights, Article 7, © United Nations. Reprinted with the permission of the United Nations; Quotes on page 240, page 270 from International Covenant on Economic, Social and Cultural Rights, Article 7, © United Nations. Reprinted with the permission of the United Nations; Quote on page 288 from International Covenant on Economic, Social and Cultural Rights, Article 10, © United Nations. Reprinted with the permission of the United Nations; Quote on page 289 from Convention on the Elimination of All Forms of Discrimination Against Women, Article 5, © United Nations. Reprinted with the permission of the United Nations; Quote on page 394 from ILO Convention 87, Copyright © International Labour Organization 1948; Quote on page 403 from ILO Convention 87, Article 2, Copyright © International Labour Organization 1948; Quotes on page 421, page 432 from ILO Convention 98, Copyright © International Labour Organization 1949; Quote on page 432 from ILO Convention 154, Copyright © International Labour Organization 1981; Quotes on page 433, page 434 from ILO Convention 135, Copyright © International Labour Organization 1971; Quote on page 459 from Article 8(1) International Covenant on Economic, Social and Cultural Rights, © United Nations. Reprinted with the permission of the United Nations.

Crown Copyright material is reproduced with the permission of the Controller of HMSO and the Queen's Printer for Scotland. Contains public sector information licensed under the Open Government Licence v2.0. European Union publications reproduced with permission from the Publications Office of the European Union. © European Union, 1995–2015.

In some instances we have been unable to trace the owners of copyright material, and we would appreciate any information that would enable us to do so.

Preface

This book is intended to be an accessible, stimulating but not overwhelming companion to an undergraduate or postgraduate course in employment or labour law. I have assumed some basic knowledge of other core subjects, particularly contract law and EU law. Each chapter seeks to set the law in its practical and political context and to draw on the relevant academic literature. There are suggestions for further reading at the end of each chapter for students who want to delve deeper into particular aspects of a topic. In a subject now heavily dominated by EU law and statute law, I have tried to avoid the common lawyer's bias towards case-law by including extensive quotations from directives and legislation, though of course there is plenty of case-law analysis too.

Although some courses may no longer include so much material on collective labour law, I have included comprehensive chapters on this topic because of its central importance to the subject's history and philosophy. Given growing academic interest in the issue, I have included a chapter on the relationship between labour law and migration (from within and outside the EU) to facilitate the inclusion of this important emerging topic on the teaching syllabus. The book considers developments up to 4 November 2014.

I have benefited enormously from working in Oxford with an outstanding group of colleagues in labour law, who have no doubt influenced my thinking on many of the topics examined in this book both directly and indirectly: Alan Bogg, Hugh Collins, Cathryn Costello, Sandy Fredman, Mark Freedland and Jeremias Prassl. Successive generations of undergraduate and graduate students have also helped to shape my thinking about how best to explain the subject and have challenged my ideas: I am grateful to them all. Anjoli Maheswaran Foster provided excellent research assistance.

I am grateful to Bill Swadling for suggesting that I write this book, and to Cheryl Cheasley and her colleagues at Pearson for her patience and support during the writing process.

I would like to thank the people who do their best to keep me sane and who help without realising: Ed Bispham, Alan Bogg, Peter, Bea, Michael and Edward Groves, Tom Krebs, Llewelyn Morgan, Bill Swadling and Stefan Vogenauer.

I dedicate this book, like the others, to my parents, without whose support none of this would be possible.

Anne Davies
Oxford

List of acronyms

ACAS   Advisory, Conciliation and Arbitration Service
ARD   Acquired Rights Directive

BERR   Department for Business, Enterprise and Regulatory Reform
BJIR   British Journal of Industrial Relations

CA   Court of Appeal
CAC   Central Arbitration Committee
CBI   Confederation of British Industry
CEACR   Committee of Experts on the Application of Conventions and Recommendations
CEDAW   Convention on the Elimination of All Forms of Discrimination against Women
CEEP   European Centre for Employers and Enterprises Providing Public Services
CFA   Committee on Freedom of Association
CJEU   Court of Justice of the European Union
CMLR   Common Market Law Review
CPRD   Convention on the Rights of Persons with Disabilities
CRC   Convention on the Rights of the Child
CiRD   Citizens' Rights Directive
CRD   Collective Redundancies Directive

DCMS   Department for Culture, Media and Sport
DBIS   Department for Business, Innovation and Skills

EA   Employment Act
EASI   Employment Agency Standards Inspectorate
EAT   Employment Appeal Tribunal
ECR   European Court Reports
ECHR   European Convention on Human Rights
ECSR   European Committee on Social Rights
ECtHR   European Court of Human Rights

EHRC   Equality and Human Rights Commission
EHRLR   European Human Rights Law Review
EHRR   European Human Rights Reports
EJIL   European Journal of International Law
EqA 2010   Equality Act 2010
ERA 1996   Employment Rights Act 1996
ERelA   Employment Relations Act 1999
ESC   European Social Charter
ETO   economic, technical or organisational
ETUC   European Trade Union Confederation
EU   European Union
EWC   European Works Council
EWCA   England and Wales Court of Appeal
EWHC   England and Wales High Court

FTER   Fixed-term Employees (Prevention of Less Favourable Treatment) Regulations 2002

GEO   Government Equalities Office
GLA   Gangmasters Licensing Authority

HL   House of Lords
HMRC   Her Majesty's Revenue and Customs
HRA   Human Rights Act
HSE   Health and Safety Executive

IANA 2006   Immigration, Asylum and Nationality Act 2006
I&C   Directive on Informing and Consulting Employees
ICCPR   International Covenant on Civil and Political Rights
ICER   Information and Consultation of Employees Regulations
ICERD   International Convention on the Elimination of All Forms of Racial Discrimination
ICESCR   International Covenant on Economic, Social and Cultural Rights

ICLQ   International and Comparative Law Quarterly
ICO   Information Commissioner's Office
ICR   Industrial Cases Reports
ICRMW   International Convention on the Protection of the Rights of All Migrant Workers and Members of Their Families
IEEAR   Immigration (European Economic Area) Regulations 2006
IJCLLIR   International Journal of Comparative Labour Law and Industrial Relations
ILJ   Industrial Law Journal
ILO   International Labour Organization

JCHR   Joint Committee on Human Rights

KB   King's Bench

LBC   London Borough Council
LEL   Lower Earnings Limit
LPC   Low Pay Commission

MLR   Modern Law Review
MPLR   Maternity and Parental Leave etc Regulations

NDPB   Non-Departmental Public Body
NGO   Non-governmental organization
NMW   National Minimum Wage
NMWA   National Minimum Wage Act 1998

ONS   Office for National Statistics
OJ   Official Journal
OJLS   Oxford Journal of Legal Studies

PCP   provision, criterion or practice
PEA   pre-existing agreement
PrWD   Pregnant Workers Directive
PTWR   Part-time Workers (Prevention of Less Favourable Treatment) Regulations 2000

PWD   Posted Workers Directive
PWED   Posted Workers Enforcement Directive

QB   Queen's Bench

SDA   Sex Discrimination Act 1975
SE   Societas Europaea
SMP   Statutory Maternity Pay
SNB   Special Negotiating Body
SOSR   some other substantial reason
SPC   service provision change
SPL   shared parental leave
SSP   Statutory Sick Pay

TEU   Treaty on European Union
TFEU   Treaty on the Functioning of the European Union
TICER   Transnational Information and Consultation of Employees Regulations
TUC   Trades Union Congress
TULRCA 1992   Trade Union and Labour Relations (Consolidation) Act 1992
TUPE   Transfer of Undertakings (Protection of Employment) Regulations

UDHR   Universal Declaration of Human Rights
UKSC   United Kingdom Supreme Court
UN   United Nations
UNICE   Union of Industrial and Employers' Confederations of Europe

WERS   Workplace Employment Relations Survey
WLR   Weekly Law Reports
WTD   Working Time Directive
WTO   World Trade Organization
WTR   Working Time Regulations 1998

Table of cases

Table of statutes

Table of statutory instruments

Table of EU legislation

Table of international conventions and treaties

1 Introduction

Learning outcomes

This chapter will enable readers to:

- understand the scope of labour law as a subject
- explain and justify the existence of a special body of law to govern work in English law
- explain why employment law is extensively regulated at EU level
- understand the role of collective bargaining in the historical development and contemporary practice of labour law
- identify some current themes in labour law policy and scholarship

1.1 INTRODUCTION

The aim of this chapter is to introduce the subject of employment or labour law and to develop some ideas or themes that will be of relevance throughout the book. We will begin by considering the justifications for having a separate body of legal doctrine to cover employment issues (section 1.2) before considering why employment law is extensively regulated at EU level (section 1.3). In section 1.4, we will examine the special role of collective bargaining as a regulatory technique in labour law. Section 1.5 identifies and explores a selection of current themes and debates in labour law scholarship which will recur in later chapters.

Before we begin, it may be helpful to consider the terminology we are using. Is the subject called labour law or employment law? In the US, for example, the choice of label is significant. Employment law denotes the law relating to individual employees' terms and conditions of employment, whereas labour law denotes the law relating to trade unions and their relationships with employers. In English law, the choice is less significant – the labels are used more or less interchangeably – though the decision to call a course 'labour law' rather than 'employment law' often indicates a greater emphasis on trade union topics than one might expect to find in a course called 'employment law'. Employment law is probably the more modern-sounding label, so it is used for the title of this book, but we will use both terms in the text.

The subject-matter of labour or employment law is fairly obvious: it is the law governing situations in which one person works for another person. Working relationships come in many different guises, so drawing a precise boundary line around labour law is fraught with difficulty. We will consider the exact location of the boundary in Chapter 4. We can then divide the subject into collective ('labour' law) and individual ('employment' law) topics (always remembering that there are important links between them). Collective topics are those dealing with relationships between *groups* of working people (usually, but not always, trade unions) and their employers. We will cover relationships between trade unions and their members in Chapter 11, collective bargaining between trade unions and employers in Chapter 12, industrial action in Chapter 13 and consultation between employers and groups of workers (which may or may not involve trade unions) in Chapter 14. Individual employment law deals with the formation and termination of the employment relationship and with terms and conditions of employment. We will examine terms and conditions in Chapters 5 (dealing with contractual matters), 7 (pay) and 8 (working time). We will consider termination in two chapters: Chapter 9, dealing with job security in general terms, and Chapter 10, focusing on business reorganisations. Chapter 6 deals with equality law, which applies across the board to prohibit discrimination at the hiring stage, during employment and when the relationship is brought to an end. Finally, Chapter 3 examines another cross-cutting topic: the treatment of working people who migrate to or from the UK in search of work.

1.2 WHY DO WE HAVE LABOUR LAW?

The decision to have a special body of doctrine governing working relationships reflects a policy choice that the 'ordinary' law of contract is not suitable (on its own, at least) to regulate these relationships. In this section, we will consider some of the main justifications for having a system of labour law: inequality of bargaining power, dignity, rights and productivity. It is important to note that a comprehensive theory of labour law might need to draw on more than one of these justifications. There are close links between dignity and rights in particular.

The law of contract takes as its central case two commercial parties striking a deal in a competitive market. Each party can negotiate for the price and other terms and conditions he or she wants. The law's role is to give effect to the parties' bargain. Contracts in the employment sphere sometimes follow this pattern, but in the vast majority of cases, they do not. Put simply, the working person generally needs a job much more than the employer needs him or her. The employer can choose from a range of job applicants, whereas the working person has to compete to be offered a job. If he or she is unhappy with the terms and conditions offered by the employer, there is limited room to negotiate because the employer can always withdraw the offer and pick another candidate instead. Once a person is employed, he or she is unlikely to be able to bargain for better terms and conditions because, again, there is a queue of other people waiting to take the job. And in all of these situations, the working person needs the job in order to put food on the table and pay the bills, whereas the employer's business is unlikely to fail for want of one worker.

Of course, there are exceptions to this. In times of very low unemployment, employers may be faced with labour shortages and may have to be more responsive to the demands of working people in order to recruit them. This may occur across the labour market as a whole, or in particular sectors. For example, if there is a shortage of IT experts, those who are looking for work may be able to command higher salaries. And sometimes, it may be the case that a particular worker has special skills that the employer values particularly highly and may be willing to pay extra for: supremely talented footballers are one example of this, but it can occur in more 'ordinary' settings too, if a particular employee makes him- or herself indispensable to the firm.

Outside these exceptional cases, inequality of bargaining power can have serious consequences for working people. They may be faced with disadvantageous terms and conditions of employment (long hours, low pay and so on) offered on a 'take it or leave it' basis. Economic necessity may force them to accept employment on that basis. The inequality of bargaining power justification for labour law, then, is to provide some protections for workers against exploitation. For example, it might be used to justify a minimum wage (banning employers from paying extremely low wages) or to justify a regime of collective bargaining, in which working people are encouraged to group together in trade unions to bargain with employers (because there is strength in numbers).

As we shall see, labour law in England traditionally placed heavy reliance on the latter technique: on combating inequality of bargaining power through collective bargaining.[1] It is important to note that this is a procedural response to the problem. Rather than giving workers a particular set of entitlements, the law provides them with a process through which they can acquire entitlements for themselves. It is no coincidence that the decline in trade union membership and thus in collective bargaining has led labour lawyers to think about other ways of justifying their subject. Inequality of bargaining power tells us that there is a problem facing working people but is less helpful when we come to design particular substantive entitlements. Ideas about rights and dignity have grown in popularity as a result.

The dignity justification for labour law is summed up in the ILO's famous slogan 'labour is not a commodity'.[2] The idea here is that when a working person supplies his or her labour, it is impossible to do this without supplying him- or herself too. Workers, unlike other factors of production (machinery, raw materials and so on) are people, so it is important that their basic human dignity is respected in their terms and conditions of employment. This type of argument might be used to justify a variety of measures, ranging from legislation banning sexual harassment at work, because this creates a hostile working environment for its victims, to legislation requiring employees to be given a hearing before they are dismissed, because this gives them an opportunity to rebut any allegations of wrongdoing.

Dignity is often used as one of the underlying justifications for human rights. Respect for the rights of working people is another way of thinking about why we have a special regime of labour law.[3] Of course, we typically think about rights as a way of protecting individuals against encroachments from the state. However, people spend a large proportion of their lives at work, so it is readily arguable that the workplace is a key location in which to consider respect for rights. This might be done either by imposing an obligation directly on employers to respect workers' rights, or by requiring the state to ensure that employers respect people's human rights when they are at work. We will consider different types of human rights instruments later in this chapter, but for now it is sufficient to note that they contain many rights either indirectly or directly relevant to work, ranging from the right to manifest one's religious beliefs, to the right to limits on working hours.

---

[1] Otto Kahn-Freund, 'Legal Framework', in Allan Flanders and Hugh Clegg (eds), *The System of Industrial Relations in Great Britain: its History, Law and Institutions* (Basil Blackwell 1954).

[2] ILO, *Declaration of Philadelphia* (1944).

[3] For an overview, see Virginia Mantouvalou, 'Are Labour Rights Human Rights?' (2012) 3 European Labour Law Journal 151; Tonia Novitz and Colin Fenwick, 'The Application of Human Rights Discourse to Labour Relations: Translation of Theory into Practice', in Tonia Novitz and Colin Fenwick (eds), *Human Rights at Work: Perspectives on Law and Regulation* (Hart 2010).

A fourth and rather different kind of justification for having a special regime of labour law focuses on the benefits of labour law to employers.[4] It is easy to assume that labour law is about protecting working people at the *expense* of employers: the more rights working people have, the more we are adding to employers' costs. However, this may be an overly simplistic viewpoint. Working hours are a good example. It might be thought that limits on working hours are bad for employers because they reduce the amount of work they can demand from their workers. They may be forced to hire more people – and thus to incur greater costs – to get the work done. However, there is good evidence to suggest that productivity declines as hours of work increase. People who work very long hours are simply too exhausted to concentrate all of the time. On this view, it may be possible to get the same amount of work done in a shorter time. Moreover, the quality of the work may improve – because workers are able to concentrate – and there is less of a risk that they will fall ill and need to take time off work.

One obvious response to arguments of this type is to say that if labour law does benefit employers, surely they will take these measures of their own accord. No rational employer would force its workers to work hours that would put their health and productivity in jeopardy. However, there are a couple of reasons why that may not be the case. One is the fear that employers who offer 'good' terms and conditions may be undercut over the shorter term (before the health and productivity benefits have been realised) by employers who exploit their workers. The other is that employers may not always recognise the advantages of, say, limited working hours, so the law can play an educational role.

Which of these justifications one finds most persuasive is very much a matter of opinion. But what this section has sought to demonstrate is that simply relying on the ordinary law of contract to offer a framework for employment relationships is unlikely to be an attractive option. Labour law is required to redress the inequality of bargaining power between workers and employers, to ensure that workers' dignity is respected, to protect workers' rights while they are at work or to maximise workers' productivity.

1.3 WHY REGULATE EMPLOYMENT LAW AT EU LEVEL?

One of the key features of employment law as a subject is that it is heavily dominated by EU law: many statutory rights implement EU directives and some claims (for example, in the field of equal pay for men and women) may be brought in reliance on directly effective provisions of EU law. The courts must construe the relevant statutory rights to give effect to EU law, and often refer questions to the Court of Justice of the European Union (CJEU) for decision. We will examine the mechanics of EU law in greater detail in Chapter 2. We will now focus on why employment law is such a big topic within EU law.

When the EU first came into being, as the European Economic Community, the Member States were attempting to create a common market in which goods and services could move freely across national boundaries. They expected that most social issues would be dealt with by national governments and did not need to be regulated

---

[4] See Simon Deakin and Frank Wilkinson, 'Labour Law and Economic Theory: a Reappraisal', in Hugh Collins *et al.* (eds), *Legal Regulation of the Employment Relation* (Kluwer 2000); and *The Law of the Labour Market: Industrialization, Employment and Legal Evolution* (OUP 2005), especially chapter 5.

at EU level.[5] The one significant exception to this was equal pay for men and women, which was included in the original Treaty of Rome.[6] France already had equal pay laws, and the French government was concerned that French firms would be disadvantaged in the common market if their competitors in other Member States could pay women less than men for the same work. Over time, the EU's competence in employment law has been expanded so that nowadays, it can regulate virtually all employment law matters except pay, freedom of association and the right to strike through the enactment of directives. And, of course, the CJEU's case-law can touch on any topic relevant to the common market (now known as the 'internal' market) between the Member States.

But why regulate employment law at EU level? One answer commonly given is the fear of triggering a 'race to the bottom'.[7] This is the idea that Member States might reduce labour standards in order to give their national firms a competitive edge in the internal market. For example, if the UK does not require firms to consult the workforce on major business decisions, that might cut the cost of doing business in the UK, enabling UK firms to price their products more cheaply and encouraging other firms to move to the UK. The 'race to the bottom' is triggered when other countries react by making corresponding cuts in their labour standards, so that all countries eventually spiral towards the lowest levels of protection. Of course, the 'race to the bottom' is an empirical claim, and there is some debate in the literature as to whether it would happen in practice.[8] Although there is some evidence of, for example, firms investing in states with lower labour standards, there is less evidence of a wholesale race to the bottom taking place in any particular context. Not surprisingly, other factors enter into governments' decision-making: even if labour law reform would bring economic benefits, for example, political opposition might make it impossible in practice.

More profoundly, many commentators would question the starting assumption of the 'race to the bottom' argument: that firms will become more competitive if they operate in an environment with lower regulatory standards. As we saw above, one of the justifications for labour law is that it can *enhance* firms' performance by weeding out destructive practices (long working hours, low pay and so on) and by encouraging firms to compete on other measures, such as quality and productivity. Indeed, it might be argued that this is of particular importance in the EU context. Since the EU is relatively wealthy in global terms, it is not plausible to suggest that products and services from the EU can compete globally on price, given that other regions and countries with a much lower cost of living can easily undercut EU firms. Thus, although the 'race to the bottom' argument was prominent in early thinking about EU labour law (as the equal pay example demonstrates), nowadays the EU itself is more focused on becoming a market characterised by its quality and productivity. On this view, the role of labour law is not to prevent a 'race to the bottom' but rather to trigger a 'race to the top', in which states use labour law to ensure that workers are highly skilled, adaptable and productive.[9]

---

[5] See Jeff Kenner, *EU Employment Law* (Hart 2003) chapter 1, for the history.
[6] Treaty of Rome (1957), art 119.
[7] Bob Hepple, *Labour Laws and Global Trade* (Hart 2005) 13–14.
[8] See, for example, Eddy Lee, 'Globalisation and Employment: Is Anxiety Justified?' (1996) 135 International Labour Review 485.
[9] See, generally, Hepple, above n 7.

Another way of justifying EU employment law focuses less on economic issues and more on political problems. In recent years, there has been a growing tide of Euroscepticism, not just in the UK, but in other Member States too. The EU institutions have responded by seeking to give the EU a more 'human' face. Developments such as the concept of EU citizenship and the increasing role of human rights within EU law can be viewed in this light. Encouraging the development of labour law at the EU level can be seen as a way of demonstrating the benefits of EU membership to citizens, by giving them rights they can exercise at work. It can also be used to encourage a sense of EU identity, rather than rivalry between Member States, through measures such as the directive on European Works Councils, which requires pan-European firms to set up a pan-European consultation mechanism with their workforces.[10] Perhaps inevitably, the EU's economic objectives sometimes exist in tension with its social objectives, with the result that the social dimension of the EU is not promoted in a consistent way. For example, during the recent economic crisis, Member States in receipt of 'bailout' funding were encouraged to reduce certain labour standards.[11] Nonetheless, developing the EU's social dimension is a key part of its role in the field of labour law.

Finally, it is important to be aware that the creation of an internal market between the Member States can intrude into domestic social policy decisions.[12] For example, the CJEU has often been called upon to determine whether a particular Member State's rules on matters like food quality are a genuine effort to protect consumers or whether they are 'protectionist' in nature: a means of shielding national firms against competition from other Member States. This is sometimes termed 'negative integration': EU law may be relevant even where the EU has not legislated (or is not able to legislate) on a particular topic, because of the extensive reach of internal market rules. To some extent, this has occurred in labour law too, with CJEU decisions playing an important role in regulating industrial action where unions in one Member State are protesting against the employer's decision to close down and move to another Member State, or to bring in workers from another Member State in order to perform certain tasks.[13] Although there can be no EU legislation on the right to strike, the Court can rule on the topic where the employer's internal market rights are affected by unions' strike action.

1.4 THE ROLE OF COLLECTIVE BARGAINING

It might be assumed that a system of labour law would be made up of legislation and case-law. Parliament would pass statutes to protect workers for some of the reasons just identified, and the courts would interpret them. The courts might also develop employment-specific doctrines at common law to address the particular circumstances of contracts in the employment sphere. While it is certainly the case

---

[10] Directive 94/45/EC on the establishment of a European Works Council or a procedure in Community-scale undertakings and Community-scale groups of undertakings for the purposes of informing and consulting employees (Official Journal L 254, 30/09/1994). See Chapter 14.

[11] See Catherine Barnard, 'The Financial Crisis and the Euro Plus Pact: a Labour Lawyer's Perspective' (2012) 41 ILJ 98.

[12] What Syrpis terms the 'integrationist' rationale for EU labour law: Phil Syrpis, *EU Intervention in Domestic Labour Law* (OUP 2007) 12–50.

[13] See Chapter 13.

that statute and common law are key modes of regulation in labour law, it is difficult to understand the subject without appreciating a third mode of regulation particular to labour law, collective bargaining.

Collective bargaining denotes a process in which trade unions, representing workers, negotiate with employers (or groups of employers in employers' associations) about terms and conditions of employment.[14] The point of collective bargaining is that it provides a way of addressing the inequality of bargaining power between workers and employers discussed above. While the employer can ignore the demands of one worker, it is much harder to ignore the demands of a group of workers expressed through an organisation like a trade union. A key element of collective bargaining is the possibility that the union might call a strike. This involves workers refusing to work until the employer meets their demands. If a big enough proportion of the employer's workers take part in the strike, it will inflict damage on the employer's business, forcing the employer to make concessions to the workers. It gives the workers a weapon – albeit an extreme one – in the bargaining process.

The trade union movement emerged in the late nineteenth century and initially struggled to gain recognition from the capitalist establishment.[15] Trade unions were regarded as conspiracies, rendering trade union leaders liable to prosecution under the criminal law. When this was removed by legislation, the courts ruled that trade unions were unlawful in the civil law because they were in breach of the doctrine of restraint of trade (that they attempted to set a price for labour rather than allowing the free play of market forces). Parliament had to intervene to make the very existence of trade unions lawful. Another area of difficulty was industrial action. Again, the criminal law was used to deal with workers who refused to work and with anyone who induced them to join a strike. Later, strikes were addressed through the civil law. A worker who refused to work was in breach of his or her contract, and the courts developed the economic torts, such as inducing breach of contract, to make strike organisers (and trade unions themselves) liable for losses caused to the employer. Parliament intervened with a system of 'immunities' for trade unions and strike organisers against these liabilities. Much the same system continues today.[16]

Over the course of the twentieth century, at least up until the late 1970s, the trade union movement gained in strength. A majority of the working population were members of trade unions, and even more people had their terms and conditions of employment governed by collectively bargained terms and conditions (since the outcome of collective bargaining was not confined to members). Commenting on the picture from the 1950s onwards, the leading scholar Otto Kahn-Freund used the term 'collective laissez-faire' to describe the uniquely English approach to labour law.[17] Instead of setting minimum wages and maximum working hours in legislation, the English system left these and other matters to be governed by collective bargaining between trade unions and employers, with legislative intervention only in those economic sectors where collective bargaining had failed to take hold. This contrasted with other European systems in which much greater emphasis was placed on regulation through statute.

[14] See Chapter 12 for more detail.
[15] For history, see Douglas Brodie, *A History of British Labour Law 1867–1945* (Hart 2003); Paul Davies and Mark Freedland, *Labour Legislation and Public Policy* (Clarendon Press 1993).
[16] See Chapter 13.
[17] Kahn-Freund, above n 1.

Although collective bargaining is an alternative to legal regulation, it is important to be aware that it can only function in a favourable legal environment.[18] We saw above that trade unions could not develop until Parliament made them lawful and provided a statutory regime to support their activities, including strikes. Kahn-Freund described this as a system of 'negative law'. Instead of providing workers with statutory rights, the law provided a framework within which they could form and join trade unions to protect their own interests.

Kahn-Freund also took the view that collective bargaining was a good thing, for a number of reasons. One of its major advantages is its flexibility. It allows workers and employers to negotiate together to achieve the rules that suit them, rather than having to deal with 'one size fits all' statutory regulation. In modern terminology, collective bargaining can be seen as a form of 'reflexive law'.[19] This is the idea that the smart way to regulate is to encourage people in a particular setting to figure things out for themselves, rather than trying to tell them how to behave, because the latter approach may not fit with their needs and thus may not work at all. Collective bargaining also makes workers' basic terms and conditions of employment somewhat less dependent on the whims of politicians, since they are set through collective bargaining rather than through statute, though this depends on there being a legislative environment favourable to collective bargaining. But there are some disadvantages too. One problem is that, even in its heyday, collective bargaining did not cover everyone in the workforce, so some people were left without protection. Moreover, collective bargaining favours the majority view, so if (for example) the majority of workers in a particular workplace wanted to work longer hours to earn more money, and a small group of workers preferred shorter, more family-friendly hours, the preferences of the minority might not be accommodated.

In the 1970s, there was increasing recognition of the need to provide some universal protections to workers even if they were not covered by collective bargaining. These included rights to be treated equally regardless of race or sex, and the right not to be unfairly dismissed. This legislation was sometimes presented as a 'floor of rights' on which collective bargaining could build, but over time, legislative protection has become very extensive leaving less and less scope for collective bargaining.[20]

Trade union membership has also declined quite considerably from the 1980s until the present day. Scholars debate the exact reasons for this but there are a few obvious candidates.[21] First, the legislative environment became hostile to trade unions with the introduction of restrictions on industrial action during the 1980s in particular. Second, large manufacturing industries such as coal and steel went into terminal decline. These were the traditional strongholds of the trade union movement. Newer service industries proved to be more difficult to unionise. Third, and perhaps most controversially, the growth of protective legislation may have reduced people's incentives to join unions and take part in their activities. If the only way to achieve protection against dismissal is through joining a union, people are much more likely to join than if there is a statutory right not to be unfairly dismissed.

---

[18] For discussion, see Alan Bogg, *The Democratic Aspects of Trade Union Recognition* (Hart 2009) chapter 1.

[19] Ralf Rogowski, *Reflexive Labour Law in the World Society* (Edward Elgar 2013) chapter 2.

[20] Lord Wedderburn, *The Worker and the Law* (3rd edn, Sweet & Maxwell 1986) 6.

[21] For analysis, see Alex Bryson and Rafael Gomez, 'Why Have Workers Stopped Joining Unions? The Rise in Never-Membership in Britain' (2005) 43 BJIR 67; Stephen Machin, 'Factors of Convergence and Divergence in Union Membership' (2004) 42 BJIR 423.

Despite the decline in trade union membership, collective bargaining remains the method of setting key terms and conditions of employment, such as pay and hours, for about one-third of the workforce.[22] It remains strong in the public sector in particular. Moreover, trade unions play an important role in campaigning for workers' rights on the political stage, particularly through their umbrella organisation, the Trades Union Congress (TUC). Indeed, at the EU level, negotiations between trade union organisations and employers' associations can be used to reach agreements which are given legislative effect as directives. Although reliance on collective bargaining is no longer the defining feature of labour law, it remains a highly important component of the subject.

1.5 THEMES

In this section, we will identify some of the most important current themes in labour law. The aim here is to provide a framework for thinking about the policy debates that will recur later in the book. The four themes to be considered are demutualisation, individualism, human rights and enforcement.

1.5.1 Demutualisation

Demutualisation is a term coined by Freedland and Kountouris to refer to the transfer of risk from employers to working people.[23] In this section, we will examine the implications of this development and how governments have reacted to it.

One of the traditional hallmarks of an employment relationship is that the employer is the party bearing the risk in the relationship.[24] A person who is an employee can expect to get paid each week or month whether there is a lot of work or very little work to do. The employer absorbs fluctuations in demand: it protects employees in a downturn (at least, until it becomes necessary to make them redundant) but does not share profits with them when there is a surge. The employer is the loss-bearing and profit-making entrepreneur; the employee just takes his or her wage. The advantage for the employer is that the employee can be relied upon: he or she is always available for work every day. Anyone who does not want this kind of employment relationship can, of course, choose the alternative and become an entrepreneur him- or herself.

The phenomenon of 'demutualisation' challenges this simple picture. Employers have begun to transfer *economic* risks of various kinds onto the workforce. We will see examples of this throughout the book.[25] One very common one involves the employer simply refusing to provide any guaranteed level of work or pay to the individual. Instead, the employer might simply call the individual in to work when his or her services are required. These arrangements have various informal labels in the labour market, like 'zero hours', casual or 'as required' working. Another is the use of fixed-term contracts: instead of making a long-term commitment to employ a

---

[22] Department for Business, Innovation and Skills, *Trade Union Membership 2013* (2014).
[23] Mark Freedland and Nicola Kountouris, *The Legal Construction of Personal Work Relations* (OUP 2011) 433–446.
[24] See Chapter 4.
[25] See, especially, Chapter 4.

particular individual, the employer simply hires him or her for a particular project or a particular period of time while the firm is busy. Yet another is the use of agency workers: in this situation, the employer contracts with an agency for the provision of labour and 'outsources' the task of finding suitable workers to the agency. Again, the agency workers may be employed on a series of short-term, unpredictable arrangements with no long-term security. The key feature of all of these arrangements is that the employer is no longer absorbing risk. If there is a downturn in demand, the employer transfers that risk to the casual worker by not calling him or her into work, to the fixed-term worker by allowing the contract to terminate, or to the agency worker by telling the agency not to send so many people. These arrangements cut the employer's costs very considerably – it only pays for the work it needs – but it leaves individuals in a precarious position with no guaranteed level of income.

Demutualisation raises two important questions, both of which have the same answer. First, although these working arrangements are cheaper for employers, they are less reliable than having always-available employees, so how do employers manage this uncertainty? Second, they are clearly disadvantageous for individuals, so why does anyone accept a job on this basis? The answer lies in the inequality of bargaining power rationale we considered above: most people need a job and the money it brings in, so they may be prepared to accept poor terms and conditions if that is the only way to find work. And if individuals are desperate for work, the employer can generally rely on them to turn up for work in practice even if they are not legally obliged to do so. Thus, particularly in times of high unemployment, demutualisation is a successful strategy for employers because it cuts their costs without generating as much uncertainty as one might expect.

Of course, it would probably be irrational for an employer to 'demutualise' its entire workforce. It makes more sense to have a 'core' of permanent employees and a 'periphery' of casual workers. This is often referred to as the phenomenon of the 'two-tier' workforce. The demutualisation phenomenon is not universal: lots of people, particularly skilled or managerial employees, still have 'employee' jobs. Demutualisation is more common among low-skilled workers. As commentators have pointed out, this means that demutualisation has a disproportionate impact on people who are already vulnerable because they are low paid.[26] There is also a significant overlap with people who experience discrimination in the labour market for other reasons, for example, because of race or gender.

A further consequence of demutualisation is the transfer of *legal* risk onto the workforce.[27] If the paradigm case of an employee is someone who bears minimal risk in the relationship, there is a strong chance that the courts will find that a person who does take risks is not an employee. This is what has tended to happen with casual work arrangements of the kind we have been considering. The employer's refusal to guarantee any hours of work is taken as a sign that the person cannot be an employee. As a result, he or she has few, or possibly no, statutory employment rights. So, for example, if the employment relationship comes to an end, it will not normally be possible to challenge the fairness of the termination of that relationship through an action for unfair dismissal. This creates a 'double whammy' for individuals: the

---

[26] Sandra Fredman, 'Labour Law in Flux: the Changing Composition of the Workforce' (1997) 26 ILJ 337; 'Women at Work: the Broken Promise of Flexicurity' (2004) 33 ILJ 299.
[27] See Chapter 4.

employer offers a work arrangement that is economically risky, so that the individual has no guaranteed income, and at the same time the courts may treat that arrangement as if it is not a legally regulated employment relationship, so that the individual also loses his or her access to statutory protections. Over time, some unscrupulous employers have exploited this aspect of demutualisation by drafting contracts which make it look as if the individual is a risk-taking entrepreneur (regardless of the reality of the situation) so that he or she is potentially denied the law's protection.

So far, we have focused on demutualisation as an employer-led phenomenon. What about the government's position? On one view, demutualisation is (in part at least) a strategy for avoiding the legal regulation of employment relationships, so one would expect governments to respond by trying to combat the problem, as they might do with any other attempt to 'get around' a particular body of law. However, while we now have some legal regulation of fixed-term and agency employment, governments have not simply sought to outlaw these practices, or the use of casual work. Of course, a government's political position is highly relevant here and we can discern two main strands of thinking.

First, some governments have thought it desirable to 'deregulate' the labour market.[28] This policy became very popular in the 1980s and early 1990s, and remains influential today. It focuses on the costs for employers associated with legal regulation and it seeks to cut them by reducing the level of regulation. 'Reducing burdens on business' is a key slogan for the advocates of deregulation. A government with a deregulatory agenda is unlikely to try to prevent employers from pursuing a similar strategy. The current coalition government is concerned to tackle the worst cases of exploitation (for example, in relation to zero-hours working) but does not regard demutualisation more generally as a problem.[29] Its deregulatory agenda is significantly constrained by EU law, to which we will now turn.

Second, at EU level, there has been a particular emphasis on a policy known as 'flexicurity'.[30] This policy advocates greater flexibility in the Member States' labour markets, with an emphasis on workers moving from job to job in accordance with demand, rather than sticking with the same job for the long term, and on workers participating in the labour market to a greater or lesser degree over their lifetimes (for example, by taking part-time or casual work while studying or in the run-up to retirement). This policy chimed particularly well with the Labour governments in office from 1997–2010.[31] It led to the enactment and implementation of a number of EU directives tackling particular forms of 'non-standard' working, such as part-time and fixed-term work.[32] These directives represent a compromise. In accordance with the flexibility agenda of flexicurity, they did not discourage 'non-standard' working. But they also sought to offer some protection to workers with these types of contract by ensuring that they would not suffer discrimination (for example, a

---

[28] Davies and Freedland, above n 15, chapter 10.

[29] See the Employment Law Review: https://www.gov.uk/government/policies/making-the-labour-market-more-flexible-efficient-and-fair/supporting-pages/reviewing-employment-law (last visited 4 November 2014); and for discussion see Bob Hepple, 'Back to the Future: Employment Law under the Coalition Government' (2013) 42 ILJ 203.

[30] Commission, *Towards Common Principles of Flexicurity: More and Better Jobs through Flexibility and Security* (COM (2007) 359 final, 2007).

[31] See Department of Trade and Industry, *Fairness at Work* (Cm 3968, 1998).

[32] See Chapter 4.

lower hourly rate of pay). Whilst this does not eliminate the 'two-tier' labour market, it does help to reduce the disparity between the different tiers.

It is important to emphasise that the advocates of deregulation and flexicurity, albeit from different political perspectives, present their policy choices as beneficial to workers. The advocates of deregulation argue that removing burdens on business will reduce costs for employers and make it cheaper to hire people. This will generate more jobs. More people will be able to find work and unemployment will be reduced. The advocates of flexicurity make similar arguments about job creation – employers may be more willing to employ people on a non-standard basis – and they also argue that people who might not otherwise be in work at all might be encouraged to enter the labour market if they can work flexibly. Again, this increases labour market participation and reduces unemployment. These are powerful claims. Those who advocate more rights for workers find themselves confronted with the argument that they are advancing the interests of one group – people already in work – at the expense of an even more disadvantaged group, the unemployed.[33]

But it is important to approach the claim that labour law might inhibit job creation with some caution. Taken to extremes, it could be argued that we should simply abandon labour law altogether in pursuit of the maximum number of jobs. However, while most people would prefer employment to unemployment, that does not necessarily mean a job under any conditions. There are good reasons, such as arguments from dignity and rights perspectives, for protecting workers against exploitation. Moreover, the argument that labour law always imposes costs on firms can be challenged, as we saw above, by the alternative view that labour law has beneficial effects on firms' productivity. Flexicurity policies pose a more subtle challenge to traditional labour law, since they are not wholly deregulatory in effect. They threaten the traditional model of the risk-bearing employer, because they encourage alternative forms of work, but at the same time, they do not allow those alternative forms of work to develop without some regulation. As we shall see in later chapters, the key question with flexicurity policies is how they are designed.

Inevitably, labour law involves striking some kind of balance between the rights or interests of workers and the needs of employers. During the years of collective laissez-faire, this balance was left to employers and unions to negotiate for themselves. Over the past 40 or 50 years, the balance has been struck, increasingly, by the government and Parliament through legislation and through the implementation of EU law. In more recent years, the balance between workers and employers seems to have been shifting so that there is less emphasis on protecting workers against risk and more emphasis on flexibility for employers. This change has been brought about by a variety of factors including employers' own endeavours, arguments about 'burdens on business' and arguments about flexicurity. Demutualisation is thus an important theme in today's labour law.

1.5.2 Individualism

A second theme in contemporary labour law is what we will term 'individualism'. It involves an emphasis on the autonomy of the individual worker to make choices about his or her working life. In some senses, it is a positive spin on demutualisation,

---

[33] See, generally, ACL Davies, 'Identifying "Exploitative Compromises": The Role of Labour Law in Resolving Disputes Between Workers' (2012) Current Legal Problems 269.

in the sense that if the individual is not an employee, he or she can be portrayed as a risk-taking entrepreneur, the master of his or her own destiny. We will discuss some manifestations of individualism in this section and some criticisms of the phenomenon.

We saw above that one of the central themes of labour law is counteracting the employer's superior bargaining power in order to protect vulnerable individuals who might otherwise be forced to work under exploitative terms and conditions. Legislation tends to do this by imposing a 'one size fits all' set of rules. The individualism trend seeks to reintroduce elements of choice into the legislative framework. For example, the Working Time Regulations impose a maximum limit of 48 hours on the working week, but they allow a worker to sign an 'opt out' in which he or she agrees with the employer that the limit will not apply.[34] This is said to give working people a choice about how many hours they work and, of course, how much money they earn. More generally, the demutualisation trend is often presented in terms of creating 'flexible' working arrangements in which individuals have a choice about how to organise their working lives and, in particular, balance work with other activities. For example, casual work is sometimes presented as a means of combining work and family time by giving workers choice over when and for how long they work. And one of the most extreme recent examples is the creation of 'employee shareholder' status, in which an employee can agree to give up significant employment rights (including the right not to be unfairly dismissed) in exchange for shares in the employer company.[35] This gives employees a choice of money or employment rights.

Obviously, it is quite difficult to be against choice: we all value being able to live our lives autonomously, the way we want to. Indeed, one of the fundamental rights in labour law is the right not to be subjected to forced labour, a right which seeks to ensure that work itself is a free choice.[36] The big problem with choice in the labour law context, though, is making sure that workers' choices are genuine. For example, does the worker really want to work more than 48 hours per week, or has he or she been told by the employer that the job offer will be withdrawn if he or she does not sign the opt-out? Does the casual worker really get a choice of when to work, or is it the case that, if he or she refuses an assignment, the employer will take him or her off the list of prospective workers? And does the employee shareholder really understand the exchange he or she is making, both in terms of the value of the shares and the nature of the rights foregone? Of course, there are two possible policy responses to these concerns. One option is to attach some safeguards to the choice in the hope of ensuring that it is genuine. The opt-out from the 48-hour working week must at least be in writing, and for employee shareholder status, it is necessary for the employee to have received independent legal advice before taking up the status. But where the safeguards are not enough to ensure that the individual's choice is genuine, it may be better to take the choice away altogether than to risk its abuse.

Individual choice poses particular challenges to collective bargaining. Collective bargaining seeks to counteract the employer's superior bargaining power through the collective strength of the workforce. Inevitably, when people bargain for something

---

[34] See Chapter 8.
[35] See Chapter 4.
[36] See Chapter 3.

as a group, the preferences of the majority are likely to prevail. So, if most of the workers want an early start to the working day, this will be the group's negotiating position, and workers who would prefer a later start will lose out. In theory at least, the distribution of workers between majority and minority opinions will vary over time, so losing out on some occasions is balanced by achieving one's goals on others. Each member is expected to show solidarity with their colleagues – even on issues they do not care about – because they will get solidarity in return on the issues that matter to them, and everyone benefits in the long term from being able to bargain with the employer. But individualistic policies prioritise the worker's choice on every occasion. For example, it is obviously the case that individuals have a free choice about joining a union, but it is also the case that they have choices about taking part in union activities.[37] Unions act unlawfully if they discipline a member who refuses to take part in a strike.

Again, it is difficult to be against some element of choice here. Although it used to be the case that some workplaces were run as 'closed shops', in which everyone had to be a union member, this would nowadays be regarded by many people as an infringement of their autonomy and it is arguably a breach of the freedom to associate (or not to associate) protected by Article 11 ECHR. But allowing members to choose their level of participation is more problematic. On the one hand, strikes involve serious personal cost for the individual, who will not be paid during the strike and may risk losing his or her job under some circumstances. On the other hand, strikes do not work very well if union leaders cannot rely on their members to obey the call to take action. Their impact on the employer is much reduced if some people continue to work. Thus, there is both an ideological and a practical conflict between the notion of solidarity underpinning trade unionism and the modern trend towards individualism.

1.5.3 Human rights

Having considered two largely negative trends for labour law, we will now turn to one that is potentially more positive: human rights. We will examine the evolving relationship between human rights and labour law, and consider some of the advantages and disadvantages of viewing labour law through a human rights lens.

Human rights instruments are generally divided into two main types: civil and political (like the European Convention on Human Rights (ECHR) or the International Covenant on Civil and Political Rights (ICCPR)) or economic, social and cultural (like the European Social Charter (ESC) or the International Covenant on Economic, Social and Cultural Rights (ICESCR)). Rights relevant to the workplace feature in both, though they tend to be more fully elaborated in the latter type of instrument. For example, in the ECHR, we find freedom of association in Article 11, including a right to form and join trade unions, but in the ESC, we find rights to fair and just conditions of work and to engage in collective bargaining.[38] Although many human rights advocates would deny that there is any hierarchy between the two, it is often the case that civil and political rights instruments are seen to carry more weight. For example, alleged breaches of the ECHR are adjudicated upon by a court, the European

---

[37] See Chapter 11.
[38] ESC 1961, arts 2 and 6.

Court of Human Rights (ECtHR), whereas the ESC is monitored by the European Committee on Social Rights, which produces reports, and it is much more common to find civil and political rights in national constitutions. Against this, critics point out that civil and political rights, such as the right to vote, are useless to people whose basic needs (food, shelter and so on) are not being met.

More generally, it is clear that there is a hierarchy in terms of the weight to be given to certain rights in moral and legal discourse. For example, it is clear that the right not to be subjected to slavery or forced labour carries greater weight than the right to holidays with pay. One way in which this is reflected in practice is in the distinction between unqualified rights (the infringement of which can never be justified) and qualified rights (which may be restricted if to do so is a proportionate means of achieving a legitimate aim). Another potentially important distinction is between rights afforded to 'everyone' and rights afforded only to people who meet certain qualifying conditions, such as rights for workers. Although it is tempting to regard all rights as 'fundamental human rights', not least because of the rhetorical force of this label, it is important not to dilute this idea. We could think instead in terms of 'labour rights', all of which carry weight in moral and legal discourse, but only some of which are properly regarded as 'fundamental', as rights that 'trump' competing considerations.[39]

Although the UK has been a long-term signatory to the main international human rights instruments, there was no real human rights tradition in English law until the enactment of the Human Rights Act 1998 (HRA). Successive governments took the view that it was for them to protect human rights by passing appropriate legislation (for example, to permit the existence and functioning of trade unions) rather than enshrining human rights themselves in English law. Any adverse rulings or reports from international bodies were for the government to address through law reform, where appropriate. During this period, labour lawyers made extensive use of human rights arguments but largely as external benchmarks against which to judge the law. For example, restrictions on industrial action in English law could be criticised as infringements of the right to strike protected by the ESC, even though this was not an argument that could usefully be made in court. As we shall see, this has changed with the enactment of the HRA. Some rights – those protected by the ECHR – can now be invoked in court.[40] Thus, while rights arguments continue to be used as external benchmarks, some of them can also be used to mount internal challenges.

There are two further dimensions to the growing relevance of human rights in English law. First, the ECtHR has become increasingly interested in referring to other human rights instruments when interpreting the Convention rights, in a phenomenon known as the 'integrated' approach to interpretation.[41] Thus, Article 11 ECHR, on freedom of association, is increasingly developed in the light of related rights in the ESC and other international instruments. This means that the scope of the right has

---

[39] For a persuasive account of the difficulties of treating labour rights as fundamental human rights, see Hugh Collins, 'Theories of Rights as Justifications for Labour Law', in Guy Davidov and Brian Langille (eds), *The Idea of Labour Law* (OUP 2011). For a counter-argument, see Mantouvalou, above n 3.

[40] See Chapter 2.

[41] See Virginia Mantouvalou, 'Labour Rights in the European Convention on Human Rights: An Intellectual Justification for an Integrated Approach to Interpretation' (2013) 13 Human Rights Law Review 529.

broadened somewhat, and that instruments with no apparent *direct* influence in the English courts might be given effect there. Second, EU law is becoming more focused on human rights. The EU Charter of Fundamental Rights, which is a comprehensive and modern statement of rights, was given legal effect by the Treaty of Lisbon. The EU is also preparing to accede to the ECHR. Although there is a debate about the exact impact of human rights in EU law, it is increasingly common for the CJEU to refer to rights in its case-law. For example, the right to paid annual leave is treated by the Court as a social right for workers and this has led it to interpret the right quite generously in a series of important cases.[42]

An interesting feature of the human rights theme within labour law is that it has not been embraced quite so strongly by scholars as might be the case in other fields of law.[43] There are three main reasons for this. First, labour lawyers have a long-standing suspicion of the courts as potentially hostile to the interests of working people. This reflects the historical development of trade union law in particular, in which it often appeared that the courts were trying to stifle the trade union movement. Placing a greater emphasis on the human rights dimension of labour law will, inevitably, mean enforcing workers' rights in court. This may result in ungenerous interpretations of the relevant rights. Second, human rights are generally regarded as individualistic in nature – they are, for the most part, the rights of individual human beings – so they are sometimes perceived as being in conflict with labour law's more collective tradition. This fear has not been realised in practice, largely because the ECtHR has adopted some quite 'collectivist' interpretations of the rights of trade unions themselves, so that human rights law has proved useful as a way of advancing trade union interests as well as those of individuals.[44] Third, as McCrudden has argued, human rights are strongly linked with dignity, which might prove to be quite a limited basis for labour law.[45] While – as we saw above – labour law can be justified in dignitarian terms, it is not clear that every infringement of a worker's interests is so severe as to amount to a breach of his or her dignity. The human rights perspective may make labour law better at dealing with serious exploitation (where *fundamental* human rights are engaged) but less effective at dealing with more everyday problems.

Throughout the book, we will draw on international human rights instruments where relevant as benchmarks, and we will identify areas in which human rights arguments might be deployed in the English courts under the HRA or through EU law. The discussion will attempt to offer a measured assessment of the pros and cons of the human rights approach to labour law. Importantly, we shall see that – since English law is, in many areas, broadly compatible with, or at least not in serious violation of, most labour rights – it can be quite difficult to make rights arguments work in court. For example, while a ban on trade unions would clearly breach Article 11 ECHR, it is harder to challenge limits on trade unions' activities. This requires a much more detailed analysis of what the right protects and what impact the limits have, and courts may not feel confident about developing this analysis on the basis of a broadly framed freedom of association guarantee.

---

[42] See Chapter 8.

[43] For example, KD Ewing, 'The Human Rights Act and Labour Law' (1998) 27 ILJ 275.

[44] For example, *ASLEF* v *UK* (2007) 45 EHRR 34, and see Chapter 11.

[45] Christopher McCrudden, 'Labour Law as Human Rights Law: A Critique of the Use of "Dignity" in Freedland and Countouris', in Alan Bogg, Cathryn Costello, ACL Davies and Jeremias Prassl (eds), *The Autonomy of Labour Law* (Hart 2015).

1.5.4 Enforcement

Our fourth and final theme is enforcement. In the heyday of collective laissez-faire, many workers' entitlements were laid down in collective agreements rather than in legislation. This meant that the mechanism used to negotiate them – collective bargaining backed by threats of industrial action – was also used to enforce them. An employer risked triggering a strike if it failed to observe the terms and conditions laid down in a collective agreement. As labour legislation has come to play a more prominent role, it is important to think about whether and how working people might enforce their statutory rights. Labour law 'in the books' is not much use if employers do not observe it.

Of course, the starting-point when thinking about enforcement is to remember that most employers are broadly law-abiding and will comply voluntarily with the law. However, enforcement is important to vindicate the rights of those whose employers do not respect the law, and to bolster the good intentions of the law-abiding majority by making it clear that if they do breach the law, litigation or other enforcement action may ensue.

In English law, most enforcement takes the form of individual litigation before specialist employment tribunals.[46] The tribunals are meant to be more accessible and user-friendly than courts, so legal aid is not available in this forum. Recently, the government has increased the fees payable by litigants before tribunals so that it is now prohibitively expensive for many people to bring a claim. The statistics suggest that the number of cases has dropped by as much as 70% since the introduction of fees.[47]

More generally, litigation is usually only a viable option when the employment relationship has come to an end. Although there are protections against detrimental treatment for asserting most statutory employment rights, most people do not want to bring proceedings against an employer for whom they are still working. This means that some rights depend heavily on the employer's willingness to respect them. For example, the right to take reasonable time off to deal with a family emergency needs to be exercised while the emergency is occurring. Litigation months after the event to claim a small amount of compensation (whilst incurring the employer's wrath) is not likely to be an attractive option in most cases.

Of course, there are alternatives to individual litigation.[48] Some rights – such as the National Minimum Wage – can be enforced by public bodies. The Equality and Human Rights Commission can support litigants whose cases raise issues of general public importance. And trade unions (where they are present) often play an important role in helping people to assert their rights at work.

The key point to remember from this discussion is that whenever a particular employment right is being discussed, it is worth considering how it could be enforced against a recalcitrant employer. This gives a good insight into the practical effectiveness of the right in question.

---

[46] See Chapter 2.

[47] In April–June 2014, there were 70% fewer single claims than in the same period in 2013, fees having been introduced in July 2013: Ministry of Justice, *Tribunals Statistics Quarterly April to June 2014* (2014) 7–9.

[48] See Chapter 2.

POINTS TO TAKE AWAY

- A system of labour law can be justified as a means of protecting workers against exploitation due to their inequality of bargaining power as against the employer, upholding workers' dignity, ensuring that workers' rights are respected, promoting workers' productivity or some combination of these arguments.

- A lot of employment law is developed at EU level. The EU's role in labour law can be justified as a means of preventing a 'race to the bottom' between Member States, encouraging a 'race to the top' or putting a 'human face' on the EU's activities.

- A key feature of English labour law is the use of collective bargaining between trade unions and employers as a regulatory technique.

- Four major themes in contemporary labour law will recur throughout this book: demutualisation, individualism, human rights and the practicalities of enforcement.

Further reading

It is useful to have some historical background before you begin studying labour law. For detailed accounts, see **Douglas Brodie, *A History of British Labour Law 1867–1945*** (Hart 2003); **Paul Davies and Mark Freedland, *Labour Legislation and Public Policy*** (Clarendon Press 1993). For the history of EU labour law, see **Jeff Kenner, *EU Employment Law* (Hart 2003)**.

The history of labour law is, of course, closely connected with the history of the trade union movement and the idea of collective laissez-faire, on which see **Otto Kahn-Freund, 'Legal Framework', in Allan Flanders and Hugh Clegg (eds), *The System of Industrial Relations in Great Britain: its History, Law and Institutions* (Basil Blackwell 1954)**. On the role of trade unions today, see **KD Ewing, 'The Function of Trade Unions' (2005) 34 ILJ 1**.

As this chapter has demonstrated, the idea of labour rights as human rights is both a possible justification for labour law and an important contemporary theme in the subject. Three very useful readings on this are: **Hugh Collins, 'Theories of Rights as Justifications for Labour Law', in Guy Davidov and Brian Langille (eds), *The Idea of Labour Law* (OUP 2011); Virginia Mantouvalou, 'Are Labour Rights Human Rights?' (2012) 3 European Labour Law Journal 151; Tonia Novitz and Colin Fenwick, 'The Application of Human Rights Discourse to Labour Relations: Translation of Theory into Practice', in Tonia Novitz and Colin Fenwick (eds), *Human Rights at Work: Perspectives on Law and Regulation* (Hart 2010)**.

On the economic justifications for labour law, see **Simon Deakin and Frank Wilkinson, 'Labour Law and Economic Theory: a Reappraisal', in Hugh Collins *et al.* (eds), *Legal Regulation of the Employment Relation* (Kluwer 2000); and *The Law of the Labour Market: Industrialization, Employment and Legal Evolution* (OUP 2005)**, especially chapter 5.

On the justifications for the EU's role in labour law, see **Phil Syrpis, *EU Intervention in Domestic Labour Law* (OUP 2007)**. For a short introduction to EU labour law, see **ACL Davies, *EU Labour Law* (Elgar 2012)**.

2 Sources of law

Learning outcomes

This chapter will enable readers to:

- understand the sources of employment law and norms relevant to employment law, including international human rights law, ILO standards, the European Convention on Human Rights, the European Social Charter, EU law, domestic statute and common law, and 'workplace law' (contracts, works handbooks and so on)
- understand the mechanisms for resolving employment disputes and enforcing employment law: Employment Tribunals, courts and public bodies

2.1 INTRODUCTION

In this chapter, we will consider the sources of employment law in the UK. This is important for three main reasons. First, it is useful to know the status of different sources. As we saw in the last chapter, employment lawyers often think about their subject in terms of human rights, so they draw on a variety of international human rights instruments in their arguments. It is important to know which of these instruments is binding on the UK, because – as we shall see – some are more influential than others. Second, it is important to know what we might call the 'hierarchy of norms' in employment law: what happens when two different sources conflict. Everyone knows that statute law trumps case-law, but it is also important to understand the relationship between EU law and national law, and between the contract of employment and statute, for example. Third, it is useful to understand on a more practical level how people experience employment law on a day-to-day basis: through works handbooks and instructions from the boss.

We will examine the sources from the 'top' down – starting with international instruments and moving down to the workplace level. This makes it easier to explain the hierarchy of norms though, as we shall see, the international instruments are in some respects less important and influential than EU or domestic sources of law. But from a practical perspective it is the wrong way round: for most people, what matters is what the workplace handbook says or what the boss says. It is worth remembering that while we, as lawyers, are interested in the law, for most people it does not form a big part of their daily life.

2.2 INTERNATIONAL LAW

We will begin by considering some aspects of 'international labour law', focusing on international human rights instruments and on the work of the International Labour Organization (ILO).

2.2.1 International human rights instruments

The international human rights regime is a large and complex body of law with three key instruments at its heart: the United Nations (UN) Universal Declaration of Human Rights (UDHR),[1] the International Covenant on Civil and Political Rights (ICCPR),[2] and the International Covenant on Economic, Social and Cultural Rights (ICESCR).[3] These three instruments are sometimes referred to as the 'international bill of rights'. The UDHR was adopted by the UN General Assembly in 1948. The ICCPR and ICESCR are international treaties dating from 1966. The UK ratified both treaties in 1976, which means that the UK government is bound in international law to uphold the rights they contain.

The ICCPR and ICESCR contain a number of rights of relevance to employment law. The ICCPR includes a right to freedom of association (including the right to form and join trade unions)[4] and several rights dealing with equal treatment.[5] The ICESCR, as a statement of economic and social rights, is more detailed, and includes a right to work,[6] a right to 'just and favourable' conditions of work[7] and a right to freedom of association with explicit reference to the right to strike.[8] Both treaties have reporting mechanisms, so states are expected to produce regular reports on how they have complied with their obligations.[9] These are received and commented upon by committees of experts.[10] The committees also produce interpretations of the various rights contained in the respective treaties.[11] Both treaties have an Optional Protocol that provides for victims of rights violations to bring complaints, but the UK has not ratified this in either case. This limits the impact of the treaties because it may be harder for the government to ignore a finding in an individual complaint than it is to ignore the committees' pronouncements on its reports.

In addition to the ICCPR and ICESCR, there are another seven international treaties on human rights that are regarded by the UN as the 'core' of international human rights law. These include three treaties in the field of equality: International Convention on the Elimination of All Forms of Racial Discrimination (ICERD),[12] Convention on the Elimination of All Forms of Discrimination against Women (CEDAW),[13] and the Convention on the Rights of Persons with Disabilities (CPRD).[14] These treaties set international standards for states' efforts to tackle discrimination and have obvious relevance to employment law, and the UK has ratified all three. The Convention on the Rights of the Child (CRC) contains a provision dealing with child

---

[1] Universal Declaration of Human Rights (adopted 10 December 1948, UNGA Res 217 A(III)).
[2] International Covenant on Civil and Political Rights (adopted 16 December 1966, entered into force 23 March 1976) 999 UNTS 171.
[3] International Covenant on Economic, Social and Cultural Rights (adopted 16 December 1966, entered into force 3 January 1976) 993 UNTS 3.
[4] ICCPR, art 22.
[5] See, for example, ibid art 26.
[6] ICESCR, art 6. For obvious reasons this does not mean that everyone who wants to work has to be given a job.
[7] ibid art 7. This includes more detailed rights about pay, working time and health and safety.
[8] ibid art 8.
[9] ICCPR, art 40(1) and ICESCR, art 16(1).
[10] ICCPR, art 40(4) and ICESCR, art 16(2).
[11] Each committee of experts publishes its interpretations in the form of 'general comments'.
[12] Adopted 21 December 1965, entered into force 4 January 1969, 660 UNTS 195.
[13] Adopted 18 December 1979, entered into force 3 September 1981, 1249 UNTS 13.
[14] Adopted 13 December 2006, UN Doc. A/61/611 (2006).

labour, in Article 32, and again has been ratified by the UK.[15] However, the UK has not ratified the International Convention on the Protection of the Rights of All Migrant Workers and Members of Their Families (ICRMW), which is the only one of the UN core human rights treaties with a predominant focus on employment.[16] We will return to this topic in Chapter 3.

Employment lawyers often draw on the international human rights instruments when analysing English law, as we saw in the last chapter. They are a well-recognised benchmark against which to judge legislation and case-law. When conducting this form of analysis, it is also important to consider the comments of the relevant expert committee: it is all too easy to assume that we can each interpret the rights for ourselves as we see fit, when in fact there is a body of 'jurisprudence' about what they mean. Of course, international human rights instruments are binding on the UK government in international law, so the government should comply with their requirements. However, governments differ in their attitudes towards human rights and some take little notice of international criticism for failing to comply. Even so, it may be a mistake to ignore human rights: as we shall see below, the various courts dealing with human rights increasingly refer to one another's judgments so a finding in one setting may have implications in another setting that the government is less prepared, or less able, to ignore.

2.2.2 The International Labour Organization (ILO)

The International Labour Organization (ILO) is the UN specialised agency dealing with labour issues. In fact, it is older than the UN itself, having been established in 1919 as part of the League of Nations arrangements after the First World War. The ILO is a key source of internationally recognised labour standards. The ILO provides forums for adjudication and technical support for its member states. Despite this, its impact on employment law in the UK has been relatively limited.

One of the special features of the ILO is its tripartite structure.[17] This means that each member state is represented not just by members of its government, but also by employer and trade union representatives. In practice, therefore, the ILO's governing body has a trade union 'block' and an employer 'block' – often with opposing views – with government representatives siding with one or the other depending on their political persuasion. Some people have criticised the ILO for its strong trade union heritage, arguing that in some countries unions may not be representative of all working people. In recent years, the ILO has sought to involve other NGOs (non-governmental organisations) in its work, for example by consulting them, as a means of addressing this concern.[18] An important consequence of the ILO's tripartite structure is the emphasis it places on freedom of association. The ILO has long assumed that all signatory states support freedom of association simply by virtue of being members.[19]

---

[15] Concluded 20 November 1989, entered into force 2 September 1990, 1577 UNTS 3.

[16] Concluded 18 December 1990, entered into force 1 July 2003, UN Doc. A/45/49 (1990). For further discussion see Einat Albin and Virginia Mantouvalou, 'The ILO Convention on Domestic Workers: From the Shadows to the Light' (2012) 41 ILJ 67.

[17] ILO Constitution, arts 3 and 7. See T Novitz and P Syrpis, 'Assessing Legitimate Structures for the Making of Transnational Labour Law: The Durability of Corporatism' (2007) 36 ILJ 367.

[18] http://www.ilo.org/pardev/civil-society/lang--en/index.htm#Statutory_0 (last visited 4 November 2014).

[19] This is based on the Preamble to the ILO Constitution.

One of the ILO's main activities is the agreement of conventions.[20] An ILO convention is an international treaty on a particular topic in employment law – working hours or maternity leave, for example – which states can choose to ratify. Once a state has ratified an ILO convention, it is bound in international law to implement its provisions in its own law. The ILO also produces recommendations (often to accompany conventions) which offer non-binding guidance. Although the ILO has enacted some 189 conventions since its creation, many have been shelved or replaced as they have become out of date, so in practice there are between 70 and 80 conventions currently open for ratification.[21]

States are required to produce regular reports on their efforts to comply with ratified conventions.[22] These are scrutinised by the ILO. Of greater significance are the various procedures for examining instances of non-compliance by states. The most important of these in practice provides for organisations of workers or employers to make 'representations' to the ILO about a member state in breach of a convention.[23] The Governing Body sets up a tripartite committee to investigate, which publishes the representation and the state's response. A similar process exists whereby employer organisations or unions can bring complaints about non-compliance with freedom of association before a special body, the Committee on Freedom of Association (CFA).[24] Because of the importance attached to freedom of association by the ILO, these complaints can be brought even where the state in question has not ratified the conventions on freedom of association. These various procedures serve two main functions. First, they seek to 'shame' states into complying with ILO norms by identifying and publicising their failures. Second, they help to develop a useful body of jurisprudence on the interpretation and application of the conventions.

In the 1990s, the ILO was subject to sustained criticism from some commentators for its ineffectiveness. It was argued that the ILO had a lot of conventions but not so many ratifications, and thus not much practical impact on labour standards around the world.[25] The ILO seemed to compare unfavourably with new and highly effective international organisations in the arena of international trade, such as the World Trade Organization (WTO). The ILO responded with the Declaration of Fundamental Rights and Principles at Work of 1998. This identified four fundamental rights in the field of labour: freedom of association, freedom from forced labour, freedom from child labour and freedom from discrimination. These were regarded as applicable in all signatory states regardless of which conventions they had ratified, and were accompanied by various reporting mechanisms.[26] The ILO also mounted a (successful) campaign to encourage states to ratify the eight conventions that underpin the four

---

[20] ILO Constitution, art 19. For discussion, see Bob Hepple, *Labour Laws and Global Trade* (Hart 2005), chapter 2; A Wisskirchen, 'The Standard-Setting and Monitoring Activity of the ILO: Legal Questions and Practical Experience' (2005) International Labour Review 253.

[21] These are available in the ILO's NORMLEX database, available at www.ilo.org (last visited 2 October 2014).

[22] ILO Constitution, art 22. There is also an obligation to report periodically on unratified conventions in Article 19.

[23] ibid arts 24 and 25. A full list is available here: http://www.ilo.org/dyn/normlex/en/f?p=NORMLEXPU B:50010:0::NO::P50010_ARTICLE_NO:24 (last visited 2 October 2014).

[24] This is a committee of the Governing Body established in 1951.

[25] P Alston, '"Core Labour Standards" and the Transformation of the International Labour Rights Regime' (2004) 15 EJIL 457; B Langille, 'Core Labour Rights – The True Story (Reply to Alston)' (2005) 16 EJIL 409.

[26] Declaration of Fundamental Rights and Principles at Work of 1998, Annex (Follow-up).

rights in the Declaration.[27] The UK has ratified all eight. The ILO further encourages states to ratify four 'governance' conventions which relate to the way in which employment law and policy are developed and enforced at the national level.[28] The UK has ratified three of these.

While the Declaration can be seen, in many respects, as a success, it reinvigorated the ILO around a very narrow set of fundamental rights. In 2008, the ILO issued another Declaration, this time on Social Justice for a Fair Globalisation.[29] This was intended as a response to the phenomenon of globalisation, which can make governments feel powerless in the face of powerful multinational enterprises in pursuit of cheap labour. This identifies four key objectives for the ILO and its members: promoting employment, promoting social protection (including job security and social security), promoting social dialogue and tripartism, and respecting fundamental rights at work. This continues the emphasis on fundamental rights but places rights in the broader context of employment policy and procedures for giving workers a voice.

Although the UK government was a key force in the creation of the ILO back in 1919, its more recent record of compliance is patchy. The law on freedom of association, collective bargaining and industrial action has been a particular problem area, as we shall see in later chapters. One example is the TUC's complaint about s. 13 Trade Union Reform and Employment Rights Act 1993 which enabled employers to offer incentives (such as pay rises) to workers if they agreed to give up collective bargaining. The ILO CFA issued a final report in 1994 stating that the legislation was in breach of Convention No. 98.[30] The government ignored this report and no action was taken until the European Court of Human Rights (ECtHR) ruled that the UK was in breach of Article 11 in *Wilson* v *UK* in 2002.[31] Again, however, this does not mean that the ILO's only role is as a benchmark for commentary on the law. The widespread recognition afforded to ILO conventions as authoritative statements of international labour standards means that they are often cited in other forums, such as the ECtHR, the Court of Justice of the European Union (CJEU) and the domestic courts. This opens up the possibility that they might have an indirect influence on the development of the law.

2.3 EUROPEAN HUMAN RIGHTS LAW

We will now turn to the European human rights regime. This consists of two main treaties, the European Convention on Human Rights (ECHR) and the European Social Charter (ESC). Both instruments exist under the auspices of the Council of Europe. It is essential to distinguish the Council of Europe, an organisation with 47 member states set up to promote human rights, democracy and the rule of law, from

---

[27] They are: Freedom of Association and Protection of the Right to Organise Convention, 1948 (No. 87); Right to Organise and Collective Bargaining Convention, 1949 (No. 98); Forced Labour Convention, 1930 (No. 29); Abolition of Forced Labour Convention, 1957 (No. 105); Minimum Age Convention, 1973 (No. 138); Worst Forms of Child Labour Convention, 1999 (No. 182); Equal Remuneration Convention, 1951 (No. 100); Discrimination (Employment and Occupation) Convention, 1958 (No. 111).

[28] Labour Inspection Convention 1947 (No. 81); Employment Policy Convention 1964 (No. 122); Labour Inspection (Agriculture) Convention 1969 (No. 129); Tripartite Consultation (International Labour Standards) Convention 1976 (No. 144).

[29] F Maupain, 'New Foundation or New Façade? The ILO and the 2008 Declaration on Social Justice for a Fair Globalization' (2009) EJIL 823.

[30] CFA, Definitive Report – Report No 294, Case No 1730 (United Kingdom) (1994).

[31] *Wilson and Others* v *United Kingdom* (2002) 35 EHRR 20.

the European Union, an organisation with 28 Member States pursuing a range of economic and social objectives through deep legal and economic integration. This does not mean to say that there are no connections between the two: all the EU Member States are also members of the Council of Europe, and there are plans afoot for the EU as an organisation to ratify the ECHR.[32] Nevertheless, it is important to be clear about the differences between the two organisations.

2.3.1 The ECHR

The ECHR is an international treaty setting out (predominantly) civil and political rights.[33] It was opened for signature in 1950 and entered into force in 1953. The ECHR is often regarded as a reaction against the Second World War and the associated atrocities: as a way of trying to prevent such things from happening in Europe again.

The ECHR contains a number of rights of relevance to employment law. The most obvious is Article 11, which protects freedom of association, including the right to form and join trade unions. Other rights also play a role, including the right to respect for private and family life (Article 8), freedom of religion (Article 9) and freedom of expression (Article 10). Although signatory states are obliged to afford equal treatment to their citizens in respect of the Convention rights under Article 14, there is no free-standing equal treatment provision in the Convention. One of the optional protocols to the Convention, Protocol No. 12, rectifies this omission, but the UK has not ratified it.

The ECHR is interpreted and applied by the European Court of Human Rights (ECtHR). This is located in Strasbourg and is sometimes referred to as 'the Strasbourg court'. The ECtHR consists of 47 judges, one from each signatory state. Any legal or natural person who considers that they are a victim of a violation of one of the Convention rights by a signatory state may make a complaint to the Court.[34] Once a complaint has been found to be admissible, the Court normally hears the case in a Chamber consisting of seven judges. Once a case has been decided by a Chamber, either the victim or the respondent state may seek to get the case re-examined by the Grand Chamber consisting of 17 judges. A panel of judges decides whether such a re-examination should take place. If a violation is found, the Court rules accordingly and may award compensation, known as 'just satisfaction', to the victim if he or she has suffered damage.[35] The signatory state is also bound by the decision in international law and is expected to make the necessary changes to its law and practice to prevent further violations. Of course, states may also choose to make changes when the outcome of a case involving another state suggests that their law may not be in compliance with Convention requirements.

One of the difficulties faced by the Court is its burgeoning case-load. Its jurisdiction – over 47 states and 800 million people – is vast. This means that it can take a long time for a case to reach a hearing. The Court has taken various steps to improve its processing times. Under Protocol No. 14, it is now possible for a single judge (instead of a committee of three judges as previously required) to declare a case inadmissible.

---

[32] TEU, art 6(2).
[33] Convention for the Protection of Human Rights and Fundamental Freedoms (ECHR).
[34] ibid art 34.
[35] ibid art 41.

This is important because it is thought that around 90% of complaints lodged at the Court are inadmissible. The Court has also adopted a priority policy, which allows it to pick the most significant cases to be heard more quickly, and a 'pilot case' procedure, which enables it to hear one test case where there are many cases on a similar issue, so that it can then dispose of the others without a full hearing.[36] Nevertheless, as noted in the conclusions of the Brighton Conference on reform of the Court, these measures may not be sufficient to solve all of the problems in this area.[37]

In later chapters, we will examine many of the Court's key employment law decisions in some detail. For now, it is worth saying something about the Court's approach to the interpretation of Convention rights. First, the Court treats the Convention as a 'living instrument'. This means that its interpretation of particular rights may develop over time in response to new technologies, changing attitudes and so on. For example, the Article 14 right to equal treatment does not mention sexual orientation as one of the prohibited grounds of discrimination, but (aided by the reference in Article 14 to 'other status') the Court has been at the forefront of developing protection for people who encounter discrimination for this reason.[38] Second, the Court has increasingly adopted what Mantouvalou has labelled the 'integrated' approach to interpretation.[39] This means that it draws on the work of other human rights bodies when deciding what the Convention rights mean. This had an important impact in the *Demir v Turkey* case, in which the Court departed from previous decisions and held that the freedom of association right in Article 11 also included some protection for the right to engage in collective bargaining and to enter into collective agreements.[40] In reaching this conclusion, the Court drew on a number of other sources, including the relevant ILO conventions.

The 'integrated approach' is controversial. On one hand, since human rights are thought of as 'universal', it makes sense for different human rights courts and bodies to work together and to develop similar interpretations of those rights. On the other hand, states are not generally bound in international law unless they have ratified a particular instrument, so one of the risks of the 'integrated approach' is that states may be obliged to accept interpretations from a source they have not ratified – an ILO convention, for example – imposed on them from a source they have ratified, such as the ECHR. Moreover, it is important to remember that while the 'integrated approach' has helped the ECtHR to broaden its interpretation of Article 11, this might not necessarily be the case on every occasion. The strategy could equally well operate to ensure that a very narrow interpretation of a right spread from one system to another.

The ECHR deserves particular attention because, of all the human rights instruments we have been considering in this chapter, it has the greatest impact in the domestic law of the UK. This is because, under the Human Rights Act 1998 (HRA), judges can take the Convention rights into account in reaching their decisions under certain circumstances. We will examine this below in our discussion of sources within the UK. For now, it is worth noting that this increases the pressure on the UK

---

[36] Rules 41 and 61 respectively, ECtHR Rules of Court.

[37] ECtHR, High Level Conference on the Future of the European Court of Human Rights, 'Brighton Declaration' (April 2012).

[38] See, for example, *SL v Austria* (2003) 37 EHRR 39.

[39] See Virginia Mantouvalou, 'Work and Private Life: *Sidabras and Dziautas v Lithuania*' (2005) 30 European Law Review 573.

[40] *Demir v Turkey* (2009) 48 EHRR 54 [153].

government to make changes to domestic law when it is found to be in breach of Convention rights, because of the possibility that further cases on the same issue might be brought at the national level under the HRA. While there are some high-profile cases in which the UK government has resisted pressure from the ECtHR,[41] it is generally the case that some effort is made to address the Court's decisions. There is usually room for interpretation about the exact nature of the changes to be made (as we shall see in later chapters), and the government's strategy on this in employment law has been criticised by some commentators.[42]

2.3.2 The ESC

We saw above that the international human rights regime divides rights into civil and political rights (under the ICCPR) and economic and social rights (under the ICESCR). A similar divide exists in the Council of Europe, in which the ECHR has a lesser-known 'sister' instrument, the European Social Charter, governing economic and social rights. There are two versions of the Charter: the original version agreed in 1961, which the UK has ratified, and the revised version of 1996, which the UK has not ratified. It is also important to note that states are not expected to accept all the Charter's provisions. They must accept six of the nine provisions designated as 'core', and may then choose among the remainder.[43]

The ESC 1961 contains a number of provisions relevant to employment law. These include the right to work (Article 1), the right to just conditions of work (Article 2), the right to healthy and safe working conditions (Article 3), the right to fair remuneration (Article 4), the right to organise (Article 5) and the right to bargain collectively (Article 6). The ESC 1996 includes these rights but adds a number of others, such as the right to information and consultation at work (Article 21), the right to protection in cases of termination of employment (Article 24) and a right to equal treatment for workers with family responsibilities (Article 27). For monitoring purposes, the various rights are grouped into four themes, two of which are relevant to employment law: group 1 on employment, training and equal opportunities, and group 3 on labour rights. Thus, work-related rights are central to the ESC regime.

Like many of the other instruments we have been considering, the ESC has a regular reporting mechanism as its main monitoring tool. States are required to report on one of the four thematic groups of rights every year, so that each group is examined once every four years.[44] The reports are considered by an independent committee of experts, the European Committee of Social Rights, which publishes 'conclusions' on states' compliance with the rights.[45] There is also a collective complaints procedure, which enables a variety of civil society organisations to submit complaints to the Committee for 'decision'.[46] These organisations include regional worker or employer associations, such as Businesseurope and the European Trade Union Confederation (ETUC), and national trade unions or employer associations in the state that is the

---

[41] See, for example, *Hirst v United Kingdom (No. 2)* (2006) 42 EHRR 41.

[42] See Chapters 11 and 12.

[43] ESC 1961, art 20; ESC 1996, Part III, art A.

[44] Decision of the Governmental Committee of the European Social Charter – New system for the presentation of reports on the application of the European Social Charter CM(2006)53.

[45] ESC 1961, art 24; ESC 1996, Part IV, art C.

[46] Additional Protocol to the European Social Charter Providing for a System of Collective Complaints (1995).

subject of the complaint. The collective complaints procedure is optional and so far only a limited number of states – not including the UK – have accepted it.

The impact of the ESC in the UK is relatively limited. The Committee's conclusions attract very little public attention and are easily ignored.[47] However, like the international human rights instruments considered above, the ESC remains a useful benchmark against which to evaluate the law, and may have practical effect through the ECHR. Although the ECtHR was initially reluctant to stray into the territory of social rights, regarding that as the province of the ESC, its adoption of the 'integrated approach' to interpretation has led it to rely on ESC materials, for example, on collective labour rights when interpreting Article 11 of the Convention.[48] The case-law of the ECtHR is far more likely to have an impact in the UK, either through legislative changes in response to adverse rulings, or via the UK courts' decisions under the HRA.

2.4 EU LAW

The most important 'external' influence on employment law in the UK is EU law, for two reasons. First, the EU has the power to regulate many different aspects of national employment law. And second, EU law is much more effective within national law than the human rights systems we have been considering, thanks to the doctrines of supremacy and direct effect, among others.[49] The aim of this section is to introduce some of the main features of EU law of relevance to the employment law field, in preparation for more detailed explanations later in the book.[50] The discussion will assume some basic knowledge of EU law. We will examine four topics here: the EU's competence in employment law matters, the process for enacting directives in the employment law field, the role of human rights in the EU, and the role of the Court of Justice in interpreting and developing EU employment law.

2.4.1 Competence

It is a basic principle of EU law that the EU only has the competences given to it in the Treaty. This means that we must look to the Treaty to see what the EU can do in the field of employment law.

A seemingly obvious starting-point is Title IX TFEU, which is entitled 'Employment'. However, this set of provisions allows the EU to work with the Member States to co-ordinate their policies on employment and related matters like training.[51] Its focus is on job creation and maintaining high levels of employment. The EU sets targets on employment levels for the Member States and their progress against these targets is assessed through an annual process known as the 'open method of co-ordination'.[52] While this is of interest to employment lawyers, it will not be our main focus here.

---

[47] KD Ewing, 'Social Rights and Human Rights: Britain and the Social Charter – the Conservative Legacy' (2000) 2 EHRLR 91.

[48] See, for example, *ASLEF* v *UK* (2007) 45 EHRR 34.

[49] See, for example, Case 6/64 *Costa* v *ENEL* [1964] ECR 585; Case 26/62 *Van Gend en Loos* [1963] ECR 1.

[50] For more detail on EU employment law, see ACL Davies, *EU Labour Law* (Elgar 2012); Catherine Barnard, *EU Employment Law* (4th edn, OUP 2012).

[51] For a detailed discussion, see Diamond Ashiagbor, *The European Employment Strategy: Labour Market Regulation and New Governance* (OUP 2005).

[52] TFEU, art 156.

The provisions on employment law are found in Title X TFEU, entitled 'Social Policy', and in various other parts of the Treaty. Article 153(1) provides the EU with competence (shared with the Member States) to adopt directives regarding:

(a) improvement in particular of the working environment to protect workers' health and safety;
(b) working conditions;
(c) social security and social protection of workers;
(d) protection of workers where their employment contract is terminated;
(e) the information and consultation of workers;
(f) representation and collective defence of the interests of workers and employers, including co-determination, subject to paragraph 5;
(g) conditions of employment for third-country nationals legally residing in Union territory;
(h) the integration of persons excluded from the labour market, without prejudice to Article 166;
(i) equality between men and women with regard to labour market opportunities and treatment at work . . .

Article 157 creates a right to equal pay between men and women. This has been held by the Court of Justice to be directly effective, so it can be invoked in litigation in the national courts regardless of any implementing measures.[53] Article 157(3) gives the EU the competence to legislate on equal pay in the form of directives.[54] Article 19(1) TFEU gives the EU competence to enact directives 'to combat discrimination based on sex, racial or ethnic origin, religion or belief, disability, age or sexual orientation'. This extends beyond employment settings but has resulted in two important directives with considerable relevance to the employment sphere.[55]

Finally, one of the central objectives of the EU is to create a 'common market' – now called the 'internal market' – in which there are no obstacles to trade between the Member States. One feature of this market is the possibility for workers to move freely from one Member State to another in search of work or to take up employment, or to be sent (or 'posted') by their employer to another Member State as part of its commercial activities.[56] These rights are guaranteed by the 'free movement' provisions of the TFEU: Article 45 (on the free movement of workers), and Articles 49 and 56, governing the employer's freedom to establish anywhere in the EU and to provide services across national borders respectively. These Treaty rights are supplemented by powers to make regulations and directives on free movement.[57] Although the right of workers to move in search of employment has economic origins, it is now reinforced (and sometimes supplanted) by broader concepts of EU citizenship (Article 20 TFEU) and by a general prohibition on discrimination on grounds of nationality (Article 18 TFEU).

[53] Case 149/77 *Defrenne v Société Anonyme Belge de Navigation Aerienne (SABENA)* [1978] ECR 1365.
[54] Directive 2006/54/EC of the European Parliament and of the Council of 5 July 2006 on the implementation of the principle of equal opportunities and equal treatment of men and women in matters of employment and occupation (recast). See Chapter 7.
[55] Council Directive 2000/78/EC of 27 November 2000 establishing a general framework for equal treatment in employment and occupation [2000] OJ L303; Council Directive 2000/43/EC of 29 June 2000 implementing the principle of equal treatment between persons irrespective of racial or ethnic origin [2000] OJ L180. See Chapter 6.
[56] See Chapter 3.
[57] For example, Directive 2004/38/EC of the European Parliament and of the Council of 29 April 2004 on the right of citizens of the Union and their family members to move and reside freely within the territory of the Member States.

By now, it should be apparent that EU law is relevant to most topics within employment law. Most of the chapters in this book will involve an examination of EU provisions alongside national ones. Indeed, EU law even creates new areas of interest for employment lawyers, such as the right for workers to move around the EU. However, there are three important matters that are outside the scope of the EU's legislative competence. Article 153(5) expressly excludes 'pay, the right of association, the right to strike or the right to impose lock-outs'. Nevertheless, even these issues are sometimes affected by EU employment law in other ways than through legislation.

2.4.2 Directives

Although a number of directly effective Treaty provisions are applicable in employment law, most EU employment law takes the form of directives. According to the definition in Article 288 TFEU:

> A directive shall be binding, as to the result to be achieved, upon each Member State to which it is addressed, but shall leave to the national authorities the choice of form and methods.

Thus, directives need to be implemented by the Member State and should, in theory at least, give some discretion in how implementation should take place.[58] In practice, the degree of discretion varies considerably as between directives, though the Member States generally get a fair degree of discretion on matters such as how a new right should be enforced, so that they can fit the new measure into their legal system. Under Article 153(3), the Member States may entrust the 'social partners' (EU jargon for trade unions and employers' associations) with the task of implementing a directive, but this is more of a tradition in the Nordic countries and rarely occurs in the UK.[59]

In employment law, the process of enacting a directive has some special features. First, under Article 154, the Commission is obliged to consult the social partners at two stages: on the 'possible direction' of EU action[60] and on 'the content of the envisaged proposal'.[61] This means that the social partners get some input into the general direction of EU policy on employment law and into proposals for directives. During the second stage of consultation, the social partners may initiate what is known as the 'social dialogue' procedure under Article 155.[62] This procedure allows them to negotiate an agreement on a particular topic instead of leaving it to the usual legislative process (involving the Member States in the Council and the European Parliament). Once the social partners have reached an agreement, there are two possible routes to implementation. One is that the social partners themselves decide to implement the agreement through collective negotiations at the national level.[63]

---

[58] Directives have vertical but not horizontal direct effect, though they can be invoked in various ways in cases between private parties.

[59] The implementation of the Directive on Temporary Agency Work (Directive 2008/104/EC) is based, in part, on an agreement between the CBI and the TUC.

[60] TFEU, art 154(2).

[61] ibid art 154(3).

[62] ibid art 154(4).

[63] ibid art 155(2).

The agreement on 'telework' (working from home) is an example of this.[64] The other possibility is that – provided that the agreement is within the EU's competence under Article 153 – the Council may give effect to the agreement by means of a directive.[65] This was used for the directives on fixed-term work, part-time work and parental leave, among others.[66]

The 'social dialogue' procedure is controversial. On the one hand, those who regard it as a legislative process worry that it suffers from a 'democratic deficit'.[67] Given declining levels of trade union and employers' association membership in many Member States, it can be argued that the European-level organisations that participate in the social dialogue are not properly 'representative' of employers and working people in the EU. Moreover, since there is only an obligation to 'inform' the European Parliament, the social dialogue process bypasses another possible source of democratic legitimacy.[68] On the other hand, it can be argued that the social dialogue should be regarded as a process with its roots in labour law.[69] Here, we tend to accept bargains between employers and unions even though it is rarely the case that the union has 100% membership in the workplace. Indeed, we regard 'free-riding' – taking the benefits of collective bargaining without taking part – as a problem suffered by unions, rather than as a problem *with* unions.

After an initial flurry of activity, the social dialogue procedure has fallen into disuse, though the social partners have recently agreed a revision to their agreement on parental leave.[70] The main reason for this is that social dialogue is much more closely related to the ordinary legislative process than it might seem at first sight. If we assume that a new directive will offer some form of protection to workers so unions want it but employers are hostile (a reasonable assumption), we can see that it is difficult to find an ideal negotiating scenario. If the Commission is unlikely to secure enactment of the directive through the ordinary legislative procedure, there is no reason for the employers to negotiate through social dialogue because they have already got what they wanted. If the Commission is likely to secure enactment, the employers have a reason to negotiate (to reduce the protection on offer) but the unions have no incentive to negotiate (unless they can improve on the Commission's proposal) because they will get what they want through the ordinary procedure. Thus, although social dialogue may seem like an alternative, in practice it is closely related to the Member States' willingness to agree.

---

[64] Framework Agreement on Telework, 16 July 2002.

[65] TFEU, art 155(2).

[66] Council Directive 1999/70/EC of 28 June 1999 concerning the framework agreement on fixed-term work concluded by ETUC, UNICE and CEEP [1999] OJ L175; Council Directive 97/81/EC of 15 December 1997 concerning the framework agreement on part-time work concluded by UNICE, CEEP and the ETUC – Annex: Framework agreement on part-time work [1997] OJ L014; Council Directive 96/34/EC of 3 June 1996 on the framework agreement on parental leave concluded by UNICE, CEEP and the ETUC [1996] OJ L145.

[67] ACL Davies, 'Should the EU Have the Power to Set Minimum Standards for Collective Labour Rights in the Member States?', in Philip Alston (ed), *Labour Rights as Human Rights* (OUP 2005).

[68] TFEU, art 155(2).

[69] Brian Bercusson, *European Labour Law* (2nd edn, CUP 2009) chapter 18.

[70] Directive 2010/18/EU of 8 March 2010 implementing the revised framework agreement on parental leave. An attempt in 2012 to negotiate a revision to the Working Time Directive (Directive 2003/88/EC) failed.

2.4.3 Human rights in EU law

We have already seen that human rights instruments have considerable relevance in employment law, since many employment rights are found in such instruments. Over time, the EU has developed a human rights dimension. We will outline this development very briefly here.

The starting-point for the EU's involvement in human rights is often traced to the Court of Justice and its decisions on the supremacy of EU law.[71] The supremacy doctrine states that where EU law and national law conflict, EU law always prevails.[72] This proved controversial, not least because it might have the effect that a provision of EU law would prevail over national constitutional guarantees. In *Internationale Handelsgesellschaft* the Court of Justice developed a doctrine of human rights as a means of reconciling national courts to the doctrine of supremacy.[73] The Court undertook to review EU law for its compatibility with human rights norms, drawn from the 'common constitutional traditions' of the Member States or from the ECHR (to which all EU Member States are parties).[74] In this way, the risk of a conflict between national human rights norms and EU law would be reduced.

In 2000, the EU 'proclaimed' the EU Charter of Fundamental Rights. This was incorporated into the Treaty architecture at Lisbon and now forms the centrepiece of the EU's human rights endeavours.[75] The Court cites the Charter in its decisions and has started to 're-base' some of its fundamental rights jurisprudence on the Charter provisions.[76] The Charter is of special importance in employment law because it is a wide-ranging statement of human rights, bridging the divide (discussed above) between civil and political rights on the one hand, and economic and social rights on the other. Thus, it replicates the rights in the ECHR,[77] and adds a number of important labour rights such as the right of workers to be informed and consulted by their employer,[78] various rights relating to working time[79] and the right to strike.[80]

Although the Charter is an important development, it is worth noting some of its limitations. First, some of the rights have a relatively 'soft' formulation, in which a right is guaranteed 'in accordance with Community law and national laws and practices'.[81] Of course, most rights are not absolute: they are limited to protect the competing interests of others, or important public interests. But this formulation tends to suggest that the right in the Charter does not have an independent existence apart from EU law and national law. Second, the Charter applies only to the EU institutions and to the Member States when they are 'implementing Union law'.[82] Nor does it increase the competences of the EU.[83] Thus, the Charter offers a means

---

[71] See, for example, Case 6/64 *Costa v ENEL* [1964] ECR 585; Case 106/77 *Simmenthal* [1978] ECR 629.

[72] *Simmenthal* [3] and [21] *et seq.*

[73] Case 11/70 *Internationale Handelsgesellschaft mbH v Einfuhr- und Vorratsstelle für Getreide und Futtermittel* [1970] ECR 1125.

[74] See now TEU, art 6(3).

[75] TEU, art 6(1).

[76] For example, Case C-297/10 *Hennigs v Eisenbahn-Bundesamt* [2011] ECR I-7965.

[77] EU Charter, Chapters I and II (with various additions).

[78] EU Charter, art 27.

[79] ibid art 31.

[80] ibid art 28.

[81] See, for example, art 34.

[82] ibid art 51(1).

[83] ibid art 51(2).

of reviewing EU law (and the Member States actions under EU law) for compatibility with human rights, but does not turn the EU into a body with power to promote human rights. We will consider the role of the Court of Justice in applying the Charter in the next section.

Finally, at the time of writing, the EU is in the process of fulfilling another commitment in the Lisbon Treaty: that it would accede to the ECHR.[84] Although the Member States are all signatories to the ECHR, it can sometimes be the case that they are faced with conflicts between the demands of EU law and the requirements of the ECHR. The EU's accession to the ECHR is meant to provide a way of addressing this problem by giving the two courts – the Court of Justice and the ECtHR – a method of resolving their differences. This has particular implications for the right to strike, a right which is (arguably) regarded very differently by the two courts.[85]

2.4.4 The role of the Court of Justice

The Court of Justice is a key player in the development of EU employment law. It hears three main types of case in this field. These are:

(1) Infringement proceedings, where the Commission argues that a Member State has failed to implement EU law correctly.[86] For example, the Court of Justice held that the UK had failed to implement the Equal Pay Directive correctly because it did not provide a possibility for the claimant to argue that she was doing work of 'equal value' to that of a man in the same employment.[87]

(2) Actions for annulment, where a Member State (or occasionally some other interested party) challenges the validity of an EU measure.[88] For example, the UK government sought annulment of the Working Time Directive, arguing that the Directive was not a 'health and safety' measure and could not therefore be based on health and safety provisions in the Treaty.[89] This argument was unsuccessful.[90]

(3) References for preliminary rulings, where a national court is hearing a case to which EU law applies and seeks the Court's advice on how to resolve those issues of EU law.[91] Most of the examples to be considered in this book fall into this category.

The Court's approach to employment law cases is, not surprisingly, quite mixed. We will consider a number of its decisions in detail in later chapters. Here it is worth noting three main points. First, the Court has on many occasions been responsible for moving the subject forward in highly significant ways. Perhaps the most obvious example is the decision in *Defrenne* that what is now Article 157 on equal pay for men and women was capable of having direct effect in the Member States (despite apparent indications to the contrary in the text of the Article).[92] This allowed the

---

[84] TEU, art 6(2).
[85] See Chapter 14.
[86] TFEU, arts 258 and 260.
[87] Case 61/81 *Commission* v *UK* [1982] ECR 2601.
[88] TFEU, art 263.
[89] Case C-84/94 *UK* v *Council of the European Union (Working Time Directive)* [1996] ECR I-5755.
[90] With the exception of art 5 of the Directive which originally provided for Sunday as the day of rest: ibid [37].
[91] TFEU, art 267.
[92] Above n 53.

Court to develop the law on equal pay through a series of test cases at a time when the EU legislature was slow to act.[93] In some cases, the Court's pro-worker stance manifests itself in a finding that a particular labour right is a fundamental social right. The right to paid annual leave is treated in this way and this has led the Court to make a number of pro-worker decisions on this topic.[94] Second, and by contrast, the Court sometimes makes more cautious decisions in employment law cases, often after a period of expansion. For example, the Court has shown itself to be quite hostile to the idea of positive discrimination – that an employer should be able to take account of the under-representation of certain groups in the workplace when it is making recruitment decisions. Positive discrimination is permitted in the Court's case-law, but only where the candidates are equally qualified and where the scheme does not operate automatically (so the 'losing' candidate gets a chance to make a case for why he or she should still get the job).[95] Third, it is sometimes the case that employment law comes into conflict with other fundamental principles of EU law, like free movement. Here, the Court tends to prioritise those principles ahead of employment law. So, for example, if a union's strike action discourages a firm from moving from one Member State to another (in EU law terms, exercising its 'freedom of establishment') the Court will tend to prioritise the firm's freedom to move over the union's right to strike.[96]

2.5 STATUTE AND COMMON LAW

Our discussion so far has already touched on statute and common law, the two main domestic sources of employment law. We have seen how they might be influenced by the UK's international and regional human rights obligations, and we have seen how, through the doctrine of direct effect in particular, EU law is thoroughly integrated into our domestic legal system. Nevertheless, it is worth examining our national sources of employment law in their own right. We will begin by considering the implications of devolution for employment law. We will then identify some important features of statute and common law as sources of employment law.

2.5.1 Devolution

The UK is made up of several different jurisdictions. Some statutes, such as the Human Rights Act 1998, apply across the whole of the UK, as does EU law. Beyond that, matters are more complex.

In Northern Ireland, many policy areas are regulated by the Northern Ireland Assembly and Executive. Employment is one of the devolved responsibilities.[97] This means that employment law and policy may develop differently in Northern Ireland to the rest of the UK, although of course the scope for this is limited by the need to comply with EU law and human rights obligations. The Northern Ireland Assembly has enacted legislation on the resolution of workplace disputes.[98]

---

[93] See Chapter 7 and Jeff Kenner, *EU Employment Law* (Hart 2003) chapter 2.

[94] Case C-131/04 *Robinson-Steele v RD Retail Services Ltd* [2006] ECR I-2531 [48]. See Chapter 8.

[95] See, for example, Case C-158/97 *Badeck* [2000] ECR I-1875. See Chapter 6.

[96] Case C-438/05 *International Transport Workers Federation v Viking Line ABP* [2007] ECR I-10779.

[97] Northern Ireland Act 1998, s 4. The NMW is a reserved (i.e. not devolved) matter under sch 3, para 21 of the Act.

[98] Employment Act (Northern Ireland) 2011.

Although devolution to the Scottish Parliament is also very extensive, employment is one of the topics 'reserved' to Westminster under the Scotland Act 1998.[99] This means that if the Scottish Parliament tried to legislate on unfair dismissal, for example, that law would be *ultra vires* and could be struck down by the courts. Similarly, the devolution of powers to Wales, which has recently been extended to give the Welsh Assembly the power to make primary legislation, does not include employment matters.[100] However, this does not mean that the Scottish Parliament and the Welsh Assembly have no say in employment issues at all. Both devolved legislatures have power over related areas, like education and training. This means that some of the decisions they take in those areas may have an impact on employment matters. For example, the Welsh Government's Redundancy Action Scheme (ReAct) helps to pay for training for people who are facing redundancy and subsidises employers who want to take on additional staff.[101]

Finally, it is important to note that statute is not the only source of difference between the law in different parts of the UK. The UK court structure is made up of three separate jurisdictions: England and Wales (still a single jurisdiction despite the possibility of Welsh legislation), Scotland and Northern Ireland. Although appeals lie from all three to the UK Supreme Court in London, which sometimes tries to act as a unifying force, there are important differences in the judge-made law applicable in each jurisdiction. Scots law is especially distinctive because it is often described as a mixed civil and common law system, having been influenced by Roman law during an important phase of its historical development. As we shall see below, some aspects of employment law are derived largely from judicial decisions – notably the law governing the contract of employment – so the rules may differ, particularly as between Scots law and the other two jurisdictions.[102]

For convenience, and with apologies to those in other jurisdictions, this book will focus primarily on the law applicable in England.

2.5.2 Statute

A large proportion of employment law is found in statute. We will give an overview here, but of course we will examine the various provisions in detail in later chapters.

Probably the two most important statutes in employment law are the Trade Union and Labour Relations (Consolidation) Act 1992 (TULRCA), which deals with most issues relating to trade unions and collective labour law, and the Employment Rights Act 1996 (ERA), which deals with most issues pertaining to individual employment law. Both statutes consolidate provisions from earlier Acts, and both have been the subject of substantial amendments over time. The government sometimes introduces new measures by amending these statutes – this is true of the law on trade union

---

[99] Scotland Act 1998, sch 5, Head H. At the time of writing, the Scottish Parliament has been promised greater powers after the independence referendum but it is not clear what these will include.

[100] Government of Wales Act 2006, sch 7.

[101] http://wales.gov.uk/topics/educationandskills/skillsandtraining/reactemployers/?lang=en (last visited 3 October 2014). The Welsh Assembly has power over economic development (ibid sch 7, para 4) and training (ibid para 5).

[102] For an example in the constructive dismissal context, see Hugh Collins, 'Constructive Dismissal and the West Lothian Question: *Aberdeen City Council* v *McNeill*' (2011) 40 ILJ 439; Douglas Brodie, 'Common Law Remedies and Relational Contracting: *McNeill* v *Aberdeen CC* (No. 2)' (2014) 43 ILJ 170.

recognition, added to TULRCA in 2000[103] – or by enacting new legislation, such as the National Minimum Wage Act 1998. Details are often spelled out in Regulations.

Where the government is implementing EU directives, it has the power to do so using Regulations under the European Communities Act 1972, instead of using primary legislation.[104] This power has been used for most employment law directives including the Working Time Directive (Working Time Regulations)[105] and the Directive on Temporary Agency Work (Agency Workers Regulations).[106] As we shall see, the government is sometimes criticised for 'gold-plating' directives: in other words, going beyond what is strictly necessary for effective implementation.[107] Sometimes, this is done to simplify matters by codifying case-law from the Court of Justice (which would be binding anyway) or to offer greater protection to workers (which is usually permitted by EU law). As we saw above, it is possible for the social partners to be involved in the implementation of directives but this is rare in the UK, though the government's implementation of the Directive on Temporary Agency Work is based on an agreement between the Confederation of British Industry (CBI) representing employers and the Trades Union Congress (TUC) representing workers.[108]

We saw above that the ECHR is an important instrument for some aspects of employment law. Most of the rights in the Convention can be applied by the English courts by virtue of the Human Rights Act 1998 (HRA). This opens up the possibility of arguing that a particular statute is incompatible with a Convention right, empowering a court to interpret the legislation to make it compatible under s. 3, or to issue a declaration of incompatibility under s. 4 if such interpretation is not possible. So far, there have been relatively few employment law cases under the HRA, and the courts have tended to adopt a cautious approach, though it remains to be seen how this will develop in the light of the ECtHR's more adventurous jurisprudence.[109]

2.5.3 Common law

The common law also plays an important role in the formulation and development of employment law. Most obviously, courts and tribunals interpret the statutes and Regulations described in the previous section. But some parts of employment law are predominantly a matter for the common law.

The courts' interpretive activities are an important way in which external influences can be brought to bear on English employment law. The courts must treat EU law as supreme in the event of a conflict with national law, and they are bound by the decisions of the Court of Justice.[110] They must apply directly effective EU law (such as Article 157, on equal pay for men and women) and even where there is no direct effect, they must interpret national law to make it compatible with EU law, insofar

---

[103] TULRCA, sch A1, inserted by the Employment Relations Act 1999.
[104] ECA 1972, s 2(2).
[105] Working Time Regulations 1998, SI 1998/1833.
[106] Agency Workers Regulations 2010, SI 2010/93.
[107] See, for example, the discussion of TUPE in Chapter 10.
[108] Above n 59.
[109] See Chapters 11, 12 and 13 in particular.
[110] Above n 49.

as it is possible to do so.[111] Thus, it is important to consider the relevant EU provisions when interpreting national measures on the same topic. The courts must also take into account ECtHR jurisprudence under s. 2 HRA, though as we shall see, this has not yet brought about any very radical changes in judicial approaches.

Some aspects of employment law are creations of the common law. The most obvious example of this is the contract of employment, which is clearly a contract but subject to a variety of special rules about interpretation and about implied terms.[112] The contract of employment is of particular importance because (in addition to the rights and duties in the contract itself) it denotes that the individual who is party to it is an employee, and may therefore avail him- or herself of all the statutory rights offered to employees.[113] In that sense, the contract of employment (a common law concept) is a 'trigger' for the application of statutory rights. In other cases, the statute is overlaid on a common law framework. This is true of the law on industrial action.[114] The common law's starting-point is that anyone who organises a strike is potentially liable in tort, but in order to provide a possibility of strike action, Parliament has stepped in to give strike organisers 'statutory immunity' from tort liability if certain conditions are met.[115]

It is important to note that, while some employment law issues arise in the ordinary courts, there is a system of specialist tribunals that deal with the vast majority of employment law cases (with a possibility of appeal to the ordinary courts). We will examine this system in the section on dispute resolution, below.

2.6 WORKPLACE LAW

As we noted at the start of the discussion, the reality of employment 'law' for most working people is far removed from international human rights instruments or even English case-law or statute. Their day-to-day activities are governed by what the boss says: in more formal terms, by 'managerial prerogative'. This is usually underpinned by their contract and perhaps by other sources such as workplace handbooks or collective agreements.

Employment law recognises that the employer cannot usually specify in advance exactly what the individual will be required to do at work each day, particularly if the employment relationship is of long duration. By entering into an employment relationship, the individual puts him- or herself at the employer's disposal. The employer is free to issue instructions, and the individual is under a duty to obey those instructions. In theory, we can think about these powers and duties as 'implied terms' of the contract of employment: the employer's implied power to direct the employee's activities, and the employee's implied duty of obedience.[116] They are terms implied by law as 'necessary incidents' of a contract of employment. It may be difficult to determine the exact limits of the employer's power to direct the employee. This power might be limited by express terms in the contract – the employee's job description,

---

[111] Case 14/83 *von Colson v Land Nordrhein-Westfalen* [1984] ECR 1891.
[112] See Chapter 5.
[113] See Chapter 4.
[114] See Chapter 13.
[115] TULRCA, s 219.
[116] See Chapter 5.

for example – or by other implied terms, such as the implied term of mutual trust and confidence (which requires the employer to avoid acting in ways that would destroy the individual's trust).[117]

Another complicating factor is the possibility that – even if the contract does limit the employer's power to make demands of the employee – the employer might be able to 'get around' such limitations by getting the contract changed. In theory at least, this can only take place with the employee's consent. However, there are two important qualifications to this in the employment context. First, the employer might opt to terminate the employee's existing contract and offer him or her re-employment on new terms and conditions.[118] This means that, if the employee does not agree to the change, he or she will be out of a job. Although it might be possible to bring an unfair dismissal claim based on these facts, tribunals will tend to find that the dismissal is fair where the employer has a good reason for making the change.[119] Second, the employer might draft the employee's contract so that the contract gives the employer the power of unilateral variation. This bypasses the need for the employee's consent (apart from his or her initial agreement to the contract). Such a power was upheld in the *Bateman* case.[120]

An employee's day-to-day existence might be governed less by the terms and conditions of his or her contract of employment, and more by some kind of 'workplace handbook'. This provides the employer with an opportunity to set out detailed requirements and procedures in informal language and in a format that can be changed and amended over time. However, the exact legal status of material in a handbook may be difficult to determine, since handbooks often contain a mixture of contract terms and non-contractual requirements.[121] In some workplaces, a collective agreement between the employer and a trade union representing the employees may also be a relevant source of norms. If certain conditions are met, some terms from the collective agreement may be incorporated into the employees' individual contracts of employment.[122]

2.7 DISPUTES AND ENFORCEMENT

In most areas of law, we assume that people are generally law-abiding and willing to comply. If we had to enforce all of the law all of the time, life would quickly become impossible. The same is true in employment: a new statute is passed, for example, containing rights for workers, and we assume that most employers will learn about it and apply it to their staff. Indeed, through the work of relevant public bodies (discussed below) and various government-supported websites, the government seeks to ensure that employers (and workers) have ready access to information about legal requirements.[123] However, problems can and do arise, because employers do not know about particular employment rights, or because they interpret the law in one

---

[117] See, for example, *Malik v Bank of Credit and Commerce International SA (In Liquidation)* [1998] AC 20 (HL).

[118] For example, *Gilham v Kent CC* [1985] ICR 227 (CA).

[119] *Iceland Frozen Foods Ltd v Jones* [1983] ICR 17, and see Chapter 9.

[120] *Bateman v Asda Stores Ltd* [2010] IRLR 370 (EAT), and see Chapter 5.

[121] *Keeley v Fosroc International Ltd* [2006] EWCA Civ 1277, [2006] IRLR 961, and see Chapter 5.

[122] *Malone v British Airways Plc* [2010] EWCA Civ 1225, [2011] ICR 125, and see Chapter 5.

[123] https://www.gov.uk/browse/employing-people (last visited 3 October 2014).

way and workers think it should be interpreted differently, or because they decide not to comply and hope that no-one will notice or complain. In this section, we will examine how employment disputes are dealt with.

2.7.1 Employment Tribunals

Many, though by no means all, employment disputes fall within the jurisdiction of the Employment Tribunals.[124] Appeal (on a point of law only) lies from the Employment Tribunal to the Employment Appeal Tribunal (EAT).[125] From the EAT, a case can be appealed (again on a point of law only) to the Court of Appeal and thence to the Supreme Court.[126] In this section, we will examine the rationale for tribunals, their jurisdiction and recent reforms to the system.

One of the distinctive features of Employment Tribunals when they were first introduced was their composition. They had three members: two lay people, one with employer expertise and one with worker or union expertise, and a legally qualified Employment Judge. The EAT had the same structure, with two lay members and a High Court or circuit judge. Employment Tribunals still have a three-member structure but it is increasingly common for cases to be heard by an Employment Judge sitting alone. This may occur either where the parties agree or in certain listed jurisdictions, such as claims for unpaid wages.[127] Controversially, unfair dismissal claims (a large part of the tribunal workload) were recently added to the list.[128] The Enterprise and Regulatory Reform Act 2013, s. 12,[129] now provides that the EAT should normally consist of a judge sitting alone though there is a discretion to sit with either two or four lay members.[130] The government argues that, in the case of tribunals, these measures cut costs, and in the case of the EAT, that it is deciding legal issues and does not need lay expertise.[131]

In general terms, Employment Tribunals have jurisdiction over most claims in the field of individual employment law. The main areas of jurisdiction are unfair dismissal and redundancy claims under ERA and discrimination claims under the Equality Act 2010, but tribunals also deal with a wide range of individual statutory rights, such as claims under the National Minimum Wage Act 1998. Importantly, Employment Tribunals also have jurisdiction to hear a claim relating to an individual's contract of employment provided that it 'arises or is outstanding on the termination' of that contract and does not relate to an excluded matter (such as personal injury[132]).[133] This avoids the need for two sets of proceedings, one in the Employment Tribunal to hear a statutory claim (such as unfair dismissal) and another in the courts for breach of contract. However, the Employment Tribunal may not order payment of more than £25,000 damages for breach of contract so a claimant with a larger value claim will

---

[124] See, generally, Employment Tribunals Act 1996.

[125] ibid s 21.

[126] ibid s 37.

[127] ibid s 4.

[128] Employment Tribunals Act 1996 (Tribunal Composition) Order 2012, SI 2012/988, art 2.

[129] Amending the Employment Tribunals Act 1996, s 28.

[130] Or one or three if the parties consent.

[131] DBIS, *Resolving Workplace Disputes: A Consultation* (January 2011).

[132] The Employment Tribunals Extension of Jurisdiction (England and Wales) Order 1994, SI 1994/1623, art 5.

[133] ibid art 4, enacted under the Employment Tribunals Act 1996, s 3.

still need to pursue it through the courts.[134] Although Employment Tribunals do not generally deal with matters relating to collective labour law, such as disputes about the lawfulness of a strike, they do have jurisdiction over claims that an employer has discriminated against an individual on grounds of trade union membership, and over some claims brought by individual union members against their union (for example, in relation to disciplinary measures imposed by the union or expulsion from the union).

Two main justifications are commonly given for the use of tribunals rather than courts: that they facilitate the use of experts to decide cases, and that they are more accessible to claimants than courts.[135] We will examine each in turn.

(1) In the Employment Tribunal system, expertise has traditionally been achieved through the use of lay members. In theory, the lay members should be well-placed to apply 'open-textured' standards like reasonableness in unfair dismissal law or proportionality in equality law because they have a good sense of 'how things are' in the workplace. However, this is increasingly undermined by the growing practice of Employment Judges sitting alone to hear cases. Of course, Employment Judges are themselves specialists: even if they are not employment law experts when they are appointed, they are bound to develop expertise over time. But their expertise is primarily legal rather than practical.

(2) The second justification for tribunals is that they are more accessible than courts. The argument is that tribunal procedures are less formal, so the parties should feel able to present their cases themselves, without the need for legal advice. This is presented as an advantage because it encourages vulnerable workers to seek redress even if they are unable to afford to pay a solicitor. The difficulty with this argument is that it is not supported by the empirical evidence.[136] Studies have shown that individuals without legal representation are significantly less likely to win their cases, particularly when the other side – the better-resourced employer – is represented by a lawyer. There are various reasons for this. One important consideration is that the law is highly complex, even if the proceedings in the tribunal are informal. Another factor is the adversarial nature of tribunal proceedings. Although tribunal members are encouraged to help claimants by asking them questions, their capacity to do so is constrained by the need to avoid allegations from the employer that they are biased in favour of the claimant.

Because of the 'accessibility' claim, it has always been the case that legal aid is not available for Employment Tribunal proceedings. This means that claimants who want legal advice but cannot afford to pay for it must obtain it by other means: for example, by retaining a solicitor on a 'no win, no fee' basis, or pro bono, or obtaining advice from organisations such as the Citizens' Advice Bureau.[137] Where the claimant is a trade union member, his or her union may provide advice or access to a lawyer. In 2011–12, it seems that about 46% of claimants had a lawyer.[138]

---

[134] ibid art 10.

[135] Sir Andrew Leggatt, *Tribunals for Users: One System, One Service* (2001) paras 1.11–1.12.

[136] Hazel Genn and Yvette Genn, *The Effectiveness of Representation at Tribunals: Report to the Lord Chancellor* (Lord Chancellor's Department 1989).

[137] An employee who wins his or her claim cannot normally recover costs from the employer (unless one of the exceptions applies, discussed below).

[138] Ministry of Justice, *Employment Tribunal and EAT statistics 2011–12 (GB)* (2012) Table 4.

A further dimension to the accessibility claim used to be that tribunals were cheap to use: there were no fees for bringing a claim, and each party bore its own costs. Although this meant that a successful claimant could not recover his or her costs from the employer, it also meant that he or she did not risk having to pay the employer's costs if he or she lost the case. Nowadays, however, there are fees for bringing claims and the possibility of costs orders, so that this justification no longer holds.

In recent years, successive governments have been concerned to reduce the number of tribunal claims.[139] There are various reasons for this. The most obvious is that the state has to provide and pay for the tribunal system. Although this is probably cheaper than having people pursue their employment claims through the ordinary courts, it is still a significant cost. Another is that employers often complain about two linked problems: vexatious litigation (where someone brings an unmeritorious claim, usually in the hope that the employer will offer a payment to settle the claim) and the costs of defending claims regardless of their merits. These two claims are difficult to evaluate. The available statistics do not enable us to identify vexatious cases. For example, in 2011–12, some 9% of unfair dismissal claims were struck out.[140] But the vexatious nature of a claim is only one of the grounds for striking out.[141] Others include failing actively to pursue the claim or failing to comply with case management orders. Thus, we cannot say with any certainty that 9% of unfair dismissal claims are vexatious. Of course, it might be suggested that some of the claims withdrawn (around 24% of unfair dismissal claims in the same period[142]) might also be vexatious, but equally this figure could include strong claims that are settled by the employer. The other common complaint from employers is that tribunal claims are costly to defend. In 2011–12, the median award for unfair dismissal compensation was a modest £4560, but this is likely to be dwarfed in many cases by the employer's legal and management expenses in preparing for and attending the hearing.[143] However, it is important to note that there is an element of employer choice here: the employer could opt to settle the claim at an earlier stage (so must perceive some benefit in defending the claim and going to a hearing) and the employer could opt (as many claimants do) not to use legal advice.[144]

Despite these various evidential difficulties, successive governments have pursued a programme of tribunal reform. This has two main elements: increasing the cost of bringing a claim, particularly (but by no means exclusively) if it has a limited prospect of success, and encouraging the use of alternative dispute resolution.[145] We will examine each in turn.

(1) Until recently, bringing an Employment Tribunal claim was free of charge, but fees were introduced in 2013.[146] The justification given for this is that the costs of the

---

[139] DBIS, above n 131.

[140] Above n 138, Table 2.

[141] Employment Tribunals (Constitution and Rules of Procedure) Regulations 2013, SI 2013/1237, sch 1, para 37.

[142] Above n 138, Table 2.

[143] ibid Table 5.

[144] The official statistics do not include information on employer representation.

[145] Above n 131.

[146] Employment Tribunals and the Employment Appeal Tribunal Fees Order 2013, SI 2013/1893. Attempts to challenge this on EU law and equality grounds have so far failed: *R (Unison)* v *Lord Chancellor* [2014] EWHC 218 (Admin), [2014] ICR 498; *R (Unison)* v *Lord Chancellor* (No. 2) [2014] EWHC 4198 (Admin).

system should be borne not just by taxpayers, but also by those who use it.[147] In simple terms, the party bringing the claim must pay a fee at the outset and a second fee prior to the hearing.[148] The purpose of this two-stage structure is to encourage the parties to resolve their dispute before the hearing. There are two different fee levels depending on the nature of the claim, so more 'complex' claims like unfair dismissal or equality involve payment of higher fees. The current fees are an issue fee of £160 or £250 and a hearing fee of £230 or £950 for Type A and Type B claims respectively.[149] It costs £400 to appeal to the EAT and £1200 for a hearing at the EAT.[150] There is a remission scheme for claimants who cannot afford fees or can only contribute in part.[151]

The statistics suggest that the fees regime is having a significant impact on the number of tribunal claims. In April–June 2014, there were 70% fewer single claims than in the same period in 2013, fees having been introduced in July 2013.[152] As critics have pointed out, it seems likely that many people with genuine grievances have been deterred from enforcing their rights as a result of the fees regime. It is implausible to suggest that 70% of claims in 2013 were vexatious.

The Employment Tribunals system also uses rules about deposits and costs to discourage people from pursuing hopeless claims. Thus, if the Employment Judge decides that a party's contentions on a particular matter have 'little reasonable prospect of success', that party may be required to pay a deposit of £1000 in order to continue.[153] And although the general rule is that each party to an Employment Tribunal claim bears its own costs, there is now a power to order one party to pay the other's costs.[154] This can be done where 'a party (or that party's representative) has acted vexatiously, abusively, disruptively or otherwise unreasonably in either the bringing of the proceedings (or part) or the way that the proceedings (or part) have been conducted; or . . . any claim or response had no reasonable prospect of success'.[155] Of course, these provisions apply equally to both sides, so they protect the employee as well as the employer, and no-one would argue that abusive litigation or behaviour should be encouraged.[156] The difficulty is in predicting when a judge might find proceedings to have had 'no reasonable prospect of success'. This might deter people from bringing legitimate claims, for example, when the arguments to be advanced are novel and untested.

The other strategy adopted by successive governments to reduce the number of claims is to encourage resort to alternative dispute resolution. Since 2014, anyone

---

[147] Ministry of Justice, *Charging Fees in Employment Tribunals and the Employment Appeal Tribunal: Response to Consultation* (CP22/2011, July 2012).

[148] SI 2013/1893, art 4.

[149] ibid sch 2.

[150] ibid arts 13 and 14.

[151] ibid art 17 and sch 3.

[152] Ministry of Justice, *Tribunals Statistics Quarterly April to June 2014* (2014) 7–9.

[153] Employment Tribunals (Constitution and Rules of Procedure) Regulations 2013, SI 2013/1237, sch 1, para 39.

[154] Employment Tribunals Act 1996, s 13; Employment Tribunals (Constitution and Rules of Procedure) Regulations 2013, SI 2013/1237, sch 1, paras 74–84. The rules on costs apply to people who are legally represented. There are 'preparation time orders' in respect of people who are not legally represented.

[155] SI 2013/1237, sch 1, para 76.

[156] The employer may be encouraged to settle the employee's claim by the new power in s 12A Employment Tribunals Act 1996 to order the employer to pay a penalty to the Secretary of State, as well as any compensation to the employee, if the claim has 'aggravating features' (for example, that the employer deliberately infringed the individual's rights).

wanting to bring an Employment Tribunal claim must first notify ACAS so that 'early conciliation' can be offered.[157] Details of the claim are passed to a conciliation officer who contacts the parties and attempts to find a solution. This service is free of charge. Any agreement reached through ACAS is binding. It is not compulsory to participate in conciliation or to accept a conciliated solution, but it is not possible to go straight to a Tribunal without notifying ACAS and obtaining a certificate to show that the time period for conciliation has elapsed. This is usually a month though it can be extended to six weeks.[158] ACAS claims a 75% success rate for the voluntary predecessor to this scheme.[159]

Prior to 2014, ACAS offered conciliation once the claimant had lodged his or her tribunal claim. This will continue to be available, though it seems less likely that it will be used if the parties have tried early conciliation and failed to reach a settlement.

Under the Employment Rights (Dispute Resolution) Act 1998, ACAS also offers arbitration in unfair dismissal and flexible working cases.[160] Again, both parties must agree to use the scheme. The arbitrator makes a binding decision after proceedings conducted in private. The arbitrator's decision can only be challenged in court in very limited circumstances under the Arbitration Act 1996. Thus, the key difference between arbitration and conciliation is that arbitration offers a binding resolution of the case and cannot be a step on the way to the tribunal. Arbitration is not suitable for complex legal issues or jurisdictional disputes (such as whether an individual has the 'employee' status required to bring an unfair dismissal claim).[161] Another option if ACAS conciliation fails is judicial mediation.[162] This may be offered by an Employment Judge at a case management hearing but will only take place if both parties agree. The mediation is conducted in private by an Employment Judge who remains neutral but tries to encourage the parties to settle. If the mediation fails, the case will proceed to a tribunal hearing. The Tribunals Service claims that over 65% of cases going through this route settle during the mediation.[163]

Taking a case to an Employment Tribunal is a stressful experience for many people. Arguably, this is exacerbated by the fact that tribunals are no longer the expert, informal and accessible forum they were originally intended to be. Alternative dispute resolution can offer a cheaper, less adversarial solution. Employers may also be attracted by the private nature of conciliation and arbitration, enabling them to avoid bad publicity. However, the current regime gives rise to two major causes for concern. First, individuals may feel pressured into accepting a conciliated solution because they do not want to pay tribunal fees, rather than because they are happy with what is being offered. And second, the development of the law may be inhibited if disputed questions are not tested in tribunals with the possibility of appeal through the courts.[164]

---

[157] Enterprise and Regulatory Reform Act 2013, s 7, which inserts s 18A and s 18B into the Employment Tribunals Act 1996.

[158] The limitation period for bringing a tribunal claim is 'paused' during early conciliation.

[159] http://www.acas.org.uk/index.aspx?articleid=2011 (last visited 4 October 2014).

[160] Inserting s 212A TULRCA.

[161] ACAS, *The ACAS Arbitration Scheme for the Resolution of Unfair Dismissal Disputes (England and Wales)* (2014).

[162] Ministry of Justice, *Judicial Mediation Employment Tribunals (England and Wales) (July 2014)*.

[163] ibid.

[164] See Linda Mulcahy, 'The Collective Interest in Private Dispute Resolution' (2013) 33 OJLS 59.

2.7.2 Courts

In this section, we will consider the role of the courts in employment law cases. We will focus on the domestic courts. The CJEU and the ECtHR both play important roles in employment law but were discussed in detail above.

Jurisdiction

Employment law issues are heard in the English courts in two main situations: where the Employment Tribunals (or other bodies) have no jurisdiction, so the case starts in court, or where the case has been heard elsewhere, usually by an Employment Tribunal and the EAT, and is appealed to the Court of Appeal (and thence to the Supreme Court). We will focus on the first kind of case in this section. As we saw above, the jurisdiction of the Employment Tribunals is laid down in statute, so we can assume that anything not so listed falls to the ordinary courts to decide. Three main types of case begin in court: cases about the contract of employment, cases in collective labour law and cases involving employment by a public body.

In principle, the employee may start any claim for breach of the contract of employment in court. As we saw above, the Employment Tribunal has limited jurisdiction to hear such claims where they arise when the employment is terminated, and where this applies it may be easier to use the Employment Tribunal. However, there are a number of possible situations in which this option will not be available. First, there are exceptions to the Tribunal's jurisdiction for certain types of contract claim, such as those relating to intellectual property.[165] Second, not all breach of contract claims arise on the termination of the employment. This might be for the very simple reason that the employee is still employed by the employer, but wants to argue that the employer is in breach of his or her contract, for example, in failing to pay wages that he or she is owed.[166] Third, the courts offer more extensive remedies. There is a limit on the damages that can be awarded by a Tribunal (currently £25,000) so higher-value claims must be brought before the courts.[167] Moreover, Tribunals have no power to award injunctions, so an employee who wants to force his or her employer to comply with a contractual disciplinary process (for example) must go to court.[168]

Another area of overlapping jurisdiction is in the field of equal pay.[169] The legal mechanism for securing equal pay for men and women is to imply an 'equality clause' into the woman's contract entitling her to equal pay with her male comparator. This can be enforced in court (as a contract claim) or in the Tribunal under s. 127 Equality Act 2010. Under s. 128 of that Act, the court may transfer a case to the Tribunal if it considers that it may be dealt with more conveniently in that forum. However, the time limit for bringing a claim before a Tribunal is shorter, usually six months (subject to some exceptions).[170] In the recent *Abdulla* case, a number of claimants had brought

---

[165] Above n 132, art 5.
[166] See Chapter 7.
[167] Above n 132, art 10.
[168] See Chapter 9.
[169] See Chapter 7.
[170] Equality Act 2010, s 129.

an equal pay claim in court after the six-month limitation period for applying to the Tribunal had elapsed.[171] By a majority, the Supreme Court held that the action should be allowed to proceed. It could not be regarded as being more 'convenient' to hear the case in the Tribunal since it could not be heard at all.

② The second type of case that arises in the ordinary courts is concerned with collective labour law.[172] Although Tribunals can hear claims relating to an individual's activities as a member of a trade union, such as an employer's refusal to hire him or her because of trade union membership, they have no jurisdiction over the activities of trade unions and strike organisers. Challenges to the lawfulness of a strike must be brought before the ordinary courts. These usually take the form of an application by the employer for an injunction to stop the allegedly unlawful strike from taking place, though it is also possible for the employer to seek damages after the event.

③ The third type of employment law case arising outside the system of Employment Tribunals is an application for judicial review or a claim under s. 6 Human Rights Act 1998. These claims can be brought where the defendant is a public body, so they are relevant to those employed in the public sector. It is important to note that, in general terms, English law does not operate a special system of employment law for public servants. Most public sector workers have contracts of employment and rights to bring claims before Employment Tribunals just like their private sector counterparts. The courts have generally been reluctant to allow public sector workers to seek judicial review of their employer's decisions where they have an alternative remedy.[173] However, judicial review is available where there is no such remedy or,[174] as the recent decision in *Shoesmith* illustrates, where the alternative remedy is much less advantageous than judicial review.[175] In that case, the applicant was the Director of Children's Services at a local authority. She was summarily dismissed after the authority's social workers had failed to prevent the death of a child who was known to be at risk of harm. She brought an application for judicial review in respect of the failure to follow proper procedures when dismissing her. Although she could have brought an unfair dismissal claim, the Court of Appeal allowed her to seek judicial review for various reasons including the possibility of getting the dismissal decision quashed. The quashing order would offer stronger vindication of her rights than a successful unfair dismissal claim, and would entitle her to pay and other benefits until such time as the local authority dismissed her in a lawful manner. Moreover, she would be able to seek an award of costs against the local authority. Another possibility for a public sector worker is to bring a claim under the HRA 1998, s. 6, against the public body in its capacity as his or her employer. This option has been used in a series of recent cases examining the applicability of Article 6 ECHR (which deals with the right to a fair trial) in employers' disciplinary procedures.[176] Although this brief discussion has focused on applications for judicial review brought by employees, it is worth noting that judicial review can be relevant in other situations too: for

---

[171] *Abdulla v Birmingham City Council* [2012] UKSC 47, [2012] ICR 1419.

[172] See Chapter 13.

[173] *R v East Berkshire Health Authority, ex p Walsh* [1985] QB 152 (CA).

[174] *R v Secretary of State for the Home Department, ex p Benwell* [1985] QB 554.

[175] *R (Shoesmith) v Ofsted and others* [2011] EWCA Civ 642, [2011] ICR 1195.

[176] *Kulkarni v Milton Keynes Hospital NHS Trust* [2009] EWCA Civ 789, [2010] ICR 101; *R (G) v X School Governors* [2011] UKSC 30, [2012] 1 AC 167; *Mattu v University Hospitals of Coventry and Warwickshire NHS Trust* [2012] EWCA Civ 641, [2013] ICR 270.

example, as a means of challenging the decisions of public bodies with an adjudicatory role in labour law, such as the Central Arbitration Committee (discussed below)[177] or sometimes as a means of challenging the UK's compliance with EU law.[178]

Approach

In English employment law, there is a tradition of suspicion of the courts. This has two (linked) causes: a worry about the courts' attitude towards working people and, in particular, towards trade unions, and a worry about the inappropriate application of doctrines from other subjects (particularly contract law) in employment settings. We will examine this tradition in this section.

One area in which the courts have, historically, shown themselves to be hostile is in relation to industrial action. When a trade union organises a strike, it generally commits one of the economic torts, such as inducing breach of contract (because a worker who is on strike is in breach of contract, and the union persuades the worker to do this). Parliament has granted unions 'immunities' against tort liability in this situation.[179] The intention is that strike action should be permitted if certain conditions are met. However, the courts have tended to construe the immunities narrowly against the unions.

One well-known example of this relates to the balloting and notice provisions. A trade union must ballot its members and give notice to the employer before calling a strike. For example, in *Metrobus*, it was held that a union had failed to notify the employer of the ballot result 'as soon as reasonably practicable' when the ballot result had been known on the afternoon of 1 September but not notified to the employer until the morning of 3 September.[180] The delay was caused in part by a fax going astray, and in part by the union's own procedures, which required the local official to wait for authorisation from the general secretary before acting on the ballot result. The court thought that it was not acceptable for the union to have such a procedure given the need to comply with the statutory duty to notify the employer. Thus, although there was a clear ballot in favour of strike action, an injunction was granted to stop it from going ahead.

In general terms, the courts have justified their strict stance by focusing on the grant of *immunities* to trade unions. They have seen the immunities as special privileges putting trade unions 'above the law'.[181] Privileges are normally construed narrowly. However, in the recent *RMT* case, Elias LJ held that the immunities should be given a neutral construction.[182] He justified this by reference to the role of Article 11 ECHR in the field of industrial action. The ECtHR has recognised industrial action as a component of the freedom of association protected by Article 11.[183]

---

[177] For example, *R (Boots Management Services Ltd) v Central Arbitration Committee* [2014] EWHC 2930 (Admin), [2014] IRLR 887.

[178] *EOC v Secretary of State for Employment* [1994] 1 All ER 910 (HL) but cf *R v Secretary of State for Employment, ex p Seymour-Smith and Perez* [1999] IRLR 253 (ECJ); [2000] IRLR 263 (HL).

[179] TULRCA 1992, s 219.

[180] *Metrobus Ltd v Unite the Union* [2009] EWCA Civ 829, [2010] ICR 173.

[181] For example, *Express Newspapers v McShane* [1979] ICR 210 (CA) 219, per Lord Denning MR.

[182] *National Union of Rail, Maritime and Transport Workers v Serco Ltd* [2011] EWCA Civ 226, [2011] ICR 848.

[183] *Enerji Yapi-Yol Sen v Turkey* (2009, unreported).

Although Elias LJ was not in a position to advocate a radical transformation of the law – being bound by *Metrobus* – he regarded neutral construction as a way of recognising the fact that the law was using the *form* of immunities to protect an important labour *right*. It remains to be seen how the law in this area will develop given that the ECtHR's attitude towards the right to strike in subsequent cases is proving to be rather ambivalent.[184]

More generally, the treatment of industrial action is a key 'battleground' in which the courts take the view that they are fulfilling the will of Parliament and balancing the interests of employers and the wider public against those of unions and their members, whereas unions (and many commentators) detect a degree of hostility. One possible interpretation of this is 'purely' political: the judges' socio-economic background makes them inherently unsympathetic to trade unionism.[185] However, the reality may be somewhat more complicated. Elias LJ sums up the issue neatly in *RMT*: 'The common law's focus on the protection of property and contractual rights is necessarily antithetical to any form of industrial action since the purpose of the action is to interfere with the employer's rights'.[186] On this view, the problem is that the judiciary may be steeped in a set of common law values that do not sit easily with the right to strike even when this is supported by Parliament.

Another area presenting similar challenges is the contract of employment. Here, the question is whether the contract of employment should be treated as a contract like any other, or whether special rules should apply to reflect the employment context.[187] This is a developing area of law and will be considered in more detail in later chapters: a key example is the *Autoclenz* decision in the Supreme Court.[188] Traditionally, when the individual had signed a written contract with the employer, the courts treated the contract document as a conclusive statement of the parties' relationship.[189] This is consistent with the ordinary law of contract.[190] However, the disadvantage of this approach is that the employer could present the individual with a contract purporting to make him or her self-employed, with few employment rights, rather than an employee or worker, entitled to a range of statutory protections. This traditional approach was rejected by the Supreme Court in *Autoclenz*, which held instead that tribunals and courts should look for the 'true agreement' between the parties.[191] Because of the inequality of bargaining power between employers and working people, this might necessitate looking beyond the contract document. Importantly, although in *Autoclenz* the adoption of a different approach in the employment setting improved the protection available to working people, this is not inevitably the case. In the *Edwards* case, the adoption of an employment-specific approach proved less protective,[192] and in the *Geys* case, the court used the ordinary

---

[184] *National Union of Rail, Maritime and Transport Workers v United Kingdom* (2015) 60 EHRR 10; Alan Bogg and KD Ewing, 'The Implications of the *RMT* Case' (2014) 43 ILJ 221. See Chapter 13.

[185] JAG Griffith, *The Politics of the Judiciary* (5th edn, Fontana 1997).

[186] *RMT* (above n 184) [9].

[187] See Chapter 5.

[188] *Autoclenz Ltd v Belcher* [2011] UKSC 41, [2011] ICR 1157.

[189] For example, *Consistent Group Ltd v Kalwak* [2008] EWCA Civ 430, [2008] IRLR 505.

[190] *L'Estrange v F Graucob Ltd* [1934] 2 KB 394.

[191] *Autoclenz* (above n 188) [29].

[192] *Edwards v Chesterfield Royal Hospital NHS Foundation Trust; Botham v Ministry of Defence* [2011] UKSC 58, [2012] 2 AC 22. See Chapter 9.

rules of contract law (as opposed to an employment-specific approach) to protect the employee.[193] Thus, the extent to which contract law should be adapted in employment settings is a highly contentious matter.

In some jurisdictions, the worry that courts might not understand or be sympathetic towards employment issues has led to the establishment of labour courts separate from the ordinary courts.[194] As we have seen, although the UK has a system of employment tribunals, they do not have jurisdiction over all employment matters, and they are bound to follow the precedents set by the Court of Appeal, Supreme Court and CJEU, and to take into account the jurisprudence of the ECtHR. It seems unlikely that there will be any reform in this area, though the advantages and disadvantages of a greater degree of separation for employment law are an interesting theme of the subject.

2.7.3 Government departments and public bodies

In this section, we will note some of the government departments and public bodies with roles in employment law. These roles include: providing advice to employers and working people, monitoring and enforcing compliance with employment law in a particular area, helping individuals to bring litigation to enforce their rights, and resolving disputes. There are two key points to note at the outset. First, there is no 'labour inspectorate' in the UK. In other legal systems, a 'labour inspectorate' would be a single body with a wide-ranging responsibility for upholding employment law.[195] In the UK, we tend to rely on individuals to enforce their rights through the tribunal system, though there are public bodies with enforcement roles in some situations. This leads to the second point: that there is a degree of historical accident about the creation of particular bodies so that the overall picture is rather confusing. It may not always be entirely clear why there are public bodies to help with some problems but not others.

The government department with primary responsibility for employment law is the Department for Business, Innovation and Skills (DBIS).[196] Most of the public bodies with roles in employment law operate under the aegis of this department. However, other departments are relevant too. For example, Her Majesty's Courts and Tribunals Service, which supports the system of Employment Tribunals, answers to the Ministry of Justice,[197] and the Government Equalities Office, which deals with equality issues, is part of the Department for Culture, Media and Sport (DCMS).[198]

---

[193] *Geys v Société Générale* [2012] UKSC 63, [2013] 1 AC 523. See Chapter 9.

[194] There is information about labour courts in some European countries on the website of The European Association of Labour Court Judges: http://ealcj.org/labour.html (last visited 4 November 2014).

[195] See, generally, International Labour Office, *Labour Administration and Labour Inspection* (report for the International Labour Conference, 100th Session, 2011).

[196] https://www.gov.uk/government/organisations/department-for-business-innovation-skills (last visited 7 October 2014).

[197] https://www.justice.gov.uk/about/hmcts (last visited 7 October 2014).

[198] https://www.gov.uk/government/organisations/government-equalities-office (last visited 7 October 2014). There is also an Office for Disability Issues within the Department for Work and Pensions https://www.gov.uk/government/organisations/office-for-disability-issues (last visited 7 October 2014).

In individual employment law, there are four main regulatory bodies:

- the Employment Agency Standards inspectorate (EAS, part of DBIS), which regulates employment agencies and businesses which supply labour to other firms;[199]

- the Gangmasters Licensing Authority (GLA, part of the Department for the Environment, Food and Rural Affairs), which regulates 'gangmasters', agencies or individuals who supply labour in the food and agriculture sector;[200]

- the Health and Safety Executive (HSE, part of the Department for Work and Pensions), which monitors employers' compliance with health and safety regulations including some of the rules on working time;[201]

- Her Majesty's Revenue and Customs (HMRC) minimum wage compliance team, which investigates alleged failures to pay the minimum wage and enforces compliance.[202]

The Pay and Work Rights Helpline is a single telephone number individuals can use to seek advice from any of these bodies.[203] Although these bodies, taken together, can hardly be described as a coherent enforcement regime, their existence does mean that help is available to secure basic rights for some of the most vulnerable working people in society. Before leaving the topic of pay, it is worth noting the existence of another important body in this area: the Low Pay Commission.[204] This body makes recommendations to the government (which need not be followed, though they usually are) about the level of the National Minimum Wage. This enables the government to draw on the advice of independent experts when deciding what rates to set.

The Equality and Human Rights Commission (EHRC) is an executive non-departmental public body of the DCMS.[205] It is the successor to the Commission for Racial Equality, the Equal Opportunities Commission and the Disability Rights Commission, with responsibility for a wide range of issues relating to equality and human rights. Its role extends beyond employment matters though employment is a key area of its activity. The EHRC has wide-ranging legal powers.[206] Much of its work involves providing general guidance on equality and human rights issues, though it no longer provides a telephone advice service for individuals, since this is run separately by the Equality Advisory and Support Service.[207] The EHRC can conduct general inquiries into particular issues or sectors.[208] It can investigate allegations that a particular person or organisation is in breach of the law, and can reach a formal 'agreement' requiring that person or organisation to take steps to

[199] Employment Agencies Act 1973.
[200] Gangmasters (Licensing) Act 2004, and see http://www.gla.gov.uk/ (last visited 7 October 2014).
[201] http://www.hse.gov.uk/ (last visited 7 October 2014).
[202] National Minimum Wage Act 1998, ss 15–19H.
[203] https://www.gov.uk/pay-and-work-rights-helpline (last visited 7 October 2014).
[204] National Minimum Wage Act 1998, ss 5–8, and see https://www.gov.uk/government/organisations/low-pay-commission (last visited 7 October 2014).
[205] http://www.equalityhumanrights.com/ (last visited 7 October 2014).
[206] Equality Act 2006.
[207] This has been commissioned by the GEO since 2012 and is run by a private firm in conjunction with a group of voluntary organisations. See https://www.equalityadvisoryservice.com/ (last visited 7 October 2014).
[208] Equality Act 2006, s 16.

prevent future breaches.[209] It is responsible for ensuring that public authorities comply with the 'public sector equality duty', which is a requirement to review their policies and practices to ensure that they do not have a discriminatory impact.[210] Finally, the EHRC has a range of powers in relation to legal proceedings.[211] It may bring test cases on equality and human rights issues, including applications for judicial review of government policy, or it may intervene in cases brought by other people in the domestic courts or the ECtHR where important human rights or equality issues are at stake. Although the EHRC uses the full range of its powers, it is probably fair to say that its main areas of activity are providing general guidance and participating in litigation, rather than investigating alleged breaches of equality or human rights law. This reflects the resource-intensive nature of investigations.

Another organisation with a wide-ranging remit is ACAS, the Advisory, Conciliation and Arbitration Service.[212] Its functions can be grouped into three main categories: advice, dispute resolution in individual cases and dispute resolution in collective cases. ACAS provides guidance on all the main employment law topics on its website, and offers a free telephone helpline for employers and working people. Its dispute resolution function in individual cases was discussed above. This includes various forms of conciliation, designed to encourage the parties to resolve their dispute informally without going to a tribunal, and an arbitration scheme for some kinds of unfair dismissal and flexible working disputes. In collective disputes, the parties (usually an employer and a trade union) may choose to use ACAS either for conciliation (to help them reach a negotiated solution to their dispute) or arbitration (in which the parties agree to abide by an arbitrator's 'award' or decision about their dispute).

In the field of collective labour law, there are two other public bodies to consider. The Certification Officer (answerable to DBIS) is responsible for maintaining a list of trade unions and employers' associations, determining whether unions are entitled to a certificate of independence (which has important consequences in law)[213] and adjudicating on trade union members' complaints that their union is in breach of either particular statutory requirements or particular union rules.[214] Because the Certification Officer has adjudicatory functions, an appeal lies on a point of law to the EAT against its decisions.[215] The Central Arbitration Committee (CAC, a tribunal NDPB of DBIS) is responsible for managing procedures and resolving disputes under a range of statutory provisions concerned with collective labour law.[216] These include: the statutory procedure for trade union recognition for collective bargaining, trade unions' rights of access to information for collective bargaining, consultation procedures under the Information and Consultation of Employees Regulations 2004, and European Works Councils.[217] Depending on the jurisdiction, CAC decisions may

---

[209] ibid ss 20 and 23.
[210] ibid s 31.
[211] ibid ss 24–30.
[212] TULRCA, ss 247–253. ACAS is an executive NDPB of DBIS. See http://www.acas.org.uk (last visited 7 October 2014).
[213] See Chapter 11.
[214] TULRCA, ss 254–258.
[215] For example, TULRCA, s 9.
[216] TULRCA, ss 259–265.
[217] See Chapters 12 and 14.

be subject to judicial review[218] or to a right of appeal to the EAT on a point of law.[219] The government has announced proposals to merge the CAC and the Certification Officer, though no timetable for this has yet been given.[220]

POINTS TO TAKE AWAY

- Most people's day-to-day life at work is governed by the boss's instructions, works handbooks and contracts.

- Employment law is a mixture of statutory and common law rules. A lot of employment law is derived from EU law (the Treaties, Directives and decisions of the Court of Justice of the European Union) though there are some gaps in the EU's legislative competence on employment law (including pay and freedom of association).

- The ECHR affects some areas of employment law (notably Article 11, on freedom of association) and can be applied in the domestic courts under the HRA.

- The ESC, international human rights instruments and many ILO norms are binding on the UK in international law but have limited influence in the domestic courts. Nevertheless, they offer a useful benchmark for evaluating domestic law.

- Most employment disputes fall within the jurisdiction of the Employment Tribunals though some begin in court. An appeal on a point of law lies from the ET to the EAT, and then to the Court of Appeal and the Supreme Court. Some aspects of employment law are enforced by public bodies.

Further reading

On EU labour law, see generally, **ACL Davies,** *EU Labour Law* **(Elgar 2012)** or, for more detail, **Catherine Barnard,** *EU Employment Law* **(4th edn, OUP 2012)**. On the ILO, see **Francis Maupain,** *The Future of the International Labour Organization in the Global Economy* **(Hart 2013)**. There are some useful chapters on specific ECHR rights and their implications for labour law in **Filip Dorssemont *et al.* (eds),** *The European Convention on Human Rights and the Employment Relation* **(Hart 2013)**. On the ESC, see generally chapters 3–6 of **Gráinne de Búrca and Bruno de Witte (eds),** *Social Rights in Europe* **(OUP 2005)**.

The interaction between these various systems is an issue of current topical interest. The ECtHR's approach to other standard-setting bodies is explored by **Alan Bogg and KD Ewing,** 'The Implications of the *RMT* Case' (2014) 43 ILJ 221; and **Virginia Mantouvalou,** 'Labour Rights in the European Convention on Human Rights: An Intellectual Justification for an Integrated Approach to Interpretation' (2013) 13 HRLR 529. On the implications of EU accession to the ECHR for labour law, see **Nicole Busby and Rebecca Zahn,** 'The EU and the ECHR: Collective and Non-discrimination Labour Rights at a Crossroad?' (2014) 30 IJCLLIR 153.

→

---

[218] For example, TULRCA, sch A1.
[219] For example, Information and Consultation of Employees Regulations 2004, SI 2004/3426, reg 35(6).
[220] Public Bodies Act 2011, sch 2.

In domestic labour law, a central theme is the 'autonomy' or otherwise of labour law: should labour law draw on common law techniques or should it develop separately? Two classic articles on this topic are **Steven Anderman, 'The Interpretation of Protective Employment Statutes and Contracts of Employment' (2000) 29 ILJ 223**; and **Bob Hepple, 'Restructuring Employment Rights' (1986) 15 ILJ 69**. This has led some to call for a separate system of labour courts, on which see another classic article: **WEJ McCarthy, 'The Case for Labour Courts' (1990) 21 IRJ 98**. Another key theme is the impact of the ECHR on domestic labour law, on which see Chapters 11, 12 and 13 of this book.

3 Migration

Learning outcomes

This chapter will enable readers to:

- understand how migrant workers may obtain a right to work in the UK, either through the rules on free movement for the nationals of other EU Member States, or through the points-based immigration system for non-EU nationals
- critically evaluate the law on irregular migrant workers' entitlement to employment rights
- understand the consequences for employers of hiring irregular migrant workers
- critically analyse the applicability of English law (both common law and statute) in cases with an international dimension, including temporary postings of workers to England from other EU Member States or from non-EU states, and 'expatriate' English employees

3.1 INTRODUCTION

Although globalisation is often seen as a modern phenomenon, people have always moved from country to country in search of work. High-skilled workers have emigrated to emerging markets in order to increase their chance of career progression, and low-skilled workers have moved from impoverished countries to richer ones in search of work of any kind. Worker movement and migration is widespread. The ILO estimates that there are some 175 million migrants around the world, of whom about half are workers.[1]

In this chapter, we will explore some of the labour law issues raised by worker movement and migration. We will divide these into three main sections. First, we will consider how individual workers from other countries can secure the right to work in the UK (section 3.3). This varies according to whether they are citizens of another EU Member State, in which case they can come to the UK to work as of right, or whether they are citizens of a non-EU state, in which case they will need to secure a visa under the points-based immigration scheme. Second, we will consider the law on irregular migrants: people who either entered the UK illegally or who entered the UK legally but subsequently lost their right to work (section 3.4). We will examine their entitlement to labour rights, and the consequences for employers of hiring someone who has no right to work. And third, we will examine what law governs a

---

[1] http://www.ilo.org/global/standards/subjects-covered-by-international-labour-standards/migrant-workers/lang--en/index.htm (last visited 7 October 2014).

person's employment if they migrate to or from the UK (section 3.5). This is a technical 'conflict of laws' or 'private international law' issue, but it is also politically controversial in EU law because it is the subject of the hotly contested Posted Workers Directive (PWD).[2]

3.2 THEORETICAL FRAMEWORK AND SOURCES OF LAW

Since this topic is quite a diverse one, it is difficult to approach it with a single theoretical framework in mind. Here, we will consider three key elements that will contribute, to different degrees, to the discussion in this chapter. These are: human rights, specific international instruments dealing with migrant workers and EU law. Towards the end of the section, we will consider these elements in the light of national policy debates.

Before we begin, it is important to get a clear understanding of the notion of a 'migrant worker'. In simple terms, this is a person who moves from his or her home country to another country in order to work there. However, while some migrants move temporarily with a view to returning to their home state after a short period of work, others may put down roots in the host country. At some point, they cease to be 'migrants' and form part of the host state's labour force. This may be formally recognised by the state, for example, if they acquire the right of permanent residence. Whilst it is important to recognise the special issues faced by migrant workers, it is equally important not to attach the label 'migrant' to people forever.

'Irregular' migrants are those who either entered the country without permission to do so, or who entered the country lawfully but then became 'irregular', for example, by overstaying or by working when they had no legal right to do so.

3.2.1 Human rights

Human rights may be relevant to migrant workers in many different ways, depending on their circumstances, but two stand out as being of particular importance: the right not to be subjected to forced labour and the right not to be discriminated against.

The right not to be subjected to forced labour is an emanation of the right not to be enslaved, as Article 8 of the ICCPR illustrates:

(1) No one shall be held in slavery; slavery and the slave-trade in all their forms shall be prohibited.

(2) No one shall be held in servitude.

(a) No one shall be required to perform forced or compulsory labour . . .

It is relevant to the topic of migrant labour because not all migrants make a free choice to travel to another state in search of work. They may be trafficked by people who force them to work against their will, often without pay, or who hold them in 'debt bondage', where they are told that they cannot earn any money until they have 'paid off' the cost of the trafficker's so-called services. The ILO's Forced Labour Convention, 1930 defines forced labour as: 'all work or service which is exacted from any person under the menace of any penalty and for which the said person has not

---

[2] Directive 96/71/EC concerning the posting of workers in the framework of the provision of services, now supplemented by Directive 2014/67/EU on its enforcement.

offered himself voluntarily'.[3] The ILO gives a number of 'indicators' to help to identify forced labour:

> Abuse of vulnerability
>
> Deception
>
> Restriction of movement
>
> Isolation
>
> Physical and sexual violence
>
> Intimidation and threats
>
> Retention of identity documents
>
> Withholding of wages
>
> Debt bondage
>
> Abusive working and living conditions
>
> Excessive overtime[4]

The right not to be subjected to forced labour also appears in the ECHR and the Court has developed case-law requiring signatory states to take positive steps to investigate allegations of forced labour and to ensure that their law prohibits it.[5] We will examine this case-law in greater detail below. Although it is important not to overstate the point (or to dilute the definition of forced labour), a key indicator that a person's work is freely chosen is his or her right to resign from a particular job. This is an important safeguard against exploitation. As we shall see, this right is not always respected in the context of migrant workers.

A second human right of particular importance to migration situations is the right not to be discriminated against. This is relevant because migrants may experience discrimination on various grounds, but particularly because of their race or nationality. Article 26 ICCPR is typical:

> All persons are equal before the law and are entitled without any discrimination to the equal protection of the law. In this respect, the law shall prohibit any discrimination and guarantee to all persons equal and effective protection against discrimination on any ground such as race, colour, sex, language, religion, political or other opinion, national or social origin, property, birth or other status.

In English law, nationality forms part of the definition of 'race' for the purposes of the Equality Act 2010, so (for example) a non-UK national who is paid less by the employer than a colleague doing the same job who is a UK national would be able to bring a discrimination claim under the Act.[6] However, the courts have been reluctant to extend the concepts of race or nationality to incorporate discrimination based on migration status itself. This is apparent from the recent decisions in *Taiwo* and *Onu*.[7] In both cases, the claimants were Nigerian women who had come to the UK on domestic worker visas and had been subjected to abuse by their employers.

---

[3] Forced Labour Convention 1930 (No. 29) (adopted 28 June 1930, entered into force 1 May 1932), art 2(1).

[4] ILO, *Indicators of Forced Labour* (October 2012).

[5] *Siliadin* v *France* (2006) 43 EHRR 16; *Rantsev* v *Cyprus and Russia* (2010) 51 EHRR 1.

[6] Equality Act 2010, s 9.

[7] *Onu* v *Akwiwu*; *Taiwo* v *Olaigbe* [2014] EWCA Civ 279, [2014] ICR 571.

At the relevant time, the domestic worker visa entitled them to change employer but only if they reapplied for the visa, making them in practice dependent on the abusive employer for their right to be in the UK. Both claimed that they had been discriminated against as vulnerable migrant domestic workers. However, the Court of Appeal held that they could not succeed on a direct discrimination claim because their status did not correspond exactly to the protected characteristic of nationality.[8] Although only non-UK nationals could be migrant domestic workers, not all non-UK nationals currently working in the UK were migrant domestic workers or shared their particular vulnerability.

More generally, the idea that migrant status should be treated as a protected characteristic for discrimination purposes is politically controversial. There are various ways in which migrant workers are treated differently to non-migrants if we consider the immigration process as a whole. For example, EU migrants find it easier to enter the EU than non-EU migrants, but temporary EU migrants may find that they have worse terms and conditions of employment than local workers. Irregular migrants have far fewer rights than lawful migrants. Thus, migration is an area in which the relationship between government policy and basic principles of equal treatment is complex and sometimes fraught.

3.2.2 Instruments relating to migrant workers

Some international instruments deal specifically with the treatment of migrant workers. For example, the European Social Charter 1961, Article 18, encourages states to liberalise their rules on worker migration. Article 19 (accepted by the UK) sets out some specific duties:

> With a view to ensuring the effective exercise of the right of migrant workers and their families to protection and assistance in the territory of any other Contracting Party, the Contracting Parties undertake:
>
> (1) to maintain or to satisfy themselves that there are maintained adequate and free services to assist such workers, particularly in obtaining accurate information, and to take all appropriate steps, so far as national laws and regulations permit, against misleading propaganda relating to emigration and immigration;
>
> (2) to adopt appropriate measures within their own jurisdiction to facilitate the departure, journey and reception of such workers and their families, and to provide, within their own jurisdiction, appropriate services for health, medical attention and good hygienic conditions during the journey;
>
> (3) to promote co-operation, as appropriate, between social services, public and private, in emigration and immigration countries;
>
> (4) to secure for such workers lawfully within their territories, insofar as such matters are regulated by law or regulations or are subject to the control of administrative authorities, treatment not less favourable than that of their own nationals in respect of the following matters:
>
> (a) remuneration and other employment and working conditions;
>
> (b) membership of trade unions and enjoyment of the benefits of collective bargaining;
>
> (c) accommodation;

[8] ibid [48]–[50].

(5) to secure for such workers lawfully within their territories treatment not less favourable than that of their own nationals with regard to employment taxes, dues or contributions payable in respect of employed persons;

(6) to facilitate as far as possible the reunion of the family of a foreign worker permitted to establish himself in the territory;

(7) to secure for such workers lawfully within their territories treatment not less favourable than that of their own nationals in respect of legal proceedings relating to matters referred to in this article;

(8) to secure that such workers lawfully residing within their territories are not expelled unless they endanger national security or offend against public interest or morality;

(9) to permit, within legal limits, the transfer of such parts of the earnings and savings of such workers as they may desire;

(10) to extend the protection and assistance provided for in this article to self-employed migrants insofar as such measures apply.

The UK has been criticised by the ECSR for non-compliance with some aspects of this provision or for failing to provide enough evidence for the Committee to make a determination.[9] Of particular relevance for our purposes is that the Committee was not prepared to accept that the UK had taken sufficient steps to combat discrimination against migrant workers within para 4 simply by providing that such discrimination is unlawful under the Equality Act 2010. The Committee was concerned with whether migrant workers had a reasonable opportunity to enforce their rights.[10] Although this is an issue for all workers, it is of particular significance for migrants because they may not be in the UK for long enough to pursue legal proceedings, and may lack information about their rights. Article 19 is similar to the provisions of ILO Convention 97, the Migration for Employment Convention (Revised), 1949, which the UK has also ratified.[11]

The provisions we have considered so far address the situation of migrants who are lawfully on the territory of the signatory states. A much more controversial instrument is ILO Convention 143, the Migrant Workers (Supplementary Provisions) Convention, 1975.[12] This has not been ratified by the UK. Article 9 provides that:

(1) Without prejudice to measures designed to control movements of migrants for employment by ensuring that migrant workers enter national territory and are admitted to employment in conformity with the relevant laws and regulations, the migrant worker shall, in cases in which these laws and regulations have not been respected and in which his position cannot be regularised, enjoy equality of treatment for himself and his family in respect of rights arising out of past employment as regards remuneration, social security and other benefits.

(2) In case of dispute about the rights referred to in the preceding paragraph, the worker shall have the possibility of presenting his case to a competent body, either himself or through a representative.

---

[9] European Committee of Social Rights, Conclusions XIX-4 (United Kingdom) arts 7, 8, 16, 17 and 19 of the Charter (2011).

[10] ibid pp 20–27.

[11] ILO Convention 97, the Migration for Employment Convention (Revised), 1949 (adopted 1 July 1949, entered into force 22 January 1952).

[12] ILO Convention 143, the Migrant Workers (Supplementary Provisions) Convention, 1975 (adopted 24 January 1975, entered into force 9 December 1978).

This requires states to ensure that *irregular* migrants are at least entitled to be paid for the work they have done. This is controversial because, in general terms, states are often reluctant to do anything that might be thought to encourage irregular migration, and national courts may be unwilling to 'condone' unlawful behaviour. However, without such a rule, irregular migrants are open to exploitation because their employers know that they cannot enforce their rights.

The UK has only accepted rights for irregular migrants in the context of people who are victims of trafficking under the Council of Europe Convention on Action against Trafficking in Human Beings.[13] This Convention requires states to take steps to combat trafficking[14] (which is narrowly defined to cover the movement of people by coercion for the purposes of exploitation) but, at the same time, to protect victims, for example, by ensuring that they can claim compensation from the perpetrators[15] and are not prosecuted for criminal offences they were forced to commit.[16]

3.2.3 Migration in EU law

Migration occupies a complex position in EU law. On the one hand, a central purpose of the EU is to promote migration *within* the EU. The free movement of workers between Member States is one of the key pillars of the internal market. On the other hand, the EU has limited competence over migration into the EU from 'third' countries, a competence the UK has been reluctant to accept.

We will discuss the free movement of workers in EU law in greater detail below. For now, it is sufficient to note that this is a right guaranteed by Article 45 of the Treaty on the Functioning of the European Union (TFEU), supplemented by various directives and regulations.[17] Although this is a right for workers, the Court of Justice has interpreted this broadly to include those seeking work,[18] and those temporarily unable to work, for example, because of pregnancy.[19] Free movement of workers is intended to bring economic benefits by ensuring that workers can move to the places where there is the greatest demand, enabling those places to thrive economically, whilst combating unemployment elsewhere. However, as the EU has expanded, levels of wealth around the EU have diverged dramatically, and Member States are increasingly divided into those 'receiving' EU migrants and those 'exporting' EU migrants. This has led to tensions, not least in relation to the Posted Workers Directive (PWD).[20] This deals with people who are sent by an employer from their home state to work temporarily in a 'host' state. The PWD limits the extent to which these workers benefit from 'host' state employment rights.[21] This means that posted workers may be significantly worse off than locally hired workers alongside whom they are working. More fundamentally, the PWD has led to accusations that it is being used

---

[13] Council of Europe Convention on Action against Trafficking in Human Beings (adopted 16 May 2005) CETS 197.

[14] ibid arts 4–8.

[15] ibid art 15(3).

[16] ibid art 26.

[17] Council Directive 2004/38/EC on the right of citizens of the Union and their family members to move and reside freely within the territory of the Member States.

[18] Case C-292/89 *R v Immigration Appeal Tribunal, ex p Antonissen* [1991] ECR 1-745.

[19] Case C-507/12 *Saint Prix v Secretary of State for Work and Pensions* [2014] All ER (EC) 987.

[20] Above n 2.

[21] ibid art 3.

to undermine 'host' state labour standards because these can be undercut by workers posted from cheaper 'home' states. Of course, firms (and sometimes workers) from cheaper home states may argue that any attempt to withdraw their competitive advantage will make it harder for them to find work.

The EU only acquired competence to legislate over migration from 'third' countries with the Treaty of Amsterdam in 1997.[22] The UK has an 'opt-out' from this aspect of EU law and only occasionally decides to participate in a particular measure. The UK tends to opt in to coercive measures designed to combat irregular migration (which are aligned with domestic policy objectives) whilst avoiding measures that grant rights to migrants.[23] An interesting example of this for our purposes is the Employer Sanctions Directive.[24] This requires the Member States to legislate for penalties for employers found to be employing workers who are not lawfully on the Member State's territory.[25] As we shall see, such penalties already exist in English law. However, the UK has not signed up to the Directive. One possible reason for this might be that it requires states to enable irregular migrants to obtain back pay from their employers.[26] English law does not permit irregular migrants to claim for unpaid wages.

This 'fault line' within EU policy is revealed particularly sharply in EU law's treatment of nationality discrimination. This is prohibited in Article 21(2) of the EU Charter of Fundamental Rights, but only insofar as the Treaties allow for this, so it is not on an equal footing with other protected characteristics such as race or sex. Similarly, nationality discrimination is excluded from the Race Directive by Article 3(2).[27]

3.2.4 National policy

These various strands come together in the UK government's current policy on immigration. This has three core components. First, the government is unable to restrict migration from the EU, though it does attempt to discourage it in various ways. It has sought to restrict EU migrants' access to benefits in ways which may not necessarily be in accordance with EU law.[28] It has also recently introduced a prohibition on the practice adopted by some employment agencies of advertising vacancies in other Member States without advertising them in Britain, to give UK nationals and others already in the country a chance of obtaining the work.[29]

---

[22] Treaty of Amsterdam, art 2(15).

[23] Cathryn Costello and Emily Hancox, *Policy Primer: The UK, the Common European Asylum System and EU Immigration Law* (May 2014); A Geddes, 'Getting the Best of Both Worlds? Britain, the EU and Migration Policy' (2005) 81 International Affairs 723.

[24] Council Directive 2009/52/EC of 18 June 2009 providing for minimum standards on sanctions and measures against employers of illegally staying third-country nationals [2009] OJ L 168/24.

[25] ibid arts 3–5.

[26] ibid art 6.

[27] Council Directive 2000/43/EC of 29 June 2000 implementing the principle of equal treatment between persons irrespective of racial or ethnic origin [2000] OJ L180/22.

[28] See https://www.gov.uk/government/news/further-curbs-to-migrant-access-to-benefits-announced (last visited 7 October 2014), and see Case C-308/14 *Commission* v *United Kingdom* (application lodged 27 June 2014).

[29] The Conduct of Employment Agencies and Employment Businesses (Amendment) Regulations 2014, SI 2014/3351, inserting new s. 27A, Conduct of Employment Agencies and Employment Businesses Regulations 2003, SI 2003/3319.

The government's review of the 'balance of competences' between the UK and the EU appears to support reform in the area of free movement of workers.[30] Second, the government seeks to restrict migration from non-EU countries to a very considerable extent, though it makes exceptions for highly skilled migrants through the 'points-based' immigration scheme, usually where a particular job cannot be filled by a UK worker. And third, the government aims to combat trafficking and other forms of abuse through measures such as the Modern Slavery Bill though, as we shall see, there is a stronger emphasis here on criminalising traffickers than there is on protecting victims. The government's overall objective is summed up in the following quotation:

> Uncontrolled, mass immigration makes it difficult to maintain social cohesion, puts pressure on our public services and forces down wages for people on low incomes.[31]

This policy is, inevitably, controversial. Critics argue that migrants who want to work in the UK are likely to contribute more to the economy through taxes than they take through their use of public services. Moreover, it is not necessarily right to assume that there is a finite number of jobs in the UK: an influx of migrants may generate additional jobs as well as taking some jobs.

We cannot resolve these controversies here. But it is worth understanding the government's agenda before examining the law, since it exists in tension with EU policy and, sometimes, with human rights instruments too.

3.3 THE RIGHT TO WORK IN THE UK

Figuring out who has the right to work in the UK is a complex task. But we can state some basic propositions with a reasonable degree of confidence. Two broad groups of people clearly have the right to work in the UK. These are, firstly, people who are UK citizens or who have indefinite leave to remain in the UK, and secondly, nationals of other EU Member States.[32] Individuals outside these two categories will either need to obtain a work visa or to establish their right to work via some other means (for example, because they are a family member of an EU national). This book is not the place for a detailed discussion of all the different ways of establishing a right to work in the UK. Instead, we will focus on two issues: the rights enjoyed by EU nationals, and the employment law issues arising from work visas.

3.3.1 Free movement of workers in EU law

One of the central concerns of the EU is the establishment of the 'internal market'. The Member States are required by the TFEU to remove barriers to intra-EU trade, allowing the free movement of goods, services,[33] companies and (crucially for our purposes) workers between Member States. As a result, individuals from other Member States have a well-established right to come to the UK to take up employment.

---

[30] HM Government, *Review of the Balance of Competences between the United Kingdom and the European Union: Single Market: Free Movement of Persons* (2014).
[31] James Brokenshire MP, 27 February 2014, press release.
[32] And EEA states.
[33] The Treaty freedom to provide services gives firms a right to 'post' workers to other EU Member States independently of whether the workers themselves have rights under art 45. We will discuss posting in more detail below.

This brings with it other related rights such as the right to come to the UK to look for work, to bring family members, and to remain in the UK once the employment has ended (if certain conditions are met). Over time, the CJEU has built links between the right of free movement for workers and the broader notion of EU citizenship, making some of these rights less closely dependent on the individual's engagement in paid work. Our primary focus will be on rights for workers.

The legal framework

The basic right to free movement for workers is contained in Article 45 TFEU:

(1) Freedom of movement for workers shall be secured within the Union.

(2) Such freedom of movement shall entail the abolition of any discrimination based on nationality between workers of the Member States as regards employment, remuneration and other conditions of work and employment.

(3) It shall entail the right, subject to limitations justified on grounds of public policy, public security or public health:

(a) to accept offers of employment actually made;

(b) to move freely within the territory of Member States for this purpose;

(c) to stay in a Member State for the purpose of employment in accordance with the provisions governing the employment of nationals of that State laid down by law, regulation or administrative action;

(d) to remain in the territory of a Member State after having been employed in that State, subject to conditions which shall be embodied in regulations to be drawn up by the Commission.

(4) The provisions of this Article shall not apply to employment in the public service.

Article 45 has direct effect, so it can be invoked in the national courts.[34]

The concept of EU citizenship is enshrined in Article 20 TFEU. EU citizenship is derived from national citizenship, in the sense that every citizen of a Member State is also a citizen of the EU.[35] Citizenship entails various political rights (set out in Articles 22–24), but for our purposes, its most important features are the right not to be discriminated against on grounds of nationality,[36] and 'the right to move and reside freely within the territory of the Member States'.[37] After some initial uncertainty, the Court has confirmed that citizens can derive movement and residence rights directly from Article 21.[38]

Thus, an individual might derive a right to move from one Member State to another either from Article 45, as a worker or work-seeker, or from Article 21, as a citizen. Article 21 grants the right to move 'subject to the limitations and conditions laid down in the Treaties and by the measures adopted to give them effect'. In theory, the relationship between the two provisions is clear: Article 45 grants better rights to people who can prove that they are workers, with all EU nationals able to derive some more basic rights from their status as citizens. In practice, the boundaries are

---

[34] Case 41/74 *Van Duyn* v *Home Office* [1974] ECR 1337.

[35] TFEU, art 20(1).

[36] ibid art 18.

[37] ibid art 21.

[38] Case C-413/99 *Baumbast* v *Secretary of State for the Home Department* [2002] ECR I-7091 [80]–[94].

somewhat blurred because the Court has interpreted 'worker' quite broadly and is also in the process of developing better rights for citizens, as the discussion below will demonstrate.[39]

Further detail is provided in the Citizens' Rights Directive (hereafter 'CiRD').[40] This Directive was intended to codify the Court's case-law and to consolidate previous legislation (with some amendments) into a single point of reference for EU citizens, whether they are economically active (as workers or self-employed people) or not. As we shall see, however, since many of the rights found in the Directive are derived from the Treaty itself, the Court is not necessarily constrained by the Directive in interpreting them.[41] We will also examine some provisions of Regulation 492/2011, which governs workers' right to equal treatment in the employment sphere.

The UK's implementation of the CiRD is the Immigration (European Economic Area) Regulations 2006 (hereafter IEEAR).[42]

Who is a worker?

For the purposes of reg. 4(1) Immigration (European Economic Area) Regulations 2006, 'worker' is given the same meaning as it has in Article 45 TFEU.

In the context of Article 45, the CJEU has defined 'worker' in the following terms: 'the essential feature of an employment relationship . . . is that for a certain period of time a person performs services for and under the direction of another person in return for which he receives remuneration'.[43] It is clear from *Levin* that the work need not be full-time, nor is it a requirement that the individual should obtain any particular level of income from the work.[44] However, in the same case, the Court stated that the free movement rules applied 'only [to] the pursuit of effective and genuine activities, to the exclusion of activities on such a small scale as to be regarded as purely marginal and ancillary'.[45] On this basis, an individual performing work as part of a therapeutic programme for recovering drug addicts was held not to be a worker for the purposes of Article 45.[46] However, the Court has also made it clear that there is no place for an argument that the individual has taken a short-term job in order to acquire 'worker' status and the benefits it brings.[47] Provided the work meets the *Levin* test, it will count.

---

[39] For a discussion of the developing law on citizenship, which is an important topic of enquiry in its own right, see H de Waele, 'EU Citizenship: Revisiting its Meaning, Place and Potential' (2010) 12 European Journal of Migration and Law 319; M Wind, 'Post-National Citizenship in Europe: The EU as a Welfare Rights Generator' (2009) 15 Columbia Journal of European Law 239.

[40] Council Directive 2004/38/EC of 29 April 2004 on the right of citizens of the Union and their family members to move and reside freely within the territory of the Member States.

[41] For an interesting discussion of the Court's approach, see KE Sorensen, 'Reconciling Secondary Legislation with the Treaty Rights of Free Movement' (2011) 36 EL Rev 339.

[42] SI 2006/1003.

[43] Case 66/85 *Lawrie-Blum* v *Land Baden-Württemberg* [1986] ECR 2121 [17]. For a critique of the Court's approach to the definition, see C O'Brien, 'Social Blind Spots and Monocular Policy Making: The ECJ's Migrant Worker Model' (2009) 46 CMLR 1107.

[44] Case 53/81 *Levin* v *Staatssecretaris van Justitie* [1982] ECR 1035 [16].

[45] ibid [17].

[46] Case C-344/87 *Bettray* v *Staatssecretaris van Justitie* [1989] ECR 1621, but see also Case C-456/02 *Trojani* v *Centre Public d'Aide Sociale de Bruxelles (CPAS)* [2004] ECR I-7573.

[47] Case C-413/01 *Ninni-Orasche* v *Bundesminister für Wissenschaft, Verkehr und Kunst* [2003] ECR I-13187 [31].

However, 'worker' status for the purposes of EU law is not co-terminous with the individual's job. At an early stage, the CJEU recognised that it would be difficult for people to obtain work in another Member State without travelling there first, so it extended the concept of 'worker' to include job-seekers.[48] And when the employment terminates, Article 45(3)(d) TFEU gives former workers a right to remain in the host Member State if certain conditions are met.[49] This helps to render free movement more attractive by ensuring that an individual does not face immediate deportation if he or she is made redundant, for example.[50] The rights of former workers are spelt out in more detail in the CiRD.[51]

If an individual is engaged in economic activity in another Member State, but does not have worker status, he or she is likely to fall within Article 56 TFEU on the provision of services or Article 49 TFEU on freedom of establishment.[52] Freedom of establishment most obviously protects companies seeking to set themselves up in other Member States, but it also covers individual working people who are self-employed and want to set themselves up in another Member State. Self-employed people who are based in one Member State and travel to another on a temporary basis to work are more likely to fall within the concept of cross-border service provision. This means that the distinction between workers and self-employed people, which is often crucial in domestic law, is not particularly important in this context.

Exit, entry and residence

The most basic aspect of free movement is the right for a person to leave his or her own country and to travel to another country to look for a job, to take up a job, or to set up a business. This involves rights against both the individual's home state and the state he or she is seeking to enter.

The citizen's right to leave one Member State is dealt with in Article 4 of the CiRD, and the citizen's right to enter another Member State is dealt with in Article 5. The key point in both cases is that a valid identity card or passport should suffice for this purpose.[53] Citizens can only be turned away for reasons of public policy, security or health, and since these are derogations from a fundamental Treaty right they have been narrowly construed by the Court.[54] Thus, nationals of other EU states do not need a visa to enter the UK.[55]

The right to reside in another Member State is best considered in three stages: short-term, long-term and permanent. Union citizens (and their family members) are entitled

---

[48] Case C-292/89 R v *Immigration Appeal Tribunal, ex p Antonissen* [1991] ECR I-745; IEEAR 2006, reg 6(4).

[49] CiRD, art 7(3); IEEAR 2006, reg 5.

[50] Or taking maternity leave: Case C-507/12 *Saint Prix* v *Secretary of State for Work and Pensions* ECLI:EU:C:2014:2007.

[51] For example, CiRD, art 17.

[52] Case 48/75 *Procureur du Roi* v *Royer* [1976] ECR 497; IEEAR 2006, reg 4.

[53] CiRD, arts 4(2) and 5(1).

[54] These derogations are set out in art 45(3) TFEU with further detail (codifying much of the case-law) in arts 27–33 CiRD. For an example of the Court's approach, see Case 30/77 R v *Bouchereau* [1977] ECR 1999. See also IEEAR 2006, regs 19 and 21.

[55] IEEAR 2006, reg 11.

as of right to reside for up to three months in another Member State.[56] This is the 'initial right of residence' in reg. 13 IEEAR. There is no requirement to be economically active in order to enjoy this right. Those who are work-seekers may be able to stay for longer. Under Article 14(4)(b) CiRD, work-seekers may not be expelled after the expiry of the three-month period 'for as long as [they] can provide evidence that they are continuing to seek employment and that they have a genuine chance of being engaged'. This forms part of the 'extended right of residence' under reg. 14 IEEAR for 'qualified persons' as defined in reg. 6 to include job-seekers.

Under Article 7 of the CiRD and reg. 14 IEEAR, individuals who are workers or self-employed have a longer-term ('extended' in UK terminology) right of residence for as long as they are working or running a business.[57] EU law takes steps to ensure that the loss of the worker's job does not result in immediate loss of the right of long-term residence. Article 7(3) CiRD therefore provides that the individual may retain worker or self-employed status even if he or she is temporarily unable to work due to sickness or injury, or is involuntarily unemployed, or embarks on vocational training.[58] This is implemented in English law via the definition of a 'qualified person' in reg. 6 IEEAR.

After five years of continuous, lawful residence in another Member State, EU citizens (and their family members) acquire the right of permanent residence under Article 16 CiRD,[59] implemented in reg. 15 IEEAR. The significance of this is that the Member State can no longer require the EU citizen either to be a worker or self-employed person, or to have sufficient resources, as it can for the right of long-term residence under Article 7 and reg. 14. People who used to have worker or self-employed status, but whose working life ended through retirement or incapacity, may be able to acquire the right of permanent residence without the need for five years' residence, under the conditions laid down in Article 17 CiRD, implemented via the definition in reg. 5 IEEAR.

Opening up the EU labour market

The right to move from one Member State to another would not be of much assistance unless the worker had a good chance of obtaining employment in the host state. To that end, EU law prohibits discrimination in the conditions on which migrant workers can access jobs in the host state: for example, they cannot usually be required to comply with extra formalities or to have extra qualifications on top of the rules applied to host state nationals. As we shall see, the Court has taken the view that simply removing discrimination may not be enough to open up the EU's labour markets. It has also subjected a broader range of 'obstacles' to the free movement of workers to scrutiny.

General The right of EU migrant workers to equal treatment with nationals of the host Member State is guaranteed by Article 45(2) TFEU. This right is fleshed out in Regulation 492/2011, which codifies earlier legislation and case-law. Individuals can

---

[56] CiRD, art 6.
[57] The Member States are permitted to require compliance with certain formalities set out in arts 8–11 CiRD.
[58] See also *St Prix*, above n 50.
[59] The relevant formalities are set out in arts 19–21.

invoke these rights directly in the English courts. Regulations do not require national implementation, but Treaty provisions do. The UK implements Article 45 by means of the Equality Act 2010, which defines nationality discrimination (against anyone, not just nationals of EU Member States) as a form of race discrimination.[60] Thus, in theory at least, an individual claiming to have been discriminated against on nationality grounds in the UK would claim under the Equality Act 2010 with the EU provisions guiding its interpretation and filling any gaps.

Section I of the Regulation prohibits discrimination based on nationality in access to employment. The basic principle is set out in Article 1(1):

> Any national of a Member State shall, irrespective of his place of residence, have the right to take up an activity as an employed person, and to pursue such activity, within the territory of another Member State in accordance with the provisions laid down by law, regulation or administrative action governing the employment of nationals of that State.

Article 3 gives more specific examples of the kinds of practices that are prohibited, including special registration requirements or recruitment procedures for workers who are not nationals. Article 4 ensures that, where a Member State requires a firm to employ a quota of its own nationals, EU citizens also count towards the quota, and Article 6 prohibits the application of medical or vocational criteria which discriminate on grounds of nationality.[61] The right not to be discriminated against also extends to employers who employ workers from other Member States.[62]

There are two major exceptions to these provisions. The first is that 'conditions relating to linguistic knowledge required by reason of the nature of the post to be filled' are not precluded.[63] In *Groener*, the Court held that it was acceptable for a teacher in an Irish school to be required to have some knowledge of Irish (subject to a proportionality test) as part of the state's policy of promoting Irish as the national language, even though the teacher would not be required to use Irish in the classroom.[64] The second is that the employer may require a non-national to take a 'vocational test' before confirming the job offer.[65]

Discrimination on grounds of nationality is, of course, a complex concept, and some examples from the case-law may help to illustrate the different ways in which discrimination can arise. The most obvious form of discrimination is direct discrimination, in which nationality is used as a criterion for employment. Thus, in *Commission v Italy*, it was held that Italy had failed to fulfil its Treaty obligations because Italian law restricted employment as a private security guard to Italian nationals.[66] Nationality criteria can only be used for jobs in the public service involving the exercise of public powers.[67]

Indirect discrimination, in which a requirement is applied equally to nationals and to migrant workers, but is more difficult for migrant workers to satisfy, is also

---

[60] Equality Act 2010, s 9(1)(b).

[61] The Regulation does not address recognition of qualifications obtained in other Member States, a topic to which we will return below.

[62] Council Regulation (EU) 492/2011 of 5 April 2011 on freedom of movement for workers within the Union [2011] OJ L141/1, art 2.

[63] ibid art 3(1).

[64] Case C-379/87 *Groener v Minister for Education* [1989] ECR 3967 [12]–[24].

[65] Regulation 492/2011, art 6(2).

[66] Case C-283/99 *Commission v Italy* [2001] ECR I-4363.

[67] TFEU, art 45(4); Regulation 492/2011, art 8.

prohibited by the Court's case-law under Article 45 and by Article 3(1)(b) of the Regulation.[68] This can be illustrated using the *Scholz* case.[69] In that case, the claimant was applying for a job in Italy. The selection process involved awarding points for previous experience. The claimant's previous experience was in Germany, but the selectors only counted experience gained in Italy. The Court held that this constituted unlawful indirect discrimination. Whilst there is a possibility of justifying such discrimination if it pursues a legitimate aim and is proportionate, the Court found that the indirect discrimination in *Scholz* itself was unjustified.[70]

The concepts of direct and indirect discrimination are familiar in the Equality Act 2010. The *Kapenova* case is a recent example of the application of indirect discrimination in the EU nationality context.[71] Medical students in the UK complete a five-year degree followed by a two-year training programme working in hospitals before qualifying as doctors. Students from countries with six-year degree programmes are not eligible to enter the first year of the two-year training programme and may find it harder to secure practical experience in the UK. It was held in *Kapenova* that this was indirectly discriminatory against the category of 'non-UK nationals' but that it was justified: it pursued the legitimate aim of ensuring that training was not wasted on people who did not need it because they had already studied for a longer period of time.

In accordance with free movement law generally, the CJEU does not always consider claims through a discrimination lens. The Court sometimes chooses to focus instead on whether or not a particular measure might hinder the worker's exercise of free movement rights and, if so, whether it can be justified. An oft-cited formulation of this test comes from the *Gebhard* case, a case involving a self-employed person's freedom of establishment:

> . . . national measures liable to *hinder or make less attractive* the exercise of fundamental freedoms guaranteed by the Treaty must fulfil four conditions: they must be applied in a non-discriminatory manner; they must be justified by imperative requirements in the general interest; they must be suitable for securing the attainment of the objective which they pursue; and they must not go beyond what is necessary in order to attain it . . .[72]

The *Terhoeve* case provides a useful example in the context of the free movement of workers.[73] The case concerned a Netherlands national who spent part of the year working in the UK. When he returned home, he was liable for a higher rate of social security contributions than if he had worked throughout the year in the Netherlands. The Court regarded this as an 'obstacle' to free movement and did not consider whether or not it was also discriminatory.[74] The Dutch government's arguments on justification were rejected.[75] Since the Equality Act 2010 is formulated in terms of direct and indirect discrimination, anyone seeking to bring a claim in the English courts would either have to present it in those terms, or rely on directly effective EU law.

---

[68] Case 152/73 *Sotgiu* v *Deutsche Bundespost* [1974] ECR 153 [11].
[69] Case C-419/92 *Scholz* v *Opera Universitaria di Cagliari* [1994] ECR I-505.
[70] ibid [11].
[71] *Kapenova* v *Department of Health* [2014] ICR 884.
[72] Case C-55/94 *Gebhard* v *Consiglio dell'Ordine degli Avvocati e Procuratori di Milano* [1995] ECR I-4165 [37] (emphasis added).
[73] Case C-18/95 *Terhoeve* v *Inspecteur van de Belastingdienst Particulieren* [1999] ECR I-345.
[74] ibid [41].
[75] ibid [43]–[47].

An area of debate in EU law is the extent to which Article 45 applies to decision-makers other than national governments: in other words, does it have horizontal direct effect? It is clear from the well-known *Bosman* case that Article 45 is applicable to non-state bodies where they play a role in regulating access to employment.[76] In that case, the claimant challenged the rules on the transfer of football players between clubs which had been laid down by the sport's governing body, UEFA. In *Casteels*, the claimant was allowed to invoke Article 45 in respect of rules on pensionable service in different Member States contained in a collective agreement between his employer and a union.[77] And it is clear from *Angonese* that discrimination by employers may also be caught.[78] Angonese applied for a job with a bank in Bolzano, an area of Italy in which both Italian and German are spoken. The bank required its employees to have a certificate of bilingualism issued by the authorities in Bolzano. Angonese was bilingual but did not have the certificate. The Court held that this was indirectly discriminatory because it was easier for workers already resident in Bolzano (the vast majority of whom were Italian nationals) to obtain the certificate. This issue is entirely unproblematic in English law since the Equality Act 2010 applies broadly to employers, unions and other bodies regulating access to employment or training.[79]

Mutual recognition of qualifications We saw above that Article 6 of Regulation 492/2011 prohibits the use of 'vocational criteria' where they discriminate on grounds of nationality. The Court has been alert to the possibility that a requirement to have qualifications to perform a particular job may not be necessary and may either be discriminatory or a hindrance to free movement.[80]

Where qualifications are required for a particular post, there is an obvious hindrance to free movement if qualifications obtained in one Member State count for nothing in another. The CJEU developed some principles for this in the *Vlassopoulou* case,[81] but it was always anticipated that the matter would be dealt with by means of directives.[82] Directive 2005/36/EC is the central measure. This consolidates several earlier directives focusing on specific professions, and three 'horizontal' or 'system' directives focusing on mutual recognition of qualifications more generally. The directive applies to 'regulated professions'[83] and to those who work as employees or on a self-employed basis.[84] According to Article 4 of the directive, it is concerned with ensuring that those who are qualified to pursue a regulated profession in one Member State have their qualifications recognised by other Member States and are thus allowed to practise their profession in those other states on the same basis as those who qualified there. The directive draws an important distinction between

---

[76] Case C-415/93 *Union Royale Belge des Sociétés de Football Association ASBL v Bosman* [1995] ECR I-4921.

[77] Case C-379/09 *Casteels v British Airways plc* [2011] ECR 1379.

[78] Case C-281/98 *Angonese v Cassa di Risparmio di Bolzano SpA* [2000] ECR I-4139.

[79] Equality Act 2010, ss 39–59.

[80] Case C-76/90 *Säger v Dennemeyer* [1991] ECR I-4221.

[81] Case C-340/89 *Vlassopoulou v Ministerium für Justiz, Bundes- und Europaangelegenheiten Baden-Württemberg* [1991] ECR I-2357.

[82] TFEU, art 53.

[83] Council Directive 2005/36/EC of 7 September 2005 on the recognition of professional qualifications [2005] OJ L255/22, art 3.

[84] ibid art 2.

those who are established in one Member State and simply want to provide services in another Member State, and those who wish to establish themselves in another Member State. In the former case, the directive makes it possible for professionals to provide services on a temporary basis without the need for the host state to recognise their qualifications, though the host state is permitted to impose various regulatory requirements.[85] In the latter case, the professional must seek recognition of his or her qualifications.[86] Consolidating the older legislation, the directive provides a three-tier approach to this. First, certain listed professions such as medicine and nursing are subject to automatic mutual recognition. Second, where the host state requires professional knowledge for the practice of a particular profession, the individual's prior experience in another Member State must be recognised provided certain conditions are met. Third, if neither of the previous two options is applicable, there are general provisions requiring the host state to recognise equivalent qualifications earned in another Member State.

In the UK, the Directive is implemented by means of the European Communities (Recognition of Professional Qualifications) Regulations 2007[87] and by specific legislation for healthcare professionals. A new directive designed to streamline the recognition process must be implemented by 2016.[88]

Rights during employment Once an EU migrant worker has obtained a job in another Member State, he or she is entitled to equal treatment 'with the nationals of that Member State within the scope of the Treaty'.[89] More precise obligations can be found in Chapter 1, Section 2 of Regulation 492/2011. The most important provision is Article 7:

(1) A worker who is a national of a Member State may not, in the territory of another Member State, be treated differently from national workers by reason of his nationality in respect of any conditions of employment and work, in particular as regards remuneration, dismissal, and, should he become unemployed, reinstatement or re-employment.

(2) He shall enjoy the same social and tax advantages as national workers.

(3) He shall also, by virtue of the same right and under the same conditions as national workers, have access to training in vocational schools and retraining centres.

(4) Any clause of a collective or individual agreement or of any other collective regulation concerning eligibility for employment, remuneration and other conditions of work or dismissal shall be null and void in so far as it lays down or authorises discriminatory conditions in respect of workers who are nationals of the other Member States.

Article 8 provides that workers should enjoy equal treatment as regards trade union membership and workplace participation. Once again, the Court has adopted a broad understanding of equality in this context, so that both direct and indirect discrimination (where the latter cannot be justified) are caught.[90] In some cases, the Court has also applied the broader *Gebhard* formula discussed above, to catch 'obstacles' to free movement.[91]

[85] ibid Title II.
[86] ibid Title III.
[87] SI 2007/2781.
[88] Council Directive 2013/55/EU, [2013] OJ L354/132.
[89] CiRD, art 24.
[90] See, for example, Case C-224/01 *Köbler* v *Austria* [2003] ECR I-10239, on the treatment of service accrued in other Member States.
[91] Above n 72.

The Commission considers that the Member States have not done enough to ensure the effective implementation of the Regulation. To that end, a new directive has been enacted to facilitate workers' exercise of their rights.[92] This must be implemented by 2016. It requires the Member States to ensure that EU migrants have access to court to enforce their rights,[93] and that there is a designated national body responsible for promoting equal treatment of EU migrants.[94]

3.3.2 Migration from outside the EU

Given that, as we have just seen, the government has limited control over migration from the EU, it has taken a much tougher line on migration from non-EU countries. It is especially difficult for unskilled workers to obtain leave to enter the UK in order to work, though there is still some scope for skilled migrants to do so. The points-based immigration system gives employers a central role as 'sponsors' of migrant workers, so it is helpful to understand – in outline at least – how it works.

The detailed arrangements for entering the UK and obtaining leave to remain are set out in the Immigration Rules.[95] Since the control of migration is a prerogative power of the Crown exercised by the executive, the legal status of the Immigration Rules is a matter for debate. The Immigration Act 1971, s. 3(2), requires the Secretary of State to lay them before Parliament, but it is clear that they are not subordinate legislation. They are a statement of the Secretary of State's policy on immigration. But in *Pankina*, the Court of Appeal held that they should be treated as if they were legal rules giving rise to justiciable rights.[96] This meant that a material change to the Rules that was not laid before Parliament was void and of no effect. Later cases have, however, confined this to substantive changes affecting individuals' entitlements.[97]

For our purposes, two main parts of the Rules are relevant. Part 5 sets out the approach to work visas outside the points-based immigration system. These include work visas for representatives of overseas businesses seeking to come to the UK to work for those businesses, and the domestic work visa, which is for domestic workers of people migrating to the UK to come with them to work in their household on a temporary basis. Part 6A sets out the points-based immigration system. Tier 1 is for so-called 'high value migrants' and Tier 2 is for 'skilled workers'. Within each tier, there are sub-categories. For example, Tier 2 is divided into four sub-categories: intra-company transfers, general, minister of religion or sportsperson.

To explain how the system works without getting into too much detail, we will focus on the arrangements for Tier 2 (General) skilled workers.[98] An employer wishing to hire a worker from outside the UK and EU must apply for and obtain a

---

[92] Council Directive 2014/54/EU of 16 April 2014 on measures facilitating the exercise of rights conferred on workers in the context of freedom of movement for workers [2014] OJ L128/8.

[93] ibid art 3.

[94] ibid art 4.

[95] HC 395, as amended. The current set of rules is available at https://www.gov.uk/government/collections/immigration-rules.

[96] *Secretary of State for the Home Department v Pankina* [2010] EWCA Civ 719, [2011] QB 376.

[97] *R (Castro) v Secretary of State for the Home Department* [2012] EWHC 281 (Admin); *R (Alvi) v Secretary of State for the Home Department* [2012] UKSC 33, [2012] 1 WLR 2208.

[98] Immigration Rules, Part 6A, paras 245H–245HF-SD.

sponsorship licence.[99] The employer risks losing the licence unless it complies with its sponsorship duties, which include checking workers' qualifications and informing the authorities if workers breach their visa conditions.[100] Once the employer has a licence, it may issue 'sponsorship certificates' to migrant workers but only if certain conditions are met.[101] The job must have a suitable skill level and rate of pay. For a Tier 2 (General) visa, there is a long list of occupations but they are, for the most part, professional or managerial occupations (doctors, nurses, teachers, engineers and so on) for which a degree might be required[102] and which attract reasonably high salaries. The current minimum salary is set at £20,500.[103] Jobs entailing a lower skill level may only be sponsored under Tier 2 (General) if they appear on a list of 'shortage' occupations where the government accepts that there are not enough people with the relevant skills in the domestic labour market. The current list includes, for example, engineers in the oil and gas industries.[104] Finally, unless the job is in a shortage occupation, the employer must prove that there are no suitable UK or EU workers to do the job by satisfying the 'resident labour market test'.[105] This involves advertising the job in specified ways for 28 days.

Once the employer has offered the worker a job and issued a 'certificate of sponsorship', the worker must apply for a Tier 2 visa. The issuance of the 'certificate of sponsorship' does not guarantee that the worker will get the visa because there are other eligibility requirements to be met. For example, the individual must have a minimum level of savings in his or her bank account prior to applying (currently £945 for the previous 90 days) and must have a minimum level of competence in English.[106] Importantly, the 'certificate of sponsorship' is only valid for the particular job with the particular employer, so if the individual's job changes significantly or if the individual wants to change employer he or she will need to reapply for the Tier 2 visa.[107]

The government argues that the extensive role given to employers under these arrangements is justified because employers benefit from the employment of migrant workers, so they should contribute to the costs of managing the immigration system by paying fees and by monitoring workers' visa compliance. However, this policy approach is controversial because it builds a link between an individual's migration status and his or her job. As we saw above, the ability to resign is an important – if drastic – safeguard against abuse and exploitation. Tier 2 visa-holders are entitled to change jobs but they must reapply for their visa if they do so. More worryingly,

---

[99] UK Visas and Immigration, *Tier 2 and 5 of the points-based system – policy guidance for sponsors* (January 2014), Section 1.

[100] ibid Section 3.

[101] ibid Section 4.

[102] UK Visas and Immigration, *Tier 2 of the Points Based System – Policy Guidance* (August 2014), para 66; *Codes of Practice for Skilled Workers: Standard Occupational Classification (SOC) Codes* (April 2014). The worker does not have to have the relevant qualification but the job must be 'pitched' at a person with that level of qualification.

[103] UK Visas and Immigration, *Codes of Practice for Skilled Workers: Standard Occupational Classification (SOC) Codes* (April 2014).

[104] UK Visas and Immigration, *Tier 2 shortage occupation list, government-approved version* (April 2014), 2–3.

[105] UK Visas and Immigration, *Tier 2 and 5 of the points-based system – policy guidance for sponsors* (January 2014), Section 28.

[106] UK Visas and Immigration, *Tier 2 of the Points Based System – Policy Guidance* (August 2014), para 154 and paras 119ff respectively.

[107] ibid paras 198–199.

individuals who enter the UK on a domestic worker visa under Part 5 of the Rules (to work temporarily in a private household) are denied the opportunity to change employer during that time.[108] The government argues that there are other safeguards for these workers, including a requirement that the employer undertake to pay the NMW, but the removal (in 2012) of the right to change job has been criticised, including by the parliamentary Joint Committee on the draft Modern Slavery Bill.[109]

Given the administrative complexity for employers associated with navigating the sponsorship rules, some might be tempted to avoid the issue altogether by refusing to consider job applicants who do not have permission to work in the UK. However, this is likely to constitute unlawful discrimination. In the *Osborne Clarke* case, a firm of solicitors adopted a policy of not considering applicants for training contracts if they required a work visa.[110] This constituted indirect discrimination because the criterion of 'not needing a visa' was harder for non-EU nationals to comply with than others. The employer failed to justify its approach: it could not claim that it would be impossible to get visas for non-EU workers because it had not even tried to do so.

3.4 IRREGULAR MIGRATION

A key element of government immigration policy is to curb 'irregular' migration. As we noted above, this may take a variety of forms, from (at one extreme) trafficking by criminal gangs, to (at the other extreme) individuals who have entered the country lawfully but have breached their visa conditions. In this section, we will focus on two aspects of irregular migration with particular relevance for labour law: the effect of irregular migration on a worker's entitlement to employment rights, and the consequences for employers of employing irregular migrants.

3.4.1 Entitlement to employment rights

In general terms, it is possible for a claim in tort or contract to be barred by the doctrine of illegality. This doctrine is founded on public policy considerations and serves to prevent the courts from being called upon to 'condone' wrongdoing by providing wrongdoers with remedies. Not having the right to work in the UK is a common example of a situation in which a worker's claim might be defeated by illegality, though it is worth remembering that there are other possibilities too, unrelated to migration, for example, where the parties agree not to pay tax in respect of the employment relationship. The application of illegality in the employment context is problematic because of the risk that (given the inequality of bargaining power between the parties) the worker may not be aware of the illegality or may be coerced by the employer into accepting an employment arrangement tainted by illegality. The law seems to distinguish between three types of claim for these purposes: claims on the contract itself, claims relating to statutory employment rights, and tort claims.

The most straightforward situation is where the employer and employee enter into a contract knowing it to be illegal. If the employee tries to bring a claim on the

---

[108] Immigration Rules, Part 5, para 159A.

[109] Joint Committee on the draft Modern Slavery Bill, *Report – Draft Modern Slavery Bill*, HL Paper 166/HC 1019 (April 2014), Part 7.

[110] *Osborne Clarke Services v Purohit* [2009] IRLR 341.

contract, it will be found to be void for illegality and the claim will fail. For example, in *Napier*, the claimant brought an action for wrongful dismissal.[111] The parties had agreed a wage of £13 per week and an 'expenses' payment of £6 per week. The judge found that the claimant was unlikely to incur any expenses in the performance of his job so the 'expenses' payment was a means of disguising his true earnings to avoid paying income tax. The contract was illegal because it defrauded the tax authorities so the claimant's wrongful dismissal action failed.

Matters are slightly more complex in relation to statutory employment rights. These rights do not usually involve enforcing the contract itself, but of course the presence of a contract (of the appropriate type) is necessary in order to demonstrate the individual's entitlement to the rights.[112] Again, then, if the parties have deliberately entered into an illegal contract, the claim will fail. In the *Tomlinson* case, the claimant was paid in cash with a view to avoiding the payment of tax.[113] The EAT held that she could not bring claims for unfair dismissal or redundancy because the claims arose from a contract of employment designed to defraud the tax authorities.

In some cases, the employee might argue that – although he or she understood the arrangements – he or she did not realise they were illegal. Such claims generally fail on the basis that ignorance of the law is no defence. The *Salvesen* case is a good example.[114] In that case, the parties had agreed that part of the claimant's wage would be paid to him directly and part to a company he ran with his wife. The claimant argued that he did not know that the arrangements were a device to avoid the payment of income tax and therefore illegal. Nevertheless, his claim was barred. One way of thinking about this is that even if the employee did not understand the law, it would have been clear to him that the arrangements did not reflect the true nature of his relationship with the employer, thus putting him on notice that there might be a problem.

However, the courts are not quick to find illegality where the parties have acted in good faith but have mischaracterised their relationship. This is quite important given the difficulties of determining employment status and identifying 'fake' arrangements.[115] In the *Enfield* case, the claimant was hired under a contract for services but, when the contract was terminated, sought to argue that he had been an employee all along for the purposes of bringing an unfair dismissal claim.[116] The employer tried to defend the claim by arguing that the fake self-employment arrangements were designed to avoid tax and should thus be regarded as 'tainted by illegality'. But the Court of Appeal allowed the employee's claim to proceed on the basis that there had not been any deliberate attempt by either party to defraud the tax authorities.

So far, we have focused on contract claims and claims to statutory employment rights based on the individual's contractual relationship with the employer. But some employment rights give rise to claims in tort, the best-known example being

---

[111] *Napier v National Business Agency Ltd* [1951] 2 All ER 264 (CA).
[112] See Chapter 4.
[113] *Tomlinson v Dick Evans 'U' Drive Ltd* [1978] ICR 639 (EAT).
[114] *Salvesen v Simons* [1994] ICR 409.
[115] See Chapter 4.
[116] *Enfield Technical Services Ltd v Payne* [2008] EWCA Civ 393, [2008] ICR 1423.

discrimination, which is treated for the purposes of awarding compensation as a 'statutory tort'.[117] In the recent *Hounga* decision, the Supreme Court used this distinction to enable a claimant to bring a race discrimination claim even though her employment was illegal.[118] With the assistance of the employer, the claimant had fraudulently obtained a visitor's visa to enter the UK, had worked despite having no right to do so, and had overstayed the visa. The Supreme Court accepted that any claims based on her contract – or based on statutory employment rights linked to the contract, like unfair dismissal – were barred by illegality.[119] But the role of illegality in relation to tort claims is less clear-cut. One view is that illegality only bars a claim in tort where there is an 'inextricable link' between the claim and the illegality. All the judges in the Supreme Court agreed that this test was not met. Ms Hounga's immigration offences 'merely provided the setting or context in which [the tort of discrimination] was committed, and to allow her to recover for that tort would not amount to the court condoning what it otherwise condemns'.[120] The majority further held that the employer's role in bringing the claimant to the UK amounted to, or came close to, 'trafficking' within the meaning of the relevant international instruments.[121] Ms Hounga had been brought to the UK whilst still a child with a promise that she would be sent to school (a promise which was not kept) and she was threatened and forced to work for no pay. On this reasoning, there was a strong public interest in enabling Ms Hounga to bring a claim, in order to satisfy the UK's international obligations, and this public interest was not outweighed by the need of the legal system to avoid condoning illegality. The minority rejected this argument, holding that the fact of having been trafficked did not absolve Ms Hounga from any consequences of immigration offences she had knowingly (and without coercion) committed.[122]

The outcome in *Hounga* is welcome because it enables irregular migrants to bring some employment claims and softens the generally tough position taken by English law on illegality. It might be argued that discrimination claims are particularly serious so it is right that they should be allowed to proceed even where other types of claim, like unfair dismissal, are barred. However, there does seem to be an element of luck in the fact that discrimination claims can be characterised as tortious, not least because they – like unfair dismissal claims – depend on the claimant having a contract of the right type with the employer.

More generally, it might be questioned as a matter of policy whether the courts' approach to illegality is helpful in this context. Although individuals sometimes profit by illegal employment arrangements – either because they do not have to pay tax on their earnings or because they are able to work in the UK when they do not have permission to do so – people in these situations are often among the most vulnerable, low-paid members of society. They might well know that what they are doing is illegal but they might be pressurised by the employer into accepting 'cash in hand' work or they might be desperate to improve their lot in life through migration. It is sometimes suggested that barring them from claiming employment rights will deter

---

[117] Equality Act 2010, s 124(6), and see *Ministry of Defence* v *Cannock* [1994] ICR 918.

[118] *Hounga* v *Allen* [2014] UKSC 47, [2014] 1 WLR 2889. For a more detailed discussion see Alan Bogg and Sarah Green, 'Rights are not just for the Virtuous: What *Hounga* Means for the Illegality Defence in the Discrimination Torts' ILJ forthcoming.

[119] ibid [24].

[120] ibid [67].

[121] ibid [46]–[52].

[122] ibid [64].

irregular migration. But the flipside is that employers face no deterrent to abusing and exploiting illegal employees, knowing that they have few enforceable rights. We saw above that at least some international instruments allow irregular migrants to bring some basic claims, such as claims for unpaid wages.[123] And, more generally, it is not clear why the status of being an irregular migrant should serve to deny an individual human rights protections. This is an area in which legislative intervention to set out some core protections for irregular migrants would be desirable (if highly unlikely in practice) rather than leaving a difficult and sensitive policy issue to the courts to grapple with using unsuitable common law tools.

3.4.2 Issues for employers

The government's crackdown on irregular migration takes two main forms. First, it is developing a regime to combat forced labour and trafficking. This is unlikely to have any impact on 'legitimate' employers but it is important to know the main provisions in outline. Second, legislation requires all employers to check that workers have the right to work in the UK before employing them. Failure to do so can have serious consequences. We will examine each aspect of the regime in turn.

Forced labour and trafficking

We will consider two offences in this section: 'slavery, servitude and forced or compulsory labour', and trafficking.[124] Forced labour does not have any necessary connection to migration. One of the most well-publicised recent convictions for this offence involved the exploitation of homeless people who were not migrants.[125] However, it is a particular risk for irregular migrants: unscrupulous 'employers' can use the threat of notifying the immigration authorities as a device to exploit workers and discourage them from seeking help. The trafficking offence deals with those who bring people to the UK in order to exploit them.

The slavery and forced labour offence is currently found in s. 71 Coroners and Justice Act 2009:

(1) A person (D) commits an offence if–

  (a) D holds another person in slavery or servitude and the circumstances are such that D knows or ought to know that the person is so held, or

  (b) D requires another person to perform forced or compulsory labour and the circumstances are such that D knows or ought to know that the person is being required to perform such labour.

(2) In subsection (1) the references to holding a person in slavery or servitude or requiring a person to perform forced or compulsory labour are to be construed in accordance with Article 4 of the Human Rights Convention (which prohibits a person from being held in slavery or servitude or being required to perform forced or compulsory labour).

---

[123] Above n 12.

[124] The UK is a signatory to the Council of Europe Convention, above n 13, but does not participate in Directive 2011/36/EU on preventing and combating trafficking in human beings and protecting its victims.

[125] *Attorney General's Reference (Nos 2, 3, 4 and 5 of 2013)* [2013] EWCA Crim 324, [2013] 2 Cr App R (S) 71.

At the time of writing, the government is proposing to consolidate this offence in the Modern Slavery Bill. The new version of the offence would carry a maximum sentence of life imprisonment, compared with 14 years at present, and would direct the courts to have regard to any particular vulnerability on the part of the individual being held, for example, if he or she was a child.[126]

The offence was introduced in response to the decision of the ECtHR in *Siliadin* v *France*.[127] Since the ECtHR's case-law is (and will remain) relevant to the interpretation of the offence, it is worth considering the Court's approach. Article 4 ECHR provides:

(1) No one shall be held in slavery or servitude.

(2) No one shall be required to perform forced or compulsory labour.

In *Siliadin*, the claimant was taken to France as a child and made to work as a 'housemaid'. She was not paid or given time off, and her passport was confiscated. Promises that her immigration status would be regularised and that she would be sent to school were never fulfilled. The Court applied the definition of forced labour from ILO Convention 29, the Forced Labour Convention of 1930: 'all work or service which is exacted from any person under the menace of any penalty and for which the said person has not offered himself voluntarily'. It found that the claimant did not work voluntarily and that she was threatened with a 'penalty' because her 'employers' put her in fear of being handed over to the police as an irregular migrant. Although the Court accepted that she was not enslaved, it held that she was held in servitude, defined as 'an obligation to provide one's services that is imposed by the use of coercion'.[128] The Court placed particular emphasis on the fact that she was a minor. The Court further held that Article 4 imposed on states a positive obligation to ensure that those responsible for violations of the Article could be convicted of appropriate criminal offences and subjected to suitable penalties. France was in breach of this obligation. The Court confirmed in *CN* that – prior to the introduction of the s. 71 offence – the UK was similarly in breach of Article 4.[129] The state's positive obligation was further developed in the *Rantsev* case to include obligations to investigate potential instances of forced labour or trafficking (either in response to a complaint or of the authorities' own motion), and to take steps to remove individuals at risk of Article 4 violations from harmful situations.[130]

The trafficking offence is currently found in the Asylum and Immigration (Treatment of Claimants, etc.) Act 2004, s. 4:

(1A) A person ("A") commits an offence if A intentionally arranges or facilitates–

(a) the arrival in, or entry into, the United Kingdom or another country of another person ("B"),

---

[126] Modern Slavery Bill, cl 1 and cl 5.

[127] *Siliadin* v *France* (2006) 43 EHRR 16. For discussion, see Virginia Mantouvalou, 'Slavery, Servitude, Forced and Compulsory Labour in the European Convention on Human Rights', in Filip Dorssemont *et al.* (eds), *The European Convention on Human Rights and the Employment Relation* (Hart 2013).

[128] *Siliadin*, above n 127, [124].

[129] *CN* v *United Kingdom* (2013) 56 EHRR 24.

[130] *Rantsev* v *Cyprus and Russia* (2010) 51 EHRR 1.

(b) the travel of B within the United Kingdom or another country, or

(c) the departure of B from the United Kingdom or another country, with a view to the exploitation of B . . .

(4) For the purposes of this section a person is exploited if (and only if)–

(a) he is the victim of behaviour that contravenes Article 4 of the Human Rights Convention (slavery and forced labour) . . .

(b) he is subjected to force, threats or deception designed to induce him–

  (i) to provide services of any kind,

  (ii) to provide another person with benefits of any kind, or

  (iii) to enable another person to acquire benefits of any kind, or

(c) a person uses or attempts to use him for any purpose within sub-paragraph (i), (ii) or (iii) of paragraph (c), having chosen him for that purpose on the grounds that–

  (i) he is mentally or physically ill or disabled, he is young or he has a family relationship with a person, and

  (ii) a person without the illness, disability, youth or family relationship would be likely to refuse to be used for that purpose.

The exploitation may be done by A or by another person, and in any part of the world. Thus, the offence is committed both where B is brought to the UK to be exploited or sent abroad to be exploited. The definition of exploitation is potentially broader than the conduct covered by Article 4 ECHR since s. 4(4)(c) may apply to less extreme situations including those perpetrated by deception. Again, the trafficking offence will be consolidated in the Modern Slavery Bill, with some amendments[131] and an increase in the maximum sentence from the current 14 years' imprisonment to life.[132]

A new development in the Modern Slavery Bill is the proposed introduction, in clause 39, of a defence for victims who have themselves committed criminal offences. It is widely believed that a major deterrent to victims seeking assistance from the authorities is fear that they may be prosecuted for offences they have committed, often under compulsion from traffickers or 'employers'. At the moment, the Crown Prosecution Service uses its discretion to decide whether or not to prosecute in these situations.[133] The defence does not apply to serious crimes listed in Schedule 3.

Despite the current political focus on forced labour and trafficking, anti-slavery advocates remain critical of the government's position. They argue that there is insufficient effort to protect victims of trafficking, for example, by enabling them to regularise their status in the UK (rather than risking deportation if they come forward)

---

[131] Modern Slavery Bill, cl 2. The new offence includes trafficking for the purposes of sexual exploitation which is currently addressed separately.

[132] Modern Slavery Bill, cl 5.

[133] The guidance is available here: http://www.cps.gov.uk/legal/h_to_k/human_trafficking_and_smuggling/#a16 (last visited 8 October 2014).

or to claim compensation for the harm they have suffered.[134] The Council of Europe's monitoring committee on the issue has also been critical of the UK's efforts under the Convention on trafficking, again noting that the UK's policies are stronger on criminalisation of trafficking than on victim protection.[135]

Penalties for employing illegal workers

A key plank of the government's policy to combat irregular migration is to make it difficult for irregular migrants to obtain work in the UK. The thinking is that this will deter irregular migrants from coming to the UK and force those already in the country to leave. Inevitably, the policy is controversial. Critics argue that irregular migrants are unlikely to be deterred by these kinds of initiatives because they may not be aware of them before they arrive in the UK, and once they are here, they are likely to be forced to take work in the informal economy without any access to basic employment rights. The policy is put into effect by targeting employers. It is a criminal offence to employ someone knowing that he or she does not have the right to work in the UK. And an employer may be required to pay a 'civil penalty' if it unwittingly employs someone without the right to work in the UK unless it can prove that it carried out a 'right to work' check. The relevant provisions are found in the Immigration, Asylum and Nationality Act 2006.

It is worth noting that the definition of employment for these purposes is 'employment under a contract of service or apprenticeship, whether express or implied and whether oral or written'.[136] Thus, the employer is only potentially liable in respect of employees, not workers or self-employed people. However, given the difficulties of accurately determining a person's employment status, employers are well-advised to comply with the 2006 Act in respect of anyone who is not clearly self-employed.

The criminal offence is found in s. 21(1) of the Act:

> A person commits an offence if he employs another ("the employee") knowing that the employee is an adult subject to immigration control and that–
>
> (a) he has not been granted leave to enter or remain in the United Kingdom, or
>
> (b) his leave to enter or remain in the United Kingdom–
>
>   (i) is invalid,
>
>   (ii) has ceased to have effect (whether by reason of curtailment, revocation, cancellation, passage of time or otherwise), or
>
>   (iii) is subject to a condition preventing him from accepting the employment.

Importantly, the employer is only guilty of an offence if it *knowingly* employs someone who does not have the right to work. The offence attracts a fine or a prison term of up to two years.[137]

---

[134] See, for example, comments by Anti-Slavery International at http://www.antislavery.org/english/press_and_news/news_and_press_releases_2009/modern_slavery_bill_draft_fails_the_victims_of_slavery.aspx (last visited 8 October 2014).

[135] Committee of the Parties to the Council of Europe Convention on Action against Trafficking in Human Beings, *Recommendation CP(2012)10 on the implementation of the Council of Europe Convention on Action against Trafficking in Human Beings by the United Kingdom* (November 2012).

[136] Immigration, Asylum and Nationality Act 2006 (IANA 2006), s 25(b).

[137] ibid s 21(1).

Under s. 15 of the Act, the employer of a person who does not have the right to work in the UK may be required to pay a civil penalty. The current maximum is set at £20,000.[138] The employer may establish an 'excuse' under s. 15(3) by showing that it did not know that the worker did not have the right to work and that it complied with the requirements of the Immigration (Restrictions on Employment) Order 2007, Articles 3–7.[139] In effect, this requires the employer to conduct a 'right to work' check on each person it employs. The employee or worker must produce documents from a prescribed list, and the employer must check their validity. The employer is not expected to identify sophisticated forgeries but is supposed to conduct basic checks such as making sure that the photograph on a passport resembles the person presenting the passport. The employer must repeat the checks if the individual only establishes the right to work in the UK for a limited period of time. If the employer has an 'excuse', it is not liable to pay a penalty. Importantly, the penalty may be issued without considering whether the employer has an 'excuse',[140] so the employer's right to object to the notice under s. 16 is an important stage in the procedure. At that point, the employer has the opportunity to establish the 'excuse'. The employer may also appeal to the court under s. 17.

There are two Codes of Practice issued under the Act. One explains how the penalty system works.[141] Of particular interest in this Code is the mechanism for calculating how much the employer has to pay in the event that it is liable under s. 15. If the employer has not been found to be employing illegal workers within the past three years, reports suspected illegal workers to the Home Office, co-operates with the investigation and has generally good 'right to work' procedures in place, the penalty may be reduced to zero and a warning notice issued instead. Where the employer can only establish some of these matters, its liability will be reduced but not eliminated. The penalty applies for each illegal worker employed.

The other Code of Practice issued under the Act attempts to reconcile employers' obligations in relation to illegal working with employers' obligations under the Equality Act 2010.[142] The Code makes clear that employers should conduct 'right to work' checks in relation to all their staff and should not single people out on the basis of stereotypical assumptions about their right to work. For example, it would clearly be discriminatory (as well as inadequate for the purposes of s. 15) for the employer only to conduct 'right to work' checks in relation to black and ethnic minority employees.

The 'right to work' regime interacts in important ways with unfair dismissal law.[143] If the employer discovers that an employee does not have the right to work, or that his or her temporary right to work has expired, it will need to terminate the employment or face civil, if not criminal, liability. Under ERA 1996, s. 98(2)(d) there is a potentially fair dismissal where 'the employee could not continue to work in the position which

---

[138] Immigration (Employment of Adults Subject to Immigration Control) (Maximum Penalty) Order 2008, SI 2008/132, art 2 (as amended).

[139] SI 2007/3290.

[140] IANA 2006, s 15(5).

[141] Home Office, *Code of Practice on Preventing Illegal Working: Civil Penalty Scheme for Employers* (May 2014).

[142] Home Office, *Code of Practice on Avoiding Unlawful Discrimination while Preventing Illegal Working* (May 2014).

[143] Unfair dismissal law is only relevant where the individual meets the qualifying conditions, e.g. being an employee with two years' continuous service: see Chapter 9.

he held without contravention (either on his part or on that of his employer) of a duty or restriction imposed by or under an enactment'. However, if the employer thinks that it is unlawful to continue employing the individual but is mistaken, its reliance on s. 98(2)(d) will fail, as in the *Kelly* case.[144] It might be able to rely on SOSR in the alternative (as suggested in *Kelly*) because of its 'genuine belief' that employing the individual was unlawful. But this is difficult to reconcile with the basic principle that the employer must give the reason that it had at the time of the dismissal.[145]

It is tempting to assume that, once it is established that the employee does not have the right to work, the employer will be found to have acted reasonably in treating this as a reason for dismissal. However, as *Kelly* makes clear, the reasonableness of the dismissal depends on the circumstances.[146] Thus, it would not be reasonable to dismiss the individual on immigration grounds if the employer was at fault or if the breach could easily be rectified. The employer may also need to follow a fair procedure, giving the employee an opportunity to explain the situation before any action is taken.

Employers must also be careful if they decide to suspend the employee while questions of immigration status are resolved. This is clear from the EAT's decision in *Okuoimose* v *City Facilities Managment (UK) Ltd*.[147] The claimant was a Nigerian national who was married to a Spanish national. She had the right to live and work in the UK as the spouse of an EU citizen. Because of difficulties with her papers she struggled to prove this to her employer. The employer suspended her until the difficulties were resolved. She brought a successful claim for unlawful deductions from wages during the period of suspension.[148] The EAT held that she had the right to work throughout. The employer's fear of liability under the civil penalty regime could not be relied upon to defend a claim for wages under a lawful contract of employment.

Overall, then, employers should proceed carefully in this area. They must conduct 'right to work' checks on all employees, both to comply with immigration law and to avoid allegations of unlawful discrimination. But the courts have, in effect, held that they may not put their fear of immigration penalties above basic fairness to the employee: for example, summarily dismissing someone because the employer suspects that he or she has lost the right to work may well be found to be an unfair dismissal.

3.5 QUESTIONS OF JURISDICTION

Most people probably assume that anyone who works in England is governed by English employment law and can bring claims in the English courts and tribunals, and that anyone who works outside England is not governed by English employment law and cannot bring claims in England. However, in cases with an international dimension, matters are considerably more complicated than this. It is important to distinguish three questions:

(1) Where can the individual bring his or her claim?

---

[144] *Kelly* v *University of Southampton* [2008] ICR 357.
[145] See Chapter 9.
[146] *Kelly*, above n 144, [56]–[66].
[147] (2011) UKEAT/0192/11.
[148] See Chapter 7.

(2) What is the law applicable to the individual's contract of employment? Is it English law or the law of some other country?

(3) Is the individual entitled to statutory rights under English law? We will consider this question for people sent to the UK from countries outside the EU, people 'posted' temporarily to the UK from other EU Member States, and people from the UK who are sent by their employer to work abroad but still wish to claim under English law.

Although this is quite a technical area of law, there are a couple of important policy issues to bear in mind. First, although private international law generally places emphasis on the autonomy of the parties to arrange their own affairs, contracts in the employment sphere require different treatment because of the inequality of bargaining power between the parties. This means that employees may need to be protected against, for example, an attempt by the employer to choose governing law for the contract that is less worker-protective than the law that would otherwise apply. Second, there are important public policy or regulatory issues at stake for the state. For example, the UK government might want to ensure that everyone working in the UK at any given time is paid the national minimum wage (NMW). If workers could come to the UK temporarily from other countries and be paid at 'home' rates instead of the NMW, the UK might face an influx of migrants from countries with lower minimum wages who would 'undercut' local workers. On one view, this is simply the exercise of a competitive advantage on their part: they get jobs by being cheaper to employ. On the other hand, from the government's perspective, this is likely to undermine the policy underlying the NMW: that it sets a 'floor' of pay for everyone. As we shall see, the state's capacity to override the parties' choices and to apply its own legislation to everyone on its territory is not always straightforward, particularly in EU law.

3.5.1 Question 1: the appropriate forum

In cases with a foreign element, there are two routes to establishing the jurisdiction of the English courts or tribunals over the matter: where the Brussels I Regulation applies and where it does not.[149] We will examine each in turn.

The Brussels I Regulation applies within the EU. It makes special provision for disputes arising out of individual contracts of employment with a view to protecting the employee as the weaker party to the relationship. Article 19 provides:

An employer domiciled in a Member State may be sued:

(1) in the courts of the Member State where he is domiciled; or

(2) in another Member State:

(a) in the courts for the place where the employee habitually carries out his work or in the courts for the last place where he did so, or

(b) if the employee does not or did not habitually carry out his work in any one country, in the courts for the place where the business which engaged the employee is or was situated.

---

[149] Regulation (EC) 44/2001 of 22 December 2000 on jurisdiction and the recognition and enforcement of judgments in civil and commercial matters [2000] OJ L12/1.

Thus, the Regulation gives the employee the option of suing the employer in the Member State where he or she normally works rather than where the employer is domiciled,[150] which is likely to be more convenient in most cases.[151]

Where the employer is not domiciled in the EU but has a branch or establishment in a Member State and the dispute relates to that branch or establishment, it is treated for these purposes as domiciled in that Member State.[152] This is intended to be facilitative but, as Grušić points out,[153] it may disadvantage employees in some fact situations, as illustrated by *Six Constructions Ltd v Humbert*.[154] In that case, the claimant was French and worked outside the EU for a non-EU employer with a branch in Belgium. Since there was no jurisdiction under Article 19(2), he was forced to proceed under Article 19(1) and bring proceedings in Belgium, even though – absent the Brussels I Regulation – he would have been able to bring proceedings in France under the ordinary rules of French law. The basic rule in English law outside the Brussels regime is that if the employer is 'present' in the jurisdiction and can be served with process, an English court will have jurisdiction.[155]

The Brussels I Regulation has been 'recast' and the new version will take effect in January 2015.[156] Article 19 becomes Article 21 and contains a significant new addition in Article 21(2). This allows the employee to sue an employer not domiciled in a Member State in accordance with the provisions of what used to be Article 19(2). So, for example, if the employer is domiciled in New York but the employee normally works in England, he or she will be able to sue in the English courts under this provision. Under the current regime, an employee who wants to sue an employer not domiciled in a Member State may only do so if the rules of that Member State allow him or her to do so.[157] However, this reform still does not address the problem in the *Six Constructions* case.

There are two points arising out of this discussion. The first is that, in general terms, it is desirable for the forum and the applicable law to be aligned, for the obvious reason that it is simpler for a court to apply the law of its own jurisdiction, with which it is familiar, rather than having to grapple with foreign law. We will consider the applicable law in the next section. But the second is that it is likely to be difficult for an employee to bring proceedings anywhere other than in a place with which he or she has close connections: his or her place of work or where he or she is domiciled.[158] The Brussels regime accommodates the former, to a certain extent, but not the latter.

---

[150] Domicile is determined in accordance with Regulation 44/2001, arts 59 and 60.

[151] Under art 21, the parties may agree on a forum but only if they do so after the dispute has arisen or if it gives the employee additional options to those afforded by the Regulation itself.

[152] Regulation 44/2001, art 18(2).

[153] Ugljesa Grušić, 'Jurisdiction in Employment Matters under Brussels I: a Reassessment' (2012) 61 ICLQ 91, 102–104.

[154] Case C-32/88 *Six Constructions Ltd v Humbert* [1989] ECR 341.

[155] Lord Collins, *Dicey, Morris & Collins on The Conflict of Laws* (15th edn, Sweet & Maxwell 2014) para 11R–101.

[156] Council Regulation 1215/2012 of 12 December 2012 on jurisdiction and the recognition and enforcement of judgements in civil and commercial matters [2012] OJ L351/1.

[157] Regulation 44/2001, art 4.

[158] Grušić, above n 153, 97–99, discusses these and other competing considerations.

3.5.2 Question 2: the applicable law

The basic starting-point in contract law is always the parties' freedom of contract: their right to choose their own arrangements.[159] Thus, the parties are in principle free to decide which country's law governs their contract: to include a 'choice of law' clause. Where the parties do not specify the law applicable to their contract, the Rome I Regulation lays down a set of rules for determining the 'objectively' applicable law.[160]

In the employment context, giving free rein to the parties' choice could give rise to difficulties because – given the inequality of bargaining power between most employees and their employers – it would be open to unscrupulous employers to insert a 'choice of law' clause to the disadvantage of the employee. A person working in England could find that his or her contract was governed by the law of a much less worker-protective state. The Rome I Regulation makes special provision for contracts of employment to address this situation.

Basic principles

Contracts of employment are dealt with in Article 8(1) of the Rome I Regulation:

> An individual employment contract shall be governed by the law chosen by the parties in accordance with Article 3.

The parties' choice of law is the primary consideration: if they state that the contract is governed by French law, English law or whatever, that is the applicable law. We will discuss the exceptions to this below.

The remaining paragraphs of Article 8 determine the 'objectively applicable' law. This is the law that applies where the parties' contract is silent on the matter. The starting-point is Article 8(2):

> To the extent that the law applicable to the individual employment contract has not been chosen by the parties, the contract shall be governed by the law of the country in which or, failing that, from which the employee habitually carries out his work in performance of the contract. The country where the work is habitually carried out shall not be deemed to have changed if he is temporarily employed in another country.

The court must begin by looking to the place 'in which' the employee works. A temporary 'posting' to another country does not override the applicable law generated by this rule. If the employee does not have a single obvious place of work, the court should consider his or her 'base'. Normally these rules will be sufficient to determine the applicable law, but if not, Article 8(3) looks to the place where the employee was hired. And under Article 8(4), if the contract is more closely connected with another country than that suggested by Article 8(2) or (3), that country's law is applicable.

---

[159] Of course, some employment claims may be made in tort. Such claims are governed by Regulation (EC) 864/2007 on the law applicable to non-contractual obligations, the Rome II Regulation, art 4 (on tort claims generally) or art 9 (on industrial action).

[160] Council Regulation (EC) 593/2008 of 17 June 2008 on the law applicable to contractual obligations (Rome I) [2008] OJ L177/6. This Regulation applies to contracts agreed from 17 December 2009 onwards. It is important to note that its effects are not confined to the Member States of the EU: an English court faced with a dispute about the applicability of English law or Delaware law to a contract must apply the rules laid down in the Regulation by virtue of art 2.

Importantly, Article 8 is confined to 'contracts of employment'. Other types of contract would fall to be governed by the general contracts provisions of the Regulation, which give greater weight to the parties' choice of law. However, since we are dealing with the interpretation of a phrase in an EU Regulation, it must be given an 'autonomous' EU meaning. Thus, the key distinction is between employment and self-employment, and the principles developed by the CJEU in other contexts, such as *Lawrie-Blum* and *Allonby*, would apply.[161] Thus, people who would not necessarily be classified as employees under English law might still benefit from Article 8 under the broader EU definition.

Overriding the parties' choice

If the parties' choice of law is different to the 'objectively applicable' law, in a way that disadvantages the employee, it may be possible for the employee to rely on the 'objectively applicable' law instead of the chosen law by virtue of Article 8(1). This provides:

> ... Such a choice of law may not, however, have the result of depriving the employee of the protection afforded to him by provisions that cannot be derogated from by agreement under the law that, in the absence of choice, would have been applicable pursuant to paragraphs 2, 3 and 4 of this Article.

This only applies to 'non-derogable' provisions of the objectively applicable law: in other words, those that do not permit contracting out.

In English law, the rights contained in the two main employment law statutes, ERA 1996 and TULRCA 1992, probably have this character. Both statutes contain provisions to the effect that any attempt by the parties to contract out of the protections they contain is void.[162] So, for example, if the employee's contract would be governed by English law except for a choice of law clause, the employee may still be able to claim unfair dismissal because this can be regarded as a 'non-derogable' provision of English law.

An interesting question is whether any of the worker-protective aspects of the common law (implied terms, the doctrine of restraint of trade and so on) might be regarded as 'non-derogable' provisions for Article 8 purposes. The leading case on this is *Duarte*, a case in which the employee's contract contained a non-compete clause applicable for two years after the end of the employment.[163] The contract was stated to be governed by the law of the US state of Maryland. The judge held that the common law rules on restraint of trade were part of the general law of contract and could not be regarded as 'non-derogable'.[164] However, as Dicey, Morris and Collins point out, the restraint of trade doctrine applies more strictly in employment cases so there is some justification for saying that *Duarte* is wrongly decided.[165]

---

[161] Case 66/85 *Lawrie-Blum* v *Land Baden-Württemberg* [1986] ECR 2121; Case C-256/01 *Allonby* v *Accrington & Rossendale College* [2004] ECR I-873. The suggested approach is supported (briefly) by the Court of Appeal in *WPP Holdings Italy Srl* v *Benatti* [2007] EWCA Civ 263, [2007] 1 WLR 2316 [45]–[51].

[162] ERA, s 203; TULRCA, s 288.

[163] *Duarte* v *Black & Decker Corporation* [2007] EWHC 2720 (QB), [2008] 1 All ER (Comm) 401.

[164] ibid [55].

[165] Above n 155, paras 33–257.

3.5.3 Question 3: statutory rights

Our third question is whether the statutory rights contained in English legislation can be invoked by the employee, sometimes described as a question of the 'territorial scope' of English law.[166] In most cases, this is a more important question than that of the law applicable to the contract because most employment rights are statutory: the employee is more likely to want to claim unfair dismissal than wrongful dismissal, for example. Most of the time, matters are straightforward: an employee working in England under a contract governed by English law will be able to invoke statutory rights found in legislation applicable to England.

But there are two (not uncommon) scenarios in which questions arise:

- In Scenario A, an individual is working in England under a contract not governed by English law. For example, the individual is temporarily sent to London from his or her main workplace in State X by a State X firm. If the contract is silent on the applicable law, the law of State X would be objectively applicable under Article 8(2) of the Rome I Regulation. But can he or she rely on rights under ERA 1996 and other employment statutes while in London? The answer to this question varies according to whether the individual is sent from an EU Member State (in which case the PWD is probably applicable)[167] or elsewhere.

- In Scenario B, an individual is hired in England by an English employer but works abroad. This might be because his or her work involves travelling (an airline pilot, for example) or because the English employer sends him or her to an overseas workplace (to work in the New York office, for example).[168] In this scenario, we will assume that English law is applicable either as a matter of choice or objectively. But what about English statutory employment rights? Can the individual bring an unfair dismissal claim if he or she is dismissed, and otherwise eligible?

These two scenarios are quite difficult to resolve, because of the complex interaction between Parliament's intentions, as expressed in the relevant statutory provisions; the parties' preferences as expressed in their contract (if any); the PWD in the case of people sent to the UK temporarily from other Member States; and the rules laid down in the Rome I Regulation. We will consider non-EU and EU versions of Scenario A before turning to Scenario B.

Scenario A

Scenario A raises the question whether a person working in England can invoke statutory provisions applicable in England even though his or her contract is (quite legitimately)[169] not governed by English law. The starting-point for this question is Article 9 of the Rome I Regulation.

---

[166] See Louise Merrett, 'The Extra-Territorial Reach of Employment Legislation' (2010) 39 ILJ 355.
[167] Above n 2.
[168] Under ERA s 1(4)(k) the employee's written statement must contain information about work to be done outside the UK.
[169] We are not here concerned with 'fake' choice of law addressed by art 8(1).

Article 9 lays down the concept of 'overriding mandatory' provisions: 'the respect for which is regarded as crucial by a country for safeguarding its public interests, such as its political, social or economic organisation, to such an extent that they are applicable to any situation falling within their scope, irrespective of the law otherwise applicable to the contract under this Regulation'. The difference between 'overriding mandatory' provisions and 'non-derogable' provisions under Article 8 is that 'non-derogable' provisions apply to contracts that would have been governed by English law in the absence of choice, whereas 'overriding mandatory' provisions can be applied by a state to all contracts[170] regardless of the parties' choice.

Interestingly, the main employment statutes purport to have this character. ERA, s. 204(1) and TULRCA, s. 289 both state:

> For the purposes of this Act it is immaterial whether the law which (apart from this Act) governs any person's employment is the law of the United Kingdom, or of a part of the United Kingdom, or not.[171]

This implies that, even if the parties have quite legitimately chosen the law of a state other than England to govern their contract, statutory rights such as the right not to be unfairly dismissed would be available to individuals working in England provided that they met the qualifying conditions.[172] Indeed, there would be little need for reliance on 'non-derogable' provisions under Article 8 because the vast majority of statutory employment rights would be of universal application regardless of choice of law under Article 9.

However, there is some doubt about whether the claim that all the rights in ERA and TULRCA apply generally by virtue of Article 9 is a plausible one. The leading textbook on conflict of laws, Dicey, Morris and Collins, questions this claim.[173] According to the authors of that work, only provisions of particular social importance can be brought within Article 9, not the whole of employment law. But the wording of Article 9 is subjective – focusing on the state's view of its own requirements – and most labour lawyers would probably argue that their subject is not divisible into mandatory and 'optional' components. The question can only be authoritatively resolved by the CJEU. The view that the Court would subject national determinations to some degree of judicial review (despite the subjective wording of Article 9) is supported by the decision in *Commission v Luxembourg* on a similarly worded provision in the Posted Workers Directive, discussed in greater detail below.[174]

'Posted' workers The Posted Workers Directive (PWD) constitutes a very important exception to the rules applicable to Scenario A where the individual is sent to work in England from another EU Member State.[175] In simple terms, a 'posted' worker is someone who is sent by his or her employer from one EU Member State

---

[170] Not just contracts of employment, though that does not concern us here.

[171] ERA used to state that it excluded those who 'ordinarily [worked] outside Great Britain' but this limitation was removed in order to afford greater protection to people posted temporarily to the UK for work.

[172] Including the qualifying period: see Chapter 9.

[173] Above n 155, paras 33–278. For a more detailed discussion, see Ugljesa Grušić, 'The Territorial Scope of Employment Legislation and Choice of Law' (2012) 75 MLR 722.

[174] Case C-319/06 *Commission v Luxembourg* [2008] ECR I-4323; and see Grušić, above n 173.

[175] Above n 2.

(the 'home' state) to another Member State (the 'host' state) to work for that employer on a temporary basis.[176] The posted worker's right to move to the host state to work is derived not from his or her own free movement rights as a worker (though he or she may have these too) but from the employer's freedom to provide services within the TFEU.[177] For reasons of administrative convenience (and often also competitive advantage), employers are likely to want to apply home state law to these workers while they are temporarily employed in another Member State. However, host states may want to apply their own laws, not least as a means of preventing their own workforce from being 'undercut' by posted workers from other Member States with lower minimum wages or levels of employment protection. The PWD sets out an uneasy compromise between these two sets of interests, and thus more generally between the economic and social dimensions of the EU.[178] We will consider the PWD itself, before examining the UK's implementation of it and the recently agreed Posted Workers Enforcement Directive.[179]

1. The Posted Workers Directive The PWD defines a 'posted worker' as 'a worker who, for a limited period, carries out his work in the territory of a Member State other than the State in which he normally works'.[180] Article 1(3) of the directive identifies three situations in which a posting will be regulated by the directive: where the individual is posted to another Member State to provide services to another firm pursuant to a contract between that firm and the employer; where the individual is posted to another Member State to work for another company in the employer's group; and where the individual is employed by an agency which posts him or her to another Member State to provide services to an end user. Importantly, then, the individual must remain in an employment relationship with the original employer in the home state, and he or she must provide services to another entity in the host state. There is no posting where the individual simply moves to another Member State to become the employee of the host undertaking or where the individual moves to another Member State to work for the home state undertaking (for example, as a travelling salesperson).[181] The applicable definition of 'worker' is that used in the host state's law.[182]

The key provision of the directive is Article 3(1), which requires the host state to ensure that posted workers benefit from the host state's norms on:

(a) maximum work periods and minimum rest periods;
(b) minimum paid annual holidays;
(c) the minimum rates of pay, including overtime rates; this point does not apply to supplementary occupational retirement pension schemes;

---

[176] ibid arts 1 and 2.
[177] The Court held in *Rush Portuguesa* that it was unlawful for a Member State to prohibit or restrict the use of posted workers. Case C-113/89 *Rush Portuguesa* v *Office national d'immigration* [1990] ECR I-1417 [12].
[178] On which see, generally, P Davies, 'Posted Workers: Single Market or Protection of National Labour Law Systems?' (1997) 34 CMLR 571; E Kolehmainen, 'The Directive Concerning the Posting of Workers: Synchronization of the Functions of National Legal Systems' (1998) 20 Comparative Labor Law and Policy Journal 71.
[179] Directive 2014/67/EU of the European Parliament and of the Council of 15 May 2014 on the enforcement of Directive 96/71/EC concerning the posting of workers in the framework of the provision of services, OJ 2014 L159/11.
[180] Directive 96/71/EC, art 2(1).
[181] Above n 178, 576.
[182] Directive 96/71/EC, art 2(2).

(d) the conditions of hiring-out of workers, in particular the supply of workers by temporary employment undertakings;

(e) health, safety and hygiene at work;

(f) protective measures with regard to the terms and conditions of employment of pregnant women or women who have recently given birth, of children and of young people;

(g) equality of treatment between men and women and other provisions on non-discrimination.

The norms may be those laid down 'by law, regulation or administrative provision'.[183] Where the posted workers are engaged in the building industry, as defined in the Annex, there is a further option of using the norms laid down in collective agreements provided that certain conditions are met.[184]

Whilst the core of Article 3 is a mandatory requirement to apply minimum standards to posted workers, it is important to note that there are also permissive provisions which appear to give the Member States the option of imposing higher standards on workers posted to their territories. However, the scope of these provisions has been significantly reduced by the Court's interpretations.

Article 3(7) states that 'paragraphs 1 to 6 shall not prevent application of terms and conditions of employment which are more favourable to workers'. This might suggest that host states are free to extend other aspects of their labour law to posted workers. However, the decisions in *Laval* and *Rüffert* make clear that this is not the case.[185] The Court held that Article 3(7) protects posted workers where the *home* state's labour law is more protective than that of the host state: in other words, posted workers should not suffer a reduction in their terms and conditions of employment as a result of the posting. The Court also held that Article 3(7) allowed the employer to agree more favourable terms with the posted workers than those provided by the host state. However, the one thing not permitted by Article 3(7) is the imposition of more protective labour law requirements by the host state.

Under Article 3(10), the Member States are given the option of applying additional standards to posted workers:

> This Directive shall not preclude the application by Member States, in compliance with the Treaty, to national undertakings and to the undertakings of other States, on a basis of equality of treatment, of:– terms and conditions of employment on matters other than those referred to in the first subparagraph of paragraph 1 in the case of public policy provisions . . .

At first sight, it might appear that this provision allowed the Member States to apply their own national labour laws to any workers posted to their territories. However, the Court held in *Commission* v *Luxembourg* that Article 3(10) constituted a derogation from the Treaty provisions on freedom to provide services and should therefore be construed strictly.[186] In particular, 'public policy may be relied on only if there is a genuine and sufficiently serious threat to a fundamental interest of society'.[187] The scope of public policy 'cannot be determined unilaterally by each

---

[183] ibid art 3(1).

[184] ibid arts 3(1) and (8).

[185] Case C-341/05 *Laval un Partneri Ltd* v *Svenska Byggnadsarbetareforbundet* [2007] ECR I-11767 [80]; Case C-346/06 *Rüffert v Land Niedersachsen* [2008] ECR I-1989 [33].

[186] Case C-319/06 *Commission v Luxembourg* [2008] ECR I-4323.

[187] ibid [50].

Member State without any control by the [EU] institutions'.[188] As a result, Luxembourg failed to establish that the labour law provisions it wanted to apply to posted workers fell within the public policy exception and indeed Barnard argues that it is hard to envisage any provisions that would pass the Court's test.[189] Thus, Article 3(1) is more of a ceiling than a floor in terms of protection for posted workers.

When it was first enacted, Davies interpreted the PWD as a confused measure, purporting to enhance firms' freedom to provide services whilst in practice offering a considerable degree of protection to the host state's labour market.[190] Subsequent interpretation by the Court has clarified matters to some extent, but perhaps not in the way labour lawyers might have hoped. It is now clear that Article 3(1) of the PWD sets both the minimum and the maximum level of protection for posted workers. This gives greater emphasis to the policy of opening up the EU labour market. However, it does not completely disregard labour considerations: Article 3(1) applies to at least some basic labour law provisions. So the Member States are allowed to adopt strategies to defend their labour markets against an influx of posted workers, but only within the confines of Article 3(1) PWD. In that sense, it appears that the 'balance' struck between economic and social considerations in the PWD strongly favours the economic.

2. Posted workers in English law Remarkably, the PWD has not been specifically implemented in English law.[191] As a result, posted workers fall to be dealt with under the rules discussed above derived from the Rome I Regulation and the various employment statutes. This probably means that the UK has failed to implement the PWD correctly.

Let us imagine a Lithuanian worker who is posted to the UK by a Lithuanian employer on a temporary basis for work. If the parties choose the applicable law for their contract, it is likely to be Lithuanian law. If the contract is silent, Lithuanian law may still apply by virtue of the general principles discussed above. The country in which the worker habitually works is Lithuania and the applicable law is not affected by a temporary posting. However, statutes such as ERA and TULRCA purport to apply regardless of the parties' choice of law. This would mean that a wide variety of rules of English employment law would be applicable to the parties' relationship even though Lithuanian law is the law of the contract, by virtue of Article 9 of the Rome I Regulation.

The difficulty with this basic position is that it does not reflect the compromise struck in the PWD, in which the host state is entitled only to enforce the rights listed in Article 3 in respect of posted workers. Thus, it is acceptable for a Member State to apply its minimum wage to posted workers on its territory but not (for example) the right to emergency family leave.

The text of the PWD suggests various ways in which the UK might avoid this conclusion. First, Article 3 purports to set minimum rather than maximum standards,

---

[188] ibid [50].
[189] Catherine Barnard, 'The UK and Posted Workers: the Effect of *Commission* v *Luxembourg* on the Territorial Application of British Labour Law' (2009) 38 ILJ 122, 127–130.
[190] Above n 178, 573.
[191] Barnard, above n 189.

and second, Article 3(10) contains a public policy exception. However, the case-law discussed above seems to have ruled out both options for justifying the more extensive protection provided in English law. A further option might be to argue that Article 9 of the Rome I Regulation prevails over the PWD in the hierarchy of EU norms, but as we have seen, the argument that the vast bulk of English statutory employment rights are 'overriding mandatory' rules is, in itself, not entirely safe.

3. New developments In response to the case-law discussed above, and the surrounding controversy, the Member States have agreed a new Directive, the Posted Workers Enforcement Directive (PWED), which must be implemented by June 2016.[192] This Directive is designed to tackle concerns that unscrupulous employers are using the PWD to undercut local workers by claiming that they are posting workers when this is not in fact the case. We will outline its main provisions here.

Article 4 of the Directive offers further guidance about how to identify a genuine posting situation. There are two aspects to this. First, Article 4(2) offers guidance on how to identify a firm engaged in 'substantial activities'. This involves looking at factors such as the undertaking's turnover. This is designed to address the situation in which, for example, workers from Member State A (with high labour standards) are hired by what is sometimes known as a 'letterbox' company in Member State B (where there are lower labour standards) and then 'posted' to Member State A to work, as a means of evading Member State A's labour standards. Second, Article 4(3) offers guidance on how to identify a genuine posted worker, looking at, for example, the temporary nature of the posting and whether the individual will return to his or her home state at the end of the posting. This is designed to tackle the situation in which the worker is, in reality, permanently employed in the so-called host state and thus should benefit from that state's labour standards in all respects. Under Article 4(5), the Member States are also directed to address 'sham' self-employment arrangements – which would take the individual outside the scope of the PWD altogether – though this is a sensitive issue since it is for the host Member State to apply its own national definition of 'worker'.

Much of the remainder of the Directive is concerned with the establishment of monitoring mechanisms within the Member States to ensure that the PWD is genuinely applicable to the situation and that its rules are enforced. These must be 'justified and proportionate'.[193] It remains to be seen how the UK will implement this aspect of the Directive since it has no such measures at the moment. The Directive also seeks to facilitate enforcement of their rights by the posted workers themselves, for example, by enabling the Member States to render the firm that has hired the posted workers' employer as a subcontractor jointly liable for unpaid wages and other infringements (subject to a defence of having carried out appropriate checks),[194] and by requiring host states to facilitate the enforcement of employers' obligations towards posted workers in the host states' courts.[195]

---

[192] Above n 2.
[193] ibid arts 9 and 10.
[194] ibid art 12.
[195] ibid art 11.

Scenario B

In Scenario B, we are concerned with an employee whose contract is governed by English law (either as a matter of choice, or objectively) but who works in another country either all or some of the time.[196] The mere fact that the contract is governed by English law does not *necessarily* trigger the application of English statutory rights. There is a separate question about their 'territorial scope'.[197]

This question is separate because it is important to look at what the statute says about its purported scope of application. For example, the National Minimum Wage Act 1998, s. 1(2)(b), makes clear that the NMW applies only to a person who 'is working, or ordinarily works, in the United Kingdom under [his or her] contract'. Thus, our individual in Scenario B cannot claim the NMW because he or she is not working in the UK and does not 'ordinarily' do so. This is the case even though his or her contract is governed by English law.

Moreover, the courts have held that even in relation to statutes which purport to apply without territorial limits, it is not possible for contracting parties with no real connection to the UK to 'buy in' to English statutes by selecting English law as the governing law of their contract. In *Financial Times* v *Bishop*, the EAT said:

> The Senegalese employee working in Peru for a Wisconsin corporation would not be enabled to bring proceedings in the Tribunals here to assert the right not to be unfairly dismissed simply because his contract of employment happened to provide that English law was the proper law of his contract.[198]

This is because of the general presumption that Parliament intends to legislate for the UK or some part of it, and does not normally intend to give extra-territorial effect to its legislation (even though, on a literal reading of s. 204, that is exactly what Parliament seems to have done).[199]

The leading case on the extra-territorial application of ERA is *Lawson* v *Serco*.[200] Two of the three claimants in that case were hired in the UK by UK-based employers but then sent to work overseas, one as a security guard on Ascension Island and the other as a youth worker with the British armed forces in Germany. These were referred to as the 'expatriate' employees, corresponding to Scenario B. The third (referred to in the case as a 'peripatetic' employee rather than an expatriate) was an airline pilot who was based at Heathrow but employed by a Hong Kong airline. All three claimed unfair dismissal.

Lord Hoffmann was concerned to limit the extra-territorial application of ERA. He held that the main focus should be on 'whether the employee was working in Great Britain at the time of [his or her] dismissal'.[201] Importantly, he rejected a 'contractual' test focusing on where the individual could be required to work under his or her contract, noting that what was agreed in the contract might either be irrelevant by the time the employee was dismissed, possibly many years later, or

---

[196] Of course, a person posted elsewhere in the EU would be able to claim rights in the host state under the PWD, but only those listed in art 3.

[197] Grušić, above n 173, 722–751; Merrett, above n 166, 355–381.

[198] (2003) UKEAT/0147/03/ZT.

[199] Grušić, above n 173, 749, notes that this scenario is unlikely but emphasises respect for the parties' choice.

[200] [2006] UKHL 3, [2006] ICR 250.

[201] ibid [27].

unhelpful because it simply allowed the employer to dictate where the work was to be done.[202]

In the case of the airline pilot, Lord Hoffmann held that he was able to bring an unfair dismissal claim because he was based in England. In the case of the expatriate employees, Lord Hoffmann gave two examples of where English law would continue to apply: 'the employee posted abroad to work for a business conducted in Britain and the employee working in a political or social British enclave abroad'.[203] Both the security guard and the youth worker were able to claim on the latter basis. Importantly, Lord Hoffmann indicated that his examples were not exhaustive and that other claims might be possible, though he was clearly concerned to confine the applicability of the right not to be unfairly dismissed to cases with a close connection with the UK.[204]

The non-exhaustive nature of Lord Hoffmann's examples has been confirmed in later cases. In *Ravat*, the employee worked for alternating periods of 28 days in Libya with 28 days at home in Scotland.[205] His employer was based in Germany and the decision to make him redundant was taken in Egypt, but all other aspects of his work (his tax arrangements and the process of consulting him about the redundancy, for example) were dealt with in Scotland. Lord Hope described him as a 'commuter' and held that his task of proving that ERA applied was easier than that of the 'expatriate' employees in *Lawson* because of his greater connection with the UK.[206] And in *Duncombe*, teachers employed by the UK government to work at European Schools in other countries were found to be protected by ERA.[207] They were not true 'expatriate' employees because they were not necessarily hired in or sent from the UK, but it was held that their employment had no real connection with the country in which they worked and instead had a much stronger connection with the UK.

An interesting feature of *Duncombe* was that it was held to be relevant (but not conclusive) to consider the law of the contract of employment when determining the reach of ERA. As Lady Hale explained:

> Although this factor is not mentioned in *Lawson v Serco Ltd*, it must be relevant to the expectation of each party as to the protection which the employees would enjoy. The law of unfair dismissal does not form part of the contractual terms and conditions of employment, but it was devised by Parliament in order to fill a well known gap in the protection offered by the common law to those whose contracts of employment were ended.[208]

Grušić criticises English law's stance on the scope of ERA, arguing that when the parties select English law as the law of their contract, they should also be treated as having selected English statute law.[209] This, he argues, would be consistent with respect for the parties' autonomy and with a proper implementation of the

---

[202] ibid [25]–[27].
[203] ibid [40].
[204] ibid. See also *Creditsights Ltd v Dhunna* [2014] EWCA Civ 1238, [2015] ICR 105.
[205] *Ravat v Halliburton Manufacturing & Services Ltd* [2012] UKSC 1, [2012] ICR 389.
[206] ibid [29].
[207] *Duncombe v Secretary of State for Children Schools and Families (No 2)* [2011] UKSC 36, [2011] ICR 1312.
[208] ibid [16], though cf *Creditsights*, above n 204, [43] (Rimer LJ).
[209] Grušić, above n 173, 749.

Rome I Regulation. However, it seems unlikely that the courts would adopt this radically different approach without a clear ruling from the CJEU requiring them to do so.

A final point to note is that the courts may be more generous if rights granted by EU law are at stake. This is illustrated by *Bleuse*.[210] In that case, the claimant was a German lorry driver working for a UK company in Germany under a contract governed by English law. The EAT held that he could not claim for unfair dismissal because his contract had no real connection with the UK. However, he could claim for holiday pay because this right was derived from the Working Time Directive.[211] Although the Working Time Regulations only applied to 'Great Britain', this limitation could be disregarded where it was necessary to give effect to rights derived from EU law.[212]

POINTS TO TAKE AWAY

- Nationals of other EU Member States have a right under Article 45 TFEU to work in the UK. This includes a right to come to the UK for at least three months to look for work. Various measures exist to facilitate the free movement of workers around the EU, such as the rules on mutual recognition of qualifications.

- Nationals of non-EU countries must obtain a visa to work in the UK. In general terms, visas are only available to highly skilled migrants who are sponsored by an employer to fill a job that cannot be filled by a local worker.

- Irregular migrants are unable to enforce their contracts of employment or statutory rights linked to the contract because of the common law doctrine of illegality, though they may be able to bring discrimination claims.

- Trafficking and forced labour are addressed by the criminal law. Employers who employ irregular migrants without conducting 'right to work' checks may be liable to pay a civil penalty.

- An employer may not use a choice of law clause in a contract of employment to deprive the employee of the protection he or she would otherwise have enjoyed by virtue of the objectively applicable law.

- Many statutory rights purport to apply to anyone working in England and thus to apply regardless of the parties' choice of the law to govern their contract. It is unclear whether this is compatible with the Rome I Regulation. The controversial Posted Workers Directive limits the extent to which national law can be applied to workers 'posted' by their employer from another Member State. This directive does not appear to have been implemented properly by the UK. 'Expatriate' workers may continue to enjoy statutory rights if their employment has a sufficiently strong connection with English law.

---

[210] *Bleuse v MBT Transport Ltd* [2008] ICR 488.
[211] ibid [52]–[61].
[212] ibid [57].

Further reading

Issues of free movement and posting in EU law are explored more fully in **ACL Davies, *EU Labour Law* (Elgar 2012), chapter 3**, and **Catherine Barnard, *EU Employment Law* (4th edn, OUP 2012), chapters 4 and 5**. There is a large literature on the PWD and associated case-law. On the directive as originally enacted, see **P Davies, 'Posted Workers: Single Market or Protection of National Labour Law Systems?' (1997) 34 CMLR 571**. And on the PWD's impact, particularly on English law, see **Catherine Barnard, '"British Jobs for British Workers": the Lindsey Oil Refinery Dispute and the Future of Local Labour Clauses in an Integrated EU Market' (2009) 38 ILJ 245** and **'The UK and Posted Workers: the Effect of *Commission* v *Luxembourg* on the Territorial Application of British Labour Law' (2009) 38 ILJ 122**. For more detail on private international law issues in employment relationships, see **Louise Merrett, *Employment Contracts in Private International Law* (OUP 2011)**.

The links between migration and labour law more generally have not been explored very much by labour lawyers, though there are some interesting contributions in **Cathryn Costello and Mark Freedland (eds), *Migrants at Work: Immigration and Vulnerability in Labour Law* (OUP 2015)**. Domestic workers have attracted a degree of scholarly attention. They are often (though not always) migrants and are especially vulnerable because they work in private homes and are dependent on the employer for accommodation as well as work. There is a recent ILO Convention on domestic work (Convention 189, 2011). For discussion, see **Einat Albin and Virginia Mantouvalou, 'The ILO Convention on Domestic Workers: from the Shadows to the Light' (2012) 41 ILJ 67**; **Deirdre McCann and Jill Murray, 'Prompting Formalisation through Labour Market Regulation: a "Framed Flexibility" Model for Domestic Work' (2014) 43 ILJ 319**; **Cliodhna Murphy, 'The Enduring Vulnerability of Migrant Domestic Workers in Europe' (2013) 62 ICLQ 599**.

4 The scope of application of labour law

Learning outcomes

This chapter will enable readers to:

- understand and critically evaluate the boundaries of labour law
- analyse the concepts of 'employee', 'worker', 'employment under a contract personally to do work' and the EU definition of 'worker', and understand their significance for an individual's entitlement to employment rights
- understand the problems facing individuals with certain types of non-standard working relationship ('zero-hours', fixed-term, agency and part-time) and critically assess the law's response

4.1 INTRODUCTION

Our focus in this chapter will be on what is sometimes called the 'personal scope' of labour law: in other words, who gets to benefit from the rights labour law has to offer. This topic is about drawing boundaries around the subject. We will start by examining why it is necessary to draw these boundaries at all (section 4.2). We will then examine the various legal concepts laid down in statute for this purpose – 'employee' and 'worker' in particular – and explore how the courts have interpreted them (section 4.3). As we shall see, the crucial question is whether the boundaries are drawn in a way that reflects the reason for having boundaries in the first place. If the point of labour law is to protect those who are in a weaker bargaining position relative to the employer, for example, then it is important to draw the boundaries so that they include everyone who fits that description. Finally, we will consider the regulation of specific forms of working arrangement, such as fixed-term or agency work (section 4.4). People with these types of working arrangement are often referred to as non-standard or atypical workers because their work deviates from the 'norm' of an indefinite contract with a single employer. They are generally thought to be vulnerable and in particular need of protection, hence the special legal regulation of these types of work.

4.2 THEORETICAL FRAMEWORK

Let us begin by imagining a world without labour law. Most people would still earn a living by supplying their labour to others, but on the basis of the ordinary law of contract. It would be up to them to bargain with the person buying their labour about the price and other terms of the contract. This system would work well for those who had a very special skill that was in great demand: talented footballers, for example. But it would work less well for those whose skills were rather more mundane. The buyer would be able to dictate the terms on which they supplied their labour because if they refused to agree, another person could easily be found to replace them. This is the problem of inequality of bargaining power between workers and employers. Labour law has emerged in response to this problem. It is designed to redress – or provide a means of redressing – this inequality of bargaining power. Of course, beyond this basic point, there are different ways of justifying and designing a system of labour law: we could focus on protecting workers' fundamental rights, or we could institute arrangements for collective bargaining so that workers could protect themselves by grouping together. These issues need not concern us here. What is important is that labour law exists to protect those who would not fare well under a system of unregulated individual contracting.

Once we have a special set of labour law rules in place, we need to decide who should benefit from them. In theory at least, this is simple: anyone who is unable to bargain for themselves should be protected by labour law. Anyone who is able to bargain does not need the protection of labour law and should be left to fend for him- or herself in the market. Some people fall obviously into one camp or the other. The owner of a large firm who supplies services to another large firm is engaging in a commercial transaction outside the remit of labour law, whereas an individual turning up for work every day in a shop or a factory is within the remit of labour law. The difficulty is that, as with any line-drawing exercise, there is always a group of people close to the boundary and it is difficult to allocate them satisfactorily to one side or the other. For example, imagine an individual who is a skilled carpenter and hires out his or her services to one building firm. He or she does not work for any other firms and accepts an hourly rate of pay set by the building firm. If there is a lot of work to do, he or she sometimes takes on a labourer to help out. On the one hand, we could say that because he or she is dependent on a single firm for his or her whole income, and because the building firm sets the rate of pay, this is an employment relationship and warrants the protection of labour law. On the other hand, we could say that because our carpenter sometimes hires another person to help out, he or she is running a (very) small business, so the relationship he or she has with the building firm is a commercial one outside the purview of labour law.

There is another factor to think about that complicates matters further. From the employer's perspective, the finding that a person is within the boundaries of labour law has a cost attached: the employer must pay for whatever rights labour law grants. Of course, there are corresponding benefits too – the employer usually gets a loyal worker who is less likely to find work elsewhere and leave it in the lurch – but the costs may seem more obvious and immediate. In recent years, there has been a growing trend of employers arranging things so that individuals fall outside the boundaries of labour law as a way of saving money. For example, the employer might dismiss a group of workers and re-employ them via an agency. This would save money because the agency would be responsible for recruiting the workers and making sure they turned up when required, and because the employer would no longer be responsible for providing a variety of benefits, such as a redundancy payment if the worker was not needed any more. Alternatively, the employer might continue the same relationship with the worker but get its lawyers to draft a contract making it look as if the worker is running a small business so that he or she might fall outside the boundaries of labour law. For many labour lawyers, these kinds of behaviour are illegitimate: firms are manipulating the boundaries in ways that disadvantage workers who may not understand what is going on and may be left considerably worse off as a result. But it is also important to recognise that whenever we draw a line in any area of law, there will always be a grey area around the line and people will always try to take advantage of it: in the cut-throat world of business we should not be surprised that some firms will do whatever they can to save money.

This process of pushing at the boundaries of labour law forms part of a broader phenomenon that Freedland and Kountouris helpfully label 'demutualisation'.[1] Traditionally, we have tended to think of the employer's role as one of shielding workers from economic risk, up to a point at least. The employer is the entrepreneur, taking the risk of loss and gaining the benefit of profit. The workers will get paid regardless of weekly or monthly fluctuations in demand. If the firm's order book is quiet, they will still expect to turn up for work, though of course eventually the employer might decide to lay some of them off. Equally, though, if the firm is doing exceptionally well, the workers might get some extra work and overtime pay but they will not expect a share of the profits made by their employer. The 'demutualisation' idea tries to capture the demise of this way of doing things. Nowadays, a firm is much more likely to transfer business risks onto its workers. This might occur in several different ways. One is to connect their pay to the firm's profit, through tips, bonuses or employee share ownership schemes. Another is to employ workers 'on demand', varying their hours according to the firm's requirements. For example, the firm might maintain a list of casual workers who can be called in at busy times and sent home when they are not needed.

It is worth noting that boundary manipulation and demutualisation do not affect everyone in the labour market equally.[2] Firms could not survive if all their staff were outside the framework of labour law and exposed to economic risk. In many firms, then, there is a 'core' of workers who are protected by labour law and shielded from risk, and a 'periphery' of workers who are not. The workers in the periphery are often referred to in the labour law literature as 'non-standard' or 'atypical' workers because their employment arrangements deviate from the 'norm' of stable, protected employment. The difficulty with this terminology is that it might imply that these workers are in a minority whereas, in some sectors at least, they probably make up the majority of the workforce, though reliable information on this issue is difficult to gather. As many commentators have pointed out, since jobs on the 'periphery' are less attractive than jobs in the 'core', they tend to be taken by people who are already disadvantaged in the labour market for other reasons. So for example we are likely to find more women, more people from ethnic minorities and more migrant workers in low-paid, unstable work. In that way, the changing shape of the labour market results in another form of discrimination against people in these groups.

Given the downsides of 'demutualisation', it might be thought that government policy and judicial interpretation would seek to reverse the change and to bring more non-standard workers back within the well-protected 'core'. The courts have only

---

[1] Mark Freedland and Nicola Kountouris, *The Legal Construction of Personal Work Relations* (OUP 2011) 439–446.
[2] See Sandra Fredman, 'Labour Law in Flux: the Changing Composition of the Workforce' (1997) 26 ILJ 337; 'Women at Work: the Broken Promise of Flexicurity' (2004) 33 ILJ 299.

started to do this relatively recently, and it remains to be seen how their approach will develop. In terms of government policy, there has been no real attempt to reverse demutualisation, largely due to the adoption both at EU level and within the UK of a policy agenda known as 'flexicurity', a portmanteau word made up of 'flexibility' and 'security'. The flexicurity agenda is about the promotion of flexible labour markets in which workers move freely to the jobs where they are most needed: they might move from one role to another within a firm (so-called functional flexibility), or from one firm to another firm (so-called numerical flexibility). The link between flexicurity and non-standard working is immediately apparent: non-standard workers are the people who are expected to move on – to be 'flexible' – when they are no longer needed.

Flexicurity has been the subject of a powerful academic critique. Its advocates argue that traditional 'job security' (a worker's right to keep his or her job unless there is a good reason for dismissal)[3] should be replaced by notions of 'employability' or 'employment security'. Government policy would support workers during times of change by providing them with training to acquire new skills and by helping them financially through the social security system while they looked for work.[4] However, critics argue that the reality is that non-standard workers experience very considerable insecurity and are offered little help to improve their situation. Its advocates also argue that flexicurity can benefit workers, because more flexible models of working enable them to combine work with other activities, such as studying or raising a family. However, this benefit depends on the type of flexible working on offer. Being able to work part-time might well help with these other life choices, but simply having an 'as required' casual job is likely to be disruptive and stressful. This chapter will consider the influence of flexicurity on two main policy areas: the introduction of the 'worker' concept alongside the traditional 'employee' concept, and the targeted regulation of various kinds of non-standard working.

4.3 ORGANISING CONCEPTS

We will now turn to examine the main organising concepts used in English employment law: employee, worker, person employed under a contract personally to do work, and person employed to provide services under the direction of another. These concepts are used in different areas of labour law to draw a boundary around who is entitled to a particular set of employment rights, so for each concept we will examine which statutory rights can be accessed by a person with that particular status. We will then consider the criteria used by the courts in order to determine whether or not an individual fits within the relevant category. Before we go into detail, it is worth making two points by way of background.

First, it is useful to understand how the four concepts fit together. Historically, the main dividing line has been drawn between employees and the self-employed. Employees benefited from all the rights employment law had to offer; the self-employed were running their own businesses so were thought not to need that protection. The 'worker' concept is a more recent addition to the legislative framework and has been used in several pieces of legislation since 1997. It reflects a recognition on the

---

[3] See Chapter 9.
[4] Commission, *Towards Common Principles of Flexicurity: More and Better Jobs through Flexibility and Security*, COM (2007) 359.

part of the legislature that there might be some people who did not fit the employee definition but were still in need of some labour law protections because they were not really running their own business either. As we shall see, workers get a subset of the rights given to employees. In the discussion below we will examine why the government chose to tackle this issue in this way, rather than simply broadening the employee definition or granting all 'employee' rights to workers, and we will link this to the 'flexicurity' agenda.

Alongside these two main organising concepts we find two others, with more clumsy labels. One is the 'person employed under a contract personally to do work'. This is the definition used in the Equality Act 2010. It is designed to ensure that equality law applies as broadly as possible. We will examine exactly how broadly in the discussion below. Finally, there is the 'person employed to provide services under the direction of another'. This is a way of rendering the definition laid down by the Court of Justice for situations in which EU law has a definition of worker, such as equality law and free movement law. This definition is relevant if a person is seeking to rely on directly effective EU law in the English courts, or if a person is seeking to challenge the UK's implementation of EU rules. But its scope of application is less than might be supposed: most of the time, EU law allows the Member States to use their own national definitions to determine who falls within the boundary of labour law when they are implementing directives. We will examine why this is the case in the discussion below.

A second general point to note before considering the various definitions – particularly employee and worker – in detail is that they are developed and applied by the courts against the background of the general law of contract. Although we have been using the term 'employee' as a shorthand, the underlying legal concept is 'employment under a contract of service'. One consequence of this is that as well as considering whether or not the contract can be characterised as one of 'service' as opposed to some other kind of contract (usually a contract 'for services' giving rise to a relationship of self-employment), the courts must also examine whether basic requirements of contract formation are met, such as offer, acceptance and consideration. But the contractual nature of employment creates a more profound tension for the courts. On the one hand, it is important to have a consistent and coherent law of contract, so the courts will want to use familiar tools when deciding whether or not someone has a contract of employment. On the other hand, one of the reasons for the emergence of labour law is that work is different to other types of market activity because of the inequality of bargaining power between workers and their employer and because of the need to protect workers' dignity at work. These considerations suggest that the ordinary law of contract – which has developed in commercial settings – may not work very well if it is applied without any adaptation to employment. As we shall see, the courts have traditionally applied a 'contractual' approach to employment situations, but in some recent cases, a more employment-focused approach has begun to emerge.

4.3.1 Employee

We will begin with the concept of 'employee'. Employees normally benefit from all the rights employment law has to offer, so from the individual's perspective, this is usually the most desirable category to be in. We will consider the main rights granted to employees, before turning to the definition developed by the courts. Towards the end of the section, we will consider a new concept, 'employee shareholder' status. This is a controversial legislative development which provides for employees to give up some of their employment rights in exchange for shares in the employer company.

Rights for employees

'Employee' is the core organising concept in employment law so a person who qualifies as an employee is entitled to anything that constitutes an employment right. These include the right not to be discriminated against and the right to the National Minimum Wage (NMW). However, these rights can also be claimed by people who do not count as employees: equality law protects a 'person employed under a contract personally to do work'[5] and the NMW applies to 'workers'.[6] To understand the significance of the employee concept, it is important to know which rights are *only* available to people in this group.

Here are the main examples:

- the right to a written statement of terms and conditions of employment;[7]
- the right not to be unfairly dismissed;[8]
- the right to claim a redundancy payment;[9]
- the right to take maternity, paternity, parental or emergency leave;[10]
- the right to request flexible working;[11]
- protection under the Fixed-term Employees Regulations.[12]

Some of these rights have 'qualifying periods'. The employee must complete a specified period of continuous employment with the employer before he or she becomes eligible to claim. Unfair dismissal has a qualifying period of two years, though there are some exceptions.[13]

Who is an employee?

Under s. 230(1) ERA 1996, 'in this Act "employee" means an individual who has entered into or works under (or, where the employment has ceased, worked under) a contract of employment'. This means that employee status depends on whether or not the individual has a 'contract of employment', a common law concept developed by the judges (sometimes also referred to as a 'contract of service'). There is a large body of case-law on the subject, not all of it consistent, so what follows is an attempt to impose a degree of clarity on the muddle.

---

[5] Equality Act 2010, s 83.
[6] National Minimum Wage Act 1998, s 54.
[7] Employment Rights Act 1996, s 1(1).
[8] ibid s 94(1).
[9] ibid s 135(1).
[10] Maternity and Parental Leave etc. Regulations 1999, SI 1999/3312; Paternity and Adoption Leave Regulations 2002, SI 2002/2788.
[11] ERA 1996, s 80F(1).
[12] The Fixed-term Employees (Prevention of Less Favourable Treatment) Regulations 2002, SI 2002/2034.
[13] ibid s 108(1).

Evidence A contract of employment may be oral or in writing. Where it is oral, the court will have to figure out from the parties' claims and the surrounding circumstances exactly what they agreed. Where it is written, the court's task seems simpler because there is a contract document to interpret and classify.[14] But labour lawyers generally argue that written contracts should be given less weight in the employment context than they are in the commercial context because of the risk of 'boundary manipulation': the use of the written contract by the employer to make it look as if the individual is in a category with fewer employment rights.

There are two important rules about written contracts in the ordinary law of contract: the signature rule and the parol evidence rule. Under the signature rule, a contracting party is bound by a contract he or she has signed, even if it is clear that he or she has not read or understood the contents.[15] And under the parol evidence rule, if the parties decide to set their contract out in writing in a comprehensive way, the courts will treat the written document as conclusive evidence of the terms of the agreement and will not normally entertain claims by one of the parties that the 'real' terms of the contract are different.[16] These two rules both serve to promote certainty, a particularly important consideration in commercial contracts. The contract will, of course, be interpreted against the appropriate factual background, but this does not allow a party to assert that the contract means what he or she subjectively intended it to mean.[17] Moreover, if one party wants to argue that a particular term is not genuine – it was included in the contract to produce particular legal consequences, for example, and was not meant to be invoked – that party would have to satisfy the test for a 'sham' laid down by Diplock LJ (as he then was) in the *Snook* case:

> if [sham] has any meaning in law, it means acts done or documents executed by the parties to the "sham" which are intended by them to give to third parties or to the court the appearance of creating between the parties legal rights and obligations different from the actual legal rights and obligations (if any) which the parties intend to create.[18]

Although Diplock LJ offered this definition in a rather tentative way, it has since been widely accepted as the leading authority on the matter.[19] It means that a sham only arises where *both* parties are aware that a term is a fake.

Traditionally, these rules have been applied to contracts in the employment setting just as they are applied to commercial contracts. The Court of Appeal's decision in *Consistent Group* is a good illustration of this.[20] In that case, the claimants' contract contained a term that they were free to refuse work when offered and free to take work with other employers. Such a term would have the effect in law of making them self-employed. The claimants sought to argue that the term did not reflect the reality of their relationship with the alleged employer, because in practice they were expected

---

[14] See Chapter 5 for discussion of the role of the statutory written statement of terms and conditions of employment.

[15] *L'Estrange* v *F Graucob Ltd* [1934] 2 KB 394.

[16] *Jacobs* v *Batavia and General Plantations Trust Ltd* [1924] 1 Ch 287.

[17] *Investors Compensation Scheme Ltd* v *West Bromwich Building Society (No 1)* [1998] 1 WLR 896; *Chartbrook Ltd* v *Persimmon Homes Ltd* [2009] UKHL 38, [2009] 1 AC 1101.

[18] *Snook* v *London and West Riding Investments Ltd* [1967] 2 QB 786 (CA) 802.

[19] See E Simpson and M Stewart, 'Introduction: "Sham" Transactions' in E Simpson and M Stewart (eds), *Sham Transactions* (OUP 2013).

[20] *Consistent Group Ltd* v *Kalwak* [2008] EWCA Civ 430, [2008] IRLR 505.

to turn up for work when required to do so. However, the Court of Appeal insisted that the written term could only be displaced by a clear finding of a 'sham' as defined in the *Snook* case:

> It is not the function of the court or an employment tribunal to re-cast the parties' bargain. If a term solemnly agreed in writing is to be rejected in favour of a different one, that can only be done by a clear finding that the real agreement was to that different effect and that the term in the contract was included by them so as to present a misleadingly different impression.[21]

The mere fact that an agreed term had not been used did not mean that it was not part of the parties' contract. The claimants were bound by the written contracts they had signed.

Decisions like that in *Consistent Group* have been the subject of long-standing criticism by labour lawyers.[22] Arguably, the court gave the employer an easy means of engaging in 'boundary manipulation'. The simple device of inserting a clause entitling the claimants to refuse to accept work converted what might have been an 'employee' relationship, with the full package of employment rights, into a self-employment relationship, with hardly any rights. The court did not recognise the possibility that the employer might have drafted the contract with legal advice in order to achieve a particular effect, and simply presented it to the individual for signature. The individual might not have negotiated its terms, participated in its drafting or even read and understood it. Rules which provide the benefit of certainty in commercial settings might generate unfairness in employment settings.

Until recently, the courts have only departed from the 'contractual' approach in one respect, by denying employers the simplest option for boundary manipulation, 'labelling'.[23] This involves inserting a clause in the contract to the effect that the relationship is of one kind rather than another (self-employed rather than employee, for example). The nature of the contract is a matter for the court to determine, so if the parties have created a contract of employment by means of the terms and conditions they have agreed, that is what the court will find. A declaration that the contract is of a different type will not affect the outcome.

But a potentially very significant change came in *Autoclenz*, in which the Supreme Court laid down a different way of approaching written contract documents in the employment sphere.[24] The claimants in that case were car valeters. Various terms of the written contract they had signed suggested that they were self-employed: the employer was not obliged to offer them work, they were not obliged to accept work if offered, and they were entitled to send a substitute instead of doing the work themselves. The Supreme Court held that the *Snook* test did not represent the *only* situation in which the courts might be entitled to disregard a written agreement.[25]

---

[21] ibid [40].
[22] See, for example, AL Bogg, 'Sham Self-Employment in the Court of Appeal' (2010) 126 LQR 166; ACL Davies, 'Sensible Thinking about Sham Transactions' (2009) 38 ILJ 318.
[23] E.g. *Ready Mixed Concrete (South East) Ltd v Minister of Pensions and National Insurance* [1968] 2 QB 497 (QB) 512–513.
[24] *Autoclenz Ltd v Belcher* [2011] UKSC 41, [2011] ICR 1157. For discussion, see AL Bogg, 'Sham Self-Employment in the Supreme Court' (2012) 41 ILJ 328.
[25] ibid [23].

There was a more general power to do so where contracts were concluded in situations of inequality of bargaining power. As Lord Clarke explained:

> [T]he relative bargaining power of the parties must be taken into account in deciding whether the terms of any written agreement in truth represent what was agreed and the true agreement will often have to be gleaned from all the circumstances of the case, of which the written agreement is only a part.[26]

Importantly, this does not mean that courts and tribunals can simply disregard written contracts. They are not being told to infer the contents of the contract from what happened on a day-to-day basis. Instead, what *Autoclenz* permits is a more rounded assessment of the evidence – the written agreement and what went on in practice – in order to identify the parties' 'true agreement'. In *Autoclenz* itself, the Supreme Court found that the valeters were employees because of the tribunal's findings that they were, in practice, obliged to turn up each day and complete their work themselves under the employer's detailed supervision.

Most commentators regard this as a considerable improvement on the 'contractual' approach. It makes it harder for employers to manipulate the boundaries between different categories of relationship – to make employees look as if they are self-employed, for example – simply by sneaking particular terms into a written contract. More attention will now focus on whether the parties' agreement (as evidenced by the contract and the surrounding circumstances) meets the tests for employee status, which we will consider next.

'Employment' In many cases, the question before the court is whether an individual is an employee or a self-employed person. In other words, there is clearly a contract between B and A but there is a dispute about whether B owes A the obligations of an employer. The courts have developed two main tests for deciding this question: 'control' and 'risk'.[27]

The 'control' test is said to be derived from the decision of the Court of Appeal in *Yewens v Noakes*, which in fact concerned the definition not of an employee but of a 'servant':

> A servant is a person subject to the command of his master as to the manner in which he shall do his work.[28]

The test was confirmed in the well-known case of *Ready Mixed Concrete*, in which MacKenna J held that a person would be an employee if:

> he agrees, expressly or impliedly, that in the performance of that service he will be subject to the other's control in a sufficient degree to make that other master.[29]

He defined 'control' in the following terms:

> Control includes the power of deciding the thing to be done, the way in which it shall be done, the means to be employed in doing it, the time when and the place where it shall be done.[30]

---

[26] ibid [35].

[27] Some cases have also used an 'integration' test but this has not proved popular: *Stevenson, Jordan & Harrison Ltd v MacDonald and Evans* [1952] 1 TLR 101.

[28] (1880) 6 QBD 530, at 532–3, per Bramwell LJ.

[29] *Ready Mixed Concrete* (n 23).

[30] ibid.

In the modern literature, the control test is sometimes expressed in terms of 'subordination', though it is necessary to take great care with this terminology because it is used to mean different things by different writers and judges, as we shall see below. The idea is that whereas a self-employed person agrees to perform a task for someone and decides when and how to go about it, an employed person is told what to do by his or her employer. This is further reflected in the implied obligation of obedience in the contract of employment: the law supports the idea that the employer is in control and the employee is subordinated by requiring the employee to obey the employer's reasonable instructions.[31]

One of the potential difficulties with the control test is that many employers employ skilled workers and give them a high degree of discretion in the performance of their tasks. For example, a doctor employed by a hospital would normally be allowed to decide how to treat patients without detailed direction from management, or a university professor might be allowed substantial freedom to determine his or her own working hours or research questions. There are two possible responses to this. One is to say that even high-discretion employees are subject to control at some level. Our doctor would be told what shifts to work, and our professor would have to give lectures and mark exams as directed by the head of department. But this may not be entirely persuasive – self-employed people might also have to comply with some minimal instructions from their clients. The other response is to look for a different test to use in high discretion cases and perhaps more generally.

The main rival to the control test is a test referred to as 'risk' or 'economic reality', or (in the literature more than the case-law) as 'dependence'.[32] The idea here is that A is an employee if B takes the risk of profit and loss in their relationship, whereas if A takes that risk, he or she is self-employed. This is designed to capture the entrepreneurial nature of self-employment. This test was used in the recent *Quashie* case.[33] Ms Quashie was a lap-dancer in a nightclub. Customers bought vouchers in the club that they could use to pay her for dances. At the end of each evening, she would present the vouchers she had earned to the cashier at the club, who would give her money in return, after deducting various fees. A key fact in the case was that Ms Quashie could be out of pocket at the end of an evening if she did not earn enough by performing for customers to cover the deductions made by the club. This assumption of economic risk was one of the factors that led the Court of Appeal to conclude that she could not be the club's employee.

Again, the risk test has its critics. One concern is that, in modern workplaces, it is more common for employers and employees to share economic risk in various ways. For example, an employer might base a proportion of an employee's pay on the performance of the company, measured by its share price or profits, or on his or her own personal performance, such as meeting sales targets. Indeed, it is arguable that in *Quashie*, the strategy of getting the customers to pay the dancers was a means of introducing a particularly grim form of 'performance-related' pay.[34] The problem is that these various mechanisms are designed to motivate employees, but they may

---

[31] See Chapter 5.
[32] *Market Investigations Ltd* v *Minister of Social Security* [1969] 2 QB 173. On the dependence/subordination terminology, see Guy Davidov, 'Who is a Worker?' (2005) 34 ILJ 57.
[33] *Quashie* v *Stringfellow Restaurants Ltd* [2012] EWCA Civ 1735, [2013] IRLR 99.
[34] See E Albin, 'The Case of *Quashie*: between the Legalisation of Sex Work and the Precariousness of Personal Service Work' (2013) 42 ILJ 180.

have the effect in law of making it appear that the employees are risk-taking entrepreneurs and not employees at all. More profoundly, there is a worry that the risk test may be a 'double whammy' for employees. If their employer *requires* them to accept a greater degree of risk against their wishes, they may face losing *both* their economic security and their statutory employment rights. There is a significant difference in practice between an individual who is an entrepreneur, positively embracing the idea of running his or her own small business, and the individual who would like to be an employee but is forced (through inequality of bargaining power) to accept work on a risky basis.

'Inconsistent terms' Another requirement of employee status is to demonstrate that there are no terms 'inconsistent' with that status in the individual's contract. In some respects, this may overlap with the control and risk tests discussed in the previous section, because the inclusion of a particular contractual term may indicate a lack of control or a decision not to assume risk on the part of the employer. However, in many cases, the courts treat this as a separate requirement.

A common example of a term inconsistent with employee status is a right for the individual to send a substitute instead of carrying out his or her work personally. This was considered in the *Express and Echo* case.[35] In that case, the contract between the parties provided that Mr Tanton was required to arrange for another person to do the work if he was 'unable or unwilling' to do it himself. The Court of Appeal held that it was impossible for the contract to be a contract of employment because employment involves personal service: the employer selects the employee and enters into a relationship of mutual trust and confidence with him or her. The requirement was softened to some extent in the *McFarlane* case.[36] Here, Ms McFarlane was a gym instructor who could send a substitute to teach her class, but only if she was ill and only if she chose another instructor from a list approved by her employer. The employer would pay the substitute direct. It was held that this term did not necessarily defeat employee status. Although the 'personal service' test can be seen as a separate requirement about the terms of the individual's contract, there are echoes of 'control' and 'risk'. If the individual can send a substitute, the employer is no longer in full control of the situation and there is more evidence that he or she is an entrepreneur running a business in which he or she hires other people.

Another example is where the contract either contains a term to the effect that the 'employer' is not obliged to pay the individual, or where it is clear that there is no contractual obligation on the 'employer' to pay the individual. Although the courts have been reluctant to say that a duty to pay the individual is always a requirement of a contract of employment, they have made it clear that this will normally be the case. This was the case in *Quashie*, discussed above, where the Court of Appeal accepted that the lap-dancer was paid by the nightclub's customers (albeit via the voucher system operated by the nightclub) rather than by the nightclub itself.[37] Similarly, in *Cheng Yuen*, the claimant was a golf caddie who was permitted by a golf club to offer his services to players.[38] The Privy Council held that he was not an

---

[35] *Express & Echo Publications* v *Tanton* [1999] ICR 693 (CA).
[36] *MacFarlane* v *Glasgow City Council* [2001] IRLR 7 (EAT).
[37] Above n 33.
[38] *Cheng Yuen* v *Royal Hong Kong Golf Club* [1998] ICR 131 (PC).

employee of the club because it was under no duty to pay him. Although players paid the club and the club paid him, the club was simply acting as an agent, collecting the players' payments on his behalf. Again, although the requirement that there be a duty to pay can be seen as a separate test, it is linked to the 'risk' test in that the 'employer' is not shouldering any economic risk in the relationship if it is not obliged to pay the individual.

The *Autoclenz* decision, discussed above, represents an important limitation on the 'terms inconsistent' test.[39] As we have seen, *Autoclenz* encourages courts and tribunals to look for the parties' 'true agreement', instead of just focusing on the written contract. This makes it harder for an employer to insert a term, such as a substitution clause, into a contract in order to trigger the result that the individual is self-employed rather than an employee. However, it would be premature to consign the 'terms inconsistent' test to the dustbin because not all 'inconsistent terms' are fakes. The *Cheng Yuen* case is, arguably, a good example of this.

Mutuality of obligation We have now reached probably the most confusing part of the employee test: mutuality of obligation. Mutuality of obligation is relatively easy to define, but there is considerable disagreement, both in the case-law and the academic commentary, as to its proper place in employment law.

According to an influential analysis by Freedland, the contract of employment consists of two layers: the wage-work bargain, and the global or umbrella contract.[40] When an employee goes to work each day, he or she enters into a wage-work bargain. The employee performs work, and the employer pays him or her for it. These separate wage-work bargains can be drawn together into a global or umbrella contract of employment if mutuality of obligation is present. Mutuality of obligation refers to a pair of promises: a promise on the part of the employer to provide the employee with future work, and a promise on the part of the employee to accept that work when offered it. Importantly, Freedland was simply seeking to analyse the structure of the contract of employment given its long-term nature.[41] He was not laying down a test for deciding whether or not a contract of employment was present in any particular case. However, the courts have tended to use mutuality of obligation in precisely that way.

A case may help to illustrate how the test works. In *O'Kelly*, the claimants were waiters in a hotel.[42] They were on a list of so-called 'regular casual' staff who could be called into work when required. In practice, many of the 'regular casuals' had no other employment and worked many hours per week at the hotel. They claimed that they were employees, arguing that they were not at liberty to turn down work if offered, and that therefore the hotel was under some obligation to offer them work. These claims failed. The Court of Appeal held that economic forces kept the relationship together – the waiters accepted work when offered because they needed the money, not because they were under a legal obligation to do so. Without mutuality of obligation, the waiters were found to be self-employed.[43]

---

[39] *Autoclenz* (n 24).
[40] MR Freedland, *The Contract of Employment* (Clarendon Press 1976).
[41] For a detailed account, see Nicola Countouris, 'Uses and Misuses of "Mutuality of Obligations" and the Autonomy of Labour Law', in A Bogg *et al.* (eds), *The Autonomy of Labour Law* (Hart 2015).
[42] *O'Kelly v Trusthouse Forte Plc* [1984] QB 90 (CA).
[43] Cf *St Ives Plymouth Ltd v Haggerty*, (2008) UKEAT/0107/08/MAA, in which a 'course of dealing' analysis was used to establish mutuality, but this approach does not seem to have proved popular.

One consequence of this approach was that it became common in some settings for employers to insert 'no mutuality' clauses into written contracts in order to trigger the result that such contracts would be found not to be contracts of employment. We saw an example of this in *Autoclenz*, discussed above.[44] In that case, the car valeters had signed a contract document stating that there was no obligation on the 'employer' to provide work and that they were free to reject work when offered. However, the Supreme Court's decision in *Autoclenz* suggests that terms of this kind will no longer work automatically to prevent tribunals from deciding that an individual is an employee. If it is clear in practice that the employer provided work on a regular basis and expected the employee to accept that work, it may be possible to draw the conclusion that the 'real agreement' between the parties was one of employment. This will be for the tribunal to decide.

However, as we saw above in relation to 'terms inconsistent', the courts' new-found willingness to look beyond the written agreement between the parties does not solve all our problems. Even taking into account the reality of the parties' relationship, it may still be the case that there is no mutuality of obligation and therefore no contract of employment between them. For this reason, it is necessary to examine mutuality of obligation in greater depth.

In the case-law and literature, there are two competing schools of thought as to the role of mutuality of obligation. Some people think that mutuality of obligation is necessary in order to show that there is a contract (of any kind) between the parties.[45] Other people think that mutuality of obligation is about showing that the contract is one of employment.[46] The 'contract' school of thought is based on the doctrine of consideration in contract law. For there to be a contract, there must be consideration: there must be some kind of exchange between the parties. A pair of promises is sufficient to constitute that exchange, so if A promises B something and B promises A something in return, they have made a contract. In many cases, the courts have held that without mutuality of obligation, there is no contract of employment because there is no *contract* at all. The alternative 'employment' view focuses on the fact that the ordinary law of contract is not fussy about *what* the parties promise each other. There is no requirement that the pair of promises have any particular content. But in employment cases, the courts have insisted that the parties' promises have particular content: the employer must promise future work and the employee must promise to accept it. If we revisit *O'Kelly*, it could be argued that there were some promises in that case. The employer promised to keep the casual waiters on a list and to give them priority when work was available, and the waiters (arguably) promised to make themselves available for that work. These 'lesser' promises do not seem to be enough to satisfy the courts that mutuality of obligation is fulfilled. In turn, this suggests that mutuality is doing more than just establishing the presence of a contract of some kind: it is helping to classify that contract as one of employment. Indeed, on this view, we can see an overlap between mutuality and the 'risk' test, a hallmark of employee status. If the employer promises the employee that there will be work, regardless of day-to-day variations in demand, the employer is accepting risk. If the employer makes no such promise, so that the individual will

---

[44] *Autoclenz* (n 24) [8], [37].
[45] For example, *Stephenson* v *Delphi Diesel Systems* [2003] ICR 471 (EAT).
[46] I explain this more fully in ACL Davies, 'The Contract for Intermittent Employment' (2007) 36 ILJ 102.

only get work when work is available, the risk lies with the individual who would be found to be self-employed.

To add to the confusion, there are two (linked) situations in which it may be possible to bring a claim as an employee without establishing a global contract. These are: where the problem arises during the wage-work bargain, and where the claimant is able to use the concept of 'statutory continuity' instead of the global contract. We will examine each in turn.

Most writers seem to agree that each particular wage-work bargain is, in itself, likely to constitute a miniature contract of employment. The *McMeechan* case is a good illustration.[47] Here, the claimant worked for an employment agency under terms which made him self-employed. When the agency became insolvent, he was not paid for his final four-day assignment with a catering company. He tried to claim the money from the Secretary of State under statutory provisions enabling employees to claim unpaid wages in insolvency situations.[48] The Secretary of State argued that he was not eligible because he was self-employed. The Court of Appeal disagreed, holding that it was entirely possible to distinguish what it termed 'the general engagement' (which made him self-employed) from the 'specific engagement' or wage-work bargain (under which he was an employee). Importantly, terms denying mutuality of obligation were held to be irrelevant to the assessment of the individual's status during the wage-work bargain:

> When it comes to considering the terms of an individual, self-contained engagement the fact that the parties are not obliged in future to offer, or to accept, another engagement with the same, or a different, client must be neither here nor there.[49]

However, the finding that a particular wage-work bargain is a contract of employment is by no means automatic, as Elias LJ confirmed in the *Quashie* case.[50] It depends on all the usual indicators – control, risk and so on – being satisfied. *Little v BMI Chiltern Hospital* illustrates the point.[51] In that case, the claimant was a hospital porter. If there was no work for him to do during his shift, he could be sent home and not paid for the remainder of the shift. The Employment Appeal Tribunal (EAT) held that his engagements were not contracts of employment because there was no mutuality of obligation *during* the shift, in the sense of no obligation to provide work and pay throughout it. On this view, a wage-work bargain is only a miniature contract of employment where the employer is obliged to pay the individual for the whole of the agreed shift.

Where the wage-work bargain does constitute a contract of employment, the individual may be able to bring a claim in respect of events during the time he or she is working. The usefulness of this will depend on the right he or she wishes to assert. For example, if the individual requested emergency time off to make provision for his or her child who was sent home from school due to illness under s. 57A ERA 1996, and the employer unreasonably refused, a claim would lie. But the individual would not be able to claim where the right in question required a period of continuous

---

[47] *McMeechan v Secretary of State for Employment* [1997] ICR 549 (CA).
[48] See Chapter 10.
[49] *McMeechan* (n 47) 565 (Waite LJ).
[50] *Quashie* (n 33) [13]–[14]. The waiters in *O'Kelly* (above n 42) were held to be self-employed during their wage-work bargains but the reasons for this are not entirely clear.
[51] (2009) UKEAT/0021/09/DA.

employment in order to establish eligibility. So, for example, the individual would not be able to claim unfair dismissal because of the requirement to work for the employer for two years.[52]

This brings us neatly to the second situation in which it may not be necessary to establish mutuality of obligation. This is where the individual can invoke the 'statutory continuity' mechanism in s. 212 ERA 1996:

(1) Any week during the whole or part of which an employee's relations with his employer are governed by a contract of employment counts in computing the employee's period of employment.

(2) Subject to subsection (4), any week (not within subsection (1)) during the whole or part of which an employee is–

    (a) incapable of work in consequence of sickness or injury,

    (b) absent from work on account of a temporary cessation of work, or

    (c) absent from work in circumstances such that, by arrangement or custom, he is regarded as continuing in the employment of his employer for any purpose, counts in computing the employee's period of employment.

(3) Not more than twenty-six weeks count under subsection (3)(a) between any periods falling under subsection (1).

This section is designed to make it more difficult for an employer to defeat a claim that an individual has continuous employment, by providing that various breaks in employment do not break the legal concept of continuity. But for our purposes what is interesting is that it provides an alternative 'glue' to mutuality of obligation for sticking a series of contracts of employment together into a continuous period of employment.[53] So an individual who has a series of wage-work bargains and can prove that they are contracts of employment in accordance with *McMeechan* may be able to go one step further and prove a long period of continuous employment under s. 212. Importantly, this may be so even if the individual does not work whole weeks (because s. 212 applies if part of a week is governed by a contract of employment) and even if there are some weeks with no contract of employment, provided that the circumstances in subsection (3) are applicable.

This use of s. 212 was first illustrated by the case of *Cornwall CC v Prater*.[54] In that case, the claimant was a teacher who provided home tutoring for school pupils who were unable to attend school. She worked for the council for 10 years under a series of different assignments of varying duration each pertaining to a particular pupil. The Court of Appeal held that each engagement was a contract of service because (once she had accepted work) she was obliged to teach the pupil and the council was obliged to pay her. These assignments could be treated as a single period of continuous employment by virtue of s. 212. Even where there were gaps in her assignments – for example, over the summer holidays – these were covered by the concept of a 'temporary cessation of work' so did not break continuity. Importantly, the Court of Appeal emphasised that it did not matter that there was no mutuality of obligation. The teacher was under no obligation to accept new assignments and

---

[52] ERA 1996, s 108(1).

[53] See H Collins, 'Employment Rights of Casual Workers' (2000) 29 ILJ 73.

[54] [2006] EWCA Civ 102, [2006] ICR 731. See ACL Davies, 'Casual Workers and Continuity of Employment' (2006) 35 ILJ 196.

the council was under no obligation to offer them, but s. 212 gave rise to statutory continuity regardless of the contractual position.

After all of this, we might ask why mutuality of obligation matters: surely the *McMeechan* rule coupled with s. 212 can solve most problems? There are two possible reasons why they might not. First, as we have seen, not all wage-work bargains are contracts of employment, thus ruling out claims while working *and* access to s. 212 in those cases. Second, even where the individual has a series of contracts of employment, s. 212 may not be able to plug *all* the gaps in an individual's relationship with the employer where it is very intermittent in nature. As we saw above, if there is a week in which the individual does not work at all, it will only count where one of the reasons in s. 212(3) applies. So in *Vernon* v *Event Management Catering*, for example, the claimant took two weeks' holiday, but the EAT held that this fell within s. 212(3)(c) because he was still 'on the books' by arrangement during that time, not least because he was exercising his right to take holiday under the Working Time Regulations 1998.[55] But if the individual does not get any work in a particular week because the employer has allocated the available work to other casual workers (rather than because there is an overall reduction in the number of workers needed), this will fall outside the concept of 'temporary cessation' in s. 212(3)(b) so the week will not count.[56]

Summary To establish employee status, the individual will need to satisfy the following tests:

- control and/or risk, to establish that the relationship is one of employment;

- no 'terms inconsistent' with employee status; (personal service)

- mutuality of obligation giving rise to a global contract (unless the claim arises during a wage/work bargain which, itself, constitutes a contract of employment, or unless statutory continuity can be invoked).

Following the *Autoclenz* decision, terms in a written contract purporting to deny any of these elements may be disregarded if they do not reflect the 'true agreement' between the parties.[57]

Employee shareholders

The Growth and Infrastructure Act 2013, inserting s. 205A into ERA, introduced a new concept into English law: the 'employee shareholder'.[58] The employee shareholder is a person who is classified as an employee, but in exchange for an allocation of shares in the employer company, agrees to give up significant rights that would normally attach to employee status.

---

[55] (2007) UKEAT/0161/07/LA.
[56] *Byrne* v *Birmingham City Council* [1987] ICR 519 (CA).
[57] Above n 24.
[58] For a detailed critique, see Jeremias Prassl, 'Employee Shareholder "Status": Dismantling the Contract of Employment' (2013) 42 ILJ 307.

Rights denied Employee shareholders give up various 'employee' rights including the following:

- the right not to be unfairly dismissed (with exceptions, for example, for discriminatory dismissals);
- the right to a redundancy payment;
- the right to request flexible working.

They may also be required to give longer notice in some circumstances, for example, when returning to work after maternity leave. A key point to note about this list is that it contains most of the statutory rights that give employee status its significance, apart from the rights to family leave. This leads to the bizarre situation in which employee shareholders have more in common with workers in terms of their access to statutory employment rights, even though they are technically employees.

Acquiring the status Employee shareholder status may be offered to existing employees or to job applicants. An individual can only become an employee shareholder if he or she agrees this status with the employer company. The employer must issue the individual with a written statement detailing various aspects of employee shareholder status, including the loss of statutory rights discussed above, and details of the rights attaching to the shares to be given to the employee as part of the status. The employee must receive independent legal or trade union advice on the change of status at the employer's expense, and can only agree to the status after a seven-day period. Existing employees of a company additionally have the right not to be subjected to detriment[59] or dismissal[60] for refusing to agree. These various rights are designed to ensure, as far as possible, that the individual makes a free and well-informed choice of employee shareholder status, though job applicants will only have the 'option' of turning down the job offer.[61]

The incentive for an employee to become an employee shareholder is, of course, the offer of at least £2000-worth of shares in the employer company, with some associated tax advantages. A key question is whether this is enough to justify the loss of employment rights. Critics have argued that it is not. A particular problem is that the government has not specified any particular rights attaching to the shares themselves.[62] Thus, the employee shareholders may not have the right to receive dividends, or to sell their shares, and may have to sell them back to the company at the end of the employment relationship at a price it determines. This may make it difficult for employee shareholders to secure any financial benefit from the shares. The employer may also decide not to give employee shareholders any voting rights with their shares, thus denying them the opportunity to participate in corporate governance.

Comment When introducing the employee shareholder provisions, the government argued that it would increase flexibility and choice in employment relationships, whilst motivating employees to commit fully to the employer company. However, the

---

[59] ERA 1996, s 47G.
[60] ibid s 104G.
[61] Unless the employer voluntarily offers the job on an employee basis.
[62] See the guidance at https://www.gov.uk/employee-shareholders (last visited 14 October 2014).

new scheme seems to fit more closely with the 'demutualisation' idea discussed above, in which employees take on greater risks (they hold shares in, as well as a job with, the employing company) in exchange for fewer employment rights. It is to be hoped that, as some have suggested, employee shareholder status will prove too complicated to interest many firms.

4.3.2 Worker

A number of statutes enacted since 1997 apply to people who are 'workers'. As we shall see, the worker concept includes everyone who is an employee but is also meant to be broader. Its introduction reflected the long-standing concern that some people fell outside the strict employee definition but could not properly be regarded as self-employed. This meant that they did not qualify for the rights normally afforded to employees, but at the same time they were not running their own businesses so were not well-placed to bargain for their own terms and conditions. Having identified the problem, the government had two options: to extend the employee definition so that more people were included, or to introduce another status. The government chose the latter option, introducing the worker concept but granting workers a subset of the employment rights afforded to employees. This choice appears to have been influenced by the flexicurity agenda: rather than trying to combat the emergence of a two-tier labour market with a core of well-protected employees and a periphery of outsiders, it reinforces that divide by creating a less protective employment status for the periphery.

Although the logic of the worker test is easy to state – it gives a subset of employment rights to people in the grey area between employee and self-employed status – it has proved much harder to apply in practice. The courts have struggled with it, for three main reasons. First, some of the early interpretations were quite narrow, drawing on the employee case-law and reducing the distinction between the two concepts. Second, relatedly but more generally, it has not been clear whether 'worker' exists on the same spectrum as employee (but with more lenient requirements) or whether it is a completely separate concept. Early decisions suggested the former, but the latter has begun to feature in recent cases. And third, the courts have started to interpret the employee concept more broadly in ways which might make 'worker' redundant. For example, in *Autoclenz*, the individuals only needed worker status to claim holiday pay but were held by the Supreme Court to be employees.[63]

What rights do workers get?

The following rights apply to workers as well as to employees:

- the right to be paid the National Minimum Wage;[64]

- rights under the Working Time Regulations 1998;[65]

- the right not to be discriminated against on grounds of trade union membership;[66]

---

[63] *Autoclenz* (n 24) [36]–[39].
[64] National Minimum Wage Act 1998, s 1.
[65] The Working Time Regulations 1998, SI 1998/1833.
[66] Trade Union and Labour Relations (Consolidation) Act 1992, Part III.

- the right not to be discriminated against because of working part-time;[67]

- rights under the Agency Workers Regulations 2010;[68]

- the right to be accompanied at a disciplinary or grievance hearing;[69]

- protection against detriment for whistleblowing.[70]

Clearly, the aim is to offer workers some core minimum protections afforded by employment law, but because the worker concept has been introduced piecemeal over time, this list of rights is, arguably, not entirely coherent. The right to the NMW and to protection against trade union discrimination fall clearly into this category. The broader coverage of the rights for part-time and agency workers reflects the fact that these are, in themselves, 'non-standard' forms of working so there may be some overlap with these categories and people who are not employees, though this makes it particularly odd that protections for people with fixed-term contracts are only available to employees. But the confinement of (to take just one example) the right to a written statement of terms and conditions to employees seems odd, given that this is a very basic protection helping individuals to know (and thus to enforce) their rights.

Who is a worker?

The worker concept is defined in s. 230(3) ERA 1996 as follows:

> In this Act "worker" . . . means an individual who has entered into or works under (or, where the employment has ceased, worked under)–
>
> (a) a contract of employment, or
> (b) any other contract, whether express or implied and (if it is express) whether oral or in writing, whereby the individual undertakes to do or perform personally any work or services for another party to the contract whose status is not by virtue of the contract that of a client or customer of any profession or business undertaking carried on by the individual;
>
> and any reference to a worker's contract shall be construed accordingly.

Paragraph (a) makes it clear that the worker concept includes everyone who is an employee. What we are interested in is paragraph (b), the definition of those who are workers but not employees. To satisfy this definition, the individual must prove that he or she:

- has a contract

- to perform work personally

- for someone who is not the customer of a business he or she is running.

We will examine each of these elements in turn. In doing so, it is important to note that the *Autoclenz* approach to construing the individual's contract – although developed in the context of a finding that the individuals in that case were employees – is also likely to be applicable in this context, so written terms purporting to deny the

---

[67] The Part-time Workers (Prevention of Less Favourable Treatment) Regulations 2000, SI 2000/1551.
[68] The Agency Workers Regulations 2010, SI 2010/93.
[69] Employment Relations Act 1999, s 10.
[70] Employment Rights Act 1996, s 43A. There are various extensions to the worker concept in s 43K.

individual worker status might be displaced where they do not reflect the 'true agreement' between the parties.[71]

First, it is important that the individual has a contract with the alleged employer in order to get the case off the ground. For example, in *Bullock*, the claimant was a foster carer who sought to argue that she was a worker for the local authority, but since there was established authority to the effect that there was no contractual relationship between a foster carer and a local authority the claim failed.[72] In some cases, notably *Byrne Brothers*, the requirement of a contract has been taken to mean that a worker must also be able to show mutuality of obligation.[73] As we saw above, this reflects the view (arguably mistaken) that promises to provide and to perform future work are necessary for the existence of a contract (as opposed to necessary in order to show that the contract is one of employment). This means that individuals who work intermittently may find it no easier to demonstrate that they are workers than to demonstrate that they are employees under a global contract. In practice, though, courts and tribunals seem to have been more generous in finding mutuality of obligation where the worker test is being applied,[74] perhaps reflecting some doubt about this aspect of the *Byrne Brothers* decision.[75]

Second, the individual must establish that he or she is under an obligation to perform the work personally. This reflects the idea that worker status – like employee status – involves a personal relationship with the employer. However, it is also open to the difficulty (discussed above) that the introduction of a substitution clause into the alleged worker's contract might defeat worker status in the same way that a substitution clause in an alleged employee's contract often defeats employee status. Here, the courts have tended to follow the *Tanton* and *MacFarlane* approach.[76] If the contract contains an unfettered power of substitution, as in *Tanton*, the individual cannot be an employee or a worker, but if the contract contains a more limited power of substitution, as in *MacFarlane*, this will not necessarily defeat employee or worker status. Importantly, this position is further qualified by *Autoclenz*, in the sense that if the individual can prove that the substitution clause in the written contract does not reflect the 'true relationship' he or she may be able to persuade the tribunal to ignore it.[77]

Third, the tribunal must find that the individual is a worker unless it can be shown that the alleged employer is, in fact, the customer or client of a business being run by the alleged worker. This appears to be designed to distinguish workers from 'genuinely' self-employed people who are thought not to be in need of the law's protection. In the *Byrne Bros* case, the EAT took a distinctly purposive approach to this aspect of the test:

> The reason why employees are thought to need . . . protection is that they are in a subordinate and dependent position vis-a-vis their employers: the purpose of the [worker test] is to extend protection to workers who are, substantively and economically, in the same position. Thus the essence of the intended distinction must be between, on the one hand, workers

---

[71] *Autoclenz* (n 24).
[72] *Bullock v Norfolk CC* (2011) UKEAT/0230/10/RN.
[73] *Byrne Brothers (Formwork) Ltd v Baird* [2002] ICR 667 (EAT).
[74] *Singh v Bristol Sikh Temple Management Committee* (2012) UKEAT/0429/11/ZT.
[75] See *Windle v Secretary of State for Justice* [2015] ICR 156 (EAT), [54]–[55] for a recent obiter statement that mutuality is not a part of the 'worker' definition.
[76] *MacFarlane* (n 36); *Tanton* (n 35).
[77] *Autoclenz* (n 24).

whose degree of dependence is essentially the same as that of employees and, on the other, contractors who have a sufficiently arm's-length and independent position to be treated as being able to look after themselves in the relevant respects . . . Drawing that distinction in any particular case will involve all or most of the same considerations as arise in drawing the distinction between a contract of service and a contract for services – but with the boundary pushed further in the putative worker's favour.[78]

This suggested that, for example, the 'control' and 'risk' tests from the employee concept might also be applied in order to determine worker status, but that an individual might qualify as a worker even if he or she had more independence and took on more risk than would be acceptable in the case of an employee.[79] However, it is difficult to see where exactly the line might be drawn in practice.

A different approach was suggested in *Hospital Medical Group* v *Westwood*.[80] Hospital Medical Group (HMG) engaged Dr Westwood to provide advice and treatment at its clinic to patients suffering from hair loss. HMG was under no obligation to pay him unless patients wanted to use his services. Dr Westwood's main job was as a GP, and he also worked for another clinic on a part-time basis, but he undertook to provide hair loss treatment exclusively through HMG. The Court of Appeal upheld the EAT's finding that he was a 'worker' on the basis of an 'integration' test drawn from *Cotswold Developments Construction Ltd* v *Williams*.[81] Although Dr Westwood was found to be running his own business, it was held that he was 'integrated' into the clinic's work, in that he was presented by HMG to patients as 'its' surgeon, and because it did not make sense to describe HMG as the customer of Dr Westwood's business. This decision can be seen as broadening the worker test because it accepts that an individual can run a business and still be a worker, provided that the recipient of the business's services cannot be described as a customer.

The most recent decision on the issue, in the *Bates van Winkelhof* case, appears to be closer to the *Westwood* approach than to that in *Byrne Brothers*.[82] The case concerned a partner in a law firm who sought to establish that she had 'worker' status in order to avail herself of the protection afforded to whistleblowers under ERA 1996, s. 47B. It was accepted that she had a contract to perform the work personally and that the law firm could not be regarded as her customer or client. However, an attempt was made to argue that she was not a 'worker' because she was not 'subordinated' to the employer. Baroness Hale rejected this as an unwarranted gloss on the statutory language:

> While subordination may sometimes be an aid to distinguishing workers from other self-employed people, it is not a freestanding and universal characteristic of being a worker.[83]

She suggested that a small firm might be 'subordinated' to the demands of a particular client, but nevertheless independent,[84] whereas an individual might be a 'worker' (like Dr Westwood) without being 'subordinated' at all.

---

[78] Above n 73, [17]. See also *Macalinden* v *Lazarov*, (2014) UKEAT/0453/13.

[79] Some doubt was cast on the purposive approach (obiter) in *Redrow Homes (Yorkshire) Ltd* v *Wright* [2004] EWCA Civ 469, [2004] ICR 1126 [21].

[80] [2012] EWCA Civ 1005, [2013] ICR 415.

[81] [2006] IRLR 181 (EAT).

[82] *Bates van Winkelhof* v *Clyde & Co LLP* [2014] UKSC 32, [2014] ICR 730. See Jeremias Prassl, 'Members, Partners, Employees, Workers: Partnership Law and Employment Status Revisited' (2014) 43 ILJ 495.

[83] ibid [39].

[84] See also *James* v *Redcats (Brands) Ltd* [2007] ICR 1006 (EAT).

These two cases suggest that, in order to apply the worker test, it is necessary to focus on the terminology used in the statute and not to approach it with preconceived ideas drawn from the employee case-law. 'Worker' is not a 'low-fat' version of employee: it is a different concept altogether. This may have the advantage of encouraging courts and tribunals to apply the worker concept more broadly and, perhaps, to abandon earlier mistakes such as the inclusion of mutuality of obligation as a requirement for worker status. However, it is important to note that the case-law in this area is likely to remain in a state of flux for some time to come, not least because of the reluctance of courts at all levels (including the Court of Appeal in *Westwood* and the Supreme Court in *Bates van Winkelhof*) to offer general guidance on the definition of worker.

4.3.3 Employment under a contract personally to do work

Equality law adopts a different definition of 'employee' and 'employment'. In theory, it offers even broader protection than the 'worker' definition, with a view to ensuring that prohibitions on workplace discrimination apply to as many people as possible, but its interpretation by the courts suggests that it may be narrower in practice.

Under s. 83(2)(a) Equality Act 2010, 'employment' means 'employment under a contract of employment, a contract of apprenticeship or a contract personally to do work'. This means that everyone who counts as an employee (discussed above) is protected (because of the reference to the contract of employment), as is everyone who counts as a 'worker' (because of the reference to a 'contract personally to do work').

What is less clear is how much broader than 'employee' and 'worker' the Equality Act definition is. The reference to 'contract personally to do work' does not include the 'client or customer' exception that is applicable in the 'worker' definition.[85] This suggests that the concept might include some people who are running their own businesses, and therefore have clients or customers, but still undertake to perform the work personally. It has long been suggested in the academic literature that someone like a self-employed plumber might be protected under the Equality Act definition provided that he or she undertook to perform the work personally.[86] While there is clearly some nervousness about making a householder liable in employment law when he or she hires a plumber, it could be argued that equality law was an exception to this because of the importance of ensuring that people did not turn away self-employed contractors for discriminatory reasons.

However, the decision of the Supreme Court in *Jivraj* v *Hashwani* has cast some doubt on this argument and on the breadth of the Equality Act definition more generally.[87] The facts of the case are unusual. The parties had entered into a commercial venture. Any disputes concerning the venture were to be subject to arbitration. The parties had agreed that the arbitrators should be members of the Ismaili community. When a dispute arose, one of the parties sought to appoint a non-Ismaili arbitrator. When this was challenged, the person appointing the arbitrator argued that the requirement to be a member of the Ismaili community was

---

[85] Nor is there any mutuality requirement: *Windle*, above n 75.
[86] For example, S Fredman, 'Marginalising Equal Pay Laws' (2004) 33 ILJ 281, 285.
[87] [2011] UKSC 40, [2011] ICR 1004.

discriminatory on grounds of religion. The question facing the Supreme Court was whether being an arbitrator fell within what is now the Equality Act definition. The Supreme Court focused on the first part of the definition and held that the phrase '*employed under* . . . a contract personally to do work' implied that a person within the definition was somehow subordinate to an 'employer'.[88] Since arbitrators are expected to act independently, they are not subordinate to an employer as a matter of principle and are not therefore within the definition.

The broader implication of *Jivraj* is that – in addition to the requirement of personal service – it is also necessary to show that there is a relationship of subordination before an individual falls within the Equality Act definition.[89] This has the bizarre consequence that the Equality Act definition may now be narrower than the worker concept, because the requirement of subordination was rejected for the worker concept in *Bates van Winkelhof*.[90] On this view, the doctor in the *Westwood* case would be entitled to (for example) the NMW but not to the protection of equality law because he provided his work personally to the hospital but was not subordinated to it. Baroness Hale in *Bates* appeared to avoid this conclusion by treating the subordination requirement in *Jivraj* as having been 'introduced in order to distinguish the intermediate category [of workers] from people who were dealing with clients or customers on their own account'.[91] She appeared to think that the worker definition and the Equality Act definition were broadly the same,[92] but this is hardly borne out by the case-law. The best solution to the problem would be to confine *Jivraj* to its unusual facts, and to return to a literal reading of the statute, which would suggest a slightly broader scope for the Equality Act than for statutes using the worker concept.

4.3.4 Worker in EU law

The meaning of worker in EU law has two dimensions. First, in some situations, EU law has its own autonomous definition of 'worker'. This applies in a limited range of areas, usually derived from articles of the Treaties, where there is a need for the law to apply uniformly across the different Member States. This definition is applicable in the law on free movement of workers across Member States' borders,[93] and in the law on equal pay for men and women.[94] Second, where national law is implementing an EU directive, EU law may be relevant to the interpretation of the national definition of 'employee' or 'worker'. Although commentators have long argued for the relevance of EU law in this second sense, there has been very little case-law on the subject, though the recent *O'Brien* litigation suggests that this may be about to change.[95]

---

[88] ibid [27], [34] (Lord Clarke). See also *Halawi* v *WDFG Ltd* [2014] EWCA Civ 1387, [2015] IRLR 50.

[89] For a detailed discussion, see Christopher McCrudden, 'Two Views of Subordination: the Personal Scope of Employment Discrimination Law in *Jivraj* v *Hashwani*' (2012) 41 ILJ 30; Mark Freedland and Nicola Kountouris, 'Employment Equality and Personal Work Relations – a Critique of *Jivraj* v *Hashwani*' (2012) 41 ILJ 56.

[90] *Bates van Winkelhof* (n 82) [39].

[91] ibid [32].

[92] See also *Windle*, above n 75, [27].

[93] Treaty on the Functioning of the European Union, art 45.

[94] ibid art 157.

[95] Case C-393/10 *O'Brien* v *Ministry of Justice* [2012] ICR 955; *Department of Constitutional Affairs* v *O'Brien* [2013] UKSC 6, [2013] ICR 499.

The EU definition of 'worker'

The Court of Justice of the European Union (CJEU) uses slightly different terminology to define 'worker' depending on the Treaty provisions in question.[96]

In the context of Article 45 Treaty on the Functioning of the European Union (TFEU), on the free movement of workers, the Court held in *Lawrie-Blum* that 'the essential feature of an employment relationship . . . is that for a certain period of time a person performs services for and under the direction of another person in return for which he receives remuneration'.[97] It is clear from *Levin* that the work need not be full-time, nor is it a requirement that the individual should obtain any particular level of income from the work.[98] However, in the same case, the Court stated that the free movement rules applied 'only [to] the pursuit of effective and genuine activities, to the exclusion of activities on such a small scale as to be regarded as purely marginal and ancillary'.[99] Thus, an individual performing work as part of a therapeutic programme for recovering drug addicts was held not to be a worker for the purposes of Article 45.[100] In the free movement context, it is more important to distinguish workers from economically inactive people, who only get the rights afforded to citizens, than to distinguish them from the self-employed, who get similar rights.[101]

There is also an EU-wide definition of worker for the purposes of equal pay for men and women under Article 157 TFEU.[102] In *Allonby*, the Court cited the *Lawrie-Blum* definition, and made it clear that Article 157 does not protect the self-employed: 'it is clear from that definition that the authors of the Treaty did not intend that the term "worker". . . should include independent providers of services who are not in a relationship of subordination with the person who receives the services'.[103] However, the Court also noted the importance of classifying individuals as workers where they were not genuinely self-employed.[104]

Fredman has criticised the Court's case-law for its focus on subordination rather than economic dependence, arguing that the latter concept would capture a broader range of non-standard workers.[105] Whilst the Court has continued to emphasise subordination in later cases, it has applied the term in a flexible way which suggests that it will not prove much of an obstacle in practice. *Danosa* is a good example of this.[106] In that case, the claimant was a company director who was dismissed from her employment on grounds of her pregnancy. She brought a claim under the Pregnant

---

[96] Case C-85/96 *Martínez Sala* v *Freistaat Bayern* [1998] ECR I-2691 [31].
[97] Case 66/85 *Lawrie-Blum* v *Land Baden-Württemberg* [1986] ECR 2121 [17].
[98] Case 53/81 *Levin* v *Staatssecretaris van Justitie* [1982] ECR 1035 [16].
[99] ibid [17].
[100] Case C-344/87 *Bettray* v *Staatssecretaris van Justitie* [1989] ECR 1621, but see also Case C-456/02 *Trojani* v *Centre Public d'Aide Sociale de Bruxelles (CPAS)* [2004] ECR I-7573.
[101] See Directive 2004/38/EC, discussed in detail in Chapter 3.
[102] See Chapter 7 for a detailed discussion. See also (in the context of competition law and collective bargaining) Case C-413/13 *FNV Kunsten Informatie en Media* v *Staat der Nederlanden* [2015] 4 CMLR 1.
[103] Case C-256/01 *Allonby* v *Accrington & Rossendale College* [2004] ECR I-873 [68].
[104] ibid [71].
[105] S Fredman, 'Marginalising Equal Pay Laws' (2004) 33 ILJ 281, 284–5.
[106] Case C-232/09 *Danosa* v *LKB Lzings* [2011] 2 CMLR 2.

Workers Directive.[107] The Court held that the application of the worker definition required a careful assessment of the context by the national court:

> The fact that Ms Danosa was a member of the Board of Directors of a capital company is not enough in itself to rule out the possibility that she was in a relationship of subordination to that company: it is necessary to consider the circumstances in which the Board Member was recruited; the nature of the duties entrusted to that person; the context in which those duties were performed; the scope of the person's powers and the extent to which he or she was supervised within the company; and the circumstances under which the person could be removed.[108]

The Court suggested that it was significant for the purposes of 'subordination' that the claimant had to report on her work to the supervisory board and could be dismissed by the shareholders.[109]

This suggests that the use of 'subordination' in EU law is less about identifying employee-like relationships and more about excluding genuine self-employment from the scope of protection. On this reading, it is closer to the Supreme Court's analysis in *Bates van Winkelhof* than that in *Jivraj*.[110]

'Worker' in implementing measures

In general terms, EU directives set out the policy objective to be achieved and allow the Member States a degree of discretion in their exact implementation. Traditionally, this discretion has extended to the 'personal scope' of the law. In other words, it is up to the Member State to decide who is protected by the EU measure. The UK government has made full use of this discretion. In English law, some measures implementing EU directives use 'employee', others 'worker', and of course the Equality Act 2010 uses a slightly different concept of 'employment under . . . a contract personally to do work'.

Nevertheless, it is important to remember that any implementation of a directive is subject to the general EU law requirement of effectiveness. For example, in *Commission* v *UK*, the UK's implementation of the Collective Redundancies Directive – requiring the employer to consult workforce representatives in the event of large-scale redundancies – was found wanting because it did not guarantee the possibility of consultation in all workplaces.[111] The UK's implementation only provided for consultation where the employer recognised a trade union, with the result that in non-unionised workplaces, there was no mechanism for consultation. This breached the requirement of effective implementation.

---

[107] Council Directive 92/85/EEC of 19 October 1992 on the introduction of measures to encourage improvements in the safety and health at work of pregnant workers and workers who have recently given birth or are breastfeeding [1992] OJ L348/1. The Court held in *Kiiski* that the term 'pregnant worker' in Article 2 of the Directive should be given an EU meaning: Case C-116/06 *Kiiski* v *Tampereen kaupunki* [2007] ECR I-7643 [24].

[108] *Danosa* (n 106), [47].

[109] ibid [49]–[50].

[110] Above n 82 and 87 respectively.

[111] Case C-383/92 *Commission* v *UK* [1994] ECR I-2479.

The same argument might be made if a Member State's choice of 'employee' or 'worker' definition excluded people who ought to receive protection. This issue was addressed in the *O'Brien* case.[112] The case concerned a barrister who sat part-time as a judge, known as a 'recorder'. The government maintained that he was not entitled to a judicial pension. He argued that this constituted discrimination on the ground that he worked part-time, contrary to the Part-Time Workers (Prevention of Less Favourable Treatment) Regulations 2000 since full-time judges were entitled to a pension.[113] In order for his claim to be heard, Mr O'Brien needed to show that he was a 'worker'.

The issue was referred to the Court of Justice.[114] The Court reiterated the general principle that the 'worker' definition was a matter for the Member State but held that the Member State's discretion was not unlimited because of the need to avoid arbitrarily excluding certain categories of person from its scope. It was for the national court to decide whether or not part-time judges were workers but the Court of Justice indicated that certain criteria were to be taken into account. Most importantly, the Court of Justice said that the 'spirit and purpose' of the directive was to protect workers as distinct from self-employed people. The Court then noted various indicators that part-time judges were not self-employed:

> With that in mind, the rules for appointing and removing judges must be considered, and also the way in which their work is organised. In that connection, it is apparent from the order for reference that judges are expected to work during defined times and periods, even though this can be managed by the judges themselves with a greater degree of flexibility than members of other professions.
>
> Furthermore, as appears from the order for reference, that judges are entitled to sick pay, maternity or paternity pay and other similar benefits.[115]

When the case returned to the UK Supreme Court, it held that in the light of these factors, part-time judges counted as 'workers'.[116]

The exact effect of *O'Brien* is difficult to discern. Since the case was brought against the government, it was not necessary for the Supreme Court to be precise about the basis for its decision. On the one hand, since the case was 'vertical' (against the state), it is possible that Mr O'Brien was allowed to rely directly on the directive. On the other hand, it may be that the Supreme Court simply reinterpreted the domestic Regulations in order to make them compatible with EU law. This would involve disapplying reg. 17, which expressly excluded part-time judges, and adopting a definition of 'worker' that included them. It was a matter of dispute between the parties whether, in the absence of reg. 17, part-time judges would have counted as 'workers' under the ordinary meaning of reg. 2.

It may be that *O'Brien* will have limited application beyond its own facts. The government had tried to exclude a specific group of people – part-time judges – from the scope of protection, and the courts (both the CJEU and the Supreme Court) found that there was no justification for the removal of this group because they had the same characteristics as people who were protected. However, *O'Brien* may

---

[112] *O'Brien* (n 95).
[113] SI 2000/1551.
[114] Case C-393/10 *O'Brien v Ministry of Justice* [2012] ICR 955.
[115] ibid [45] and [46].
[116] *Department of Constitutional Affairs v O'Brien* [2013] UKSC 6, [2013] ICR 499.

turn out to stand for a broader proposition: that when implementing a directive, the UK government must define its personal scope so that the directive's objective (of protecting people who are not self-employed) is met. If that were to be the case, it would cast serious doubt on the UK's implementation of some directives, particularly where the narrower 'employee' definition has been used instead of 'worker'.

4.3.5 Self-employment

It may be helpful to conclude this section by thinking very briefly about people who are self-employed, since much of the focus of the discussion so far has been about excluding them from the scope of labour law.

A self-employed person works under a contract for services rather than a contract of service. This relationship is governed by the ordinary law of contract rather than by labour law. The thinking behind this is that a self-employed person is an entrepreneur capable of *bargaining* with anyone who wishes to use his or her services. So, for example, a self-employed electrician would tell a householder how much a particular job would cost, rather than the householder telling the electrician how much he or she intends to pay.

The genuinely self-employed are often thought to have two other key characteristics that ought to exclude them from the scope of labour law. One is that they may employ other people to help them do their work. It might seem odd to give them the protection of labour law when they are, themselves, the employers of others. It is also inconsistent with the general assumption within labour law that someone who is an employee or worker provides *personal* service and cannot send someone else to do his or her job. The other is that they may have numerous customers or clients for whom they work. This suggests that they are able to *spread* their economic risks across those different customers or clients. For example, if one customer takes his or her business elsewhere, the self-employed person will be able to take on more work for other customers or find new customers to fill the shortfall. The self-employed person is not dependent on one source of income.

However, these various assumptions can be quite problematic in practice. Imagine that the electrician works for a major house-building firm on a building site. He or she is allowed to (and does) employ an assistant to help out, but the work on the building site is full-time so there is no real opportunity to take on other jobs. The firm has a standard rate for all the electricians working on the site. Once a particular building project is finished, the work is at an end, unless the house-building firm sets up another project in the local area at which the electrician might be able to get work. On these facts, the electrician does not bargain for his or her own rate of pay and does not have an obligation of personal service, but cannot spread his or her risk very easily across multiple jobs and does not have a stable income.

The point of the example is not to revisit the discussion, above, about classification as an employee or a worker. It seems likely, in this case, that the electrician would be found to be self-employed because there is no obligation to do the work personally, a factor that defeats the application of all the domestic law definitions we have considered. This is so even without introducing any attempt by the house-building firm to ensure that the electricians will be treated as self-employed through a cleverly drafted contract. The point is simply to highlight the fact that we should be wary about our assumptions about the self-employed. This category covers a wide variety of different types of relationship, and not everyone within the category is capable of bargaining for protection or spreading risk. Thus, the boundary between employment and self-employment remains highly contested, despite attempts to broaden the notion of employment through various types of worker concept.

4.4 NON-STANDARD WORKING

In this section, we will consider various different types of 'non-standard' working arrangement: so-called 'zero hours', fixed-term, part-time and agency working. These arrangements all attract special regulation in law. It is important to note that the umbrella label of 'non-standard' working is not in any sense 'official' terminology and is simply used as shorthand. It implies that there is a 'standard' form of working – perhaps an employee on an indefinite, full-time contract with an employer – and that anything else is a deviation from the norm. But in today's labour market, non-standard working is becoming increasingly common. Our discussion will focus on two issues: the problems faced by individuals with each type of non-standard arrangement, and whether the law addresses those problems, and the intersection between each type of arrangement and the organising concepts (employee and worker) we discussed in the previous section.

With the exception of the law on 'zero-hours' working, much of the regulation to be considered in this section comes from EU law and reflects the 'flexicurity' policy discussed in section 2. This is the idea that EU labour markets – and therefore workers – need to become more flexible and adaptable to change, whilst maintaining some kind of protection (or security) for workers. The directives on non-standard forms of work seek to strike this balance by encouraging the availability of non-standard forms of work (because they are more flexible for firms, and provide job opportunities for workers), whilst ensuring that people doing non-standard jobs do not suffer from discrimination (so that the difference between typical and atypical forms of work is reduced). Not surprisingly, this approach is controversial among those who take the view that some forms of atypical work – like agency work – are inherently unstable and therefore disadvantageous to workers, and for that reason should not be encouraged at all. And it is controversial among those who believe that regulating non-standard forms of work, like agency work, will make them less attractive to firms, thereby making it even harder for the unemployed to find work. Importantly, since EU law generally gives Member States a discretion to determine questions of personal scope when transposing directives, there is a complex and not always satisfactory interaction between the employee and worker concepts and the protective regimes derived from the relevant directives.

4.4.1 'Zero hours'

Zero-hours work is an increasingly common label for a particular kind of casual working arrangement. It refers to the situation in which an individual has an arrangement with an employer under which the employer does not promise any particular level of work to the individual. This type of working may also be referred to as casual or intermittent or 'as required' work, but it is important to remember that none of these terms is a term of art so they may denote different types of arrangement.

Of course, in some cases, the individual's contract may purport to be a 'zero-hours' arrangement when in fact he or she has regular working hours, but the *Autoclenz* decision should help to address this.[117] We will examine the problems associated with 'genuine' 'zero-hours' working before considering a recent proposal by the government to regulate a particular facet of these arrangements.

Problems

There are two main problems faced by people with 'zero-hours' working: they do not have any guaranteed level of income, and their employment status (and thus access to employment rights) is uncertain.

The first problem is quite obvious. If the employer does not promise any particular level of work, the individual's income may vary from week to week and may be zero in some weeks. This makes it difficult to manage financially, not least because the benefits system may take some time to catch up with fluctuations in the individual's income. One response to this might be to suggest that the individual could supplement his or her income by taking on a second job. However, there are two problems with this. One possibility is that the employer may include an 'exclusivity' clause in their agreement, providing that the individual must offer his or her services exclusively to that employer and may not work elsewhere. But the more likely possibility in practice is that the individual may feel unable to take a second job because then he or she would not necessarily be available for work when called in by the first employer. This might lead to the individual either not being called upon again or being 'demoted' in the pecking order which often exists in this kind of work, in which those who work regularly are more likely to be offered work when it becomes available.[118] Thus, the individual may feel that taking a second job will put the first one at risk.

The second problem flows from the employee and worker definitions we considered above. While the individual is at work – during the wage/work bargain – it is strongly arguable (though not inevitable) that he or she is an employee, entitled to employee and worker rights (like the NMW) where they are applicable during work. However, it is unlikely that someone with a zero-hours arrangement would be able to establish employee status over the longer term (for example, in order to claim unfair dismissal or a redundancy payment when the employment was terminated). This is because – without a promise on the part of the employer to provide work – there is no mutuality of obligation. And if there are significant gaps in the employment, statutory continuity may not work to fill them. Although the government's consultation on zero-hours working suggests that some individuals in these relationships may be employees, the case cited, *Pulse Healthcare*, involved a finding that the zero-hours term in the contract did not reflect the true arrangement between the parties and that the employees in the case had in fact regular working hours.[119]

---

[117] For an example see *Borrer* v *Cardinal Security* (2012) UKEAT/0416/12/GE.

[118] For further discussion, see ACL Davies, 'The Contract for Intermittent Employment' (2007) 36 ILJ 102.

[119] *Pulse Healthcare Ltd* v *Carewatch Care Services Ltd* (2012) UKEAT/0123/12/BA, cited in Department for Business, Innovation and Skills, *Zero Hours Employment Contracts: Consultation* (BIS/13/1275; 2013), Annex 2.

Proposed reforms

The government's consultation on zero-hours working has been condemned by commentators for its acceptance that zero-hours working is, in principle, a legitimate form of arrangement which brings flexibility to the labour market to the benefit of working people as well as employers.

The only reform it suggests is a ban on exclusivity clauses in zero-hours contracts. This is to be implemented in cl. 139 Small Business, Enterprise and Employment Bill, inserting a new s. 27A into ERA 1996:

(1) In this section "zero hours contract" means a contract of employment or other worker's contract under which–

   (a) the undertaking to do or perform work or services is an undertaking to do so conditionally on the employer making work or services available to the worker, and

   (b) there is no certainty that any such work or services will be made available to the worker.

(2) For this purpose, an employer makes work or services available to a worker if the employer requests or requires the worker to do the work or perform the services.

(3) Any provision of a zero hours contract which–

   (a) prohibits the worker from doing work or performing services under another contract or under any other arrangement, or

   (b) prohibits the worker from doing so without the employer's consent, is unenforceable against the worker.

There are two problems with this provision. First, it does not address the more general problems associated with zero-hours working, discussed above. Second, even within the confines of its limited ambitions, it may fail. As drafted, it only applies to zero-hours contracts defined as contracts of employment or worker contracts. As we have seen, zero-hours contracts have uncertain status. Proposed new s. 27B contains a regulation-making power which would allow the Secretary of State to ban exclusivity clauses for 'individuals who work under non-contractual zero hours arrangements' which may – if exercised – help with this problem. But even without exclusivity clauses, zero-hours arrangements will continue to be held together by the economic forces described above. In most cases, the employer does not need to ban the individual from taking other work because the individual's *availability* is crucial to being offered work when there is any to do.

4.4.2 Fixed-term

Fixed-term working is the name given to work with a definite end-point. For example, the individual is employed for a set number of months, or for the duration of a particular project. As a form of non-standard working it is implicitly contrasted with 'standard' employment under an indefinite contract, which continues until it is lawfully terminated by either party. Again, we will consider some of the problems with fixed-term working before examining the legislative response.

Problems

It is important to be clear from the outset that fixed-term working offers flexibility to employers which may often be quite legitimate. The employer might be engaged in a seasonal business, for example, and might take on extra staff on a fixed-term basis to cover busy periods. It is hard to imagine a functioning labour market without some fixed-term working.

Fixed-term working is often portrayed as offering flexibility to the individual as well as the employer. He or she can take on a temporary job (a student working over the summer, for example) knowing that it will end when he or she needs to do something else (go back to university). However, this advantage is easy to overstate. It is a straightforward matter to resign from an indefinite contract, by giving the employer the appropriate length of notice. Given the choice, there is no obvious reason for the individual to prefer a fixed-term arrangement.[120]

The main problem with fixed-term working is uncertainty. This may seem odd, since the point of a fixed-term contract is that it has a clear end date. Indeed, it may be more certain in that regard than an indefinite contract, which looks as if it will last forever but may be terminated by the employer (provided it complies with the law on wrongful and unfair dismissal) at any time. The uncertainty with fixed-term work arises in two ways. First, there is the uncertainty of looking for another job when the fixed-term job ends. This may make it difficult to achieve a stable income or to plan financially. Second, there is the uncertainty associated with the fact that – in many cases – the employer may renew the contract. Of course, on one level, this is a good thing, because the individual keeps his or her job, but on another level, it may mean that the individual works for a long time for the employer without ever acquiring the long-term commitment from the employer associated with an indefinite contract. More worryingly, a series of fixed-term contracts might be used in an abusive way to deny the individual employment rights. For example, the employer might use a discontinuous series of fixed-term contracts to ensure that the individual never becomes entitled to unfair dismissal protection.

The regulatory response

The main response to fixed-term work comes from the EU in the shape of the social partners' Agreement on fixed-term work which was given legal effect in Directive 99/70.[121] This has been implemented in English law by means of the Fixed-term Employees (Prevention of Less Favourable Treatment) Regulations 2002 (FTER).[122] This regime affords fixed-term employees a right not to be discriminated against and protection against the abuse of successive fixed-term contracts.

A fixed-term worker is defined in the Agreement as 'a person having an employment contract or relationship entered into directly between an employer and a worker where the end of the employment contract or relationship is determined by objective

---

[120] A point made forcefully by Jill Murray, 'Normalising Temporary Work: the Proposed Directive on Fixed-Term Work' (1999) 28 ILJ 269.

[121] See, generally, ibid.

[122] SI 2002/2034.

conditions such as reaching a specific date, completing a specific task, or the occurrence of a specific event'.[123] FTER, reg. 2(1) adopts the same definition with slightly different wording. However, a key feature of the FTER is that they apply only to employees (because a fixed-term contract is defined as a contract of employment) and not to any broader category such as worker. On one view, this may not matter very much, since the focus will be on the individual's status whilst working during the fixed-term contract, when it may be easier to establish employee status. But it may exclude some people, for example, highly skilled individuals taken on to complete a project who are given discretion over their work and may thus fail the 'control' test.

Fixed-term employees are protected against discrimination when compared with the employer's permanent employees, by virtue of cl. 4 of the Agreement (which has direct effect)[124] and reg. 3 FTER. The intention here is to ensure that, for example, a fixed-term employee cannot be paid less per hour than a permanent employee performing the same tasks. The permanent employees must be 'comparable' within reg. 2:

(1) For the purposes of these Regulations, an employee is a comparable permanent employee in relation to a fixed-term employee if, at the time when the treatment that is alleged to be less favourable to the fixed-term employee takes place,

    (a) both employees are–

        (i) employed by the same employer, and

        (ii) engaged in the same or broadly similar work having regard, where relevant, to whether they have a similar level of qualification and skills; and

    (b) the permanent employee works or is based at the same establishment as the fixed-term employee or, where there is no comparable permanent employee working or based at that establishment who satisfies the requirements of sub-paragraph (a), works or is based at a different establishment and satisfies those requirements.

(2) For the purposes of paragraph (1), an employee is not a comparable permanent employee if his employment has ceased.

The technique of comparison is familiar from equality law more generally, but it is worth noting that the provisions for fixed-term employees are less generous. For example, the comparable permanent employee must be real (not hypothetical) and employed at the same time as the fixed-term employee. It is not difficult to envisage a situation in which the employer uses fixed-term employees for certain types of work so that there are no permanent employees engaged on the 'same or broadly similar' work to act as comparators.

It must be established that any difference in treatment between the fixed-term employee and his or her comparator is because he or she is a fixed-term employee, under reg. 3(3)(a). Under reg. 3(3)(b), the employer has an 'objective justification' defence. In other words, the employer can argue that the difference in treatment is for legitimate business reasons. This is facilitated by reg. 4, which provides that an objective justification is established where the terms of the fixed-term employee's contract taken as a whole are 'at least as favourable' as those of the comparator even

[123] Council Directive 1999/70/EC of 28 June 1999 concerning the framework agreement on fixed-term work concluded by ETUC, UNICE and CEEP, [1999] OJ L175/43, Annex, cl 3(1). This excludes agency workers: see SI 2002/2034, reg. 19, and the discussion of agency work below.
[124] Case C-268/06 *Impact v Minister for Agriculture and Food* [2008] ECR I-2483 [59]–[68].

if there are differences in relation to particular terms. This 'package' comparison would not be permitted in equal pay law, for example, where a woman is entitled to a line-by-line comparison between her contract and that of her male comparator.[125]

Although the non-discrimination provision has not been much litigated in the UK, it has been used by the CJEU to combat various forms of discrimination against fixed-term workers, for example, a rule precluding them from obtaining pay increments for length of service afforded to permanent workers,[126] and a rule that previous experience as a fixed-term worker did not count in a competition for civil service jobs.[127]

The second element of protection afforded by the Agreement and the FTER tackles the problem of successive fixed-term contracts. Clause 5 of the Agreement requires the Member States to take steps to prevent the 'abuse' of successive fixed-term contracts, but gives them the choice of requiring the employer to have objective reasons for renewing a fixed-term contract, limiting the maximum total duration of successive fixed-term contracts, limiting the number of renewals or some combination of these measures. Because this clause gives the Member States a discretion, it has been found to be insufficiently precise for the purposes of direct effect.[128]

The provision is transposed into English law by reg. 8 FTER. This is quite a complex provision but its effect is to convert a fixed-term contract into a permanent one where the employee has been employed on more than one fixed-term contract for four years or more, unless the employer has provided objective justification for the continuation of the relationship on a fixed-term basis. The CJEU has held that these reasons must involve 'objective factors relating to the particular features of the activity concerned and to the conditions under which it is carried out'.[129] There are two points to note about reg. 8. First, it does not preclude the use of a single fixed-term contract with a duration longer than four years. This is because it only applies to an employee who is on a second, or renewed, fixed-term contract. Second, the choice of four years as the period for achieving a permanent contract is relatively long compared to other Member States, many of which have opted for two years.[130]

It is worth noting that, under s. 95 ERA 1996, the expiry of a fixed-term contract constitutes a 'dismissal' for the purposes of unfair dismissal law. This prevents employers from evading the unfair dismissal provisions by employing people on fixed-term contracts and simply allowing the contracts to expire. It also means that, if an employer does allow a fixed-term contract to expire, it must have a reason for the dismissal within the list of potentially fair reasons and it must act reasonably if it is to avoid unfair dismissal liability.[131] However, the value of this protection is limited, since courts and tribunals have held that, if the employer's need for an employee is genuinely temporary and this is made clear to the employee from the

---

[125] Case C-262/88 *Barber* v *Guardian Royal Exchange Assurance Group* [1990] ECR I-1889.

[126] Case C-444/09 *Gavieiro Gavieiro* v *Consellería de Educación e Ordenación Universitaria de la Xunta de Galicia* [2010] ECR I-14031.

[127] Case C-177/10 *Santana* v *Consejería de Justicia y Administración Pública de la Junta de Andalucía* [2011] ECR I-7907 [63]–[84], though it was for the national court to determine whether experience as an interim civil servant was comparable to experience gained as a permanent civil servant.

[128] *Impact*, above n 124, [69]–[80].

[129] Case C-212/04 *Adeneler* v *ELOG* [2006] ECR I-6057 [72].

[130] Commission, *Report by the Commission Services on the Implementation of Council Directive 1999/70/EC of 28 June 1999 concerning the Framework Agreement on Fixed-term Work Concluded by ETUC, UNICE and CEEP (EU-15)* (SEC(2006) 1074) (2006).

[131] *Tansell* v *Henley College Coventry* [2013] IRLR 174 (EAT).

outset, the expiry of the fixed-term contract may constitute 'some other substantial reason' for dismissal and is thus potentially fair.[132] Moreover, an employee would need two years' continuous service in order to qualify to bring a claim. A creative argument that the termination of a fixed-term contract amounted to discrimination within FTER (compared to the treatment of permanent employees) failed in *Webley* v *Department for Work and Pensions*, on the grounds that it would effectively abolish the concept of a fixed-term contract.[133]

The one element of protection missing from English law – but common in other EU Member States – is a requirement on the employer to have a justification for the first use of a fixed-term contract.[134] This does not feature in the social partners' Agreement either. This approach involves making a much stronger normative claim that indefinite contracts should be regarded as the normal type of employment relationship with fixed-term contracts being used only in special circumstances where the employer can show a genuinely temporary need for additional workers.

4.4.3 Agency work

Many people use an agency to help them find work.[135] Sometimes, the role of the agency is simply to act as a recruiter on behalf of the employing entity. In that case, the worker gets a contract of some kind with the employing entity and the agency drops out of the picture. Our focus in this section will be on agencies which *supply* workers to other entities (usually referred to as 'end users'). In this situation, the end user contracts with the agency for the supply of workers, and the agency provides suitable people who are 'on its books' looking for work. Although the workers will normally perform their tasks under the careful supervision of the end user, they are usually paid via the agency. When the assignment comes to an end, the workers will generally be without work until the agency finds another assignment for them to do. Around 5% of the total UK workforce has this kind of employment arrangement.[136] Agency work is often referred to in the literature as 'triangular' in the sense that the worker has a relationship with the agency and a relationship with the end user though, as we shall see, the legal nature of the worker's relationships with these two organisations may be difficult to discern.

Issues

Firms use agency work for a variety of different reasons. It is a good source of temporary labour – to cover a sudden surge in demand for the firm's products, for example – and it saves on recruitment costs, because the agency takes responsibility

---

[132] *Terry* v *East Sussex County Council* [1976] ICR 536 (EAT); *Nash* v *Governors of Binstead Primary School* (2003) UKEAT/0120/03/LA.

[133] [2004] EWCA Civ 1745, [2005] ICR 577.

[134] Commission, above n 130.

[135] There is also some regulation of agencies themselves under the Employment Agencies Act 1973 and the Conduct of Employment Agencies and Employment Businesses Regulations 2003, SI 2003/3319. We will not examine these rules in detail here. A key principle is that agencies may not charge workers a fee for their services unless an exception applies.

[136] Department for Business, Enterprise and Regulatory Reform, *Agency Working in the UK* (2008), 19. For an analysis of the problems facing agency workers, see TUC, *Hard Work, Hidden Lives: Report of the Commission on Vulnerable Employment* (2008).

for finding suitable workers. From the worker's perspective, agency work might be a good way to get a range of experience, and might lead on to a permanent job, or it might just be the only kind of work available. A particular disadvantage of agency work for the worker is its precarious nature: because it is flexible for end users, it is inherently risky for the worker. He or she may experience long gaps between assignments, usually with no obligation on the agency to pay him or her when there is no work to be done.

Agency workers face two main sets of legal difficulties. First, it can be difficult to tell who, if anyone, is their employer. They may be self-employed, with no-one against whom to claim any employment rights. Second, agency workers may experience less favourable terms and conditions than people who are employed directly by the end user. The Agency Workers Regulations 2010, which implement the Temporary Agency Work Directive, tackle the second problem but not the first.[137] We will examine each in turn.

Identifying the employer

In this section, we will consider who – if anyone – might be the employer of an agency worker. There are, of course, two candidates: the agency and the end user.

In order to show that an agency worker is an employee or a worker as regards the agency, it is necessary to apply the tests discussed above to the particular fact situation. In the past, many agencies used contracts which described individuals as self-employed and contained other clauses designed to suggest that status. Since the Supreme Court's decision in *Autoclenz*, these clauses may no longer be effective because it is open to tribunals and courts to disregard them where they do not reflect the reality of the agreement between the parties.[138] However, this does not solve all the difficulties in this area because the individual must still meet the tests in practice.

We saw above that it is generally easier to establish employee status during the wage/work bargain: in other words, when the individual is working.[139] This should also be true of agency workers. One possible problem, though, is that it is arguable that agency workers do not work under the 'control' of the agency. Although the agency might assign them to a particular end user for a particular task, their detailed day-to-day activities are supervised by the end user. We shall see, below, that the Agency Workers Regulations 2010 tackle this problem in the definition that they employ, but the control test may prove to be a problem outside that context. In theory at least, it should be easier to establish that the individual is a worker during the wage/work bargain. There will usually be a contract of some kind containing an obligation to work personally. And it is hard to see how (at least under normal circumstances) the agency could be regarded a customer of the individual's business.

Outside the wage/work bargain, it is much more difficult for agency workers to establish a long-term contract of employment with the agency because of the requirement to show 'mutuality of obligation'. It is unlikely to be the case that an

---

[137] Above n 68; Directive 2008/104/EC on temporary agency work.
[138] *Autoclenz* (n 24).
[139] *Quashie* (n 33), [13]–[14].

agency worker is guaranteed any work by the agency. If no suitable assignment is available, the individual will have no work to do and no pay from the agency. It is important to emphasise that – in this context – such an arrangement is unlikely to be in any sense a 'sham'. The purpose of the agency is to match people with available assignments, not to guarantee them work and pay regardless of demand. This may also defeat claims to worker status outside the wage/work bargain.[140]

Some agency workers – usually where they are unable to show employee or worker status as against the agency – have tried to argue for a contract with the end user, either as an employee or a worker. Again, the normal tests would apply, but in this case there is a further hurdle: showing that there is a contractual relationship with the end user. In most cases, the worker has a contract (of whatever kind) with the agency and the agency contracts with the end user to provide suitable workers. Thus there is no direct relationship between the worker and the end user. The worker must therefore persuade the court that a contract can be *implied* between him or her and the end user. Although this argument was successful in some early cases,[141] the courts' more recent approach has been to hold that it is only appropriate to imply a contract where the 'business necessity' test is satisfied: in other words, where implying a contract is the only way to make sense of the arrangements.[142] This test is unlikely to be satisfied in agency work cases because the worker's provision of labour to the end user can be explained by reference to the agency's contract with the end user and the worker's contract with the agency. Therefore there is no need to imply an additional contract between the worker and the end user.

Agency workers and particular employment rights

In this section, we will consider those statutes that make specific provision for agency workers. These are designed to overcome some of the difficulties with agency workers' 'triangular' situation and, in particular, uncertainties about their contractual status.

One of the most radical statutory approaches to agency workers is found in the National Minimum Wage Act 1998. This Act ensures that anyone who meets the 'worker' definition is entitled to the National Minimum Wage.[143] However, as we saw above, an agency worker is unlikely to have a contract with the end user and (depending on the circumstances and the courts' approach) may not be a worker as regards the agency. Where this is the case, s. 34 of the Act states that whoever is responsible for paying the individual (or whoever pays the individual in practice) – the end user or the agency – must ensure that he or she receives the NMW unless he or she is running a business and is contracting with them as a customer or client. This approach aims largely to avoid technicalities about contract and status by providing, in effect, that anyone who works through an agency and is not genuinely running a business is entitled to receive the NMW.

---

[140] *Byrne Brothers* (n 73).
[141] *Dacas v Brook Street Bureau UK Ltd* [2004] EWCA Civ 217, [2004] ICR 1437 [52]–[53].
[142] *James v Greenwich London Borough Council* [2008] EWCA Civ 35, [2008] ICR 545; *Smith v Carillion (JM) Ltd* [2014] IRLR 344 (EAT).
[143] NMWA 1998, s 1.

The Equality Act 2010 seeks to ensure that employment agencies do not discriminate against people who seek to use their services.[144] However, this still leaves open the possibility of discrimination by the end user. For example, the individual might be sent by the agency to perform a particular assignment but be turned away by the end user on religious or racial grounds. This is addressed in s. 41 of the Act, which subjects the end user (referred to as the 'principal') to duties not to discriminate against agency workers (referred to as 'contract workers'). It covers discrimination broadly defined, harassment and victimisation, and requires the end user to comply with the duty to make reasonable adjustments where the individual has a disability. However, there is a difficulty with the scope of the provision. It defines the end user (or principal) in the following terms:

A "principal" is a person who makes work available for an individual who is–

(a) employed by another person, and

(b) supplied by that other person in furtherance of a contract to which the principal is a party (whether or not that other person is a party to it).[145]

There are two elements here. The agency worker must be employed by another person, and must be supplied under a contract with the end user. Importantly, the second of these elements is broadly defined, so it does not matter if the agency has no direct contractual relationship with the end user (which might happen in complex situations where the end user contracts with agency A which fulfils the contract by obtaining workers from agency B). The first limb of the test is more problematic. The term 'employed by' references the s. 83(2) definition discussed above and therefore applies when the person is 'employed under a contract personally to do work'. While this is one of the broader definitions of 'worker' in English law, it is still possible for an agency worker to fall outside it, for example, because he or she has the right to send a substitute or does not meet the requirement of subordination in *Jivraj*. Where the individual is not 'employed by' the agency in this sense, he or she will not be eligible for the protection afforded by s. 41. This could result in a gap in protection.[146]

Our final example is the right to (paid) time off for ante-natal care. This is an interesting example of a right that is difficult to exercise in the agency work context because the agency worker may need the permission of both the agency and the end user in order to exercise the right, and is unlikely to be entitled to any pay unless she is actually working.[147] Sections 57ZA to 57ZD ERA 1996 have recently been introduced in order to extend the right to paid time off for ante-natal care to agency workers. The right imposes a duty on *both* the hirer and the agency to permit the worker to take time off for ante-natal appointments during working time, defined as time when the worker is required to be working for the end user. The agency worker is entitled to be paid by the agency for the time off, in accordance with provisions in s. 57ZB for calculating the appropriate rate. The definition of agency worker for these purposes is the same as that used in the Agency Workers Regulations 2010, to be discussed in detail below.

---

[144] Equality Act 2010, s 55.
[145] ibid s 41(5).
[146] A point illustrated by *Muschett v HM Prison Service* [2010] EWCA Civ 25, [2010] IRLR 451.
[147] This right is normally only available to employees under s 55 ERA 1996.

The Temporary Agency Work Directive and the Agency Workers Regulations 2010

The Temporary Agency Work Directive was agreed using the normal legislative process, not the social dialogue, in 2008, after protracted negotiations over many years.[148] It is transposed into English law by the Agency Workers Regulations 2010.[149] Of all the directives governing non-standard working, this one offers the strongest promotion of the 'flexicurity' agenda. Like the Agreement on fixed-term work, its main focus is on discrimination even though this may not be the most important problem facing agency workers, in English law at least.

The flexicurity agenda is apparent from Article 4(1) of the Directive:

> Prohibitions or restrictions on the use of temporary agency work shall be justified only on grounds of general interest relating in particular to the protection of temporary agency workers, the requirements of health and safety at work or the need to ensure that the labour market functions properly and abuses are prevented.

This reflects a desire to encourage greater use of agency work in the EU labour market, despite the disadvantages of precariousness for workers noted in the discussion above. The UK government did not need to review restrictions on agency work under Article 4(2) because no such restrictions existed.

The scope of application of the Directive is set out in Article 1(1):

> This Directive applies to workers with a contract of employment or employment relationship with a temporary work agency who are assigned to user undertakings to work temporarily under their supervision and direction.

This is translated into English law's terminology in reg. 3:

(1) In these Regulations "agency worker" means an individual who–

    (a) is supplied by a temporary work agency to work temporarily for and under the supervision and direction of a hirer; and

    (b) has a contract with the temporary work agency which is–

        (i) a contract of employment with the agency, or

        (ii) any other contract with the agency to perform work or services personally.

(2) But an individual is not an agency worker if–

    (a) the contract the individual has with the temporary work agency has the effect that the status of the agency is that of a client or customer of a profession or business undertaking carried on by the individual; or

    (b) there is a contract, by virtue of which the individual is available to work for the hirer, having the effect that the status of the hirer is that of a client or customer of a profession or business undertaking carried on by the individual.

---

[148] Above n 137. For background, see Emma L Jones, 'Temporary Agency Labour: Back to Square One?' (2002) 31 ILJ 183; Loredana Zappala, 'The Temporary Agency Workers' Directive: an Impossible Political Agreement?' (2003) 32 ILJ 310.

[149] Above n 68. For discussion, see Nicola Countouris and Rachel Horton, 'The Temporary Agency Work Directive: Another Broken Promise?' (2009) 38 ILJ 329; ACL Davies, 'The Implementation of the Directive on Temporary Agency Work in the UK: A Missed Opportunity' (2010) 1 European Labour Law Journal 303.

The effect of this is that the Regulations apply where the individual is an employee or a worker as regards the agency. The extent to which this might turn out to be a problem in English law depends on how the courts interpret the relevant tests, as discussed above. One positive feature of reg. 3 is that it acknowledges that an agency worker works under the supervision of the hirer rather than the agency, which removes the possibility of arguing that the individual is not an employee or worker because the agency does not control the individual's work.

The basic entitlement under Article 5 of the Directive and reg. 5 of the Regulations is to equal treatment with the hirer's directly employed workers. According to reg. 5(1):

> . . . an agency worker (A) shall be entitled to the same basic working and employment conditions as A would be entitled to for doing the same job had A been recruited by the hirer–
>
> (a) other than by using the services of a temporary work agency . . .

In simple terms, an agency worker should not get (among other things) less pay per hour for the same job than a directly hired worker. However, the provisions are quite complicated and we need to consider several elements in greater detail. These are: the qualifying period for bringing a claim, the definition of 'basic working conditions' and the process of proving unequal treatment.

In most Member States, the equal treatment provisions apply from the start of the employment. However, the UK government refused to agree to this and managed to block the enactment of the Directive for many years as a result. The Directive was eventually passed on the basis of a compromise. The UK 'social partners' – the TUC and the CBI – reached an agreement that agency workers would be entitled to equal treatment after a 12-week qualifying period. The government then negotiated a provision in the Directive – Article 5(4) – allowing Member States to fulfil their obligations under the Directive by implementing social partner agreements, even if they derogated from the basic principle of equal treatment. The presence of the 12-week qualifying period serves to exclude agency workers on shorter assignments from the protection of the Directive.

The Regulations define the qualifying period in the following terms: 'the agency worker must work in the same role with the same hirer for 12 continuous calendar weeks, during one or more assignments'.[150] A key point to note about this provision is that the focus is on the hirer, not the agency or the assignment, so the worker might meet the 12-week requirement by means of more than one assignment from the same agency, or by means of assignments from different agencies. Further detail on the meaning of 'the same role' is given in reg. 7(3). The effect of this is to ensure that only quite significant changes in the worker's role are sufficient to 'stop the clock' on the 12-week period. Since Member States are obliged to take steps to prevent abuse under Article 5(5), the Regulations contain complex provisions designed to make it more difficult for hirers to prevent workers from acquiring the necessary 12 weeks of continuous employment. Probably the most important is reg. 7(8)(a), which states that there must be a gap of more than six weeks between assignments or during an assignment with the same hirer for continuity to be broken. There is also a targeted provision against abuse in reg. 9.

[150] AWR 2010, reg 7(2).

Although it is difficult to criticise the formulation of the qualifying period – which is quite carefully designed to prevent abuse – there is nothing in English law to tackle the most obvious form of abuse. This is simply to hire agency workers on assignments shorter than 12 weeks so that they never complete the qualifying period. This may inconvenience the hirer – who has to train a new batch of workers every couple of months – but in unskilled work this may not matter very much.

The right to equal treatment applies to 'basic working and employment conditions', defined in Article 3(1)(f) of the Directive to cover various aspects of working time, and pay. In the Regulations, this is implemented in reg. 6(1) to cover:

(a) pay;
(b) the duration of working time;
(c) night work;
(d) rest periods;
(e) rest breaks; and
(f) annual leave.

It is worth noting that, since the agency worker must be a worker as regards the agency in order to fall within the Regulations, he or she will already have the protection of the Working Time Regulations and the National Minimum Wage, so these provisions are significant primarily where the hirer offers its directly employed workers more than the statutory minimum: for example, a longer rest break or higher pay.

The test for establishing unequal treatment laid down by Article 5(1) of the Directive is to inquire how the agency worker would have been treated if he or she 'had been recruited directly by [the user] undertaking to occupy the same job.' This involves a hypothetical comparison. In contrast to other equal treatment laws, there is no objective justification defence – it is not open to the employer to argue that there was a good reason for treating agency workers unequally – so litigation is bound to focus closely on whether or not unequal treatment is established.

The Regulations begin by setting out the hypothetical comparison:

. . . an agency worker (A) shall be entitled to the same basic working and employment conditions as A would be entitled to for doing the same job had A been recruited by the hirer–

(a) other than by using the services of a temporary work agency; and
(b) at the time the qualifying period commenced.[151]

Confusingly, the tribunal must factor into this comparison whether the individual would have been recruited as an employee or a worker.[152] This seems unnecessarily complicated. In reg. 5(3)–(5), the hypothetical comparison is supplemented by what we might term the 'real comparator defence'. This means that the employer will be 'deemed to have complied with' reg. 5(1) where the agency worker has the same terms and conditions as a comparable employee. The employee is comparable if the conditions in reg. 5(4) are met. A possible risk here is that the employer will use a 'token' employee to defeat agency workers' claims. It is also unclear whether this is a legitimate implementation of the Directive.

---

[151] ibid reg 5(1).
[152] ibid reg 5(2).

It should be noted that agency workers are entitled to equal access to 'collective facilities', like workplace canteens and crèches, from 'day one' of their employment with the hirer, without the need to fulfil a qualifying period. This is implemented in reg. 12. The agency worker's right of equal treatment in relation to collective facilities and amenities is subject to an objective justification defence.[153] This is consistent with Article 6(4) of the Directive.

4.4.4 Part-time work

A final form of non-standard work sometimes considered together with casual, fixed-term and agency work is part-time work. Many of the issues affecting part-time workers are to do with the hours that they work and who controls them, so they are more a matter of working time than non-standard working.[154] But we will consider equal treatment for part-time workers very briefly in this section.

Issues

Part-time work differs from other forms of non-standard working in that its benefits to workers are much easier to discern. Some people may prefer to work fewer hours than a standard full-time working week, perhaps because they are easing into retirement or need to fit their work in around other activities like childcare or study. Of course, it is important to many part-timers that they have predictable working hours. Part-time work that is also casual in nature may be more difficult to fit around the individual's other commitments. And it is worth remembering that some people may be forced to take part-time jobs when they would prefer full-time working, particularly during recessions when employers may decide to cut the number of hours of work on offer rather than going through the process of making some people redundant.

The main difficulty for employers in hiring part-time workers is that there may be additional administrative costs associated with having lots of people working part-time rather than fewer people working full-time. Nevertheless, there are benefits to employers too: part-timers may be used to cover busy times, and in some sectors it may be difficult to recruit or retain enough workers without offering part-time opportunities.

Historically, it was quite common to discriminate against part-time workers on the assumption that they were less dependent on, or committed to, their jobs than full-time workers. Since part-time working is much more common among women than men, it was often possible to challenge discriminatory measures using sex discrimination arguments. So, for example, it could be argued that it was indirectly discriminatory against women for an employer to dismiss part-timers before full-timers in a redundancy situation,[155] or for the state to impose a longer qualifying period for unfair dismissal rights on part-timers.[156] However, these arguments were not normally open to male part-time workers.

---

[153] ibid reg 12(2).
[154] See Chapter 8.
[155] *Clarke v Eley (IMI) Kynoch Ltd* [1983] ICR 165.
[156] *R v Secretary of State for Employment, ex p EOC* [1995] 1 AC 1.

The Directive on Part-time Work and the Part-time Workers (Prevention of Less Favourable Treatment) Regulations 2000

Directive 97/81/EC implements the social partners' framework Agreement on part-time work, concluded in 1997.[157] It is transposed into English law by the Part-time Workers (Prevention of Less Favourable Treatment) Regulations 2000 (PTWR).[158]

The most important worker-protective right in the Agreement is the right not to be discriminated against by reason of working part-time.[159] A part-time worker is defined as 'an employee whose normal hours of work, calculated on a weekly basis or on average over a period of employment of up to one year, are less than the normal hours of work of a comparable full-time worker'.[160] A comparable full-time worker is defined as someone 'in the same establishment having the same type of employment contract or relationship, who is engaged in the same or a similar work/occupation, due regard being given to other considerations which may include seniority and qualification/skills'.[161] The agreement also provides for a broader range of comparison where there is no comparable full-time worker in the 'same establishment', either using a collective agreement (where relevant) or other approaches provided for in national law or practice.[162] Clause 4(1) of the agreement lays down the right not to be discriminated against: 'in respect of employment conditions, part-time workers shall not be treated in a less favourable manner than comparable full-time workers solely because they work part time unless different treatment is justified on objective grounds'. There is no distinction here between direct and indirect discrimination, so in contrast to most other areas of discrimination law, it is theoretically possible to justify direct discrimination against part-time workers. The Court of Justice has held that clause 4 of the Agreement is directly effective.[163]

English law contains no established definitions of full- and part-time working, so under reg. 2(2) the following definition of a part-time worker is used:

> A worker is a part-time worker for the purpose of these Regulations if he is paid wholly or in part by reference to the time he works and, having regard to the custom and practice of the employer in relation to workers employed by the worker's employer under the same type of contract, is not identifiable as a full-time worker.

The definition of a full-time worker is in similar terms. Under reg. 2(4):

> A full-time worker is a comparable full-time worker in relation to a part-time worker if, at the time when the treatment that is alleged to be less favourable to the part-time worker takes place–
>
> (a) both workers are–
>
>   (i) employed by the same employer under the same type of contract, and
>
>   (ii) engaged in the same or broadly similar work having regard, where relevant, to whether they have a similar level of qualification, skills and experience; and

---

[157] See, generally, Mark Jeffery, 'Not Really Going to Work? Of the Directive on Part-Time Work, "Atypical Work" and Attempts to Regulate It' (1998) 27 ILJ 193.

[158] SI 2000/1551. See Mark Bell, 'Achieving the Objectives of the Part-Time Work Directive? Revisiting the Part-Time Workers Regulations' (2011) 40 ILJ 254.

[159] Directive 97/81/EC, Annex, cl 4.

[160] ibid cl 3(1).

[161] ibid cl 3(2).

[162] ibid.

[163] Case C-486/08 *Zentralbetriebsrat der Landeskrankenhäuser Tirols v Land Tirol* [2010] 3 CMLR 30 [25].

(b) the full-time worker works or is based at the same establishment as the part-time worker or, where there is no full-time worker working or based at that establishment who satisfies the requirements of sub-paragraph (a), works or is based at a different establishment and satisfies those requirements.

Importantly, the part-time worker must find a person with the same type of contract to be his or her comparator, so if he or she is an employee, the comparator must be an employee, and if he or she is a worker, the comparator must be a worker.[164] More encouragingly, where the individual becomes part-time or returns to work part-time after an absence, regs 3–4 enable him or her to compare with the terms and conditions he or she enjoyed while full-time.

The right to equal treatment is set out in reg. 5:

(1) A part-time worker has the right not to be treated by his employer less favourably than the employer treats a comparable full-time worker–

  (a) as regards the terms of his contract; or

  (b) by being subjected to any other detriment by any act, or deliberate failure to act, of his employer.

(2) The right conferred by paragraph (1) applies only if–

  (a) the treatment is on the ground that the worker is a part-time worker, and

  (b) the treatment is not justified on objective grounds.

Importantly, the pro-rata principle applies, so a part-time worker cannot claim discrimination if he or she earns less in total than a full-time worker, but a claim would lie if he or she was paid a lower hourly rate (subject to the employer's justification defence).

We saw above that part-timers might want predictable hours to balance work with other commitments. The Agreement does not tackle this, and in the *Wippel* case, the CJEU rejected a creative argument which sought to develop the Agreement in that direction.[165] The claimant had a casual work arrangement with her employer. She could be called in to work when needed and had the right to refuse particular assignments. She argued that she was being discriminated against on grounds of part-time work (and on grounds of sex) because, unlike full-time workers (and other non-casual part-time workers) who had fixed weekly hours, her earnings were unpredictable. The Court rejected this argument on the basis that there was no 'comparable full-time worker' within the meaning of the Agreement, because all the full-time workers had fixed hours.

POINTS TO TAKE AWAY

- An employee is a person who satisfies the control or risk test, whose contract has no terms inconsistent with a contract of employment, and who can show mutuality of obligation. A worker is a person employed under a contract to do work personally for another person who is not his or her customer or client. Employees are entitled to all the rights labour law has to offer, whereas workers are entitled to a smaller subset of rights.

[164] PWR 2000, reg 2(3).
[165] Case C-313/02 *Wippel* v *Peek & Cloppenburg* [2004] ECR I-9483.

- It seems that employee and worker are best regarded as different concepts rather than as different points on the same spectrum, though the matter is not entirely clear from the case-law.

- The courts will disregard terms in a written contract in the employment sphere where they do not reflect the 'true agreement' between the parties.

- Equality law simply requires employment under a contract to do work personally but its scope may have been unduly narrowed by the Supreme Court's decision in *Jivraj*.

- People who work on an intermittent basis face particular difficulties with the employee and worker tests, but should at least be able to establish employee status while working. Proposed legislation to address 'zero-hours' contracts is seriously misguided.

- People who work on fixed-term contracts experience unstable working relationships. Legislation prohibits discrimination by employers against fixed-term employees and the abuse by employers of successive fixed-term contracts.

- People who find work via an employment agency may find it difficult to establish employee or worker status. Legislation prohibits discrimination by end users or hirers against agency workers but (in general) only after a 12-week qualifying period.

- Part-time work is a potentially attractive form of work for some workers, but part-timers have historically experienced discrimination. Legislation now prohibits this.

Further reading

There is a large literature noting the emergence of a 'two-tier' workforce: for example, **Hugh Collins, 'Independent Contractors and the Challenge of Vertical Disintegration to Employment Protection Laws' (1990) 10 OJLS 353; Sandra Fredman, 'Labour Law in Flux: The Changing Composition of the Workforce' (1997) 26 ILJ 337.** For a detailed account of the historical development of regulation in this area, see **Paul Davies and Mark Freedland, *Towards a Flexible Labour Market: Labour Legislation and Regulation since the 1990s* (OUP 2007) chapter 2.**

Some have responded to the 'two-tier' workforce by challenging the contractual basis of employment (for example, **Bob Hepple, 'Restructuring Employment Rights' (1986) 15 ILJ 69**); others, by arguing for broader understandings of the personal scope of employment (for example, **Mark Freedland and Nicola Kountouris, 'The Legal Characterisation of Personal Work Relations and the Idea of Labour Law' in G Davidov and B Langille (eds), *The Idea of Labour Law* (OUP 2011)**, elaborated more fully in **Mark Freedland and Nicola Kountouris, *The Legal Construction of Personal Work Relations* (OUP 2011)**).

EU policy in this area is firmly rooted in the concept of flexicurity, on which see **Commission, *Towards Common Principles of Flexicurity: More and Better Jobs through Flexibility and Security* (2007) COM 359.** For critiques, see **Sandra Fredman, 'Women at Work: the Broken Promise of Flexicurity' (2004) 33 ILJ 299**; and **Jeffrey Kenner, 'New Frontiers in EU Labour Law: From Flexicurity to Flex-Security' in M Dougan and S Currie, *50 Years for the European Treaties: Looking Back and Thinking Forward* (Hart 2009).** For more detail on the various directives, see **Catherine Barnard, *EU Employment Law* (OUP 2012) 426–453; ACL Davies, *EU Labour Law* (Elgar 2012) chapter 6.**

5 Contract terms

Learning outcomes

This chapter will enable readers to:

- understand and critically evaluate the role of the contract of employment or worker's contract as a source of norms governing the employment relationship
- understand the role of the statutory written statement of an employee's terms and conditions
- identify different sources of contractual terms: terms expressly agreed between the parties (including terms incorporated from other instruments, like collective agreements), terms implied by statute and terms implied at common law
- understand how contracts may be varied
- understand the circumstances in which an employee may continue to owe certain contractual obligations after the employment relationship has ended

5.1 INTRODUCTION

Although nowadays it is probably true to say that a majority of employment disputes concern statutory employment rights (the National Minimum Wage or the right not to be unfairly dismissed, for example), it is important not to lose sight of the fact that employment is also a contractual relationship. The contract between the employer and the individual is, in itself, an important source of norms governing the parties' behaviour. The simplest of contracts is likely to set out some basic duties for the employer – to pay the employee at the agreed wage, for example – and for the employee – identifying the place of work and the normal working hours, among other things. The parties' contractual rights and obligations sit alongside any statutory rights and obligations triggered by the classification of the contract as a contract of employment or a worker's contract.

Although there are some important intersections between contract and statute to be discussed in this chapter, much of the material has been developed by the courts at common law. Inevitably, this material refers primarily to employees employed under contracts of service, the traditional common law construct. Other types of employment relationship have been developed by statute in more recent times, such as the worker's contract and the 'contract personally to do work'.[1] The relationship

---

[1] See Chapter 4.

between these contracts and the contract of service or employment is uncertain. This means that the applicability of some of what we are discussing in this chapter to working people who are not employees is unclear. We will highlight this issue at various points during the chapter.

After a discussion of theory (section 5.2), we will examine express contractual terms in section 5.3, with a particular focus on the role of the statutory written statement of terms and conditions for employees, before turning to terms implied by (or prohibited by) statute in section 5.4 and terms implied at common law in section 5.5. Section 5.6 considers how contracts in the employment sphere may be varied, and section 5.7 examines employees' obligations after the employment has ended. Section 5.8 addresses some issues of enforcement.

5.2 THEORETICAL FRAMEWORK

Historically, employment was not thought of in contractual terms. Instead, the parties typically entered into a relationship of 'master and servant'.[2] The employer could invoke the criminal law, enforced by local magistrates, to discipline servants and to prevent them from leaving their employment before the end of the term of service, usually one year.[3] Although, in theory, the employer was obliged to pay the servant for the duration of the contract (even in the event of a downturn), claims by servants rarely succeeded and deductions of various kinds from wages were common.[4] The contractual approach to employment emerged gradually.[5] In the late 19th century, the courts began to use a contractual model for high-status employees such as those in managerial roles.[6] It was not until the early 20th century that the courts began to apply the same reasoning to employees engaged in manual work.[7] In this section, we will explore what it means to think about employment as a contractual relationship.

A useful starting-point is to think about the law of contract in its own terms. This body of law is primarily concerned with facilitating and regulating commercial transactions. The notion of 'freedom of contract', which emerged very strongly from the 19th century case-law, reflected the understanding that the contract represents the freely negotiated agreement of two equal parties in the market.[8] The courts' role is to enforce the parties' bargain, not to make it fair. If the contract disadvantages one of the parties, he or she must live with the consequences of his or her own lack of commercial acumen. The only options available are to comply with the contract or to breach it and pay damages to the other party.

From this perspective, the employment relationship differs from the ordinary commercial contract in two very significant respects. First, in most cases, there is significant inequality of bargaining power between the parties.[9] The employee needs

---

[2] See Simon Deakin and Frank Wilkinson, *The Law of the Labour Market* (OUP 2005) chapter 2.

[3] The system originated in the Statute of Artificers 1562 (5 Elizabeth I c. 4), but was updated and reinforced by a series of Master and Servant Acts from 1747–1867.

[4] Deakin and Wilkinson, above n 2, 65, 71–74.

[5] The Employers and Workmen Act 1875 removed the criminal law from the employment sphere but gave employers significant civil sanctions against workers.

[6] Deakin and Wilkinson, above n 2, 78–80, and see, for example, *Yewens v Noakes* (1880) 6 QBD 530.

[7] ibid 80–82, and see *Devonald v Rosser & Sons* [1906] 2 KB 728.

[8] PS Atiyah, *The Rise and Fall of Freedom of Contract* (Clarendon Press 1979), especially chapters 14 and 15.

[9] See Chapter 1.

a job in order to make money and to survive. The employer needs a workforce, but (unless the job is particularly specialised) it is likely that many different people would be able to perform the required tasks. Thus, it is usually the case that the employee needs the particular job much more than the employer needs the particular employee. In this situation, any agreement between the parties is unlikely to be the result of a negotiating process between equals. Second, although some commercial transactions are long-term in nature, such as major construction projects, the law of contract tends to take as its paradigm the 'discrete' contract.[10] This is a one-off transaction in a market full of choices: A buys a ton of grain from B because B's price on the relevant day is cheaper than C's or D's. Although some employment relationships are casual – the individual works briefly for the employer and then moves on – most are long-term. They are often described as 'relational' in nature.[11] This means that the parties' relationship may change and develop over time, and is likely to play a much more significant role in the employee's life than a one-off transaction.

Thus, although there are notable exceptions on both sides, we can characterise the commercial contract as a discrete transaction between equals, and the employment contract as a relational contract between parties with unequal bargaining power. This means that significant problems are likely to arise if we apply legal rules developed for the first type of transaction to relationships of the second kind. For example, the rule that a party is bound by a contract document he or she has signed may be an efficient approach to commercial transactions, but problematic in the employment setting.[12] The employer may have drafted the document and presented it to the individual on a 'take-it-or-leave-it' basis, without ensuring that it is a fair reflection of their relationship, and even if it did reflect the relationship at the beginning, it might not do so if it has evolved over time. How might this difficulty be addressed?

One option is to downplay the role of contracts in the employment context as the vehicle for setting terms and conditions of employment, and to rely instead on collective bargaining.[13] By grouping together in trade unions, employees may be able to enhance their bargaining power relative to that of the employer. The employer may be able to do without a particular employee, but will find it much harder to run a business if the entire workforce is on strike. On this view, the role of the contract of employment is simply to provide a convenient legal vehicle to give effect to collectively agreed terms and conditions of employment.

Another option is to use statute to regulate the content and operation of contracts in the employment setting. On this approach, it is the responsibility of Parliament to set out what kind of employment relationships it wants people to have – the balance of advantages and disadvantages for the employer and employee – and to legislate accordingly. Depending on the extent of the legislation, the parties may be left more or less space within which to negotiate terms and conditions for themselves. For example, the National Minimum Wage sets a 'floor' below which wages may not fall, but there is scope for the employer (perhaps in negotiation with the employee as an individual, or with a trade union representing employees) to determine higher rates

---

[10] For the development of the 'discrete' and 'relational' terminology, see Ian R Macneil, 'Contracts: Adjustment of Long-term Economic Relations under Classical, Neoclassical and Relational Contract Law' (1978) 72 Northwestern University Law Review 854.

[11] For discussion, see Douglas Brodie, 'How Relational is the Employment Contract?' (2011) 40 ILJ 232.

[12] *L'Estrange* v *F Graucob Ltd* [1934] 2 KB 394.

[13] See Chapter 1.

of pay.[14] Of course, in order for statutory regulation to apply, it is necessary to classify the contractual relationship as a contract of employment or a worker's contract, each of which 'triggers' a different set of statutory rights and duties.[15] On this view, then, the contract becomes the mechanism by which we identify who is entitled to a particular set of statutory protections.

A third option is for the contract of employment (and possibly also the worker's contract) to be the subject of special regulation at common law. We noted above that the 'classical' version of contract law may not be very helpful in this regard. However, there are other strands of thinking within the common law. For example, the courts might recognise the inequality of bargaining power inherent in consumer contracts, and require the party with superior bargaining power to spell out any unusually disadvantageous terms in a particularly clear way.[16] Or they might be willing to fill in the gaps in complex, long-term contracts through the use of implied terms. Contracts in the employment context have proved to be a key area for the use of the latter technique, leading to an interesting debate – which we do not need to resolve here – about whether there is a special law of the employment contract, or whether (more fundamentally) the classical view is no longer the dominant version of contract law.[17] On this view, the contract becomes a vehicle for the courts' view of the proper balance of advantages and disadvantages between employer and employee or worker. Importantly, since common law development is piecemeal in nature, and since different judges may have widely differing views about employment, it may be difficult to pin down a clear view of the courts' 'model' of the contract at any given point in time. As we shall see, some decisions are highly worker protective, whereas others reinforce managerial prerogative. It may also be difficult to determine whether the courts' 'model' does or should prevail over any express terms agreed by the parties (in the way that statutory regulation normally would) or whether it should be regarded merely as supplementary to their agreement and open to exclusion by the parties.[18]

In practice, all three of these approaches feature in English law. Many contracts remain subject to collective bargaining, there is extensive statutory regulation, and terms implied at common law play a significant role in some areas. This means that the contract of employment performs a clever conjuring trick: it manages to be both a source of rights and duties in itself, and a vehicle through which other sources of rights and duties can operate. These other sources of rights and duties may operate either inside or outside the contract: they may involve implying additional terms into the contract (like the common law implied terms) or they may affect the parties' agreement indirectly (for example, by providing a floor of rights to underpin negotiations).

Before we discuss the content of contracts in detail, it is worth noting two broader points. First, although this area might seem to be quite technical, there are important underlying policy issues. A decision to allow free rein to the classical

---

[14] National Minimum Wage Act 1998, and see Chapter 7.

[15] See Chapter 4.

[16] *Thornton v Shoe Lane Parking* [1971] 2 QB 163 (CA).

[17] See Hugh Collins, 'Contractual Autonomy', in Alan Bogg *et al.* (eds), *The Autonomy of Labour Law* (Hart 2015).

[18] See Hugh Collins, *Regulating Contracts* (OUP 1999) 78–79; 'Legal Responses to the Standard Form Contract of Employment' (2007) 36 ILJ 2, 7–10.

model of contract in the employment sphere is a decision to favour the employer since, in most cases, it will have superior bargaining power and will be able, for the most part, to set its preferred terms and conditions. A decision to encourage collective bargaining arguably favours the workforce, since it allows unions to redress the imbalance as against employers. Regulatory interventions by the courts or by Parliament inevitably involve applying some theory of the appropriate balance of advantages and disadvantages between employer and employee. So it is important to be aware that a person's underlying view of what labour law is for is likely to influence his or her thinking in this area as much as in any other.

Second, at various points in time, it has been suggested that we ought to replace the contractual analysis of employment with some kind of employment 'status'.[19] This might seem like a retrograde step – back to the old law of master and servant – but its advocates point to the fact that the contractual understanding of employment offers an impression of negotiation between equal parties that is, for most people, quite false. Moreover, the contractual approach is particularly susceptible to the courts' tendency to apply rules from the general law of contract which might not work well in employment settings. For example, the courts have (until very recently) been reluctant to admit evidence that a written contract of employment is not a true reflection of the bargain between the parties, even though in practice such contracts are often drafted by the employer and presented to the employee for signature.[20] The suggestion is that a status-based approach would offer the chance for Parliament to devise new tests for when a person should be treated as an employee or a worker and to set out the key incidents of each relationship. The courts would have to interpret these rules without reference to the general law of contract. However, such a move – which seems unlikely to occur in practice – would also remove any opportunity for the courts to use the relational strand of contract law in order to protect employees and workers.[21]

5.3 EXPRESS TERMS

In the general law of contract, a contract is formed by offer, acceptance and consideration (which may consist of a pair of promises). The same is true in the employment setting. Normally the employer makes a job offer – to provide work and to pay for it – and the individual promises to make him- or herself available for work. This is sufficient to constitute a contract. Indeed, the contract need not be express: the parties might conduct themselves in such a way that a court might be willing to imply a contractual relationship between them.

In this section, we will examine contracts in the employment sphere and how they are identified and interpreted (exploring the differences between oral, written and implied contracts). We will then assess how the law deals with the incorporation of terms from other sources such as collective agreements and works handbooks. Finally, we will turn to the role of the statutory written statement: this is a statement of terms and conditions for employees which now implements an EU directive. Its relationship with the contract of employment is somewhat unclear.

[19] Bob Hepple, 'Restructuring Employment Rights' (1986) 15 ILJ 69; Alain Supiot, *Beyond Employment: Changes in Work and the Future of Labour Law in Europe* (OUP 2001).
[20] See, for example, *Consistent Group Ltd* v *Kalwak* [2008] EWCA Civ 430, [2008] IRLR 505.
[21] See ACL Davies, 'The Contract for Intermittent Employment' (2007) 36 ILJ 102, 117–118.

5.3.1 Types of contract

There are three main types of contract in the employment setting: an implied contract, an express oral contract and an express written contract. In this section, we will focus on how the courts identify the terms of the contract between the parties in the event of a dispute. This is an important task because it determines not only the parties' rights and obligations under the contract itself, but also the individual's statutory rights (depending on the classification of the contract as a contract of employment, a worker's contract or a contract for services).[22]

The existence of – and the exact terms of – an implied contract can only be identified by looking at all the facts and circumstances surrounding the parties' relationship. The courts are reluctant to imply contracts unless it is the only way to make sense of what is going on. This can be illustrated by the *James* case.[23] The claimant in that case was supplied by an agency to work for the defendant council. When she returned to work after a period of sickness absence, she was told that her services were no longer required because the agency had sent another worker in her place. She tried to bring an unfair dismissal claim against the council. However, she failed to show that she was the council's employee. The Court of Appeal held that it was not necessary to imply a contract between the claimant and the council. The claimant worked for the council because she had a relationship with the agency which had a contract to provide workers to the council. A contract could only be implied where it was 'necessary to give effect to the business reality of a relationship'.[24]

An express oral contract is likely to be fairly simple in nature: perhaps the individual agrees to work a certain number of hours for a particular wage. Such contracts are, of course, particularly open to dispute about what exactly the parties agreed. In the event of a dispute, the court will need to examine all the facts and circumstances in order to identify the terms of the contract.

An express written contract is, superficially, the most straightforward type because it is possible to look to the contract document in order to identify the terms of the contract (and thus to classify it). To minimise the scope for disagreement, the general law of contract holds that a person who signs a written contract is usually bound by his or her signature[25] and that, where a written contract purports to be a complete statement of the parties' relationship, oral evidence to contradict the terms of the written contract may not be admitted in court.[26] However, there are two problems with the application of these strict rules in the employment context. First, as we saw above, contracts in the employment setting are often long-term relationships. Thus, the contract document agreed at the outset may cease to reflect the reality of the parties' evolving relationship over time. Second, contracts in the employment setting tend to be drafted by employers or their lawyers and presented to individuals to sign on a 'take-it-or-leave-it' basis. The inequality of bargaining power between the parties

---

[22] See Chapter 4.

[23] *James v Greenwich London Borough Council* [2008] EWCA Civ 35, [2008] ICR 545, departing from *Dacas v Brook Street Bureau (UK) Ltd* [2004] EWCA Civ 217, [2004] ICR 1437.

[24] ibid [48] (Mummery LJ).

[25] *L'Estrange v F Graucob Ltd* [1934] 2 KB 394.

[26] *Jacobs v Batavia and General Plantations Trust Ltd* [1924] 1 Ch 287.

in most cases means that the individual either may not understand what he or she is signing or may not have the chance to object to disadvantageous terms.

The 'long-term relationship' problem may be dealt with in one of two ways. First, it is always possible for the parties to vary their contract so that it 'catches up' with the reality of their relationship. We will discuss the law on this in section 5.6, below. Second, and more likely in practice, the law encourages a degree of vagueness in contracts in the employment sphere, by invoking the notion of 'managerial prerogative'.[27] The written contract might include details about the individual's pay and hours, and perhaps a job title, but it will not normally set out in very much detail what the individual's work tasks are. In practice, it would probably be quite expensive and time-consuming to do this, even for a relatively simple job. The courts address this by working on the assumption that the individual makes him- or herself available for work *as directed by* the employer. As we shall see, this is reinforced by various implied terms, not least that the individual should obey the employer's reasonable instructions.[28] Although this approach offers considerable flexibility for employers, it reduces the employee's ability to refuse to accept a change in his or her work activities, as we shall see below.

The issue of inequality of bargaining power was, for many years, a problem that the courts were unwilling to recognise. Claimants often argued that terms in written contracts were not a true reflection of their relationship with the employer, and had been included deliberately to make the relationship look like something it was not. So, for example, the employer might include a clause to the effect that it did not guarantee to provide any particular level of work to the individual. Taken literally, this would have the effect of denying 'mutuality of obligation' and would make it difficult for the individual to establish that the contract was one of employment.[29] In other words, written contracts sometimes included terms that were, in an everyday sense, 'fake'. However, the problem facing claimants (and the courts) was that the law had a very particular understanding of when it was possible to set aside a written contract as a 'sham'. This understanding was laid down in the *Snook* case:

> It means acts done or documents executed by the parties to the 'sham' which are intended by them to give to third parties or to the court the appearance of creating between the parties legal rights and obligations different from the actual legal rights and obligations (if any) which the parties intend to create . . . all the parties thereto must have a common intention that the acts or documents are not to create the legal rights and obligations which they give the appearance of creating.[30]

While this made sense in some contexts – for example, in tax law, where both parties might agree to commercially pointless contracts to evade tax – it did not help very much in the employment context, where the most likely scenario was that the employer would impose a written document which did not reflect the reality of the relationship on the unwitting employee.[31] An important change of approach came

---

[27] For discussion, see Deakin and Wilkinson, above n 2.

[28] *Cresswell and Others v Board of Inland Revenue* [1984] ICR 508 (Ch), discussed further below.

[29] *Carmichael v National Power Plc* [1999] 1 WLR 2042 (HL).

[30] *Snook v London and West Riding Investments Ltd* [1967] 2 QB 786 (CA) 802 (Diplock LJ).

[31] See, for example, *Consistent Group Ltd v Kalwak* [2008] EWCA Civ 430, [2008] IRLR 505.

about in the *Autoclenz* case, in which the Supreme Court rejected an overly rigid focus on the written agreement:

> [T]he relative bargaining power of the parties must be taken into account in deciding whether the terms of any written agreement in truth represent what was agreed and the true agreement will often have to be gleaned from all the circumstances of the case, of which the written agreement is only a part.[32]

On this view, it may be possible to disregard some terms of the written contract between the parties where they do not reflect the 'true agreement'. Importantly, the task of the court or tribunal is still to identify the parties' contract – the 'true agreement' – but they may use a wider range of evidence than just the written contract when doing so. For example, in the case itself, the Supreme Court held that a 'substitution clause' (which purported to allow the individual to send a substitute if he or she did not want to work) could be disregarded because the 'true agreement' between the parties was that the individuals would do their work personally.[33] This was one of the factors that helped to demonstrate that they were employees (with all the associated rights) and not self-employed.[34] It remains to be seen how much impact the *Autoclenz* ruling will have in practice.

5.3.2 Incorporating terms from other sources

Sometimes, the parties' contract might refer to other sources of norms to govern their relationship. The two main possibilities are collective agreements negotiated between the employer and a trade union representing the workforce, or some kind of 'workplace handbook' maintained by the employer. We will consider the treatment of each in turn.

Collective agreements

When a trade union and an employer agree to regulate terms and conditions at the workplace by means of collective bargaining, the product of their negotiations (if successful) is a collective agreement.[35] The collective agreement may, for example, set out the hourly rates to be paid to workers in different job grades, or standard hours of work. The collective agreement is presumed by statute not to be legally enforceable as between the union and the employer.[36] But there is generally a clear intention on the part of the employer and the union that the firm's workers should be entitled to the collectively agreed wages, hours and so on. Because it would be disruptive (and probably unlawful) to do otherwise, the collectively agreed terms are normally applied to everyone in the relevant work group, not just those who are union members.[37] In this section, we are concerned with how the law gives effect to collective agreements in individuals' contracts of employment.

---

[32] *Autoclenz v Belcher* [2011] UKSC 41, [2011] ICR 1157 [35] (Lord Clarke).
[33] ibid [37]–[38].
[34] ibid [39].
[35] TULRCA, s 178.
[36] ibid s 179(1).
[37] Non-members are protected against discrimination by s 146 TULRCA.

What is required is a term in each individual's contract that 'incorporates' elements of the collective agreement into that contract. This is sometimes referred to as a 'bridging' term. Obviously, the simplest way to do this is to include it, expressly, in the individual's contract.[38] If there is no express bridging term, it may be possible to imply one, for example, where this is clearly how the parties intended their relationship to operate in practice.[39] Importantly, the bridging term may be 'static' or 'dynamic' in operation: it may refer to a particular collective agreement,[40] or it may state that the individual's terms and conditions are governed by whatever collective agreement is 'in force for the time being' between the employer and a particular union.[41]

Once the bridging term has been established, it is clear that not all parts of the applicable collective agreement will be incorporated into individual contracts. The courts always consider whether a term is 'suitable' for, or was intended for, incorporation. In general, terms governing the negotiating procedure between the union and the employer are unsuitable, whereas terms governing substantive matters like pay and hours are suitable.[42] However, this simple dichotomy is sometimes hard to apply in practice, and it can seem as if the courts, in focusing on what the employer might have intended, are in fact protecting the employer against a bad bargain. For example, in the *Kaur* case, the employer had agreed a 'no compulsory redundancies' deal with the union, but the Court of Appeal held that an individual threatened with redundancy could not argue that the deal had been incorporated into her contract of employment. The deal with the union was found to be no more than an 'objective'.[43] Similarly, in the *Malone* case, there was a term in a collective agreement setting out the number of crew to be employed on different types of aircraft operated by the defendant employer.[44] When the employer sought unilaterally to reduce crew numbers, the claimants argued that the term formed part of their individual contracts of employment. They argued that operating a flight with a reduced crew would increase their workload. Smith LJ in the Court of Appeal accepted that this pointed towards the term's suitability for incorporation,[45] but then said:

> Set against that are the disastrous consequences for BA which could ensue if this term were to be individually enforceable. It seems to me that they are so serious as to be unthinkable. By that I mean that, if the parties had thought about the issue at the time of negotiation, they would have immediately said it was not intended that [the provision] could have the effect of enabling an individual or a small group of cabin crew members to bring a flight to a halt by refusing to work under complement. So, if I apply the rule by which a term of uncertain meaning is to be construed, that of asking what, objectively considered in the light of the factual matrix against which the agreement was made, the parties must be taken to have intended the provision to mean, I am driven to the conclusion that they did not mean this term to be individually enforceable.[46]

[38] See, for example, *National Coal Board v Galley* [1958] 1 WLR 16 (CA).
[39] *Henry v London General Transport Services Ltd* [2001] IRLR 132 (EAT).
[40] *Robertson v British Gas Corp* [1983] ICR 351 (CA).
[41] *Glendale Managed Services Ltd v Graham* [2003] EWCA Civ 773, [2003] IRLR 465; though there is now an exception to this in the transfer of undertakings context following the CJEU's decision in Case C-426/11 *Alemo-Herron v Parkwood Leisure Ltd* [2014] 1 CMLR 21.
[42] *National Coal Board v National Union of Mineworkers* [1986] ICR 736 (Ch).
[43] *Kaur v MG Rover Group Ltd* [2004] EWCA 1507, [2005] ICR 625 [32] (Keene LJ).
[44] *Malone v British Airways Plc* [2010] EWCA Civ 1225, [2011] ICR 125 (see Roseanne Russell, '*Malone and others v British Airways plc*: Protection of Managerial Prerogative?' (2011) 40 ILJ 207).
[45] ibid [61] (Smith LJ).
[46] ibid [62] (Smith LJ).

The last sentence of this quotation states the orthodox approach to contractual interpretation. However, with respect, the court's application of this approach appears to focus less on the objective meaning of the words in the collective agreement and more on the balance of advantages and disadvantages for each party, suggesting that the court is in fact rewriting the parties' bargain.

More generally, the case-law highlights one of the difficulties with the incorporation of terms from collective agreements into individual contracts of employment. Collective agreements are not, themselves, contracts, and are not drafted as such. Some matters may be left ambiguous because the parties cannot in fact reach an agreement and each side can claim a victory: the union to its members and the employer to its shareholders. Problems are bound to ensue when agreements of this nature are considered for enforcement through individual contracts of employment by courts with a limited understanding of collective bargaining. In other legal systems, the collective agreement plays a much stronger regulatory role so there is less scope for judicial discretion in deciding which aspects of the agreement should or should not be enforced.[47]

Workplace handbooks; custom and practice

Two other possible sources of contract terms are workplace handbooks, and custom and practice. We will consider each in turn.

Many employers have some kind of 'handbook' to govern the workplace. This document may include rules on a wide range of different matters, from the procedure for booking holidays to the company's policy on harassment. It is convenient for the employer to set out some of these rules and procedures in a single document which can be made available to all employees (probably online nowadays) and revised from time to time. However, the existence of such handbooks can lead to ambiguity about the extent to which the handbook contains rights and obligations which are contractually binding. And the employer may want to have its cake and eat it: sometimes, it might want to say that handbook terms are binding on an employee (for example, to deny him or her a benefit because he or she did not claim it in the proper way) and sometimes, it might want to retain flexibility for itself by denying that certain terms are binding (for example, by withdrawing certain benefits if the firm is in financial difficulties).

A statement in a handbook that a particular benefit is or is not a contractual entitlement is not conclusive. In the event of a dispute, it is for the courts to determine what is or is not a part of the individual's contract by looking at what the parties, objectively, can be taken to have agreed. For example, in *Keeley v Fosroc International Ltd*, the claimant's contract of employment referred to a staff handbook which made provision for an enhanced redundancy payment over and above the statutory minimum. The employer argued that it was not contractual. The Court of Appeal disagreed, pointing to the clear language of the provision, expressed as an entitlement, and its inclusion in the 'employee benefits' section of the handbook along with other clearly contractual rights.[48] It was distinguishable from other aspirational or discretionary elements of the handbook.

---

[47] See, generally, Peter Sheldon *et al.*, 'Collective Bargaining: Globalizing Economies and Diverse Outcomes' in Roger Blanpain (ed), *Comparative Labour Law and Industrial Relations in Industrialized Market Economies* (11th edn, Kluwer 2014).

[48] [2006] EWCA Civ 1277, [2006] IRLR 961.

Another possible source of terms is 'custom and practice'. This phrase used to be taken to refer to the customs of a particular industry, which might possibly be given contractual effect if they were reasonable, well-known (though not necessarily to every employee) and certain.[49] Nowadays, it tends to refer more to practices adopted by the employer over time which have not been reduced to writing either in contract documents or works handbooks. A recent example is the *Park Cakes* case, in which the claimants argued that they were contractually entitled to a redundancy payment beyond the statutory requirement because of the employer's long-standing practice of making additional redundancy payments.[50] After reviewing the authorities, Underhill LJ stated:

> Taking that approach, the essential question in a case of the present kind must be whether, by his conduct in making available a particular benefit to employees over a period, in the context of all the surrounding circumstances, the employer has evinced to the relevant employees an intention that they should enjoy that benefit as of right . . .[51]

The relevant circumstances would include how often the employer had made the payments and how they had been presented to the employees. The employer's subjective intention that the payments should be discretionary rather than contractual is not relevant because the existence of a contract term is approached objectively. If the employer does not want a practice to have contractual effect, it is very important that this is made clear to the employees whenever the practice is invoked.

5.3.3 The statutory written statement

Where the individual is classified as an employee and has been employed for at least a month, he or she is entitled to a 'written statement' of the terms and conditions of the employment.[52] This must be provided within two months of the start of the job (even if the employment ends during the second month).[53]

The written statement traces its origins to the Contracts of Employment Act 1963. Davies and Freedland explain that the Act's purpose was to reduce the number of disputes about terms and conditions, particularly where the employer had entered into an oral contract with the employee.[54] The legislation has been amended on several occasions, including to ensure that it implements Directive 91/533/EEC on an employer's obligation to inform employees of the conditions applicable to the contract or employment relationship.

The best way to understand the content of the written statement is simply to consider ERA 1996, s. 1(3) and (4), which list the requirements:

> (3) The statement shall contain particulars of–
>> (a) the names of the employer and employee,
>> (b) the date when the employment began, and

---

[49] *Sagar v H Ridehalgh and Son Ltd* [1931] 1 Ch 310 (CA).
[50] [2013] EWCA Civ 974, [2013] IRLR 800.
[51] ibid [35].
[52] Council Directive 91/533/EEC of 14 October 1991 on an employer's obligation to inform employees of the conditions applicable to the contract or employment relationship [1991] OJ L288/32, art 1(2)(a); ERA 1996, s 198.
[53] Directive 91/533/EEC, art 3(1); ERA 1996, s 1(2).
[54] Paul Davies and Mark Freedland, *Labour Legislation and Public Policy* (Clarendon Press 1993) 145.

(c) the date on which the employee's period of continuous employment began (taking into account any employment with a previous employer which counts towards that period).

(4) The statement shall also contain particulars, as at a specified date not more than seven days before the statement (or the instalment containing them) is given, of–

(a) the scale or rate of remuneration or the method of calculating remuneration,
(b) the intervals at which remuneration is paid (that is, weekly, monthly or other specified intervals),
(c) any terms and conditions relating to hours of work (including any terms and conditions relating to normal working hours),
(d) any terms and conditions relating to any of the following–

   (i) entitlement to holidays, including public holidays, and holiday pay (the particulars given being sufficient to enable the employee's entitlement, including any entitlement to accrued holiday pay on the termination of employment, to be precisely calculated),
   (ii) incapacity for work due to sickness or injury, including any provision for sick pay, and
   (iii) pensions and pension schemes,

(e) the length of notice which the employee is obliged to give and entitled to receive to terminate his contract of employment,
(f) the title of the job which the employee is employed to do or a brief description of the work for which he is employed,
(g) where the employment is not intended to be permanent, the period for which it is expected to continue or, if it is for a fixed term, the date when it is to end,
(h) either the place of work or, where the employee is required or permitted to work at various places, an indication of that and of the address of the employer,
(i) any collective agreements which directly affect the terms and conditions of the employment including, where the employer is not a party, the persons by whom they were made, and
(j) where the employee is required to work outside the United Kingdom for a period of more than one month–

   (i) the period for which he is to work outside the United Kingdom,
   (ii) the currency in which remuneration is to be paid while he is working outside the United Kingdom,
   (iii) any additional remuneration payable to him, and any benefits to be provided to or in respect of him, by reason of his being required to work outside the United Kingdom, and
   (iv) any terms and conditions relating to his return to the United Kingdom.

This corresponds to the list of requirements in Article 2 of the Directive, with some minor variations in terminology. Under s. 3, the employer must also include in the statement information about disciplinary rules and procedures applicable to the employee, and details of the person to whom the employee may apply if he or she has a grievance or wishes to appeal a disciplinary decision.[55] This is not required by the Directive, though the Directive allows Member States to introduce more favourable provisions.[56]

---

[55] This has its origins in the Employment Act 2002, which required employers to have such procedures.
[56] Above n 52, art 7.

What is rather more complicated is the form in which the statement is to be provided. Under s. 2(4), the employer must provide a single document containing all the information except: sickness absence, pensions, notice periods, the end date of a fixed-term contract, collective agreements and information about working abroad. Since employers often simply issue employees with a letter of engagement or a written contract of employment, either before the contract starts or soon afterwards, this may be relied upon to fulfil the duty to provide the statement if it includes all the information that the employer was required to provide in the single document under s. 2(4).[57]

The other items of information not required to be included in the single document may be provided 'in instalments'.[58] In some cases, the employer need not provide the information in the statement itself but may refer the employee to another 'reasonably accessible' document containing the information.[59] This is true of matters relating to sickness absence and pensions,[60] and disciplinary rules and procedures.[61] The statement may refer the employee to the general law or to a collective agreement for information about notice periods.[62]

Where any aspect of the information provided to the employee changes, the employer must give the employee 'a written statement containing particulars of the change'.[63] Under s. 4(3), this statement 'shall be given at the earliest opportunity and, in any event, not later than . . . one month after the change in question'.[64]

If the employer fails to provide a written statement at all, or provides one that does not comply with the statutory requirements, the matter may be referred to the Employment Tribunal 'to determine what particulars ought to have been included or referred to in a statement' so as to comply with the requirements'.[65] Under s. 12, the tribunal may determine the proper content of the statement which is then treated as having been issued by the employer. There is no independent right to compensation for a breach of the right to a written statement. However, if the employee brings other proceedings against the employer, the employer's failure to comply with the written statement requirement is taken into account in calculating the award of compensation.[66] The tribunal must increase the award by two weeks' pay and may increase the award by four weeks' pay if it considers it 'just and equitable' to do so.[67] It is not clear how effective these remedies are. On the one hand, it seems unlikely that many people currently in employment would sue their employer for failing to provide a written statement, even if compensation was available. On the other hand, the failure to provide any independent remedy reduces any possible deterrent effect of the legislation.

---

[57] Above n 52, art 3; ERA, ss 7A and 7B.

[58] ERA, s 1(2).

[59] For the definition, see ERA, s 6.

[60] ERA, s 2(2).

[61] ibid s 3.

[62] ibid s 2(3).

[63] ibid s 4(1).

[64] Reflecting above n 52, art 5(1).

[65] ERA, s 11(1). The employer may also invoke the Tribunal's assistance to determine the proper content of the statement under s 11(2) though this seems unlikely in practice.

[66] Employment Act 2002, s 38.

[67] The week's pay is subject to a maximum, currently £464, set out in ERA, s 227.

A final point to note about the written statement is its complex relationship with the contract of employment. Conceptually, the two are quite distinct: the contract of employment is the legally binding source of the terms on which the individual is employed, whereas the statement simply reports the terms on which the individual is employed. But in practice, confusion may arise, not least because – as we saw above – the contract of employment may be used in place of the statement.

One question is what happens if the contract does not make provision for some of the matters required to be covered by the statement. This is addressed by s. 2(1), which provides that there is no need for the employer to provide information where there is none to provide.[68] So, for example, if there are no contract terms on place of work or sick pay or pensions, the employer does not need to address these matters in the statement. Some commentators have suggested that this is not sufficient to comply with the Directive, which requires in Article 2(1) that the employer notify the employee 'of the essential aspects of the contract or employment relationship'. However, it is worth remembering that the individual is only entitled to a written statement if he or she is an employee. Given the tests for establishing employee status, it seems unlikely that a person with a very minimal contract would in fact qualify as an employee.[69] For example, if there are no terms about pay and hours, it may be difficult to prove that the control or risk tests, or the mutuality of obligation requirement, are satisfied.[70] Thus, it is highly unlikely to be the case that a person who counts as an employee could legitimately be given a largely 'empty' written statement.

The other key question is what happens when there is a dispute about the statement. Either party – employer or employee – might argue that the statement is not a true reflection of their contractual relationship. The Court of Justice addressed this question in the *Kampelmann* case.[71] In simple terms, the employees in the case argued that they were entitled to be promoted to the next job grade, but the employer denied the promotions by saying that their initial job grading – as set out in the written statement – had been incorrect. The Court held that, although the written statement was not intended to alter national rules on the burden of proof, it would be pointless if employees could not rely on it at all.[72] Thus, the written statement should be presumed to be correct unless the employer could prove that it was not. English law's position was set out by the EAT in the *System Floors* case:

> [The written statement] provides very strong prima facie evidence of what were the terms of the contract between the parties, but does not constitute a written contract between the parties. Nor are the statements of the terms finally conclusive: at most, they place a heavy burden on the employer to show that the actual terms of contract are different from those which he has set out in the statutory statement.[73]

This makes good sense. The statutory written statement cannot be conclusive because it is only the employer's view of what the terms of the contract are. However, the

---

[68] See *Morley v Heritage plc* [1993] IRLR 400 (CA).

[69] This appears to be the point being made in *Eagland v British Telecommunications Plc* [1993] ICR 644 (CA) 652 (Parker LJ).

[70] See Chapter 4.

[71] Cases C-253–258/96 *Kampelmann and others v Landschaftsverband Westfalen-Lippe* [1997] ECR I-6907.

[72] ibid [11].

[73] *System Floors (UK) Ltd v Daniel* [1982] ICR 54 (EAT) 58 (Browne-Wilkinson J), approved by the Court of Appeal in *Robertson v British Gas Corporation* [1983] ICR 351 (CA).

courts should not be quick to accept a situation in which the employer is allowed to go back on what it has said in the statement. In the *Robertson* case, the Court of Appeal rejected the idea that it should be equally difficult for the employee to contest the accuracy of the statement.[74] This is an important safeguard for the employee, who would otherwise be bound by the employer's opinion of their contract.

This brings us to a further, more technical problem. Employment Tribunals have jurisdiction over the statutory written statement, as we saw above.[75] If the employer fails to issue a statement at all, or issues one that is incomplete or incorrect, the tribunal may determine what the statement should have contained. Because the statutory statement is not, in itself, normative, this requires the tribunal to identify the contract terms on which the statement should have been based and to summarise them for the statement. However, Employment Tribunals do not have jurisdiction over contractual disputes (except, in limited circumstances, if they arise in the context of a dismissal claim).[76] The *Southern Cross* case illustrates the problem to which this may give rise.[77] In that case, the employees were given an extra five days' holiday as a reward for long service on top of a basic entitlement of 20 days. When the statutory holiday entitlement was increased to 28 days, the employer refused to continue providing the extra five days. The Employment Tribunal held that the employees were contractually entitled to the extra five days (which should then have been reflected in the holiday section of the written statement).[78] However, the Court of Appeal held that the tribunal had exceeded its jurisdiction.[79] The dispute between the parties related to the terms of the contract and this dispute should have been heard in court. While this is an accurate reflection of the respective roles of the courts and tribunals in employment cases, it is highly problematic in practice. If any of the terms of the contract of employment are disputed, it appears that the employee may need to bring proceedings in court to resolve the matter before going to the tribunal to obtain an accurate written statement. This is obviously unrealistic for most people.

5.4 STATUTORY REGULATION

Contracts in the employment setting are, of course, very heavily regulated by statute. The interaction between contract and statute is a major theme throughout this book. But in this section, we are concerned with a more precise form of interaction: where statute impacts directly on the contract, either by implying or prohibiting particular terms.

5.4.1 Terms implied by statute

In practice, Parliament operates by implying terms into contracts in the employment setting much less frequently than might be supposed. Most statutory employment rights do not take the form of contractual terms. Instead, they are free-standing rights for the individual or duties for the employer. In this section, we will consider the main

[74] *Robertson*, above n 73, 355.
[75] Above n 65.
[76] Employment Tribunals Act 1996, s 3; see Chapter 2.
[77] *Southern Cross Healthcare Co Ltd* v *Perkins* [2010] EWCA Civ 1442, [2011] ICR 285.
[78] *Southern Cross Healthcare Co Ltd* v *Perkins* (2010) UKEAT/0276/09/JOJ [56]–[64].
[79] *Southern Cross*, above n 77, [32]–[34].

examples of those that do take the form of contractual terms: the 'equality clause', the minimum wage, and notice to terminate the contract of employment.

Probably the most well-known of these is the 'equality clause' originally found in the Equal Pay Act 1970 and now contained in s. 66(1) Equality Act 2010 (EqA):

> If the terms of A's work do not (by whatever means) include a sex equality clause, they are to be treated as including one.

This applies to the contracts of workers broadly defined.[80] However, the operation of the equality clause is quite complex.[81] It works by changing or adding to the claimant's contract terms until the requirements of equal pay are fulfilled. According to s. 66(2):

> A sex equality clause is a provision that has the following effect–
>
> (a) if a term of A's is less favourable to A than a corresponding term of B's is to B, A's term is modified so as not to be less favourable;
> (b) if A does not have a term which corresponds to a term of B's that benefits B, A's terms are modified so as to include such a term . . .

Thus, although the equality clause is, itself, imposed by legislation, it also has the effect of modifying other terms of the claimant's contract or implying additional terms into that contract.

Another example of a term implied by statute is the right, under s. 17 National Minimum Wage Act 1998, to recover the shortfall between what a worker was in fact paid by the employer and what the worker would have been paid by the employer had he or she been paid the NMW. In order to protect vulnerable claimants, this right may be enforced by an enforcement officer under s. 19D or by the worker him- or herself. The statutory language makes clear that this is a right 'under [the individual's] contract'.[82]

Our third example consists of the statutory minimum notice periods set out in s. 86 ERA 1996. This provision details how much notice the employer (and the employee) must give in order to terminate the contract of employment. Under s. 86(3), '[a]ny provision for shorter notice in any contract of employment with a person who has been continuously employed for one month or more has effect subject to' the minimum notice periods. Thus, the parties to the contract are free to agree longer periods of notice but any contractual term containing a shorter period of notice is ineffective. The section preserves some of the ordinary rules of contract law such as the right of either party to waive his or her entitlement to notice,[83] and the right of either party to terminate the contract immediately because of the other party's repudiatory breach.[84] Section 91(5) makes clear that the employer's failure to provide the required notice is actionable as a breach of contract.

An interesting feature of these disparate provisions is that they have different personal scopes. The entitlement to a minimum period of notice under s. 86 is for employees, the NMW is for workers, and the equality clause is for workers broadly defined. Thus, terms implied by statute are by no means the preserve of employees.

---

[80] EqA 2010, s 83(2)(a).
[81] Mark Freedland, *The Personal Employment Contract* (Clarendon Press 2003) 123.
[82] NMWA, s 17(1).
[83] ERA, s 86(3).
[84] ibid s 86(6).

Nevertheless, they are relatively unusual and it is worth considering why this route is chosen in some cases. A key factor is enforcement. By making a particular provision a term of someone's contract, it can be enforced by contractual means. Thus, an employer's failure to equalise a woman's contractual terms with those of her male comparator, or to pay the minimum wage, or to give proper notice of termination, are all breaches of contract and actionable accordingly.

However, contractual enforcement has advantages and disadvantages and the balance can vary from case to case. One potential advantage is the longer limitation period attaching to claims in contract: six years, as opposed to three months for an employment tribunal claim. This advantage was confirmed by the Supreme Court in the *Abdulla* case, in which the claimant brought an equal pay claim (relying on the equality clause) in court because she was out of time at the tribunal.[85] The employer argued that the claim should not be heard, but the Supreme Court held that the equality clause was a term of the claimant's contract and could be enforced accordingly. A potential disadvantage is that contract damages are (in general) about compensating the innocent party for his or her lost expectations. So where the employer has terminated the contract without giving notice, all the claimant can expect is to have worked out his or her notice period and earned a wage during that time.[86] Moreover, the normal rules on mitigation of damages are applicable in this context so if the claimant got – or could have got – a new job during that time, his or her damages will be reduced accordingly.[87]

So far, we have focused on terms implied into contracts in the employment context by legislation which is clearly intended to have contractual effect. But there is another interesting possibility: that the courts might interpret statutory rights as having contractual effect even where that is not expressly stated in the legislation itself. An example of this is the ruling in *Barber* v *RJB Mining*.[88] The case concerned reg. 4(1) Working Time Regulations 1998 (WTR), which lays down a maximum working week (on average) of 48 hours, but with the possibility of an individual opt-out from the limit. The workers in the *Barber* case refused to sign an opt-out, but the employer insisted that they continue working over the limit. The judge held that the 48-hour limit, apparently because of the mandatory language in which it was expressed, was intended by Parliament to be a term of the workers' contracts.[89] This opened up the possibility of an injunction to stop the employer from insisting on longer working hours, though the judge refused to grant the injunction because he did not regard it as appropriate on the facts.[90]

There are no obvious examples of cases following *Barber* by giving contractual effect to statutory rights, either in the working time context or elsewhere. On one view, the *Barber* decision is to be welcomed. The courts have a legitimate role in filling in the gaps in enforcement – particularly in areas in which Parliament has not provided a remedy for individuals. The idea that the WTR do not provide a comprehensive statutory scheme for working time enforcement was upheld in the

---

[85] *Abdulla* v *Birmingham City Council* [2012] UKSC 47, [2012] ICR 1419.
[86] *Gunton* v *Richmond-upon-Thames LBC* [1981] Ch 448 (CA), 469 (Buckley LJ).
[87] ibid. See Chapter 9.
[88] [1999] ICR 679 (QB).
[89] ibid 690.
[90] ibid 692–693.

Stringer case, in which the House of Lords held that the (separate) statutory regime for challenging unlawful deductions from wages could be used to tackle a problem about holiday pay under the WTR.[91] On another view, the *Barber* decision is to be criticised because it subverts the statutory enforcement mechanisms provided in the WTR. In the case of the maximum working week, the Regulations provide for administrative enforcement by the Health and Safety Executive,[92] and perhaps it was a deliberate choice not to provide for individual enforcement as well. The House of Lords' decision in *Johnson* and Supreme Court's decision in *Edwards* (discussed in the enforcement section, below) suggest that this view may be gaining ground, because in these cases the courts were concerned not to use the law of contract to provide alternatives to the statutory law of unfair dismissal.[93] Thus, it seems unlikely – but by no means impossible – that *Barber* will spark a new trend.

5.4.2 Terms prohibited by legislation

A key problem with a system in which employment is contractual but most employment rights are statutory is to determine the relationship between the parties' freedom to contract – to reach an agreement of their own choosing – and the statutory rights. Are the parties allowed to 'contract out' of statutory rights? In general terms, given that statutory rights are designed to protect the individual, who is the weaker party to the contract, it is quite important that freedom of contract is restricted in employment settings. The relevant statutory provisions tackle both specific and general problems of contracting out.[94]

An example of a specific prohibition is s. 77 Equality Act 2010.[95] This tackles the inclusion in some people's contracts of a clause barring them from asking their colleagues what they get paid, or telling their colleagues what they themselves get paid. This makes it difficult for people to know whether they are being discriminated against (for example, because of their gender) in relation to pay. The provision is as follows:

(1) A term of a person's work that purports to prevent or restrict the person (P) from disclosing or seeking to disclose information about the terms of P's work is unenforceable against P in so far as P makes or seeks to make a relevant pay disclosure.

(2) A term of a person's work that purports to prevent or restrict the person (P) from seeking disclosure of information from a colleague about the terms of the colleague's work is unenforceable against P in so far as P seeks a relevant pay disclosure from the colleague; and "colleague" includes a former colleague in relation to the work in question.

(3) A disclosure is a relevant pay disclosure if made for the purpose of enabling the person who makes it, or the person to whom it is made, to find out whether or to what extent there is, in relation to the work in question, a connection between pay and having (or not having) a particular protected characteristic.

---

[91] *Revenue and Customs* v *Stringer* [2009] UKHL 31, [2009] ICR 985. Such claims are now subject to a two-year limit: see the Deduction from Wages (Limitation) Regulations 2014, SI 2014/3322, reg 2.

[92] Working Time Regulations 1998, SI 1998/1833, reg 28.

[93] *Johnson* v *Unisys Ltd* [2001] UKHL 13, [2003] 1 AC 518; *Edwards* v *Chesterfield Royal Hospital NHS Foundation Trust* [2011] UKSC 58, [2012] 2 AC 22.

[94] The employer is also precluded from using choice of law to contract out of employment rights: see Chapter 3.

[95] See also the Fixed-Term Employees (Prevention of Less Favourable Treatment) Regulations 2002, SI 2008/2034, reg 8, on terms limiting the duration of a contract if the conditions for permanence are met.

Importantly, this provision does not prohibit employers from including non-disclosure clauses, nor does it render such clauses void. If P discloses his or her pay to a journalist or a competitor firm, for example, the employer can enforce the clause against P. But they do protect individuals who have a pay discussion with a work colleague in order to find out whether there is any discrimination taking place by rendering a non-disclosure clause unenforceable by the employer in that situation. In keeping with the broad personal scope of the Equality Act, these provisions apply to contracts of employment and to 'contracts to do work personally'.[96]

More generally, many employment statutes provide that the employer and the individual may not 'contract out' of the statutory rights they contain. In other words, the parties may not agree in the contract that statutory rights, like unfair dismissal, are not applicable. For example, ERA 1996, s. 203(1) states that:

(1) Any provision in an agreement (whether a contract of employment or not) is void in so far as it purports–

(a) to exclude or limit the operation of any provision of this Act, or

(b) to preclude a person from bringing any proceedings under this Act before an employment tribunal . . .

This precludes 'contracting out' in any form. However, it is subject to some exceptions, the most important being for 'settlement' agreements. These arise when the parties are in dispute but choose to reach a compromise rather than pursuing the matter to a tribunal hearing. Settlements are generally seen as a good thing because they save on costs and stress for both parties, but it is important that the individual is not bullied into accepting a bad deal. To this end, a settlement is only binding if it clearly states the particular claims to which it relates, and the individual receives independent legal advice before signing the agreement.[97]

The leading case on s. 203 is *Igbo*.[98] In that case, the employee wanted to take additional leave beyond her normal entitlement to visit family in Nigeria. The employer allowed this but required her to sign an agreement to the effect that if she did not return to work on a specified date, her contract would terminate automatically. She returned to the UK in time but was ill on the relevant date so could not go to work. The employer therefore treated the employment relationship as having come to an end. However, the Court of Appeal held that the agreement was void as an attempt to contract out of the law of unfair dismissal.[99] An interesting question is whether an employer could avoid s. 203 altogether by inserting a clause in an 'agreement' with the employee that their relationship was not intended to give rise to legal relations. This issue arose (on unusual facts) in the *M&P Steelcraft* case.[100] The EAT held that a 'no legal relations' clause would infringe s. 203, provided that the parties' agreement – absent the clause – would have given rise to a contract of employment or a worker's contract giving rise to employment rights under the 1996

---

[96] Above n 80.

[97] ERA 1996, s 203(3). It is worth noting that the protections in s 203 only apply to the settlement of statutory claims, not contractual ones, so a settlement may be ineffective for the former but effective in relation to the latter: *Sutherland v Network Appliance Ltd* [2001] IRLR 12 (EAT).

[98] *Igbo v Johnson, Matthey Chemicals* [1986] ICR 505 (CA).

[99] ibid 512–513.

[100] *M&P Steelcraft Ltd v Ellis* [2008] ICR 578 (EAT).

Act. However, it is worth noting that this leaves untouched the broader problem of employers drafting contracts in ways which make it appear that the individual is not an employee or a worker in order to avoid statutory employment rights. While the *Autoclenz* ruling can be used to tackle artificial clauses that do this without reflecting the 'true agreement' between the parties,[101] *M&P Steelcraft* appeared to suggest that s. 203 did not have a role to play in tackling this problem.[102]

A final point to note is that it seems unlikely that the Unfair Contract Terms Act 1977 has any application to contracts of employment.[103] Had it applied, it would have enabled the courts to apply a reasonableness test to certain types of contract term under s. 3(2). According to s. 3(1), the reasonableness test applies 'as between contracting parties where one of them deals as consumer or on the other's written standard terms of business'. In *Commerzbank v Keen*, it was held that an employee could not rely on either of these elements, the first because he could not be regarded as a consumer,[104] and the second because the employer's *business* was something else (in the case in question, banking) and not making contracts of employment with employees.[105] Although on a literal reading of the statute this must be correct, it overlooks the fact that many contracts of employment are 'standard form' and many employees are in no better position than consumers.[106]

5.5 TERMS IMPLIED AT COMMON LAW

Implied terms are used by the courts to fill in the gaps in contracts. They are particularly important in the employment setting because of the special features of contracts of employment noted above: they may be long-term in nature, and the parties may not be able to (or may not even try to) set out full details of their rights and obligations in advance. Thus, contracts in the employment setting may have some particularly big gaps for the courts to fill.

In the ordinary law of contract, the courts imply terms in two situations. The first (a term 'implied in fact') sets out something that was obviously intended as a term of the contract by the parties at the time of the agreement. The courts use the 'officious bystander'[107] or 'business efficacy'[108] tests for this purpose. In *AG for Belize v Belize Telecom*, Lord Hoffmann stated that the traditional approach:

> is best regarded not as a series of independent tests which must each be surmounted, but rather as a collection of different ways in which judges have tried to express the central idea that the proposed implied term must spell out what the contract actually meant, or in which they have explained why they did not think that it did so.[109]

The courts are keen to state that they are not writing the parties' contract for them: instead, they are trying to give effect to the parties' intentions, objectively determined.

---

[101] *Autoclenz*, above n 32, and see Chapter 4.
[102] *M&P Steelcraft*, above n 100, [48]–[50].
[103] Hugh Collins, 'Legal Responses to the Standard Form Contract of Employment' (2007) 36 ILJ 2.
[104] Doubting *Brigden v American Express Bank Ltd* [2000] IRLR 94.
[105] [2006] EWCA Civ 1536, [2007] ICR 623.
[106] Collins, above n 103, 15. The Law Commission proposed reform but this aspect of its proposals has not been implemented: Law Commission, *Unfair Terms in Contracts* (Law Com No 292, 2005).
[107] *Southern Foundries (1926) Ltd v Shirlaw* [1939] 2 KB 206 (CA), 227 (MacKinnon LJ).
[108] See, for example, *Luxor (Eastbourne) Ltd v Cooper* [1941] AC 108, 137 (Lord Wright).
[109] [2009] UKPC 10, [2009] 2 All ER 1127 [27].

We are concerned with the second type of implied term: a term 'implied in law'. Terms of this type are implied as 'necessary incidents' of a particular kind of contract, such as the relationship between landlord and tenant or, in our case, employer and employee.[110] The implied terms we will consider in this section – mutual trust and confidence, fidelity and obedience – are of this character. If the parties create a contract of employment, they can assume that it will come with a certain set of implied terms: it is more of an 'off the peg' contract than a bespoke one. This is important because, as we saw above, contracts of employment are generally incomplete. What is not entirely clear is the test to be used in the event that a court is called upon to imply a new term not supported by prior case-law into a particular kind of contract, such as a contract of employment. In some cases, the 'business efficacy' test has been used, but nowadays, judges tend to accept that terms implied in law reflect judicial understandings of what would be fair and reasonable in the relevant relationship.[111]

For obvious reasons, it is not possible to imply a term in fact where it would conflict with the express terms of the contract agreed by the parties. But matters are less clear in relation to terms implied in law. If they are necessary to make the relationship fair, surely it should not be possible for the parties to exclude them? However, it is difficult for the courts to achieve this result given that contract law is about giving effect to the parties' agreement.[112] For example, if there is a 'no mutual trust and confidence' clause, this may be an indication that the parties did not intend to create a contract of employment. This not only contradicts the implied term, but also takes away the justification for having the implied term in the first place. The *Autoclenz* decision, discussed above, may be helpful here because it offers a route for the courts to classify a contract as one of employment (with all the implied terms that would entail) even if there are terms in the written agreement that appear to contradict this.[113]

A further difficulty that arises nowadays is whether to regard implied terms as features only of contracts of employment or also of workers' contracts.[114] This problem is particularly acute in this area because most of the case-law has concerned the contract of employment. Should workers benefit from the same set of implied terms, or is the nature of the worker relationship different? We will consider this issue after our discussion of the implied terms themselves, which will be divided into duties placed on the employer and duties placed on the employee.

5.5.1 The employee's duties

The employee's duties fall into three main groups: skill and care; obedience, co-operation or trust and confidence; and loyalty or fidelity.

---

[110] See, for example, *Liverpool City Council v Irwin* [1977] AC 239 (HL).
[111] *Geys v Société Générale* [2012] UKSC 63, [2013] 1 AC 523 [56] (Baroness Hale); and see Hugh Collins, 'Implied Terms: The Foundation in Good Faith and Fair Dealing' (2014) 67 Current Legal Problems 297.
[112] *Johnstone v Bloomsbury HA* [1992] QB 333 (CA).
[113] *Autoclenz*, above n 32.
[114] This distinction is explained in Chapter 4. See also Freedland, above n 81, Chapter 3.

Skill and care

There is an implied term in the contract of employment that the employee owes a duty of care towards his or her employer. This means that the employee must exercise appropriate skill and care in his or her work, and is liable to indemnify the employer if he or she causes loss by his or her negligence.

The implied duty to exercise care and skill has two elements. First, any employee is obliged to exercise reasonable care when carrying out his or her work.[115] Second, an employee who purports to have a particular skill, trade or profession impliedly promises that he or she is reasonably competent in that regard.[116]

The employee's duty of care towards the employer means that, in theory at least, the employer may sue the employee for damages in the event that the employee causes loss to the employer. The leading case on this is *Lister v Romford Ice and Cold Storage Co Ltd*.[117] In that case, the employee lorry driver took his father with him in the lorry and injured him in an accident. The father obtained an award of damages against the employer on the basis that it was vicariously liable for its employee's negligence. The employer then sued the employee, seeking to recover from him the money it had paid to his father. The House of Lords held that the employee was in breach of the implied term of his contract of employment requiring him to exercise reasonable care in the performance of his duties. The employer was, of course, insured. Counsel for the employee tried to argue that it was an implied term of the employee's contract that he or she should not have to indemnify the employer where the employer was insured against the loss. However, the House of Lords rejected this argument for a variety of reasons, including a general reluctance to take account of insurance in developing the law of tort, and a concern that it would not give employees an incentive to be careful.[118] Thus, an employee may be required to compensate the employer for any loss he or she causes. In practice, though, most employers do not sue their employees in these circumstances because an employee is unlikely to have the resources to compensate the employer. There is also an understanding that employers' insurers will not pursue claims against employees.[119] Nevertheless, the basic rule has been much-criticised by commentators because of the risk that an employer or insurer might depart from the 'normal' practice and sue an employee who would be ill-equipped to meet the claim.

Obedience, co-operation, maintaining trust and confidence

We saw above that a key area of incompleteness in contracts of employment relates to the work the employee is hired to do. This is resolved by means of managerial prerogative: the courts accept that the employer (or, more usually, the boss employed by the employer) will tell the employee what to do on a day-to-day basis. After all, an employee is traditionally someone who is under the 'control' of the employer.[120] Of course, managerial prerogative only works if the employee does as he or she is

---

[115] *Lister v Romford Ice and Cold Storage Co Ltd* [1957] AC 555 (HL).
[116] *Harmer v Cornelius* (1858) 5 CBNS 236, 141 ER 94 (QB).
[117] Above n 115.
[118] ibid 576–579.
[119] Employers are obliged to have insurance under various pieces of legislation including the Employers' Liability (Compulsory Insurance) Act 1969.
[120] See Chapter 4.

told. The implied duty of obedience is the means by which the law gives effect to managerial prerogative.[121]

Over time, the basic duty of obedience has evolved into something more elaborate. The correct label for this development is open to debate. One option is to identify a duty of co-operation, but the language of co-operation is rarely used by the courts and maintaining the employer's trust and confidence may be a more appropriate label.[122] A simple example of the developing case-law is the *ASLEF* case, in which the union instructed its members to 'work to rule' as part of industrial action.[123] The question before the court was whether a 'work to rule' constituted a breach of contract. Working to rule involves obeying the employer's instructions but in a very literal way so as to cause disruption. So, for example, if the employer requires particular safety equipment to be present in the workplace, the employee might cause disruption by checking the safety equipment more frequently or elaborately than normal. Although the three judges in the Court of Appeal gave slightly different reasons, the thrust of their ruling was that employees were in breach of contract if they obeyed the employer's orders in a perverse way.[124] Buckley LJ held that there was 'an implied term to serve the employer faithfully within the requirements of the contract'.[125]

The duty to co-operate or to maintain the employer's trust can generate quite broadly framed obligations. A key example of this is the *Sim* case, in which teachers refused to provide cover for colleagues who were off work, as part of industrial action.[126] The judge held that 'teachers have a contractual obligation under their contracts to discharge their professional obligations as teachers towards their pupils and their school'.[127] This meant that they were obliged to obey the head teacher's reasonable instructions on matters such as the timetabling of lessons and the provision of cover for absent colleagues. This approach offers considerable flexibility to the employer to insist on a wide range of 'professional' activities as a matter of contractual obligation, even though in some cases the employees involved might have assumed that they were engaging in those activities voluntarily, as a matter of professional pride.

The employee may refuse to obey an instruction from the employer that is unreasonable or unlawful. In relation to unlawful orders, this is relatively straightforward. For example, in *Gregory v Ford*, the employer sent the employee lorry driver out in an uninsured vehicle.[128] It is clear that, had the driver known there was no insurance policy in place, he could have refused to drive the lorry without breaching his contract of employment. Unreasonable orders are more difficult to spot. The broader the employee's duty of co-operation, the harder it is to say that an instruction to do a particular task does not form part of the individual's job. In *Sim*, the judge noted that there was agreement between the school and the teachers that

---

[121] *Turner* v *Mason* 153 ER 411.
[122] Freedland, above n 81, 140–170; and see *Smith* v *London Metropolitan University* [2011] IRLR 884 (EAT) [77].
[123] *Secretary of State for Employment* v *ASLEF (No 2)* [1972] 2 QB 455 (CA).
[124] ibid 490–493 (Lord Denning MR), 498 (Buckley LJ), 508–509 (Roskill LJ).
[125] ibid 498.
[126] *Sim* v *Rotherham Metropolitan Borough Council* [1987] Ch 216.
[127] ibid 251.
[128] [1951] 1 All ER 121.

it was not part of their professional obligations to supervise pupils during the lunch break, so that an order to do so would have been unreasonable and could have been disobeyed.[129] In the *Bull* case, a fire authority instructed its employee firefighters to respond to emergency calls where an ambulance was required but could not be deployed quickly enough.[130] The Court of Appeal held that the fire authority had no right to do this because, although the firefighters had first aid skills, their job was to fight fires and responding to ambulance calls could not be regarded as a part of this job. Thus, the employer's instruction was not reasonable.

A particularly grey area relates to changes in the work the employee is required to do. As we shall see below, a change in the employee's contractual obligations requires his or her consent. This offers some protection for the employee, who cannot be hired to do one thing and then made to do something completely different without his or her agreement (though, of course, his or her need of a job may make it difficult to resist). However, it is also important that the employer has some flexibility because, particularly in long-term contracts, the needs of the business may change or develop over time. A key question is therefore whether the employer's general managerial prerogative can be used to effect changes in the employee's duties. In the *Cresswell* case, the employees were clerical workers at the Inland Revenue.[131] They objected to the introduction of a computer system for storing tax records because it would put some of them out of a job. However, it was held that they could not legitimately refuse to operate the new system because it was their duty to co-operate with the employer's instructions. These instructions did not change the nature of their job but simply required them to do the same job in a new way, using new technology. This can be contrasted with *Bull*, discussed above, in which the court distinguished *Cresswell*, holding that the fire authority's instruction went beyond a change in the manner of doing the job and instead required the employees to do another job entirely.[132] This strikes a reasonable balance between protecting the employee and preserving the employer's flexibility, though there are bound to be some difficult cases in between these two extremes.

Loyalty, fidelity

A third set of obligations imposed on the employee at common law require him or her to be loyal or faithful to the employer. In simple terms, this means that during the contract of employment, the employee must work for the employer and may not use information, skills or opportunities gained as part of his or her job for his or her own profit. However, this obligation is not absolute: the law acknowledges that the employee is an economic actor in his or her own right, and may want to earn extra money in his or her spare time. Since some of the information obtained by an employee in the course of his or her employment may be confidential, obligations in the law of confidentiality (which apply generally, not just to employees) are also relevant here.

---

[129] *Sim*, above n 126, 249.
[130] *Bull v Nottinghamshire and City of Nottingham Fire and Rescue Authority* [2007] EWCA Civ 240, [2007] ICR 1631.
[131] *Cresswell*, above n 28.
[132] *Bull*, above n 130, 1641–1642.

A simple example of the implied term of fidelity in action is the *Hivac* case.[133] In that case, the employees worked five and a half days per week for the claimant employer, and in their spare time worked for one of its business rivals doing the same kind of work. The Court of Appeal held that this was a breach of the implied term of faithful service. While the judges were keen to stress that the employees were entitled to use their free time as they wished, including by taking a second job to earn extra money,[134] they held that this did not extend to working, in secret, for a rival firm, and thus inflicting 'great harm' on the employer's business.[135] Similarly, in the *Thomas Marshall* case, the defendant set up his own business while working for the claimant company.[136] His business was in direct competition with the company and had dealings with the same suppliers and customers. This was held to be a breach of the implied duty (as well as of other express terms of his contract of employment).

Of course, a problem with this approach is that – for most employees – the obvious way to earn extra money outside their 'main' job is to do a similar kind of work. Not many people have earning power in two radically different sectors of the economy. While the decisions in *Hivac* and *Thomas Marshall* seem entirely justifiable on their facts, it is potentially very easy to argue that any extra work performed by the employee in the same sector as the employer involves harming the employer's interests. However, the *Fishel* case applied some limits to the extent of the employee's duty of fidelity.[137] In that case, the employee, Dr Fishel, was an embryologist who conducted research and ran a fertility clinic for the employer university. He also provided his services for payment at other clinics around the world. The university argued that he was in breach of his contract of employment in respect of his 'outside' work. However, Elias J held that since it was not part of Dr Fishel's job to attract contracts from overseas clinics, he was not acting in breach of his duty of fidelity when he accepted those contracts for himself.

A particular area of confusion in the law – also tackled by Elias J in *Fishel* – is the relationship between the implied term of fidelity and the more general concept of acting as a fiduciary. Fiduciaries owe particularly extensive obligations towards those on whose behalf they act. They are obliged to put the other person's interests above their own. Some employees, such as company directors, are treated by the law as fiduciaries.[138] Thus, a company director must always put the company's interests above his or her own and must (among other things) disclose any personal gains he or she has made arising from his or her position, even if this amounts to confessing to his or her own wrongdoing. Unfortunately, the terminology commonly used to identify when a fiduciary relationship arises – where one person owes an obligation of loyalty or trust and confidence towards another – is very similar to that used to describe the employee's duties in the employment field. However, as Elias J argued with some force in *Fishel*, it is not necessarily appropriate to equate the two situations or to assume that all employees are fiduciaries.[139] As Elias J explained:

---

[133] *Hivac Ltd v Park Royal Scientific Instruments Ltd* [1946] Ch 169 (CA).

[134] Of course, an employer could seek to prevent this by including an express 'exclusive service' clause in the employee's contract.

[135] *Hivac*, above n 133, 178 (Lord Greene MR).

[136] *Thomas Marshall (Exports) Ltd v Guinle* [1979] Ch 227 (Ch).

[137] *University of Nottingham v Fishel* [2000] ICR 1462 (QB).

[138] See, generally, Paul L Davies and Sarah Worthington, *Gower and Davies' Principles of Modern Company Law* (9th edn, Sweet & Maxwell 2012), chapter 16.

[139] Approved by the CA in *Customer Systems Plc v Ranson* [2012] EWCA Civ 841, [2012] IRLR 769.

There are many cases which have recognised the existence of the employee's duty of good faith, or loyalty, or the mutual duty of trust and confidence – concepts which tend to shade into one another. As I have already indicated, Lord Millett has used precisely this language when describing the characteristic features which trigger fiduciary obligations. But he was not using the concepts in quite the same sense as they tend to be used in the employment field. Lord Millett was applying the concepts of loyalty and good faith to circumstances where a person undertakes to act solely in the interests of another. Unfortunately, these concepts are frequently used in the employment context to describe situations where a party merely has to take into consideration the interests of another, but does not have to act in the interests of that other.[140]

Thus, an 'ordinary' employee must 'take into consideration' the interests of the employer, whereas an employee who is also a fiduciary must put the employer's interests first. According to Elias J, fiduciary obligations only arise where the terms of the contract and the surrounding circumstances so indicate.[141] Thus, the employee may be a fiduciary where he or she is in possession of confidential information, or the employer's money or property. But there should be no general assumption that all employees owe fiduciary obligations to their employer. This is an important safeguard for employees as independent economic actors.

A particular concern for many employers relates to confidential information. Many employees have access to confidential information during the course of their work.[142] For example, a restaurant employee might know the employer's secret recipe for a speciality dish, or a sales employee might have access to the customer database. The implied obligation of fidelity, as we have seen, will serve to prevent the employee from using that information to set up a rival business or to work for a rival employer in his or her spare time. That same obligation – or the employee's fiduciary obligations, which arise when he or she is in receipt of confidential information, or a tort action for breach of confidence, will also serve to make it unlawful in most situations for the employee to disclose the confidential information to others. However, there may be an exception where it is in the public interest for disclosure to be made. For example, in *Lion Laboratories Ltd* v *Evans*, the defendants were former employees of the employer which manufactured breathalyser equipment used by the police.[143] They disclosed documents to a newspaper which suggested that the breathalysers were defective. The court held that it was in the public interest for this disclosure to be made because of the risk that some people might be wrongly convicted of drink-driving offences.[144] Nowadays, 'whistleblowers' enjoy specific statutory protection against detriment or dismissal for making a 'protected disclosure' either within the firm or (if certain conditions are met) externally.[145]

Often, employers want the duty of fidelity to continue after the employment relationship has ended – they do not want employees to leave and set up rival businesses – but in this situation matters are more complicated because the employee (who no longer has a job) has a stronger interest in making money. We will consider

---

[140] *Fishel*, above n 137, 1492.
[141] ibid 1493.
[142] But the employee must know the information for any duties to apply: *Vestergaard Frandsen S/A (now called MVF3 APS)* v *Bestnet Europe Ltd* [2013] UKSC 31, [2013] 1 WLR 1556.
[143] [1985] QB 526 (CA).
[144] ibid 551 (Griffiths LJ).
[145] See Chapter 9.

post-employment restraints separately below. For now, it is sufficient to note that the courts will not normally imply post-employment restraints at common law, so the employer must include them expressly in the contract.[146]

5.5.2 The employer's duties

The employer's duties can be divided into two main types: the duty of care, and the duty to maintain trust and confidence.

Care

We saw above that contracts of employment contain implied terms that employees will exercise reasonable care and skill in the performance of their tasks. The employer also owes a duty of care towards the employee. In this section, we will examine the legal basis of the duty of care before considering its content. We will then briefly examine the role of statute in promoting health and safety at work.

Tort or contract? For historical reasons, the employer's duty of care developed in the law of tort, though nowadays the courts also recognise it as an implied term in contracts of employment.[147] According to Lord Steyn in the *Frost* case:

> The rules to be applied when an employee brings an action against his employer for harm suffered at his workplace are the rules of tort . . . The duty of an employer to safeguard his employees from harm could also be formulated in contract. In that event, and absent relevant express provisions, a term is implied by law into the contract as an incident of a standardised contract . . . But such a term could not be wider in scope than the duty imposed by the law of tort.[148]

In many cases, it does not matter whether the employee frames his or her claim in contract or tort, though there are some situations in which it may be advantageous to pursue one route rather than the other. For example, the employee may claim damages in tort but not in contract for loss of future earnings. But if the employee wishes to resign from the job and claim that he or she has been unfairly (constructively) dismissed, the claim must, of course, be framed in terms of the employer's repudiatory breach of contract in not providing a safe workplace.[149]

As the above quotation indicates, in a contract claim, the implied duty of care may come into conflict with the express provisions of the contract. This was the case in *Johnstone v Bloomsbury HA*.[150] The claimant was a doctor whose standard working week was 40 hours and who could also be required under his contract to be available for another 48 hours per week on call. He regularly worked in excess of 88 hours per week and sued his employer for damages when he became physically ill, arguing that it was in breach of its duty of care towards him. By a majority, the Court of Appeal held that his claim should not be struck out. How could the employer's duty of care be reconciled with the claimant's express contractual duty to work up to

---

[146] *Faccenda Chicken Ltd v Fowler* [1987] Ch 117 (CA).
[147] *Matthews v Kuwait Bechtel Corp* [1959] 2 QB 57 (CA).
[148] *Frost v Chief Constable of South Yorkshire Police* [1999] 2 AC 455 (HL) 497–498.
[149] *Nicolas UK Ltd v Troquet* (2004) UKEAT/0923/03/TM.
[150] [1992] QB 333 (CA).

88 hours per week? Browne-Wilkinson VC solved the problem by focusing on the fact that the employer had a discretion to require the additional on-call working, and that therefore there was no inconsistency in requiring the employer to exercise its discretion compatibly with the employee's health and safety.[151] Stuart-Smith LJ appeared to take a broader view, holding that only the clearest of language would exclude the employer's duty of care, and that the express term about hours should be read together with the implied duty of care.[152] The latter approach would potentially aid the employee even where the contract fixed the exact hours to be worked, whereas Browne-Wilkinson VC suggested, obiter, that the employee would be unable to claim in that situation.[153] Given the inequality of bargaining power between the parties when the contract is drafted, it is highly undesirable to allow the employer to 'contract out' of its duty of care simply by specifying long working hours in the contract. More generally, it is worth remembering that under s. 2(1) Unfair Contract Terms Act 1977, it is not possible to use a contract term to exclude or limit liability for death or personal injury due to negligence.

Content of the duty The employer's duty of care in its current form originates in the decision of the House of Lords in *Wilson & Clyde Coal Co Ltd v English*.[154] At common law, the employer owes a duty of care to the employee in respect of the provision of: a safe working environment, adequate equipment (though this is now the subject of extensive statutory intervention), competent colleagues and a safe system of work. As with any duty of care, the employer is not liable where it can show that it took reasonable steps to ensure its employees' safety. To give a simple example, in the *Corus* case, the employees were required to use pneumatic tools at work for significant periods of time.[155] These tools generated high levels of vibration, so that the employees contracted a condition known as Hand/Arm Vibration Syndrome (HAVS), resulting in numbness or pain in their hands and arms. It was held that within a reasonable time of the risks associated with excessive exposure to vibration becoming known, in the mid-1970s, the employer should have taken reasonable steps to reduce the employees' exposure. The case was remitted to the county court for the assessment of damages.

Although there is still a steady stream of cases in which claimants have suffered physical injuries at work, many claims nowadays relate to psychiatric injury caused by long working hours, stress, harassment or bullying. The employer's duty of care in respect of the employee's mental health was first established in the case of *Walker v Northumberland CC*.[156] The claimant was a senior social worker who suffered a nervous breakdown due to overwork. When he returned to work, he was given extra support, but this was quickly withdrawn and his workload continued to increase. He became ill again and was eventually dismissed. He sued his employer for damages. Colman J stated:

> It is clear law that an employer has a duty to provide his employee with a reasonably safe system of work and to take reasonable steps to protect him from risks which are reasonably

[151] ibid 350–351.
[152] ibid 343–344.
[153] ibid 350.
[154] [1938] AC 57 (HL).
[155] *Brown v Corus (UK) Ltd* [2004] EWCA Civ 374, [2004] PIQR P30.
[156] [1995] ICR 702 (QB).

foreseeable. Whereas the law on the extent of this duty has developed almost exclusively in cases involving physical injury to the employee as distinct from injury to his mental health, there is no logical reason why risk of psychiatric damage should be excluded from the scope of an employer's duty of care or from the co-extensive implied term in the contract of employment.[157]

The judge held that the employer was in breach of its duty after the claimant's first breakdown, because from that point onwards it was reasonably foreseeable that he would suffer further psychiatric injury if he did not receive extra support. This was so even though the extra support would cost money and might impair, to some extent, the council's provision of services to the public. The decision in *Walker* has been affirmed by the House of Lords in later cases, notably *Barber v Somerset CC*.[158] The House of Lords cited with approval the following summary of the standard of care: 'the conduct of the reasonable and prudent employer, taking positive thought for the safety of his workers in the light of what he knows or ought to know'.[159] The employer's duty is towards the employee as an individual, so if the employer knows that the employee is especially vulnerable because of a past history of depression, for example, the employer must take extra care.

It is not just overwork that can cause psychiatric harm to an employee. Harassment and bullying by colleagues may also cause such harm. This can be illustrated by the case of *Waters v Metropolitan Police Commissioner*.[160] The claimant police officer alleged that she had been raped by a colleague. She complained to her superiors and was then subjected to a campaign of harassment by other colleagues aimed at getting her to resign. The House of Lords allowed her case to go to trial. Lord Slynn said:

> If an employer knows that acts being done by employees during their employment may cause physical or mental harm to a particular fellow employee and he does nothing to supervise or prevent such acts, when it is in his power to do so, it is clearly arguable that he may be in breach of his duty to that employee. It seems to me that he may also be in breach of that duty if he can foresee that such acts may happen and, if they do, that physical or mental harm may be caused to an individual.[161]

As Freedland notes, this case suggests a strong positive obligation on the employer to look out for the well-being of its employees.[162]

Another area in which the employer's duty of care may be relevant is where the employer is engaged in disciplinary action against the employee. In the recent *Yapp* case, the employee was a diplomat who was withdrawn from his overseas posting in response to allegations made against him, pending further investigation.[163] He argued that the act of suspending him without investigating the allegations first had caused him psychiatric injury. However, the Court of Appeal rejected the claim on remoteness grounds, finding that it was not reasonably foreseeable that the suspension would cause psychiatric injury. Underhill LJ held that the suspension was not serious enough in itself to trigger the injury even though some aspects of the employer's conduct had

[157] ibid 710.
[158] [2004] UKHL 13, [2004] ICR 457.
[159] ibid [65] (Lord Walker), citing *Stokes v Guest, Keen and Nettlefold (Bolts and Nuts) Ltd* [1968] 1 WLR 1776, 1783 (Swanwick J).
[160] [2000] ICR 1064.
[161] ibid 1068.
[162] Freedland, above n 81, 144.
[163] *Yapp v Foreign and Commonwealth Office* [2014] EWCA Civ 1512, [2015] IRLR 112.

been unfair, and that the claimant had no history to suggest to the employer that he was prone to psychiatric injury. This case suggests that it is difficult to bring a claim in respect of a 'one-off' act of unfairness unless it is very extreme or unless the employer knows that the employee is vulnerable.

It is sometimes suggested that the employer also owes a duty of care towards its employees in respect of their economic well-being. The case-law does not support any such general duty,[164] though the employer may have specific duties of care in certain narrowly defined fact situations. One such situation is when the employer is writing a reference for the employee. This proposition was laid down by the House of Lords in *Spring* v *Guardian Assurance*.[165] The employee in that case was dismissed by the defendant but needed a reference in order to get regulatory approval to work at another firm. The approval was refused – and the job offer withdrawn – after the defendant supplied a reference containing various inaccuracies. The House of Lords held that although the employer is not required to guarantee the accuracy of everything in the reference, it must take reasonable care in gathering the facts and preparing the reference. The employer's duty could be framed either in tort or as an implied term of the contract of employment. The duty has been further elucidated in later cases so that it is now well-established that the reference must not give an unfair impression when read as a whole, even if particular factual statements within it are accurate.[166] However, the reference need not be 'full and comprehensive'.[167]

Another situation in which the employer may owe a duty of care in respect of the employee's financial well-being relates to matters such as pensions and other benefits. The leading case on this matter is *Scally*.[168] In that case, the employer provided a pension scheme which gave maximum benefits after 40 years' service. Employees who were not going to be able to accumulate 40 years' service before retirement could purchase additional 'years' in the pension scheme, but they could only do so on favourable financial terms if they met a particular deadline. The House of Lords rejected the idea of a claim in tort but held that a term could be implied into their contracts that the employer was under an obligation to take reasonable steps to publicise the conditions for claiming the benefit to which they were entitled. This term was to be implied as a necessary incident of the contract of employment, and was to be defined narrowly. Lord Bridge was concerned to confine it to the situation in which the employee could not easily have found out about the benefit him- or herself, as in *Scally* itself, where the scheme had been agreed through collective bargaining and not with the employees as individuals.[169]

Where the employee approaches the employer with questions about his or her entitlements, the employer must give accurate information in response to employee requests, but need not provide help or advice.[170] For example, in *Eyett*, the claimant asked his employer for a pension calculation because he wished to take early retirement.[171] The calculation was accurate but he was not told that a slightly later

---

[164] *Crossley* v *Faithful & Gould Holdings Ltd* [2004] EWCA Civ 293, [2004] ICR 1615.
[165] [1995] 2 AC 296 (HL).
[166] *Bartholomew* v *Hackney LBC* [1999] IRLR 246 (CA).
[167] *Kidd* v *Axa Equity & Law Life Assurance Society Plc* [2000] IRLR 301.
[168] *Scally* v *Southern Health and Social Services Board* [1992] 1 AC 294 (HL).
[169] ibid 307.
[170] *Outram* v *Academy Plastics Ltd* [2001] ICR 367 (CA).
[171] *University of Nottingham* v *Eyett* [1999] ICR 721.

retirement date would generate a bigger pension. It was held that the employer was not in breach of any duty towards the employee in that case.

Statute The employer's duty of care towards the employee is now overlaid by a complex set of statutory obligations relating to working time and health and safety.[172] Health and safety is a complex topic best left to specialist books, but we will give a brief overview here.

The main sources of law in this area are Directive 89/391/EEC on the introduction of measures to encourage improvements in the safety and health of workers at work and the Health and Safety at Work etc Act 1974. These general measures are supplemented by a series of directives and domestic rules on specific types of activity, such as dealing with hazardous chemicals. Employers have three main duties in health and safety law: to conduct risk assessments to identify risks;[173] to take such steps as are 'reasonably practicable' (for the most part) to mitigate risks facing employees and others;[174] and to consult employees on health and safety matters at the workplace.[175] The law is enforced by a public body, the Health and Safety Executive.

Trust and confidence

The implied term of mutual trust and confidence recognises the relational nature of the contract of employment. Using this term, the courts encourage the parties to behave in ways that will maintain a functioning relationship over the longer term. Although the term is applicable to both parties, a number of more well-established terms govern employee behaviour, as we have seen, so it is of greater significance in relation to the employer. As we shall see, the implied term has a close relationship with broader ideas of good faith and fair dealing, and these are used interchangeably in some circumstances.

General The implied term of mutual trust and confidence was first stated in its modern form in the case of *Malik* v *BCCI*.[176] The claimants in that case were employees of a bank. The bank was run fraudulently and was eventually closed down. The claimants argued that it was difficult for them to find new jobs because of their association with the bank. Lord Nicholls explained that:

> the bank was under an implied obligation to its employees not to conduct a dishonest or corrupt business. This implied obligation is no more than one particular aspect of the portmanteau, general obligation not to engage in conduct likely to undermine the trust and confidence required if the employment relationship is to continue in the manner the employment contract implicitly envisages.[177]

The employees could therefore seek damages for breach of contract, including damages in respect of the financial loss they had suffered as a result of not being able to find new jobs, subject to the usual principles such as causation, remoteness and mitigation.

---

[172] See Chapter 8.
[173] Management of Health and Safety at Work Regulations 1999, SI 1999/3242, reg 3(1).
[174] Health and Safety at Work etc. Act 1974, s 2(2).
[175] Health and Safety at Work etc. Act 1974, s 2(6).
[176] [1998] AC 20 (HL).
[177] ibid 34–5.

Lord Steyn gave a useful overview of what he regarded as the purpose of the implied term of mutual trust and confidence:

> the implied obligation as formulated is apt to cover the great diversity of situations in which a balance has to be struck between an employer's interest in managing his business as he sees fit and the employee's interest in not being unfairly and improperly exploited.[178]

Lord Steyn emphasised the point that only conduct 'likely to destroy or seriously damage' trust and confidence would give rise to a breach of the term.[179]

Another illustration of the implied term in action is provided by the *Gogay* case.[180] The claimant worked with vulnerable children in a residential home. She was suspended when a child in her care accused her of abuse. She suffered severe depression and was unable to work. The Court of Appeal held that the employer was in breach of the implied term because, although it owed duties towards the children in its care, it had over-reacted to the allegations of abuse, which were imprecise, and should have taken further steps to investigate them before suspending the employee, given the seriousness of being accused of abuse.

However, some doubt has been cast on this ruling by the decision in the *Yapp* case, discussed above, in which a diplomat argued that he had suffered depression as a result of being withdrawn from his overseas posting on disciplinary grounds.[181] The Court of Appeal rejected his claim for breach of the implied term of mutual trust and confidence as being too remote, holding that it was not within the reasonable contemplation of the parties that he would suffer psychiatric injury as a result of his suspension. The remoteness issue had not been explored fully in *Gogay*, and its use in *Yapp* adds a new obstacle to employees' claims because the test in contract is more stringent than that for breach of the duty of care in tort (on which the claimant also failed, as we saw above). This suggests that claims for breach of the implied term of mutual trust and confidence will only succeed if the facts are quite extreme.

Relationship with unfair dismissal law Particular difficulties have arisen because of the relationship between the implied term and the law of unfair dismissal.[182] One of the significant limitations of the law of unfair dismissal is that the compensation available is limited to a year's salary or £76,574, whichever is the lower.[183] This means that well-paid employees in particular may not regard the compensation available as sufficient. As a result, various attempts have been made to use the implied term to challenge dismissals – to create what might be thought of as a common law action in respect of the fairness of a dismissal – but the courts have been reluctant to permit this development.

---

[178] ibid 46.

[179] ibid 47.

[180] *Gogay v Hertfordshire CC* [2000] IRLR 703.

[181] Above n 163.

[182] See Chapter 9. For discussion, see Lizzie Barmes, 'Common Law Implied Terms and Behavioural Standards at Work' (2007) 36 ILJ 35; Douglas Brodie, 'Legal Coherence and the Employment Revolution' (2001) 117 LQR 604; 'Mutual Trust and Confidence: Catalysts, Constraints and Commonality' (2008) 37 ILJ 329; Judy Fudge, 'The Spectre of *Addis* in Contracts of Employment in Canada and the UK' (2007) 36 ILJ 51.

[183] ERA 1996, s 124.

The leading authority in this area is the decision in *Johnson* v *Unisys*.[184] The claimant, who had already recovered the then maximum compensation for unfair dismissal, sought to argue that the manner of his dismissal had been in breach of the implied term of trust and confidence. It had made him depressed and unable to work, thereby causing him economic loss. The House of Lords rejected his claim. Lord Hoffmann gave three main reasons for his decision. First, he held that an implied obligation to dismiss the employee only with proper cause and after a fair procedure would be inconsistent with the employer's express power to dismiss the employee with four weeks' notice.[185] Second, although the first problem could be overcome by judicial creativity in the design of the implied term, to do so would go beyond incremental common law development and would potentially impose very substantial liability on employers.[186] Third, Parliament had created a remedy for employees in the law of unfair dismissal, with a limitation on the damages to be awarded, so it was not appropriate to develop the common law to 'get around' Parliament's wishes.[187]

In many cases, the employer's alleged breach of the implied term of trust and confidence occurs prior to the dismissal, for example, in the conduct of a disciplinary or grievance process leading up to dismissal. The effect of *Johnson* on such claims was clarified in the *Eastwood* case.[188] Here, it was held that what is often referred to as the '*Johnson* exclusion area' related only to the dismissal itself. Employees who already had a cause of action for breach of the implied term prior to the dismissal could still claim, even if they were subsequently dismissed. Thus, in *Eastwood* itself, the claimants were employees who had been dismissed after very inadequate investigations or disciplinary procedures conducted by their employers. Provided that they could demonstrate economic loss flowing from these procedures (as opposed to the dismissal), they could claim. However, a shadow has been cast over the *Eastwood* decision by the more recent decision of the Supreme Court in the *Edwards* case.[189] This case did not concern the implied term of mutual trust and confidence, but it did consider the so-called '*Johnson* exclusion area' in relation to alleged infringements of express contractual disciplinary procedures. Mr Edwards argued that the disciplinary panel which decided to dismiss him was improperly constituted and did not follow a fair procedure. The majority held that any harm to Mr Edwards caused by these problems did not arise independently of the decision to dismiss him so his claim was precluded by *Johnson*.[190] Arguably, this makes it more difficult for future claimants to bring *Eastwood*-style claims where the breach of the implied term arises close to the dismissal itself.

These decisions have been the subject of much criticism, particularly because they stifle the potentially interesting development of a common law action in respect of the manner of dismissal.[191] For present purposes, what is important is to note that the implied term of mutual trust and confidence remains an important aspect of the contract of employment governing the employer's behaviour but it can only be invoked during the life of the contract and not around the time of termination.

---

[184] [2001] UKHL 13, [2003] 1 AC 518.
[185] ibid [42].
[186] ibid [47]–[49].
[187] ibid [58].
[188] *Eastwood* v *Magnox Electric Plc* [2004] UKHL 35, [2005] 1 AC 503.
[189] *Edwards* v *Chesterfield Royal Hospital NHS Foundation Trust* [2011] UKSC 58, [2012] 2 AC 22.
[190] ibid [57] (Lord Dyson).
[191] See Chapter 9.

Relationship with express terms Contracts of employment often contain express terms which give the employer a discretion of some kind, for example, to pay the employee a bonus. In some cases, the courts have been willing to hold that these discretions must be exercised reasonably or in good faith, often drawing on the *Wednesbury* test in public law.[192] Although the language of mutual trust and confidence is less common here, the overall effect is quite similar and the courts often use the terminology interchangeably.[193]

For example, in *Clark* v *Nomura*, the claimant was an equities trader who was not paid a discretionary bonus in respect of his final year of employment, even though he had made a large profit for the employer in that time.[194] The court held that the employer could not act unreasonably or perversely in assessing the claimant's performance and awarded him substantial damages. This offers significant protection to the employee.

Of course, there is a broader debate within contract law as to whether the parties to any contract owe each other duties to act in good faith.[195] This is a normal feature of many continental European legal systems, but has traditionally been rejected in English law. In the recent *Yam Seng* case, it was suggested that the courts should be more willing to imply a good faith requirement into long-term commercial contracts, albeit as a term implied in fact.[196] The judge stopped short of suggesting that all contracts could contain a good faith requirement as a default term required by law, though he did indicate that certain types of contract already contained such a requirement. Importantly for our purposes, he noted that contracts of employment were a kind of contract that already contained a good faith requirement.[197]

5.5.3 Implied terms in workers' contracts

Most of the case-law just considered concerns contracts of employment. This is not surprising, because the contract of employment is a long-established common law concept and the jurisprudence on its content has built up over many years. Nowadays, statute also uses the concept of a 'worker's contract', in which the individual undertakes to perform work personally for the employer who is not his or her customer or client.[198] The scope of the worker concept is highly uncertain. A further difficulty is that it is unclear to what extent the common law content of the contract of employment – the implied terms we have just been discussing – might also apply to the worker's contract. There is very little case-law to go on.

It is clear that terms implied by law into the contract of employment may also be implied into analogous contracts. This is evident from the case of *Tullett Prebon*, in which trust and confidence was found to be a feature of a 'forward' contract, in

---

[192] *Associated Provincial Picture Houses Ltd* v *Wednesbury Corp* [1948] 1 KB 223 (CA). For discussion, see ACL Davies, 'Judicial Self-Restraint in Labour Law' (2009) 38 ILJ 278.

[193] See e.g. *IBM United Kingdom Holdings Ltd* v *Dalgleish* [2014] EWHC 980 (Ch).

[194] [2000] IRLR 766 (QB). See also *Horkulak* v *Cantor Fitzgerald International* [2004] EWCA Civ 1287, [2005] ICR 402.

[195] See, generally, Collins, above n 111, and in the employment context, Douglas Brodie, 'Beyond Exchange: the New Contract of Employment' (1998) 27 ILJ 79; 'Fair Dealing and the World of Work' (2014) 43 ILJ 29.

[196] *Yam Seng Pte Ltd* v *International Trade Corporation Ltd* [2013] EWHC 111 (QB), [2013] 1 All ER (Comm) 1321.

[197] ibid [132].

[198] See, for example, ERA 1996, s 230(3).

which the individuals in question had promised to go and work for a rival firm when they were free to leave their current employment.[199] The courts have, however, rejected the implied term of trust and confidence in commercial contracts[200] and franchising agreements.[201] This suggests that the key question is whether a worker's contract is more closely analogous to a commercial or business arrangement or to a contract of employment. This is a difficult question to answer because of the variety of different arrangements that might be covered by a worker's contract.[202] Nor can it be correct to say that the role of implied terms might vary from case to case, because terms like trust and confidence are implied in law into particular kinds of relationship and do not depend on the intentions of the contracting parties in the case.

Freedland argues strongly that the courts should use worker-protective implied terms in worker cases as well as employee ones. He notes that terms like trust and confidence have evolved to protect 'the dignity, autonomy and personal security and integrity' of individuals, concerns which are valid in worker cases as well as employee ones.[203] However, it is also important to consider the implied terms governing the worker's obligations. If one of the distinguishing features of a worker's contract is that the worker is less shielded from risk by the employer than an employee would be, it is important that the worker is able to protect him- or herself by spreading his or her economic activities across multiple employers. This would suggest (as Freedland also argues) that implied obligations of loyal service to the employer are not appropriate in this context.[204] Indeed, the government's recent enquiry into so-called 'zero-hours' contracts has resulted in a recommendation that employers should not be allowed to demand exclusive service from people who are not guaranteed any particular level of work.[205]

This leaves us in the difficult position of arguing that the employer's duties towards workers should be more extensive than workers' duties towards employers. Since the parties are in unequal bargaining positions, this makes perfect sense as a matter of policy, but it may be difficult for the courts to accept given that many of the implied terms, such as the duty of care and the duty to maintain trust and confidence, have developed as obligations on *both* parties to the contract.

5.6 VARIATION

Because of the long-term nature of some employment relationships, it may be necessary to vary the contract of employment over time. For example, the employer might want to redefine the employee's job to adjust to new technology, or change the employee's working hours to reflect new opening hours, or cut the employee's pay to deal with a downturn in the business. Against this must be set the employee's preference (in some cases, at least) for maintaining the status quo: the employee may not want

[199] *Tullet Prebon Plc* v *BGC Brokers LP & Ors* [2011] EWCA Civ 131, [2011] IRLR 420 [37]–[45].
[200] *Bedfordshire CC* v *Fitzpatrick Contractors Ltd* (1998) 62 Con LR 64.
[201] *Jani-King (GB) Ltd* v *Pula Enterprises Ltd* [2007] EWHC 2433 (QB), [2008] 1 All ER (Comm) 451.
[202] See Chapter 4.
[203] Freedland, above n 81, 170.
[204] ibid 177–178.
[205] Department for Business, Innovation and Skills, *Consultation on Zero Hours Employment Contracts* (December 2013), and see now Small Business, Enterprise and Employment Bill, cl 139.

to do job A instead of job B, or to work in the evenings, and is unlikely to want to take a pay cut. Of course, any discussions between employer and employee take place against the background of inequality of bargaining power and the employee's need for a job, so in most cases the employee's power to resist change – even if it exists in law – may be limited in practice. In this section, we will consider the various legal routes by which the contract of employment may be changed.

Before we get into the detail, it is worth noting that many changes in the employee's day-to-day activities can be brought about without changing his or her contract. This flows from the fact, noted above, that employment contracts tend not to contain very much detail about what it is that the employee is employed to do. Because of the implied term of obedience, the employee must obey the employer's reasonable instructions.[206] These may include instructions bringing about major changes in working methods, as in the *Cresswell* case, discussed above,[207] though the decision in *Bull* suggests that the employer cannot use this technique to change the employee's job entirely.[208]

Let us now assume that it is necessary to vary the contract because it contains express terms about pay and hours, or a job description, that the employer wants to alter. The simplest option is for the employer and employee to agree to vary the contract. Since they agreed the contract in the first place, according to basic contractual principles, they can agree to change it. In theory at least, this serves to protect the employee against unwanted variations, by giving him or her an opportunity to refuse or to bargain for some kind of concession in return. But in practice, the employee may be too worried about losing his or her job to refuse, or to try to bargain.

The employer may decide to raise the stakes by dismissing the employee and offering immediate re-employment on fresh terms and conditions. This makes it very clear to the employee what the consequences of refusal will be. A key question is whether an employee who is unhappy with the change could refuse the offer of new employment and successfully sue the employer for unfair dismissal or redundancy instead. Although this is unlikely to mean that the individual would get his or her old job back, it would at least generate some compensation. The case-law on this is highly context sensitive and (in general) not particularly sympathetic towards the employee's position. It is important to note that workers are not eligible to make unfair dismissal or redundancy claims.

Redundancy occurs where the employer's requirements for employees to do 'work of a particular kind' or at a particular place 'cease or diminish'.[209] For example, in *Johnson v Nottinghamshire Combined Police Authority*, the claimants worked 9.30 to 5.30.[210] The employer sought to introduce a new shift system that would involve either starting at 8am or finishing at 8pm. The claimants refused to accept the change because of childcare obligations and were dismissed. They argued that they had been made redundant on the basis that the employer's need for people to do 'work of a particular kind' had ceased or diminished. However, the Court of Appeal rejected the claim, holding that the replacement employees were doing work of the same 'kind',

---

[206] Above n 121.
[207] *Cresswell*, above n 28.
[208] *Bull*, above n 130. See also *Smith v London Metropolitan University* [2011] IRLR 884 (EAT) [77].
[209] ERA 1996, s 139. See Chapter 10 for more detail.
[210] [1974] ICR 170 (CA).

just at different times.[211] In the *Butterwick* case, the employee was a car mechanic.[212] When the garage at which he worked was taken over by a new owner, he was required to do more administrative tasks and less 'hands-on' repair work. He was not very good at these tasks and was dismissed. He claimed that he was redundant, but the court rejected the claim, holding that the requirements of the business for 'work of a particular kind' had not changed, and that he was obliged to adapt to new working methods.

An alternative route is for the employee to argue that he or she has been unfairly dismissed. In an unfair dismissal claim, attention focuses on whether the employer has a legitimate reason (within the statute) for the dismissal, and has acted within the 'band of reasonable responses' in dismissing the employee.[213] The reason is a relatively low threshold: if the employer needs to reorganise the business, this will normally be treated as 'some other substantial reason' for dismissal. The key question then is whether the dismissal is reasonable. The definition of the reasonableness test – the 'band of reasonable responses' – is a question of law, but its application to the facts of the case is a question of fact for the tribunal.[214] This is important because it means that this aspect of a tribunal's ruling cannot be overturned on appeal. As a result, cases of dismissal and re-employment on new, usually worse, conditions of employment each turn on their own facts and it is difficult to generalise about them. Indeed, in *Gilham*, the Court of Appeal refused to intervene where a tribunal had found a local authority's dismissal (and offer of re-employment on lower pay) of its school dinner ladies to be unreasonable when other tribunals had found similar dismissals by other local authorities to be fair.[215]

Although it is difficult to generalise, two themes emerge from the case-law. First, according to the decision in *Catamaran Cruisers*, the tribunal must consider the balance of advantages to the employer and set that against the disadvantages to the employee.[216] Where the employer is making a large-scale change, the fact that other employees have accepted the new terms or that their trade union has not objected will count in favour of the employer's actions being fair.[217] But where the change involves significant disadvantages to the employee, the courts tend to be more inclined in their favour. For example, in *Docherty*, the employer was in financial difficulties and put its employees onto so-called 'zero hours' contracts for a two-month period.[218] They were required to remain available for work but were not guaranteed any particular level of work and pay. The case was remitted to the tribunal for further consideration in light of (among other things) the serious disadvantage associated with this type of contract, not least the possible loss of employment rights, as the affected individuals might no longer count as employees in law.[219] Second, the tribunal will consider the employer's process for informing and consulting the employees

---

[211] In *Alford Group of Doctors* v *Thornalley* (2000) UKEAT/1077/99/1611 similar facts were held not to give rise to an unfair dismissal claim.
[212] *North Riding Garages* v *Butterwick* [1967] 2 QB 56.
[213] *Iceland Frozen Foods* v *Jones* [1983] ICR 17 (EAT) 24. See Chapter 9 for more detail.
[214] *Gilham* v *Kent County Council (No 2)* [1985] ICR 233 (CA).
[215] ibid.
[216] *Catamaran Cruisers Ltd* v *Williams* [1994] IRLR 386 (EAT).
[217] *Sandford* v *Newcastle upon Tyne Hospitals NHS Foundation Trust* (2013) UKEAT/0324/12/DM.
[218] *Docherty* v *SW Global Resourcing Ltd* [2013] IRLR 874.
[219] ibid [23].

about the proposed change. If the process is unfair, the dismissal may be unfair on procedural grounds. For example, in the *Willow Oak* case, the employer had sought to impose new post-employment restrictions on its employees.[220] It gave them limited time to consider the change and did not warn them that it intended to dismiss them if they refused to agree. The Court of Appeal upheld the tribunal's finding that the dismissals were unfair.[221]

A final question to consider is whether the employer can include an express variation clause in the contract of employment. This would give the employer the power to vary the contract unilaterally. Having agreed to the variation clause in the first place, the employee would have lost the chance to refuse his or her consent to any subsequent changes. Since the law of contract is based so clearly on consent, the courts have tended to be nervous about powers to vary unilaterally, so as a matter of general contract law they have insisted that the power be expressed in clear and unambiguous language, and that the party using the power should not do so unreasonably. The need for some kind of control seems even stronger in the employment context, because of the inequality of bargaining power between employer and employee. The issue arose in the *Bateman* case.[222] The employer had an express right to vary the content of its staff handbook unilaterally. This included contractual matters such as pay and hours. The employer imposed a new pay structure. The EAT held that it was entitled to do this under the variation clause. In a brief judgment, the EAT found that the clause was clear and unambiguous, and rejected claims based on arbitrariness or breach of the implied term of mutual trust and confidence because they had not been raised before the tribunal.[223] It also rejected arguments that the clause should be construed in the light of *Autoclenz* in the sense that the written handbook might not have reflected the 'true agreement' between the parties.[224] Although, as we have seen, the employee's opportunity to refuse to agree to changes is of limited practical value, it is important in principle and it seems unfortunate that the EAT in *Bateman* was quite quick to reject any possible avenues of challenge to the express variation clause.

Some hope is offered by the decision in *Attrill*.[225] In that case, the employer investment bank promised to pay its employees a bonus as a means of retaining them during the financial crisis, when the future of the bank was in doubt. According to the employee handbook, it had the power unilaterally to vary the employees' terms and conditions of employment. The employer announced the change orally. Because of public hostility towards bankers' bonuses, the employer subsequently changed its mind about the payment of bonuses and wrote to the employees saying that the bonuses were subject to possible change. When the bonuses were eventually paid, they were much reduced from the level originally offered. The employer argued that it had not given a contractually binding promise to pay the bonuses because it had not followed the procedure for varying the contract laid down in the staff handbook, which required variation in writing. However, the court held that the variation was

---

[220] *Willow Oak Developments Ltd (t/a Windsor Recruitment) v Silverwood* [2006] EWCA Civ 660, [2006] ICR 1552.

[221] ibid [29].

[222] *Bateman v Asda Stores Ltd* [2010] IRLR 370 (EAT), discussed by Frederic Reynold and John Hendy, 'Reserving the Right to Change Terms and Conditions: How Far Can the Employer Go?' (2012) 41 ILJ 79.

[223] ibid [26].

[224] ibid [23].

[225] *Attrill and others v Dresdner Kleinwort Ltd and another* [2013] EWCA Civ 394, [2013] ICR D30.

effective because it had been announced clearly and there was no doubt that the employer intended it to be legally binding. Moreover, the employer had breached the implied term of mutual trust and confidence by going back on its original promise to pay the bonuses when it introduced the statement that the bonuses were subject to possible change. Although this decision does not regulate the initial variation, it does indicate that an attempt by an employer to go back on a variation to the advantage of the employees will be subject to scrutiny using mutual trust and confidence.

5.7 POST-EMPLOYMENT RESTRAINTS

We saw above that the employee owes the employer a duty of loyal and faithful service during the contract of employment. Once the contract has come to an end, the implied obligation ceases to apply. However, in some cases, the employer may be concerned about employees (particularly more senior staff with specialist skills and knowledge) leaving to set up rival businesses of their own, or to work for the employer's competitors. It is open to the employer to include an express term in the contract to address this situation. Such terms are subject to careful scrutiny by the courts because they restrict competition, in breach of the doctrine of 'restraint of trade'. They also limit the ex-employee's ability to earn a living.

The basic starting-point is that a clause restricting the ex-employee's activities is void – because it is in restraint of trade – unless it can be shown to be reasonable. Thus, the employer cannot enforce a term that simply forbids the ex-employee from competing. The employer must show that it is protecting a specific interest, such as its trade secrets or its list of customers. For example, in the *Roger Bullivant* case, there was a clause in the ex-employee's contract prohibiting him from contacting the former employer's customers with a view to doing business with them for 12 months after the termination of his employment.[226] When the employee left, he took with him a list of customers. The employer successfully obtained an injunction to stop the ex-employee using the list for his own rival business for 12 months.

The *Roger Bullivant* case also highlights the importance of considering the scope of the clause, both geographically and temporally. The employer is more likely to succeed if the clause only applies to a limited area for a limited time. So a clause prohibiting the ex-employee from setting up a rival business in the same town for a year is more likely to be upheld than one prohibiting the ex-employee from setting up a rival business anywhere in the UK for five or 10 years. For example, in the recent case of *Safetynet Security Ltd* v *Coppage*, a six-month restriction on soliciting the former employer's clients was found to be reasonable.[227] But in *CEF Holdings Ltd* v *Mundey*, the court refused to grant the former employer an injunction restraining ex-employees from competing, in part because the former employer had not sought to limit the geographical area in which the injunction would have applied.[228]

Finally, the impact of the clause on the employee is relevant in some cases. In the recent *Sunrise Brokers* case, the employee refused to continue working for the employer during the period of the restraint, so he was not earning any money during that time.[229] He argued that it would be 'oppressive' to grant the employer an

---

[226] *Roger Bullivant Ltd* v *Ellis* [1987] ICR 464 (CA).
[227] [2013] EWCA Civ 1176, [2013] IRLR 970.
[228] *CEF Holdings Ltd* v *Mundey* [2012] EWHC 1524 (QB), [2012] IRLR 912.
[229] *Sunrise Brokers LLP* v *Rodgers* [2014] EWCA Civ 1373, [2015] IRLR 57.

injunction to enforce the restraint because the effect would be to force him to go back to work for the employer. However, the Court of Appeal held that the employee had not demonstrated that the injunction would cause him 'hardship' on the facts.

5.8 ENFORCEMENT

We will conclude the chapter by noting a few brief points about the enforcement of contracts in the employment sphere. The aim here is to highlight special rules governing contracts of employment as compared to other contracts, and special rules governing contractual claims as opposed to other types of employment claim.

5.8.1 Court or tribunal?

Employment cases are generally heard in the Employment Tribunals, with a possibility of appeal to the EAT and thence to the Court of Appeal on a point of law. The original policy behind the tribunal system was to create a more user-friendly, specialist forum for employment claims. However, contract claims belong in the ordinary courts. What about claims relating to employment contracts?

The basic starting-point is that the normal divide applies in employment cases: contractual claims belong in court, whereas other types of claim belong in the employment tribunal. We saw above that this has given rise to difficulties in relation to the written statement, where it is the courts' job to determine the content of the contract of employment but the tribunal's job to decide what the written statement should contain.

By virtue of the Employment Tribunals Extension of Jurisdiction Order 1994, SI 1994/1623 the employee may bring a claim for damages for breach of contract or for a sum due under the contract in the employment tribunal if it is outstanding when his or her employment is terminated. The employer may counter-claim. Some types of breach of contract claim are excluded by Article 5, such as those relating to breaches of confidence or restraint of trade. Under Article 10, the tribunal may not award more than £25,000 in a contract claim. This allows an employee to proceed in the employment tribunal in relation to a small-value contract-claim and is particularly valuable where the employee is already claiming unfair dismissal and can bring the contract claim at the same time. However, its scope of application is relatively limited.

It is important to remember that, in one respect, dealing with contractual issues is a day-to-day occurrence for tribunals. Statutory employment rights depend upon the classification of the contract as a contract of employment or a worker's contract. Tribunals decide these classification issues all the time in order to determine people's eligibility to bring claims to enforce their statutory rights.

5.8.2 Claims by employees

In general terms, a claim by an employee against an employer for breach of contract is subject to the same legal rules as any other type of breach of contract claim, but the courts have proved reluctant to award substantial damages in some employment contract claims and have instead pushed employees towards their statutory remedies.

One problem with a claim for breach of contract is that the courts will, in general, award expectation damages. Traditionally, the courts have held that employees' expectations are limited by the fact that – at common law at least – an employee can only expect to be employed until such time as the employer can lawfully terminate the contract by giving notice.[230] What are sometimes referred to as 'stigma' damages – damages for harm to reputation or hurt feelings – are not recoverable in a wrongful dismissal claim,[231] though they may be recoverable in other types of breach of contract claim, as in the *Malik* case.[232] These rules seem ripe for reconsideration. First, employees (in a world with unfair dismissal law) may expect to work for longer than simply their notice period. The courts could use the normal rules on remoteness to assess their expectation damages. Second, although damages for hurt feelings may well be inappropriate in commercial contexts, this may be an area in which a different and more generous rule for employees would be justified, overruling the muddled decision in the *Addis* case.[233]

More worryingly, the intersection between contractual and statutory claims may limit employees' contractual rights. We saw above that the implied term of trust and confidence – although a well-recognised feature of contracts in the employment sphere – cannot be used to 'get around' the limits on unfair dismissal law by developing a stronger action for wrongful dismissal at common law. This is the effect of the ruling in *Johnson*.[234] More worryingly, in *Edwards*, the same reasoning was used to deny enforceability (in damages at least) to a contractual disciplinary procedure expressly agreed by the parties.[235] The majority reasoned that the procedure had only been included in the parties' contract in order to satisfy the requirements of unfair dismissal law, so that the parties did not intend a breach of it to sound in damages at common law. This reasoning rests on a misapprehension of the legal effect of the statutory written statement (that it is virtually indistinguishable from the contract, a point rebutted above) and is hard to reconcile with the ordinary rules of contract law.[236]

A further bizarre consequence of *Edwards* is that a contractually agreed disciplinary procedure cannot be enforced by bringing a claim for damages but can be enforced by means of an injunction to require the employer to comply with it.[237] This remedy does not exist in unfair dismissal law so the Supreme Court took the view that it could continue to exist without any 'incompatibility' with the statute.

The key point to take away from this discussion is that an action by an employee for breach of contract may be affected by the courts' perception of the relationship between that claim and any statutory rights the employee may have. The courts appear to take the view that Parliament has the primary responsibility for regulating employment matters and may sometimes be reluctant to use the normal rules of contract law where they might interfere with Parliament's perceived objectives.

---

[230] *Gunton*, above n 86.
[231] *Addis v Gramophone Co Ltd* [1909] AC 488 (HL).
[232] *Malik v Bank of Credit and Commerce International SA (In Liquidation)* [1998] AC 20, [1997] ICR 606.
[233] ibid.
[234] Above n 184.
[235] *Edwards*, above n 189.
[236] Hugh Collins, 'Compensation for Dismissal: In Search of Principle' (2012) 41 ILJ 208.
[237] *Edwards* (n 189) [44] (Lord Dyson).

5.8.3 Claims against the employee

As we have seen, employees owe a number of duties towards their employer. In general terms, these are enforced by the simple expedient of inequality of bargaining power. The employee wants to keep his or her job and therefore does what he or she is told.

At common law, a repudiatory breach of contract would normally entitle the employer to terminate the contract with immediate effect. The statute law of unfair dismissal does not hinge on the parties' contract, though a serious breach of that contract might well enable the employer to argue that the individual could be fairly dismissed, for example, for misconduct.[238] The employer is much more likely to terminate the contract than to seek damages for the obvious reason that most employees would not have the resources to pay a substantial award. As we saw above, this explains why employers do not normally seek to recover from employees who have breached their duty of care.

Because of the very basic principle that forced labour is a serious infringement of human rights, it is not possible to obtain an injunction to force someone to work. This is the effect of s. 236 TULRCA:

> No court shall, whether by way of–
>
> (a) an order for specific performance . . . of a contract of employment, or
> (b) an injunction . . . restraining a breach or threatened breach of such a contract,
>
> compel an employee to do any work or attend at any place for the doing of any work.

However, as we saw above, it is possible to obtain an injunction to *stop* an employee from working (whether in his or her own business or for a rival), where there is a valid post-employment restriction in place. Since this could leave the individual in financial difficulties, it is important that there are safeguards. As we saw above, the restriction must be express and must be limited in scope. This should mean that the employee is aware of the issue and able to find alternative employment that does not infringe the restriction.

POINTS TO TAKE AWAY

- Contracts in the employment sphere may be express or implied, oral or in writing. Written contracts may incorporate terms from other sources such as collective agreements and workplace handbooks. The statutory statement of an employee's terms and conditions is evidence of the employer's views as to the content of the contract but is not, in itself, contractual.

- Most statutory rights operate outside the contractual relationship between the parties, though sometimes they function as implied terms. Statutes often bar the parties from 'contracting out' of the protective provisions they contain.

- Implied terms at common law perform an important role in filling the gaps in the parties' contract, placing obligations on both employer and employee, though they have not developed into a comprehensive common law scheme of protection. Their applicability to non-employee contracts is unclear.

[238] See Chapter 9.

- Where the contract of employment is vague, the employer may use managerial prerogative to change the individual's work without varying the contract. Where the contract is more specific, it may be varied by agreement, by dismissal and re-engagement on new terms, or by an express power to vary reserved to the employer.

- The employer may include a clause in a contract of employment to restrain the employee from competing with it after the termination of the employment relationship, provided its scope is limited.

- Employees may not be able to recover substantial damages for breaches of contracts of employment.

Further reading

For a more detailed account of the contract of employment, and related contracts, see **Mark Freedland, *The Personal Employment Contract* (OUP 2003), especially chapters 3 and 5.**

We noted at the outset that contracts of employment are often described as 'relational'. For an in-depth account of the advantages and limitations of this characterisation, see **Douglas Brodie, 'How Relational is the Employment Contract?' (2011) 40 ILJ 232.** Another major area of intersection between the general contract law literature and the contract of employment literature is the concept of 'good faith'. This concept might provide a way of unifying or underpinning the various implied terms used in employment contracts by the courts. It might also build links between employment law and the less commercially orientated strands of reasoning within contract law. For development of this set of ideas, see **Douglas Brodie, 'Beyond Exchange: the New Contract of Employment' (1998) 27 ILJ 79; 'Fair Dealing and the World of Work' (2014) 43 ILJ 29; Hugh Collins, 'Implied Terms: The Foundation in Good Faith and Fair Dealing' (2014) 67 Current Legal Problems 297.**

Not surprisingly, the *Johnson* and *Edwards* line of case-law has given rise to a substantial literature. See **Lizzie Barmes, 'Common Law Implied Terms and Behavioural Standards at Work' (2007) 36 ILJ 35; Douglas Brodie, 'Legal Coherence and the Employment Revolution' (2001) 117 LQR 604; 'Mutual Trust and Confidence: Catalysts, Constraints and Commonality' (2008) 37 ILJ 329; Hugh Collins, 'Compensation for Dismissal: In Search of Principle' (2012) 41 ILJ 208; Judy Fudge, 'The Spectre of *Addis* in Contracts of Employment in Canada and the UK' (2007) 36 ILJ 51.**

6 Equality

6.1 INTRODUCTION

In this chapter, we will consider equality or anti-discrimination law. This body of law first developed in the 1970s to tackle sex and race discrimination. Over time, it has developed (primarily through legislation but sometimes also through case-law) to address a much wider range of protected characteristics, including religion or belief, sexual orientation, disability and age. The EU has been particularly active in this field so we will be examining the interaction between EU law and domestic law throughout the chapter. It is important to note at the outset that equality law does not just apply in the workplace: it is relevant to many aspects of life, such as the provision of goods and services. However, our focus will be on equality law in the workplace.

The chapter is organised as follows. We will begin by examining the theoretical underpinnings of the topic, focusing in particular on the uncertainties surrounding the meaning of equality (section 6.2). We will then turn to a brief history of how the law has developed, in order to clarify the relationships between EU law, domestic law and the ECHR (section 6.3). The remaining sections of the chapter will consider the legal provisions. To establish that discrimination has taken place, it is necessary to show that the employer has:

- discriminated (directly or indirectly) or committed an act of harassment

- because of a protected characteristic (age, disability, gender reassignment, marriage and civil partnership, pregnancy and maternity, race, religion or belief, sex, sexual orientation)

- at work (for example, when making a hiring or promotion decision).

We will consider each of these elements in turn in sections 6.4 and 6.5, though it is important to remember how they fit together. We will then examine some issues relating to enforcement in section 6.6.

6.2 THEORETICAL FRAMEWORK

In this section, we will consider some theoretical perspectives on equality law. This body of law can be justified through rights arguments or through arguments about business productivity. But before we get into the detailed justificatory arguments, it is worth probing the concept of equality itself.

6.2.1 Equality

The concept of equality sounds simple. At its most basic, it refers to the idea of treating like cases alike. This appeals to our most deep-rooted sense of fairness. However, this straightforward approach may conceal a more complex reality. Perhaps the selection criteria for a job (being able to carry heavy loads or to work full-time) are easier for some people than others to meet. And perhaps the candidates who are competing for the job did not have the same opportunities to acquire qualifications and experience. More complex conceptions of equality are required to address these situations. We will examine these first. However, some writers argue that as our understanding of equality becomes more complex, it also becomes less coherent. These writers suggest alternative theories to underpin the law which we will examine below.

Conceptions of equality

The simple 'treating like cases alike' version of equality is referred to in the literature as 'formal equality'.[1] The key to applying this concept lies in identifying a 'like case'. The aim is to exclude from the decision-making process characteristics that are irrelevant to a person's job performance. So, to take a simple example, imagine that a man and a woman are performing exactly the same job to the same standard. The difference in their genders is irrelevant to their work, so we can regard their cases as being 'like'. Therefore, they should be treated 'alike' in that they should be paid the same wage.

One problem with 'treating like cases alike' is that it is not very helpful in the situation where the people involved have not had equal starting-points. For example, the employer might require that candidates for the job of architect are fully qualified architects. This criterion applies equally to everyone and is entirely justifiable given the nature of the job. However, it might be the case that the opportunity to train as an architect is not available equally to all groups in society, with the result that the profession is predominantly male, or predominantly white. The concept of 'equality of opportunity' is often invoked in this context. This focuses on the chances people have had to get to the point at which they can benefit from an employer making selection decisions on a formally equal basis. So, for example, equality of opportunity might require a wide range of public policies in fields such as education and training to help people to acquire the skills they need to compete on an equal footing in the job market. Sometimes, employers can contribute to this by offering additional training themselves,

[1] For an overview, see Sandra Fredman, *Discrimination Law* (2nd edn, OUP 2011) chapter 1.

or by encouraging people to try out a particular career, but equality of opportunity tends to prescribe policy choices that go well beyond the employment context.

A third version of equality is 'equality of results' or 'substantive equality'. This is a more complex concept because it can be defined in various ways and thus might be manifested in the law in different forms. The starting-point for this concept is to focus on what we want to achieve by having equality law in the workplace: a society in which all social groups are equally represented in all workplaces. Proponents of this version of equality identify at least three flaws in formal equality and suggest solutions based on equality of results.

First, formal equality does nothing to tackle situations in which the employer uses criteria that apply equally to everyone but have a different effect on different groups of people. For example, the employer might require all its employees to be able to lift heavy weights. This would exclude some people (women, and some older or younger workers, perhaps) from jobs with that employer. By thinking about equality in terms of outcomes, we can see that the formally equal criterion is generating unequal results. We can then turn our attention to why the employer has adopted the requirement. If the employer can show a genuine business need for a physically strong workforce, it should be able to continue to use the weight-lifting test. But if the employer cannot demonstrate this, the test should be abandoned. It is important to note that this version of equality of results does not *guarantee* greater diversity in workplaces: it simply operates to remove criteria that are neutral on the surface but discriminatory in their impact. This gives workers in previously disadvantaged groups a better chance of getting a job with that employer. So it also has much in common with the idea of 'equality of opportunity' discussed above.

Second, formal equality does nothing to tackle situations in which the individual's characteristic cannot simply be disregarded in the work context. Pregnancy is a good example. Formal equality helps where the employer discriminates against a woman because she is pregnant – demoting or dismissing her, for example – when it would not have treated a man, or a woman who was not pregnant, in the same way. But formal equality cannot generate a right to take maternity leave or to return to the same job afterwards, because there are no obvious comparable situations. Different or special treatment is required, in order to achieve the *result* that women are not disadvantaged at work by their reproductive capacity. The same point can be made about other characteristics, including disability (where the employer may need to adapt the workplace or the job to the worker) and perhaps religious belief (where the worker may seek time off for religious observance, for example). Formal equality tackles employer prejudice against people with disabilities, or particular beliefs, but does not do anything to accommodate them at work.

Third, critics argue that formal equality is inadequate to address deep-seated problems of discrimination in society. This claim focuses on the fact that although equality law usually applies universally, the problems it seeks to tackle are historic ones affecting some people more than others. So, for example, while the law might enable people of any sexual orientation to bring a discrimination claim, gay people are more likely to encounter discrimination than straight people are. Placing reliance on formal equality – or even equality of opportunity – against a background of injustice will not bring about a swift solution to the problem. Critics in this tradition argue that we should abandon formal equality in favour of 'positive discrimination' or 'affirmative action', in which members of historically disadvantaged groups are given extra help to secure particular jobs.[2] This extra help might take different forms. For example, the employer might be allowed or required to choose a member of an under-represented group when choosing between otherwise equally qualified candidates for a job, or to have preferential shortlisting arrangements for members of disadvantaged groups, or to apply quotas for recruiting a certain number of people from a particular background.

'Equality of results' is thus a relatively simple idea in terms of the goal we are pursuing, but much more complex in terms of the policy prescriptions it generates. A particular problem is its relationship with formal equality. The first option – dealing with apparently neutral but in practice discriminatory criteria – can be reconciled relatively easily with formal equality. It remains focused on treating like cases alike, but adopts a richer understanding of what that might entail, by looking not just at how the employer formulates criteria but also at how they apply in practice. The second option – dealing with situations in which different treatment is required – is a bit more difficult, because it does conflict with the idea of treating like cases alike. However, since its use is generally confined to certain protected characteristics, where formal equality does not make sense, it can be accommodated as an exception to the rule. Indeed, it is important to remember that the law rarely gives effect to formal equality in absolute terms. A person's characteristics may sometimes be relevant to his or her ability to do the job – where a male actor is required to play a male character in a film, for example – so it is not unthinkable to develop more nuanced exceptions. The third option – positive discrimination – is generally regarded as more controversial because it contradicts formal equality and would operate instead of it. For example, a quota system for under-represented groups would entail permitting discrimination against 'majority' groups in the formal sense. Critics argue that the third option should be discarded for this reason: it departs too radically from most people's basic understanding of fairness in how jobs and other opportunities should be allocated, and thus undermines public support for the broader cause of developing a more equal society. Advocates argue that true equality in the substantive sense can only be achieved by making some temporary sacrifices in terms of formal equality, and note that the people who would lose out are people who have been advantaged in the past (even though they may not have been personally responsible for the discriminatory treatment of others).[3]

As we shall see, English law includes the concepts of formal equality, equality of opportunity and equality of results, but in respect of the latter, accepts only a very narrow version of positive discrimination. Thus, it gives greater weight to formal equality than some critics would like.

Alternatives to equality

It may seem odd to consider alternatives to equality as the basis for 'equality' law. However, given the potential for conflicts within our understanding of equality, some commentators have suggested that equality should be replaced with some other concept, such as dignity or social inclusion. We will examine each in turn.

---

[2] ibid chapter 5.
[3] For an excellent overview, see Aileen McHarg and Donald Nicolson, 'Justifying Affirmative Action: Perception and Reality' (2006) 33 Journal of Law and Society 1.

Dignity is a rather nebulous concept and is used in different ways in international human rights instruments, national constitutions and in political philosophy more generally. McCrudden identifies three core elements from the wealth of material.[4] First, dignity focuses on the 'intrinsic worth' of every human being.[5] Second, 'this intrinsic worth should be recognized and respected by others'.[6] And third, particularly in the human rights context, 'the state should be seen to exist for the sake of the individual human being'.[7] Thus, a body of equality law that was based on dignity would focus on recognising the 'intrinsic worth' of every worker. Some aspects of equality law do draw heavily on the concept of dignity, as we shall see. One example is harassment. This is defined, in part, as conduct that 'violates [the claimant's] dignity'.[8] It is less focused on unequal treatment compared with others, and more focused on treatment that falls below acceptable standards of respect.

However, the mere presence of dignity considerations within equality law does not help us to determine whether it would offer a better theoretical basis for the law. Its advocates point to two main advantages. First, a focus on whether a worker's dignity has been violated would overcome some of the technicalities associated with equality law.[9] As we shall see, the claimant in an equality case generally needs to compare him- or herself with a similarly situated person not sharing his or her protected characteristic in order to show that there is unequal treatment. Although it is usually possible to do this on a hypothetical basis – to imagine how such a person would have been treated – dignity avoids this altogether by asking the simple question whether the individual has been treated with respect. Second, one of the inherent problems in equality is that it protects equal treatment but not necessarily good or fair treatment.[10] So, for example, if an employer is found to have discriminated by providing a benefit to one group of workers but not to another, equality allows the employer to respond by withdrawing the benefit altogether instead of providing it to everyone. Proponents of dignity argue that it would not allow 'levelling down' in this way. Against these advantages, critics identify one major disadvantage with dignity: its inherent vagueness. Equality gives the court a yardstick against which to judge an employer's treatment of an individual or group. Dignity does not: it would be for the court to decide what amounted to fair treatment. In relation to economically sensitive areas such as pay, it would be particularly difficult for courts to do this and the application of the law might become difficult to predict. Thus, Fredman suggests that we should use dignity in combination with, rather than in place of, equality.[11]

Another alternative to equality sometimes proposed in the literature is the concept of social inclusion. Collins explains this in the following way:

> The group of the socially excluded is defined . . . as people who are effectively prevented from participating in the benefits of citizenship or membership of society owing to a combination of barriers, of which poverty is merely one. Other barriers include poor

[4] Christopher McCrudden, 'Human Dignity and Judicial Interpretation of Human Rights' (2008) 19 EJIL 655.
[5] ibid 679.
[6] ibid.
[7] ibid.
[8] Equality Act 2010, s 26(1)(b)(i).
[9] Gay Moon and Robin Allen, 'Dignity Discourse in Discrimination Law: a Better Route to Equality?' (2006) 6 EHRLR 610.
[10] For example, Case C-408/92 Smith v Avdel Systems Ltd [1994] ECR I-4435.
[11] Above n 1, 19–25.

educational opportunities, membership of a disfavoured racial minority, an inaccessible location, responsibility for family dependants, or, more commonly a combination of such factors.[12]

He argues that existing equality law may be better understood (and improved) by analysing it in terms of promoting the inclusion of previously excluded groups. For example, he suggests that the law's strong focus on the employment context can be explained because of the close link between having a job and avoiding social exclusion.[13] Not only are people in work better off financially (in general terms), they may also have a greater sense of self-worth and an important source of social contact with other people. Collins accepts that not all aspects of the law reflect his preferred objective, but argues that social inclusion can be used to identify areas for reform.[14] For example, he notes that being a single parent is not a protected characteristic under the current law but ought to be under a social inclusion framework, because of the strong association between this characteristic and social exclusion.[15] However, there are two difficulties with the social inclusion approach. First, it does not have anything to say to people who are in work but are experiencing some form of unequal treatment. A female investment banker who is earning a smaller bonus than her male colleague may not attract much sympathy, and is certainly not socially excluded, but she is being treated unfairly and unequally and she ought to have access to a legal remedy. Second, the concept of social inclusion has a particular resonance for centre-left politics and was closely associated with the 'third way' politics of the late 1990s.[16] Although the issues it sought to address remain highly relevant today, its lack of universal appeal may make it problematic as a basis for the law.

6.2.2 Justifying equality law

In this section, we will turn to the human rights instruments that may be used to underpin equality law. As we shall see, these do not always attempt to resolve the inherent tension within the concept of equality.

A right to equal treatment features in all the major international human rights instruments. However, in older instruments, it tends to be 'parasitic' on the other rights in the relevant text: the state undertakes to secure the human rights of everyone in its territory without distinction. Article 2(1) International Covenant on Civil and Political Rights (ICCPR) is typical:

> Each State Party to the present Covenant undertakes to respect and to ensure to all individuals within its territory and subject to its jurisdiction the rights recognized in the present Covenant, without distinction of any kind, such as race, colour, sex, language, religion, political or other opinion, national or social origin, property, birth or other status.

More modern instruments, such as the EU Charter, provide a free-standing right not to be discriminated against.[17] This is more helpful in terms of analysing employment

---

[12] Hugh Collins, 'Discrimination, Equality and Social Inclusion' (2003) 66 MLR 16, 21.
[13] ibid 28–30.
[14] ibid e.g. 34.
[15] ibid 27.
[16] See Anthony Giddens, *The Third Way* (Polity 1998) chapter 4.
[17] Charter of Fundamental Rights of the European Union, Article 21(1). Protocol 12 ECHR provides a free-standing right not to be discriminated against but it has not been ratified by the UK.

situations because it avoids the need to find that another recognised human right has been violated before addressing the discrimination question. Paying a woman less than a man for equal work is clearly discriminatory but does not necessarily violate any other human right of hers.

A second important difference between instruments lies in the number of different protected characteristics they recognise. Again, this tends to reflect the date of the instrument because societies have acknowledged new forms of discrimination over time. One of the most comprehensive lists is Article 21(1) EU Charter:

> Any discrimination based on any ground such as sex, race, colour, ethnic or social origin, genetic features, language, religion or belief, political or any other opinion, membership of a national minority, property, birth, disability, age or sexual orientation shall be prohibited.[18]

Many instruments deal with changing perceptions of what constitutes a protected characteristic by maintaining an 'open' list to which new characteristics can be added by interpretation. Thus, the EU Charter's list is illustrative ('such as') and the ICCPR uses the phrase 'or other status'.[19] This has proved particularly important in relation to the ECHR.[20] Although this is an older instrument, it has an open list so the ECtHR has added several new characteristics through its case-law.[21]

A third feature to consider is the definition of 'discrimination'. Most instruments leave this vague, so do not grapple with the problem of competing and sometimes conflicting conceptions of equality discussed in the previous section. Specialist anti-discrimination instruments tend to adopt a broad definition. For example, Convention on the Elimination of All Forms of Discrimination against Women (CEDAW) defines discrimination in Article 1 as 'any distinction, exclusion or restriction made on the basis of sex which has the *effect or purpose* of impairing or nullifying the recognition, enjoyment or exercise by women . . . of human rights and fundamental freedoms in the political, economic, social, cultural, civil or any other field'.[22] The phrase 'effect or purpose' does not fit precisely with the equality concepts analysed above but does capture the idea that discrimination may be deliberate or unintentional. As a result, it is broad enough to cover (for example) an employer's use of neutral criteria which have a discriminatory effect in practice. Article 4(1) permits states to use positive discrimination as a temporary measure to achieve equality, and Article 4(2) provides that different treatment because of pregnancy and maternity should not be regarded as discrimination.

In summary, then, the UK government is under a number of international human rights obligations with regard to equality. While these reinforce the importance of having a body of equality law at the national level, they are unlikely to offer very precise guidance as to its content. As always, particular attention is likely to focus on the ECHR because of its close relationship with domestic law through the Human Rights Act. However, in this area, the ECHR's impact is limited by the fact that Article 14 is an example of a 'parasitic' equality right. So far at least, the biggest role

---

[18] Article 21(2) deals with nationality discrimination which is sensitive in the EU context because EU law clearly prohibits discrimination against nationals of other Member States but the EU has limited competence over migration into the EU from third countries.

[19] International Covenant on Civil and Political Rights, art 2(1).

[20] European Convention on Human Rights, art 14.

[21] See, for example, *Inze* v *Austria* (1988) 10 EHRR 394, which added 'children born in and children born out of wedlock' as a new characteristic.

[22] Emphasis added.

for the ECHR has been in the field of religious freedom which is expressly protected under Article 9. We will explore this in more detail in what follows.

6.3 HISTORY

Before we tackle the detailed law, it may be helpful to have a brief overview of how the law has developed. There is a complex interaction between UK and EU law in this context, together with the ECHR.

6.3.1 EU law

The right of women to equal pay with men doing 'like work' was enshrined in the Treaty of Rome when the original European Economic Community was established in 1957. The French government was concerned that its own legislation on the matter would put it at a competitive disadvantage compared to other Member States with no such legislation, because firms in those Member States would have access to a pool of cheap female labour.[23] It seems likely that, at the time, no-one recognised the impact the provision would have.

In the seminal *Defrenne (No. 2)* decision, the Court of Justice held that Article 119 (which it regarded not just as a market measure but as a fundamental social right) could have direct effect.[24] This meant that it could be invoked in the national courts in cases brought by women against the state and against private employers. This generated an important body of case-law that we will examine in more detail in Chapter 7. Around the same time, the Member States made first use of their legislative competence under Article 119, to enact Directive 75/117/EEC on equal pay, and Directive 76/207/EEC on equal treatment in other aspects of employment. The first of these directives broadened the equal pay principle to work of equal value,[25] and the second broadened the equality principle beyond pay to other aspects of the employment relationship.[26] The Member States agreed another important directive on the burden of proof in sex discrimination cases[27] in response to a series of Court decisions beginning with *Danfoss*.[28] These and other measures are now consolidated into the Recast Directive, Directive 2006/54. EU law on sex discrimination also extends to self-employed people. This legislation is currently contained in Directive 2010/41/EU.

The Court used the Treaty provisions and directives on sex discrimination to develop a body of rules on pregnancy discrimination.[29] The Member States did not

---

[23] Article 119, and see Jeff Kenner, *EU Employment Law* (Hart 2003) chapter 1.

[24] Case 149/77 *Defrenne v Société Anonyme Belge de Navigation Aerienne (SABENA)* [1978] ECR 1365.

[25] Council Directive 75/117/EEC of 10 February 1975 on the approximation of the laws of the Member States relating to the application of the principle of equal pay for men and women (1975) OJ L45/19, art 1.

[26] Council Directive 76/207/EEC of 9 February 1976 on the implementation of the principle of equal treatment for men and women as regards access to employment, vocational training and promotion, and working conditions (1976) OJ L39/40, art 1.

[27] Council Directive 97/80/EC of 15 December 1997 on the burden of proof in cases of discrimination based on sex.

[28] Case C-109/88 *Handels-og Kontorfunktionærernes Forbund I Danmark v Dansk Arbejdsgiverforening (Danfoss)* [1989] ECR 3199.

[29] For example, Case C-179/88 *Handels-og Kontorfunktionaererernes Forbund i Danmark (Hertz) v Dansk Arbejdsgiverforening (Aldi Marked K/S)* [1990] ECR I-3979.

legislate on this issue until the enactment of the Pregnant Workers Directive (92/85/ EEC). The Court also extended the law to cover transgender discrimination in *P v S and Cornwall CC*.[30] Nevertheless, the EU's elaborate body of law on sex discrimination stood in marked contrast to its lack of competence to legislate on other grounds of discrimination. This changed with the Treaty of Amsterdam (which entered into force in 1999). This inserted a new Article 13 into the EC Treaty which is now Article 19(1) TFEU, giving the EU legislative competence 'to combat discrimination based on sex, racial or ethnic origin, religion or belief, disability, age or sexual orientation'.

The Member States used this new provision to enact two directives, one on race discrimination[31] and the so-called 'framework directive' covering the other new grounds (religion, disability, sexual orientation and age).[32] So far at least, it looks as if the Court of Justice is not inclined to treat the grounds of discrimination listed in Article 13 as an open list to which other grounds might be added. This issue arose in *Chacón Navas*, in which an attempt was made to add 'sickness' to the list.[33] However, the argument in this case was not a particularly strong one and it remains to be seen what the Court might do in the future.

Overall, then, it can be seen that the EU has arrived at a reasonably comprehensive treatment of equality, albeit that the law on sex discrimination is much more well-established. This is reinforced by the rights contained in the EU Charter. Although the Court of Justice has drawn on its sex discrimination case-law in interpreting the new grounds, some differences between the grounds have begun to emerge, as we shall see below.

6.3.2 English law

The common law does very little to combat discrimination at work because the principle of freedom of contract has traditionally allowed employers to make choices (for example, when hiring employees) for any reason, including discriminatory reasons. Thus, equality law in the UK has a statutory source.

The government's first major intervention in the field of equality at work was the Race Relations Act 1968. This Act purported to tackle race discrimination but it was narrowly drafted and created a cumbersome and ineffective enforcement mechanism.[34] It was replaced by the Race Relations Act 1976, which employed a more modern definition of discrimination and allowed claimants to bring actions in the employment tribunal to enforce their rights. Gender inequality was addressed through the Equal Pay Act 1970 (dealing with pay, as the name suggests), which did not come into force until 1975, and the Sex Discrimination Act 1975 (which addressed sex discrimination in areas other than pay). Interestingly, although the UK joined the EU in 1972, it appears that UK equality law developed largely independently of the EU measures enacted at roughly the same time.[35] For example, the concept of equal pay for work

---

[30] Case C-13/94 [1996] ECR I-2143.

[31] Council Directive 2000/43/EC of 29 June 2000 implementing the principle of equal treatment between persons irrespective of racial or ethnic origin (2000) OJ L180/22.

[32] Council Directive 2000/78/EC of 27 November 2000 establishing a general framework for equal treatment in employment and occupation [2000] L303/16.

[33] Case C-13/05 *Chacón Navas v Eurest Colectividades SA* [2006] ECR I-6467.

[34] For history, see Paul Davies and Mark Freedland, *Labour Legislation and Public Policy* (Clarendon Press 1993) 220–230, 380–385.

[35] Christopher McCrudden, 'Institutional Discrimination' (1982) 2 OJLS 303.

of equal value (not just like work) was not included in the 1970 Act and did not feature until the Court of Justice found the UK to be in breach of EU law on the matter in the early 1980s.[36] The US civil rights movement is thought to have been more influential, particularly in the development of the concept of 'indirect discrimination', known as 'disparate impact' in the US, which we shall discuss in more detail below. However, as EU law evolved (for example, when the Court of Justice decided that remedies in English law were inadequate),[37] the UK government tended to extend the same principles to race discrimination law,[38] so that the two developed in parallel.

The first significant legislative intervention in relation to disability at work was the Disabled Persons (Employment) Act 1944, which set up a quota system for the employment of people with disabilities by larger firms. In the 1980s, there was a long-running campaign to replace this old-fashioned (and not particularly effective) approach with an anti-discrimination measure. The government finally succumbed to pressure with the enactment of the Disability Discrimination Act 1995 (DDA).[39] Although this drew on the equality concepts used in sex and race discrimination law, its drafting was weaker. It required amendment to bring it into line with the more rigorous provisions of the EU Framework Directive.[40]

The remaining elements of UK legislation on equality were enacted in response to the Framework Directive. Provisions on religion and sexual orientation were enacted in 2003 and on age in 2006.[41] The Member States were given a longer implementation period for age discrimination law because of the prevalence of age-related rules in the employment sphere, such as upper and lower age limits on particular jobs, and retirement ages. These various developments in equality law prompted the decision to create the Equality and Human Rights Commission (EHRC) with a variety of responsibilities including promoting equality, conducting research and supporting litigation.[42] This replaced three predecessor bodies from the 'original' anti-discrimination statutes: the Equal Opportunities Commission, the Commission for Racial Equality, and the Disability Rights Commission. The government argued that a single body would be a more efficient use of resources, but the decision was controversial, with critics arguing that it would lose direction and might pursue some issues more vigorously than others.[43]

By 2006, the law had become highly complex, with a multitude of different instruments tackling different grounds of discrimination. After consultation, this led to the enactment of the Equality Act 2010, which is the current source of

[36] Case 61/81 *Commission* v *UK* [1982] ECR 2601; Equal Pay (Amendment) Regulations 1983, SI 1983/1794.

[37] Case C-271/91 *Marshall* v *Southampton and South-West Hampshire Area Health Authority (No 2)* [1993] ECR I-4367.

[38] Sex Discrimination and Equal Pay (Remedies) Regulations 1993, SI 1993/2798; Race Relations (Remedies) Act 1994.

[39] HM Government, *The Equality Bill – Government Response to the Consultation* (Cm 7454, 2008).

[40] Above n 32.

[41] Employment Equality (Religion or Belief) Regulations 2003, SI 2003/1660; Employment Equality (Sexual Orientation) Regulations 2003, SI 2003/1661; Employment Equality (Age) Regulations 2006, SI 2006/1031.

[42] Equality Act 2006.

[43] See, generally, Colm O'Cinneide, 'The Commission for Equality and Human Rights: a New Institution for New and Uncertain Times' (2007) 36 ILJ 141.

equality law in Britain.[44] Two points are worth noting at this stage. First, the government adopted a relatively conservative approach to the 2010 Act. Although it might have been expected to bring all the grounds of discrimination into a unified framework, it maintains a number of traditional distinctions. One of the most puzzling of these is the decision to continue with separate provisions on equal pay for men and women, even though pay discrimination on other grounds does not attract special treatment.[45] The government argued that well-understood provisions should be maintained, but critics argue that opportunities to simplify and clarify the law were missed.[46] Second, the 2010 Act coincided with a change of government from Labour to the Conservative–Liberal Democrat coalition. Some of the more radical provisions of the 2010 Act had not been brought into force at this point, and the new government opted not to do so.[47] This further limited the impact of the Act.

6.3.3 The relationship between EU law and national law

Given that there is a comprehensive body of both EU and national law on equality, it may be worth reminding ourselves of how the two bodies of law fit together.

The first and most obvious point is that the UK is obliged to give effect to EU law and may face infringement proceedings brought by the Commission (and perhaps also *Francovich* actions brought by individuals)[48] if it does not. There are a number of important examples of this, such as the Court's ruling that the Equal Pay Act 1970 did not give effect to the principle of equal pay for work of equal value because it only allowed an equal value claim where the employer had voluntarily arranged a job evaluation study at the workplace.[49]

From the perspective of the individual litigant, a more important consideration is the potential for direct effect: the ability to invoke EU law to fill in any gaps in national law. In an equal pay claim, it is possible to rely directly on what is now Article 157 in both vertical (against the state) and horizontal (against private parties) cases. This means that a woman can sue her employer based on Article 157 if domestic law does not address the problem. However, in this chapter, our focus is on other forms of discrimination (non-pay discrimination in relation to sex, and discrimination generally in relation to the other grounds) which are prohibited by EU directives rather than by Treaty provisions. This means that the directives can potentially be invoked in vertical cases (assuming the provision in question meets the conditions for direct effect) but not in horizontal ones, because of the Court's general prohibition on the horizontal direct effect of directives.[50]

Nonetheless, directives are still relevant in horizontal cases, in at least two respects. First, under the *Marleasing* rule, national legislation implementing a directive must

---

[44] Discrimination Law Review, *A Framework for Fairness: Proposals for an Equality Bill for Great Britain* (2007); HM Government, *The Equality Bill – Government Response to the Consultation* (Cm 7454, 2008).

[45] EA 2010, ss 64–71. See Chapter 7.

[46] See, generally, Bob Hepple, *Equality: The Legal Framework* (2nd edn, Hart 2014); and articles in (2011) 40(4) Industrial Law Journal, a special issue on the Act.

[47] For example, EA 2010, s 14 (dual discrimination) and s 78 (gender pay gap information).

[48] Case C-6/90 *Francovich v Italy* [1995] ECR I-3843.

[49] Above n 36.

[50] Case 152/84 *Marshall v Southampton and South West Hampshire AHA* [1986] ECR 723.

be interpreted to give effect to it, insofar as it is possible to do so.[51] Thus, even in a case against a private employer, the Equality Act 2010 must be interpreted in the light of the various directives to which it gives effect. Second, and more controversially, there may be scope for 'incidental direct effect' in some cases.[52] Where a national court cannot interpret national law compatibly with a directive, it may be obliged to 'disapply' the inconsistent national provisions.

More generally, the Court of Justice has begun to speak of non-discrimination in employment as a 'general principle' of EU law. On this view, the relevant EU directives elaborate – but do not lay down – this principle. This approach first arose in the controversial *Mangold* case, in which the Court was called upon to examine provisions of German law allowing employers to employ older workers on fixed-term contracts.[53] Although this was intended as a means of improving the employment prospects of older workers, it also had the potential to reduce their job security. The Court found that it was discriminatory on grounds of age, but could not apply the Framework Directive in the case because the transposition period had not expired. It 'got around' this problem by relying on age equality as a general principle of EU law and invoking the concept of 'incidental direct effect'. In later cases, the Court has not returned to the strategy of ignoring the transposition deadline,[54] but it has re-iterated the idea of equality (and not just on grounds of age) as a general principle of EU law.[55] It remains to be seen what impact this will have in future cases.

6.3.4 The role of the ECHR

The ECHR contains an equality right in Article 14. As we noted above, since this is one of the older human rights instruments, it does not contain as comprehensive a list of protected characteristics as we would recognise today. However, it is an open list and the ECtHR has added new characteristics through interpretation.[56]

More problematic in terms of using Article 14 in the employment context is the fact that it is a 'parasitic' right, applicable only when the victim's other rights have been violated in a discriminatory way. One example of a successful Article 14 claim is the case of *Smith and Grady* v *UK*, in which the claimants challenged the UK government's policy of excluding gay people from the armed forces.[57] Because this was also an infringement of their private life, under Article 8, it was possible to invoke Article 14. However, in most cases, it is rather more difficult to identify the violation of another right on which Article 14 can bite.

However, Article 14 is not the only right of relevance to equality. Two other rights worth considering are Article 9, which protects freedom of thought, conscience and religion, and Article 10, which protects freedom of expression. These rights may be relevant to people who are discriminated against at work because of their religious

---

[51] Case C-106/89 *Marleasing SA* v *La Comercial Internacional de Alimentacion SA* [1990] ECR I-4135.
[52] Case C-194/94 *CIA Security International SA* v *Signalson SA and Securitel Sprl* [1996] ECR I-2201.
[53] Case C-144/04 *Mangold* v *Helm* [2005] ECR I-9981.
[54] Case C-427/06 *Bartsch* v *Bosch und Siemens* [2008] ECR I-7245.
[55] Case C-555/07 *Kücükdeveci* v *Swedex GmbH & Co* [2010] ECR I-365; Case C-297/10 *Hennigs* v *Eisenbahn-Bundesamt* [2011] ECR I-7965.
[56] Above n 21.
[57] (2000) 29 EHRR 493.

or other beliefs or political opinions.[58] Both have limitations. One is that both rights are applicable to the state, so anyone who has a grievance against a private employer must be able to show that the state is in breach of its duty to protect him or her against the employer's infringement. The other is that both rights are subject to exceptions where the state (or employer) is pursuing a proportionate means of achieving a legitimate aim. This means that the individual's claim may be defeated by competing considerations.

Under the HRA, the domestic courts are required to take into account the Strasbourg case-law and to interpret domestic law compatibly where it is possible to do so.[59] The ECHR is worth considering in equality cases but it is not so influential in this area of law than it is in some other fields.

6.4 CORE CONCEPTS

In this section, we will examine the main concepts used in equality law: direct discrimination, positive discrimination, indirect discrimination and harassment. In order to bring a successful discrimination claim, the claimant must show that the employer:

- discriminated (directly or indirectly) or committed an act of harassment

- because of a protected characteristic (race, sex, age and so on)

- at work (for example, when making a hiring or promotion decision).

Thus, our focus will be on the first of these components in this section. It may help to give a brief definition of each of the core concepts before we get into the detail:

- Direct discrimination occurs where an individual is treated less favourably than another because of his or her protected characteristic.

- Indirect discrimination occurs where the employer applies a seemingly neutral requirement which puts the individual and other people at a disadvantage because of their protected characteristic, unless the employer can justify the use of the requirement.

- Harassment occurs where the individual is subject to unwanted behaviour that violates his or her dignity because of his or her protected characteristic.

We will also examine positive discrimination in this section. This occurs where the employer selects a person for a job or a promotion because people with that person's protected characteristic are under-represented in the workplace. Although this would normally be unlawful direct discrimination against the unsuccessful candidates, the law permits it in some circumstances as a means of advancing substantive equality.

6.4.1 Direct discrimination

In this section, we will consider direct discrimination: less favourable treatment because of a protected characteristic. We will begin with the concept itself, before turning to some of its broader manifestations (based on a person's association with

---

[58] For example, *Eweida v UK* (2013) 57 EHRR 8; *Redfearn v UK* (2013) 57 EHRR 2.
[59] Human Rights Act 1998, s 2.

others or on a person's perceived characteristics) and exceptions where it is not unlawful.

The basic concept

The basic concept of direct discrimination is the employer's failure to 'treat like cases alike'. It is defined in Article 2(2)(a) of the Framework Directive as occurring:

> where one person is treated less favourably than another is, has been or would be treated in a comparable situation on any of the [protected] grounds.

In EA 2010, it is defined in s. 13(1) as follows:

> A person (A) discriminates against another (B) if, because of a protected characteristic, A treats B less favourably than A treats or would treat others.

This applies to obvious cases of discrimination: for example, where an employer only hires men because he assumes that women are not physically strong enough to do the job in question. The use of the word 'would' in both provisions is significant. There is no need for the claimant to show that he or she was treated differently to a real person (sometimes called a 'comparator'). It is sufficient for the claimant to show that had he or she not had the characteristic in question, his or her treatment would have been different. However, in practice, this may involve imagining how a hypothetical comparator would have been treated.

Although direct discrimination seems relatively straightforward to understand, the courts sometimes find it difficult to determine whether the employer's treatment of a person was 'because of a protected characteristic'. In *James* v *Eastleigh BC*, the council adopted a rule that people of pensionable age could use its swimming pools free of charge, with a view to helping those whose incomes were limited.[60] At the time, the pension age was 60 for women and 65 for men. The claimant was a man aged 61. He argued that the rule discriminated against him because of his sex. The court held that the council's benign motive of helping pensioners was irrelevant. It used a 'but for' test. Since, 'but for' being a man, the claimant would have been able to go swimming for free, the court found that the council had discriminated directly against him. Some other more recent cases have used a 'reason why' approach, focusing more directly on the employer's reason for the treatment. An example of this is *Shamoon*, in which a police officer was given a reduced role after complaints were made about her conduct.[61] It was held that the tribunal should have considered whether her role was changed because of the complaints or because she was a woman (in that a man who had been the subject of similar complaints would have been treated differently). Again, though, the employer's underlying motive is irrelevant: it is possible to engage in direct discrimination against someone without subjectively intending to do so.

The key question is whether a prohibited characteristic features in the employer's reasoning process. In *Hall* v *Bull*, the owners of a hotel refused to allow unmarried couples to have double rooms because of their religious beliefs relating to marriage.[62]

---

[60] [1990] 2 AC 751.
[61] *Shamoon* v *Chief Constable of the Royal Ulster Constabulary* [2003] UKHL 11, [2003] ICR 337.
[62] [2013] UKSC 73, [2013] 1 WLR 3741.

The claimants were a gay couple in a civil partnership who were refused a room. The hotel owners argued that they had not discriminated because their reason was that the couple were unmarried, a policy they applied equally to gay and straight couples. However, the Supreme Court rejected this argument because, at the time, marriage was not an option for gay couples. This meant that the hotel owners' different treatment of the claimants compared to a married couple was because of their sexual orientation. The fact that they would have treated an unmarried heterosexual couple in the same way was regarded by the majority as irrelevant.

Finnis challenges the courts' approach to direct discrimination on the basis that it fails to analyse employers' reasoning processes properly.[63] He claims that something only features in the employer's reasoning process if the employer acts because of it. In *James*, for example, the council acted because of the pension age, and this act was only discriminatory because a third party (Parliament) had set that age differently for men and women. This approach would reduce the scope of direct discrimination quite considerably, with the result that more cases would fall under the concept of indirect discrimination (which has a justification defence). The courts have cast the net wider by looking beyond the employer's stated reason where – objectively – that reason differentiates on prohibited grounds.

Association and perception

EA 2010 uses the phrase 'because of a protected characteristic'. It is important to note that it does not say 'because of the claimant's protected characteristic'.[64] This has the effect of broadening the law to include discrimination by association and discrimination by perception.

Associational discrimination occurs where the employer discriminates against the claimant because of his or her association with a person with a protected characteristic. The leading case is *Coleman*, in which the claimant was discriminated against by her employer because of her caring responsibilities in relation to her son, who had a disability.[65] A similar approach would apply where, for example, the employer did not like the employee's friends or family because of their race or religion.

A 'perception' claim is not very satisfactory shorthand for a case in which the claimant is discriminated against on the grounds of a particular characteristic, regardless of whether or not he or she in fact has that characteristic. It gets its name from the idea that the employer might discriminate against someone because it 'perceives' him or her to be of a particular religion, for example, even though that is not the case. But this type of claim can arise even where the employer *knows* that the person does not have the characteristic in question. An illustration is the *English* case, in which the claimant was subjected to homophobic harassment by his work colleagues, who knew that he was heterosexual.[66] The harassment nevertheless took place 'because of' sexual orientation.

---

[63] John Finnis, 'Intention in Direct Discrimination' in *Intention and Identity: Collected Essays Volume II* (OUP 2011).

[64] This *is* required in relation to marriage and civil partnership under EA 2010, s 13(4).

[65] *ERB Attridge Law LLP* v *Coleman* [2010] ICR 242 (EAT).

[66] *English* v *Thomas Sanderson Blinds Ltd* [2008] EWCA Civ 1421, [2009] 2 All ER 468.

Occupational requirements

In general terms, direct discrimination does not have a justification defence: the employer cannot argue that it discriminated against a person on the grounds of his or her sex but had a good reason for doing so. Age discrimination is an exception to this, as we shall see below.[67] But there are (relatively rare) situations in which a protected characteristic is relevant to a person's capacity to do the job, for example, where the director of a film wishes to cast female actors to play the female characters. This is dealt with using the concept of an 'occupational requirement' (known in the old law as a 'genuine occupational qualification'):

> A person (A) does not contravene [the law] by applying in relation to work a requirement to have a particular protected characteristic, if A shows that, having regard to the nature or context of the work–
>
> (a) it is an occupational requirement,
>
> (b) the application of the requirement is a proportionate means of achieving a legitimate aim, and
>
> (c) the person to whom A applies the requirement does not meet it (or A has reasonable grounds for not being satisfied that the person meets it).[68]

This test includes a proportionality requirement and is quite strict. Thus, for example, organisations providing services to women would not necessarily be able to insist that all their staff should be female, unless there was a particular reason for this. The EHRC guidance gives the example of a women's refuge, in which the provision of an all-female environment might be regarded as an important means of enabling the residents to feel safe.[69]

6.4.2 Indirect discrimination

Although the prohibition of direct discrimination is important both practically and symbolically, the idea of 'treating like cases alike' only goes so far in combating deep-seated inequalities in society. Indirect discrimination tackles the situation in which like cases are being treated alike – the employer has a rule that applies to everyone – but when we probe more deeply, we can see that the rule is harder for some groups to comply with than it is for others. To take some obvious examples, a requirement to work on Sundays may be a problem for some Christians (compared with those of other faiths or none); a requirement to lift heavy loads may be a problem for women (compared with men) or older people (compared with younger people); and a requirement to have perfect vision would be a problem for people with visual disabilities. In other words, certain groups are put 'at a particular disadvantage' by the rule in question.

However, an important contrast between direct and indirect discrimination is that, in cases of indirect discrimination, the employer may be able to invoke a justification defence. In cases of direct discrimination, the law regards it as illegitimate for the

---

[67] EA 2010, s 13(2).
[68] EA 2010, sch 9, para 1.
[69] EHRC, *Equality Act 2010 Code of Practice: Employment Statutory Code of Practice* (EHRC 2011) para 13.8.

employer to make a decision based on a protected characteristic (unless it is an occupational requirement). In cases of indirect discrimination, though, it may be lawful for the employer to apply the neutral rule, even though it puts certain groups at a disadvantage, where the employer can show that it is a proportionate means of achieving a legitimate aim. So, to return to our examples, a requirement to work on Sundays may be justified where the employer's business is open on Sundays; a requirement to lift heavy loads may be justified where the employer's business is a removals firm; and a requirement to have perfect vision may be justified where the employer is hiring airline pilots. However, it is important to look closely at the employer's argument: a requirement to lift heavy loads may not be necessary in a different type of business where (for example) the employee would only be required to lift heavy loads occasionally or where lifting equipment could be provided.

The basic concept

When examining indirect discrimination, it is worth remembering that the precise formulation of the test has changed over time. Some of the older cases are based on different legislative wording and got quite bogged down in technicalities. The modern formulation is designed to overcome some of these problems.

According to the Framework Directive, Article 2(2)(b):

> indirect discrimination shall be taken to occur where an apparently neutral provision, criterion or practice would put persons having a particular [protected characteristic] at a particular disadvantage compared with other persons . . .

This is implemented in s 19 EA 2010:

(1) A person (A) discriminates against another (B) if A applies to B a provision, criterion or practice which is discriminatory in relation to a relevant protected characteristic of B's.

(2) For the purposes of subsection (1), a provision, criterion or practice is discriminatory in relation to a relevant protected characteristic of B's if–

    (a) A applies, or would apply, it to persons with whom B does not share the characteristic,

    (b) it puts, or would put, persons with whom B shares the characteristic at a particular disadvantage when compared with persons with whom B does not share it,

    (c) it puts, or would put, B at that disadvantage, and

    (d) A cannot show it to be a proportionate means of achieving a legitimate aim.

This provision applies to all the protected characteristics except pregnancy, though a pregnant woman may be able to present her case as a sex discrimination claim.[70] We will consider sub-paragraph (d), on justification, below, and will concentrate for now on establishing indirect discrimination.

The first step is to identify the 'provision, criterion or practice' (sometimes abbreviated to PCP) being used by the employer. The old law required the claimant to identify a specific 'requirement or condition' applied by the employer, a hurdle which could sometimes be difficult to satisfy where the claimant could not formulate his or her problem in terms of a particular demand being made by the employer.[71]

---

[70] EA 2010, s 19(3), and see *Commissioner of Police of the Metropolis* v *Keohane* [2014] Eq LR 386 (EAT) [10].
[71] For example, *Perera* v *Civil Service Commission* (No 2) [1983] ICR 428.

The Court of Justice of the European Union (CJEU) adopted a broader, non-technical understanding[72] which is reflected in the drafting of the Framework Directive and in EA 2010. Although a 'criterion' used by the employer is covered, the terms 'provision . . . or practice' are wider.

The next step is to show that the PCP has a discriminatory impact. This involves a group comparison. The claimant is treated as part of a group sharing his or her particular characteristic, and the effect of the rule on this group is then compared with the effect of the rule on others who do not share the characteristic. So, for example, a female claimant might try to persuade the court that the rule puts women at a 'particular disadvantage' as compared with men. The claimant must also show that he or she is in fact disadvantaged by the rule.

Again, this is an improvement on the old law, which required the claimant to show that a considerably smaller proportion of people sharing his or her characteristic could not comply with the employer's requirement or condition and that he or she could not comply with it. This test was problematic because of the 'non-compliance' and 'considerably smaller proportion' elements.

The 'non-compliance' requirement made it difficult to prove indirect discrimination where people in the claimant's group were disadvantaged by a rule but could – in theory – comply with it. A good example is *Price v Civil Service Commission*, in which the employer placed an upper limit of 35 on a civil service job.[73] A female applicant sought to challenge this as sex discrimination (the case pre-dates the age discrimination law) because women were more likely to take career breaks to have children during their twenties and thirties. On a strict construction, women 'could' comply with the age limit, but the court adopted a more generous purposive approach, recognising women's role in childbearing (and generally also in child-care), and held that the rule was indirectly discriminatory. This type of case is much easier to address under EA 2010 because it is sufficient to prove that the PCP puts people with the claimant's characteristic at a 'particular disadvantage'.

The old law also required the claimant to show that a 'considerably smaller proportion' of people with his or her characteristic could comply with the rule. This led the courts into some quite complex statistical enquiries, particularly where the case involved discrimination by the state in its choice of legislative rules rather than discrimination by a particular employer. Often, the way in which the court structured the comparison dictated the outcome of the case. A good example of this is the *Rutherford* case.[74] In that case, which again predates the age discrimination law, a group of men challenged a rule (no longer in force) that employees dismissed when they were 65 or over could not claim unfair dismissal. They argued that the rule indirectly discriminated against men because slightly more men than women continued in work after the age of 65. The House of Lords rejected the claim. Different judges took different approaches, but the majority held that there was no discrimination because men in work over the age of 65 got the same treatment (no unfair dismissal protection) as women in work over the age of 65. On this view, it did not matter that more men than women were in this situation. Nowadays, the case would be much easier to argue because it is an example of direct age discrimination and the government has repealed the offending rule.

---

[72] Case C-127/92 *Enderby v Frenchay HA* [1993] ECR I-5535.
[73] [1978] ICR 27.
[74] *Rutherford v Secretary of State* [2006] UKHL 19, [2006] ICR 785.

A further problem with the old law was that it was quite 'data hungry', even though in many cases statistical evidence to establish indirect discrimination might not exist. This was particularly a problem at the employer level, because employers might not gather data about their workforce at all and, even if they did, would be reluctant to share it with potential claimants. Moreover, with the addition of some of the newer protected characteristics, accurate data may be hard to come by. For example, a transgender person may place particular value on *not* revealing his or her transgender status at work for privacy reasons, making it difficult to collect information about that characteristic.

The approach in EA 2010 places less emphasis on statistics and proportions because it uses the phrase 'particular disadvantage' rather than 'considerably smaller proportion'. This was recognised by Baroness Hale in *Homer*:

> [T]he new formulation was . . . intended to do away with the need for statistical comparisons where no statistics might exist. It was intended to do away with the complexities involved in identifying those who could comply and those who could not and how great the disparity had to be. Now all that is needed is a particular disadvantage when compared with other people who do not share the characteristic in question.[75]

Although statistics may still be useful where they are available, it is important that lower courts follow this common-sense approach.

So far, we have noted that indirect discrimination is about 'group' comparisons: the claimant must show that he or she is a member of a group sharing a protected characteristic, and that members of the group are put at a 'particular disadvantage' by the PCP. However, the courts may need to modify their approach in response to recent ECtHR decisions in the area of religious freedom. In *Eweida* and *Chaplin*, the Court considered employers' uniform policies which prohibited employees from wearing crosses or crucifixes at work.[76] The Court found that these policies were indirectly discriminatory. In *Chaplin*, the policy was found to be justified on health and safety grounds (because the employee was a nurse) whereas in *Eweida* it was found not to be justified in relation to an airline check-in employee. As Pitt explains, in neither case did the Court require the employee to show any form of group disadvantage.[77] It is clear that not all Christians feel obliged to or even wish to wear a cross or crucifix, nor was there any evidence that employees other than the claimants had been adversely affected at work by the employer's rules. Pitt suggests that the courts will have to use s. 3 HRA to interpret EA 2010 to bring it into line with this approach.

However, it may be that existing indirect discrimination law is already sufficiently flexible to accommodate these decisions. An example is *London Underground* v *Edwards*.[78] The claimant in that case was a single mother who was adversely affected by the employer's decision to move to a flexible shift pattern because she could not find suitable child-care. Women were in a very small minority in her workplace and, of the women, she was the only one who could not cope with the new shifts. Nevertheless, her claim succeeded. The Court of Appeal held that it would be unfair to deny the claim because of the claimant's inability to point to other affected women

---

[75] *Chief Constable of West Yorkshire Police* v *Homer* [2012] UKSC 15, [2012] ICR 704 [14].
[76] *Eweida* v *United Kingdom* (2013) 57 EHRR 8.
[77] Gwyneth Pitt, 'Taking Religion Seriously' (2013) 42 ILJ 398.
[78] [1999] ICR 494.

since – given the poor gender balance in the workplace – this was probably a result of discrimination in itself. As the law's range of protected characteristics increases, it seems likely that the requirement of group disadvantage will diminish in importance because it will be difficult for many claimants to satisfy, particularly in small or non-diverse workplaces. However, for reasons of clarity, it would be desirable for the legislation to be amended to reflect this.

Justification

Once the claimant has established that there is a PCP which puts him or her at a particular disadvantage (and puts others with his or her characteristic at a particular disadvantage), attention is likely to turn to the employer's justification defence. This is designed to ensure that where the PCP is genuinely necessary to do the job, the employer is still able to rely on it even though it has an indirectly discriminatory effect.

The approach to justification is the proportionality test, initially developed by the Court of Justice in the *Bilka-Kaufhaus* case, and now codified in the relevant directives and EA 2010.[79] Thus, there is discrimination under the Framework Directive unless:

> [the] provision, criterion or practice is objectively justified by a legitimate aim and the means of achieving that aim are appropriate and necessary . . .[80]

and more succinctly under EA 2010 where the defendant 'cannot show [the PCP] to be a proportionate means of achieving a legitimate aim'.[81] In general terms, the proportionality test is quite strict, though as we shall see, there are some variations.

To take a simple example, in the *Homer* case, the claimant's employer adopted a new promotion structure which required employees to have a law degree in order to be promoted to the highest grade.[82] The claimant met the other criteria for promotion but did not have a law degree. He was aged 61, and because there was an expectation that he would retire at 65, it was not practical for him to obtain a degree by part-time study before retirement. The Supreme Court held that the employer's aim of improving recruitment and retention of staff of an appropriate calibre was legitimate. Moreover:

> To be proportionate, a measure has to be both an appropriate means of achieving the legitimate aim and (reasonably) necessary in order to do so.[83]

So in *Homer*, the case was remitted to the tribunal on the justification point because it had not considered recruitment and retention as separate aims, or assessed whether the law degree requirement was appropriate for retention, or examined whether there were any non-discriminatory alternatives (such as a different set of rules for staff recruited before a law degree became a requirement).

However, the courts (both the domestic courts and the CJEU) tend to take a less rigorous approach where the case involves a challenge to the compatibility of national legislation with EU directives or Treaty provisions on equality. For example, in the *Seymour-Smith* case, it was established that the two-year qualifying period for

---

[79] Case 170/84 *Bilka-Kaufhaus GmbH* v *Weber von Hartz* [1986] ECR 1607.
[80] Directive 2000/78/EC, art 6(1).
[81] EA 2010, s 19(2)(d).
[82] *Homer* (n 75).
[83] ibid [22] (emphasis added).

bringing an unfair dismissal claim was indirectly discriminatory against women because they were more likely than men to take career breaks and to work on short-term contracts.[84] The Court of Justice held that encouraging recruitment was a legitimate social policy aim[85] and the House of Lords then held that the measure was proportionate, noting the difficulty of obtaining 'hard evidence' relating to the impact of the law on employers' recruitment plans.[86]

6.4.3 Harassment

In the early years of equality law, there was no special provision for harassment. In a series of cases, the courts gradually developed the idea that harassment because of a protected characteristic could constitute unlawful direct discrimination.[87] Nowadays, harassment is dealt with separately in EU Directives and in EA 2010.

According to the Framework Directive, Article 2(3):

> Harassment shall be deemed to be a form of discrimination . . . when unwanted conduct related to any of the [protected characteristics] takes place with the purpose or effect of violating the dignity of a person and of creating an intimidating, hostile, degrading, humiliating or offensive environment. In this context, the concept of harassment may be defined in accordance with the national laws and practice of the Member States.

EA 2010, s. 26(1), adopts very similar language:

> A person (A) harasses another (B) if–
>
> (a) A engages in unwanted conduct related to a relevant protected characteristic, and
>
> (b) the conduct has the purpose or effect of–
>
>   (i) violating B's dignity, or
>
>   (ii) creating an intimidating, hostile, degrading, humiliating or offensive environment for B.

Importantly, this provision does not create a free-standing right not to be harassed at work, because the conduct must be 'related to' a protected characteristic (although this is a broad formulation). All the protected characteristics are covered except marriage and civil partnership, the government having taken the view that there was no need for protection on this ground.[88] Specific provision is made for conduct 'of a sexual nature' in s. 26(2).

A particularly noteworthy feature of s. 26(1) is that it makes express use of the concept of dignity. As we saw above, critics of equality often champion dignity as an alternative basis for the law in this area. The harassment provision shows how dignity might be used. However, it might be thought that harassment is a rather different kind of wrong to other forms of discrimination, because the focus is on the hostile treatment meted out to the individual rather than on how this compares to the treatment of others. If this is the case, though, there would be some force in the argument that tying the provision to the protected characteristics is unnecessary.

---

[84] Case C-167/97 *R v Secretary of State for Employment, ex p Seymour-Smith* [1999] ECR I-623.
[85] ibid [71].
[86] *R v Secretary of State for Employment, ex p Seymour-Smith (No 2)* [2000] ICR 244 (HL) 451.
[87] *Porcelli v Strathclyde Regional Council* [1986] ICR 564.
[88] EA 2010, s 26(5).

Of course, hostile treatment related to a protected characteristic is particularly bad, but it might be thought to be undesirable to tolerate hostile treatment for any reason.

A particular difficulty in harassment cases is striking a balance between the objective and subjective views of the hostile treatment. If the individual's view is ignored, his or her dignity is not upheld. However, if a purely subjective view were to be taken, there is the risk that an individual might be able to base a claim on what would generally be regarded as normal social behaviour. This is addressed in s. 26(4), which requires the court or tribunal to consider both points of view:

> In deciding whether conduct has the effect referred to in subsection (1)(b), each of the following must be taken into account–
>
> (a) the perception of B;
> (b) the other circumstances of the case;
> (c) whether it is reasonable for the conduct to have that effect.

We noted above that s. 26 does not provide a general protection against harassment unrelated to the protected characteristics. Another option may be to rely on the Protection from Harassment Act 1997. Section 1(1) provides:

> A person must not pursue a course of conduct–
>
> (a) which amounts to harassment of another, and
> (b) which he knows or ought to know amounts to harassment of the other.

Harassment is not defined in the Act, other than to say that it includes 'alarming the person or causing the person distress'.[89] Thus, it is for the courts to decide what is covered by the concept. The Act was intended to tackle the problem of stalking, but in the *Majrowski* case, the House of Lords held that there was no reason why it could not apply in the workplace.[90] In that case, the claimant successfully sued his employer for damages under s. 3 of the Act because he had been bullied at work by his manager in breach of s. 1 of the Act. The employer was vicariously liable for the manager's actions.

6.4.4 Positive discrimination

As we saw above, positive discrimination or affirmative action is one of the more controversial areas of equality law. Proponents argue that favouring historically disadvantaged groups is the only way to secure 'true' equality, given that employers' decisions might be influenced by subconscious biases of various kinds. Opponents argue that positive discrimination is unfair to those in non-disadvantaged groups and liable to create resentment in the workplace. English law permits positive discrimination in three quite limited sets of circumstances.

First, it is lawful to discriminate in favour of people with disabilities, for example, by reserving a particular job for a disabled person. This is not stated explicitly in EA 2010, but follows from the fact that there is no protection for non-disabled people under the Act.[91] Thus, a person who does not have a disability could not complain

---

[89] Protection from Harassment Act 1997, s 7(2).
[90] *Majrowski* v *Guy's and St Thomas's NHS Trust* [2006] UKHL 34, [2007] 1 AC 224.
[91] EA 2010, s 4.

of discrimination if an employer preferred a disabled person when hiring. This contrasts with the other protected characteristics, which are universal or symmetrical in application. Thus, if an employer gave preferential treatment to a female job applicant, a male job applicant could complain of sex discrimination (unless one of the other forms of positive discrimination applied to the case).

The second type of positive action permitted in English law can be viewed as an 'equality of opportunity' measure. It has a long history and is currently to be found in s. 158 EA 2010:

(1) This section applies if a person (P) reasonably thinks that–

(a) persons who share a protected characteristic suffer a disadvantage connected to the characteristic,

(b) persons who share a protected characteristic have needs that are different from the needs of persons who do not share it, or

(c) participation in an activity by persons who share a protected characteristic is disproportionately low.

(2) This Act does not prohibit P from taking any action which is a proportionate means of achieving the aim of–

(a) enabling or encouraging persons who share the protected characteristic to overcome or minimise that disadvantage,

(b) meeting those needs, or

(c) enabling or encouraging persons who share the protected characteristic to participate in that activity . . .

There are three features to note about this provision. First, it is not compulsory for the employer to invoke it. This limits its impact very considerably, since only employers with a particular interest in equality (or employers facing public or workforce pressure to act) are likely to make use of it. Second, the employer must 'reasonably think' that one of the conditions in subsection (1) is met. The EHRC guidance makes clear that this can be done in a variety of ways and does not necessarily require the gathering of sophisticated statistical evidence.[92] Third, the measures taken must fulfil a proportionality test. Examples of appropriate measures might be offering internships to people from a particular ethnic group who are underrepresented in the workplace, or drafting job adverts to encourage people from a particular age group to apply.

The third form of positive action permitted by English law is the newest and most controversial. It was introduced by EA 2010 in response to the criticism, discussed above, of the limitations of the existing direct and indirect discrimination concepts in achieving equality. Its drafting reflects the CJEU's case-law on positive action, which imposes quite strict limits on what the Member States may do in this area. We will examine the CJEU's case-law first, before analysing the EA 2010 provision.

The CJEU's case-law arose in relation to Article 2(4) of the Equal Treatment Directive, which provided that the principle of equal treatment should be applied 'without prejudice to measures to promote equal opportunity for men and women, in particular by removing existing inequalities which affect women's opportunities'.[93]

[92] Above n 69, para 12.14.
[93] Directive 76/207/EEC.

Initially, in *Kalanke*, the Court took the view that Article 2(4) was an exception to the principle of equal treatment and should therefore be construed strictly.[94] It rejected a German scheme which allowed an employer to promote a female candidate in preference to a male candidate where women made up less than 50% of the grade in question and both candidates were equally qualified. However, the Court retreated from this much-criticised decision in the *Marschall* case, recognising that there was a role for positive action:

> [I]t appears that even where male and female candidates are equally qualified, male candidates tend to be promoted in preference to female candidates particularly because of prejudices and stereotypes concerning the role and capacities of women in working life and the fear, for example, that women will interrupt their careers more frequently, that owing to household and family duties they will be less flexible in their working hours, or that they will be absent from work more frequently because of pregnancy, childbirth and breastfeeding . . . For these reasons, the mere fact that a male candidate and a female candidate are equally qualified does not mean that they have the same chances.[95]

The positive discrimination scheme at issue in *Marschall* was regarded by the Court as acceptable because, although it allowed an employer to promote a female candidate in preference to a male candidate where women made up less than 50% of the grade in question and both candidates were equally qualified, it differed from the scheme in *Kalanke* because the preference did not operate automatically. There was an opportunity to consider whether some special (non-discriminatory) consideration relating to the male candidate meant that the preference for the female candidate should not apply. This might apply, for example, where the male candidate had a protected characteristic of his own, such as a disability.[96]

Although the decision in *Marschall* has been welcomed, the Court has stuck fairly closely to this ruling and has not been willing to expand the range of permissible schemes. For example, in *Abrahamsson*, a scheme provided that where women were under-represented, the employer could appoint or promote a woman who was 'sufficiently' qualified for the job, even if there was a male candidate who had better qualifications and experience.[97] The Court held that this was not acceptable because it departed too radically from the principle of making selection decisions on merit. The Court's approach has been criticised for its timidity.[98] The power of an 'equal qualifications' scheme to effect change is, arguably, limited, because members of a disadvantaged group may find it difficult to acquire the qualifications and experience they need in order to benefit from the scheme. However, it can also be argued that such schemes offer minimal interference with the principle of appointment on merit – if two candidates are equally qualified, they cannot be separated on merit so it is appropriate to use some other means of choosing between them – and are less likely to generate serious resentment.

Historically, English law did not permit positive discrimination. This was because of the symmetrical or universal nature of the protected characteristics, noted above: a

---

[94] Case C-450/93 *Kalanke v Freie und Hansestadt Bremen* [1995] ECR I-3051.
[95] Case C-409/95 *Marschall v Land Nordrhein-Westfalen* [1997] ECR I-6363 [29]–[30].
[96] Case C-158/97 *Badeck* [2000] ECR I-1875 [35].
[97] Case C-407/98 *Abrahamsson v Fogelqvist* [2000] ECR I-5539.
[98] Catherine Barnard, 'The Principle of Equality in the Community Context: *P, Grant, Kalanke* and *Marschall*: Four Uneasy Bedfellows?' (1998) 57 CLJ 352; Sandra Fredman, 'After *Kalanke* and *Marschall*: Affirming Affirmative Action' (1998) 1 CYELS 199.

scheme favouring women would discriminate against men, and vice versa. However, EA 2010, s. 159, introduced a positive action provision for the first time:

(1) This section applies if a person (P) reasonably thinks that–

    (a) persons who share a protected characteristic suffer a disadvantage connected to the characteristic, or

    (b) participation in an activity by persons who share a protected characteristic is disproportionately low.

(2) Part 5 (work) does not prohibit P from taking action within subsection (3) with the aim of enabling or encouraging persons who share the protected characteristic to–

    (a) overcome or minimise that disadvantage, or

    (b) participate in that activity.

(3) That action is treating a person (A) more favourably in connection with recruitment or promotion than another person (B) because A has the protected characteristic but B does not.

(4) But subsection (2) applies only if–

    (a) A is as qualified as B to be recruited or promoted,

    (b) P does not have a policy of treating persons who share the protected characteristic more favourably in connection with recruitment or promotion than persons who do not share it, and

    (c) taking the action in question is a proportionate means of achieving the aim referred to in subsection (2).

Like s. 158, this provision is permissive rather than mandatory: employers are allowed, not obliged, to use positive action. This is likely to limit the utility of the provision, not least because employers may fear litigation from disappointed candidates. It allows the employer to decide when a group is under-represented, provided that the employer acts 'reasonably'. The drafting of subsection (4)(a) and (b) reflects EU law: the two candidates must be equally qualified, and the employer may not apply a blanket policy. However, English law adds a proportionality requirement in subsection (4)(c): the employer must be able to show that giving preference to the candidate from the under-represented group is a proportionate means of addressing the disadvantage. This is potentially quite problematic. Instead of adopting a clear, general policy that positive action is an appropriate means of tackling under-representation, the legislation instead requires that question to be addressed at the level of the particular workplace. This exposes employers to further uncertainty and potential litigation. And it remains to be seen how the courts will apply the test. For example, under-representation could be tackled less intrusively – but less effectively – by measures under s. 158, raising the question whether the courts might require the employer to exhaust those opportunities before turning to s. 159. All of this suggests that the provision is unlikely to be used.

6.5 PROTECTED CHARACTERISTICS

Discrimination is only prohibited where it takes place because of a 'protected characteristic' (referred to in the old law as a 'ground' of discrimination). These are listed in s. 4 EA 2010:

The following characteristics are protected characteristics–

age;

disability;

gender reassignment;

marriage and civil partnership;

pregnancy and maternity;

race;

religion or belief;

sex;

sexual orientation.

This list reflects the UK's obligations under EU law, with the exception of marriage and civil partnership, which is largely domestic in origin. We will examine each of the characteristics in turn, before considering whether there is anything missing from the list.

6.5.1 Age

Age discrimination is addressed by the Framework Directive, Article 1, and by EA 2010, s. 5. It is a relative newcomer to the law, since the UK government took advantage of the longer implementation deadline of 2006 permitted by Article 18 of the Directive. Age discrimination applies where a particular age or an age group is used in decision-making. So, for example, requiring a person to retire at the age of 65 or stating that a job is only open to people aged 25–45 are both examples of age discrimination. Both older and younger workers are protected by the law on age discrimination.

A special feature of the law on age discrimination is that direct age discrimination can be justified.[99] This contrasts with the normal position which is that the employer only has a general justification defence in relation to indirect discrimination. This reflects an argument that sometimes a person's age may be relevant in the employment context. However, critics argue that too great a willingness to accept justifications for direct age discrimination may undermine the law's underlying objective of securing equality on this ground.

The Directive tackles the issue of justification in Article 6(1):

> Notwithstanding Article 2(2), Member States may provide that differences of treatment on grounds of age shall not constitute discrimination, if, within the context of national law, they are objectively and reasonably justified by a legitimate aim, including legitimate employment policy, labour market and vocational training objectives, and if the means of achieving that aim are appropriate and necessary.

Such differences of treatment may include, among others:

(a) the setting of special conditions on access to employment and vocational training, employment and occupation, including dismissal and remuneration conditions, for young people, older workers and persons with caring responsibilities in order to promote their vocational integration or ensure their protection;

(b) the fixing of minimum conditions of age, professional experience or seniority in service for access to employment or to certain advantages linked to employment;

(c) the fixing of a maximum age for recruitment which is based on the training requirements of the post in question or the need for a reasonable period of employment before retirement.

The phrasing of Article 6(1) differs slightly from that of Article 2(2), on justification for indirect discrimination, which was held to be significant in the *Seldon* case,

---

[99] EA 2010, s 13(2).

discussed below.[100] The possibility of justifying direct age discrimination is confirmed by EA, s. 13(2):

> If the protected characteristic is age, A does not discriminate against B if A can show A's treatment of B to be a proportionate means of achieving a legitimate aim.

There is a growing body of case-law before the Court of Justice on how to apply the proportionality test in the age discrimination context. In general terms, the Court is more willing to accept the use of retirement ages than it is to accept age limits relating to younger workers. The UK courts are, of course, bound by this case-law, but so far at least, have decided fewer cases.

The *Kücükdeveci* case is a good example of the Court's treatment of age rules applying to younger workers. In that case, the claimant received notice of termination calculated on the basis of three years' service for her employer.[101] She had worked for the firm for 10 years, but national law provided that service before the age of 25 did not count. The national government argued that the rule protected the job security of older workers and reflected the greater flexibility of younger workers. The Court disagreed, pointing out that the rule did not apply equally to younger workers because it disadvantaged those who entered the labour market early. And it operated to reduce the notice given to workers who entered the labour market before the age of 25 regardless of their age at the time of dismissal, so it did not protect the job security of older workers. More generally, the ruling suggests that length of service criteria (which are often used to determine pay rises, promotions and even redundancy selection) may now fall to be scrutinised quite closely for their impact on younger workers.

Policies adversely affecting older workers (other than retirement ages) have also been subject to fairly rigorous scrutiny by the Court. In *Mangold*, national law allowed firms to conclude successive fixed-term contracts with workers over the age of 52.[102] It was argued that this would promote employment among older workers. But the Court rejected this claim, pointing out that the legislation did not apply only to those who were unemployed and seeking to enter the labour market, but also to those who were already in work. The legislation deprived workers in the latter group of job security and was found not to be proportionate.

In relation to retirement ages, the Court has insisted that they must be scrutinised (despite Recital 14 of the Directive, which states that it is 'without prejudice' to compulsory retirement ages). Nevertheless, the Court's review has been relatively light touch. In *Palacios*, the Court accepted the argument that retirement ages were necessary in order to share employment opportunities across the generations.[103] It appears that there may be two possible qualifications to this. First, in *Palacios*, the retiring employees were eligible for a pension. The Court saw this as a safeguard for them and would probably be unsympathetic to the compulsory retirement of workers who would not receive a pension, though in *Rosenbladt* it rejected an argument that the pension on offer was insufficient.[104] Second, in *Palacios* and *Rosenbladt*, the retirement rules were determined by collective agreement. The Court seemed attracted to this because it allowed for the specific situation of particular types of job to be

---

[100] *Seldon v Clarkson Wright & Jakes* [2012] UKSC 16, [2012] ICR 716.
[101] Above n 55.
[102] *Mangold* (n 53).
[103] Case C-411/05 *Palacios de la Villa v Cortefiel Servicios* [2007] ECR I-8531 [72]–[75].
[104] Case C-45/09 *Rosenbladt v Oellerking Gebäudereinigungsges* [2010] ECR 9391.

taken into account.[105] More generally, the Court seems to be at pains to avoid generalisations in this area and to encourage context-specific decision-making. In *Age Concern*, the Court was keen to stress that the final decision on proportionality lay with the national court and did not try to dictate the outcome.[106]

These issues came before the Supreme Court in the *Seldon* case, which concerned a partner in a firm of solicitors who was forced to retire at the age of 65.[107] This case differed from the retirement age cases considered by the CJEU because it concerned a provision in an individual contract of employment, rather than national policy or a collective agreement. As Baroness Hale explained, this gave rise to particular difficulties of interpretation because Article 6 (quoted above) is aimed at the Member States. She said:

> It seems, therefore, that the United Kingdom has chosen to give employers and partnerships the flexibility to choose which objectives to pursue, provided always that (i) these objectives can count as legitimate objectives of a public interest nature within the meaning of the Directive and (ii) are consistent with the social policy aims of the state and (iii) the means used are proportionate, that is both appropriate to the aim and (reasonably) necessary to achieve it.[108]

This means that a narrower range of arguments will be admissible under Article 6 than would be the case when justifying indirect discrimination under Article 2(2). Baroness Hale noted that the CJEU had identified two legitimate aims: intergenerational fairness (which might include encouraging older people to retire in order to create opportunities for younger people), and 'dignity', in the sense of avoiding the embarrassment of having to force older workers out using arguments about incompetence.[109] As Baroness Hale pointed out, the latter risks stereotyping older workers as incompetent, contrary to the broader aim of equality law to encourage individual assessment rather than stereotyping. She held that the firm in question had pursued legitimate aims but remitted the question of whether the choice of 65 as the retirement age was proportionate in the circumstances. The tribunal's decision to accept the employer's reasoning on this point was recently upheld by the EAT.[110] Although the range of arguments open to an employer here is limited by the social policy objectives of the state, the aims accepted by the CJEU are wide-ranging and appear easy for employers to satisfy. As a result, it seems likely that compulsory retirement will remain a feature of English employment law for some time to come.

6.5.2 Disability

This section will consider the definition of disability before introducing some additional discrimination concepts which apply to the protected characteristic of disability: disability-related discrimination and the duty to make reasonable adjustments. It is worth remembering that the law on disability discrimination is not symmetrical – it does not protect non-disabled people in the same way that

---

[105] ibid [49].
[106] Case C-388/07 *Incorporated Trustees of the National Council on Ageing (Age Concern England)* v *Secretary of State for Business, Enterprise and Regulatory Reform* [2009] ECR I-1569 [52].
[107] *Seldon* v *Clarkson Wright & Jakes* [2012] UKSC 16, [2012] ICR 716.
[108] ibid [55].
[109] ibid [56]–[58].
[110] *Seldon* v *Clarkson Wright & Jakes* [2014] IRLR 748.

sex discrimination law protects men and women – so there is no restriction on an employer *favouring* disabled people in employment.

Definitions

The literature identifies two main types of definition of disability.[111] 'Medical' definitions focus on what the individual cannot do because of mental or physical impairment. 'Social' definitions focus on the interaction between the individual's impairment and socially constructed barriers. For example, an individual with a physical impairment would not experience difficulties at work if the workplace was designed to be accessible to people with physical impairments. Social definitions are generally regarded as more helpful because they focus less on what a particular disabled person cannot do (compared with others) and more on society's responsibility to accommodate people with a range of different abilities.

The EU Framework Directive does not contain a definition of disability and in the early case of *Chacon Navas*, the Court appeared to adopt a medical definition.[112] This decision was heavily criticised and was difficult to reconcile with the UN Convention on the Rights of Persons with Disabilities, which the EU ratified in 2010.[113] This states, in Article 1, that:

> Persons with disabilities include those who have long-term physical, mental, intellectual or sensory impairments which in interaction with various barriers may hinder their full and effective participation in society on an equal basis with others.

In the recent *HK Danmark (Ring)* case, the Court revisited its approach, noting that the Framework Directive fell to be interpreted in the light of the UN Convention and adopting the UN definition.[114]

The UK definition is long-established, predating both the Framework Directive and the Convention. It is currently found in s. 6(1) EA 2010:

> A person (P) has a disability if–
>
> (a) P has a physical or mental impairment, and
> (b) the impairment has a substantial and long-term adverse effect on P's ability to carry out normal day-to-day activities.

It seems likely that this definition will have to be interpreted expansively in the light of the evolving EU definition. There is also some detailed guidance on the meaning of 'disability' in Schedule 1 EA 2010 and the Equality Act 2010 (Disability) Regulations 2010.[115] In terms of interpreting the basic definition, the two key points are that a 'long-term' effect is defined as having lasted, or being likely to last, for at least 12 months,[116] and a person is regarded as having a disability if he or she would suffer a 'substantial . . . adverse effect' without medical treatment or other help he

---

[111] DL Hosking, 'Great Expectations: Protection from Discrimination because of Disability in Community Law' (2006) 31 EL Rev 667; Lisa Waddington, 'Case C-13/05, *Chacon Navas* v *Eurest Colectividades SA*' (2007) 44 CML Rev 487.

[112] Case C-13/05 *Chacón Navas* v *Eurest Colectividades SA* [2006] ECR I-6467.

[113] Gráinne de Búrca, 'The European Union in the Negotiation of the UN Disability Convention' (2010) 35 EL Rev 174.

[114] Case C-335/11 *HK Danmark (Ring)* v *Dansk almennyttigt Boligselskab* [2013] ICR 851.

[115] SI 2010/2128.

[116] EA 2010, sch 1, para 2.

or she is receiving.[117] The Schedule extends the definition of disability to protect people with progressive conditions. Cancer, HIV and multiple sclerosis are all deemed to be disabilities by para 6, regardless of the effect these conditions are currently having on a particular individual, and under para 8, a person with a progressive condition is protected if the condition has some effect on his or her abilities even if that effect has not yet become substantial. In these respects, English law is much more protective than the basic definition might suggest. The Regulations exclude certain conditions from protection. These include alcohol and nicotine addiction under reg. 3 (though, importantly, not consequential conditions like liver disease or lung cancer), and tendencies to commit certain criminal acts under reg. 4.

A question of some current interest is the treatment of obesity within disability discrimination law. The CJEU in the recent *Kaltoft* case has held that obesity is not a disability in itself but may amount to a disability where it impedes the individual's participation in the workplace, for example, because it reduces his or her mobility.[118] The EAT in *Walker v Sita Information Networking Computing Ltd* reached a similar conclusion.[119] The claimant was not disabled simply because he was obese, but his obesity (coupled with other factors) meant that he had impairments which amounted to disabilities.

Additional concepts for disability discrimination cases

The protected characteristic of disability attracts special treatment in the legislation. This is because – in contrast to the other characteristics – disability is more likely to have an impact on a person's ability to do a particular job. So, for example, while we generally think of someone's race as being irrelevant to their work, the same could not be said of a serious visual impairment, or bipolar disorder (of course, always depending on the job in question). The law supplements direct and indirect discrimination where the protected characteristic is disability with two additional concepts – discrimination arising from disability and the duty to make reasonable adjustments – in order to achieve a better balance between the interests of people with disabilities and employers. We will see in later sections that these approaches (particularly the duty to make adjustments) might usefully be extended to other protected characteristics too.

Discrimination arising from disability Discrimination arising from disability is addressed in s. 15 EA 2010:

(1) A person (A) discriminates against a disabled person (B) if–

    (a) A treats B unfavourably because of something arising in consequence of B's disability, and

    (b) A cannot show that the treatment is a proportionate means of achieving a legitimate aim.

(2) Subsection (1) does not apply if A shows that A did not know, and could not reasonably have been expected to know, that B had the disability.

---

[117] ibid para 5.
[118] Case C-354/13 *Fag og Arbejde (FOA) (Kaltoft) v Kommunernes Landsforening (Billund)* [2015] IRLR 146.
[119] [2013] Eq LR 476.

This deals with the situation in which the employer discriminates not simply because of the person's disability but because of 'something arising in consequence' of it.[120] It would apply where, for example, the employer dismisses an employee who has a disability because he or she is less productive or off sick more often than other employees. The employer has two defences: that its action was proportionate or that it did not know about the disability. It remains to be seen how strictly the proportionality test will be applied here. To continue our example, it is not clear how much of a difference in productivity or attendance might be required before a court would be willing to accept an employer's argument that the employee should be dismissed.

The duty to make reasonable adjustments The duty to make reasonable adjustments is an important special feature of disability discrimination law. It acknowledges the fact that, in many instances, people with disabilities are disadvantaged because jobs and workplaces are not adapted to their needs, and it requires employers to make adaptations unless it is unreasonable to expect them to do so. It reflects the need to remove 'barriers' emphasised by the social definition of disability discussed above.

The duty operates in three situations.[121] First, it applies where the employer adopts a PCP which puts a disabled person 'at a substantial disadvantage'.[122] For example, the employer might insist that a particular job can only be done on a full-time basis, but this would disadvantage an employee with a disability that makes him or her tire easily who can only work part-time. Second, it applies where a physical feature of the employer's premises puts the disabled person 'at a substantial disadvantage'.[123] The obvious example here is a workplace with steps that is inaccessible to wheelchair users. Third, it applies where the disabled person would be 'at a substantial disadvantage' unless the employer provides an 'auxiliary aid'.[124] For example, this could be used to get the employer to provide software to voice documents for a visually impaired employee. In all three situations, the duty is qualified by a 'reasonableness' test. This means that the employer may be able to refuse to make an adjustment where, for example, it would be prohibitively expensive to do so. But where the adjustment is reasonable, a failure to make it constitutes discrimination.[125]

Perhaps one of the most important functions of the duty to make reasonable adjustments has been to require the employer to consider redeploying an employee who becomes disabled and remains able to work but not in his or her original job. A leading example of this is the decision of the House of Lords in *Archibald*.[126] In that case, the claimant was a road-sweeper who was unable to walk because she suffered a complication after undergoing surgery. She applied for numerous office jobs but was unsuccessful because she did not have relevant experience. It was held that it would be a reasonable adjustment for her employer simply to transfer her to an appropriate office job when it fell vacant without forcing her to compete against other candidates.

---

[120] This reverses *Malcolm v Lewisham LBC* [2008] UKHL 43, [2008] 1 AC 1399.

[121] It cannot be relied on in an 'associational' way: see *Hainsworth v Ministry of Defence* [2014] EWCA Civ 763, [2014] IRLR 728.

[122] EA 2010, s 20(3).

[123] ibid s 20(4).

[124] ibid s 20(5).

[125] See, further, the Equality Act 2010 (Disability) Regulations 2010, SI 2010/2128.

[126] *Archibald v Fife Council* [2004] UKHL 32, [2004] ICR 954. See also *Chief Constable of South Yorkshire v Jelic* [2010] IRLR 744.

6.5.3 Gender reassignment

The law's protection of transgender people at work developed from the law on sex discrimination at EU level, but gender reassignment is now regarded as a protected characteristic in its own right. The ECHR has also been influential in bringing about broader legislative change in this area.

In *P v S and Cornwall CC*, the Court of Justice held that EU law on sex discrimination should be interpreted to protect transgender people.[127] It stated:

> Such discrimination is based, essentially if not exclusively, on the sex of the person concerned. Where a person is dismissed on the ground that he or she intends to undergo, or has undergone, gender reassignment, he or she is treated unfavourably by comparison with persons of the sex to which he or she was deemed to belong before undergoing gender reassignment.[128]

The UK government amended the Sex Discrimination Act 1975 (SDA) in response to this decision. The relevant provision today is s. 7(1) EA 2010:

> A person has the protected characteristic of gender reassignment if the person is proposing to undergo, is undergoing or has undergone a process (or part of a process) for the purpose of reassigning the person's sex by changing physiological or other attributes of sex.

The Act uses the term 'transsexual person' to refer to someone protected by s. 7(1). The provision offers comprehensive protection against discrimination when a person 'proposes' to undergo gender reassignment, against discrimination during the process, and against discrimination because an individual has, in the past, undergone gender reassignment. It is important to note that this provision is broader than its SDA predecessor, in that it does not refer to a process 'under medical supervision'. This means that a person is protected by the section if he or she simply chooses to live as his or her target gender without undergoing any medical treatment.

The core concepts of direct discrimination, indirect discrimination and harassment all apply to this characteristic. Specific provision is made in s. 16 for the situation in which a person is absent from work because of gender reassignment. The employer may not treat him or her less favourably than a person who is absent for other reasons.

For many years, transgender people experienced serious difficulties because the law did not allow them to change their birth certificates and other official documents to reflect their target gender. This was changed by the Gender Recognition Act 2004 which was introduced as a result of the ECtHR's ruling in *Goodwin v UK*.[129] This may make it easier for those people who do not wish to disclose their transgender status at work to keep the matter private.

6.5.4 Marriage and civil partnership

Individuals are protected against discrimination under s. 8 EA 2010 if they have the characteristic of being married or being a civil partner. It appears that the impetus for protecting this characteristic is largely domestic in origin. 'Marital or family status' was mentioned as a form of sex discrimination in the 1976 Equal Treatment Directive

---

[127] Case C-13/94 *P v S and Cornwall CC* [1996] ECR I-2143.
[128] ibid [21].
[129] (2002) 35 EHRR 18.

(though the UK did not take any action to implement the 'family status' element) but this provision was not carried forward into the Recast Directive.

The original underlying motivation for this characteristic is linked to sex discrimination. Historically, women were required by law to give up certain jobs when they got married, and even after this had been abolished, there was often a social expectation to that effect.[130] Thus, the treatment of marriage as a protected characteristic was largely intended to protect married women, though the protection is available to any married person. Nowadays, marriage is available to opposite- and same-sex couples,[131] and civil partnership to same-sex couples.[132] The protection afforded to people who are married or in civil partnerships may be an important additional layer of protection against discrimination because of a person's sexual orientation. ·

It is worth noting that the provision is not 'symmetrical' in the sense that it does not protect people with other types of family status (single, engaged, divorced, widowed or cohabiting, for example) against discrimination for those reasons. In these cases, the ECHR may have some relevance because of the protection afforded by Article 8 ECHR (the right to respect for private and family life). It might be possible to challenge the limited nature of s. 8 EA 2010 before the ECtHR, or perhaps to persuade a domestic court to interpret it broadly using s. 3 HRA.

There are two important variants to the usual equality concepts in relation to marriage and civil partnership. First, under s. 13(4), a person who is married or in a civil partnership is only protected against direct discrimination because of that characteristic if he or she in fact has the characteristic. It is not possible to bring a claim of discrimination by association or perception in relation to this characteristic. Second, it is not possible for a person to claim that he or she has been harassed because of his or her marriage or civil partnership status.[133] These differences add unnecessary complexity to the law.

In practice, it seems plausible to suggest that, in many cases, an employer might treat a person less favourably not because of his or her marriage or civil partnership as such, but because of the identity or characteristics of his or her spouse or partner. Where those characteristics are, in themselves, protected, this may be actionable as associational discrimination on another ground. So, for example, where the employer treats an employee less favourably because his or her spouse has a disability, or is of a particular religion, the employee could challenge this as discrimination because of disability or religion. However, the law is much less clear on whether an employer discriminates because of marriage or civil partnership where the employer has a problem with the identity of the individual's spouse or partner. In the *Hawkins* case, the claimant was dismissed because her husband was the chief executive of the company employing her, and he had appointed her in breach of an instruction not to employ members of his own family.[134] Her claim failed because the EAT found that she had been dismissed because of their close relationship and not because of the fact that they were married. By contrast, in the *Dunn* case, the claimant and her

---

[130] Sex Disqualification (Removal) Act 1919.
[131] Marriage (Same Sex Couples) Act 2013.
[132] Civil Partnership Act 2004.
[133] EA 2010, s 26(5).
[134] *Hawkins* v *Atex Group Ltd* [2012] ICR 1315 (EAT).

husband were employed by the same employer.[135] She complained of discrimination because she was married when the employer raised concerns relating to her husband during grievance proceedings she had brought. The EAT in that case held that discrimination because of being married included discrimination because of being married to a particular person. It is submitted that the approach in *Hawkins* is preferable. An employer may have various legitimate reasons for treating an employee differently because he or she is in a close relationship with another employee (as in *Hawkins* itself, to prevent accusations of favouritism) and it would be unfortunate if this were actionable when they were married or in a civil partnership but not when they were in any other type of relationship. The fact that the claimant in *Hawkins* would have been treated the same way if she had been the chief executive's partner or sister suggests that their marriage was not the 'reason' for the treatment.

6.5.5 Pregnancy and maternity

The law on pregnancy and maternity is closely linked with the law on sex discrimination. In the early years of equality law, pregnancy and maternity discrimination was not addressed explicitly in the legislation, so cases brought by women because of this characteristic had to be framed as sex discrimination claims.

The SDA 1975 as originally enacted did not specifically address pregnancy, so it was left to the courts to determine whether this should be treated as a form of sex discrimination. In some early rulings, the English courts held that different treatment because of pregnancy could not be different treatment because of sex, because no male comparator was available.[136] The courts reversed this approach but devised a comparator by comparing a pregnant woman with a man who was unavailable for work because of illness.[137] The CJEU held in the *Dekker* case that, since pregnancy could only affect women, pregnancy discrimination claims should be treated as sex discrimination claims without the need to find a male comparator.[138] The Court has also extended the protection afforded to pregnancy to cover pregnancy-related illness, during the pregnancy itself and up to the end of maternity leave.[139] Attempts by employers to argue that decisions to dismiss pregnant women were due to their unavailability for work at the required time, rather than to the pregnancy itself, have been roundly rejected by the Court.[140] Although there is no obligation on the state to arrange for a woman to receive full pay while she is on maternity leave, her other terms and conditions must be maintained, and she should benefit from any improvements, such as pay rises, occurring while she is away.[141]

---

[135] *Dunn v Institute of Cemetery and Crematorium Management* [2012] ICR 941 (EAT).

[136] *Turley v Allders Department Stores Ltd* [1980] ICR 66 (EAT).

[137] *Hayes v Malleable Working Men's Club and Institute* [1985] ICR 703 (EAT).

[138] Case C-177/88 *Dekker v Stichting Vormingscentrum voor Jonge Volwassenen Plus* [1990] ECR I-3941.

[139] Case C-394/96 *Brown v Rentokil Ltd* [1998] ECR I-4185; Case C-179/88 *Handels-og Kontorfunktionaererernes Forbund i Danmark (Hertz) v Dansk Arbejdsgiverforening (Aldi Marked K/S)* [1990] ECR I-3979.

[140] Case C-32/93 *Webb v EMO Air Cargo (UK) Ltd* [1994] ECR I-3567; Case C-109/00 *Tele Danmark A/S v Handels-og Kontorfunktionaererernes Forbund i Danmark* [2001] ECR I-6993.

[141] Case C-342/93 *Gillespie v Northern Health and Social Services Board* [1996] ECR I-475.

The developing case-law eventually brought about an amendment to what was then the Equal Treatment Directive, and the Recast Directive now provides that discrimination because of pregnancy or maternity leave is a form of sex discrimination.[142] The Pregnant Workers Directive provides for maternity leave[143] and for protection against dismissal.[144] The right to return to work after maternity leave is found in the Recast Directive, Article 15.[145]

EA 2010, s. 18, now deals explicitly with pregnancy and maternity discrimination:

(2) A person (A) discriminates against a woman if, in the protected period in relation to a pregnancy of hers, A treats her unfavourably–

(a) because of the pregnancy, or

(b) because of illness suffered by her as a result of it.

(3) A person (A) discriminates against a woman if A treats her unfavourably because she is on compulsory maternity leave.

(4) A person (A) discriminates against a woman if A treats her unfavourably because she is exercising or seeking to exercise, or has exercised or sought to exercise, the right to ordinary or additional maternity leave.

(5) For the purposes of subsection (2), if the treatment of a woman is in implementation of a decision taken in the protected period, the treatment is to be regarded as occurring in that period (even if the implementation is not until after the end of that period).

(6) The protected period, in relation to a woman's pregnancy, begins when the pregnancy begins, and ends–

(a) if she has the right to ordinary and additional maternity leave, at the end of the additional maternity leave period or (if earlier) when she returns to work after the pregnancy;

(b) if she does not have that right, at the end of the period of 2 weeks beginning with the end of the pregnancy . . .

This reflects the EU materials discussed above, for example, in the express reference to illness and in the absence of any requirement to find a comparator, captured by the idea of 'unfavourable' treatment. However, it is limited to direct discrimination: it does not cover discrimination by association or perception, indirect discrimination or harassment. These claims must still be brought as sex discrimination claims, as must any claims relating to the pregnancy but arising outside the 'protected period'.[146] Claims relating to breast-feeding are deemed to constitute sex discrimination claims under s. 13(6) EA 2010.

Also by virtue of s. 13(6), men cannot challenge special treatment afforded to women on grounds of pregnancy as a form of sex discrimination against them. This is an example of one of the problems we highlighted with equality in section 6.2 above: that different treatment may be required to achieve equal results.

---

[142] Directive 2006/54, art 2(2).
[143] Pregnant Workers Directive, Directive 92/85/EEC, art 8.
[144] ibid art 10.
[145] Directive 2006/54.
[146] Claims relating to pay are addressed separately in EA 2010, ss 72–76.

6.5.6 Race

The Race Directive prohibits discrimination on the ground of 'racial or ethnic origin'.[147] These terms are not defined. English law is wider than this. EA 2010, s. 9(1), provides that:

Race includes–

(a) colour;
(b) nationality;
(c) ethnic or national origins.

The Enterprise and Regulatory Reform Act 2013, s. 97, amends the Act so that there is an obligation on a minister to amend s. 9 to include caste as an aspect of race. The EHRC has recently published two reports on the issue which will contribute to the government's consultation on the new caste provisions.[148] This will remedy a gap in the current law.[149]

As the definition makes clear, English law treats nationality discrimination as a form of race discrimination. But the EU Race Directive does not cover nationality discrimination. This is because EU law is ambivalent on the matter. On the one hand, a key objective of the EU is to create an internal market in which workers can move freely between the Member States. Thus, discrimination against citizens of EU Member States on the grounds of their nationality is clearly prohibited by the EU law on free movement of workers.[150] On the other hand, although the EU has developed some measures relating to migration into the EU from third countries, this is an area that remains largely under the Member States' control. The EU measures are limited in scope and several Member States (including the UK) have opted not to participate in most of them.[151] Thus, EU law requires a prohibition on nationality discrimination, but only in relation to people from the EU, and not by virtue of the Race Directive.

Another area of ambiguity is the relationship between race discrimination and religious discrimination. In some cases, there is significant overlap between the two categories, with a particular group sharing a race and a religion, though this is by no means always the case. In the early years of the equality legislation, religious discrimination was not prohibited, so the courts adopted a broad definition of race so that some religious groups with a shared ethnic heritage were also protected. In the *Mandla* case, for example, it was held that Sikhs were an ethnic group for the purposes of a race discrimination claim.[152] Now that religious discrimination is prohibited by law, there is less need to manipulate the distinction between the two types of claim. However, the distinction may still be relevant in some instances. Although some commentators may want to resist the conclusion that there is a hierarchy between different protected characteristics, it seems likely that an employer's justification for indirect race discrimination would be scrutinised more strictly than an employer's justification for indirect religious discrimination. The issue arose in the

---

[147] Directive 2000/43, art 1.
[148] M Dhanda *et al.*, *Caste in Britain: Socio-legal Review* (Research Report No. 91; EHRC 2014); *Caste in Britain: Experts' Seminar and Stakeholders' Workshop* (Research Report No. 92; EHRC 2014).
[149] In some cases, caste discrimination might be addressed via provisions on religious discrimination, but most forms of caste system do not have religious origins.
[150] See Chapter 3.
[151] See Chapter 3.
[152] *Mandla* v *Dowell Lee* [1983] ICR 385 (HL).

JFS case, in which a student was denied admission to a faith school because he did not meet the Chief Rabbi's criterion for being Jewish.[153] The criterion was that the student's mother should be Jewish, either by descent or by conversion according to Orthodox principles. The claimant's mother had converted to Judaism but not according to Orthodox principles. A majority in the Supreme Court held that the school's application of the criterion constituted discrimination on grounds of race. Applying the test for ethnicity drawn from *Mandla*, Jewish people could be identified as an ethnic group based on a 'long shared history' and a 'cultural tradition'. Although the school's criterion identified a different (but overlapping) group of people as Jewish when compared with the *Mandla* test, that criterion relied to some extent on descent and was thus to be regarded as a criterion of ethnic origin. The school argued that its intention was to identify students as Jewish on religious grounds, but the majority rejected this argument because of the irrelevance of motive in direct discrimination cases.

The three main discrimination concepts apply to the protected characteristic of race. Specific provision is made in s. 13(5) EA 2010 to confirm that segregation constitutes direct race discrimination.

6.5.7 Religion or belief

Religion or belief discrimination is addressed by the Framework Directive, Article 1, and by EA 2010, s. 10. Freedom of thought, conscience and religion is also guaranteed by Article 9 ECHR.[154] There are three main issues to consider in relation to this characteristic: the definition of 'religion or belief', the treatment of 'manifestations' of religious belief, particularly where these clash with the rights of others, and the exemptions for religious organisations.

EA 2010, s. 10 defines religion or belief as follows:

(1) Religion means any religion and a reference to religion includes a reference to a lack of religion.

(2) Belief means any religious or philosophical belief and a reference to belief includes a reference to a lack of belief.

These definitions make clear that agnosticism and atheism are protected as well as religious beliefs, but beyond that, they leave it to the courts to determine what counts as a religion and what counts as a philosophical belief that must be protected under the Act. In undertaking this task, the courts are bound by the HRA to take into account the ECtHR's Article 9 jurisprudence on the matter.

The most recent judicial attempt to define 'religion' is that of the Supreme Court in *R (Hodgkin) v Registrar-General*.[155] Although this case arose in a different context, and Lord Toulson was at pains to emphasise that he was not seeking to lay down a universal definition, his formulation is helpful:

I would describe religion in summary as a spiritual or non-secular belief system, held by a group of adherents, which claims to explain mankind's place in the universe and relationship

---

[153] *R (E) v JFS Governing Body* [2009] UKSC 15, [2010] 2 AC 728.
[154] We saw above that art 9 may also affect the approach to the concept of indirect discrimination, particularly because the ECtHR does not appear to require group disadvantage.
[155] [2013] UKSC 77, [2014] AC 610.

with the infinite, and to teach its adherents how they are to live their lives in conformity
with the spiritual understanding associated with the belief system. By spiritual or non-
secular I mean a belief system which goes beyond that which can be perceived by the senses
or ascertained by the application of science ... Such a belief system may or may not involve
belief in a supreme being, but it does involve a belief that there is more to be understood
about mankind's nature and relationship to the universe than can be gained from the senses
or from science.[156]

It is important to note that, even if an individual's belief system might not warrant
the label 'religion' (for example, because it is not spiritual in nature or is not shared
by other people), this is unlikely to matter very much if the individual can show that
his or her belief is protected as a 'philosophical belief'. The requirements for
protection as a philosophical belief derived from the ECtHR case-law[157] were
helpfully summarised in the *Grainger* case:

(i) The belief must be genuinely held. (ii) It must be a belief and not . . . an opinion or
viewpoint based on the present state of information available. (iii) It must be a belief as to
a weighty and substantial aspect of human life and behaviour. (iv) It must attain a certain
level of cogency, seriousness, cohesion and importance. (v) It must be worthy of respect in
a democratic society, be not incompatible with human dignity and not conflict with the
fundamental rights of others . . .[158]

In *Grainger* itself, the individual's sincerely held belief in the dangers of climate
change and the moral duty of everyone to take steps to address it was held to qualify
as a philosophical belief for the purposes of equality law.

An interesting question is whether an individual's political opinions are
protected under this set of provisions. It seems unlikely that, in most cases, an
individual's political opinions would qualify as a 'belief' rather than as an 'opinion'
within the definition just given, though there might be some exceptions to this in
individual cases. Even if an individual cannot argue discrimination based on
political opinion or affiliation, the law does offer limited protection on this ground
in the dismissal context. An employee who claims to have been dismissed for this
reason has the possibility of bringing unfair dismissal proceedings without the
need to fulfil the two-year qualifying period, and might be able to invoke other
Convention rights (either freedom of expression under Article 10 or freedom of
association under Article 11) to reinforce his or her claim.[159] However, in the
public sector, some jobs carry with them restrictions on an individual's political
activities with the aim of maintaining the neutrality of certain civil servants and
local government officials.[160]

Although some employers might discriminate directly on grounds of religion or
belief (for example, because of prejudice against people of a particular faith), in many
cases problems are likely to arise at work because of an individual's 'manifestation'
of his or her religious belief. There are various possible examples of this, but obvious
ones include wishing to observe a particular dress code (which might conflict with

---

[156] ibid [57].
[157] *Campbell v UK* (1982) 4 EHRR 293 [36]; *Eweida*, above n 58, [81].
[158] *Grainger Plc v Nicholson* [2010] ICR 360 (EAT) [24].
[159] Enterprise and Regulatory Reform Act 2013, s 13, inserting new s 108(4) ERA 1996. This responds
to the ruling in *Redfearn v UK*, above n 58.
[160] For example, the Local Government Officers (Political Restrictions) Regulations 1990, SI 1990/851.

an employer's uniform policy), not wishing to work on certain days or at certain times because of the requirements of religious observance (which might conflict with an employer's work schedule), and not wishing to perform certain job requirements because they conflict with religious beliefs. In general terms, these cases constitute examples of indirect discrimination: the claimant argues that the employer is imposing a PCP which is harder for members of his or her religious group to comply with than it is for others who do not share his or her beliefs. In the domestic courts, cases of this kind are likely to be argued under EA 2010, but this must be interpreted compatibly with Article 9 ECHR, so the ECtHR's jurisprudence is also relevant, and of course claimants who are dissatisfied with the outcome in the domestic courts may pursue their cases to the ECtHR. The CJEU's jurisprudence on this topic has yet to develop.

Initially, the ECtHR was unsympathetic towards claimants who argued that their employer had interfered with their right to manifest their religious beliefs. In the *Stedman* case, a dispute about working hours, the Court held that the individual was free to resign his or her job and seek alternative employment that could be reconciled with his or her religious duties.[161] However, in the more recent *Eweida* group of cases, the Court accepted that this was a harsh position to adopt (given the difficulty of finding alternative employment).[162] It held instead that it was appropriate to examine whether the UK had fulfilled its positive obligation to ensure that national law enabled a balance to be struck between the individual's right and the employer's interests.[163] This achieves a degree of alignment between the approach under Article 9 and the approach under EA 2010, because in both contexts, the proportionality of the employer's interference with the individual's right plays a decisive role.

The facts of the *Eweida* group of cases offer some useful illustrations of how proportionality operates in this area. Two of the claimants, Ms Chaplin and Ms Eweida, challenged their employer's refusal, as part of a uniform policy, to allow them to wear crosses at work. The Court recognised this as a manifestation of religious belief even though it is not generally regarded as a duty by Christians (and was not so regarded by the claimants). The Court then considered the employer's reason for banning the wearing of crosses. In *Chaplin*, the Court held that the employer's policy was proportionate because the claimant was a nurse and there were health and safety objections to the wearing of loose jewellery while working with patients.[164] In *Eweida*, the Court held that the employer's policy (which had been changed by the time of the hearing anyway) was disproportionate because its aim was to maintain a certain corporate image, and because this was insufficient to outweigh the claimant's Article 9 rights, not least because people of other faiths had been permitted to wear certain items of religious clothing.[165]

The *Ladele* and *McFarlane* cases (also part of the *Eweida* group) offer useful illustrations of the approach to be taken where the individual in question refuses on grounds of conscience to perform a certain aspect of his or her job. Mr McFarlane

---

[161] *Stedman v UK* (1997) 23 EHRR CD 168.
[162] *Eweida* (n 58), [83]–[84].
[163] Or, in public sector cases, whether the state itself had struck a proportionate balance.
[164] *Eweida* (n 58), [98]–[100].
[165] ibid [94]–[95].

worked for the counselling organisation Relate, and refused to provide counselling to same-sex couples in contravention of Relate's equality policy. Ms Ladele worked for Islington LBC as a registrar and refused to perform civil partnership ceremonies for same-sex couples in contravention of the Council's equality policy. Both argued that this was because they did not agree with same-sex relationships because of their particular Christian beliefs. The only significant difference between the two cases was that Mr McFarlane had been aware of Relate's requirement to provide services to same-sex couples when he took the job, whereas the civil partnerships legislation had been introduced some time after Ms Ladele had started working for Islington LBC. However, in both cases, the Court held that (although the individuals suffered the serious consequence of losing their jobs) the employer's policy was proportionate because it pursued the important objective of providing a service without discrimination on grounds of sexual orientation.[166]

A final point to note is that religious organisations may themselves wish to discriminate both on religious grounds (to ensure that people holding positions of authority within the religion are believers) and other grounds (for example, where the religion does not allow women to hold positions of authority). This is addressed by two provisions in EA 2010, Schedule 9. Under para 3, employers with a religious 'ethos' (which does not just include religions but also covers related organisations, like faith schools) are allowed to use religious belief as an occupational requirement:

> A person (A) with an ethos based on religion or belief does not contravene a provision mentioned in paragraph 1(2) by applying in relation to work a requirement to be of a particular religion or belief if A shows that, having regard to that ethos and to the nature or context of the work–
>
> (a) it is an occupational requirement,
> (b) the application of the requirement is a proportionate means of achieving a legitimate aim, and
> (c) the person to whom A applies the requirement does not meet it (or A has reasonable grounds for not being satisfied that the person meets it).

In general terms, the proportionality test serves to ensure that there is a reasonably close link between the religious requirement and the person's job. So, for example, while a Christian church would be able to require its clergy to be Christians, it would not be able to apply the same requirement to cleaners or caterers, because their beliefs are not relevant to their job performance.

The other type of requirement – where the religion includes requirements that discriminate on other grounds – is addressed in para 2. This applies where the employment is 'for the purposes of an organised religion'. This is narrower than the concept of an employer with a religious 'ethos' under para 3. It allows the employer to discriminate where it is necessary either to 'comply with the doctrines of the religion' or 'to avoid conflicting with the strongly held religious convictions of a significant number of the religion's followers'. The application of these requirements may raise some sensitive issues in practice, particularly where a court is called upon to determine what religions require or what their followers believe. Paragraph 2 allows the employer to discriminate on a variety of grounds, including sex, sexual orientation and marital status (including, in this instance, being divorced).

---

[166] ibid [102]–[110].

6.5.8 Sex

The law on sex discrimination is well-established. A requirement to ensure that women could claim equal pay for equal work was included in the original Article 119 of the Treaty of Rome, and the UK has had sex equality law since the Equal Pay Act 1970 and the Sex Discrimination Act 1975. The current requirements are found in Article 157 TFEU, the Recast Directive, Directive 2006/54, and s. 11 and ss. 64–71 EA 2010. The term 'sex' in this context refers to being a man or a woman.[167]

One of the particular features of sex discrimination law is the historic distinction between pay discrimination and other forms of discrimination. In relation to the other protected characteristics it is, of course, unlawful to pay someone less than another person doing the same job because of his or her race, religious belief and so on. But this is dealt with through the ordinary concepts of discrimination and not through a special body of equal pay law. The reason for the distinction seems to be the particular prevalence of pay discrimination on gender grounds. For example, prior to the Equal Pay Act 1970, it was common for firms to have separate pay grades for women. Often, these grades were similar to or lower than the grades for men doing unskilled work, even where the women's work required special skills. Employers were given five years' notice of the Act to give them time to address this deep-seated differentiation. When the EA 2010 was enacted, some commentators regarded it as a good opportunity to bring sex into line with the other protected characteristics by abandoning the separate treatment of pay discrimination. However, the government chose not to take this route, so pay is still dealt with through separate provisions (in ss. 64–71).[168] There are some important differences between equal pay law and other kinds of discrimination law. For example, equal pay law generally requires a woman to compare herself with a real, not hypothetical, man doing like work or work of equal value (though there are exceptions), but it has a longer limitation period for bringing a claim (six years rather than three months). Although separate 'women's grades' are a thing of the past, statistics show that women earn, on average, about 80% of what men earn, so the 'gender pay gap' remains unresolved.[169]

A key issue in sex discrimination law has long been the treatment of pregnancy, maternity and child-care responsibilities. We examined the treatment of pregnancy discrimination and its relationship to sex discrimination in the section on pregnancy, above. Here, we will focus on child-care and career breaks.

After maternity leave, a woman may want to return to work part-time, or to organise a job-share, in order to balance work and family time. In general terms, the courts have been willing to acknowledge that the burden of child-care tends to fall more heavily on women than on men. This means that a woman is generally able to argue that a requirement to do a particular job full-time is indirectly discriminatory: it is a PCP that puts women at a particular disadvantage compared with men.[170] The outcome of the case will then depend on whether the employer can put forward a proportionate justification for the PCP. While this type of claim is an important recognition of the current reality of many women's lives, it is regarded by some commentators as problematic because of its potential to entrench the stereotype that

---

[167] The law in this context does not recognise the possibility of an individual's gender being indeterminate.
[168] See Chapter 7.
[169] David Bovill, *Patterns of Pay: Results from the Annual Survey of Hours and Earnings, 1997 to 2012* (Office for National Statistics 2013) 10.
[170] *Home Office v Holmes* [1984] ICR 678 (EAT).

child-care is women's responsibility and its limited capacity to promote the cause of 'equal parenting' in couple families. It is worth noting that there is also a right (now available to anyone) to request flexible working, which could also enable an individual to do a job part-time.[171] However, it is relatively easy for an employer to refuse such a request. As a result, the indirect sex discrimination claim remains the stronger option because of the proportionality test. Discrimination against a woman because she is a part-time worker can also be addressed as a form of indirect sex discrimination (because more women than men work part-time),[172] though there is also a right not to be discriminated against on grounds of working part-time under the Part-Time Workers Regulations which is available to men and women.[173]

Because of maternity (and child-care), women are more likely than men to take career breaks during their working lives. This makes it more difficult for those women to build up long periods of service. Length of service (which is also potentially discriminatory on age grounds, as we saw above) is often used as a factor in employers' decisions on pay rises, promotions and redundancy selection. The CJEU addressed the matter in *Cadman*.[174] It held that the employer did not need to justify the use of a length of service criterion, but if the claimant could cast doubt on whether it truly reflected the need to gain experience, the burden would shift to the employer to prove that it was proportionate under the circumstances. This would apply where, for example, the employer insisted on a particular number of years of service to secure a promotion even though the relevant experience could be acquired much more quickly.

6.5.9 Sexual orientation

Discrimination because of sexual orientation was first prohibited in English law in 2003,[175] implementing the relevant provisions of the Framework Directive.[176]

Attempts to extend the protection of sex discrimination law to sexual orientation cases (by analogy with *P v S and Cornwall CC*, discussed above)[177] were unsuccessful. In *Grant*, the claimant challenged her employer's policy of providing concessionary travel to its employees' different-sex partners but not to its employees' same-sex partners.[178] The Court held that this was not sex discrimination because the relevant comparison was with a man with a same-sex partner (rather than a woman with a different-sex partner) who would also have been denied the travel benefit by the employer.

Discrimination because of sexual orientation is now addressed in EA 2010, s. 12(1):

Sexual orientation means a person's sexual orientation towards–

(a) persons of the same sex,
(b) persons of the opposite sex, or
(c) persons of either sex.

---

[171] ERA 1996, s 80F.
[172] For example, *R v Secretary of State for Employment, ex p EOC* [1995] 1 AC 1 (HL).
[173] Part-time Workers (Prevention of Less Favourable Treatment) Regulations 2000, SI 2000/1551.
[174] Case C-17/05 *Cadman v Health and Safety Executive* [2006] ECR I-9583.
[175] Employment Equality (Sexual Orientation) Regulations 2003, SI 2003/1661.
[176] Directive 2000/78, art 1.
[177] Above n 30.
[178] Case C-249/96 *Grant v South West Trains Ltd* [1998] ECR I-621.

All the different types of discrimination identified in the previous section are applicable to the characteristic of sexual orientation.

6.5.10 Anything missing?

As the discussion so far has shown, equality law has developed over time as new protected characteristics have been added to the list. It is worth considering whether this process has ended, or whether there is scope for further expansion.

Several characteristics may be suggested as possible candidates for inclusion in the law. Some campaigners argue for the inclusion of genetic characteristics, fearing that employers will discriminate against workers (particularly at the hiring stage) because they have a genetic predisposition to a certain condition. This characteristic is protected in the US under the Genetic Information Nondiscrimination Act of 2008.[179] However, a significant difference between the US and the UK is the greater role of US employers in providing health insurance as a key employment benefit to their workers. This may make them more likely to investigate employees' potential to suffer health problems. Another possible candidate is an individual's socio-economic background or status, since there is clear evidence to suggest that this may have a negative impact on educational opportunities and job prospects. EA 2010, s. 1 placed a duty on public authorities (but not private employers) to have regard to this characteristic when exercising their functions, but the provision had not been brought into force when the government changed in 2010 and the current government has announced that it does not intend to bring it into force.[180] A third option is political opinion. As we saw above, this is not protected under the existing law unless it amounts to a 'belief' equivalent to a religious or philosophical belief.

Of course, any change in the protected characteristics could be brought about by legislation, either at EU level or domestically. But it is also worth considering whether a court could extend the list. The CJEU has indicated its reluctance to do so in the *Chacón Navas* case, holding that the protected characteristics in the Framework Directive are a closed list.[181] The Court in *Kaltoft* reiterated this view holding that although there is a general principle of non-discrimination in EU law, this does not support the extension of the grounds of discrimination beyond those represented in the relevant directives.[182] By contrast, the non-discrimination right in Article 14 ECHR is 'open', because it uses the phrase 'or other status'. This gives the ECtHR the ability to add new characteristics to the list. The Court has done this on several occasions, for example, in relation to sexual orientation, which is not listed.[183]

In theory at least, this opens up the possibility that an English court might be called upon to interpret EA 2010 broadly to extend its protection, relying on the Court's case-law and the interpretive obligation in s. 3 HRA 1998. This could occur in relation to a ground listed in Article 14 but not addressed in English law, such as political opinion or property, or in relation to a new ground added by the Court at a later date. However, this seems unlikely to be successful, for two reasons. First, as we have seen,

---

[179] William J McDevitt, 'I Dream of GINA: Understanding the Employment Provisions of the Genetic Information Nondiscrimination Act of 2008' (2009) 54 Villanova L Rev 91.
[180] Theresa May, 'Equality Strategy Speech', 17 November 2010, available at https://www.gov.uk/government/speeches/theresa-mays-equality-strategy-speech (last visited 21 October 2014).
[181] Above n 112.
[182] Above n 118.
[183] For example, *Smith and Grady* v *UK* (2000) 29 EHRR 493.

Article 14 ECHR is parasitic on other Convention rights and is not a free-standing right to equal treatment, thus limiting its applicability. Second, EA 2010 is precise in its identification of protected characteristics, making it difficult to extend them through legitimate interpretation. The best that might be hoped for is a declaration of incompatibility under s. 4 HRA if the law failed to provide a remedy to a victim of a type of discrimination recognised under the ECHR but not under English law.

Of course, in many cases, the law's reach can be extended not by adding new grounds but by adopting an expansive interpretation of existing ones, as we saw above in relation to the treatment of obesity as part of disability. This type of argument is much more likely to succeed in court.

6.6 APPLICATION AND ENFORCEMENT

We are now in a position to consider when equality law applies and how it is enforced. Equality law is, of course, much broader than employment law, applying to a variety of other fields of activity such as education and public transport. Our focus in the first section below will be on explaining how equality law applies at work, looking at the definition of 'worker' and the different types of employer action that are covered by the law. An important critique of equality law challenges its emphasis on enforcement through individual litigation. In the second section below, we will examine some of the ways in which the law tries to support and facilitate individual litigation (for example, through rules reversing the burden of proof) and in the third section below, we will briefly examine what the alternatives to individual litigation might look like.

6.6.1 Discrimination at work

Discrimination at work is addressed in Part 5 EA 2010. We will consider the 'employee' definition used in the legislation before examining the types of employer action that are covered.

For the purposes of this part, employment is broadly defined to include 'employment under a contract of employment, a contract of apprenticeship or a contract personally to do work'.[184] This extends the definition beyond employees to include others who are obliged to work 'personally' and who have some degree of subordination to the employer in accordance with the controversial ruling in the *Jivraj* case.[185] In most cases, the EA definition falls to be interpreted compatibly with EU law, which adopts a broad definition of 'worker' for the purposes of equality law which is largely designed to exclude the genuinely self-employed from the law's protection.[186]

The employer is liable for discrimination at all stages in the employment relationship: at the hiring stage, during the relationship and when the employment is terminated. This is the effect of s. 39 EA 2010:

(1) An employer (A) must not discriminate against a person (B)–

    (a) in the arrangements A makes for deciding to whom to offer employment;

    (b) as to the terms on which A offers B employment;

    (c) by not offering B employment.

---

[184] EA 2010, s 83(2)(a). See Chapter 4 for more detail.
[185] *Jivraj* v *Hashwani* [2011] UKSC 40, [2011] ICR 1004.
[186] Case C-256/01 *Allonby* v *Accrington & Rossendale College* [2004] ECR I-873.

(2) An employer (A) must not discriminate against an employee of A's (B)–

  (a) as to B's terms of employment;

  (b) in the way A affords B access, or by not affording B access, to opportunities for promotion, transfer or training or for receiving any other benefit, facility or service;

  (c) by dismissing B;

  (d) by subjecting B to any other detriment . . .

(5) A duty to make reasonable adjustments applies to an employer.

Harassment of employees and job applicants is addressed separately in s. 40 EA 2010.

In many cases, the discriminatory act at issue may have been committed by a manager or a colleague of the claimant, and not by his or her employer. This issue is addressed by s. 109 EA 2010:

(1) Anything done by a person (A) in the course of A's employment must be treated as also done by the employer . . .

(3) It does not matter whether that thing is done with the employer's . . . knowledge or approval.

(5) In proceedings against A's employer (B) in respect of anything alleged to have been done by A in the course of A's employment it is a defence for B to show that B took all reasonable steps to prevent A–

  (a) from doing that thing, or

  (b) from doing anything of that description.

This provision means that the claimant will normally be able to bring proceedings against the employer for discriminatory acts of other employees, so the employer may be vicariously (as well as, or instead of, personally) liable for discrimination. This benefits claimants because the employer is much more likely to be able to pay compensation than an individual. However, the employer has a defence under subsection 4. Although this reduces the claimant's prospect of recovery, it may have the beneficial effect of encouraging employers to give clear instructions and appropriate training to their workforce about equality issues.

Under s. 111, it is unlawful to instruct, cause or induce someone to discriminate against a third party. This means that, for example, it is unlawful for an employer to instruct a manager to discriminate against job applicants with particular characteristics. This is actionable by the third party or by the person receiving the instruction if he or she has suffered a detriment as a result. To continue our example, if the manager refused to comply with the instruction and was then demoted, he or she would be able to bring proceedings against the employer.

Although we cannot consider the provisions in detail here, it is worth noting that the law also prohibits discrimination by trade unions[187] and by a variety of other work-related bodies such as organisations providing training and employment agencies.[188]

---

[187] EA 2010, s 57.
[188] ibid ss 53 and 55.

6.6.2 Enforcement

The main method for enforcing equality law at work is by making a complaint to the employment tribunal. There are two main remedies currently available under s. 124: a recommendation and an award of compensation.

Compensation is awarded using tort principles in accordance with s. 119. It is important to note that the tort measure of compensation is quite generous, so for example, whereas it is generally assumed that compensation for lost future earnings is limited in contract law (because of the employer's ability to terminate the contract with notice)[189] it may be a substantial head of damages in tort law.[190] Moreover, compensation for injury to feelings is available in tort (in contrast to contract law[191] and unfair dismissal law[192]), a point made explicit by s. 119(4). At one time, there was a cap on the damages available in discrimination law, but this was removed after an adverse ruling in the CJEU in a sex discrimination case.[193] This means that there is a significant advantage to challenging a dismissal through equality law rather than unfair dismissal law wherever possible, because there is no upper limit on the damages available.

Under s. 124(3):

> An appropriate recommendation is a recommendation that within a specified period the respondent takes specified steps for the purpose of obviating or reducing the adverse effect of any matter to which the proceedings relate–
>
> (a) on the complainant;
> (b) on any other person.

The point of this provision is to force the employer to take steps to rectify the problem both for the complainant and for the workforce more generally. The provision could be used to require the employer to review its policies and practices more generally or to institute equality monitoring in the workplace, among other things. Where the recommendation relates to the claimant, and the employer fails to comply 'without reasonable excuse', the tribunal may make an award of compensation to the claimant if it had not done so already, or increase the award already made, under s. 124(7).

Under the Deregulation Bill currently before Parliament, cl. 2 would amend s. 124(3) so that the tribunal could only make recommendations in relation to the complainant and not the wider workforce. The government argues that employers who have lost a case will take steps to change their policies anyway, so that the provision is unnecessary 'red tape'. However, the risk is that employers will simply pay compensation to the individual, and fail to learn wider lessons, thereby reducing the impact of the litigation.

A long-standing criticism of equality law is that it may be very difficult for individual claimants to gather the evidence they need to prove their case, because employers will be reluctant to admit to having discriminated. The CJEU recognised this problem in the

---

[189] See Chapters 5 and 9 for more detail.
[190] *Ministry of Defence* v *Cannock* [1994] ICR 918 (EAT).
[191] *Addis* v *Gramophone Co Ltd* [1909] AC 488 (HL).
[192] *Dunnachie* v *Kingston upon Hull City Council* [2004] UKHL 36, [2005] 1 AC 226.
[193] Case C-271/91 *Marshall* v *Southampton and South West Hampshire AHA (No 2)* [1993] ECR I-4367.

Danfoss case.[194] The employer had a system of basic pay plus bonuses. The female claimants in the case could show that women in the firm earned less than men in general, but could not explain why this was so. The Court held that, since the pay system lacked transparency, the burden of proof shifted to the employer to demonstrate that no discrimination was taking place. This prompted the Member States to agree a Directive on the burden of proof, a measure they had not supported until that point.[195] This is now codified in the relevant equality directives. EA 2010 addresses the matter in s. 136:

(2) If there are facts from which the court could decide, in the absence of any other explanation, that a person (A) contravened the provision concerned, the court must hold that the contravention occurred.

(3) But subsection (2) does not apply if A shows that A did not contravene the provision.

EA 2010, s. 14 contains another provision designed to facilitate claims, on dual discrimination. This would allow an individual to establish a direct discrimination claim based on two protected characteristics (race and sex, for example) without the need to prove that a claim based on either one taken alone would have succeeded. However, this provision has not been brought into force.

Individuals who bring discrimination claims often find that this prompts an adverse reaction by the employer, who then subjects them to further detriment because of the claim. This is dealt with by the provision on victimisation in s. 27:

(1) A person (A) victimises another person (B) if A subjects B to a detriment because–

(a) B does a protected act, or

(b) A believes that B has done, or may do, a protected act.

(2) Each of the following is a protected act–

(a) bringing proceedings under this Act;

(b) giving evidence or information in connection with proceedings under this Act;

(c) doing any other thing for the purposes of or in connection with this Act;

(d) making an allegation (whether or not express) that A or another person has contravened this Act.

(3) Giving false evidence or information, or making a false allegation, is not a protected act if the evidence or information is given, or the allegation is made, in bad faith.

This provision has sometimes proved difficult to apply in practice.[196] According to the *St Helens* case, the central focus should be on the detriment to the claimant.[197] In that case, the employer was faced with equal pay claims. A large proportion of the claimants agreed to a settlement offered by the council but some refused to accept the deal. The council then sent a letter to all the relevant employees stating that if the claimants continued with the litigation, the employer might have to make cutbacks which would involve large-scale redundancies. The House of Lords held that this constituted victimisation because it went beyond normal settlement negotiations and was an attempt to intimidate the claimants into dropping their claims.

---

[194] Above n 28.
[195] Above n 27.
[196] For example, *Chief Constable of West Yorkshire* v *Khan* [2001] UKHL 48, [2001] ICR 1065 has been doubted by the House of Lords itself in *St Helens MBC* v *Derbyshire* [2007] UKHL 16, [2007] ICR 841.
[197] *St Helens MBC* v *Derbyshire* [2007] UKHL 16, [2007] ICR 841.

Under s. 108 EA 2010, discrimination and harassment are prohibited where they arise out of a past relationship, for example, where an employer continues to discriminate against or harass an employee after the end of the employment. This provision does not mention victimisation, but in the recent *Jessemey* case, the Court of Appeal held that it should be interpreted to include victimisation in order to comply with the UK's EU law obligations.[198] This is important because, as in *Jessemey* itself, an employer might be tempted to supply an unfavourable reference to prospective future employers of someone who has brought proceedings against it, thereby damaging the individual's future employment prospects.

6.6.3 Alternatives to individual litigation

It is sometimes argued that individual litigation is not the best way of enforcing equality law, for a variety of reasons. It places a considerable burden on the claimant to find resources to fund the litigation, to gather evidence and to endure the stress of the proceedings. And it may be ineffective at securing wider change in the workplace or in society, despite the possibility of the remedy of a recommendation noted above.

The Equality and Human Rights Commission has the power to support individual litigation brought under the EA 2010.[199] However, the Commission's resources are limited and it can only hope to involve itself in a tiny fraction of cases. It also has a wide range of powers to investigate alleged incidents of discrimination, for example, at a particular firm,[200] but these have never been used extensively, not least because – in the early years of the legislation – firms were able to use judicial review to challenge decision-making by the Commission's predecessor bodies.[201]

Another option, advocated by Fredman in particular, is to use a 'mainstreaming' approach in which employers are encouraged to review their policies and activities to ensure that they comply with equality norms. This approach already exists in the public sector because of the 'public sector equality duty' under EA 2010.[202] It also applies to employers in Northern Ireland in respect of community background (Protestant, Catholic or other) and sex.[203] This more proactive approach has the advantage over individual litigation that it may prevent discrimination by spotting problems before they occur, and fixing them for the entire workforce. However, there is a risk that 'mainstreaming' approaches may be applied in a superficial, 'tick-box' way without bringing about any real change. Whether it would be beneficial to extend the 'mainstreaming' approach to private employers in England is unclear.

---

[198] *Rowstock Ltd v Jessemey* [2014] EWCA Civ 185, [2014] ICR 550.

[199] Equality Act 2006, s 28. For discussion of problems facing the Commission, see Bob Hepple, 'Enforcing Equality Law: Two Steps Forward and Two Steps Backwards for Reflexive Regulation' (2011) 40 ILJ 315; *Equality: the Legal Framework* (2nd edn, Hart 2014) chapter 7.

[200] ibid s 20.

[201] For example, *Re Prestige Group plc* [1984] ICR 473.

[202] EA 2010, ss 149–157. For discussion, see Sandra Fredman, 'The Public Sector Equality Duty' (2011) 40 ILJ 405; Tom Hickman, 'Too Hot, Too Cold or Just Right? The Development of the Public Sector Equality Duties in Administrative Law' [2013] PL 325.

[203] Fair Employment (Northern Ireland) Act 1989, and see Christopher McCrudden *et al.*, 'Regulation of Affirmative Action in Northern Ireland: An Empirical Assessment' (2004) 24 OJLS 363.

POINTS TO TAKE AWAY

- The concept of equality is multifaceted – including formal equality, substantive equality and equality of opportunity – and its various facets may conflict. Alternative bases for equality law advocated by some commentators include dignity and social inclusion.

- Equality law is a complex mix of EU and domestic law, with some interventions by the ECtHR.

- Direct discrimination involves less favourable treatment because of a protected characteristic. Indirect discrimination occurs when a 'provision, criterion or practice' puts the claimant and people sharing his or her protected characteristic 'at a particular disadvantage'. In general terms, direct discrimination cannot be justified by an employer (though there are exceptions) whereas indirect discrimination may be justified if the employer is engaged in the proportionate pursuit of a legitimate aim.

- Positive discrimination in favour of a person from an underrepresented group is only permitted in very limited circumstances where both candidates (for the job or promotion, for example) are equally qualified.

- Discrimination is only unlawful where it relates to a recognised 'protected characteristic'. These are age, disability, gender reassignment, marriage and civil partnership, pregnancy and maternity, race, religion or belief, sex, and sexual orientation.

- Equality law is enforced primarily by individual litigation leading to a 'recommendation' and (usually) an award of compensation. Various measures exist to support individual litigation, but critics argue that it is not an effective means of enforcing equality law.

Further reading

Making distinctions between people is a normal part of life – we distinguish between people we like and people we don't like, and between people with different levels of qualifications – so it is important to think about what makes certain types of distinction-making morally wrong. There is a large philosophical literature on this. Three of the more accessible contributions are **John Gardner, 'On the Ground of Her Sex(uality)' (1998) 18 OJLS 167**; **Deborah Hellman, *When is Discrimination Wrong?* (Harvard University Press 2008), chapters 1 and 2**; and **Sophia Moreau, 'What is Discrimination?' (2010) 38 Philosophy and Public Affairs 143.**

Lawyers have tended to focus on ways of defining (and critiquing) equality, and linking it to the concepts used in legislation. For a critical analysis of different conceptions of equality as a basis for equality law, see **Sandra Fredman, *Discrimination Law* (2nd edn, OUP 2011), chapter 1.** On dignity, see **Gay Moon and Robin Allen, 'Dignity Discourse in Discrimination Law: a Better Route to Equality?' (2006) 6 EHRLR 610**; and **Denise Réaume, 'Dignity, Equality and Comparison' in Deborah Hellman and Sophia Moreau (eds), *Philosophical Foundations of Discrimination Law* (OUP 2013)**; and on social inclusion, see **Hugh Collins, 'Discrimination, Equality and Social Inclusion' (2003) 66 MLR 16.**

As we have seen, EU law is central to this topic, so for a more detailed account of the EU measures, see **Catherine Barnard, *EU Employment Law* (4th edn, OUP 2012), chapters 6–10.** For a more detailed discussion of English law, with a particular focus on EA 2010, see **Bob Hepple, *Equality: the Legal Framework* (2nd edn) (Hart Publishing 2014).**

For many writers, the enforcement of equality law is a particular concern. They worry that, despite a long history of equality law (for the protected characteristics of sex and race, at least) inequalities are persistent. The concern is that individual litigation is not an efficient or reliable way of bringing about social transformation. On positive discrimination, see **Catherine Barnard, 'The Principle of Equality in the Community Context: *P*, *Grant*, *Kalanke* and *Marschall*: Four Uneasy Bedfellows?' (1998) 57 CLJ 352; Sandra Fredman, 'After *Kalanke* and *Marschall*: Affirming Affirmative Action' (1998) 1 CYELS 199; and *Discrimination Law* (2nd edn, OUP 2011), chapter 5.** On the EHRC, see **Bob Hepple, 'Enforcing Equality Law: Two Steps Forward and Two Steps Backwards for Reflexive Regulation' (2011) 40 ILJ 315.** On 'mainstreaming' in the public sector, see **Sandra Fredman, 'The Public Sector Equality Duty' (2011) 40 ILJ 405; *Discrimination Law* (2nd edn, OUP 2011), chapter 6;** and **Tom Hickman, 'Too Hot, Too Cold or Just Right? The Development of the Public Sector Equality Duties in Administrative Law' [2013] PL 325.**

7 Pay

Learning outcomes

This chapter will enable readers to:

- understand the employer's contractual duty to pay the employee or worker (including the law's treatment of performance- and profit-related pay schemes), and the employer's right to make deductions from pay as a disciplinary measure, and analyse what happens to the employer's duty to pay when the employee or worker is not working (because of industrial action, illness or because there is not enough work to do)

- critically evaluate the National Minimum Wage (NMW), and how it is set, applied and enforced

- understand the law on equal pay for men and women, and how it is applied and enforced

7.1 INTRODUCTION

Pay is at the heart of the employment relationship. The most basic kind of employment relationship is the 'wage/work bargain', in which the individual supplies his or her labour in exchange for a wage. Although people's motivations for working are many and varied, for the vast majority of people getting paid for what they do is essential.

Pay can take a variety of forms. The two most obvious forms are hourly pay and salary. Those who are paid by the hour are simply paid at an agreed rate for each hour they work. In many workplaces, the concept of 'overtime' is common: when a worker is asked to do extra hours beyond his or her normal obligation, the work may be paid at a higher hourly rate. Those who are paid a salary are paid a certain amount per week, or month. Of course, salaried workers are expected to work a certain number of hours, but their pay does not generally relate precisely to the number of hours worked.

Employers have long sought to use pay as a means of motivating the workforce and improving productivity. Perhaps the oldest example of this is the payment of 'piece rates', where workers are paid for each item they produce (each garment they sew, or each punnet of strawberries they pick) rather than for the time they have worked. Nowadays, it is common for workers to be able to earn 'bonus' payments of various kinds. These might be linked to the individual's performance (such as a salesperson receiving 'commission' for each product sold) or to the performance of a particular group of workers (the sales team, for example) or to the profits of the firm itself. Some firms pay workers in part by giving them shares in the business.

Since the value of the shares will usually increase if the firm performs well, this gives workers an added incentive to work hard. A difficulty with these kinds of arrangements is that they transfer risk from the employer to the individual, and can sometimes cast doubt on whether he or she is an 'employee' or a 'worker' for the purposes of employment rights.[1]

In this chapter, we examine the three main areas of law relating to pay. We begin in section 7.2 by considering the individual's basic entitlement to remuneration. This is derived from his or her contract. We will focus in particular on the avenues of redress open to the individual if the employer does not pay the money to which he or she is entitled, and on the circumstances in which the employer might be permitted to make deductions from the individual's pay. In section 7.3, we examine the National Minimum Wage (NMW). This is a statutory minimum hourly rate to which all workers in the UK are entitled. We consider some of the details of how the NMW is calculated and enforced. And in section 7.4, we turn to the issue of equal pay for men and women. Even today, women's average hourly earnings are much lower than those of men, at around 80%.[2] We examine the statutory framework enabling women to claim equal pay with men, and assess some of the reasons for the persistence of the 'gender pay gap'.

7.2 CONTRACTUAL REMUNERATION

According to ILO Convention 95,[3] wages should be paid in legal tender[4] at regular intervals,[5] and should only be subject to deductions where these are permitted by national laws or collective agreements.[6] The UK ratified this Convention in 1951 but denounced it in 1983. The English law on wages is a complex patchwork of common law rules (many of which were developed a long time ago) with some statutory overlay. We will begin by examining the basics of the wage/work bargain before examining the statutory regime on 'deductions' from pay. We will then examine some particular situations in which disputes about pay can arise because the employee or worker is not working: either on purpose, because of industrial action, or through no fault of his or her own, because of illness and shortages of work (known as 'lay-off'). Finally, we will look at some of the emerging legal issues surrounding performance-related and profit-related pay, where the individual's pay is tied to his or her own performance or to the performance of the firm.

7.2.1 The wage/work bargain

So far, we have been using the phrase 'wage/work bargain' as if its meaning is obvious. However, the worker's obligation to 'work' can be formulated in different ways. It is important to get this clear because it affects the worker's ability to enforce his or her contract in the event of a dispute. It also matters (as we shall see below) if the worker

---

[1] See Chapter 4.
[2] David Bovill, *Patterns of Pay: Results from the Annual Survey of Hours and Earnings, 1997 to 2012* (Office for National Statistics 2013) 10.
[3] ILO, The Protection of Wages Convention, 1949 (No. 95).
[4] ibid art 3.
[5] ibid art 12.
[6] ibid art 8.

is prevented from working in circumstances which are not his or her fault, such as illness. In this section, we will focus on the position at common law.

The worker may be paid piece rates, a wage expressed as a rate per hour, or a salary for a particular period of time. If the worker is employed on piece rates, the employer is only liable to pay in respect of each product completed by the worker. If the worker is paid by the hour, it is normally the case that the employer is only liable to pay for each hour of completed work. This has both good and bad consequences from the worker's perspective. If the worker is sent home at lunchtime because of a lack of work, he or she is entitled to pay for the hours worked in the morning, but gets nothing for the afternoon. If the worker is paid a salary (on a monthly basis, for example) the connection between hours worked and pay is more obscure. This has created difficulties. In some cases, the courts have held that salaried workers get paid simply for being ready and willing to work.[7] This would mean that in a 'lack of work' situation, the salaried worker – unlike the hourly paid worker – would continue to get paid. In the *Miles* case, Lord Templeman cast doubt on the validity of this distinction in modern times given its tendency to treat well-paid workers (who are more likely to be salaried) much more generously than low-paid workers (who are more likely to be hourly paid).[8] However, the reverse is also true. If salaried workers are treated as entitled to be paid only when they have completed a period of work, this could mean that a person who worked three weeks out of four in a month would not be entitled to that month's salary payment.[9] For this reason, the courts have used various techniques, including the doctrine of substantial performance, s. 2 of the Apportionment Act 1870 or simple construction of the contract, in order to reach the result that the salaried worker's right to payment accrues on a daily basis.[10] This seems to be a fair compromise between the two extremes, but in practice, it is still not entirely clear that this is the law.

Of course, it is important to note that there is a distinction between accruing a right to payment and getting paid. Even if payment accrues by the day or by the hour, most people have to wait until the end of the week or the month to receive any money from the employer, because this is either a term of their contract or the normal practice in the workplace.

The employer's duty to pay can be enforced in two ways at common law: through the action for an agreed sum or through an action for damages. The advantage of the former is that the worker is simply claiming the money due under the contract and is not under any obligation to mitigate his or her loss.[11] However, this action is only available where the worker has performed his or her side of the bargain and the duty to pay has arisen, so that the court can simply order the employer to perform. In all other cases, an action for damages is the appropriate route. This requires the court to quantify the loss suffered by the worker and to apply the normal principles of mitigation (for example, by deducting any welfare benefits received by the worker during the period of non-payment by the employer). As we shall see in the next section, ERA 1996 also offers some statutory protection to employees in the event of

---

[7] AT Denning, 'Wages During Sickness' (1939) 55 LQR 353, 355; and see *Cuckson* v *Stones* 120 ER 902.
[8] *Miles* v *Wakefield Metropolitan District Council* [1987] AC 539 (HL).
[9] For example, *Boston Deep Sea Fishing and Ice Co* v *Ansell* (1888) 39 Ch D 339.
[10] See, for example, *Sim* v *Rotherham Metropolitan Borough Council* [1987] Ch 216, 255.
[11] *White and Carter (Councils) Ltd* v *McGregor* [1962] AC 413.

unlawful deductions from wages – which can include a failure to pay the employee altogether – and this provides an alternative route to enforcement in the Employment Tribunal.

7.2.2 Statutory protection against unlawful deductions

There are a number of different situations in which the employer might seek to make deductions from the worker's pay. In general terms, the employer's right to make deductions is a matter for the common law, but there is some minimal statutory regulation of the procedure for doing so. We will examine this regime in this section. To keep matters simple, we will focus on the situation in which the employer wants to make a deduction for disciplinary reasons: for example, because the worker has arrived late on several occasions or has damaged some equipment.[12]

Under ERA 1996, s. 13, the employer is only permitted to make a deduction where it has a statutory or contractual right to do so, or the worker's prior written consent. Where the employer seeks to rely upon a contractual right, it can only do so where the worker has been made aware of it, in accordance with s. 13(2):

> In this section "relevant provision", in relation to a worker's contract, means a provision of the contract comprised–
>
> (a) in one or more written terms of the contract of which the employer has given the worker a copy on an occasion prior to the employer making the deduction in question, or
> (b) in one or more terms of the contract (whether express or implied and, if express, whether oral or in writing) the existence and effect, or combined effect, of which in relation to the worker the employer has notified to the worker in writing on such an occasion.

In most cases, workers have limited bargaining power relative to the employer, so it is not realistic to assume that there would be any meaningful negotiation about these kinds of terms. Thus, the main effect of the statute is to ensure that workers have advance warning of the situations in which they might face deductions by their employer. To go back to our lateness example, at least this would enable the worker to avoid a deduction by turning up on time.

However, as Deakin and Morris have argued, the statutory scheme offers little substantive protection.[13] For example, there is no requirement that the employer should give the worker a hearing before making a deduction, or that deductions may only be made for particularly serious infringements. It is possible that the implied term of mutual trust and confidence may be of some assistance in this context, though there is no case-law on the point and it is difficult to rely on an implied term in the face of clear and express rights on the part of the employer to make deductions.[14]

The only area in which the common law has intervened in recent years is where the amount of the deduction is excessive relative to the loss suffered by the employer. Where that is the case, the worker may be able to argue that the deduction is

---

[12] Another significant use of the deductions regime is to challenge an employer's failure to fulfil a worker's entitlements, for example, to holiday pay. See *Revenue and Customs* v *Stringer* [2009] UKHL 31, [2009] ICR 985.

[13] Simon Deakin and Gillian Morris, *Labour Law* (6th edn, Hart Publishing 2012) para 4.73.

[14] See Chapter 5.

unenforceable as a penalty clause.[15] This argument succeeded in *Giraud*, where the employer had an unlimited contractual right to make deductions if the worker failed to work out his notice period after resigning.[16] The EAT was influenced by the fact that the worker, who was a driver, could easily be replaced, so that any losses suffered by the employer would probably be minimal. However, each case must be considered on its facts so, for example, in *Tullett Prebon* v *El-Hajjali*, a clause requiring a newly hired worker with highly specialist skills to make a substantial payment if he failed to start work was upheld as a valid attempt to pre-estimate the employer's losses.[17]

7.2.3 Industrial action

One important situation in which the employer might want to make deductions is where workers have engaged in industrial action. This might take the form of a strike (a complete stoppage of work for a period of time) or action short of a strike (continuing to work but causing some disruption through strategies such as a 'work to rule', a 'go slow' or a refusal to carry out certain duties).[18] A strike is a repudiatory breach of contract, and in general the courts have found that action short of a strike is too. This means that the worker has little right to complain if his or her pay is docked.

Where the worker is on strike, it is settled law that he or she is not entitled to be paid because he or she is in repudiatory breach of contract: not working and not ready and willing to work.[19] Under s. 14(5) ERA 1996, the employer is entitled to make deductions in respect of the worker's participation in industrial action without giving prior notice or seeking the worker's agreement, so there is no statutory protection in this setting. The calculation of how much pay the employer is entitled to deduct is obviously easiest where the worker is paid on an hourly or daily basis, since it is relatively straightforward to match the deduction to the missed work. Where the worker is paid a weekly or monthly salary, it might be argued that the employer is entitled to refuse to pay anything in respect of the salary period if the worker was on strike for some days during that period. However, as we saw above, the modern view is that salaried workers accrue their earnings on a daily basis so a deduction for each day (or part of a day) not worked would seem more appropriate.[20]

Matters are more complex in relation to action short of a strike, because although the courts generally regard this as a repudiatory breach of contract too, the worker may still be performing a substantial part of his or her normal job. In the early cases, employers simply sought to make deductions from the worker's pay to reflect the work not done. The courts upheld employers' right to do so and engaged in some examination of whether or not the amount deducted was appropriate. Thus, in the *Sim* case, the court upheld the employer's deduction in respect of a teacher's refusal

---

[15] *Dunlop Pneumatic Tyre Co Ltd* v *New Garage & Motor Co Ltd* [1915] AC 79 (HL).
[16] *Giraud UK Ltd* v *Smith* [2000] IRLR 763 (EAT).
[17] *Tullett Prebon Group Ltd* v *El-Hajjali* [2008] EWHC 1924 (QB), [2008] IRLR 760.
[18] See Chapter 13.
[19] *Secretary of State for Employment* v *ASLEF* (No 2) [1972] 2 QB 455 (CA) 491–492 (Lord Denning MR).
[20] *Miles*, above n 8.

to provide cover for absent colleagues,[21] whereas in *Royle*, the court substituted a smaller deduction for a teacher's refusal to teach larger classes.[22] In *Miles* v *Wakefield*, the House of Lords went a bit further.[23] The case concerned a registrar who took industrial action by refusing to conduct weddings on Saturday mornings. The employer divided his monthly salary by the number of hours he normally worked, and deducted three hours' pay per week (to cover Saturday mornings) in respect of this refusal. It was held that, although the registrar did other duties on Saturdays, the employer was entitled to refuse to accept less than full performance. However, as Freedland points out,[24] some of the judges suggested that the employer might have been entitled to refuse to pay him any of his monthly salary.[25] This suggestion bore fruit in *Wiluszynski*.[26] Here, the claimant was a council worker who refused to reply to councillors' queries during a period of industrial action. This amounted to a few hours' work over a period of several weeks. The council made clear that it would not accept or pay for anything other than full performance of his duties, and that any work he did during the industrial action would be regarded as voluntary. When the industrial action ended, the claimant brought a claim for his salary, but the Court of Appeal upheld the employer's right to refuse any payment. The claimant argued that the council had benefited from his work. But it was held that the council had done nothing to undermine its statement that it would not accept partial performance (because it had not actively given him work or instructed him during the industrial action) and that there was no obligation on the council to prevent him from working (for example, by instituting a lock-out).

Mead questions whether the analysis in *Wiluszynski* is correct as a matter of contract law.[27] The employee's repudiatory breach entitles the employer to terminate the contract and dismiss the employee. But if the employer elects not to do this, the employer must be ready and willing to perform its side of the bargain. This would suggest that, unless the action short of a strike deprives the employer of substantially what it bargained for, it should still make some payment to the employee. Since the employer is entitled to damages for breach from the employee, the employer would be entitled to reduce the payment to reflect the damages. In some situations, this would mean that no pay was due, but of course this would depend on the facts of the case. In a case like *Wiluszynski*, where the harm to the employer was small, it might be arguable that some payment was still owed to the employee. Another option suggested by the courts and by some commentators is that the employee could bring a claim in unjust enrichment.[28] However, this is difficult for various reasons, not least because it is hard to argue that the employer is 'unjustly' enriched when it makes clear that it does not want the employee to perform.[29]

Of course, in practice, questions of pay during an industrial dispute are more likely to be resolved through bargaining than through litigation. The employer might decide

[21] Above n 10.
[22] *Royle* v *Trafford Borough Council* [1984] IRLR 184.
[23] Above n 8.
[24] Mark Freedland, *The Personal Employment Contract* (OUP 2003) 219–223.
[25] *Miles*, above n 8, 552–3 (Lord Brightman), 561–2 (Lord Templeman).
[26] *Wiluszynski* v *London Borough of Tower Hamlets* [1989] ICR 493.
[27] Geoffrey H Mead, 'Employer's Right to Withhold Wages' (1990) 106 LQR 192, 193–194; and in greater detail, in 'Restitution within Contract' (1991) 11 LS 172.
[28] Above n 25. For discussion, see Andrew Burrows, *The Law of Restitution* (3rd edn, OUP 2011) 360.
[29] It is also generally thought to be impossible to bring a restitutionary claim while the contract is still in force: Mead, above n 27, 195.

simply to make deductions, in order to maintain a better atmosphere at the end of the dispute, or the employer might decide to take a strong line, as in *Wiluszynski*, in order to force the workers back to the negotiating table and to end the dispute.[30] Nonetheless, many commentators regard the courts as unduly willing to allow the employer to 'have its cake and eat it' in this context.

7.2.4 Lay-off

The term 'lay-off' is used to describe the situation in which the employer does not have any work for its employees to do, so sends them home temporarily until the firm is busy again. Nowadays, employers might anticipate this situation by employing some or all staff on a casual basis so that they do not owe them any obligations.[31] But one of the characteristics of being an employee is that some protection is available in this situation.

At common law, the position depends on the construction of the contract. Traditionally, this has meant that salaried employees are still entitled to their salary because they are paid simply for being 'ready to work'.[32] But in the *Devonald* case, the court extended protection to other groups of employees by developing the idea that it is the employer's responsibility to provide employees with work so that they have an opportunity to earn money.[33] In that case, employees who were paid piece rates were able to recover damages in respect of a period of lay-off. This reflects a more general hostility on the part of the courts towards lay-off within the contract of employment because a central characteristic of the contract of employment is that the employer protects the employee against economic risk.[34]

Since 1975, statute has provided employees with a right to 'guarantee pay' in the event of a lay-off, if certain conditions are met.[35] The relevant provisions are now found in ERA 1996. If the employee has a month's qualifying service, he or she is entitled to a payment in respect of a 'workless day', which is a day on which he or she was contractually obliged to work but no work (either his or her normal work or a suitable alternative offered by the employer) was available, for reasons relating to the employer's business.[36] The payment is calculated by working out the employee's normal hourly pay, though since it is subject to a relatively low statutory maximum limit per day, most people would end up with less than they would normally have earned.[37] In any three-month period, the employee may only claim guarantee pay for up to five days.[38]

The rules on guarantee pay seem rather old-fashioned now that employers routinely use agency staff or casual workers to deal with fluctuations in demand. But they are a useful reminder that one way to think about the employment relationship – and

---

[30] Above n 26.

[31] See Chapter 4.

[32] Above n 7.

[33] *Devonald* v *Rosser & Sons* [1906] 2 KB 728, though cf *Browning* v *Crumlin Valley Collieries Ltd* [1926] 1 KB 522, in which the employer was allowed to withhold pay. Freedland, above n 24, 476–7, distinguishes *Browning* on the basis that the cause of the lay-off in *Browning* was (arguably) not the employer's fault.

[34] See Chapter 4.

[35] Employment Rights Act 1996, s 28(1).

[36] ibid s 29(1).

[37] ibid s 30.

[38] ibid s 31(2), (3).

the one that still obtains, up to a point, for employees – is that the employer acts as a 'buffer' to protect the employee against a volatile economic situation.

7.2.5 Illness

The traditional common law distinction between salaried and hourly paid workers meant that salaried workers would get sick pay (they were seen as ready and willing to work but prevented through no fault of their own) whereas hourly paid workers would not (they were only entitled to be paid for work done).[39] In some cases, the courts began to adopt a more generous construction of the contracts of workers in the latter category, so that they were also entitled to sick pay.[40] However, the employer can easily defeat claims to sick pay by making it clear in the contract that it does not provide a sick pay scheme. The only way a worker can be sure of getting sick pay is if he or she has an express contractual right to it.

Since the 1980s, employees have been entitled to Statutory Sick Pay (SSP) if certain conditions are met.[41] The government's policy objective in introducing this scheme was to shift the burden of supporting people who were temporarily off work away from the social security system and onto employers, though in some situations the employer can recover some of the cost from the state. The current amount of SSP is £87.55 per week.[42] If the employer is also under a contractual obligation to provide sick pay, the first £87.55 of this per week discharges the liability to pay SSP.[43] The scheme is complex, but broadly the employee qualifies if he or she has been off work for more than four consecutive days and notifies the employer that he or she is sick.[44] If the employee is off sick for more than seven days, he or she will need to get a doctor's note.[45] SSP is available for up to 28 weeks (after which time the employee would potentially be eligible for social security benefits).[46] If the employee is off sick for a long time, the employer may seek to terminate his or her employment, subject to the rules on unfair dismissal.[47]

7.2.6 Performance- and profit-related pay

Nowadays, performance- and profit-related pay are common in many sectors and workplaces. Performance-related pay is used to refer to the situation in which the individual's pay is linked to his or her own performance, so for example a salesperson might get a bonus for achieving monthly or annual targets. Profit-related pay is used to refer to schemes in which the pay of the workforce (or a section of it) is linked to the firm's performance. This might involve the payment of bonuses or the creation of a scheme whereby employees are given options to buy shares in the company. The

---

[39] Compare *Cuckson*, above n 7, with *O'Grady* v *M Saper Ltd* [1940] 2 KB 469 (CA) and *Mears* v *Safecar Security Ltd* [1983] QB 54 (CA); discussed in Freedland (above n 24), 212–218.

[40] For example, *Orman* v *Saville Sportswear* [1960] 1 WLR 1055, concerning an employee on a weekly wage: see Freedland, above n 24, 218.

[41] Social Security Contributions and Benefits Act 1992, ss 151–163.

[42] ibid s 157.

[43] ibid sch 12, para 2.

[44] ibid ss 152–156.

[45] Statutory Sick Pay (General) Regulations 1982, SI 1982/894.

[46] ibid s 155.

[47] See Chapter 9.

government has encouraged the latter type of scheme by offering tax breaks (for example, reducing the amount of tax payable when the worker sells the shares). The thinking behind these schemes is that they help to motivate staff to do their best for the firm. Importantly, they are to be distinguished from the new concept of 'employee shareholder' status in which the employee gives up certain employment rights in exchange for shares.[48] In this section, we will consider some of the legal issues surrounding performance- and profit-related pay.

The design of a performance-related pay scheme is very much a matter for the employer: the law does not address this issue. Nevertheless, it is worth considering whether an employee who is unhappy with his or her bonus has any possibility of legal recourse. The most obvious route is to argue for an implied term that the employer's discretionary power to award a bonus should be exercised rationally.[49] For example, in *Clark v Nomura*, the claimant was an equities trader who was not paid a discretionary bonus in respect of his final year of employment, even though he had made a large profit for the employer in that time.[50] The court held that the employer could not act unreasonably or perversely in assessing the claimant's performance and awarded him substantial damages. This offers significant protection to the employee, though it is worth noting that the courts tend to use a high threshold for unreasonableness in this context, similar to the *Wednesbury* test in administrative law.[51] Another possibility in some circumstances may be to use equality law. For example, a female employee might be able to challenge her bonus using equal pay law if she can show that she is doing work of equal value to that of a male comparator who is receiving a bigger bonus. As the Court of Justice's landmark decision in *Danfoss* shows, the employer would be well-advised to ensure that its bonus decisions are based on objective criteria because it may be called upon to justify them.[52]

Another potential area for dispute is what happens to shares and bonuses if the individual's employment is terminated. Since these schemes are about motivating employees, employers might be reluctant to make large payouts at the end of someone's contract. In relation to bonuses, one way of achieving this is to terminate the employee's contract before the bonus payment becomes due. Whether this amounts to a wrongful or an unfair dismissal depends on the circumstances. At common law, the employer may well be able to dismiss the employee for no reason at all, provided that the proper notice is given.[53] However, if the employer fails to give proper notice, two possibilities arise. One, revealed by the recent decision in *Geys*, is that the employee might be able to refuse to accept the employer's repudiatory breach of contract until after his or her bonus has become payable.[54] The other is that (depending on the terms of the contract) the employee may be able to persuade the court to award damages in respect of the bonus payment he or she has lost.[55]

---

[48] See Chapter 4.

[49] For discussion, see Freedland, above n 24, 223–230.

[50] [2000] IRLR 766(QB), approved by the Court of Appeal in *Horkulak v Cantor Fitzgerald International* [2004] EWCA Civ 1287, [2005] ICR 402.

[51] *Commerzbank v Keen* [2006] EWCA Civ 1536, [2007] ICR 623. For discussion, see ACL Davies, 'Judicial Self-Restraint in Labour Law' (2009) 38 ILJ 278.

[52] Case C-109/88 *Handels-og Kontorfunktionærernes Forbund I Danmark v Dansk Arbejdsgiverforening (Danfoss)* [1989] ECR 3199.

[53] See Chapter 9, and *Reda v Flag Ltd* [2002] UKPC 38, [2002] IRLR 747.

[54] *Geys v Société Générale* [2012] UKSC 63, [2013] 1 AC 523.

[55] *Horkulak v Cantor Fitzgerald International* [2004] EWCA Civ 1287, [2005] ICR 402.

Of course, a dismissal designed to prevent someone from getting a bonus may also be unfair under the statutory scheme, because the employer is unlikely to be able to point to a legally acceptable reason for dismissing the employee. However, for the very well-paid employees who usually benefit from bonus schemes, this action is unattractive because there is an upper limit on the damages that can be claimed.[56] In the case of options to buy shares, it is common to find that the employer's scheme contains a rule barring people from exercising their options after their employment has been terminated.[57] This means that when someone loses his or her job, he or she may lose valuable share options at the same time.

Bonuses and share schemes are regarded as an important motivational tool in some sectors of the economy. They challenge the basic idea that, in an employment setting, the employer protects the employee against economic risk. By transferring some of that risk back to the employee, the thinking is that his or her objectives will be better aligned with those of the firm. However, there are disadvantages too. From the employee's perspective, the transfer of risk may be substantial, particularly when a large chunk of his or her pay is contingent on performance (which may not always be objectively assessed) or where his or her savings (invested in shares) and job both depend on the success of one firm. Even the motivational advantage can turn into a disadvantage where the desire to win bonuses prompts employees to behave inappropriately: for example, in the financial services sector, instances of 'mis-selling' (where a customer is sold a product that is unsuitable) are often explained by the salesperson's interest in obtaining commission.[58]

7.3 NATIONAL MINIMUM WAGE

In contractual terms, an individual's pay – like any other contract price – is a matter for negotiation between the contracting parties. However, because of the inequality of bargaining power inherent in most employment relationships, the employer is usually able to set the rate of pay. Only people with special skills or talents of considerable value to the employer (footballers, top executives and so on) have a real prospect of negotiating their own pay and other benefits. Of course, the employer's wage-setting activity takes place within a market setting. This means that there will usually be a 'going rate' for the job in question, so the employer will need to pay at or above that rate in order to attract applicants. The 'going rate' will reflect factors such as the skills required to do the job and the cost of living in the relevant area. When the economy is booming and unemployment is low, employers may well have to offer higher wages in order to attract and retain workers, whereas when the economy is struggling and unemployment is high, wages tend to fall because there are many candidates for every available job.

One way in which ordinary workers might be able to influence their wage levels is to group together to bargain with the employer under the auspices of a trade union. 'Collective bargaining' helps to mitigate the inequality of bargaining power between

---

[56] See Chapter 9.

[57] *Thompson* v *Asda-MFI Group Plc* [1988] Ch 241, though cf *Mallone* v *BPB Industries Ltd* [2002] EWCA Civ 126, [2002] ICR 1045, in which the employer had a discretion and was obliged to exercise it reasonably in accordance with *Clark* (above n 50).

[58] For example, Competition Commission, *Market Investigation into Payment Protection Insurance* (January 2009).

workers and their employer because it is much harder for the employer to ignore the demands of a trade union representing many workers than it is to ignore a request for a pay rise from one worker.[59] In collective bargaining, the workers may back up their demands by threatening to go on strike, thereby increasing their leverage even further. Although collective bargaining is in decline, some 64% of public sector workers and 17% of private sector workers had their pay set by this method in 2013.[60]

A legally binding minimum wage acts as a 'floor' below which people's pay cannot fall. While this can be a useful 'backstop' in workplaces covered by collective bargaining, its real value is for the majority of people not covered by collective bargaining. Particularly in times of high unemployment, there is a risk that employers will drive down the wages of these workers to very low levels indeed. In the UK, a legally binding minimum wage was introduced for the first time in the National Minimum Wage Act 1998.[61] Around 5% of the UK workforce earns the NMW,[62] though its impact is broader because changes in the rate also affect those who earn slightly more than the NMW.

In the next section, we will consider some of the arguments for and against minimum wage laws in general terms. We will then turn to the NMW itself, examining who is eligible, what the rates are and how they are set, how entitlement to the NMW is calculated, and how it is enforced.

7.3.1 Minimum wages – policy issues

Let us begin with the arguments in favour of minimum wage laws. These fall into three main groups: arguments from dignity and human rights, economics arguments and arguments relating to social security policy.

One key argument in favour of minimum wage laws is that they preserve workers' dignity by ensuring that their labour is suitably rewarded. Article 23(3) of the UDHR states that pay should be sufficient to ensure 'an existence worthy of human dignity'. Article 7 ICESCR states that there is a right to 'remuneration which provides all workers, as a minimum, with . . . a decent living for themselves and their families'. However, it is important to note that the human rights instruments do not generally insist that all of a worker's 'decent wage' should come from the employer.[63] A state may satisfy its human rights obligations by supplementing the incomes of very low paid workers with social security benefits. Nevertheless, the claim that a worker should be able to provide for basic necessities from his or her earnings is a powerful one. Moreover, the rights-based argument in favour of minimum wages can be supplemented by an equality argument. Low pay does not affect everyone equally:

---

[59] See Chapter 12.

[60] Department for Business, Innovation and Skills, *Trade Union Membership 2013* (2014) 43.

[61] Prior to this, there was a system of sectoral Wages Councils, first introduced under the Trade Boards Act 1918, and finally abolished by the Trade Union Reform and Employment Rights Act 1993. For analysis of the Act and subsequent case-law, see Bob Simpson, 'A Milestone in the Legal Regulation of Pay: the National Minimum Wage Act 1998' (1999) 28 ILJ 1; 'Implementing the National Minimum Wage – the 1999 Regulations' (1999) 28 ILJ 171; 'The National Minimum Wage Five Years On: Reflections on some General Issues' (2004) 33 ILJ 22; 'The Employment Act 2008's Amendments to the National Minimum Wage Legislation' (2009) 38 ILJ 57.

[62] Low Pay Commission, *The National Minimum Wage Low Pay Commission Report 2014* (Cm 8816, 2014) para 2.6.

[63] UDHR, art 23(3); ILO, Minimum Wage Fixing Convention (No 131, 1970) art 3 (not ratified by the UK).

there is a correlation between low pay and characteristics that may result in discrimination, so that (for example) women or individuals with disabilities are more likely to find themselves in lower pay brackets.[64] A minimum wage will raise the pay of these groups and (unless everyone else's pay goes up too) may help to reduce inequality in society.

Although (as we shall see below) many economists oppose minimum wage laws, they can be supported from this perspective. One possible role for such laws is to bring more people into the labour market by making work more attractive, thereby broadening the pool of talent from which employers can hire. Another claim is that minimum wage laws enhance productivity: if workers are well-paid, so the argument goes, they will work harder and produce more, with benefits for the economy as a whole.[65] Of course, minimum wage laws also increase employers' costs, with the possibility of putting some firms out of business, but some schools of economic thought argue that this is a good thing, in the sense that a firm that can only compete by paying very low wages is probably not a very successful firm and therefore not worth preserving.[66] Minimum wage laws force firms to think about the quality of their products and to compete on that basis rather than by exploiting workers.

A final argument in favour of minimum wage laws links back to the point we considered earlier about social security benefits. Where wages do not provide workers with enough money to live on, governments may need to help out through housing benefit, tax credits and so on. In effect, the state 'subsidises' low-paying employers by ensuring that workers with very low wages still have basic necessities like food and shelter. Thus, one argument for introducing a minimum wage is that it shifts the cost of supporting these workers away from the state and onto employers, who are deriving an advantage from their labour.

The arguments against minimum wage laws tend to come from economists who think that it is best not to interfere in the workings of the market. Their main claim is that minimum wage laws will cause unemployment.[67] They argue that wages are determined by market forces: the employer will pay exactly what it needs to in order to attract the right number of workers with the right skills. When the minimum wage is introduced or increased, employers' costs will go up but they will still be getting the same amount of work from the workers.[68] In order to stay competitive, the rational employer will seek to reduce its costs back to the original level. Since wages can no longer be reduced, the only way to do this is to make some workers redundant. In extreme cases, the firm may go out of business. In that way, minimum wage laws end up harming those they are intended to protect by reducing the *number* of jobs available in the economy.

---

[64] Above n 62, 2.18–2.24.

[65] An application of the 'efficiency wage' theory: see R Solow, 'Another Possible Source of Wage Stickiness' (1979) 1 Journal of Macroeconomics 79; C Shapiro and T Stiglitz, 'Equilibrium Unemployment as a Worker Discipline Device' (1984) 74 American Economic Review 433.

[66] An application of the 'shock theory': see A Rees, *The Economics of Work and Pay* (Harper & Row 1973) 80–83.

[67] See, for example, J Stigler, 'The Economics of Minimum Wage Legislation' (1946) 36 American Economic Review 358; J Mincer, 'Unemployment Effects of Minimum Wages' (1976) 84 Journal of Political Economy S87; P Linneman, 'The Economic Impacts of Minimum Wage Laws: a New Look at an Old Question' (1982) 90 Journal of Political Economy 443. For counter-arguments, cf David Card and Alan B Krueger, *Myth and Measurement: the New Economics of the Minimum Wage* (Princeton University Press 1995); Simon Deakin and Frank J Wilkinson, 'The Law and Economics of the Minimum Wage' (1992) 19 Journal of Law and Society 379.

[68] These theorists tend to reject the efficiency wage argument considered above.

On a macro-economic level, the introduction of a minimum wage and subsequent increases in the level of the wage may also contribute to the problem of inflation. In a sense, the minimum wage can be regarded as good for the economy because it increases workers' spending power. They can buy more goods and services with their new, higher earnings. However, the costs of those goods and services may also increase because the people producing them are also earning more. So worker X might decide to buy new shoes with his or her extra pay, only to find that the price of shoes has gone up because the wage costs of the shoe shop have also increased. The result of this may be that no-one is better off in a 'real' sense as a result of the wage rise. Or, more worryingly, it may trigger an inflation spiral as people demand yet more pay in order to keep up with the rise in prices.

When the NMW was introduced in the UK in 1998, the government made two main arguments in its favour: the dignity argument and the social security argument.[69] Its aim was to ensure that workers had a decent standard of living in return for their efforts, and to reduce the need for the state to subsidise low-paying firms. But it also took account of the worry about unemployment by setting the rate at a relatively low level, at least initially.

7.3.2 Eligibility

Under s. 1(2) National Minimum Wage Act 1998 (NMWA), an individual qualifies for the NMW if he or she is a 'worker' as defined in s. 54(3).[70] The intention of the Act was to extend the protection of the NMW broadly to anyone who was under a contract to perform work personally and was not running his or her own business, though the breadth of the 'worker' definition depends on the courts' interpretations.

An interesting feature of the NMWA is that it includes various provisions designed to ensure the breadth of its application. Agency workers may find it difficult to demonstrate that they have a worker's contract with either the end user or the agency. But s. 34 NMWA states that they must be paid the minimum wage by whichever of the end user or agency is either contractually or in practice responsible for paying them. Similarly, home workers may find it difficult to show that they perform work 'personally' – since they are normally paid for completed work and the employer may not know or care who has done the work – but s. 35 removes the requirement to do work 'personally' in the case of home workers. Perhaps most radically, s. 41 NMWA empowers the Secretary of State to make regulations applying the NMW to persons who would not otherwise qualify as workers, thereby affording a potential safeguard to groups excluded by difficulties with the worker definition. However, no regulations have been issued under the section.

There is a list of workers excluded from the NMW but this is relatively narrow, covering only family workers,[71] share fishermen, unpaid voluntary workers, resident workers in religious communities, prisoners, those working to discharge fines, and those detained under immigration legislation.[72]

---

[69] See, generally, Low Pay Commission, *The National Minimum Wage: First Report of the Low Pay Commission* (Cm 3976, June 1998); and the government's response: statement by Margaret Beckett, HC Deb 18 June 1998 cc 507–519.

[70] See Chapter 5.

[71] National Minimum Wage Regulations 1999, SI 1999/584, reg 2(2). The issues surrounding this exclusion are illustrated by *Nambalat v Taher* [2012] EWCA Civ 1249, [2013] ICR 1024.

[72] NMWA 1998, ss 43–45B.

7.3.3 The rate

The NMW is expressed as an hourly wage and is currently set at the following rates:

> The adult rate (for workers aged 21 and over): £6.50[73]
>
> The development rate (for workers aged between 18 and 20): £5.13[74]
>
> Workers under 18: £3.79[75]
>
> The apprentice rate: £2.73

The special apprentice rate, introduced in 2010, applies to apprentices who are under 19 and to apprentices of any age during the first year of their apprenticeship.[76] The justification for this is that apprentices are receiving training during this time.

Under s. 1(3) NMWA, the NMW is 'such single hourly rate as the Secretary of State may from time to time prescribe'. Importantly, then, the Secretary of State has a free hand in setting the rate and is under no obligation to review the rate on a regular basis. However, the Act also provides for the creation of an independent body called the Low Pay Commission (LPC).[77] The Secretary of State invites this body to make a recommendation once a year on the appropriate level for the NMW. If the Secretary of State chose not to follow the LPC's recommendation, he or she would have to set out the reasons for doing so in a report to be laid before Parliament.[78] In practice, the LPC's recommendations are usually followed and the rates are altered in October each year.

The government's decision to vary the NMW by reference to age – and not to vary it by reference to other factors – was controversial. The government argued that the lower rate would combat youth unemployment, because when young workers decided to enter the labour market, they would be cheap for employers to hire and would therefore find it easier to get work.[79] If they had to be paid the same as older workers, employers would choose people with more experience who would be more productive. This would expose young workers to the risk of never finding a job. The law now prohibits discrimination on grounds of age,[80] but since (unusually) direct age discrimination is subject to a justification defence, the retention of age-related NMW rates may be less anomalous than it seems.[81]

Although the NMW varies by age, it does not vary by sector of the economy or by region of the UK. Thus, although the cost of living is far higher in London than it is in, say, South Wales, the NMW rate is the same. The government's claim here was that the NMW would be simpler to publicise and enforce if it was a single rate. There is no need for complex jurisdictional rules to determine which of several rates applies in any given case. However, this does make the task of setting the rate rather more complex.

---

[73] NMWR 1999, SI 1999/584 reg 11. This was for workers aged 22 and over until 2010.

[74] NMWR 1999, reg 13. This was for workers aged between 18 and 21 until 2010.

[75] ibid. This was introduced for the first time in 2003. Before then, workers under the age of 18 were not covered by the NMW.

[76] ibid.

[77] NMWA 1998, s 8.

[78] ibid s 6(3).

[79] See Malcolm Sargeant, 'The Employment Equality (Age) Regulations 2006: A Legitimisation of Age Discrimination in Employment' (2006) 35 ILJ 209.

[80] See Chapter 6.

[81] Under sch 9, para 11 Equality Act 2010, an employer has a defence to an age discrimination claim if it differentiates between younger and older workers in its pay scales by basing those scales on the NMW.

Of course, a key question with any minimum wage is whether it offers workers a decent standard of living – whether it meets the dignity justification set out above. The Living Wage Foundation, a non-governmental organisation with a focus on this issue, argues that the hourly wage needed for a decent living is £9.15 in London and £7.85 in the rest of the UK.[82] It seeks to persuade public bodies and firms to agree to pay these rates, which are considerably in excess of the NMW. However, as we have seen, the government may supplement the NMW with social security in order to guarantee a decent standard of living, and it is also important to bear in mind competing considerations such as the fear of increasing unemployment levels.

7.3.4 Calculations

The NMW is expressed as a set of hourly rates depending primarily on age. In this section, we will consider how the law works out whether or not someone is being paid the NMW. For those who are paid by the hour (known as 'time work' in this context), this is a relatively simple task, but even here there are some complications. Those who are not paid by the hour count as 'salaried workers', 'output workers' or 'unmeasured workers' for NMW purposes and different rules apply in each case.

Time work

Time work is defined in the National Minimum Wage Regulations (NMWR), reg. 3 as work paid for by reference to the time worked or to the worker's output per hour, that is not salaried work.[83] The simplest case of time work is someone paid by the hour. In order to determine whether a time worker is receiving the minimum wage, it is necessary to calculate how many hours he or she has worked over the 'pay reference period', which is one month (or the period for which he or she is paid, if shorter than a month) and to divide his or her earnings for that period by the number of hours worked.[84] So if the individual is paid weekly and has worked ten hours in a particular week, the employer must pay him or her £65 to comply with the NMW.

Inevitably, difficulties might arise where the individual is, for example, travelling between work sites or 'on call' (available for work but not working). Regulation 15 helps to unravel some of these problems. Thus, the worker is *not* entitled to the NMW for:

- time when he or she is absent from work, unless this is for the purposes of attending a training course;

- time when he or she is on strike;

- rest breaks;

- time 'on call' if he or she is at home or if he or she is provided with sleeping accommodation and is not required to be awake;

- time spent travelling to work.

---

[82] http://www.livingwage.org.uk/ (last visited 5 November 2014). The NMW rate has been criticised by the ECSR: European Committee of Social Rights, *Conclusions XIX-3 (United Kingdom)* (2010).
[83] NMWR 1999, reg 3.
[84] ibid reg 14.

But the worker is entitled to the NMW for:

- 'on call' time, defined as time spent being available at or near the place of work for the purpose of doing time work (even if not actually working);

- travel time where it is part of the job (for example, a bus driver);

- travel time where the worker is travelling between assignments (for example, a computer repair person travelling from one job to the next).

'Salaried hours' work

Salaried hours work is defined in reg. 4 as where the individual is paid in weekly or monthly instalments in respect of his or her basic contractual hours. The difference between salaried hours and time work is that in salaried hours work, the worker's pay does not vary according to the exact number of hours worked, and he or she is not entitled to extra payments beyond salary in respect of the hours actually worked, such as overtime payments.

In order to calculate a salaried hours worker's entitlement to the NMW, the law provides a method for converting his or her work to time work.[85] So, for example, if the individual is contracted to work 1040 hours per year and is paid weekly, the figure of 1040 should be divided by 52 (the number of weeks per year) to give a figure of 20 hours' work in each pay reference period.[86] Provided that the individual is earning at least £130 per week, the employer is in compliance with the minimum wage.

Again, though, there are some additional factors to consider. The treatment of 'on call' time, travelling time and training is the same as it is for people doing time work, as discussed above.[87] Regulation 22 deals with the situation in which a salaried worker works more than his or her basic hours in the year. This is designed to close the loophole that would arise if an employer was entitled to specify the individual's contractual hours for the purposes of NMW calculation but then insist in practice that he or she worked lots of extra hours, so that his or her 'real' earnings would drop below the NMW. It does this in a rather complex way but, put simply, seeks to ensure that the extra hours worked are taken into consideration when working out whether or not the individual has been paid the NMW.

Output work

Under reg. 5, output work is defined as work paid for by reference to the amount of work done by the worker rather than the time worked. The most obvious example is 'piece work', where the individual is paid for the number of items produced, but the definition also covers people who are paid on a commission basis for the number of sales they make.

There are two different ways in which output work can be dealt with under the Regulations. One possibility is simply to convert it to time work, so the worker's

---

[85] NMWR 1999, reg 21.
[86] If the worker is absent (through industrial action or some other cause) and therefore loses some entitlement to pay, the figure for the pay reference period can be reduced under reg 21(3) and (4).
[87] NMWR 1999, reg 16.

entitlement is calculated based on the time it takes him or her to perform the task for which he or she is paid.[88] But this does not apply where the worker is engaged in 'rated output work'.[89] This option allows the employer to base its NMW calculations on the average time taken by workers to perform the task in question. The provisions here are complex. The employer must first conduct a test to determine the speed at which either all the workers or a representative sample of workers can perform the relevant task. This is used to determine the 'mean hourly output rate' – the average number of tasks that can be performed in an hour, which in turn is used to convert the number of tasks actually performed by the claimant worker into hours worked, on the basis of 120% of the average hours.[90] So, let us assume that the average worker can produce 10 handmade greetings cards in an hour. The claimant worker is paid weekly and has produced 100 cards in a week. This amount of work would take the average worker 10 hours, but we apply the 120% multiplier to give a figure of 12 hours' work. Thus, the claimant worker is receiving the NMW if he or she is getting £78 per week. The employer can only invoke the 'rated output work' provisions if it does not control the workers' working time in practice and if it gives the worker a notice in advance, in the appropriate form, that it will be paying him or her on this basis.[91]

The 'rated output work' provisions are designed to strike a balance between the employer's desire to use piece rates as a way to motivate workers whilst ensuring that the NMW is still paid to those workers. The use of the 120% multiplier ensures that at least some of the workers who are slower than average should still be paid the NMW in respect of the time they work. The real difficulty with these provisions relates to the employer's calculation of the average time taken to perform the relevant task.[92] Although the legislation is detailed and seeks to ensure that the calculation is done fairly, there is always a risk that the employer may overestimate the speed at which workers can perform the task, leaving some earning well below the NMW. And while the employer's calculation is open to challenge, it is hard to imagine a tribunal overturning it in practice.

Unmeasured work

Our fourth category is unmeasured work, defined in reg. 6. This is a default category, so it applies when the work does not fall within any of the other categories. As the name suggests, it is especially relevant when the worker does not have fixed hours and is required to work when work is available.

As with output work, there are two approaches to calculating the NMW for unmeasured workers. One option is to work out how many hours the individual has actually worked during the pay reference period, and to ensure that he or she is paid the NMW for those hours.[93] But this approach can be displaced if the employer chooses the alternative: a 'daily average' agreement under reg. 28. This is a written

[88] NMWR 1999, reg 24.
[89] ibid reg 24(2); regs 25–26A.
[90] ibid reg 26.
[91] ibid reg 25.
[92] Simpson, 'The National Minimum Wage Five Years On', above n 61, 32–35.
[93] NMWR 1999, reg 27.

agreement between the employer and the worker setting out, in advance, how many hours he or she is likely to work per day. The agreement must be 'realistic'.[94] The employer may then calculate the individual's NMW entitlement by reference to the agreement. So, for example, if the agreement specifies five hours per day, and the individual worked for two days in a pay reference period of one week, the employer would need to pay £65 for that week in order to satisfy the NMW. This would be the case regardless of whether, in practice, the individual had worked more or less than 10 hours in that week.

'On call' time

Before we move on, it is worth noting that what we might characterise, informally, as 'on call' work has given rise to particular difficulties in relation to the NMW. The term 'on call' is not used in the NMWR, but it is a useful shorthand for the situation in which a person is required to be available for work if needed during a particular period of time, but may not be actively working for the whole of that time. Often, 'on call' workers are provided with sleeping accommodation and are entitled to go to sleep if there is no work to do. Examples include a night porter in a hotel or a warden in a care home. From the worker's perspective, it can be argued that he or she is at the employer's disposal and should therefore be paid for his or her time. In most jobs, it is not a condition of getting paid that the worker is actively working for the whole shift: for example, a worker in a call centre would still expect to get paid even if he or she did not spend the whole of any given hour on the phone. From the employer's perspective, though, it can be argued that it is unreasonable to pay people the NMW for time spent asleep. The courts have adopted divergent approaches in the case-law and it is not always easy to explain the distinctions drawn.

One option is to treat the 'on call' time as time work and to require the employer to pay the NMW for each hour spent 'on call'. In the *British Nursing* case, the claimants were nurses who worked night shifts dealing with telephone enquiries.[95] They worked from home, so while they were required to be available to answer the telephone all night, they were free to do as they chose if there were no calls. The Court of Appeal upheld the tribunal's finding that they were engaged in time work and should therefore be paid the NMW for the whole shift. Similar results were reached in *Scottbridge*, concerning a nightwatchman who was permitted to sleep during his shift,[96] *Burrow Down Support Services*, concerning a night sleeper in a care home who was required to attend to emergencies but permitted to sleep for the remainder of the shift,[97] and *Esparon*, in which the employer was under a statutory duty to have someone on the premises overnight.[98]

The contrasting approach is to apply reg. 15(1A) or reg. 16(1A) (depending on whether the individual is doing time work or salaried work) which state that when the worker is provided with sleeping accommodation, he or she is only entitled to be

---

[94] ibid reg 28(2).
[95] *British Nursing Association v Inland Revenue* [2002] EWCA Civ 494, [2003] ICR 19.
[96] *Scottbridge Construction Ltd v Wright* 2003 SC 520, 2002 SLT 1356; Court of Session (Inner House, First Division).
[97] *Burrow Down Support Services Ltd v Rossiter* [2008] ICR 1172.
[98] *Esparon v Slavikovska* [2014] ICR 1037.

paid the NMW for time spent awake and working. A good example here is *South Manchester Abbeyfield Society*.[99] The claimant was a housekeeper in a nursing home. She worked during the day and was required to be 'on call' on the premises overnight for four nights per week. She was provided with sleeping accommodation and was permitted to sleep during the nights unless there was an emergency. The EAT held that in this situation, she was only entitled to be paid the NMW for any hours spent actively working during the 'on call' periods. A similar result was reached in *Lauder*, concerning a warden in sheltered accommodation with a working arrangement very like the one just described,[100] and in *Wray*, concerning a pub manager who was required to sleep on the premises overnight for security reasons.[101]

Another way of achieving a similar result is to use the 'unmeasured work' option and to pay the worker on the basis of a 'daily average' agreement.[102] This was the approach taken by the employer in *Walton*.[103] In that case, the claimant was a care worker who spent three days per week living in the home of the person for whom she was caring. She had to be available for the full 24 hours on each of the days she worked, but there was a written agreement in place to the effect that her duties took, on average, six hours and 50 minutes per day. She argued that her work should be treated as 'time work' and that she should be paid for the 14 hours she spent awake and either caring for or supervising the client each day. But the Court of Appeal accepted the tribunal's finding that she was paid by reference to the tasks performed, not by reference to time. This meant that her work was 'unmeasured' and she could be paid according to the 'daily average' agreement reached with her employer.

These different lines of case-law seem hard to reconcile. The *Burrow Down* and *South Manchester* cases seem to have fundamentally similar facts, and the worker in *Walton* received much lower pay for a more onerous job than that in *British Nursing*, for example. One possible explanation – advanced in *Lauder* in particular – is the distinction between 'on call' work as the worker's main job, and 'on call' work on top of the worker's main job.[104] In that case, it was suggested that the worker's main job was his daytime work during the week. The extra 'on call' time should only be remunerated when the worker was called upon to work. It was argued that this contrasted with cases like *British Nursing* and *Scottbridge* because, in those cases, the worker's only job was to work the shift in question and it was in the nature of the work that it might be intermittent, therefore it was appropriate to regard the whole shift as working time attracting the NMW. However, this distinction does not account for cases like *Walton*, in which the carer's main job was to be available for the three-day period, or *Burrow Down*, in which the night sleeper was found to be entitled to the NMW for the whole shift.

The problem is exacerbated by the fact that the Working Time Regulations 1998 adopt a different view of time spent 'on call', treating all such time as working time regardless of whether the worker is awake or asleep.[105] So, as the EAT explained in *South Manchester*, the housekeeper was entitled to be treated as working for working

[99] *South Manchester Abbeyfield Society Ltd* v *Hopkins* [2011] ICR 254.
[100] *Edinburgh City Council* v *Lauder* (2012) UKEAT/0048/11/BI.
[101] *Wray* v *JW Lees & Co (Brewers) Ltd* [2012] ICR 43.
[102] NMWR 1999, reg 28.
[103] *Walton* v *Independent Living Organisation Ltd* [2003] EWCA Civ 199, [2003] ICR 688.
[104] *Lauder* (n 100) [33].
[105] See Chapter 8.

time purposes for the whole of the time she spent on call, whereas she was only entitled to the NMW if she had to get up in the night and work in response to an emergency.[106] There is a straightforward explanation for the different treatment of on call time for working time and NMW purposes: the two pieces of legislation have different sources. The Working Time Regulations implement an EU directive and the approach to on call time taken in that field reflects decisions of the Court of Justice of the European Union (CJEU), whereas the NMW is a domestic measure so the UK government and courts are free to adopt a different construction. It might also be argued that their purposes are different: working time is about protecting the health and safety of workers, whereas the NMW is designed to ensure that workers are fairly remunerated for the work they have done. On this view, it might be thought that long periods of time spent at the employer's disposal do pose a potential threat to the worker's well-being, whereas (if they do not involve work) they need not be remunerated. Nevertheless, even this is difficult to reconcile with the different approaches the courts have taken to people who are required to be at the employer's premises but who are not working for all of the time that they are there.

Perhaps the problem here is that the NMW – as a single rate – is too unsubtle to deal with complex situations like 'on call' time. One option might be to have a lower rate for time when the individual is not actively working but is at the employer's disposal, to reflect the fact that his or her freedom is limited during that time. However, the difficulty is that this would be open to abuse. Employers might argue that individuals were merely 'available for work' and therefore only entitled to the lower rate during quiet times, thereby leaving many people worse off just because (through no fault of their own) there is less work for them to do.

Payments and deductions

So far, we have focused on different ways of calculating the hours worked by the worker in order to judge whether or not he or she is in receipt of the NMW. The other factor to consider is the amount of money paid by the employer to the worker in respect of the pay reference period. Part IV of the NMW Regulations 1999 deals with payments and deductions in detail.

In simple terms, money paid by the employer in respect of the pay reference period, whether it is paid during the pay reference period or in the next pay reference period, 'counts' for NMW purposes.[107] Money paid later may also count if the worker was late in submitting his or her timesheet for the pay reference period.[108] However, it is important that the money comes from the employer. In the *Annabel's* case, the tips paid by customers in a restaurant were paid by the employer into a bank account belonging to a 'troncmaster', a manager working for the employer.[109] The troncmaster calculated each worker's share of the tips and paid the workers monthly. The employer sought to rely on the tronc money in order to show that the workers were being paid the NMW, but the Court of Appeal held that the money was not 'paid by the employer to the worker' so could not be relied upon in satisfaction of the

---

[106] *South Manchester* (n 99) [38].
[107] NMWR 1999, reg 30.
[108] ibid reg 30(c)(iii).
[109] *Revenue and Customs Commissioners v Annabel's (Berkeley Square) Ltd* [2009] EWCA Civ 361, [2009] ICR 1123.

employer's obligations.[110] Under reg. 31(1)(e), as amended, it is now clear that tips do not count towards payment of the NMW even where the employer pays them directly to the workers.

The treatment of tips forms part of a more general approach in the NMW Regulations to 'extra' payments. The Regulations pursue the policy that it is the worker's basic pay that must satisfy the NMW.[111] So, for example, additional payments (such as an allowance for working anti-social hours) or overtime payments (where the hourly rate is higher than normal for doing extra work or working at particular times, such as public holidays) must be subtracted from the total paid by the employer to the worker before calculating whether or not the NMW is being paid.[112]

However, there are some circumstances in which the employer is entitled to make deductions from the worker's pay which are ignored in the NMW calculation. Thus, for example, if the employer has given the worker an advance on his or her wages or is recovering previously overpaid wages, the NMW calculation is performed as if these deductions had not been made.[113] In some sectors, it is common for the employer to provide workers with accommodation near the workplace. This is true for agricultural workers, for example. The Regulations control the amount of money that can be deducted in respect of accommodation, limiting it to £5.08 per day.[114] Any additional accommodation charges deducted by the employer would serve to reduce the worker's total remuneration for NMW purposes.[115] In theory, this means that employers cannot undermine the NMW by deducting large sums for accommodation, though it is easy enough to evade by requiring the workers to pay rent for their accommodation to a legally separate entity.

7.3.5 Enforcement

Individuals are, of course, entitled to bring legal action to enforce the NMW themselves. But – unusually in English employment law – there are also possibilities for enforcement by the state. A public body – Her Majesty's Revenue and Customs (HMRC), better known for enforcing the tax system – may investigate employers (either of its own motion or based on a tip-off from workers) to see whether they are complying with the NMW. If they are not, HMRC may take legal action to compel them to do so and to secure payment of arrears to the affected workers. A deliberate failure to pay the NMW is a criminal offence and may lead to prosecution. These measures acknowledge the vulnerability of low-paid workers, who may not be well-placed to litigate to enforce their own rights, and also constitute a clear statement by the government that compliance with the NMW by employers is regarded as a particularly important duty.

The 1998 Act gives power to 'officers' appointed by the Secretary of State – in practice HMRC – to seek information from employers in order to determine whether

---

[110] ibid [40].
[111] See *Smith* v *Oxfordshire Learning Disability NHS Trust* [2009] ICR 1395.
[112] NMWR 1999, reg 31.
[113] ibid reg 33.
[114] ibid reg 36.
[115] This also includes related charges such as for gas and electricity at the accommodation: *Leisure Employment Services Ltd* v *Revenue and Customs Commissioners* [2006] ICR 1094.

or not they are paying the NMW.[116] Employers are obliged to keep records in accordance with s. 9 of the Act. If HMRC finds that an employer is not paying the NMW, it may issue a 'notice of underpayment'.[117] There is provision for an employer to appeal against the notice.[118] The notice provides that the employer must pay arrears to the affected workers, and a penalty to the Secretary of State, within 28 days.[119] The penalty is currently a sum equal to the arrears, subject to a minimum of £100 and a maximum of £20,000.[120] Employers are also 'named and shamed' on the Department for Business, Innovation and Skills website.[121] Clause 138 of the Small Business, Enterprise and Employment Bill currently before Parliament would increase the maximum penalty to £20,000 *per worker* rather than per notice. If the employer does not comply with the notice, HMRC may take legal action to enforce both the payment of the arrears and the payment of the penalty.[122] In 2011–12, HMRC identified 17,000 workers who were not being paid the NMW and who were owed £3.6 million in arrears.[123] While this sounds impressive, it is difficult to judge how effective HMRC is because no-one knows how many workers are doing jobs that do not pay the NMW. These jobs generally exist outside the formal economy, so the workers concerned are paid in cash with no tax or National Insurance deductions, and are therefore difficult to detect. And of course an employer who is not paying the NMW is unlikely to advertise that fact given the risk of enforcement action or even prosecution.

The use of the criminal law in the employment law field is relatively unusual. However, under the NMWA, there are five main offences. The first and most important is committed where an employer 'refuses or wilfully neglects' to pay the NMW.[124] It is worth emphasising that this offence is only committed where the employer *deliberately* does not pay the NMW. An accidental failure – for example, because of a misunderstanding of how to calculate the worker's hours – would only be a civil wrong. The other offences are supplementary and deal with: failing to keep records,[125] falsifying records,[126] providing false records (for example, to HMRC)[127] or obstructing an officer who is conducting an investigation.[128] These act as an important deterrent to employers and reinforce the government's original policy objective that the Act should be 'self-enforcing': in other words, its provisions would be so well-known and well-accepted that employers would comply without the need for action by workers or HMRC.

Under s. 17 NMWA, the worker's entitlement to the NMW is treated as contractual. This means that the worker can use the common law or statutory actions discussed

---

[116] NMWA 1998, s 14(1).
[117] ibid s 19.
[118] ibid s 19C.
[119] ibid s 19(2) and s 19A(1).
[120] National Minimum Wage (Variation of Financial Penalty) Regulations 2014, SI 2014/547. If the employer pays within 14 days, the penalty is halved.
[121] DBIS, *Policy on HM Revenue & Customs Enforcement, Prosecutions and Naming Employers who Break National Minimum Wage Law* (March 2014).
[122] NMWA 1998, s 19D.
[123] DBIS/HMRC, *Delivering Results: National Minimum Wage Compliance & Enforcement, Report for 18 month period to 30 September 2012* (January 2013) 2.
[124] NMWA 1998, s 31(1).
[125] ibid s 31(2).
[126] ibid s 31(3).
[127] ibid s 31(4).
[128] ibid s 31(5).

above in order to obtain payment from the employer. Several features of the Act support the worker in bringing a claim. Under s. 10, if the worker has reasonable grounds for suspecting that he or she is not getting the NMW, he or she is entitled to inspect the records kept by the employer under s. 9. And under s. 28, the burden of proof is reversed so that it is to be presumed that the worker was entitled to the NMW unless the employer proves to the contrary. However, one of the major criticisms of the NMWA is that the provision in s. 12 that workers should be provided with a statement explaining how they are being paid the NMW (for example, on their payslip each week or month) has not been put into effect by the government.[129] This would have helped workers to understand their pay and would have operated as another encouragement to employers to comply with the Act.

7.4 EQUAL PAY FOR MEN AND WOMEN

In this section, we will consider the issue of equal pay for men and women. Of course, any pay inequality between different groups on discriminatory grounds is unlawful.[130] But pay inequality between men and women has a particularly long history and remains a significant problem in today's society, despite legislation to address the issue since the 1970s. Since equal pay for men and women has always been dealt with separately by the law – and continues to be dealt with separately today, to a large extent – we will consider it separately here. We will start with an examination of the 'gender pay gap' and some of its causes. We will then consider how equal pay law fits into the broader scheme of EU law and equality law, before examining the relevant provisions of the Equality Act 2010 in detail. Since it is usually women who bring equal pay claims, we will refer to the claimant as 'she' in this section.

7.4.1 The 'gender pay gap'

The 'gender pay gap' refers to the difference in what men and women earn, on average. The Office for National Statistics (ONS) calculates the gap by examining the median hourly earnings of men and women excluding overtime.[131] This generates a gap of 9.6% for full-time employees (so women earn, on average, 90.4% of what men earn) and 19.7% for both full- and part-time employees (so women earn, on average, 80.3% of what men earn). The figures are, at least, improving over time. The equivalent ONS figures for 1997 were 17.4% and 27.5% respectively.

The causes of the gender pay gap are many and complex. Of course, one reason might just be prejudice – there may still be some employers out there who think that women are just worth less than men – but there are less obvious causes too. We will focus on two here: the hours women work and the jobs women do.

One of the most significant issues – as the ONS statistics suggest – is working hours. The gender pay gap is relatively narrow if we only look at full-time employees, but it widens substantially when part-timers are also taken into account. This reveals a fundamental problem: that of working time. Women make up the majority of the

---

[129] Simpson, 'The National Minimum Wage Five Years On', above n 61, 35–36.
[130] See Chapter 6.
[131] Bovill, above n 2, 10–12.

part-time workforce.[132] This is generally thought to be explained by the fact that the responsibility for bringing up children still tends to fall more heavily on women than it does on men, leaving women with less time available for paid work. Of course, it is obvious that people working fewer hours will tend to earn less *in total* than people working full-time. But the problem we are seeing here is a more subtle one: it is that people working part-time tend to earn less *for each hour they work* than people working full-time. There are a couple of possible explanations for this. One is that there is discrimination against part-time workers because they are part-time. Although the Part-Time Workers Regulations should help to tackle this problem, instances of discrimination may well persist.[133] The other – more intractable – explanation is that employers tend to be reluctant to make high-paid jobs available on a part-time basis. For example, it is probably much easier to obtain part-time work on the supermarket checkout (on low pay) than it is as a solicitor or a manager (on higher pay). Employers tend to argue that people in higher-paid jobs need to be available for the whole of the working week (and more) in order to deal with problems as they arise or meet clients at any time.

Another reason for the gender pay gap is the uneven distribution of women in the labour market. Women are over-represented in low-paid occupations (caring for the elderly, child-care, cleaning) and under-represented in well-paid occupations (judges, chief executives, investment bankers). This problem is linked to the working time issue just discussed, but there are some other factors to consider too. Feminist writers argue that some types of work that were historically performed in the home (rather than in the labour market) by women tend to be regarded as less skilled and less valuable than they really are.[134] For example, child-care is notoriously low-paid, perhaps because it is seen as something that women are 'naturally' able to do without any need for training, even though arguably it should be regarded as a highly responsible job requiring a range of educational and caring skills. And there are economic explanations too: if women 'crowd' into certain jobs, the sheer number of women looking for work in those fields will drive down wage levels.[135]

In the literature on equal pay, there is an important debate about what we can reasonably expect equal pay legislation to achieve. Some economists argue that equal pay laws are unnecessary because the market will sort itself out over time: if women are cheaper to hire, rational employers will hire them, firms that discriminate will go out of business, and women's wages will rise as the rational employers increase their market share.[136] Critics point out, however, that the gender pay gap persists, showing that real-life labour markets do not always work as the theory would predict. Leaving this issue aside, it is clear that equal pay laws only tackle some aspects of pay inequality. For example, equal pay laws have helped to dismantle the practice of 'women's grades', where women were paid less than men doing the same work simply because of their gender. They have also helped to address more subtle forms of discrimination, for example, by encouraging employers to evaluate jobs against objective, non-discriminatory criteria rather than making assumptions about the value of different types of work. However, the explanations for the gender pay gap

---

[132] Office of National Statistics, *Labour Market Statistics, June 2014* (2014) 9.
[133] The Part-time Workers (Prevention of Less Favourable Treatment) Regulations 2000, SI 2000/1551.
[134] For example, Sandra Fredman, *Women and the Law* (Clarendon Press 1997) chapter 3.
[135] BR Bergmann, *The Economic Emergence of Women* (Basic Books 1986) chapters 5 and 6.
[136] GS Becker, *The Economics of Discrimination* (2nd edn, University of Chicago Press, 1971).

discussed above suggest that other initiatives – such as encouraging men to play a greater role in child-care, providing affordable nursery places, encouraging women to train for jobs not traditionally done by women, and requiring employers to make a range of jobs available on a part-time basis – might also be needed in order to solve the problem properly.

7.4.2 Equal pay laws in context

In this section, we will examine three issues concerning the 'fit' between equal pay laws and other areas of law. We will begin by considering the treatment of equal pay in human rights instruments. We will then examine the relationship between EU law and domestic law on equal pay. And finally, we will consider the relationship between equal pay law and discrimination law.[137]

Before getting into the detail, it is worth pausing for a moment to consider why equal pay for men and women has attracted particular attention. Surely pay discrimination is just one form of discrimination, and gender is just one ground of discrimination? It is certainly true that women may experience many other forms of discrimination, and that other social groups may encounter pay discrimination. But the particular focus on equal pay for men and women has deep roots in our history, at least in the UK. Although women have always worked outside the home, there has been a tendency for policy-makers and others to focus on a social 'ideal' of the family in which the man is the breadwinner and the woman stays at home to run the household and bring up the children.[138] This had the consequence that it was common for women's pay to be much lower than men's because their money was perceived as somehow 'supplementary' to the family's main income. Of course, in practice this perception was often incorrect: single or widowed women generally had to support themselves, and even within a couple the woman might be the breadwinner if her husband was ill or unemployed, for example. Nevertheless, the pay disparity was a well-established phenomenon, with separate 'women's grades' in operation in many workplaces until the 1970s, when equal pay legislation was introduced. In view of the history, then, we should not be surprised at the special focus on equal pay for men and women. Towards the end of this section, we will consider whether the law should work differently today.

Equal pay (with particular reference to equal pay for men and women) is often regarded as a fundamental right, or at least a core part of the right not to be discriminated against. Article 23(2) of the Universal Declaration of Human Rights (UDHR) provides that 'everyone, without any discrimination, has the right to equal pay for equal work'. Most civil and political rights instruments contain a right not to be discriminated against, which is broad enough to include pay discrimination,[139] but for more specific references to equal pay it is necessary to turn to economic and social rights instruments. The ESC, the ICESCR, the EU Charter and (obviously) CEDAW make specific reference to equal pay for men and women.[140] Most instruments

---

[137] See Chapter 6.
[138] Fredman, above n 134, chapter 3.
[139] See, for example, European Convention on Human Rights, art 14.
[140] European Social Charter, art 4(3); International Covenant on Economic, Social and Cultural Rights, art 7(a)(i); Charter of Fundamental Rights of the European Union, art 23; Convention on the Elimination of All Forms of Discrimination against Women, art 11(1)(d).

use the phrase 'equal pay for work of equal value'. This is significant because it suggests that women may be entitled to equal pay with men not just for doing the same work but also for doing different work which is equally valuable in an objective sense. As we shall see when we examine the law, this is highly important in practice.

Equal pay also has a special status in EU law. When the Treaty of Rome was first agreed in 1957, the right to equal pay for men and women was included in Article 119. The current provision (after very slight alterations) is Article 157 TFEU:

(1) Each Member State shall ensure that the principle of equal pay for male and female workers for equal work or work of equal value is applied.

(2) For the purpose of this Article, 'pay' means the ordinary basic or minimum wage or salary and any other consideration, whether in cash or in kind, which the worker receives directly or indirectly, in respect of his employment, from his employer . . .

Article 119 had the distinction of being the main social provision in what was otherwise a treaty focused largely on trade. It was included primarily for economic reasons.[141] France had already enacted equal pay legislation, so the French government was concerned that French products would be undercut by those of firms based elsewhere in the new European Economic Community using cheaper female labour. Article 119 was intended to create a level playing field between France and other countries. Initially, Article 119 did not have much impact, but in the foundational case of *Defrenne*, the Court of Justice held that it was capable of having direct effect.[142] As a Treaty provision, that direct effect could be both vertical (against the state) or horizontal (against another private party, such as a private sector employer).[143] This opened the way for a series of cases in which the Court of Justice developed a body of rules on equal pay that women could invoke in the courts of their own Member States against their employers. The Court has been responsible for some big developments in the field of equal pay, such as the adoption of a broad definition of 'pay' to include workplace pensions.[144] In 1975, the Member States agreed the Equal Pay Directive,[145] which fleshed out some aspects of the developing law on equal pay. Equal pay is now dealt with in Article 4 of the Recast Directive,[146] which simply provides that:

For the same work or for work to which equal value is attributed, direct and indirect discrimination on grounds of sex with regard to all aspects and conditions of remuneration shall be eliminated.

In particular, where a job classification system is used for determining pay, it shall be based on the same criteria for both men and women and so drawn up as to exclude any discrimination on grounds of sex.

When bringing an equal pay claim, it is possible for a woman to argue her case both in domestic law (relying on the provisions of the Equality Act 2010) and in EU law (relying on the directly effective Article 157). In most cases, this will not be necessary because the Equality Act 2010, interpreted in the light of EU law, will elicit the same approach. However, just occasionally there are benefits to invoking Article 157 and we will note these in the discussion below.

---

[141] See Jeff Kenner, *EU Employment Law* (Hart 2003) chapters 1 and 2.
[142] Case 43/75 *Defrenne v Sabena (No 2)* [1976] ECR 455.
[143] ibid [24].
[144] Case C-262/88 *Barber v Guardian Royal Exchange Assurance Group* [1990] ECR I-1889.
[145] Directive 75/117/EEC.
[146] Directive 2006/54/EC.

A final piece of the equal pay jigsaw is the relationship between equal pay law and domestic equality law more generally under the 2010 Act. In the early years of the legislation, equal pay was dealt with using a separate statute – the Equal Pay Act 1970 – whereas other types of claim fell under the Sex Discrimination Act 1975. Although all the legislation has now been consolidated into the Equality Act 2010, the Act still contains a separate group of provisions on equal pay.[147] It is therefore important to know when to use these provisions and when to bring an 'ordinary' discrimination claim. Where the claim concerns a term of the woman's contract, the equal pay provisions must be used; all other claims should be brought as discrimination claims.[148] This means that it is something of an oversimplification to speak of 'equal pay' claims, since claims relating to unequal treatment in other aspects of the woman's contract are dealt with in the same way. The Equality Act 2010 has introduced one exception to this, for claims involving direct discrimination in contractual pay (the 'women's grade' scenario).[149] This can be dealt with as a discrimination claim. The importance of all of this is that in an equal pay claim, the woman must compare her terms and conditions with those of a real man working for the employer (a 'comparator'),[150] whereas in a discrimination claim, the court may look hypothetically at how she would have been treated had she been a man.[151] Thus, it is harder to bring an equal pay claim because of the need to identify a real comparator.

7.4.3 Bringing an equal pay claim

In simple terms, the law on equal pay allows a woman to identify a male comparator doing the same or equivalent work, and to compare the terms of her contract with his. If he has more favourable terms, and if the employer cannot justify the difference in treatment, her contract can be changed to match his. We will examine the various elements of the claim in turn.

The comparator

The claimant's first challenge is to identify a suitable comparator. For equal pay purposes – unlike gender equality more generally – this must be a real person of the opposite sex, not a hypothetical person.[152] It is only possible to look at what a man is being paid for the job, not at what a man would have been paid. There are two main routes to identifying a comparator.

The first is to choose someone working at the same establishment.[153] The person must be employed by the claimant's employer or by an associated employer.[154] Employers are 'associated' for this purpose if either:

(a) one is a company of which the other (directly or indirectly) has control, or

(b) both are companies of which a third person (directly or indirectly) has control.[155]

---

[147] EA 2010, ss 64–80.
[148] ibid s 70.
[149] ibid s 71.
[150] ibid s 64(1).
[151] ibid s 13(1) for direct discrimination ('treats or would treat') and s 19(2)(b) for indirect discrimination ('puts or would put').
[152] ibid s 79.
[153] ibid s 79(3)(b).
[154] ibid s 79(3)(a).
[155] ibid s 79(9).

The second is to choose someone working for the same employer or an associated employer (defined in the same way) at a different establishment, but where 'common terms apply at the establishments', either between the claimant and the comparator or more generally.[156] This phrase was given a broad construction by the House of Lords in the *Leverton* case.[157] Any broadening of the scope of comparison is to be welcomed because it increases the chances that a woman will be able to find a suitable comparator for the purposes of bringing a claim. 'Cross-establishment' comparisons are particularly useful where the employer is signed up to a collective agreement laying down 'common terms' for multiple establishments. However, with the decline in collective bargaining, such collective agreements are relatively unusual nowadays.

The comparator need not be employed at the same time as the claimant. This is clear from s. 64(2). This allows a woman to bring an equal pay claim where, for example, she discovers that her male predecessor in the job had better terms and conditions. Such claims were not permitted in the Equal Pay Act 1970 but in *Macarthys* the Court of Justice ruled that they could be brought under the Treaty.[158] The Equality Act 2010 brings UK law into line with this ruling.

Some commentators believe that the scope of comparison is drawn too narrowly because it still requires the comparator to be employed by the same employer or an associated employer. It does not permit comparisons with other firms in the same market, for example. In the *Lawrence* case, the claimants attempted to use EU law to broaden the scope of comparison.[159] The claimants in that case were dinner ladies and school cleaners who were transferred to the private sector when their previous employer, the local authority, contracted out these services. Their new private employer offered lower pay than the council. They sought to bring an equal pay claim using as their comparators people doing equivalent work who were still employed by the council. The Court of Justice accepted that there was nothing in the wording of Article 157 to limit equal pay claims to claimants and comparators employed by the same employer. But the Court then introduced a decisive limitation on the scope of claims:

> [W]here . . . the differences identified in the pay conditions of workers performing equal work or work of equal value cannot be attributed to a single source, there is no body which is responsible for the inequality and which could restore equal treatment. Such a situation does not come within the scope of [Article 157].[160]

Because the inequality was attributable to the actions of two separate employers, the claim failed. This means that neither national law nor EU law permits cross-industry comparisons. Of course, this limits the possibility for women to bring equal pay claims by limiting them to a comparison with people employed by the same or an associated employer. However, cross-industry comparisons might be quite difficult to manage in practice, not least because there could be a variety of reasons – other than discrimination – why one employer might pay more than another for a particular job.

[156] ibid s 79(4).
[157] *Leverton* v *Clwyd County Council* [1989] AC 706, 744–6 (per Lord Bridge of Harwich). See also *North* v *Dumfries and Galloway Council* [2013] UKSC 45, [2013] ICR 993.
[158] Case 129/79 *Macarthys Ltd* v *Smith* [1980] ECR 1275.
[159] Case C-320/00 *Lawrence* v *Regent Office Care Ltd* [2002] ECR I-7325.
[160] ibid [18].

Equal work

The next element of the claim is to establish that the claimant and her comparator are doing equal work. There are three ways to do this: 'like' work, work 'rated as equivalent', or work 'of equal value'.

The concept of 'like' work is defined in s. 65(2) as 'the same or broadly similar', with any differences being 'not of practical importance in relation to the terms of [the claimant and the comparator's] work'. In s. 65(3), tribunals are directed to have regard to 'the frequency with which differences between their work occur in practice' and 'the nature and extent of the differences'. The point here is that the claimant can bring a 'like' work claim even if there are some differences between her work and that of the comparator, provided that those differences are not significant.

The concept of 'work rated as equivalent' under s. 65(4) applies where the claimant's job is given equal value to that of her comparator under a job evaluation study. These studies measure the 'demands' made of a worker. The 'work rated as equivalent' option is of limited value as a basis for an equal pay claim because it depends upon the employer arranging for a job evaluation study to be conducted. In the unlikely event that the job evaluation study is blatantly discriminatory – 'sex-specific', defined as setting 'values for men different from those it sets for women'[161] – it can be disregarded. Under s. 65(4)(b), the claimant's work can be 'rated as equivalent' where it would achieve the same score if the job evaluation study was not sex-specific.

The third option is 'work of equal value'.[162] This was introduced into UK law in 1983 after the Court of Justice ruled that the UK was in breach of its European law obligations by only providing for the two options we have just considered.[163] The 'work of equal value' claim only applies if neither of the other two options is applicable but the claimant's work is 'equal to [the comparator's] work in terms of the demands made on [the claimant] by reference to factors such as effort, skill and decision-making'.[164] This is for the tribunal to determine, but provision is made for it to appoint an expert (from a panel maintained by ACAS) to prepare a report on the matter.[165] Where the employer has already arranged for a job evaluation study which ranked the claimant's job lower than that of her comparator, this may put a stop to the equal value claim unless the tribunal has reasonable grounds to suspect that the study was discriminatory or otherwise unreliable.[166] Importantly, this is broader than the 'sex-specific' provision discussed above, so it allows the claimant to use an equal value claim to challenge a job evaluation study that is discriminatory but not blatantly so.

The importance of equal value claims is that they broaden out the scope of comparison very considerably, looking beyond the details of the jobs people do and focusing instead on the characteristics of those jobs. For example, in the *British Coal* case, the claimants worked in the canteen at a coal mine.[167] They brought an equal value claim by comparing themselves to male surface mineworkers. We saw above

---

[161] EA 2010, s 65(5).
[162] ibid s 65(6).
[163] Case 61/81 *Commission v United Kingdom* [1982] ECR 2601.
[164] EA 2010, s 65(6).
[165] EA 2010, s 131; Employment Tribunals (Constitution and Rules of Procedure) Regulations 2013, SI 2013/1237, sch 3.
[166] ibid s 131(6).
[167] *British Coal Corporation v Smith* [1996] ICR 515.

that one of the reasons for the persistence of the gender pay gap is women working in certain occupations not normally chosen by men. For these women, a 'like' work claim is impossible, but an 'equal value' claim may be available.

7.4.4 The employer's justification defence

In equality law generally, the employer gets an opportunity to justify indirect but not direct discrimination.[168] The same is true in the field of equal pay. However, the means of achieving that result has always been rather more complex since, as we saw above, the starting-point of an equal pay claim is the establishment of unequal pay with a suitable comparator, rather than the establishment of direct or indirect discrimination. This led to a lot of litigation and confusion in the courts over many years.[169] The Equality Act 2010 has sought to resolve the problem by explaining the justification defence (known as the 'material factor' defence in this context) in terms of direct and indirect discrimination, in s. 69:

(1) The sex equality clause in A's terms has no effect in relation to a difference between A's terms and B's terms if the responsible person shows that the difference is because of a material factor reliance on which–

    (a) does not involve treating A less favourably because of A's sex than the responsible person treats B, and

    (b) if the factor is within subsection (2), is a proportionate means of achieving a legitimate aim.

(2) A factor is within this subsection if A shows that, as a result of the factor, A and persons of the same sex doing work equal to A's are put at a particular disadvantage when compared with persons of the opposite sex doing work equal to A's.

(3) For the purposes of subsection (1), the long-term objective of reducing inequality between men's and women's terms of work is always to be regarded as a legitimate aim.

Section 69(1)(a) deals with direct discrimination: where this is established, no defence is available to the employer. So, for example, if the reason for the pay inequality is that the employer has separate grades for men and women the employer will not be able to argue that this is justified. Section 69(2) deals with indirect discrimination: where this is established, the employer may justify the discrimination provided that its claims satisfy the proportionality test set out in s. 69(1)(b). Pay arrangements are indirectly discriminatory where they have a disproportionate impact on people of the claimant's sex. As is the case for non-pay claims, the dividing line between direct and indirect discrimination is not always clear and there may be a debate in some cases as to whether the employer's pay scale is 'tainted by sex' and unjustifiable, or indirectly discriminatory and therefore potentially justifiable.[170]

    The proportionality test does a lot of work in equal pay claims for two reasons. First, examples of direct pay discrimination are relatively rare nowadays, and second, the reversed burden of proof under s. 136 Equality Act 2010 places the onus on the employer to defend itself once the claimant has established unequal pay between herself and her comparator (or between a group of women workers, of which she is

---

[168] See Chapter 6.
[169] For example, *Gibson v Sheffield City Council* [2010] EWCA Civ 63, [2010] ICR 708.
[170] See *North Yorkshire County Council v Ratcliffe* [1996] ICR 515.

one, and a group of male workers).[171] The proportionality test derives originally from the very famous decision of the Court of Justice in the *Bilka Kaufhaus* case,[172] and although in principle the application of the proportionality test to the facts of cases is a matter for the national courts, the Court often gives detailed guidance on the correct approach to take. In some cases, the employer's argument may be personal to the claimant and her comparator: he is paid more because he has better qualifications or more experience, for example.[173] Here we will focus on three broader arguments that have arisen in the case-law: that the pay differential is justified because the employer is responding to market forces, rewarding length of service or making a transition to a fairer pay system.

An employer makes a 'market forces' argument when it claims that male workers were paid more than female workers because the labour market required it. Such claims are potentially problematic because they could amount to saying that a woman is precluded from bringing an equal pay claim simply because she accepted the job offer at a lower rate of pay than her male comparator was prepared to accept.[174] This would do little to tackle the problem of unequal pay. However, where the employer can show that the pay inequality results from specific recruitment difficulties, the market forces argument might succeed. For example, in *Rainey*, the NHS sought to expand its prosthetics service.[175] To do this, the employer needed to recruit workers from the private sector. In order to persuade these workers (who were all men) to join, the employer decided that it needed to match their private sector pay, which was higher than that normally offered to prosthetists in the NHS. A woman who was employed on the normal NHS wage brought an equal pay claim. The House of Lords held that the employer could justify the difference in pay. The Court of Justice reached a similar conclusion in the *Enderby* case: 'The state of the employment market, which may lead an employer to increase the pay of a particular job in order to attract candidates, may constitute an objectively justified economic ground.'[176] However, the Court also emphasised the role of proportionality in judging the employer's claim, so the employer must be able to show that the extra pay is no more than is necessary in order to attract suitable candidates.[177]

Length of service is a very common basis for setting pay and is thought to reward loyalty and encourage the acquisition of firm-specific skills. But critics argue that it disadvantages women because they are more likely to take career breaks to have children and thus find it harder than men do to build up long periods of service with the same employer. According to the Court of Justice's ruling in the *Cadman* case, length of service is in principle a legitimate criterion for an employer to use in setting pay and does not need to be justified in itself.[178] But if the claimant can show that the pay scale goes beyond what is necessary to reward experience and better job performance, the burden shifts to the employer to justify its use in the particular context. This might occur where, for example, the pay scale rewards very long periods

---

[171] See Chapter 6.
[172] Case 170/84 *Bilka-Kaufhaus GmbH v Weber von Hartz* [1986] ECR 1607.
[173] *Clay Cross (Quarry Services) Ltd v Fletcher* [1979] ICR 1.
[174] ibid 5 (Lord Denning MR).
[175] *Rainey v Greater Glasgow Health Board* [1987] AC 224.
[176] Case C-127/92 *Enderby v Frenchay HA* [1993] ECR I-5535 [26].
[177] ibid [27].
[178] Case C-17/05 *Cadman v Health and Safety Executive* [2006] ECR I-9583.

of service even though it is quite clear that after a couple of years' service, everyone is equally good at doing the job and no-one's performance improves significantly.

Finally, we turn to situations in which the employer is seeking to redress past inequality. This may seem rather odd, but in practice it has proved to be a significant problem. Imagine that the employer reviews its pay arrangements and discovers that there are significant past inequalities in those arrangements. It seeks to rectify this by putting in place new structures. However, this means that men who have benefited from the old structures will suffer significant pay cuts. The employer decides to keep the men happy by allowing them to stay on a higher rate until the women catch up. The difficulty here is that, while this may help to secure the workforce's acceptance of the new arrangements, it means that the new 'equal' pay scheme is nothing of the sort, because the women are still paid lower rates. In the *Bainbridge* case, the Court of Appeal held that a 'pay protection' arrangement of this kind could potentially be justified by an employer but only in very limited circumstances, for example, where it was clearly a short-term measure.[179] The Equality Act 2010 (which post-dates *Bainbridge*) addresses this situation directly for the first time. Section 69(3) provides that the aim of securing equal pay over the long term is to be regarded as legitimate by the courts. However, the significance of this is limited because the employer must still be able to demonstrate that the transitional arrangements are a *proportionate* means of achieving the aim. Thus, many of the issues considered in *Bainbridge* remain relevant.

7.4.5 The 'equality clause'

Once the claimant has established that she is doing work that is equal to that of her comparator, and the employer has been unable to make out a defence, her equal pay claim takes effect through the device of an 'equality clause' implied by statute into her contract.[180] The effect of the equality clause is to bring any terms in her contract that are less favourable than those in her comparator's contract into line with his, and to insert into her contract any beneficial terms that are in her comparator's contract but not in hers. One of the special features of equal pay law is that it requires a line-by-line comparison of the contracts of the woman and her comparator. It is not open to the employer to argue that the overall effect of the two contracts is broadly similar.[181] This detailed comparison may be one of the reasons why equal pay law insists on a real comparator and does not allow claimants to use a hypothetical comparator.

7.4.6 Evidence, time limits and arrears

Equal pay law has some interesting procedural features. In this section, we will think about how people find out about pay inequalities, the time limit for bringing a claim, and the remedies available.

Most people regard their pay as a private matter and, in many cases, have no idea what their colleagues earn. This gives rise to a significant problem with equal pay claims: how do women find out what potential comparators earn and thus whether

---

[179] *Redcar and Cleveland BC* v *Bainbridge* [2008] EWCA Civ 885, [2009] ICR 133.
[180] EA 2010, s 66.
[181] *Hayward* v *Cammell Laird Shipbuilders Ltd (No 2)* [1988] AC 894 (HL); *Barber*, above n 144.

they have any basis for a claim? Sometimes employers actively discourage their staff from discussing their pay. The Equality Act 2010, s. 77, seeks to address this issue by making terms banning workers from discussing their pay unenforceable if certain circumstances are met. Thus, it is not open to an employer to preclude a person from asking a colleague or former colleague about their pay – or to preclude a person from answering such a request – where the request is made in order to find out whether or not pay discrimination might be taking place. Importantly, this still allows employers to ban workers from discussing pay in other situations, for example, with people working for a competitor. Under s. 138 of the Act, there was a procedure by which a claimant could send her employer a questionnaire to determine whether she had a potential claim. There were deadlines for the employer's response. This has been replaced by non-statutory guidance with no formal deadlines with the aim of cutting 'red tape'.[182] However, tribunals may still draw adverse inferences if the employer gives incomplete or evasive answers.[183]

Section 78 of the Act as originally enacted would have gone further. This provision enabled the Secretary of State to make regulations requiring larger firms (with 250 or more employees) to publish an annual report on the pay of men and women within the firm. It is not clear whether this report would have contained enough information to enable women to identify potential equal pay claims. It is more likely that the report would have worked as a 'naming and shaming' device, prompting firms with big gender pay gaps to take steps to tackle the problem. However, it has not yet been brought into force because of the change of government since the 2010 Act was passed. The Coalition government took the view that it would impose unnecessary 'burdens' on businesses and has instead adopted a two-pronged strategy: an equal pay audit scheme for all firms which operates on a voluntary basis,[184] and a power for tribunals to require an employer to conduct an equal pay audit when it *loses* an equal pay claim, unless certain exceptions apply.[185]

Another important procedural issue is the time limit for bringing claims. This is linked to the information issue in the sense that, if it is difficult to find out about pay inequalities, a longer limitation period may give more scope for women to vindicate their rights. Under s. 129 of the 2010 Act, the time limit for bringing an equal pay claim in the employment tribunal is six months from the end of the employment. This period can be extended if certain conditions are met. However, the Supreme Court's decision in the *Abdulla* case has opened up a much longer limitation period.[186] We saw above that equal pay law operates through the device of an equality clause implied by statute into the contract of employment. The claimants in *Abdulla* were outside the limitation period for tribunal claims but sought instead to bring a contract claim in court, relying on the six-year limitation period normally available for such claims. By a majority, the Supreme Court held that this was permissible and was not limited to situations in which the claimant had a good reason for failing to bring the claim in time to the tribunal. In general terms, there are significant advantages to bringing a claim in a tribunal, so most people will probably continue to proceed in

---

[182] Enterprise and Regulatory Reform Act 2013, s 66(1); ACAS, *Asking and Responding to Questions of Discrimination in the Workplace* (January 2014).

[183] EA 2010, s 138(4).

[184] This is called Think, Act, Report: https://www.gov.uk/government/policies/creating-a-fairer-and-more-equal-society/supporting-pages/think-act-report (last visited 27 October 2014).

[185] EA 2010, s 139A; Equality Act 2010 (Equal Pay Audits) Regulations 2014, SI 2014/2559.

[186] *Abdulla* v *Birmingham City Council* [2012] UKSC 47, [2012] ICR 1419.

that way, but the *Abdulla* case means that employers are still at risk of equal pay litigation for six years after a person leaves.

7.4.7 Assessment

We saw earlier that the problem of the gender pay gap is unlikely to be resolved by reforming equal pay legislation alone. Nevertheless, it is worth considering what contribution might be made by law reform.

One possibility would be to integrate equal pay law with equality law more generally. Equal pay for men and women has always been dealt with separately because of its special status and history in EU law, but it could be argued that nowadays it seems anomalous to single out one ground of discrimination (gender) and one type of discrimination (pay) within the comprehensive framework of EU equality law. An integrated approach would have practical consequences, too. It would not make sense to treat equal pay as part of equality law more generally whilst maintaining its exceptional features. So, for example, since hypothetical comparators are permitted elsewhere in equality law, it could be argued that they should be allowed for equal pay law too. This would help to broaden out the scope of comparison in some cases, for example, where women are 'crowded' into a particular job and do not have a real male comparator to invoke. However, the proposal is not without its disadvantages: it could be argued that the court's task in judging what someone would have been paid had she been a man is much harder than assessing her pay against that of a real comparator.

Other reform proposals also seek to broaden the scope of equal pay law so that more claims might be brought. One example is the possibility of cross-industry comparisons. We saw above that the 'single source' rule means that women may only choose a comparator who has the same employer: the 'single source' of inequality who can rectify that inequality. Some commentators have suggested that women should be able to identify comparators doing the same job at other firms.[187] This would enable women to use comparators at more 'enlightened' female-friendly employers to challenge their own pay. However, this proposal is fraught with difficulty. It would be hard for women to find out about pay at other firms, and any such claims would be open to quite strong arguments that the pay differentials were attributable to other factors (the other firm's profitability or generosity, for example) rather than gender. This could result in protracted and ultimately unsuccessful litigation. Judges may not be best qualified to determine 'fair' rates of pay for particular jobs. Another option would be to allow so-called 'proportionate' pay claims. At the moment, as we have seen, the law focuses on equal pay. If a woman manages to show that her work is of greater value than that of her comparator, her claim is still limited to equal pay with what he earns. And if she shows that her work is valued at 80% of her comparator's work, but she only gets 60% of his pay, her claim fails outright, because she cannot show that she is doing equally valuable work. A move to proportionate pay claims would enable women to achieve 'accurate' – not just 'equal' – pay. Again, though, critics argue that this would make the courts' task more complex.

A final point to consider is the issue of gender pay audits, discussed above. One of the current trends in equality law is to make greater use of proactive obligations

---

[187] See Sandra Fredman, 'Reforming Equal Pay Laws' (2008) 37 ILJ 193.

requiring public bodies (and potentially employers) to review their policies and practices with a view to identifying and rectifying inequalities.[188] The government's decision to confine audits to firms that have lost an equal pay claim can be justified as a means of not burdening 'good' businesses with additional obligations. However, a general audit requirement on all firms would provide an opportunity to identify and correct pay inequalities without requiring individuals to engage in expensive, lengthy and stressful litigation.

POINTS TO TAKE AWAY

Contractual and statutory entitlements:

- A working person's entitlement to pay stems from his or her contract. People may be paid piece rates, an hourly wage, or a salary.

- The employer may make deductions from wages (for example, as a disciplinary measure) provided that the employee knows in advance that this is a possibility. The employer has a largely unfettered power to make deductions when working people take part in a strike or action short of a strike.

- Employees enjoy some statutory protection for their pay in the event of a shortage of work (lay-off) or illness.

The National Minimum Wage:

- The NMW is intended to protect workers' dignity and to reduce their reliance on state benefits. Some economists regard it as harmful because it interferes with market forces.

- All 'workers' broadly defined are entitled to be paid the NMW. The 'adult' rate is £6.50 per hour with lower rates for young workers. The legislation contains mechanisms for calculating a worker's entitlement in situations where he or she is not paid by the hour. Time spent 'on call' has proved particularly difficult for the law to deal with.

- The NMW can be enforced by workers themselves or by HMRC. A deliberate failure to pay the NMW is a criminal offence.

Equal pay for men and women:

- Women earn, on average, less per hour than men. The causes of the 'gender pay gap' are complex but include the concentration of women in part-time work and the low value often attributed to jobs traditionally done by women. Equal pay laws can only offer a partial solution to the problem.

- Equal pay is addressed in Article 157 TFEU and the Equality Act 2010.

- To bring an equal pay claim a woman must be doing the same work, work rated as equivalent or work of equal value to that of a real male comparator, usually employed at her workplace. The court will compare each term of her contract with his. The employer cannot justify direct pay discrimination but may be able to justify indirect pay discrimination if it is proportionate.

[188] ibid and see Chapter 6.

Further reading

For a more detailed account of the contractual issues surrounding pay, see **Mark Freedland,** *The Personal Employment Contract* **(OUP 2003), chapter 4**. The *Wiluszynski* decision remains highly controversial and the best analysis of the legal issues surrounding deductions in industrial action situations is **Geoffrey H Mead, 'Restitution within Contract' (1991) 11 LS 172**.

The NMW has been analysed in detail in a series of articles by **Bob Simpson: 'A Milestone in the Legal Regulation of Pay: the National Minimum Wage Act 1998' (1999) 28 ILJ 1; 'Implementing the National Minimum Wage – the 1999 Regulations' (1999) 28 ILJ 171; 'The National Minimum Wage Five Years On: Reflections on some General Issues' (2004) 33 ILJ 22**; and **'The Employment Act 2008's Amendments to the National Minimum Wage Legislation' (2009) 38 ILJ 57**. The oft-repeated claim that minimum wage laws are ultimately harmful to workers because they increase unemployment is challenged by **Simon Deakin and Frank J. Wilkinson, 'The Law and Economics of the Minimum Wage' (1992) 19 Journal of Law and Society 379**; or in greater detail using US data, by **David Card and Alan B Krueger,** *Myth and Measurement: the New Economics of the Minimum Wage* **(Princeton University Press 1995)**.

For more detail on equal pay law, see **Bob Hepple,** *Equality: the New Legal Framework* **(Hart 2011), chapter 4**. Although it is now out of date on some of the detail, **Sandra Fredman,** *Women and the Law* **(OUP 1997)**, contains useful background information about women at work (chapters 1–3) and equal pay issues (chapter 6). Social scientists continue to try to unravel the exact causes of the gender pay gap (which is important in working out what kind of law, if any, we need to tackle it). Two interesting recent studies are **Marie Drolet and Karen Mumford, 'The Gender Pay Gap for Private-Sector Employees in Canada and Britain' (2012) 50 BJIR 529**; and **David N Barron and Elizabeth West, 'The Financial Costs of Caring in the British Labour Market: Is There a Wage Penalty for Workers in Caring Occupations?' (2013) 51 BJIR 104**.

8 Working time

8.1 INTRODUCTION

Working time regulation might take a variety of different forms. It might focus on the total number of hours people work, on when they work or on when they are able to take time off from work. A policy of regulating working time might be motivated by several different considerations, from the need to protect workers against risks to their health and safety caused by excessive working hours, to the need to enable parents to spend more time with their children.

This chapter will assess three main forms of working time regulation: general limits on working time in the Working Time Directive and Working Time Regulations (section 8.3), the right to request flexible working (section 8.4), which gives employees a say in their working time arrangements, and rights to time off for family reasons (section 8.5). These three forms of regulation are motivated by different policy agendas but they all have in common their capacity to affect when and for how long people work.

This topic is a complex mix of EU law and domestic law, with the unusual feature that, in some cases, English law is more generous to workers than EU law. Although the Working Time Regulations follow the Working Time Directive quite closely, English law provides more generous maternity and shared parental leave rights than EU law requires. The right to request flexible working is a home-grown right, although it now features (in an attenuated form) in the revised EU Parental Leave Directive.

8.2 THEORETICAL FRAMEWORK

This section will explore some of the different ways in which working time might be regulated, and the reasons for doing so. As a basic starting-point, there are two broad issues to consider: when the worker is required to work, and how long he or she is required to work for (which might include entitlements to holidays and other forms of time off as well as limits on weekly working hours).

The difficulty with regulating working time is the variety of perspectives we might take on the topic. Traditionally, the focus has been on *excessive* working time: employers expecting workers to work very long days or weeks with little or no rest. However, while this is still a significant issue in many workplaces, the casualisation of the labour market has generated a new set of concerns.[1] Nowadays, some employers expect workers to make themselves available for work but without any guaranteed hours – on a so-called 'zero hours' contract, for example – so the problem for those workers is *uncertainty* about both when and for how long they might be required to work. This leaves them with no guaranteed level of income and potentially large fluctuations in working hours from week to week. Moreover, although time spent 'on call' is not time spent working, it is not free time either because the worker needs to be available for work if required by the employer.

Although the practical situations of casual workers with unpredictable hours and full-time workers with long hours are quite different, they do have a common theme: control. In both cases, the employer exercises control over the worker's life, either by insisting on long hours or by refusing to commit to a particular working time arrangement. Of course, some degree of employer control over working hours is necessary to the running of a successful business: it would be bizarre if, for example, workers in a nightclub could insist on doing all their hours during the day. The key question is how to strike a fair balance between the employer's legitimate business interests and the needs or preferences of workers.

In order to explore this question in greater depth, it is helpful to consider some of the different ways in which rules to protect workers might be justified. We will examine four possible arguments here: protecting workers' health and safety, helping workers to balance work and family life, promoting workers' dignity and autonomy, and promoting high productivity.[2] As we shall see, it may be necessary to draw on more than one of these arguments in order to generate a comprehensive regulatory regime.

The health and safety justification for regulating working time can be formulated in different ways. As Bercusson explains, the traditional British understanding of health and safety focuses on avoiding accidents at work and preventing work-related disease.[3] This type of argument might serve to justify limits on maximum working hours and required rest periods, particularly in sectors such as transport where tiredness can lead to accidents. However, health and safety can also be understood more broadly. In this regard, the Court of Justice has adopted the World Health Organization's definition of health: 'a state of complete physical, mental and social well-being that does not consist only in the absence of illness or infirmity'.[4] As we shall see, the EU Working Time Directive was originally enacted using a Treaty provision on health and safety as its legal basis, because the UK was opposed to the measure and health and safety directives did not require unanimity among the Member States.[5] When the UK challenged the lawfulness of the Directive before the Court of Justice, the Court used the idea of health as 'well-being' in order to uphold it.[6]

---

[1] See Chapter 4.

[2] For more detail, see Jean-Yves Boulin *et al.*, *Decent Working Time* (ILO 2006), especially chapters 1 and 16.

[3] Brian Bercusson, *European Labour Law* (2nd edn, CUP 2009).

[4] Case C-84/94 *United Kingdom* v *Council of the European Union (Working Time Directive)* [1996] ECR I-5755 [15].

[5] EC Treaty (Treaty of Rome, as amended), art 118a.

[6] Above n 4.

This has important consequences for the formulation of legal rules, because 'well-being' suggests a greater degree of intervention to protect workers. For example, while a relatively long working week might not be dangerous in the sense of liable to cause illness or accidents, it might be inconsistent with the worker's 'well-being'. Moreover, 'well-being' might be used to justify different types of rule, such as paid holidays. Time away from work might not be necessary to prevent illness or accidents, but it might play a role in promoting 'well-being'.

Another argument in favour of regulating working time draws on the concept of 'work/life balance'. This is the idea that working people may want to engage in other socially valuable activities outside the workplace. Perhaps the most obvious of these is raising a family. The work/life balance argument can be used to support a range of different types of control on working time. For example, work/life balance clearly suggests that workers' hours should be limited so that they have time and energy for other activities. But it can be taken further: for example, in order to combine work with family obligations, a worker might need predictable working time so that he or she can arrange child-care, or time off during school holidays. Work/life balance is often regarded as having particular relevance to women, since it is still the case that the responsibility for child-care tends to fall more heavily on women either as single parents or in couples. Thus, the argument can be presented in feminist terms as a means of enabling women to participate in the labour market or, more radically, as a means of encouraging 'shared parenting' in which both partners in a couple use their work/life balance rights in order to take responsibility for child-care. However, although the work/life balance argument initially found its expression in so-called 'family-friendly' policies, there is an increasing recognition nowadays that it is a relevant issue for all workers, not just those with children.

So far, we have focused on two arguments that are particularly relevant to working time. However, it is possible to justify controls on working time using more general arguments about workers' rights. The ILO's principle that 'labour is not a commodity' is particularly relevant here, and reminds us of the importance of respecting workers' dignity and autonomy. Other factors of production, such as machines, can be used 24 hours a day, seven days a week, but workers need time to sleep and time to do other things. Very long working hours can raise issues about forced labour, a severe infringement of a worker's dignity. Autonomy focuses on workers' ability to make choices about their lives. This idea could be taken in various directions. For example, it could be argued that workers need stable and predictable working hours in order to plan other aspects of their lives, or that workers should be given some choice over when to do their work where this is possible. The right to request flexible working could be justified on the latter basis. However, a complication with autonomy is that it might also suggest that workers should be allowed to choose very long working hours if they want. As we shall see, English law on the regulation of working time tends to adopt the position that workers should be able to make this choice, but there is a difficulty about ensuring that the choice is genuine, given the inequality of bargaining power between workers and their employer.

Another, rather different, method of justifying working time regulation is to consider the link between hours worked and productivity. It is often suggested that very long working hours are damaging from this perspective.[7] Workers may simply

---

[7] M White, *Working Hours: Assessing the Potential for Reduction* (ILO 1987).

be too tired to perform well, or they may resent the long hours spent at work and find ways of carving out some 'leisure' time during the working day. Relatedly, workers who are worried about their other responsibilities, such as child-care, may be distracted while they are at work. On this view, shorter working hours organised around the worker's needs are the best way of getting people to make a good contribution while they are at work.

A final point to consider when designing a working time regime is the relationship between working time and pay. This is most obvious for those who are paid an hourly rate: the more hours they work, the more money they will earn. For salaried workers, the link may be more indirect: a worker may feel that his or her promotion prospects (and thus his or her capacity to earn more) depend on working long hours and thus showing 'commitment' to the employer. The relationship between working time and pay affects the government's capacity to control people's working hours. For example, if legislation applies a strict limit to the maximum number of hours people can work in a week, that puts pressure on either the minimum wage, or the minimum wage in combination with the social security system, to ensure that workers have enough money to live on.

8.3 GENERAL LIMITS ON WORKING HOURS

In this section, we will discuss the role of the Working Time Directive (WTD)[8] and the Working Time Regulations 1998 in setting general limits on people's working hours.[9] The WTD is an ambitious attempt to set limits on the working week and the working day, and to provide a right to paid annual leave, across most sectors of the economy.[10] A particular feature of the working time regime is its odd mix of rigidity and flexibility.[11] On the one hand, the WTD sets 'one size fits all' standards, such as a maximum limit of 48 hours on the working week. It is not necessarily obvious that working for longer than this will, in all cases, prove damaging to a worker's well-being, but of course in some industries, where high levels of physical effort or concentration are required, it may be far too long. On the other hand, the WTD seeks to provide various tools for flexibility – the individual opt-out, collective derogations and a wide range of exceptions of different kinds. Critics argue that these tools have rendered the WTD ineffective because it is too easy for an employer to use its superior bargaining power to get round the standards it purports to impose.

8.3.1 International instruments

Rights to limited working hours and paid holidays are the preserve of economic and social rights instruments, such as the International Covenant on Economic, Social and Cultural Rights (ICESCR), Article 7:

---

[8] Originally Directive 93/104/EC [1993] OJ L307/18; now Directive 2003/88/EC concerning certain aspects of the organisation of working time [2003] OJ L299/9. See, generally, Catherine Barnard, *EU Employment Law* (4th edn, OUP 2012) chapter 12.

[9] Working Time Regulations 1998, SI 1998/1833. See, generally, C Barnard, 'The Working Time Regulations 1998' (1999) 28 ILJ 61; 'The Working Time Regulations 1999' (2000) 29 ILJ 167.

[10] There are 'sectoral' directives for different forms of transport which we will not be able to consider in detail here.

[11] Catherine Barnard, 'EC "Social" Policy', in Paul Craig and Gráinne de Búrca (eds), *The Evolution of EU Law* (OUP 1999).

The States Parties to the present Covenant recognize the right of everyone to the enjoyment of just and favourable conditions of work which ensure, in particular:
... (d) Rest, leisure and reasonable limitation of working hours and periodic holidays with pay, as well as remuneration for public holidays.

Article 31 of the EU Charter is in similar terms, making the link to the health and safety and dignity arguments discussed in the previous section:

(1) Every worker has the right to working conditions which respect his or her health, safety and dignity.

(2) Every worker has the right to limitation of maximum working hours, to daily and weekly rest periods and to an annual period of paid leave.

For more precise international standards, it is necessary to look to the relevant ILO conventions. These set a maximum working week of 48 hours and a maximum working day of eight hours,[12] though with an aspiration to reduce the working week even further to 40 hours.[13] ILO conventions also lay down a right to 24 hours off in every seven days,[14] and a right to three weeks' paid annual leave for a year of service.[15] The UK has not ratified any of these conventions.

8.3.2 The WTD/WTR regime

After considering eligibility under the WTD/WTR, we will examine the main rights in the regime – paid annual leave, controls over the working week and controls over the working day – before considering exceptions and derogations. We will conclude by examining how rights under the WTR may be enforced.

Eligibility

The WTD leaves its scope of application to the Member States to define. The WTR use the 'worker' definition, giving them a broader scope of application than legislation confined to 'employees'.[16] The rights apply from the first day of employment.[17]

In some instances, a distinction is drawn between 'adult' workers who are 18 or over, and 'young' workers, who are aged between 15 and 17. Young workers are afforded extra protections. Special provision is also made for people who work at night. For reasons of space, we will not be able to consider the treatment of young workers or night workers in depth in this chapter.

Paid annual leave

The right to paid annual leave was a long-held ambition for the labour movement in its early years. A basic right to a week or two weeks off would enhance workers' dignity by allowing them a brief period of respite during which they were not at the

---

[12] Hours of Work Industry Convention 1919 (No 1) (adopted 28 November 1919, entered into force 13 June 1921).

[13] Forty-Hour Week Convention 1935 (No 37) (adopted 22 June 1935, entered into force 23 June 1957).

[14] Weekly Rest (Industry) Convention 1921 (No 14) (adopted 17 November 1921, entered into force 19 June 1923).

[15] Holidays with Pay Convention (Revised) 1970 (No 132) (adopted 24 June 1970, entered into force 30 June 1973).

[16] WTR, reg 2.

[17] The right to paid annual leave accrues at the rate of one-twelfth of the annual entitlement per month: WTR, reg 15A.

employer's beck and call. A similar claim can be made today, though nowadays the legal entitlement is rather longer and people might use their time off in a variety of ways, not just for 'holidays': these might include spending time with their children during school holidays or waiting in for a delivery. Paid annual leave is an area in which the Court of Justice of the European Union (CJEU) has had a particular impact. It has interpreted the right to paid annual leave in the WTD as a 'particularly important principle of Community social law'.[18] This has had important consequences for the way the right is implemented in the UK.

Article 7 WTD sets out the basic right:

(1) Member States shall take the measures necessary to ensure that every worker is entitled to paid annual leave of at least four weeks in accordance with the conditions for entitlement to, and granting of, such leave laid down by national legislation and/or practice.

(2) The minimum period of paid annual leave may not be replaced by an allowance in lieu, except where the employment relationship is terminated.

In the UK, the annual leave entitlement is 5.6 weeks but this is subject to a calculation relating to the worker's normal working week.[19] So if the worker works a five-day week, 5.6 multiplied by 5 gives an annual leave entitlement of 28 days. If the worker works part-time, his or her entitlement is calculated pro rata so, for example, a worker with a three-day week would be entitled to 16.8 days of paid annual leave (5.6 multiplied by 3). However, there is a statutory maximum leave entitlement of 28 days, so a worker who works a six-day week does not get any more time off than a worker who works a five-day week. The entitlement is to time off, so the employer may not offer the worker money instead ('allowance in lieu') unless the employment relationship comes to an end before the worker has used his or her entitlement.[20] Importantly, the legislation lays down minimum periods so an employer may choose to offer workers additional holiday entitlements. Any extra holiday offered by the employer is a contractual matter so it is subject to whatever rules the employer chooses to lay down, and need not conform to the statutory scheme.[21]

Although Article 7(1) WTD gives a role to national law in determining the 'conditions for entitlement' to paid annual leave, the Court of Justice has taken a strict line on this. The UK initially implemented the right with a 13-week qualifying period. This was challenged before the Court of Justice in the *BECTU* case, in which a trade union argued that many of its members would not be able to take leave because they were usually employed on short-term contracts.[22] The Court of Justice upheld this complaint on the basis that the conditions for entitlement laid down in national law could not be such as to deprive workers of their rights. Since then, the UK has adopted a different approach in which workers in the first year of their employment accrue one-twelfth of the annual leave entitlement for each month that they work.[23]

---

[18] Case C-173/99 R v *Secretary of State for Trade and Industry, ex p BECTU* [2001] ECR I-4881 [43].
[19] WTR 1998, regs 13 and 13A.
[20] ibid reg 14.
[21] ibid reg 17.
[22] *BECTU*, above n 18.
[23] WTR 1998, reg 15A.

A worker must take his or her leave entitlement within the 'leave year' in which it has accrued,[24] and is in principle entitled to decide which days to take off.[25] However, by giving notice, the employer may require the worker to take leave on particular days or require the worker to work on particular days.[26] This enables the employer to manage the workforce, for example, by insisting that workers take leave when the workplace would be closed anyway – for example, at Christmas – or preventing too many workers from taking leave at the same time. In the *Russell* case, it was held that offshore workers could be required to take annual leave during their 'shore time'.[27] The workers in question worked on an oil rig on a 'two weeks on, two weeks off' basis and argued that since leave meant time off when they would otherwise be working, they were entitled to take leave during the 'on' periods. The Supreme Court rejected this argument on the basis that 'rest time' simply meant time away from work, and it did not matter if the time in question was fixed by the employer at a time when no work would have been taking place anyway. It noted that people in many occupations – teachers, for example – are required to take time off at particular times of year when they would not necessarily be working anyway. However, this ruling is problematic. As the Supreme Court noted, there appears to be nothing to stop an employer from requiring an employee to work Monday to Friday, to treat Sunday as the statutory rest day (see below) and to take annual leave every Saturday, when he or she would not be working anyway, thereby denying the worker an opportunity to take leave in any meaningful sense.[28]

It is important to note that although workers are *entitled* to leave, they may choose not to take it or not to take all of it. The Court of Justice criticised the UK government for publishing guidance stating that rest breaks did not have to be taken, but nevertheless, there is no element of compulsion.[29] This can be seen as a reflection of workers' autonomy – they may choose not to exercise their rights – though there is always a risk that unscrupulous employers may discourage workers from taking time off.

An important feature of the right to annual leave is that it is a right to *paid* leave.[30] The Court of Justice has taken the view that if workers are worried about money, they will not feel inclined to exercise their right to take leave, and as a result it has adopted a strict construction of the 'paid' element of paid leave. Two cases – both from the UK – illustrate the point. In the *Williams* case, a dispute arose concerning paid holiday for airline pilots.[31] The pilots' pay was made up of three elements: basic pay, flying pay and 'time away from base' allowance. The employer argued that the

---

[24] ibid reg 13(9)(a).

[25] ibid reg 15(1).

[26] ibid reg 15(2).

[27] *Russell* v *Transocean International Resources Ltd* [2011] UKSC 57, [2012] ICR 185.

[28] See *Sumsion* v *BBC (Scotland)* [2007] IRLR 678 (EAT).

[29] Case C-484/04 *Commission* v *UK* [2006] ECR I-7471. The case concerned daily and weekly rest periods, though the point is more generally applicable.

[30] WTR 1998, reg 16. An employer's failure to pay workers the holiday pay to which they are entitled can be challenged as an unlawful deduction from wages under ERA 1996, ss 13–27, but this has recently been made subject to a two-year limit: Deduction from Wages (Limitation) Regulations 2014, SI 2014/3322, reg 2.

[31] Case C-155/10 *Williams* v *British Airways plc* [2011] ECR I-8409. See also the CJEU's decision on commission in Case C-539/12 *Lock* v *British Gas Trading Ltd* [2014] ICR 813; and the EAT's decision on the inclusion of overtime pay in *Bear Scotland Ltd* v *Fulton* [2015] IRLR 15 (EAT).

pilots should receive basic pay during annual leave, whereas the pilots argued that they should also receive flying pay and a proportion of 'time away from base' allowance so that their holiday pay would be closer to their 'normal' pay. The Court of Justice held that pay must enable the worker 'to enjoy, during his period of rest and relaxation, economic conditions which are comparable to those relating to the exercise of his employment'.[32] This meant that flying pay should be included, and any proportion of 'time away from base' allowance that was not genuinely attributable to the costs of living away from home (and was therefore, in reality, a part of salary) should also be included. The Supreme Court remitted the latter point to a tribunal to decide.[33] The other illustrative case is *Robinson-Steele*.[34] This case concerned the practice of paying 'rolled-up' holiday pay. Instead of paying workers when they took holiday, the employer in that case paid a small extra sum per hour in respect of holiday pay. This formed part of a collective agreement with a trade union, perhaps because the higher hourly rate was attractive to the workers. It also offered a way of implementing the holiday entitlements of casual workers for whom paid leave may seem to be an odd concept, given the sporadic nature of their work. However, the Court of Justice held that this method of paying holiday pay was unacceptable. The workers might not manage to save the extra money to cover their holidays, which would deter them from taking the time off.

A final point to consider relates to the relationship between paid annual leave and other forms of time off, such as sick leave. There are several different issues to think about here. First, a worker who is on sick leave may want to take some of that time as annual leave, for example, because this may attract better pay. The UK courts were sceptical about this, on the grounds that a person who was not fit to work did not need to 'rest' from work,[35] but the Court of Justice disagreed.[36] It held that this was a matter for the Member State, which could choose to permit or prohibit this practice. In the UK, it is permitted by virtue of reg. 17 WTR, which allows a worker with more than one statutory right to exercise whichever is the most favourable. Second, a worker who is on sick leave but then returns to work might be unable to take his or her full annual leave entitlement before the end of the leave year. In this situation, the Court of Justice has held that the worker should be allowed to carry the unused annual leave over into the next leave year.[37] A Member State may limit for how long this unused leave can accumulate,[38] though in most cases it seems likely that the employer will terminate the employment relationship of a worker who is off sick for a long time (in which case the worker will be entitled to a payment in lieu).[39] Third, a worker who is scheduled to take annual leave may be sick before or during that leave, in which case he or she may take sick leave instead and postpone the annual leave to a later date.[40]

---

[32] ibid [23].
[33] *British Airways Plc v Williams* [2012] UKSC 43, [2012] ICR 1375 [32].
[34] Case C-131/04 *Robinson-Steele v RD Retail Services Ltd* [2006] ECR I-2531.
[35] *Inland Revenue Commissioners v Ainsworth* [2009] UKHL 31, [2009] ICR 985.
[36] Joined Cases C-350/06 and C-520/06 *Schultz-Hoff v Deutsche Rentenversicherung Bund* and *Stringer v Revenue and Customs* [2009] ECR I-179; Case C-282/10 *Dominguez v Centre informatique du Centre Ouest Atlantique* [2012] IRLR 321.
[37] *Schutz-Hoff*, above n 36, [43].
[38] Case C-214/10 *KHS AG v Schulte* [2011] ECR I-11757.
[39] WTR 1998, reg 14.
[40] Case C-277/08 *Pereda v Madrid Movilidad SA* [2009] ECR I-8405.

The working week

The WTD and WTR contain various rules limiting the number of hours a worker may be required to work during any particular week. We will begin with an overview of the rules before examining the two main controversies to which they have given rise: the treatment of time spent 'on call', and the individual worker's right to 'opt out' of the maximum limit on the working week.

Under Article 6 WTD and reg. 4 WTR, the working week is limited to an average of 48 hours. This is normally averaged over 17 weeks (though a collective agreement or workforce agreement may increase the averaging period to 52 weeks). It is worth noting that this is less strict than the ILO standard which is an absolute limit, only allowing for averaging in exceptional cases.[41] Within each 24-hour period, the worker is entitled to a 'rest period' of 11 consecutive hours under Article 3 WTD and reg. 10 WTR. And within each seven-day period, the worker is entitled to an 'uninterrupted rest period' of 24 hours under Article 5 WTD and reg. 11 WTR. The employer may change this to a rest period of 48 hours in a 14-day period.

If we take a seven-day period as our starting-point, the worker is entitled to 24 hours off, plus an uninterrupted 11 hours off in each of the remaining six 24-hour periods. This leaves 78 hours potentially available for work. But the maximum working week, as laid down in reg. 4, is 48 hours. Since this is an *average* limit, in practice a worker might work substantially more hours in some weeks, provided that he or she works substantially fewer hours in other weeks.

So far, we have assumed that there is a clear divide between 'working time' and 'time off'. However, many workers spend a proportion of their working week 'on call'. This term has no technical meaning and can denote different degrees of restriction on a worker's freedom. Some 'on call' workers are merely required to be contactable by phone in case of an emergency, or to wait at home in case they are called in to work. Other types of 'on call' work require the worker to be at the employer's premises. For example, a hospital doctor might be 'on call' overnight in case of an emergency, but provided with somewhere to sleep, or a resident warden in a hall of residence might be required to stay in for a certain number of nights per week and to deal with fire alarms or other problems. For the purposes of the 48-hour limit on the working week, then, it is necessary to be able to say when someone is 'working' and when he or she is not. The WTD and the WTR both define working time using the same phrase: 'any period during which he is working, at his employer's disposal and carrying out his activity or duties'.[42]

The CJEU has played a key role in applying this definition to 'on call' cases. In the *SIMAP* case, the Court held that if the worker was required to be at the employer's premises during 'on call' time, he or she was 'working' for working time purposes.[43] This was reaffirmed in *Jaeger*, even though in that case, the worker was provided with somewhere to sleep when not required to work.[44] This means that the EU law definition of working time for the purposes of the WTD is

[41] Hours of Work Industry Convention 1919 (No 1) (n 12), art 2.
[42] WTD, art 2; WTR 1998, reg 2.
[43] Case C-303/98 *Sindicato de Medicos de Asistencia Publica (SIMAP)* v *Conselleria de Sanidad y Consumo de la Generalidad Valenciana* [2000] ECR I-7963.
[44] Case C-151/02 *Landeshauptstadt Kiel* v *Jaeger* [2003] ECR I-8389.

different to the domestic definition of working time for NMW purposes.[45] For example, in *South Manchester Abbeyfield Society* v *Hopkins*, the claimant was a housekeeper in a residential home.[46] She lived on the premises and was expected to be 'on call' overnight during the working week. She was only paid for her work during the day. It was held that the nights spent 'on call' counted for determining the claimant's working time but not her entitlement to the NMW. While this can be explained by the different legal regimes applicable in the two cases, it does seem rather odd that the law should deem someone to be working but with no entitlement to be paid.

The most controversial aspect of the rules on the working week is the 'opt-out' identified in the first phrase of reg. 4(1): the limit does not apply if the worker signs a written agreement to that effect with the employer.[47] The Court of Justice has emphasised the point that the opt-out is an individual matter and cannot be agreed collectively.[48] In the UK, employers in some sectors have made widespread use of the opt-out.[49] It appears that there are two main reasons for this. One is that UK workers tend to work longer hours, on average, than their counterparts elsewhere in Europe.[50] It is not surprising that a maximum limit on the working week that is, in effect, voluntary has not brought about a radical change. The other reason is that once a worker has opted out, the employer has fewer record-keeping obligations and is not at risk of accidentally infringing the limit.[51] Thus, in some firms, it may be normal practice to get workers to sign the opt-out 'just in case'. Although the opt-out was included in the WTD because of pressure from the UK government, it is worth noting that it has since been invoked in many other countries, in part because of the Court of Justice's strong approach towards on-call time, discussed above.[52]

Critics of the opt-out generally argue that it is inconsistent with the health and safety rationale for the WTD. If 48 hours represents a safe working week, why should workers be able to choose to work unsafe hours? However, the opt-out is likely to be popular with at least some workers: it gives them choice over their working hours, thus respecting their autonomy, and in some cases, they may need the extra money to make ends meet. If the opt-out is to be retained, a key issue is how to ensure that a worker's consent is genuine, given that most workers are in a situation of inequality of bargaining power with their employer. Although a worker can withdraw his or her opt-out, he or she is particularly vulnerable at the start of the employment where the employer may make it seem as if the job offer is conditional on signing. The protection against detrimental treatment in the WTR applies to workers, so on a literal reading would not be applicable at this stage.

[45] See Chapter 7.

[46] [2011] ICR 254 (EAT).

[47] The term 'opt out' is potentially ambiguous because it is also used to refer to art 22 of the Directive which is often regarded as the UK's 'opt out' from the requirement to enforce the 48-hour limit. However, it is important to note that the UK is not the only country now using art 22.

[48] Case C-397/01 *Pfeiffer* v *Deutsches Rotes Kreuz* [2004] ECR I-8835 [84].

[49] For empirical evidence, see Catherine Barnard *et al.*, 'Opting Out of the 48-Hour Week: Employer Necessity or Individual Choice? An Empirical Study of the Operation of Article 18(1)(b) of the Working Time Directive in the UK' (2003) 32 ILJ 223.

[50] Martin Teichgraber, *European Union Labour Force Survey – Annual Results 2012* (Eurostat 2013).

[51] Barnard, above n 49, 242. Compare WTR 1998 reg 4(2) with reg 9.

[52] Commission, *Report on Implementation by Member States of Directive 2003/88/EC ('The Working Time Directive')* (COM(2010) 802 final, 2010) para 3.7.

The Commission has been seeking for some time to reform the WTD, though so far without success.[53] In relation to 'on call' time, it proposes to maintain the *SIMAP* principle[54] – that 'on call' time spent at the employer's premises counts as working time – but to allow derogations in certain sectors, such as healthcare. The derogation would allow the 'on call' time to be counted differently to time spent working in the normal sense. In relation to the opt-out, the Commission is no longer trying to remove it altogether (though most unions would support this) but proposes various safeguards instead, such as barring the employer from introducing the opt-out at the start of the employment, and placing an upper maximum limit of 65 hours per week on the working time of an opted-out worker. The prospects of reaching an agreement on these matters seem remote.

The working day

During the working day, the worker is entitled to a rest break in accordance with Article 4 WTD and reg. 12 WTR:

(1) Where a worker's working time is more than six hours, he is entitled to a rest break.

(2) The details of the rest break to which a worker is entitled under paragraph (1), including its duration and the terms on which it is granted, shall be in accordance with any provisions for the purposes of this regulation which are contained in a collective agreement or a workforce agreement.

(3) Subject to the provisions of any applicable collective agreement or workforce agreement, the rest break provided for in paragraph (1) is an uninterrupted period of not less than 20 minutes, and the worker is entitled to spend it away from his workstation if he has one.

This provision entitles the worker to a 20-minute rest break for every six hours worked. Although many employers do pay workers during breaks, there is no legal obligation to do so.

Another much less well-known provision relating to the working day is that in reg. 8:

Where the pattern according to which an employer organizes work is such as to put the health and safety of a worker employed by him at risk, in particular because the work is monotonous or the work-rate is predetermined, the employer shall ensure that the worker is given adequate rest breaks.

This is intended to implement Article 13 of the WTD:

Member States shall take the measures necessary to ensure that an employer who intends to organise work according to a certain pattern takes account of the general principle of adapting work to the worker, with a view, in particular, to alleviating monotonous work and work at a predetermined workrate, depending on the type of activity, and of safety and health requirements, especially as regards breaks during working time.

There does not appear to have been any litigation on reg. 8 in the UK. However, it would seem arguable that the provision as implemented does not fully capture the

---

[53] The latest document is Commission, *Reviewing the Working Time Directive (Second-Phase Consultation of the Social Partners at European Level under Article 154 TFEU)* (COM(2010) 801 final, 2010), but the social partners were unable to agree.

[54] Above n 43.

concern addressed by Article 13. This is what Bercusson calls the principle of the 'humanisation of work': the idea that work should be organised around the worker, rather than around the employer.[55] He suggests that this principle has the potential to transform the way we think about working time. But reg. 8 treats it as another (vaguer) entitlement to rest breaks. Section 4 will explore other ways in which workers might be able to gain control over their working time outside the WTR/WTD framework.

Exceptions and derogations

Inevitably, the generality of the WTD/WTR regime means that it is necessary to make exceptions to the rights it contains. As we shall see, these exceptions apply to particular types of work and to particular sectors of the economy. The key question here is whether these exceptions are justified or whether they undermine the effectiveness of the regime. The WTD and WTR also make provision for the employer to negotiate a collective or workforce agreement to vary or derogate from certain rights. The thinking here is that this is a 'reflexive' mechanism enabling the social partners to agree arrangements which better reflect their needs, though again the risk is that the employer may use its superior bargaining power to undermine workers' rights.

Exceptions There are at least four groups of exceptions to some or all of the rules in the WTR. For the most part, these are 'copied out' from the WTD.

First, workers in some sectors or types of activity are excluded from some or all of the rights.[56] Under reg. 18 WTR, members of the armed forces and the police and other emergency services lose most of the protection where their work 'inevitably conflict[s]' with the various rights. This reflects the need for people in these jobs to deal with emergencies even if this means missing rest breaks. More surprisingly, domestic workers in private households are excluded from the maximum working week and night work protections by virtue of reg. 19. This is unfortunate because domestic workers are especially vulnerable and the fact that they are often resident in the employer's household should not be treated as a reason for failing to restrict their working hours.

Second, there are 'special cases' in reg. 21.[57] These people lose their rest periods and rest breaks. They include 'security and surveillance' workers, workers whose activities involve the need for 'continuity of service' (for example, people working in hospitals or utility companies), situations in which there is a foreseeable 'surge of activity', and unexpected accidents or emergencies. While the last of these is clearly justifiable – it would be difficult for the employer if workers could disappear to take a break in the middle of a crisis – the others are potentially problematic, since they do not encourage the employer of workers in these high-stress environments to think creatively about ways of enabling staff to enjoy reasonable working hours.

---

[55] Brian Bercusson, *European Labour Law* (Butterworths 1996) 332; and see Alan Bogg, 'Of Holidays, Work and Humanisation: a Missed Opportunity?' (2009) 34 ILJ 738.
[56] WTD, art 17.
[57] ibid.

However, under reg. 24, where a worker is required to work through a rest period or a rest break under reg. 21:

(a) his employer shall wherever possible allow him to take an equivalent period of compensatory rest, and

(b) in exceptional cases in which it is not possible, for objective reasons, to grant such a period of rest, his employer shall afford him such protection as may be appropriate in order to safeguard the worker's health and safety.[58]

This provision was analysed by the Court of Appeal in the *Hughes* case.[59] Mr Hughes was a security guard who worked a 12-hour shift, so he was entitled to a rest break. However, he was always on duty alone, so this meant that his breaks were often interrupted – for example, if a visitor arrived at the gate. If this happened, he was permitted to restart his interrupted break from the beginning. The Court of Appeal accepted that reg. 21(b) was applicable in the case: the exception for security guards where a 'permanent presence' is required. Attention then turned to reg. 24(a). Here, the question was whether the 'equivalent' period had to be an uninterrupted 20-minute break in accordance with reg. 12, or whether some other arrangement was sufficient. The Court of Appeal upheld the EAT's finding that the break need not be in accordance with reg. 12. Thus, the arrangement applicable to Mr Hughes – that he could restart his break if it was interrupted – fell within reg. 24(a). As the Court of Appeal explained, although Mr Hughes could not always expect an uninterrupted break, he might sometimes end up with a much longer period of time away from work than 20 minutes if his break was interrupted and he began it again from the beginning. The Court further held that even if the arrangement was not within reg. 24(a) it would be within reg. 24(b) as a form of 'appropriate protection'. While this seems reasonable on the facts, it highlights the limited transformative potential of the regime: the Court of Appeal rejected any suggestion that the employer should change its shift system so that another person could cover Mr Hughes's break.[60]

Third, under reg. 22, there are special arrangements for shift workers.[61] The entitlements to daily and weekly rest do not apply where a worker changes shift (so, for example, when he or she switches from the day shift to the night shift and cannot fit in a break in between). Nor do they apply to people on 'split shift' systems who work twice a day (for example, in catering or cleaning). But reg. 22 is subject to the reg. 24 requirement to provide compensatory rest.

Fourth, and perhaps most importantly, most of the rules do not apply to workers whose working time is 'unmeasured': defined as where 'the duration of his working time is not measured or predetermined or can be determined by the worker himself'.[62] This is a potentially wide-ranging exception because it covers anyone who has control over his or her working hours. Thus, many people in professional or managerial occupations are not covered. Of course, it can be argued that these workers do not need the law's protection because they have the freedom to manage their own work/life balance. However, workers in these groups often have very long working hours and the exclusion of 'unmeasured' work means that the WTR have not tackled this at all.

[58] WTD, art 17(2).
[59] *Hughes v Corps of Commissionaires Management Ltd* [2011] EWCA Civ 1061, [2011] IRLR 915.
[60] Brenda Barrett, 'When is a Work Break not a Statutory Rest Break?' (2012) 41 ILJ 363.
[61] WTD, art 17(4).
[62] WTR 1998, reg 20; WTD, art 17(1).

Collective or workforce agreements Under Article 18 WTD:

> Derogations may be made . . . by means of collective agreements or agreements concluded between the two sides of industry at national or regional level or, in conformity with the rules laid down by them, by means of collective agreements or agreements concluded between the two sides of industry at a lower level . . .
>
> The derogations . . . shall be allowed on condition that equivalent compensating rest periods are granted to the workers concerned or, in exceptional cases where it is not possible for objective reasons to grant such periods, the workers concerned are afforded appropriate protection.

Under the WTR, reg. 23(a), a collective or workforce agreement may 'modify or exclude' the following entitlements:

- the eight-hour limit on night work in reg. 6;

- the 11-hour rest period in every 24 hours in reg. 10;

- the 24-hour rest period in every seven days (or 48-hour rest period in every 14 days) under reg. 11;

- the rest break in a working day of more than six hours in reg. 12.

Under reg. 12(3), the rest break is set at a default 20 minutes away from the worker's workstation, but this is subject to any provisions of a collective or workforce agreement specifying the details of the break.

Under the WTR reg. 23(b), a collective or workforce agreement may 'for objective or technical reasons or reasons concerning the organization of work' substitute any period of up to 52 weeks for the default reference period of 17 weeks used to calculate a worker's weekly working hours for the purposes of the 48-hour limit under reg. 4. This is of limited significance given that many workers sign individual opt-outs from the 48-hour limit.

There are two points to note about these provisions. First, they allow the union or workforce representatives to reach an agreement with the employer that excludes – not just modifies – workers' rights. In theory, they will only do this where the employer is offering something in return, because there is no reason to give up rights which will take effect as a matter of law if the union or workforce representatives simply refuse to agree. However, matters may not be so simple in practice, particularly if the employer is able to pressure the representatives into signing an agreement. Second, while it is necessary to provide for workforce representatives as an alternative to unions in non-unionised workplaces, there is always a worry that they may not have the independence to stand up to the employer or access to any sources of information about their role. This may reduce their capacity to negotiate effectively.

Enforcement

As Barnard explains, the broad scheme of the Regulations is to make employers criminally liable for infringing limits, and to allow workers to enforce entitlements in the Employment Tribunal.[63]

---

[63] Barnard, above n 9.

Criminal liability exists in respect of:

- the 48-hour week (though, as usual, this is irrelevant where there is an opt-out);
- the night work limits;
- record-keeping obligations;
- the provision of compensatory rest under reg. 24.[64]

Responsibility for enforcement is divided between various public bodies, primarily local authorities and the Health and Safety Executive, depending on the sector.

Under reg. 30, the worker may complain to the employment tribunal if the employer has refused to permit him or her to exercise any of the following rights:

- daily rest;
- weekly rest;
- rest breaks;
- annual leave;
- compensatory rest (in some situations).

The worker may also bring a complaint in respect of the employer's failure to pay him or her during annual leave. The tribunal may award such compensation as it considers 'just and equitable' and may require the employer to pay any money owing in respect of annual leave.

One of the quirks of this system is that it does not give the worker a remedy in respect of the 48-hour week. This gap was filled by the ruling in *Barber v RJB Mining*.[65] The workers in that case refused to sign an opt-out, but the employer insisted that they continue working over the limit. The judge held that the 48-hour limit, apparently because of the mandatory language in which it was expressed, was intended by Parliament to be a term of the workers' contracts.[66] This opened up the possibility of an injunction to stop the employer from insisting on longer working hours, though the judge refused to grant the injunction because he did not regard it as appropriate on the facts.[67]

Where a worker is forced to work particularly long hours to the extent that his or her health is damaged, it may be possible to bring a claim against the employer in tort (outside the WTR altogether) where it can be shown that the employer breached its duty of care towards the worker.[68]

8.4 GETTING CONTROL OVER WORKING TIME

So far, we have focused on the WTD and WTR, which seek to limit the number of hours people work on grounds of health and safety, broadly defined. Although they offer workers some control over their working time, for example, by giving them the 'choice' of whether or not to sign an opt-out from the 48-hour week, that is not their

[64] WTR, reg 29.
[65] [1999] ICR 679 (QB).
[66] ibid 690.
[67] ibid 692–693.
[68] See Chapter 5.

main focus. They assume that the employer will set the individual's working hours, and that the law's main role is to place some boundaries around what the employer can do.

However, a more radical approach to working time would give working people some say in when and for how long they work. For example, they might be allowed to choose part-time working over full-time working, or to work flexible hours (agreeing a total number of hours but working them at times of the individual's choosing), or to work some hours from home. A choice of this kind might be justified in one of two main ways. One is to argue that choice is necessary to enable workers with family responsibilities to 'reconcile' work and family life. The other is to focus on some more general principle – perhaps the principle of the humanisation of work – and thus to treat working time as a matter of choice for all working people, not just those with families.

The discussion in this section will focus on various legal mechanisms by which an individual might gain control over his or her working hours, the most important of which is the right to request flexible working. This is designed to prompt a negotiation between employer and employee about the employee's working arrangements, including his or her working hours. Although initially this right was introduced for employees with child-care responsibilities, and then extended to those with caring responsibilities, it is now available to all employees, so it has broken free of its moorings in family friendly justifications.

Of course, the individual's involvement in choosing his or her working times or hours is potentially very intrusive upon the employer's managerial prerogative: its capacity to run the business as it sees fit and to have the workforce available for work when required. As a result, the right to request flexible working is not particularly strongly framed.

8.4.1 International instruments

The idea that the individual might be able to have a say in his or her working hours – beyond the basic, but often unrealistic, opportunity to negotiate a contract – is too radical for the international instruments. The closest they come to the issue is through the regulation of part-time work or through a more general right to 'reconcile' work and family life.

The ILO Convention on part-time work states that 'where appropriate, measures shall be taken to ensure that transfer from full-time to part-time work or vice versa is voluntary in accordance with national law and practice'.[69] However, this is quite limited. It clearly requires states to prohibit a situation in which an individual is forced to transfer from full-time to part-time work (or vice versa) against his or her wishes. But while it could support a right to do a job on a part-time or full-time basis at the individual's choice, this would be quite a radical interpretation of the provision.

Rights to 'reconcile' work and family life are more promising. One of the most detailed is Article 27 of the revised ESC (not ratified by the UK):

> With a view to ensuring the exercise of the right to equality of opportunity and treatment for men and women workers with family responsibilities and between such workers and other workers, the Parties undertake:

---

[69] Part-time Work Convention 1994 (No 175) (adopted 24 June 1994, entered into force 28 February 1998), art 10. This has not been ratified by the UK.

to take appropriate measures:

(a) to enable workers with family responsibilities to enter and remain in employment, as well as to re-enter employment after an absence due to those responsibilities, including measures in the field of vocational guidance and training;

(b) to take account of their needs in terms of conditions of employment and social security . . .

Although this does not specifically entail a right to control over working hours, it is arguable that such a right is an important aspect of enabling workers with family responsibilities to remain in the labour market. However, any right justified on this basis would, inevitably, be confined to working parents.

8.4.2 Equality law

One route to obtaining control over working hours is to argue that the employer's inflexibility on the matter amounts to indirect sex discrimination, based on women's greater responsibility for child-care. Some claimants have used this argument in order to secure the right to work part-time.

For example, in *Home Office v Holmes*, the EAT held that the employer had discriminated against the claimant because it had declined her request to return to work part-time after taking maternity leave.[70] The EAT accepted the claimant's argument that it was harder for women than men to comply with the requirement to work full-time, and found that the employer had not done enough to justify its alleged need for full-time working. Similarly, in *London Underground v Edwards (No. 2)*, the claimant, who was a single mother, was able to challenge the employer's proposal to offer its employees new contracts which would have required her to work shifts incompatible with her child-care responsibilities.[71] However, not all courts are sympathetic to these kinds of arguments. For example, in *Clymo*, the claimant wanted to job-share her role as a librarian with her husband after returning from maternity leave.[72] The EAT in that case cast doubt on the *Holmes* decision as laying down any general principle.[73] It placed particular emphasis on the point that it was for the employer – not the tribunal – to decide whether or not full-time working was a requirement of the job, and accepted the employer's argument that part-time working was inappropriate in a senior management role. Interestingly, the EAT also made the point that, as a well-paid employee, the claimant could afford child-care as an alternative to job-sharing.

There are three main difficulties with the equality law approach. First, because each case turns on its own facts, it is hard to draw out any general principles. This makes it difficult for a woman who wants to work part-time – but does not want to or cannot afford to sue her employer – to assert that she has a legal right to work part-time. Second, equality law does not offer much help to men with family responsibilities unless the employer provides special benefits to women but does not offer the same benefits to similarly situated men. Nor does it offer any help to people who might want to work part-time for reasons unrelated to family. And third, the law is based on a factual finding that women take a greater responsibility for

---

[70] [1984] ICR 678 (EAT).
[71] [1999] ICR 494 (CA).
[72] *Clymo v Wandsworth London Borough Council* [1989] ICR 250 (EAT).
[73] See also *Hardy & Hansons Plc v Lax* [2005] EWCA Civ 846, [2005] ICR 1565.

child-care than men. While this is often true – most notably in the case of a single mother like Ms Edwards – it might have a tendency to reinforce that stereotype rather than bringing about greater equality in parenting (at least in couple families) over the longer term.

8.4.3 The Part-time Workers Regulations 2000 (PTWR)

A second possible source of a right to work part-time comes from the Directive on Part-Time Work[74] and the relevant implementing Regulations.[75] This measure is designed primarily to combat discrimination against part-time workers and thus forms part of a group of measures on different types of 'non-standard' or 'atypical' working.[76] In this chapter, our focus is on whether the Directive and Regulations offer any help to people who want to take control over their working hours. It is important to emphasise that any rights we can identify here would be applicable to anyone for any reason, not just to those with family responsibilities.

The social partners' agreement on part-time work, implemented by the Directive, provides in cl. 5(3):

As far as possible, employers should give consideration to:

(a) requests by workers to transfer from full-time to part-time work that becomes available in the establishment;
(b) requests by workers to transfer from part-time to full-time work or to increase their working time should the opportunity arise;
(c) the provision of timely information on the availability of part-time and full-time positions in the establishment in order to facilitate transfers from full-time to part-time or vice versa;
(d) measures to facilitate access to part-time work at all levels of the enterprise, including skilled and managerial positions, and where appropriate, to facilitate access by part-time workers to vocational training to enhance career opportunities and occupational mobility . . .

But when we turn to the PTWR, there is no equivalent of cl. 5. This is because the government took the view that it was largely aspirational in its wording and did not create any legally binding obligations. Bell argues that the government's interpretation of cl. 5 may be mistaken because the Court of Justice has already given legal effect to it in some cases.[77] For example, in *Michaeler*, it was held that additional administrative requirements relating to part-time contracts were contrary to EU law because, in breach of cl. 5(1), they made it more onerous for employers to hire part-timers.[78] It remains to be seen how the Court's case-law will develop. But as things stand, a UK worker who wants to transfer from full-time to part-time work cannot derive any help from the Regulations because the only legal right they contain – not to be discriminated against on grounds of working part-time – has no application to a full-time worker who is *seeking* to work part-time.

---

[74] Directive 97/81/EC.
[75] Part-Time Workers (Prevention of Less Favourable Treatment) Regulations 2000, SI 2000/1551. For discussion, see Mark Bell, 'Achieving the Objectives of the Part-Time Work Directive? Revisiting the Part-Time Workers Regulations' (2011) 40 ILJ 254.
[76] See Chapter 4.
[77] Above n 75, 265–272.
[78] Case C-55/07 *Michaeler v Amt fur sozialen Arbeitsschutz* [2008] ECR I-3135.

8.4.4 The right to request flexible working

A third possible source of a right to control one's own working hours is the right to request flexible working. This was initially introduced as a right for parents, but is now available to any qualifying employee so is no longer tied to family friendly justifications. It is important to note at the outset that the concept of 'flexible working' is not just about working time – it may also include working from home, for example – but since in many cases it will involve adjustments to working time, this chapter is the best place to examine it. The right is set out in s. 80F ERA 1996 and the Flexible Working Regulations 2014.[79]

Background

The right to request flexible working was initially introduced in the Employment Act 2002 for parents of children under the age of five. It was subsequently extended to apply to parents of older children (up to the age of 17, or 18 if the child was disabled) and to people with caring responsibilities for an adult. These limitations were repealed by the Children and Families Act 2014.

Directive 2010/18/EU, the revised Parental Leave Directive, includes a right to request flexible working in cl. 6(1) of the social partners' Agreement:

> In order to promote better reconciliation, Member States and/or social partners shall take the necessary measures to ensure that workers, when returning from parental leave, may request changes to their working hours and/or patterns for a set period of time. Employers shall consider and respond to such requests, taking into account both employers' and workers' needs.
>
> The modalities of this paragraph shall be determined in accordance with national law, collective agreements and/or practice.

This is a very limited right because it only applies to parents returning from parental leave, so it has not had much impact on English law.

Eligibility

The right to request flexible working is available to an employee (not a worker) who has completed a period of 26 weeks' continuous employment with the employer.[80] The right is not available to agency workers, except in the situation where the agency worker is returning to work after parental leave, to comply with the revised Parental Leave Directive.[81]

Content

The right to request flexible working offers the employee three possibilities:

> A qualifying employee may apply to his employer for a change in his terms and conditions of employment if–

---

[79] SI 2014/1398.
[80] ibid reg 3.
[81] Parental Leave (EU Directive) Regulations 2013, SI 2013/283, reg 2.

(a) the change relates to–

    (i) the hours he is required to work,

    (ii) the times when he is required to work,

    (iii) where, as between his home and a place of business of his employer, he is required to work . . . [82]

There is a power for the Secretary of State to add further possibilities by regulations but this has not been exercised.[83] Thus, the most obvious requests would be to work fewer hours in total, to work at different times (for example, starting later or finishing earlier to fit around school hours, or working during term-time only), or to work from home some or all of the time.

Reasons for refusal

The strength of the right to request flexible working turns on the extent of the employer's power to decline the employee's request. The employer must 'consider' that one or more reasons from the list in s. 80G(1)(b) is applicable to the situation. The permitted reasons are:

  (i) the burden of additional costs,

  (ii) detrimental effect on ability to meet customer demand,

  (iii) inability to re-organise work among existing staff,

  (iv) inability to recruit additional staff,

  (v) detrimental impact on quality,

  (vi) detrimental impact on performance,

  (vii) insufficiency of work during the periods the employee proposes to work,

  (viii) planned structural changes . . .

Commentators have pointed out that these reasons are quite broadly framed and would not be difficult for an employer to invoke.[84] For example, it is relatively easy to identify additional costs associated with a change in an employee's working patterns. As we shall see below, any judicial scrutiny of the employer's reasons is likely to be light touch.

Procedures

Under the legislation as originally introduced, there was a formal procedure to be followed by the employee in making a request and by the employer in considering it. The employer's duties were set out in the Flexible Working (Procedural Requirements) Regulations 2002.[85] These Regulations have been revoked with a view to simplifying the process.

---

[82] ERA 1996, s 80F(1).

[83] ibid s 80F(1)(a)(iv).

[84] See Lucy Anderson, 'Sound Bite Legislation: The Employment Act 2002 and New Flexible Working "Rights" for Parents' (2003) 32 ILJ 37.

[85] SI 2002/3207.

The current requirements are minimal. The employee's application must be in writing[86] and must specify the change being requested and 'explain what effect, if any, the employee thinks making the change applied for would have on [the] employer and how, in his opinion, any such effect might be dealt with'.[87] The employer's duty under s. 80G(1)(a) is to 'deal with the application in a reasonable manner'.[88] The employer must reach a decision within three months of the employee's request, though there is scope to extend this period by agreement.

Once the employee has made an application, he or she may not apply again until a year has elapsed since the previous request.[89] This protects employers against repeated requests (for example, by employees whose first attempt was unsuccessful, or by employees who are unhappy with the new arrangements they have been given).

Enforcement

The employee has a right to complain to the employment tribunal under s. 80H(1) about two things:

(a) that his employer has failed in relation to the application to comply with section 80G(1) . . .

(b) that a decision by his employer to reject the application was based on incorrect facts . . .

At first sight it appears that the employee may be able to challenge the employer's decision on both procedural and substantive grounds. However, some caution is required. Section 80G(1) only requires the employer to act 'reasonably' when considering the request, and allows the employer to refuse the employee's application where it 'considers' that one of the listed reasons applies, a subjective test.

Section 80H(1)(b) was discussed in *Commotion Ltd v Rutty*.[90] There, the EAT rejected both an argument that the tribunal had to take the employer's assertions at face value, and an argument (at the opposite extreme) that the tribunal could consider the fairness or reasonableness of the employer's refusal. The tribunal's primary role was to check the facts, as s. 80H(1)(b) indicated. The EAT also suggested, obiter, that review of the employer's decision on the grounds of bad faith might be a possibility in a future case. This would be consistent with the requirement that the employer should 'consider' that a permitted reason is applicable, since an employer acting in bad faith would not be able to demonstrate this.

The remedy for a breach of s. 80H is set out in s. 80I(1):

Where an employment tribunal finds a complaint under section 80H well-founded it shall make a declaration to that effect and may–

(a) make an order for reconsideration of the application, and

(b) make an award of compensation to be paid by the employer to the employee.

The compensation is what the tribunal considers to be 'just and equitable', subject to a maximum of eight weeks' pay.[91]

---

[86] Flexible Working Regulations 2014, SI 2014/1398, reg 4.

[87] ERA 1996, s 80F(2).

[88] There is an ACAS Code of Practice on this but it does not offer much detail: ACAS, *Handling in a Reasonable Manner Requests to Work Flexibly* (Code of Practice 5, June 2014).

[89] ERA 1996, s 80F(4).

[90] *Commotion Ltd v Rutty* [2006] ICR 290 (EAT).

[91] FWR 2014, reg 6. This is subject to the statutory cap in s 227 ERA 1996.

Under the ACAS (Flexible Working) Arbitration Scheme (Great Britain) Order 2004,[92] it is possible for the parties to refer their dispute to an arbitrator appointed by ACAS instead of going to the tribunal. This option is only available where both parties agree. The role of the arbitrator is to determine whether the employer has complied with the rules, not to substitute his or her judgment for that of the employer on the feasibility of agreeing to the employee's request. The scheme cannot be used for technical disputes such as whether the individual was an 'employee' and therefore entitled to make a request. The arbitrator has the power to award the same remedies as the tribunal. The main difference between arbitration and a tribunal hearing is that arbitration takes place in private. This may be particularly attractive to employers because it offers a way of avoiding bad publicity. Arbitration hearings may also be less formal than tribunal hearings. However, the government's latest policy to minimise tribunal claims is to encourage conciliation when a claim is brought, so it is not clear what the future of the arbitration alternative might be.[93]

Conclusion

The right to request flexible working is a step in a potentially radical direction, reflecting the idea that working time might sometimes be organised around the worker rather than around the employer. The extension of the right to all employees with the requisite qualifying service is to be welcomed. However, it is important to remember that some firms may provide flexible working schemes voluntarily,[94] and in any case it is always open to an employee to discuss working time with his or her employer and to negotiate a variation to his or her contract, outside the statutory framework. So the key question is whether the right to request flexible working adds anything to the basic contractual position. In particular, does the right help to overcome the inequality of bargaining power that prevents most people from negotiating their terms and conditions of employment in a meaningful way with their employer? As we have seen, it is doubtful whether the right makes any significant moves in that direction. It requires the employer to consider the request in a 'reasonable' way, but no longer gives the employee any explicit procedural rights (to have a meeting with the employer, for example)[95] and the list of possible reasons for refusal is broadly framed and subject to light touch scrutiny by tribunals.

8.5 TIME OFF FOR FAMILY REASONS

The WTD and WTR, and the right to request flexible working, deal with weekly working time. As we have seen, limiting and controlling weekly working time are important tools in enabling people to balance work with family life. However, in some instances, workers may want time away from the workplace for family reasons without having to give up work altogether. In this section, we will examine the four main rights the law grants in this area: maternity leave, paternity leave, parental leave

---

[92] SI 2004/2333.
[93] See Chapter 2.
[94] On the relevance of firms' attitudes see Richard Croucher and Clare Kelliher, 'The Right to Request Flexible Working in Britain: the Law and Organisational Realities' (2005) 21 International Journal of Comparative Labour Law and Industrial Relations 503.
[95] Though the ACAS Code, above n 88, recommends this.

and emergency leave.[96] Each right involves several components: the right to take time off, rights during the leave, the right to return afterwards and rights not to be penalised for having taken the leave. We will consider the international human rights instruments before examining the various rights to leave in English law. It is worth noting at the outset that although there are EU directives on maternity leave and parental leave, English law has tended to develop in advance of these directives and offers more generous provision.

8.5.1 International instruments

The international instruments on family leave illustrate the historical development of rights in this area. Initially, the focus was on protecting pregnant women at work, largely on health and safety grounds. Over time, the focus shifted towards granting more generous rights to women, recognising that they faced the 'double burden' of work and a greater share of the responsibility for child-care. On this view, rights to leave were about helping women to reconcile their family role with working life and thus to participate more fully in the labour market. More recently, there has been a growing focus on 'shared parenting': the idea that – in couple families at least – both parents might want to be (or should be) involved in child-care. This suggests a reduced emphasis on rights for mothers, confining maternity leave to what is strictly required by biological needs, and a much greater emphasis on rights for both parents to take time off for child-care.

The ICESCR provides a basic right to maternity leave in Article 10(2):

> Special protection should be accorded to mothers during a reasonable period before and after childbirth. During such period working mothers should be accorded paid leave or leave with adequate social security benefits.

The ESC 1961, which has been ratified by the UK, specifies that maternity leave should be for a minimum duration of 12 weeks.[97] The revised ESC 1996[98] and the ILO Maternity Protection Convention[99] specify a minimum of 14 weeks. The right to maternity leave itself implies a right to return to work, but the Convention on the Elimination of All Forms of Discrimination against Women (CEDAW) expressly states that the woman should be able to return without loss of seniority.[100] Some instruments, including the ILO Convention[101] and the ESC 1996,[102] also provide that a woman who returns to work while she is still breastfeeding should be given time off for this purpose. Several instruments state that pregnancy or the taking of maternity leave should not be permitted as grounds of dismissal.[103] Finally, it is common to find a requirement that pregnant women or women who are breastfeeding should not be required to engage in hazardous work or night work.[104]

---

[96] The law also provides rights to adoption leave but space precludes a detailed consideration of them in this chapter.

[97] Art 8.

[98] Art 8.

[99] Maternity Protection Convention 2000 (No 183) (adopted 15 June 2000, entered into force 7 February 2002). This convention has not been ratified by the UK.

[100] Art 11(2)(b).

[101] Maternity Protection Convention (n 99), art 10.

[102] Art 8.

[103] ESC 1961, art 8; ESC 1996, art 8; CEDAW, art 11(2)(a).

[104] ESC 1961, art 8; ESC 1996, art 8; ILO, above n 99, art 3; CEDAW, art 11(2)(d).

Modern human rights instruments have begun to look beyond the basic provision of maternity leave and to consider the longer-term problems of balancing work and family life faced by working parents of both sexes. Article 27(2) of the revised ESC obliges signatory states to:

> provide a possibility for either parent to obtain, during a period after maternity leave, parental leave to take care of a child, the duration and conditions of which should be determined by national legislation, collective agreements or practice.

The right to parental leave is also recognised in the EU Charter, Article 33(2), and is expressed to be available to 'everyone'. Although CEDAW focuses on maternity rights and the provision of child-care facilities rather than parental leave, one of its more general provisions, Article 5, is of considerable interest in relation to this topic. Article 5(a) requires states to work towards the elimination of stereotypical assumptions about men's and women's roles. It is coupled with Article 5(b), which states:

> To ensure that family education includes a proper understanding of maternity as a social function and the recognition of the common responsibility of men and women in the upbringing and development of their children, it being understood that the interest of the children is the primordial consideration in all cases.

This provision encapsulates the key distinction between the biological function of giving birth and the shared responsibility of both parents within a couple for child-care.[105]

8.5.2 Maternity leave

In this section, we will focus on the right to take maternity leave and to return afterwards. In EU law, these rights can be found in the Pregnant Workers Directive (PrWD).[106] This is an individual directive within the meaning of Article 16(1) of Directive 89/391/EEC, the Framework Directive on Health and Safety, so its primary justification is to protect the health and safety of pregnant workers. In English law, the rights are contained in the Employment Rights Act 1996, and implementing regulations, the Maternity and Parental Leave etc Regulations (MPLR) 1999, as amended.[107] A version of the right to take maternity leave was first introduced into English law in 1975, so significantly in advance of the EU's intervention in this area.

It is important to bear in mind during this discussion that it is unlawful to discriminate against a woman because she is pregnant (or, in some circumstances, because she is suffering from an illness related to pregnancy) under EU law and the Equality Act 2010.[108] This means that when employers are applying the detailed rules on leave, they must also be alert to the possibility that their actions may be challenged under equality law too. The rights to be discussed in this section are available to employees only, so the right not to be discriminated against acquires particular importance for pregnant workers who are not employees, since it is their primary source of protection.

[105] Of course nowadays many same-sex couples have children; the provision assumes a different-sex couple.
[106] Directive 92/85/EEC.
[107] SI 1999/3312.
[108] See Chapter 6.

Entitlement and duration

Article 8 of the PrWD requires Member States to provide a right to 14 weeks' maternity leave. When the leave can be taken is to be determined in accordance with national law and practice.[109] In 2008, the Commission proposed an amendment to the Directive that would have seen maternity leave increased from 14 weeks to 18 weeks. The European Parliament supported this move and indeed proposed that leave should be set at 20 weeks. However, these plans were rejected by the Council.

English law offers much more generous leave than the minimum standard set by the Directive. A woman may take up to 52 weeks' leave though, as we shall see below, the possibility of doing so in practice is likely to be heavily influenced by her financial circumstances. For various technical reasons, the 52-week period is divided into two: ordinary maternity leave of 26 weeks, and additional maternity leave of 26 weeks.[110] There is also a compulsory maternity leave period of two weeks from the date of childbirth during which it is a criminal offence for the employer to permit the employee to work.[111]

As we have already noted, the entitlement to maternity leave applies only to employees. It arises if the following relatively straightforward conditions are met:

An employee is entitled to ordinary maternity leave and to additional maternity leave provided that she satisfies the following conditions–

(a) no later than the end of the fifteenth week before her expected week of childbirth, or, if that is not reasonably practicable, as soon as is reasonably practicable, she notifies her employer of–

(i) her pregnancy;

(ii) the expected week of childbirth, and

(iii) the date on which she intends her ordinary maternity leave period to start, and

(b) if requested to do so by her employer, she produces for his inspection a certificate from–

(i) a registered medical practitioner, or

(ii) a registered midwife,

stating the expected week of childbirth.[112]

The employee may not specify a start date for the maternity leave that is earlier than the 11th week before the expected week of childbirth.[113] Although the law allows the employee to choose when to start her maternity leave, this choice may be overridden during the four weeks prior to the expected week of childbirth. Under reg. 6(1), if the employee is absent from work for a reason 'wholly or partly because of pregnancy' during that time, her maternity leave starts the following day. If the employee gives birth without having started her maternity leave, reg. 6(2) provides that her leave begins the following day. In both of these cases, the employee risks losing her right to maternity leave unless she notifies the employer under reg. 4(3) and (4).

---

[109] Art 1(3) contains a non-regression clause, so if a Member State already provides more than 14 weeks' leave, it may not treat the Directive as a reason to reduce this.
[110] MPLR 1999, reg 7.
[111] ERA 1996, s 72(5); MPLR 1999, reg 8.
[112] MPLR 1999, reg 4(1).
[113] ibid reg 4(2).

Rights during leave

Under the PrWD, the pregnant worker must either receive pay or an 'adequate' allowance during the leave which is at least equivalent to that she would receive if she was off work due to illness.[114] Apart from pay, the worker's other rights under her employment contract must be maintained during the leave.[115]

We will consider pay first. This is dealt with through the concept of Statutory Maternity Pay (SMP). A woman who is eligible for maternity leave but not SMP may be eligible instead for a benefit called Maternity Allowance. We will not consider this in detail because benefits are beyond the scope of this book.

A woman is eligible for SMP if she has worked for a 26-week qualifying period ending in the 15th week before the week the baby is due and if, in the last eight weeks of the qualifying period, her normal weekly earnings were above the Lower Earnings Limit (LEL).[116] The LEL varies from year to year and is the point at which a worker becomes obliged to make National Insurance contributions.

For the first six weeks, the claimant is entitled to be paid at the rate of 90% of her normal weekly earnings in the last eight weeks of the qualifying period.[117] After that, she is entitled to be paid the SMP rate, at the time of writing fixed at £138.18 per week,[118] or 90% of her normal weekly earnings where this is lower. The relevant statute obliges the Secretary of State to set the SMP rate no lower than the statutory sick pay rate, which reflects the requirement in the PrWD that the allowance paid to a woman on maternity leave should be no worse than that for employees who are off sick.[119] The maximum total duration of payment (including the first six weeks) is 39 weeks.[120] This means that if a woman chooses to take the whole 52-week entitlement to maternity leave, the final 13 weeks will attract no payment at all.

The obligation to pay SMP lies with the claimant's employer prior to her maternity leave. This remains so even if she resigns her job at the start of the maternity leave, or if it can be shown that the employer tried to dismiss her in order to avoid paying SMP.[121] The obligation to pay SMP shifts to the Secretary of State if the employer becomes insolvent.[122] Of course, while the employee is on maternity leave, the employer faces the additional cost of hiring, training and paying a temporary replacement. The legislation recognises this by providing for employers to be reimbursed by HMRC for the SMP payments they make.[123] Smaller firms are fully reimbursed, and larger firms are reimbursed in respect of 92% of the payments.[124] Although firms still face administrative costs when an employee takes maternity leave, the bulk of the financial burden is shouldered by the state.

---

[114] ibid art 11(2) and (3). The Member States may make this conditional. Conditions may include a qualifying period of employment but this may not exceed 12 months.

[115] ibid art 11(2).

[116] Social Security Contributions and Benefits Act 1992 (SSCBA 1992), s 164.

[117] ibid s 166.

[118] Statutory Maternity Pay (General) Regulations 1986, SI 1986/1960 (SMPGR), reg 6.

[119] SSCBA 1992, s 166(3); PrWD, art 11.

[120] SMPGR 1986, reg 2(2).

[121] ibid regs 2 and 3.

[122] ibid reg 7.

[123] SSCBA 1992, s 167.

[124] This is worked out by determining how much an employer paid in Class 1 employer's and employees' National Insurance contributions in the previous tax year. If the sum is below £45,000, the employer will be reimbursed SMP in full; if it is above that figure, the reimbursement is at 92%.

Before leaving the subject of pay, it is important to emphasise that the legislation only sets minimum standards, so it is always open to an employer to offer a better deal to employees taking maternity leave. The employer might do this as a means of demonstrating that it offers a 'family friendly' working environment, which in turn might help it to recruit and retain workers more effectively.

We noted above that the PrWD requires that the worker's contractual rights (other than pay) must be maintained during her maternity leave. This is addressed in reg. 9(1) of the Maternity and Parental Leave etc. Regulations 1999 as follows:

> An employee who takes ordinary maternity leave or additional maternity leave–
>
> (a) is entitled, during the period of leave, to the benefit of all of the terms and conditions of employment which would have applied if she had not been absent, and
>
> (b) is bound, during that period, by any obligations arising under those terms and conditions . . .

For these purposes, pay is excluded from para (1)(a), and obligations that would be inconsistent with the employee's right to be absent from work are not covered by para (1)(b).

The right to return to work

The right to take maternity leave is a rather hollow concept if it is not accompanied by a right to return to work at the end of the leave. In EU law, an express right to return was a relative late-comer in the legislative framework. It was inserted into the Equal Treatment Directive in 2002,[125] and can now be found in the Recast Directive, Article 15:

> A woman on maternity leave shall be entitled, after the end of her period of maternity leave, to return to her job or to an equivalent post on terms and conditions which are no less favourable to her and to benefit from any improvement in working conditions to which she would have been entitled during her absence.[126]

The obligation to ensure that the worker benefits from improvements, such as pay rises, awarded during her absence codifies some of the Court's case-law on the matter.

The distinction between ordinary and additional maternity leave becomes important in relation to the right to return. Under reg. 18(1), an employee who has taken ordinary maternity leave is entitled to return to the same job, whereas under reg. 18(2), an employee who has taken additional maternity leave 'is entitled to return from leave to the job in which she was employed before her absence or, if it is not reasonably practicable for the employer to permit her to return to that job, to another job which is both suitable for her and appropriate for her to do in the circumstances'.

The right to return is reinforced by reg. 18A(1):

> An employee's right to return under regulation 18(1) or (2) is a right to return–
>
> (a) with her seniority, pension rights and similar rights as they would have been if she had not been absent, and

---

[125] Directive 2002/73/EC amending Council Directive 76/207/EEC on the implementation of the principle of equal treatment for men and women as regards access to employment, vocational training and promotion, and working conditions, art 2.

[126] Directive 2006/54/EC.

(b) on terms and conditions not less favourable than those which would have applied if she had not been absent.

An employee who intends to return to work before the end of the additional maternity leave period must give the employer eight weeks' notice in accordance with reg. 11.

An area of particular controversy in practice is what happens if the employer needs to make redundancies while an employee is on maternity leave. Under reg. 10, there is a right to be offered a suitable alternative vacancy where one exists. The employer must also take considerable care to observe a fair selection procedure and to ensure that it does not discriminate against employees who are pregnant or taking maternity leave. However, in the *Eversheds* case, a male employee who was made redundant in preference to a colleague who was on maternity leave was able to challenge the employer's decision-making process as discriminatory against him on grounds of sex.[127] The absent employee was given top scores for the selection criteria that could not be measured while she was away. The EAT held that the employer had gone beyond what was necessary to protect the absent employee.

Dismissal and detriment

Article 10 PrWD requires the Member States to provide pregnant workers and workers taking maternity leave with protection against dismissal:

> Member States shall take the necessary measures to prohibit the dismissal of workers, within the meaning of Article 2, during the period from the beginning of their pregnancy to the end of the maternity leave referred to in Article 8(1), save in exceptional cases not connected with their condition which are permitted under national legislation and/or practice . . .

Article 10 is directly effective[128] and has been held to apply to fixed-term as well as indefinite contracts.[129] This is significant because in some cases, employers had sought to argue (albeit unsuccessfully) that it was legitimate to dismiss a worker on a fixed-term contract who became pregnant because she would not be available for work at the required time.[130]

In English law, there is protection against detrimental treatment on grounds of pregnancy and maternity leave under s. 47C ERA 1996 and reg. 19 MPLR. It is automatically unfair to dismiss an employee on these grounds.

Time off for ante-natal care

Article 9 of the PrWD requires the Member States to grant a right to time off to attend ante-natal examinations where these take place during working hours. This time off must be paid.

The right to time off for ante-natal care in English law is set out in s. 55 ERA 1996. It applies to an employee who is pregnant and who has made an appointment for

---

[127] *Eversheds Legal Services Ltd v De Belin* [2011] ICR 1137 (EAT).
[128] Case C-438/99 *Melgar v Ayuntamiento de Los Barrios* [2001] ECR I-6915.
[129] See Case C-109/00 *Tele Danmark A/S v Handels- og Kontorfunktionaerernes Forbund I Danmark* [2001] ECR I-6993, and Case C-438/99 *Melgar v Ayuntamiento de Los Barrios* [2001] ECR I-6915.
[130] For example, Case C-32/93 *Webb v EMO Air Cargo (UK) Ltd* [1994] ECR I-3567.

ante-natal care on the advice of a doctor, nurse or midwife. Unless it is the employee's first appointment for ante-natal care, the employer may require her to produce a medical certificate to show that she is pregnant and to produce written evidence of the ante-natal appointment. The right to be paid for the leave is governed by s. 56.

The right can be enforced by making an application to the employment tribunal under s. 57. If the employer 'unreasonably refuses' to permit the employee to take the time off, the tribunal can make a declaration to that effect and can order the employer to pay the employee any money she would have been entitled to had she taken the time off. This increased to twice the money from October 2014.[131] If the employee was permitted to take time off, but there is a dispute about payment, the tribunal may order the employer to pay the employee any money it considers she is owed.

The reference to the employer's 'unreasonable' refusal is puzzling. As we saw above, the employee must meet certain conditions in order to get the time off, so perhaps this simply denotes the fact that the employer is not obliged to permit the employee to take time off if she fails to show an appointment card. However, it seems to imply that a tribunal might find that the employer was not liable for a refusal to permit the employee to take time off because it had acted reasonably, for example, because the employee had made her appointment at a particularly busy time.

More problematic is the reliance on enforcement through the tribunal system. It seems highly unlikely that a pregnant worker would bring proceedings in order to enforce her right to time off for ante-natal appointments. The sums of money involved are small and by the time the case had reached the tribunal the worker would probably have had her baby. Thus, the employer's willingness to comply with the law voluntarily is crucial in this area.

From October 2014, an employee in a 'qualifying relationship' to the mother is entitled to take time off work to accompany her to two ante-natal appointments.[132] This applies to the mother's spouse, civil partner, partner or the father of the child.

8.5.3 Shared parental leave

As we saw above, while maternity leave is an important element in any scheme of family leave, extensive maternity rights can reinforce the idea that child-care is the mother's responsibility. Thus, there has been growing interest in creating a mechanism by which parents in a couple can share leave once the mother has recovered from the birth. Initially, this was developed through the concept of 'additional paternity leave', but from 2015 there will be a new regime of 'shared parental leave'. For simplicity, we will refer to the person taking this leave as the 'partner'.

The right to take additional paternity leave is detailed in the Additional Paternity Leave Regulations 2010.[133] Despite the name, the leave is available to the father of the child or to the mother's spouse, civil partner or partner, provided that the person expects to have responsibility for the child. Additional paternity leave is a right to take between two and 26 weeks of leave. The leave must be taken in whole weeks, and the weeks must be consecutive, so the employee cannot take, for example, five and a half weeks of leave or two separate blocks of four weeks. The leave must be

[131] Children and Families Act 2014, s 130(1).
[132] ERA 1996, s 57ZE.
[133] SI 2010/1055.

taken during the period between 20 weeks and 12 months from the date of the child's birth. An employee is eligible for additional paternity leave if three main conditions are met. He or she must have 26 weeks' continuous employment, give the appropriate notice, and the child's mother must have returned to work. Pay equivalent to SMP is available where the mother would have been entitled to SMP had she not returned to work.

The government regards the system of Additional Paternity Leave as unduly rigid, because it is only available once the baby is 20 weeks old, and because the mother faces a one-off choice between continuing her leave or returning to work. Shared parental leave (SPL) is designed to overcome these problems.[134] The right is found in new s. 75E ERA 1996 inserted by the Children and Families Act 2014 and the Shared Parental Leave Regulations 2014.[135]

To share the leave, both the mother and the partner must satisfy the eligibility conditions, which include a 26-week qualifying period. The shared parental leave period is whatever leave is left over after the mother has taken maternity leave. So, if the mother only takes the two-week compulsory leave, 50 weeks will be available for sharing, but if the mother takes, say, 10 weeks, 42 weeks will be available for sharing. The mother must trigger the shared parental leave either by returning to work or by giving eight weeks' notice to the employer that she intends to terminate her maternity leave.[136] Once either of these things has happened, the partner may start taking shared parental leave (even if the mother is still on maternity leave).[137] This allows both parents to take time off together during the first few weeks after the birth, though of course that will have the consequence that the leave will run out more quickly. Both the mother and her partner must give notice to the employer including a statement of how much leave is available to them in total and how they intend to share it.[138]

The employer must be given eight weeks' notice of the proposed start date of the leave.[139] The employee may propose a single period of continuous leave or a series of discontinuous periods (though each must be at least a week long).[140] However, whereas the employer is *entitled* to take the continuous leave, any discontinuous leave is subject to the employer's agreement and may be replaced by a single period of continuous leave if no agreement can be reached.[141] This means that the system of shared parental leave may turn out to be much less flexible in practice than it appears, since employers may not permit their employees to take the leave in the format they propose.

Under the SPL regime, any of the 39-week entitlement to SMP that has not been taken by the mother can be paid to either the mother or the partner as SPL pay at the same rate.[142] This means that some of the SPL (like some maternity leave) may be unpaid. For example, if both partners take 26 weeks' leave together, the mother will use 26 weeks' SMP, leaving 13 weeks' SPL pay for the partner (plus two weeks of

[134] DBIS, *Employers' Technical Guide to Shared Parental Leave and Pay* (September 2014) 4.
[135] Shared Parental Leave Regulations 2014, SI 2014/3050.
[136] SPLR 2014, reg 4(2)(d).
[137] ibid reg 5.
[138] ibid regs 8–9.
[139] ibid reg 12.
[140] ibid regs 13–14.
[141] ibid regs 14(2) and 14(4).
[142] Statutory Shared Parental Pay (General) Regulations 2014, SI 2014/3051.

paid paternity leave). This leaves the partner with no pay for 11 weeks while the mother gets SMP. Since SMP is not particularly generous, many families will not be able to survive on this level of income, making SPL unrealistic in practice.

The usual rights to protection against detriment and to protection against dismissal apply to people taking shared parental leave.[143]

8.5.4 Paternity leave

The law also provides a right to paternity leave (currently called 'ordinary paternity leave' to distinguish it from 'additional paternity leave', but it will revert once SPL takes effect). This is a right to two weeks' leave when the baby is born. The right to ordinary paternity leave is set out in regulations made under ERA 1996, ss. 80A and 80C. The current regulations are the Paternity and Adoption Leave Regulations 2002.[144]

The right is to take either one continuous week or two continuous weeks of leave, at the employee's choice.[145] The leave must normally be taken within 56 days of the birth of the child, but the employee may decide when the leave should start. The entitlement to paternity leave is granted to those who fulfil the conditions laid down in reg. 4 and who provide the relevant notices and evidence to the employer in accordance with reg. 6. The eligibility requirements are similar to those for SPL, discussed above, the most important being that the individual must be an employee with 26 weeks' continuous employment and (again despite the name) may be the spouse, civil partner or partner of the mother. The leave is paid at a rate equivalent to basic SMP.

The government has considered increasing the entitlement to paternity leave but has postponed this in the light of the introduction of SPL.

8.5.5 Parental leave

Maternity and paternity leave and SPL are, as we have seen, available when a child is born. Parental leave, by contrast, can be used at a later date. Its main disadvantage is that it is unpaid, which may make it difficult in practice for some parents to make use of it.

EU law

The Parental Leave Directive was enacted in 1996 under the social dialogue procedure.[146] The social partners negotiated a revised Agreement on the subject in 2009, and a new Directive was enacted in 2010 to give effect to this.[147]

---

[143] SPLR 2014, regs 42 and 43.
[144] SI 2002/2788.
[145] ibid reg 5(1).
[146] Directive 96/34/EC of 3 June 1996 implementing the Framework Agreement on parental leave concluded by UNICE, CEEP and the ETUC, OJ L145/4, extended to the UK by Council Directive 97/75/EC, OJ L10/24.
[147] Council Directive 2010/18/EU of 8 March 2010 implementing the revised Framework Agreement on parental leave concluded by BUSINESSEUROPE, UEAPME, CEEP and ETUC and repealing Directive 96/34/EC, OJ L68/13.

The Agreement applies equally to male and female workers. Although the definition of 'worker' is a matter for national law,[148] one of the new features of the revised Agreement is that it applies explicitly to part-time, fixed-term and agency workers.[149] Many of the practical details of taking leave are for the Member States to determine, such as the imposition of a qualifying period of service (which may not exceed one year), the circumstances in which the employer can postpone the leave for business reasons, and the form in which leave can be taken (in longer or shorter blocks of time, for example).[150]

The original Agreement required the Member States to give every parent a right to three months' parental leave. The revised Agreement has increased that to four months' leave.[151] Member States are obliged to ensure that at least one month out of the four is not transferable to the other parent, as a means of encouraging both parents to make use of the leave.[152]

Clause 5 of the Agreement requires that workers taking parental leave be afforded the right to return to the same or an equivalent job afterwards. Their contractual rights should be maintained, so that, for example, any pay rises awarded during their leave should be applied to them on their return. The clause also requires the Member States to ensure that those taking or seeking to take parental leave are protected against dismissal and other detrimental treatment on this ground (the latter being a new addition to the revised Agreement).

English law

The right to parental leave is set out in ERA s. 76 and the MPLR, as amended.[153]

An employee is eligible for parental leave if he or she expects to have responsibility for a child and has been employed by the employer for a one-year qualifying period. The entitlement was increased from 13 to 18 weeks in 2013 to comply with the revised Directive.[154] At the moment, the leave is only available in respect of children under five (or disabled children under 18),[155] though the government has announced an intention to increase this to 18 in 2015.[156] The leave is for each child so a parent with two children may, in theory at least, take 36 weeks' leave.

The arrangements for taking parental leave are set out in MPLR Schedule 2, though they may be displaced by a workforce agreement or a collective agreement. The employee must give 21 days' notice of his or her intention to take leave. The employer may require the employee to take leave at a different time to the one he or she has proposed if it 'considers that the operation of [the] business would be unduly disrupted'.[157] Under para 7, the leave must be taken in minimum blocks of one week but under para 8, it may not be taken in blocks of more than four weeks.

---

[148] ibid Annex, cl 1(2).
[149] ibid cl 1(3).
[150] ibid cl 3.
[151] ibid cl 2.
[152] ibid cl 2(2).
[153] The Parental Leave (EU Directive) Regulations 2013, SI 2013/283.
[154] MPLR 1999, reg 14(1).
[155] ibid reg 15.
[156] The Maternity and Parental Leave etc. (Amendment) Regulations 2014, SI 2014/3221.
[157] MPLR 1999, sch 2, para 6.

The main disadvantage of parental leave is that it is unpaid. This limits the take-up of the right because it is unaffordable for most people. It may also have the effect of discouraging the higher earner in a couple from taking the leave.

8.5.6 Emergency leave

The Parental Leave Directive (in both the original and revised versions) requires the Member States to put in place a right to 'emergency leave'. This is currently contained in cl. 7(1) of the Annex to the revised Directive:

> Member States and/or social partners shall take the necessary measures to entitle workers to time off from work, in accordance with national legislation, collective agreements and/or practice, on grounds of force majeure for urgent family reasons in cases of sickness or accident making the immediate presence of the worker indispensable.

The Member States may place conditions on this form of leave, which may include limiting it to a certain period of time per year or per situation. Since the right is framed in very general terms, making reference to national legislation, there is limited scope to challenge restrictions placed on the right at national level.

The right is implemented in English law by s. 57A ERA 1996. Crucially, the right is to take 'a reasonable amount of time off' so there is scope for debate between the employer and the employee about *how much* time the employee needs to deal with the emergency he or she faces. Moreover, the leave is available for the employee to 'take action which is *necessary*' (emphasis added) to deal with one of the listed emergencies, so there is also scope for argument about whether or not the employee's presence is really required.

The directive refers loosely to 'sickness or accident' but the legislation spells out in greater detail the types of situation in which the right arises, as follows:

(a) to provide assistance on an occasion when a dependant falls ill, gives birth or is injured or assaulted,
(b) to make arrangements for the provision of care for a dependant who is ill or injured,
(c) in consequence of the death of a dependant,
(d) because of the unexpected disruption or termination of arrangements for the care of a dependant, or
(e) to deal with an incident which involves a child of the employee and which occurs unexpectedly in a period during which an educational establishment which the child attends is responsible for him.[158]

Dependant is defined in subsections 3, 4 and 5 and includes people who 'reasonably' rely on the employee and members of his or her household as well as his or her parent, child or spouse or civil partner.

Finally, subsection 2 sets out the conditions under which the right can be exercised:

> Subsection (1) does not apply unless the employee–
>
> (a) tells his employer the reason for his absence as soon as reasonably practicable, and
> (b) except where paragraph (a) cannot be complied with until after the employee has returned to work, tells his employer for how long he expects to be absent.[159]

---

[158] ERA 1996, s 57A(1).
[159] On the importance of complying with the notification requirements see *Ellis v Ratcliff Palfinger Ltd* (2014) UKEAT/0438/13/BA.

Under s. 57B, the employee may enforce the right by taking a case to the Employment Tribunal, which has the power to make an award of compensation that is 'just and equitable' in relation to the employer's breach of the law and any losses suffered by the employee as a result.

This means of enforcement is practically useless. It is in the nature of emergency leave that the employee needs to take the time off when the emergency occurs. Financial compensation at a later date is of limited value. In practice, it seems likely that many employers provide this type of leave voluntarily, regardless of the law. If an employee is upset about a crisis at home, he or she is unlikely to focus on work and it is usually kinder and more efficient to allow him or her to go and sort it out. The most the law can do here is to encourage employers to do the right thing.

POINTS TO TAKE AWAY

- The WTD is based on a health and safety justification, broadly defined to include the principle of 'humanisation' of work. The WTD/WTR entitle workers to paid annual leave, a 48-hour maximum working week, and rights to daily and weekly rest periods. However, the 48-hour week is subject to an individual opt-out and the other rights are the subject of various exceptions and derogations.

- The right to request flexible working enables an employee to ask the employer to vary his or her working hours. The employer must consider the request and may only refuse it if it thinks that one of a list of business reasons applies. This right has the potential to give employees a greater say in their working arrangements but the right is not particularly strong in practice.

- Employees enjoy a range of rights to leave for family reasons. There is a right to up to 52 weeks' maternity leave, though from 2015 most of this may be taken as 'shared parental leave' shared between the mother and her partner. There is a right to two weeks' paternity leave, and to 18 weeks unpaid parental leave per child. There is also a right to emergency leave for family reasons.

Further reading

For more detail on the EU dimensions of this topic, see **Catherine Barnard, *EU Employment Law* (4th edn, OUP 2012), chapters 9 and 12.**

As we noted at the start of this chapter, the regulation of working time is a complex exercise given the variety of different issues and preferences at stake. For an overview, see **Jean-Yves Boulin et al, *Decent Working Time* (ILO 2006), especially chapters 1 and 16.** There are important intersections between the regulation of working time for 'standard' employees, the emergence of various forms of non-standard working (see Chapter 4), and ideas about work/life balance. These are well explained by **Hugh Collins, 'The Right to Flexibility', in Joanne Conaghan and Kerry Rittich (eds), *Labour Law, Work and Family* (OUP 2005).** The lack of 'fit' between the WTD and the modern labour market is also discussed by **Jeff Kenner in 'Regulating Working Time – Beyond Subordination?' in Stephen Weatherill (ed), *Better***

→

Regulation (Hart 2007). The importance of giving working people some control over their working hours is discussed by **Mark Bell in 'Achieving the Objectives of the Part-Time Work Directive? Revisiting the Part-Time Workers Regulations' (2011) 40 ILJ 254**.

In relation to so-called 'family-friendly' policies, there is a strong feminist critique of the EU's approach. See, for example, **Eugenia Caracciolo di Torella, 'Is there a Fundamental Right to Reconciling Work and Family Life in the EU?', in Nicole Busby and Grace James (eds),** *Families, Care-giving and Paid Work: Challenging Labour Law in the 21st Century* **(Edward Elgar 2011); and Clare McGlynn, 'Work, Family and Parenthood: The European Union Agenda' in Joanne Conaghan and Kerry Rittich (eds),** *Labour Law, Work and Family* **(OUP 2005).**

9 Job security

Learning outcomes

This chapter will enable readers to:

- critically evaluate the idea of job security: should we protect employees against unjustified dismissal, and if so, what are the policy options?
- understand the statute law of unfair dismissal: the situations covered by unfair dismissal law, automatically unfair dismissals (reasons that the employer cannot lawfully rely on to dismiss someone), potentially fair dismissals (reasons that the employer may lawfully rely on to dismiss someone provided that the employer acts reasonably and follows a fair procedure), the procedure for making an unfair dismissal claim and the remedies available
- understand the common law of wrongful dismissal: the possibilities for bringing a claim in contract based on a failure to give the employee notice of dismissal, a breach of the implied term of mutual trust and confidence, or a breach of disciplinary procedures in the employee's contract

9.1 INTRODUCTION

People's jobs are, generally, very important to them. Most obviously, this is because they need money to live on. But there are other factors too. People spend a large proportion of each day at work, and work can be a significant source of personal satisfaction, and of friendships. People who lose their jobs not only suffer financially; they may also experience a sense of failure or a loss of self-esteem. For these reasons, the law tries to provide a degree of 'job security' to the workforce.

Set against the job security agenda are the interests of employers. From the employer's point of view, it is important to have an efficient and productive workforce. Thus, for example, if the employer's trade declines because of a downturn in the economy, it will no longer need so many workers. Or if the employer finds out that a particular individual is not doing a good job, perhaps because he or she is always late or spends too much time surfing the web instead of working, the employer may want to dismiss him or her and hire a more productive employee instead.

In this chapter, we will consider how the law balances the competing interests of employers and employees. The main mechanism for this is the statutory law of unfair dismissal. But, as we shall see, it may sometimes be worthwhile for the worker to bring a claim for breach of contract at common law – usually known as a claim for 'wrongful dismissal' – as well.

9.2 THEORETICAL PERSPECTIVES

Before we delve into the details of the law, it is worth spending some time considering competing theories of how the balance should be struck between the interests of workers and employers on the matter of dismissal.

9.2.1 A spectrum

In some legal systems, notably that of the US, there are no job security laws to limit employers' ability to dismiss their workers. This approach is known as 'employment at will'.[1] The employer can dismiss a worker for any reason at any time. Subject to some exceptions, the worker does not have any opportunity to challenge his or her dismissal in court. This system has obvious benefits for employers. It allows the employer to alter the size of the workforce as the need arises, and to get rid of unproductive workers quickly and with the minimum of fuss. Moreover, the fear of being dismissed may encourage workers to work harder. Interestingly, the advocates of employment at will argue that it is not as bad for workers as it sounds.[2] A sensible employer would not dismiss a productive worker because it would be too costly to do so: the employer would lose the worker's output and would have to train someone else. So although there are no legal guarantees of job security, the effect in practice might be quite similar.

At the other extreme, we find 'job property' theories.[3] These theories treat a job as something a worker can 'own'. And, like any other form of property, only the strongest possible reasons would be considered sufficient for taking the worker's job away from him or her. From the perspective of the worker, this is an attractive theory because it gives great importance to keeping one's job. However, taken to its logical conclusion, job property would mean that a worker would be able to sell his or her job to the highest bidder, or leave it to someone else when he or she died. This would take away the employer's ability to select the most suitable candidate for the job. A true job *property* approach would be unworkable in practice. Thus, it seems more likely that theorists who speak of 'property' in a job are thinking instead of a strong version of job security.[4]

9.2.2 Job security – justifications

In between employment at will and job property, there is a middle ground occupied by a variety of different job security theories. These theories have in common a desire to place some limits on the employer's power to dismiss a worker in order to give workers some degree of security at work. Where they differ is on exactly how strict those limits should be, and what form they should take. We will examine each of these issues in turn.

---

[1] Steven L Willborn *et al.*, *Employment Law: Cases and Materials* (5th edn, LexisNexis 2012) chapters 3–7.
[2] RA Epstein, 'In Defence of the Contract at Will' (1984) 51 University of Chicago Law Review 947.
[3] For example, DHJ Hermann and YS Sor, 'Property Rights in One's Job: the Case for Limiting Employment-at-Will' (1982) 24 Arizona Law Review 763.
[4] Wanjiru Njoya, *Property in Work: The Employment Relationship in the Anglo-American Firm* (Ashgate 2007).

To determine how strict the limits should be, we need to find a way of balancing the competing interests of the employer and the employee. To do this properly, we need to weigh up what is at stake for each of them. There are lots of different ways of doing this, so we will focus on three main examples here.

First, we could think about job security as a right in itself. This is the approach adopted in the European Social Charter 1996, Article 24. This Article requires states to ensure that workers can only be dismissed for a valid reason, that they have a right to challenge their dismissal before an 'impartial body', and that compensation is available if the dismissal is found to be unfair. Of course, this leaves a number of unanswered questions: the Article only gives a vague outline of 'valid' reasons, nor is it clear how much compensation should be on offer. But it does suggest that we should strike the balance towards the 'job security' end of the spectrum. However, the UK has not signed up to the 1996 version of the Charter so this right is unlikely to have significant influence in our law.[5]

Second, we could think about job security in more general terms as a means of protecting employees' dignity and autonomy. One of the most persuasive versions of this argument is put forward by Collins.[6] He suggests that the law should provide a strong version of job security where the employer's dismissal decision would constitute a serious breach of the individual's dignity, for example, where it infringes an important right such as the right to join a trade union or the right not to be discriminated against.[7] In less serious situations, Collins argues that the focus should be on protecting the individual's dignity and autonomy through fair procedures.[8] For example, in a disciplinary situation, it is fair to dismiss an employee provided that the rules are clearly laid out in advance and he or she is given a hearing. Of course, other people might interpret the requirements of dignity and autonomy in different ways. Collins thinks that employees do not need much protection in cases of economic dismissal, because it is clear that they are losing their job through no fault of their own,[9] but critics have suggested that the law should intervene to ensure that such job losses only occur when they are really necessary.[10]

Third, we could think in terms of 'flexicurity'. This idea is popular in the European Commission's thinking on these issues.[11] Although it can be a bit difficult to pin down, flexicurity seems to involve striking a balance more towards the flexibility end of the spectrum than the security end. The underlying theory is that workers should be encouraged to move from one job to another in accordance with the needs of employers. They should think in terms of 'employment security' – having *a* job – rather than 'job security' – having *this* job – though the Commission is keen to stress that job security laws need not be abandoned altogether.[12] In some countries, this

---

[5] Interestingly it was not cited by the ECtHR in *Palomo Sanchez* v *Spain* (2012) 54 EHRR 24, a case in which some workers challenged their dismissals on art 10 ECHR grounds.

[6] Hugh Collins, *Justice in Dismissal* (Clarendon Press 1992), especially chapter 2.

[7] ibid chapter 6.

[8] ibid chapter 4.

[9] ibid chapter 5.

[10] Gwyneth Pitt, 'Justice in Dismissal: a Reply to Hugh Collins' (1993) 22 ILJ 251.

[11] Commission, *Towards Common Principles of Flexicurity: More and Better Jobs through Flexibility and Security* (COM(2007) 359 final, 2007). Although the EU has competence to legislate on termination of employment, it has not exercised this competence, though it has intervened in some related areas, such as redundancy consultation.

[12] ibid 4–6.

approach is supported by strong social security regimes which help to maintain individuals' standard of living while they are between jobs. Flexicurity stems from a worry that labour markets in the EU are inefficient because they are too rigid – workers are not deployed in accordance with demand – so this makes it harder for the EU to compete in the global economy. Thus, although individual workers might find the greater emphasis on flexibility unattractive, it might support economic growth at the macro level.

So far, we have assumed that employers have an interest in flexibility: that their preference will be for as little job security as possible so that they are free to make changes to their workforce. However, there is another school of thought on this issue too. Some economists think that job security laws can benefit firms.[13] They argue that workers who are insecure in their jobs will not perform to the best of their ability. For example, they might do work that is more 'visible' to the boss instead of more useful but less obvious activities. Job security laws can create a more productive working environment. Such laws can also discourage employers from making irrational decisions, for example, dismissing a productive employee because of a false belief that he or she has done something wrong. Although most employers will want to avoid doing this because of the costs of losing the employee's contribution and training a replacement, things can sometimes go wrong. On this view, the law has a role to play in educating employers about the need to have good reasons for dismissal and to use fair procedures.

9.2.3 Job security – types of control

As well as thinking about how to justify job security laws, it is also important to consider what form such laws should take. Those who are in favour of strong job security are likely to support a range of substantive and procedural controls on employers' decision-making with strong remedies for unfairly dismissed employees to act as a deterrent. Those who are in favour of a weaker version of job security may only want to pick and choose among different techniques. We will consider some of the options in this section.

One important dividing line is between procedural and substantive limits. A relatively 'light touch' limit on the employer's dismissal power would be to require the employer to follow a fair procedure before making a decision. If the employee was accused of theft, for example, the employer would be required to give the employee an opportunity to explain him- or herself before taking the decision to dismiss. A more intrusive limit on the employer's power is to require the employer to have a good reason for the dismissal: for example, that the employee's performance is poor or that the business needs to make cuts for economic reasons. And, of course, both types of limit could be combined, so that the employer would need to have a good reason and to follow a fair procedure before dismissing someone.

Within these general approaches, further subdivisions are possible. Requiring the employer to have a good reason for dismissing a worker could involve more or less intense scrutiny of the employer's decisions. For example, the law could simply prohibit certain reasons for dismissal, such as discrimination, whilst leaving employers free to make their own choices outside those reasons. Alternatively, the

---

[13] Alan Fox, *Beyond Contract: Work, Power and Trust Relations* (Faber 1974) chapter 1.

law could list a set of permitted reasons for dismissal so that employers are required to prove that one of these reasons exists in order for a dismissal to be lawful.

Of course, any unfair dismissal law assumes that the worker has the possibility of challenging his or her dismissal in court or through some other procedure. This may also influence the degree of job security in a particular legal system. If the court applies a very strict form of scrutiny to employers' decisions, this will increase the degree of job security, whereas a test focusing on the reasonableness of employers' actions will allow them a greater degree of discretion. The remedies available to the disgruntled employee are also significant: a small award of compensation may not deter many dismissals, whereas an award of reinstatement or a large amount of compensation may make employers think twice.

9.3 RESIGNATION

Before we explore dismissal in detail, it is worth noting that an employment relationship may come to an end at the initiative of the worker or employee, rather than the employer.

In relation to employees, according to s. 86(2) ERA 1996:

> The notice required to be given by an employee who has been continuously employed for one month or more to terminate his contract of employment is not less than one week.

This is so even if the employee's contract provides for a shorter notice period, though it is possible for the employer to waive the right to notice.[14] The employee is entitled to be paid for the notice period.[15] The contract may provide for a longer period of notice: for example, teachers are often required to give a term's notice. In practice, notice periods are difficult to enforce. It is not possible for the employer to get an order forcing the employee to work,[16] and whilst it is possible for the employer to sue the employee for damages, the sums involved are small and such litigation is unlikely to be worthwhile.[17] Finally, it is worth noting that if the employer commits a repudiatory breach of contract, the employee is legally entitled to resign without giving notice.[18] As we shall see below, this situation may give rise to a claim for unfair dismissal often known as 'constructive dismissal'.

In relation to workers who are not employees, there is no statutory regulation of resignation. Thus, any duty to give notice must be found in the worker's contract. Since many people who are not employees work on a casual basis anyway, it seems unlikely that a decision on their part to move on would give rise to any particular legal difficulties.

9.4 UNFAIR DISMISSAL

According to s. 94(1) ERA 1996, 'An employee has the right not to be unfairly dismissed by his employer'. This apparently simple statement is underpinned by a complex body of law.

---

[14] ERA 1996, s 86(3).
[15] ERA 1996, ss 87–91.
[16] TULRCA 1992, s 236.
[17] Damages would only be available for the notice period because the employee could lawfully resign after giving notice.
[18] ERA 1996, s 86(6).

9.4.1 Who is protected, and in what circumstances?

The law provides a remedy for an employee who has been dismissed. Both of these concepts require some explanation. Most of the time, an employee can only bring an action for unfair dismissal if he or she has been employed by the employer for a continuous period of two years.[19]

Employee

The definition of the term 'employee' is a complex matter requiring the application of a set of tests derived from the case-law.[20] People who are 'workers' but not employees do not have any rights in unfair dismissal law.

Dismissal

A dismissal can occur in one of three ways:

    (a) the contract under which he is employed is terminated by the employer (whether with or without notice);

    (b) he is employed under a limited-term contract and that contract terminates by virtue of the limiting event without being renewed under the same contract; or

    (c) the employee terminates the contract under which he is employed (with or without notice) in circumstances in which he is entitled to terminate it without notice by reason of the employer's conduct.[21]

Paragraph (a) is what we would normally think of as a dismissal: the employer says to the employee, 'you're fired'. Paragraphs (b) and (c) are a bit more complicated and warrant further discussion.

Limited-term contracts Paragraph (b) deals with the expiry and non-renewal of a limited-term contract.[22] The simplest example of a limited-term contract is one for a fixed period of time, but the concept also includes contracts to perform a specific task and contracts that terminate when a specific event occurs. So, if the employee is employed on a contract for two years, and the employer decides not to renew it at the end of the two years, it must treat the situation as a dismissal. This means that it must have a reason for not renewing the contract, and must follow appropriate termination procedures, as detailed below. This was introduced to ensure that employers could not avoid the application of unfair dismissal law by the simple strategy of employing people on fixed-term contracts.

Since 2002, employees on fixed-term contracts have had additional rights under the Fixed-Term Employees (Prevention of Less Favourable Treatment) Regulations 2002, reg. 8.[23] If the employee is employed under successive fixed-term contracts for a period of more than four years, he or she is to be treated as a permanent employee (in other words, the contractual term limiting the duration of the contract no longer

---

[19] ERA 1996, s 108(1).

[20] See Chapter 4.

[21] ERA 1996, s 95(1). Under s 95(2), there is also a dismissal where the employer gives the employee notice of dismissal but the employee resigns during the notice period.

[22] Defined in ERA 1996, s 235(2A) and (2B).

[23] SI 2002/2034. See Chapter 4 for further discussion.

has effect). Importantly, the provision targets successive fixed-term contracts, so it has no application where the employee is employed on a single fixed-term contract for, say, five years. The employer can defeat the employee's claim to be permanent if it provides objective justification for the use of a fixed-term contract when entering into or renewing the employee's contract. The provision implements the Directive on Fixed-Term Work and is designed to tackle the abuse of successive fixed-term contracts: where the employer takes someone on, effectively on a permanent basis, but gives them fixed-term contracts as a way of maintaining its own flexibility.[24]

These two sets of provisions sit rather uncomfortably together. Since the termination of a fixed-term contract counts as a dismissal, individuals on such contracts (at least if they have two years' continuous employment) arguably have as much job security as individuals on indefinite contracts, because the employer should comply with unfair dismissal law in bringing either form of contract to an end.[25] However, the value of this protection is limited, since courts and tribunals have held that, if the employer's need for an employee is genuinely temporary and this is made clear to the employee from the outset, the expiry of the fixed-term contract may constitute 'some other substantial reason' for dismissal and is thus potentially fair.[26] Moreover, there may be other benefits associated with becoming permanent. For example, a permanent employee may find it easier to obtain a mortgage than someone on a fixed-term contract.

Constructive dismissal Paragraph (c) of the definition, above, deals with the situation in which the employee resigns in response to the employer's conduct. This is often referred to informally as 'constructive dismissal': 'an act which is not an explicit dismissal but which in law has the same effect'.[27] If this were not included, employers would have a simple route to evade the legislation: instead of firing people, employers could just make them miserable until they resigned.

The crucial question in applying this paragraph is how bad does the employer's conduct have to be in order for the employee to be able to resign and bring an unfair dismissal claim? The courts have approached this issue using reasoning drawn from the law of contract.[28] The leading authority is *Western Excavations (ECC) Ltd* v *Sharp*,[29] reaffirmed by the Court of Appeal in *Bournemouth University Higher Education Corp* v *Buckland*.[30] The employee is entitled to resign and bring proceedings for unfair dismissal where the employer has committed a repudiatory breach of a fundamental term of the contract of employment.

In the *Buckland* case, the employee was a university professor who failed a significant number of the students who had taken his course. The exam papers were re-marked by other colleagues on two occasions without Professor Buckland's

---

[24] Council Directive 1999/70/EC of 28 June 1999 concerning the framework agreement on fixed-term work concluded by ETUC, UNICE and CEEP, cl 1.

[25] *Tansell* v *Henley College Coventry* [2013] IRLR 174 (EAT).

[26] *Terry* v *East Sussex County Council* [1976] ICR 536 (EAT); *Nash* v *Governors of Binstead Primary School* (2003) UKEAT/0120/03/LA.

[27] *Bournemouth University Higher Education Corp* v *Buckland* [2010] EWCA Civ 12, [2011] QB 323 [19] (Sedley LJ).

[28] Steven Anderman, 'The Interpretation of Protective Employment Statutes and Contracts of Employment' (2000) 29 ILJ 223.

[29] [1978] QB 761 (CA).

[30] *Buckland* (n 27). See Alan L Bogg, '*Bournemouth University Higher Education Corporation* v *Buckland*: Re-establishing Orthodoxy at the Expense of Coherence?' (2010) 39 ILJ 408.

involvement, and some of the marks were changed. Professor Buckland thought that this process undermined his authority and breached the implied term of mutual trust and confidence in his contract of employment.[31] The tribunal agreed with Professor Buckland so, since this term is a fundamental term of the contract of employment, a constructive dismissal was established.

As we shall see below, the fairness or unfairness of a dismissal is assessed using a 'reasonableness' test. This has given rise to some confusion, because it is tempting to say that a repudiatory breach occurs when the employer behaves unreasonably, thereby rolling the two tests into one. However, in *Buckland*, Sedley LJ was concerned to emphasise that while a constructive dismissal will often also be unreasonable, the two tests should be kept separate.[32] We will consider the reasonableness aspects of constructive dismissal in more detail below.

The contractual approach to constructive dismissal has one further consequence: once the employer has committed a repudiatory breach, it cannot 'cure' that breach. In *Buckland*, the university organised an internal enquiry into the remarking of Professor Buckland's exam scripts. This enquiry vindicated Professor Buckland and criticised the conduct of his colleagues, though he was not happy with the enquiry and resigned anyway. The university argued that he was not in a position to resign and claim constructive dismissal because the enquiry had 'cured' its initial breach. Again, though, in accordance with ordinary contractual principles, the Court of Appeal held that this was not possible.[33] Once a repudiatory breach has been committed, it is entirely up to the injured party to decide whether to terminate or affirm the contract.[34] Professor Buckland did not lose this right by waiting to see what would happen at the enquiry. This does not mean that employers should not try to put things right if they have inadvertently committed a repudiatory breach: it may still persuade a valued employee not to resign.[35] But the employer's efforts make no difference to the employee's rights in law.

Terminations not amounting to dismissal Are there any situations in which an employee's contract might terminate without it falling within the definition of dismissal? The answer is yes, although it is not clear whether that was Parliament's original intention.

The Act does not permit the employer and employee to contract out of its provisions. This is an important safeguard for employees, who might otherwise be persuaded to agree to disadvantageous terms:

> Any provision in an agreement (whether a contract of employment or not) is void in so far as it purports—
>
> (a) to exclude or limit the operation of any provision of this Act, or
>
> (b) to preclude a person from bringing any proceedings under this Act before an [employment tribunal].[36]

---

[31] See Chapter 5.
[32] *Buckland*, above n 27, [28] (Sedley LJ).
[33] ibid [36]–[38] (Sedley LJ).
[34] On which see *Geys v Société Générale* [2012] UKSC 63, [2013] 1 AC 523.
[35] Or prevent a situation escalating into one of repudiatory breach: *Assamoi v Spirit Pub Company (Services) Ltd* (2012) UKEAT/0050/11/LA.
[36] ERA 1996, s 203(1).

If a dispute arises between an employee and his or her employer, this provision does not preclude the parties reaching a 'settlement agreement', in which the employee agrees not to litigate his or her claim, provided that certain safeguards (most importantly, independent legal advice for the employee) are met.[37]

The operation of this provision was examined in detail in the *Igbo* case.[38] In that case, the employer allowed the employee to take leave from work beyond her normal holiday entitlement in order to visit family abroad. The employer required the employee to sign an agreement stating that her employment would terminate automatically if she did not return to work on the agreed date. When the time came for her to return, she was unwell and could not go to work, so the employer treated her employment as at an end. She claimed that she had been unfairly dismissed. The Court of Appeal upheld her claim, holding that the automatic termination agreement was void as an attempt to contract out of the Act.

However, it is still possible for a contract to come to an end without a dismissal taking place by virtue of the operation of the doctrine of frustration. This was confirmed by the Court of Appeal in the *Notcutt* case.[39] In that case, the employee had become seriously ill and it was apparent that he would never be able to work again. The Court held that, applying the ordinary rules of contract law, the contract was frustrated. This is a problematic ruling because it is possible to dismiss a person for incapacity under unfair dismissal law, as we shall see below. For the employee, the benefit of the dismissal route is that the employer must follow a fair procedure and must act reasonably in reaching its decision. These protections are lost if the contract is held to be frustrated instead. Having said that, reliance on the doctrine of frustration may be unwise given that the employer may also have obligations under the Equality Act 2010 in respect of disability discrimination in this type of case too.

Qualifying period

It is usually necessary for the employee to complete a qualifying period of employment with the employer before he or she is eligible to bring a claim for unfair dismissal or to seek a redundancy payment.

At the time of writing, the qualifying period for an unfair dismissal claim (laid down in s. 108 of the Act) and for a redundancy payment (laid down in s. 155) are both set at two years. The requirement is for a period of continuous employment, but it is worth noting that the statute contains detailed provisions on continuity designed to help the employee.[40] Gaps of various kinds do not necessarily serve to break the employee's continuous employment in the statutory sense.

The qualifying period has varied over the life of the legislation, from six months, to one year, to the current two years. It is thus a subject of some controversy. One of the main advantages of the qualifying period from the employer perspective is that it gives some time within which to assess the employee's suitability for the job, safe in the knowledge that the relationship can be terminated with less risk of litigation.[41]

---

[37] ERA 1996, s 203(3).

[38] *Igbo v Johnson, Matthey Chemicals Ltd* [1986] ICR 505.

[39] *Notcutt v Universal Equipment Co (London)* [1986] 1 WLR 641. A contract of employment may also be frustrated where the employee is imprisoned: see *Hare v Murphy Bros* [1974] ICR 603 (CA).

[40] ERA 1996, ss 210–219.

[41] It is important to note that there is always some risk of litigation because of the various reasons for dismissal to which no qualifying period applies.

Another claimed advantage is that the qualifying period encourages job creation by reducing employers' exposure to liability in the event that, for example, the extra workers are no longer needed. Whatever view you take of the purpose of the qualifying period, it is still necessary to consider how long a time the employer might need either to assess the suitability of the individual or the business need for the job.

There are some exceptions to the two-year qualifying period. For the most part, these overlap with the 'automatically unfair' reasons for dismissal: reasons singled out by the law as unacceptable in any circumstances. We will examine these in the next section. However, the overlap is not exact. An employee dismissed because of his or her political opinions need not satisfy the qualifying period but is not automatically unfairly dismissed;[42] whereas an employee who is dismissed because of a change in the ownership of the employing entity is automatically unfairly dismissed but must satisfy the qualifying period.[43] The significance of this is that all employees have *some* unfair dismissal protection from 'day one' of the employment.

9.4.2 Judging the fairness of dismissal

There are two main routes to a finding that an employee has been unfairly dismissed. One is to demonstrate that the employer's reason for dismissal fell into the category of 'automatically unfair' reasons for dismissal. The other is to show that, although the employer's reason fell into the category of 'potentially fair' reasons for dismissal, the employer acted unreasonably. This second route might involve showing either that the employer overreacted to the problem (for example, by treating a minor mistake as grounds for termination) or that the employer did not follow a fair procedure leading up to the dismissal.

Automatically unfair dismissals

There are a number of situations in which it is 'automatically unfair' to dismiss an employee. If one of these reasons applies, the employer does not get an opportunity to defend itself by arguing that it acted reasonably in dismissing the employee.

To explain the law more easily, we will divide it into three categories: asserting individual rights, trade union activities, and other forms of collective consultation.[44] But it is important to note that the law does not approach automatically unfair dismissal in this way. The legislature has chosen to make separate provision in relation to each right, each aspect of trade union activity and each consultation process. This approach seems unnecessarily complicated and there is always a risk that it might fail to provide comprehensive protection.

One important category of automatically unfair dismissals is where the employee has asserted or exercised his or her rights under other legislation. It is important to be aware that the drafting varies between these various provisions so it is worth looking at the rights to see exactly which activities are covered, though we do not have the space to do so in this chapter. The purpose of this category is clear: there is

---

[42] ERA 1996, s 108(4). See Hugh Collins and Virginia Mantouvalou, '*Redfearn* v *UK*: Political Association and Dismissal' (2013) 76 MLR 909.

[43] Transfer of Undertakings (Protection of Employment) Regulations 2006, SI 2006/246, reg 7.

[44] There is some overlap between the second and third categories because trade union representatives may be involved in consultation, for example, in relation to collective redundancies.

little point in affording employees an array of statutory rights if they can simply be dismissed for asserting them, though of course this may not deter some employers in practice. Rights protected in this way include:

- any right in the Employment Rights Act 1996,[45] such as the right to notice of dismissal under s. 86;

- pregnancy, childbirth, taking maternity leave or parental leave;[46] paternity leave or adoption leave,[47] invoking the right to request flexible working;[48]

- taking various actions under health and safety laws, or refusing to work in dangerous situations;[49]

- asserting rights under working time legislation;[50]

- claiming the National Minimum Wage (NMW);[51]

- whistleblowing (making a 'protected disclosure');[52]

- asserting rights under legislation protecting part-time, fixed-term or agency employees.[53]

It is worth noting here that whilst dismissal on grounds of pregnancy is automatically unfair, dismissal on other discriminatory grounds – for example, because of a person's race or religion or sexual orientation – is not. However, discriminatory dismissals are also unlawful under the Equality Act 2010.[54] It is hard to imagine a case in which a discriminatory dismissal would not also count as unfair – because the employer would not be able to identify a legitimate reason for dismissal under the provisions to be discussed below – but there are advantages to bringing a claim under the Equality Act 2010. These include the burden of proof, which favours the claimant, and the absence of a statutory limit on compensation payments.

Another area in which employers might be tempted to be hostile towards their employees is where those employees get involved in collective activities which might challenge the employer's authority.[55] In relation to trade unions, it is automatically unfair to dismiss an employee because he or she:

- is a trade union member or has engaged in trade union activities (in certain circumstances);[56]

- was taking part in an official, lawful strike;[57]

---

[45] ERA 1996, s 104.
[46] ERA 1996, s 99 and Maternity and Parental Leave etc. Regulations 1999, SI 1999/3312, reg 20.
[47] ERA 1996, s 99 and Paternity and Adoption Leave Regulations 2002, SI 2002/2788, reg 29.
[48] ERA 1996, s 104C.
[49] ibid s 100.
[50] ibid s 101A.
[51] ibid s 104A.
[52] ibid s 103A.
[53] Part-time Workers (Prevention of Less Favourable Treatment) Regulations 2000, SI 2000/1551, reg 7(1); Fixed-term Employees (Prevention of Less Favourable Treatment) Regulations 2002, SI 2002/2034, reg 6(1); Agency Workers Regulations 2010, SI 2010/93, reg 17(1).
[54] Equality Act 2010, s 39(2)(c).
[55] See Chapters 11–13.
[56] TULRCA 1992, s 152. As we shall see below, there are special remedies for breaches of this provision.
[57] TULRCA 1992, s 238A. Importantly, this protection usually only applies within the first 12 weeks of the action.

- asserted his or her statutory right not to be subject to detrimental treatment on grounds of trade union membership or activities;[58]

- asserted his or her statutory right not to have an offer made by the employer to induce him or her to give up trade union membership or collective bargaining;[59]

- asserted his or her statutory right to time off for trade union activities or duties as a trade union representative;[60]

- was dismissed because of information obtained by the employer from a 'blacklist' of trade union members or activists;[61]

- took part in the trade union recognition procedure under Schedule A1 of TULRCA 1992.[62]

In relation to other forms of collective activity, legislation tends to provide protection for those who 'put their heads above the parapet' by becoming employee representatives, and for those who participate in the process, for example, by asserting rights to be consulted or participating in elections for representatives.[63] Much of our law on non-union collective activity stems from EU law, and the directives in these areas generally require Member States to protect representatives as they would do under national law. The main provisions are:

- working time;[64]

- collective redundancies or transfers of the undertaking,[65] cross-border mergers;[66]

- the information and consultation regime;[67]

- European Works Councils;[68]

- European Companies[69] and European Co-Operative Societies.[70]

A final point to note here is that these special protections for employees highlight the two-tier nature of the modern labour market.[71] Nowadays, some statutory rights are afforded to workers as well as to employees. But if a worker's contract is terminated for asserting these rights, there is no possibility of claiming unfair dismissal, because this is only applicable to employees. One way round this is for the worker to claim

---

[58] ERA 1996, s 104, in respect of TULRCA 1992, s 146.
[59] ibid ss 145A and B.
[60] ibid ss 168–170.
[61] ERA 1996, s 104F.
[62] TULRCA 1992, sch A1, para 161.
[63] See Chapter 14.
[64] ERA 1996, s 101A.
[65] ibid s 103.
[66] Companies (Cross-Border Mergers) Regulations 2007, SI 2007/2974, regs 46 and 47.
[67] Information and Consultation of Employees Regulations 2004, SI 2004/3426, reg 30.
[68] Transnational Information and Consultation of Employees Regulations 1999, SI 1999/3323, reg 28.
[69] European Public Limited-Liability Company Regulations 2004, SI 2004/2326, reg 42; European Public Limited-Liability Company (Employee Involvement) (Great Britain) Regulations 2009, SI 2009/2401, reg 29.
[70] European Cooperative Society (Involvement of Employees) Regulations 2006, SI 2006/ 2059, reg 31.
[71] See Chapter 4.

for detriment, where the statute protects against this, and to argue that the termination of the contract is a form of detriment.[72] In practice, this may be just as effective, but it does not send out quite such a strong signal to employers.

Potentially fair dismissals 1 – reasons

Most dismissal cases proceed through a rather different route: they are 'potentially fair'. The employer argues that the dismissal was for a legitimate reason permitted by the statute. If the reason is established, the tribunal then goes on to consider whether the employer acted reasonably (both substantively and procedurally) in dismissing the employee for that reason. If the dismissal is found to be for a permitted reason, and reasonable, it will be fair. In this section, we will examine the potentially fair reasons for dismissal before turning, in the next few sections, to the substantive and procedural aspects of the reasonableness test.

There are five 'potentially fair' reasons for dismissal: capability or qualifications, conduct, redundancy, statutory requirements or 'some other substantial reason of a kind such as to justify the dismissal of an employee holding the position which the employee held'.[73] The burden of proving the reason or principal reason for the dismissal is placed on the employer.[74] At this stage, the focus is simply on establishing the employer's motive, not on testing whether or not the employer has acted fairly. We will consider each of these reasons in turn.

Capability dismissals must 'relate to the capability or qualifications of the employee for performing work of the kind which he was employed by the employer to do'.[75] Capability is further defined as 'capability assessed by reference to skill, aptitude, health or any other physical or mental quality' and qualifications means 'any degree, diploma or other academic, technical or professional qualification relevant to the position which [the employee] held'.[76] Capability dismissals allow the employer to get rid of poorly performing employees. This is obviously important in order to ensure that workplaces are as productive as possible. However, the capability category is broadly framed and addresses two quite different reasons why an employee might perform badly: ill health and skills. As we shall see, these may give rise to different requirements at the reasonableness stage.

The second ground is 'conduct'. This allows the employer to dismiss employees who, for example, disobey the employer's instructions or the rules of the workplace. Of course, conduct may involve very different degrees of seriousness. This is considered at the reasonableness stage. For minor misconduct, it may only be fair to dismiss an employee if he or she persists in the misconduct after being warned and told to improve, whereas for very serious misconduct, it may be fair to dismiss the employee without warnings.

A third ground is redundancy.[77] This covers the situation in which the employer needs to reduce the size of its workforce on economic grounds, though the statutory definition of a redundancy situation is somewhat more precise:

---

[72] See, for example, National Minimum Wage Act 1998, s 23.
[73] ERA 1996, s 98(1) and (2).
[74] ibid s 98(1).
[75] ibid s 98(2)(a).
[76] ibid ss 98(3)(a) and (b).
[77] Redundancy is dealt with more fully in Chapter 10.

For the purposes of this Act an employee who is dismissed shall be taken to be dismissed by reason of redundancy if the dismissal is wholly or mainly attributable to–

(a) the fact that his employer has ceased or intends to cease–

   (i) to carry on the business for the purposes of which the employee was employed by him, or

   (ii) to carry on that business in the place where the employee was so employed, or

(b) the fact that the requirements of that business–

   (i) for employees to carry out work of a particular kind, or

   (ii) for employees to carry out work of a particular kind in the place where the employee was employed by the employer,

have ceased or diminished or are expected to cease or diminish.[78]

This definition has given rise to some litigation, for two reasons. On the one hand, the employer might want to argue that the employee is not redundant, for example, by saying that he or she has been dismissed fairly for 'some other substantial reason' (SOSR). This is because redundancy has a special feature not shared by the other potentially fair reasons for dismissal. Even if a dismissal on redundancy grounds is fair, the employee is entitled to a compensation payment. This reflects the fact that a dismissal on economic grounds is not the employee's fault. On the other hand, the employee might want to contest the idea that he or she is redundant, either with a view to keeping his or her job or to challenging the employer's procedure for selecting people for redundancy. A case will help to illustrate the point.

In *Murray* v *Foyle Meats*, the claimants worked at an abattoir.[79] They usually worked in the slaughter hall but under their contracts they could be required to work elsewhere in the factory too, and sometimes they did so. For economic reasons the employer decided to cut down its slaughtering activities and therefore made the claimants redundant. They argued that the concept of diminishing requirements for employees to do 'work of a particular kind' should be construed to include the work they could be required to do under their contracts. This would mean that a much larger proportion of the employer's workforce – not just those in the slaughter hall – would be potential candidates for redundancy. On this view, there would have been a strong argument for unfairness because the employer would not have considered the right 'pool' of people when deciding who was redundant. However, the House of Lords rejected this argument, holding that tribunals should focus primarily on what the employees did in fact, and not on their work as defined in their contracts of employment.[80]

Where the strict definition of redundancy is not met, SOSR usually comes to the rescue. An employer might respond to a downturn in the business not by making some employees redundant, but by cutting their terms and conditions of employment to save money. In this situation, the employer might dismiss the employees and offer them re-employment on reduced terms and conditions, or the employees might resign and claim constructive dismissal in response to a proposal from the employer to force

---

[78] ERA 1996, s 139(1).
[79] [2000] 1 AC 51 (HL).
[80] ibid 56–58 (Lord Irvine), 58–60 (Lord Clyde).

changes to their contracts.[81] Provided that it is plausible to claim that the employer's plans will save money, the SOSR threshold will usually be met. The reasonableness of cutting the employees' terms and conditions will be addressed later.

A fourth 'potentially fair' reason for dismissal is contravention of a statutory duty.[82] One important illustration of this is where statute requires that people who do certain jobs have certain qualifications. For example, gas-fitters and electricians are required to complete certain qualifications and to do regular refresher courses. If an employer hired someone to work as an electrician but he or she failed the courses and lost the right to do certain types of electrical work, this would give grounds for a potentially fair dismissal.

Finally, the employer may dismiss an employee for SOSR, 'some other substantial reason'. As we saw above, this is often used in cases where the employer is dismissing people for economic reasons but these do not fall within the precise definition of redundancy. But it is by no means confined to these situations and can be used for any reason not covered by those we have already discussed.

Potentially fair dismissals 2 – reasonableness

Once the employer has established the reason for the dismissal, attention shifts to determining whether or not the employer has acted reasonably. This test is set out in s. 98(4):

Where the employer has fulfilled the requirements of subsection (1), the determination of the question whether the dismissal is fair or unfair (having regard to the reason shown by the employer)–

(a) depends on whether in the circumstances (including the size and administrative resources of the employer's undertaking) the employer acted reasonably or unreasonably in treating it as a sufficient reason for dismissing the employee, and
(b) shall be determined in accordance with equity and the substantial merits of the case.

There are two important points to note about this definition. First, s. 98(4)(b) means that the burden of proof is neutral. In other words, there is no burden on the employee to prove that the dismissal was unfair, but nor is there any burden on the employer to prove that the dismissal was fair.[83] Second, the statute directs that the reasonableness test should be sensitive to the 'size and administrative resources' of the firm. This suggests that smaller firms will not be held to such high standards as larger firms.

For a proper understanding of the reasonableness test, we need to examine the case-law. Although the statute simply directs tribunals to ask whether the employer 'acted reasonably or unreasonably', the *Iceland* case put an important gloss on this phrase.[84] The EAT said:

The function of the . . . tribunal, as an industrial jury, is to determine whether in the particular circumstance of each case the decision to dismiss the employee fell within the band of reasonable responses which a reasonable employer might have adopted.

---

[81] For example, *Gilham v Kent CC (No 2)* [1985] ICR 233 (CA).
[82] ERA 1996, s 98(2)(d).
[83] Originally, the burden was on the employer, but it was made neutral by the Employment Act 1980.
[84] *Iceland Frozen Foods Ltd v Jones* [1983] ICR 17.

If the dismissal falls within the band the dismissal is fair: if the dismissal falls outside the band it is unfair.[85]

Despite some attempts to displace this formulation in later case-law, the Court of Appeal has upheld it as the correct approach to the reasonableness test.[86]

One of the important consequences of the use of the *Iceland* test is that, as Collins has pointed out, dismissals may be fair even though some people might see them as 'harsh'.[87] For example, imagine a situation in which an employee asks the boss if he can leave early because his wife is ill. The boss agrees, but later on, another member of staff sees the employee in the pub. Although the employee has never done anything wrong before, the employer takes the view that the employee is not to be trusted and dismisses him.[88] On the one hand, many people would agree with this decision. It is clearly not appropriate to leave work early to go to the pub, nor is it appropriate to abuse the boss's goodwill by giving a false reason for asking to leave early. On the other hand, it might be argued that if the employee has an unblemished record, perhaps it would be more appropriate to give him one last chance: a final warning that, if he offends again, he will be dismissed. The 'band of reasonable responses' test means that once a tribunal has found that some employers would dismiss in this situation, the dismissal is not unfair, even if other employers (or even most other employers) would have imposed a lesser penalty.

The 'band of reasonable responses' test has been the subject of considerable academic criticism, for two related reasons.[89] First, it is argued that the test does not allow tribunals to set standards for employers' behaviour. It encourages them to reflect what 'some employers' would do, rather than making an independent determination of what is fair or unfair. This limits the effectiveness of the legislation in regulating employers' decisions and allows 'harsh' practices to continue if enough employers use them. Second, it is often pointed out that the statute itself uses the phrase 'reasonably or unreasonably' and does not make any mention of a 'band of reasonable responses'. Thus, the *Iceland* test is wrong because it does not reflect the true meaning of the statute.

Against this, it is important to recognise that the *Iceland* test does have advantages. The use of a reasonableness test in the statute indicates that tribunals are not supposed to overturn employers' decisions just because they disagree with them. The *Iceland* formulation helps to remind tribunals of their proper role. It also makes the system more predictable: employers know that if they stay in line with generally accepted practices, their dismissal decisions are likely to be upheld.

One situation in which a more stringent standard of review might apply is where the employee's human rights are affected by the dismissal. In the *Redfearn* case, the claimant was dismissed when he was elected to the local council as a British National Party (BNP) candidate.[90] Although there was no criticism of his work, the employer feared that his BNP activities would damage its reputation and upset its customers.

---

[85] ibid 25.

[86] *Foley v Post Office; HSBC Bank v Madden* [2000] ICR 827.

[87] Collins, above n 6, chapter 1.

[88] The facts here are similar to those in *Foley v Post Office* (n 86) though it is important to note that Mr Foley denied that he had been to the pub other than to call a taxi to get home.

[89] See the notes by Mark Freedland and Hugh Collins, 'Finding the Right Direction for the Industrial Jury' (2000) 29 ILJ 288, discussing the EAT decisions in *Foley* and *Madden*, above n 86.

[90] *Redfearn v Serco Ltd* [2006] EWCA Civ 659, [2006] ICR 1367.

He had no remedy in unfair dismissal law because he had not worked for the employer for the requisite qualifying period. He took his case to the ECtHR, arguing that his Article 11 right to freedom of association had been infringed.[91] The ECtHR stated that:

> [T]here is also a positive obligation on the authorities to provide protection against dismissal by private employers, where the dismissal is motivated solely by the fact that an employee belongs to a particular political party (or at least to provide the means whereby there can be an independent evaluation of the proportionality of such a dismissal in the light of all the circumstances of a given case).[92]

Importantly, the Court did not hold that the employer's decision to dismiss Mr Redfearn was disproportionate; rather that there should have been an opportunity for him to have the matter addressed by a tribunal. We saw above that the government has made an exception to the qualifying period for political dismissals,[93] though it has failed to do so for all dismissals in breach of human rights, even though it seems clear that the Court's reasoning would be more generally applicable.[94]

For present purposes, *Redfearn* is particularly significant for its reliance on the proportionality test as the means of assessing the fairness of the employer's decision.[95] This is generally thought to be more searching than a reasonableness test such as the 'band of reasonable responses'.[96] In fact, the English courts had already taken some steps in this direction in the *Pay* case.[97] Mr Pay was a probation officer who performed in fetish clubs and ran a website dedicated to bondage in his spare time. His employer asked him to give up these activities because it took the view that they were incompatible with his job, but he refused. He was dismissed. He brought an unfair dismissal claim, arguing that his Article 10 (freedom of expression) rights had been infringed. Under s. 3 Human Rights Act 1998, courts and tribunals are obliged to read statutes so that they are compatible with Convention rights, insofar as it is possible to do so.[98] It was held in *Pay* that if an employer's dismissal decision contravened the employee's human rights, this would generally fall outside the 'band of reasonable responses'.[99] In order to determine this question, the court or tribunal would have to consider whether or not the employee's right had been infringed and, in the case of a qualified right, whether the employer's interference with that right was justified using the proportionality test.

However, it is important to be cautious about this development, for two reasons. First, the ECHR does not contain very many rights of relevance to employment settings so it seems unlikely that many employees will be able to access the proportionality test by arguing that their dismissal infringed their human rights. Second, as the *Pay* case itself illustrates, the courts' reluctance to interfere too much with employers' decision-making may influence their approach to proportionality reasoning too. The EAT held that any interference with Mr Pay's Article 10 right to

---

[91] *Redfearn* v *United Kingdom* (2013) 57 EHRR 2.
[92] ibid [43].
[93] Above n 42.
[94] Collins and Mantouvalou, above n 42.
[95] See also *Palomo Sanchez* v *Spain* (2012) 54 EHRR 24; *Matúz* v *Hungary*, (ECtHR, 21 October 2014).
[96] ACL Davies, 'Judicial Self-Restraint in Labour Law' (2009) 38 ILJ 278.
[97] *Pay* v *Lancashire Probation Service* [2004] ICR 187.
[98] Note that this obligation applies in cases between private parties as well as in cases brought against the state, though the EAT in *Pay* is confused on the point.
[99] Above n 97, [32]–[35].

freedom of expression was justified because of the potential impact of Mr Pay's activities on his employer's reputation.[100] Mr Pay's attempt to argue his case before the ECtHR was also unsuccessful.[101]

Potentially fair dismissals 3 – procedures

So far, we have focused on the substantive fairness of a dismissal. But it is also possible for a dismissal to be unfair because of the procedure adopted by the employer leading up to the dismissal. A dismissal may be unfair because of the substance of the employer's decision, because of the procedure followed, or both. Although the ultimate guide for tribunals here is still the reasonableness test, as interpreted in *Iceland*, some detailed law has developed on what constitutes procedural fairness.

One source of information about procedures is the ACAS Code of Practice.[102] This is a statutory code of practice and tribunals are obliged to take it into account in reaching their decisions.[103] The Code identifies some core principles of procedural fairness, as follows:

- Employers and employees should raise and deal with issues promptly and should not unreasonably delay meetings, decisions or confirmation of those decisions.
- Employers and employees should act consistently.
- Employers should carry out any necessary investigations, to establish the facts of the case.
- Employers should inform employees of the basis of the problem and give them an opportunity to put their case in response before any decisions are made.
- Employers should allow employees to be accompanied at any formal disciplinary or grievance meeting.
- Employers should allow an employee to appeal against any formal decision made.[104]

These must be adapted to deal with different types of dismissal case. For example, misconduct cases may require a different approach to ill-health dismissals. The Code gives some further guidance on this, though it is primarily focused on misconduct cases. And the principles must be adapted to deal with different types of employer. For example, a large organisation may be able to provide employees with the chance to appeal against their line manager's decision to a person in another department who has not been involved in the case before, whereas a small firm may only have one person who can take disciplinary and dismissal decisions. As we saw above, the reasonableness test reflects a firm's 'size and administrative resources'.

There is also a considerable body of case-law on procedural fairness upon which tribunals may draw. This puts employers in a risky situation because they might think that by relying on the Code, which is readily available, they have done everything possible to avoid a finding of procedural unfair dismissal, but in practice this may not be the case. For example, as we shall see below, the Code does not cover redundancy issues, but there is detailed case-law on procedural fairness in this area.

---

[100] Though cf *Smith v Trafford Housing Trust* [2012] EWHC 3221 (Ch), [2013] IRLR 86.
[101] *Pay v United Kingdom (Admissibility)* (2009) 48 EHRR SE2.
[102] ACAS, *Code of Practice 1 – Disciplinary and Grievance Procedures* (2009).
[103] TULRCA 1992, s 207.
[104] ACAS, above n 102, para 4.

Nevertheless, it remains important to follow the Code where it applies because if a tribunal considers that an employer has unreasonably failed to comply with the Code, it may increase the employee's compensation by up to 25%.[105] It is also important to note that if an employee unreasonably fails to comply with the Code, his or her compensation may be reduced by up to 25%.[106] It is difficult to predict how bad a failure would have to be to count as 'unreasonable' on either side, though a large firm with good legal advice would probably be acting unreasonably if it ignored the Code altogether.

Sometimes, employers argue that the employee's actions were so bad that it was acceptable to dismiss him or her without conducting any kind of procedure at all. For example, the employee might be caught red-handed in an act of gross misconduct, such as stealing or punching a customer. The decision in the *Polkey* case supports this theory, stating that it all turns on the reasonableness test: if other employers would have dismissed the individual without conducting any kind of procedure, then it may be within the band of reasonable responses to do so.[107] However, the ACAS Code discourages this, noting that while gross misconduct may entitle the employer to dismiss the employee without giving notice and without prior warnings, it does not entitle the employer to dispense with the investigation or hearing.[108] It remains to be seen how the law in this area will develop.

Potentially fair dismissals 4 – examples

So far, we have established that for a dismissal to be fair, the employer must show a potentially fair reason for the dismissal, must be found to have acted reasonably in dismissing the employee for that reason, and must have followed a fair procedure in reaching the dismissal decision. If one or more of these elements is not met, the dismissal will be found to be unfair. In this section, we will put all of these ideas together and consider some examples of different types of dismissal: for misconduct, for incapability, on economic grounds and in constructive dismissal cases. The aim is to highlight some of the particular considerations which arise in these different types of case, and to show how unfair dismissal cases develop on a practical level.

Misconduct In misconduct cases, procedural fairness is particularly important because the facts of the case may be disputed. The employer may allege serious wrongdoing but the employee may deny it or may have a different explanation for the events. He or she may also want to argue that dismissal is too severe a sanction for the wrongdoing.

The ACAS Code sets out in some detail the procedures to be followed in misconduct cases.[109] The first step is for the employer to investigate the case, which may include holding a meeting with the employee. Then, the employer should give the employee notice of the case against him or her and time to prepare for the hearing. The employer should hold a disciplinary meeting at which the employee is given an opportunity to challenge the case against him or her. The employee has a statutory right to be

---

[105] TULRCA 1992, s 207A(2), inserted by EA 2008, s 3.
[106] ibid s 207A(3), inserted by EA 2008, s 3.
[107] *Polkey* v *AE Dayton Services Ltd* [1998] AC 344 (HL).
[108] ACAS, above n 102, para 22.
[109] ACAS, above n 102, paras 5–30.

accompanied by a colleague or union representative at that meeting.[110] If the employer decides after the meeting that the employee should be disciplined or dismissed, it must provide the employee with the possibility of appealing against that decision. Ideally, the tasks of investigating, hearing the case and hearing the appeal should be done by different people, but this may not be possible in smaller firms.

Where there is a factual dispute, the employer is not expected to get to the 'truth' of the matter or even to establish what has happened beyond reasonable doubt. Instead, the reasonableness test informs the employer's obligations:

> What the tribunal have to decide every time is, broadly expressed, whether the employer who discharged the employee on the ground of the misconduct in question (usually, though not necessarily, dishonest conduct) entertained a reasonable suspicion amounting to a belief in the guilt of the employee of that misconduct at that time. That is really stating shortly and compendiously what is in fact more than one element. First of all, there must be established by the employer the fact of that belief; that the employer did believe it. Secondly, that the employer had in his mind reasonable grounds upon which to sustain that belief. And thirdly, we think, that the employer, at the stage at which he formed that belief on those grounds, at any rate at the final stage at which he formed that belief on those grounds, had carried out as much investigation into the matter as was reasonable in all the circumstances of the case.[111]

This means that a dismissal may be fair even if the employee did not in fact commit the misconduct in question or if the employer could have reached a different view by conducting additional investigations, provided that the employer's procedural actions fell within the 'band of reasonable responses'.[112] However, the employer cannot rely on evidence which has come to light after the dismissal in order retrospectively to justify its decision to dismiss.[113]

In the *Turner* case, an attempt was made to use the HRA to argue that tribunals should scrutinise the procedural fairness of misconduct dismissals more closely.[114] The employer dismissed the claimant for alleged acts of dishonesty. She argued that this infringed her Article 8 rights because it damaged her reputation and made it more difficult for her to get another job. She therefore argued that the tribunal should scrutinise the fairness of her dismissal using the proportionality test. However, the Court of Appeal rejected the claim, holding that any concerns were already addressed by the 'band of reasonable responses' test. Elias LJ said:

> I accept that where article 8 interests are engaged, matters bearing on the culpability of the employee must be investigated with a full appreciation of the potentially adverse consequences to the employee. But the band of reasonable responses test allows for a heightened standard to be adopted where those consequences are particularly grave.[115]

Of course, it is also possible to challenge the substantive fairness of the decision to dismiss. Sometimes, the employer may establish after proper investigation facts which justify the dismissal of a previously blameless employee, as we saw above. But in

---

[110] Employment Relations Act 1999, s 10. For interpretation, see *Roberts* v *GB Oils Ltd* [2014] ICR 462 (EAT).
[111] *British Home Stores Ltd* v *Burchell* [1980] ICR 303.
[112] *Sainsbury's Supermarkets Ltd* v *Hitt* [2002] EWCA Civ 1588, [2003] ICR 111.
[113] *W Devis & Sons* v *Atkins* [1977] AC 931 (HL), though this might affect the level of compensation awarded.
[114] *Turner* v *East Midlands Trains Ltd* [2012] EWCA Civ 1470, [2013] ICR 525.
[115] ibid [52].

many cases, it will not be appropriate to dismiss the employee for a first offence, or for minor but repeated instances of misconduct (such as regularly turning up late for work). Such dismissals would fall outside the 'band of reasonable responses'.[116] In these situations, it is common practice to give the employee a series of warnings.[117] The employer might start with a verbal warning, and then proceed to a written warning, before issuing a final written warning. The aim is to give the employee notice of the problem and a reasonable period of time within which to improve. If the employee continues to be late, even after a final written warning, the employer may decide to dismiss him or her. In determining the fairness of the dismissal, the tribunal will have regard both to whether the employer has gone through the system of warnings and to the process for issuing those warnings. So, if the employee wanted to challenge a warning (for example, because the employer had wrongly recorded the number of times he or she had been late) but was not given the chance to do so, the fairness of the eventual dismissal might be called into question.

Capability We saw above that capability cases fall into two categories: incompetence and ill health.

In incompetence cases, it remains important for employers to follow fair procedures and the ACAS Code.[118] But the aim is rather different to that in misconduct cases. It is to ensure that the employee is given proper notice of the ways in which he or she falls short of the required standards, and a chance to improve, before a decision to dismiss is taken. As with misconduct, it is normally appropriate to give the employee a series of warnings (with an opportunity to discuss and challenge the warnings) before dismissing him or her. These warnings should include a reasonable time within which to improve. The employee has the right to be accompanied to disciplinary hearings and should be given the chance to have his or her say, and to appeal against the employer's decision.

In cases of dismissal on grounds of ill health, it is unlikely to be reasonable to dismiss an individual for being off sick for a week with flu. But dismissal may be reasonable as a last resort where the individual has been off sick for a long period of time. There are two important factors for the employer to bear in mind in this situation.

First, there is a potential overlap between illness and disability. Under the Equality Act 2010, a disability is defined as a long-term impairment which has a substantial effect on a person's ability to perform day-to-day activities.[119] For example, an employee who is off sick because of workplace stress might eventually be diagnosed with depression. If this is likely to last for more than 12 months and has a serious impact on his or her daily functioning, it may well fall within the definition of disability under the Act. If this is the case, the employer is under a duty not to discriminate against the disabled person, and is also under a duty to make 'reasonable adjustments' to enable the disabled person to work.[120] This has important consequences if the employer is considering dismissal. In particular, the employer should consider whether any changes, such as a phased return to work, alterations

---

[116] For example, *Salford Royal NHS Foundation Trust v Roldan* [2010] EWCA Civ 522, [2010] ICR 1457.
[117] ACAS, above n 102, paras 18–22.
[118] ACAS, above n 102.
[119] EA 2010, s 6.
[120] See Chapter 6.

to working hours or the provision of additional support, might enable the individual to work.

Second, whether or not there is a disability, the employer must follow a fair procedure. Although the ACAS Code is relevant here too, the Code itself notes that it may need to be adapted for this type of case.[121] In general terms, the employer should warn an employee before dismissing him or her on grounds of ill-health, so that he or she has notice that the situation is becoming serious, and should hold discussions with the employee before taking the final decision to dismiss. These discussions should include consideration of whether there is any way in which the employee can be helped to return to work – in practice, rather like the duty to make reasonable adjustments – otherwise there is a risk that the dismissal will be found to be unfair.

Economic dismissals As we saw above, many dismissals take place for economic reasons.[122] The employee is not at fault; the employer just needs fewer people. Such dismissals might fall within the statutory definition of redundancy, discussed above, and if not, they will usually count as SOSR dismissals. Tribunals are generally reluctant to question the employer's view of what its business requires so, for example, it is highly unlikely that a tribunal would rule that a dismissal was unfair because the employer did not need to make cutbacks, or that reductions in the employees' terms and conditions (unless very extreme in nature) were unfair.[123]

In practice, the focus tends to be on the employer's selection procedure.[124] In most cases, there will be a pool of employees who might be dismissed on economic grounds (the whole workforce, or the people in a particular department, for example), so the employer will have to make a choice among them. There are various ways in which this choice might be challenged in an unfair dismissal claim.

One possibility is to challenge the selection criteria adopted by the employer, or their application in practice. There are three main issues to bear in mind here. First, the various 'automatically unfair' grounds for dismissal discussed earlier are also applicable in the context of redundancy selection. This means that, for example, if the employer selects trade union activists as a priority group for redundancy, this will be unfair and there will be no opportunity for the employer to argue otherwise. Second, the employer must avoid discriminatory selection criteria. In the *Clarke* case, it was held that a decision to make part-timers redundant before full-timers (which used to be a common practice) was unlawful because it was indirectly discriminatory against women, who are more likely than men to work part-time.[125] Nowadays, discrimination against part-timers is expressly prohibited so such a rule would also be problematic on that ground.[126] Third, whatever criteria the employer does use must be objective and must be applied fairly.[127] Thus, the employer cannot select people just on the basis of dislike. If the employer uses a scoring system, it may be

---

[121] ACAS, above n 102, para 1.
[122] This topic is covered in more detail in Chapter 10.
[123] See, for example, *James W Cook & Co (Wivenhoe) Ltd* v *Tipper* [1990] ICR 716 (CA); *St John of God (Care Services) Ltd)* v *Brooks* [1992] ICR 715.
[124] See, generally, *Williams* v *Compair Maxam* [1982] ICR 156 (EAT).
[125] *Clarke* v *Eley (IMI) Kynoch Ltd* [1983] ICR 165.
[126] Part-time Workers (Prevention of Less Favourable Treatment) Regulations 2000, SI 2000/1551.
[127] *Williams*, above n 124.

obliged to disclose how the aggrieved employee fared relative to other employees in the pool, though the courts have been reluctant to go too far in ordering widespread disclosure of other employees' scores.[128]

The other possibility is to challenge the redundancy procedure. When the employer is dismissing 20 or more employees on economic grounds, there is a duty to consult with representatives of the workforce under EU law.[129] However, even where this duty does not arise, for example, because the employer is not making so many people redundant, it is still necessary to follow a fair procedure. For example, this might include giving notice of impending redundancies and allowing employees an opportunity to appeal against the score they have been given under the employer's selection criteria.[130]

Constructive dismissal We saw above that a constructive dismissal occurs where the employer commits a repudiatory breach of the contract of employment, entitling the employee to treat the relationship as at an end. This gives rise to some difficulties in applying the reasonableness test, and has its own set of procedural fairness issues too.

A first problem with the reasonableness test is the temptation to muddle it up with the question of whether or not there has been a constructive dismissal at all: in other words, whether the employer's behaviour is such as to amount to a repudiatory breach of contract. However, as we saw in the *Buckland* case, above, these are two separate enquiries.[131] Although a repudiatory breach of contract will often also be unreasonable, it is not impossible to think of cases in which the employer might breach a fundamental term of the contract but might not be acting unreasonably in the statutory sense. In *Buckland*, Sedley LJ gave as an example a case in which the employer failed to pay the employee's wages. This would be a constructive dismissal on ordinary contractual principles, because it is a breach of the fundamental obligation to pay the employee, but might be fair if the employer had a good reason, for example, an unexpected cashflow problem.[132]

A second issue with the application of the reasonableness test in constructive dismissal cases is that they may not fit into the neat two-stage enquiry we have been considering in other types of case. If the employer just behaves badly towards the employee, in breach of the contract of employment, it may not direct its mind to the question of dismissing the employee so may not have a clear reason for dismissal at all. This was the case in *Buckland* itself. Although the university undermined the relationship of mutual trust and confidence with Professor Buckland, and thus breached his contract, it did not intend to dismiss him. According to Sedley LJ in *Buckland*, the best way to solve this problem will usually be to infer that the employer acted unreasonably because it is in no position to justify its actions.[133]

Constructive dismissal cases also have a special procedural dimension. Under the ACAS Code, the employer is expected to have a grievance procedure in place to enable employees to raise their concerns.[134] The employee should communicate his

[128] *British Aerospace Plc* v *Green* [1995] ICR 1006 (CA).
[129] TULRCA, s 188(1). See Chapter 14.
[130] *Williams*, above n 124.
[131] *Buckland* (n 27), and see Bogg, above n 30, for a detailed commentary.
[132] ibid [28].
[133] ibid [47].
[134] Above n 102, paras 31–44.

or her grievance to an appropriate person. The employer should arrange a meeting to discuss the grievance (at which the employee is entitled to be accompanied) and should report the outcome back to the employee promptly. If the employee is unhappy with the employer's attempt to resolve the grievance, he or she should be able to appeal within the employing organisation. Importantly, an employee who unreasonably fails to comply with the ACAS Code may have his or her compensation reduced by up to 25% by the tribunal.[135] Since it is not clear what tribunals will find to be an 'unreasonable failure', it is therefore advisable for an employee to raise a grievance even if it is apparent – as may well be the case in a constructive dismissal scenario – that the employer will not take it seriously. In turn, this may lead to an increase of up to 25% in the compensation awarded since a failure by the employer to comply with the Code may also be taken into account by the tribunal, as we saw above.[136]

9.4.3 Procedure and remedies

We are now in a position to consider the procedure for bringing an unfair dismissal claim and the remedies available to the successful claimant. It is easy to assume that the key determinants of job security in English law are the tests for the procedural and substantive fairness of dismissal just discussed. But remedies are important too. Although they are designed to compensate the employee and not to punish the employer, they send out important signals about the seriousness of an unfair dismissal.

Procedure

We will begin with a brief overview of the process of an unfair dismissal claim.

Under s. 92(1) ERA 1996, an employee (with two years' continuous employment) is entitled to a written statement of the reasons for his or her dismissal:

> An employee is entitled to be provided by his employer with a written statement giving particulars of the reasons for the employee's dismissal–
>
> (a) if the employee is given by the employer notice of termination of his contract of employment,
>
> (b) if the employee's contract of employment is terminated by the employer without notice, or
>
> (c) if the employee is employed under a limited-term contract and the contract terminates by virtue of the limiting event without being renewed under the same contract.[137]

This must be provided within 14 days of receipt of the employee's request for a written statement. Where the employee is dismissed while she is pregnant or on maternity leave, she is entitled to a written statement without having to request it and regardless of her length of service.[138] There is a remedy of two weeks' pay for an 'unreasonable' failure to provide a statement or for the provision of reasons which

---

[135] Above n 106.
[136] Above n 105.
[137] Notice that this does not cover constructive dismissal situations.
[138] ERA 1996, s 92(4).

are 'inadequate or untrue'.[139] In theory, the written statement should provide the starting-point for the employee's claim by identifying the reason for the dismissal. However, the right to a written statement does not apply outside the qualifying period, even though many automatically unfair dismissal claims (not just pregnancy) are available from 'day one'. Nor is the employer bound by the written statement if the case reaches a tribunal hearing: it may later argue a different reason when defending the employee's claim.[140]

An unfair dismissal claim must be brought to a tribunal within three months of the 'effective date of termination', calculated in accordance with s. 97 ERA 1996.[141] Initially, ACAS must be notified so that 'early conciliation' can be offered.[142] Details of the claim are passed to a conciliation officer who contacts the parties and attempts to find a solution. This service is free of charge. Any agreement reached through ACAS is binding. It is not compulsory to participate in conciliation or to accept a conciliated solution, but it is not possible to go straight to a tribunal without notifying ACAS and obtaining a certificate to show that the time period for conciliation has elapsed. Under the Employment Rights (Dispute Resolution) Act 1998, ACAS also offers an alternative to a tribunal hearing – arbitration – in unfair dismissal cases. Again, both parties must agree to use the scheme. The arbitrator makes a binding decision after proceedings conducted in private. The arbitrator's decision can only be challenged in court in very limited circumstances under the Arbitration Act 1996. In their different ways, both conciliation and arbitration represent attempts to reduce the number of claims proceeding to a tribunal hearing: conciliation by encouraging the parties to settle, and arbitration by providing a different route altogether.[143]

Remedies

The unfair dismissal legislation as originally enacted envisaged that re-employment would be the main remedy in an unfair dismissal claim. However, re-employment is very rarely requested or ordered, and in practice, most claimants receive an award of compensation.[144] We will examine each in turn.

Re-employment Re-employment is a useful non-technical term for two statutory concepts: 'reinstatement', defined in s. 114 ERA 1996, and 're-engagement', defined in s. 115. Reinstatement involves putting the employee back into the position he or she would have been in had he or she not been dismissed. This involves giving him or her back his or her old job, together with arrears of pay and other benefits, such as pay rises, which have occurred in the meantime. Re-engagement involves giving the employee a 'comparable' job or 'other suitable employment'.

---

[139] ERA 1996, s 93.

[140] *Abernethy* v *Mott, Hay and Anderson* [1974] ICR 323 (CA). This must be a reason the employer had at the time of the dismissal.

[141] ERA 1996, s 111, unless it was not 'reasonably practicable' to bring the claim within that time.

[142] Enterprise and Regulatory Reform Act 2013, s 7, which inserts s 18A and s 18B into the Employment Tribunals Act 1996.

[143] As we saw in Chapter 2, the introduction of tribunal fees has resulted in a dramatic reduction in the number of claims.

[144] ERA 1996, s 112.

The tribunal must first consider the possibility of reinstatement, having regard to the following considerations:

(a) whether the complainant wishes to be reinstated,
(b) whether it is practicable for the employer to comply with an order for reinstatement, and
(c) where the complainant caused or contributed to some extent to the dismissal, whether it would be just to order his reinstatement.[145]

If the tribunal does not order reinstatement, it must proceed to consider re-engagement on much the same basis.[146] The fact that the employer has already hired a permanent replacement for the dismissed employee may only be taken into account in determining the 'practicability' question in limited circumstances.[147] If the employer does not comply with the re-employment order, the tribunal must make an award of compensation (under the principles to be discussed below), plus an 'additional award' of between 26 and 52 weeks' pay.[148]

In principle, a requirement to take the employee back constitutes a strong statement that unfair dismissal is wrong. It 'overturns' the employer's decision and is similar in effect to a quashing order in administrative law.[149] However, it can hardly be regarded as a central feature of unfair dismissal law because it is rarely used. In part, this is because employees themselves rarely request it: it must be difficult to return to a workplace from which one has been fired. But it also reflects structural weaknesses in the legislation. First, the employer is able to argue that it is not practicable to take the employee back. Tribunals are unlikely to question this for fear of interfering too much with managerial prerogative. Second, the consequences of not complying with a re-employment order are limited to the payment of the 'additional award'. Because tribunals are not courts, they do not have the power to issue an injunction to force the employer to comply with the order. Third, with the exception of trade union and worker representative cases, there is no power to order interim relief – to encourage the employer to keep the employee on while the dispute is resolved – a mechanism which may make it easier for the employee to return to work afterwards.[150]

Compensation For most claimants, compensation is the normal remedy for unfair dismissal. This is made up of two elements: the basic award and the compensatory award.[151] In redundancy cases, the claimant is entitled to a redundancy payment, calculated in the same way as the basic award, even if the redundancy is fair, and to a compensatory award in addition if the redundancy is unfair.[152]

The basic award is designed to reflect the employee's length of service with the employer. It reflects the fact that an employee who has worked for the employer for a long time may find it harder to get another job (because his or her skills are specific to the firm) and will lose any 'perks' that come with seniority at a particular workplace. Nowadays, people tend to change jobs more often, so for many people, the basic award is a small sum. Under s. 119 ERA 1996, it is calculated by working

---

[145] ERA 1996, s 116(1).
[146] ibid s 116(2) and (3).
[147] ibid s 116(5) and (6).
[148] ibid s 117. This is subject to the statutory limit on a week's pay in ERA 1996, s 227.
[149] This remedy may be available to public sector employees in some circumstances.
[150] TULRCA 1992, ss 161–166; ERA 1996, ss 128–132.
[151] ERA 1996, s 118.
[152] See Chapter 10 for more detail.

out how many years the employee has worked for the employer, and then applying the following formula:

(a) one and a half weeks' pay for a year of employment in which the employee was not below the age of forty-one,

(b) one week's pay for a year of employment (not within paragraph (a)) in which he was not below the age of twenty-two, and

(c) half a week's pay for a year of employment not within paragraph (a) or (b).[153]

A maximum of 20 years' service may be counted for this purpose.[154] The concept of a week's pay is subject to a maximum of £464, so anyone who earns more than this will not be fully compensated.[155] The maximum available under this heading is thus £13,920, but most people are entitled to far less than this. In trade union and worker representative dismissal cases, a minimum basic award of £5676 is applicable to reflect the seriousness of dismissal on this ground.[156]

The other element of the award is the compensatory award. This is calculated in accordance with s. 123 ERA as follows:

(1) . . . the amount of the compensatory award shall be such amount as the tribunal considers just and equitable in all the circumstances having regard to the loss sustained by the complainant in consequence of the dismissal in so far as that loss is attributable to action taken by the employer.

(2) The loss referred to in subsection (1) shall be taken to include–

(a) any expenses reasonably incurred by the complainant in consequence of the dismissal, and

(b) . . . loss of any benefit which he might reasonably be expected to have had but for the dismissal.

Crucially, there is an upper limit on the sum available under this heading, in s. 124(1ZA):

The amount specified in this subsection is the lower of–

(a) £76,574, and

(b) 52 multiplied by a week's pay of the person concerned.

In this situation, the week's pay is not subject to a maximum limit so the compensation awarded here reflects the employee's actual earnings. This means that anyone earning below £76,574 per year will receive no more than a year's pay in compensation, and anyone earning above that figure will receive no more than that figure in compensation. This change was introduced in 2013.[157] The government argued that the previous limit, which was simply set at £74,200, was much higher than the awards most claimants in fact received. It suggested that the limit caused unnecessary concern to employers and misled claimants into believing that they would receive very large compensation payments.[158] However, coupled with the introduction of tribunal

---

[153] ERA 1996, s 119(2).

[154] ibid s 119(3).

[155] ibid s 227.

[156] TULRCA 1992, s 156; ERA 1996, s 120. In blacklisting cases, the sum is £5000 under ERA 1996, s 120(1C).

[157] Unfair Dismissal (Variation of the Limit of Compensatory Award) Order 2013, SI 2013/1949, art 2.

[158] DBIS, *Unfair Dismissal Compensatory Awards: Final Impact Assessment* (January 2013).

fees,[159] there is a risk that some claimants will no longer consider it worthwhile to challenge their dismissal, thus enabling employers to act unfairly with impunity. There is no upper limit on the compensation available in discriminatory dismissal cases brought under the Equality Act 2010.[160]

It is important to be aware that although the tribunal may award such compensation as it considers 'just and equitable' up to the applicable limit, tribunals do in practice observe certain key principles in making awards. For example, it is highly unlikely that an employee would be able to claim for loss of future earnings until retirement because the employer might have terminated the employment lawfully at an earlier date.[161] Nor is it possible to claim damages for hurt feelings or other forms of non-economic loss arising out of the dismissal.[162] This reflects the approach to damages in contract law, though it is not clear whether it is appropriate to extend that same approach into unfair dismissal law. Finally, the tribunal may increase (or reduce) the award by up to 25% to reflect a failure by the employer (or employee) to observe the procedural fairness requirements of the ACAS Code, as discussed above.[163]

According to the Ministry of Justice's statistics, the median award in unfair dismissal cases (including both basic and compensatory elements) in 2011–12 was £4560.[164] This is a salutary reminder that, despite the debates about the appropriate maximum limits, in practice most claimants receive quite small sums of compensation for the loss of their job. This does not send out a particularly strong signal about the importance of job security.

9.5 WRONGFUL DISMISSAL

The term 'wrongful dismissal' is shorthand for a dismissal in breach of contract. Employment relationships are contractual, so it has always been possible for the individual to sue in contract in respect of his or her dismissal.[165] In the 1960s, wrongful dismissal law came to be perceived as inadequate to provide a remedy for ordinary employees who were dismissed. At that time, the workforce was much more highly unionised than it is today, so dismissals often led to strikes. The introduction of unfair dismissal law in 1971 was seen as a way of making up for the deficiencies of wrongful dismissal law, and (indirectly) of reducing the number of strikes relating to dismissals.[166] Nowadays, dismissals are rarely the subject of strike action, though it is important to bear in mind that this may reflect the decline in trade union strength as much as it does the success of unfair dismissal law.

In recent years, the tide has turned somewhat in the other direction. Wrongful dismissal law has been seen by some people as a way of remedying some of the perceived defects of unfair dismissal law. There are two main 'defects'. One is that although unfair dismissal is heavily focused on procedural fairness, it usually only provides the employee with compensation for the employer's procedural failings: it

---

[159] See Chapter 2.
[160] See Chapter 6.
[161] For discussion see *Contract Bottling Ltd v Cave* [2015] ICR 146 (EAT).
[162] *Dunnachie v Kingston upon Hull City Council* [2004] UKHL 36, [2005] 1 AC 226.
[163] Above nn 105–106.
[164] Ministry of Justice, *Employment Tribunal and EAT Statistics 2011–12* (September 2012) Table 5.
[165] See Chapter 5.
[166] For the history, see Paul Davies and Mark Freedland, *Labour Legislation and Public Policy* (Clarendon Press 1993) 194–211.

does not offer a way of forcing the employer to act fairly or preventing an unfair dismissal. The other is that (except in discrimination cases) there is a cap on the total amount of damages the unfairly dismissed employee can recover.[167] People in highly paid jobs may not regard this as sufficient to compensate them fully for all their losses. This has led to some interesting test cases in which individuals have tried to use wrongful dismissal law to improve on the remedies available to them under the statute. As we shall see, the courts have been worried about the idea of getting round the limits on unfair dismissal law and have not generally been receptive to these claims.

To explain the law, we will proceed in three stages. First, we will examine a straightforward wrongful dismissal claim in order to illustrate why it was thought necessary to introduce unfair dismissal law. In the second and third sections, we will consider two routes that have been adopted in recent times to try to enhance the remedies available in wrongful dismissal law: the use of the implied term of mutual trust and confidence, and reliance on disciplinary procedures in the contract of employment. Logically, we should probably consider arguments based on express terms of the contract before arguments based on implied terms, but the courts' rulings in the former cases now turn quite heavily on the views they have taken in the latter, so on this occasion it is better to follow the chronological order of the case-law.

9.5.1 Wrongful dismissal – the basic claim

At common law, the courts generally regard a contract of employment (or a worker's contract) as terminable with notice. This means that the employer can bring the relationship to an end by telling the employee or worker that he or she is dismissed from a particular date: perhaps a week away, or two weeks away, or longer. Although this does not give the individual any job security, it is a weak form of procedural protection. It gives him or her a chance to start looking for another job and to prepare for the loss of income.

Notice

Statute now provides a mechanism for calculating the minimum notice to which an employee is entitled, depending on how long he or she has worked for the employer:

> The notice required to be given by an employer to terminate the contract of employment of a person who has been continuously employed for one month or more–
>
> (a) is not less than one week's notice if his period of continuous employment is less than two years,
> (b) is not less than one week's notice for each year of continuous employment if his period of continuous employment is two years or more but less than twelve years, and
> (c) is not less than twelve weeks' notice if his period of continuous employment is twelve years or more.[168]

These are minimum periods, so if the parties include a shorter period of notice in their contract it will not be effective.[169] However, they are free to include a longer

---

[167] ERA 1996, s 124(1ZA).
[168] ERA 1996, s 86(1).
[169] ibid s 86(3).

period of notice if they wish. Higher-paid, managerial employees may well be given a contractual entitlement to longer notice.

The statutory notice periods can be disregarded where the employee commits a repudiatory breach,[170] where the employee accepts a payment in lieu of notice, or where the employee agrees to waive his or her notice.[171] The last two are straightforward. The first applies where the employee is in breach of a fundamental term of the contract. This entitles the employer to accept the employee's breach and bring the contract to an end. In practice, this is often said to occur when the employee commits 'gross misconduct'.

If none of these exceptions applies, but the employer purports to dismiss the employee without given notice (often referred to as a 'summary dismissal'), the employee is entitled to bring a claim for breach of contract.

The statutory notice periods only apply to employees.[172] People with other types of work contract must therefore fall back on any notice clause contained in their contract. If the contract is silent on the matter, the courts would imply an appropriate notice period.[173] The length of the notice is traditionally worked out by reference to the individual's pay period, so if the individual is paid weekly, a week's notice would be required in order to terminate the contract. If a worker commits a repudiatory breach of contract, the employer is entitled to bring the contract to an end without giving notice under the ordinary rules of the law of contract. Since most of the case-law relates to employees, we will use the term 'employee' for the remainder of the discussion.[174]

Remedies

In a wrongful dismissal claim, in accordance with normal contractual principles, the employee is entitled to expectation damages: to the wages he or she could have expected to receive if the contract had been performed in accordance with its terms. Since the employer could have dismissed the employee lawfully with notice, the most he or she could have expected was to work out the notice period. If the employee was entitled to a month's notice, he or she could obtain damages of a month's wages.

Also in accordance with normal contractual principles, the rules of mitigation are applicable.[175] In an employment case, the way to mitigate the loss is to look for another job. So, if the court takes the view that the employee could have found another job after the termination, it may reduce the employee's damages to reflect his or her failure to mitigate. And if the employee does find another job, the damages will be reduced. So, to continue with our example, if the employee entitled to a month's notice finds a job after three weeks, he or she will only be entitled to three weeks' wages in damages.

Finally, it appears that it is not possible to claim for hurt feelings or mental distress as a result of the dismissal or the manner in which the dismissal took place (for

---

[170] ERA 1996, s 86(6).

[171] ibid s 86(3).

[172] ibid s 86.

[173] *Richardson v Koefod* [1969] 1 WLR 1812 (CA).

[174] In practice, wrongful dismissal claims are only worthwhile if the individual has a long notice period, and this seems more likely to be the case for employees than for workers.

[175] *Gunton v Richmond-upon-Thames London Borough Council* [1981] Ch 448 (CA) 469 (Buckley LJ).

example, where the employer terminates the contract in a way that is humiliating to the employee). This is said to be precluded by the famous decision in *Addis*:

> If there be a dismissal without notice the employer must pay [damages]; but [those damages] cannot include compensation . . . for the injured feelings of the servant.[176]

This reflects a more general principle of contract law that a breach does not give rise to a claim for damages in respect of hurt feelings. Although there are some exceptions to this principle, employment contracts do not seem to fall within any of them.[177]

Problems

From a job security perspective, wrongful dismissal is seriously deficient. It does not involve any control over the employer's reason for dismissal and it results in minimal awards of damages for most employees (except those who are highly paid and have long periods of notice). Unfair dismissal was intended to respond to these problems by providing substantive and procedural protection for employees, meaningful remedies, and an accessible route for making a claim.

9.5.2 The implied term of mutual trust and confidence

Now that we have seen the basic operation of a wrongful dismissal claim, we can examine some of the ways in which people have tried to develop that claim into a more powerful form of redress for aggrieved employees. As we shall see, these attempts have had varying degrees of success. This section will focus in particular on the implied term of mutual trust and confidence.

The implied term of mutual trust and confidence requires both parties to behave in a way which maintains a relationship of trust between them.[178] A breach of this term can give rise to a claim in damages. In the *Malik* case, the claimants worked for a bank.[179] It was discovered that the bank was being run fraudulently. The bank closed down and the claimants lost their jobs. The claimants found it difficult to obtain fresh employment in the banking sector because they said that they were 'tainted by association' with the fraudulent bank, even though they were entirely innocent of the fraud. They brought a case against their former employers alleging that they had suffered economic loss due to their inability to find work. The House of Lords held that this type of claim could potentially succeed, provided that the claimants could overcome the hurdles of causation and remoteness at trial.

The *Malik* case is not, strictly speaking, a dismissal case. Although the claimants were made redundant, the breach of the implied term arose while they were still working for the bank (although they did not find out about it until later). But *Malik* opened up the possibility of arguing that the implied term of mutual trust and confidence could be relied upon at the time of dismissal, to enable employees to recover substantial damages for a breach of that term flowing from the manner in which they were dismissed.

---

[176] *Addis v Gramophone Co Ltd* [1909] AC 488 (HL) 491 (Lord Loreburn LC).
[177] For example, *Jarvis v Swans Tours Ltd* [1973] QB 233 (CA), though there is a debate about whether this is a true exception or a reflection of the purpose of the contract.
[178] See Chapter 5.
[179] *Malik v Bank of Credit and Commerce International SA (In Liquidation)* [1998] AC 20 (HL).

This issue arose for decision in *Johnson v Unisys*.[180] In that case, Mr Johnson had brought a successful claim for unfair dismissal. He won on the ground that the employer had failed to follow an appropriate procedure when dismissing him and he secured compensation up to the statutory maximum.[181] He then argued that he had not been fully compensated for the losses he had suffered (he was depressed and had been unable to find another job) and he brought a wrongful dismissal claim, arguing that the employer had breached the implied term of mutual trust and confidence, both in respect of the fact of his dismissal and the manner in which the dismissal had taken place. By a majority, the House of Lords held that his claim could not succeed.

One argument against Mr Johnson's claim was that it was precluded by the decision in *Addis*. The majority rejected this argument.[182] They took the view (obiter) that *Addis* only precluded claims for hurt feelings and damage to reputation arising from the fact of dismissal itself. Since Mr Johnson was claiming for a breach of the implied term of mutual trust and confidence, the *Addis* ruling did not govern his case.

However, Mr Johnson's claim was rejected on several other grounds. First, there was some suggestion that the implied term of mutual trust and confidence was about the maintenance of the relationship between the parties and was therefore inherently unsuitable for application to a dismissal situation, in which that relationship was being brought to an end.[183] Second, it was held that the implied term could not override the express term governing dismissal in Mr Johnson's contract, which provided that his employment could be terminated by the employer with four weeks' notice.[184]

Third, and perhaps most importantly, the majority rejected Mr Johnson's claim on policy grounds.[185] It was held that Parliament had remedied the deficiencies in the law of wrongful dismissal by enacting the unfair dismissal legislation. It was therefore inappropriate for the courts to develop the common law action in a way that would circumvent the limits placed by Parliament on employees' ability to recover, notably the cap on the amount of damages. Moreover, it was suggested that the common law action would be uncertain in scope and might lead to large and unpredictable damages awards against employers.

The decision in *Johnson* has been the subject of much academic criticism,[186] and in the case itself, Lord Steyn delivered a powerful dissenting judgment.[187] The three points made by the majority can be met with the following counter-arguments. First, the implied term can be regarded as a means of ensuring good behaviour throughout the parties' relationship. It therefore has an important role to play during termination in particular, when there is a particular risk of harsh behaviour by the employer to the detriment of the employee.[188] Second, there is no conflict between the implied

---

[180] [2001] UKHL 13, [2003] 1 AC 518.

[181] At the time, this was £11,000.

[182] *Johnson*, above n 180, [44] (Lord Hoffmann), [77] (Lord Millett). Lord Bingham agreed with Lord Hoffmann and Lord Millett.

[183] ibid [46] (Lord Hoffmann), [78] (Lord Millett).

[184] ibid [42] (Lord Hoffmann).

[185] ibid [2] (Lord Nicholls), [56]–[58] (Lord Hoffmann), [80] (Lord Millett).

[186] See Lizzie Barmes, 'Common Law Implied Terms and Behavioural Standards at Work' (2007) 36 ILJ 35; Douglas Brodie, 'Legal Coherence and the Employment Revolution' (2001) 117 LQR 604; 'Mutual Trust and Confidence: Catalysts, Constraints and Commonality' (2008) 37 ILJ 329; Judy Fudge, 'The Spectre of *Addis* in Contracts of Employment in Canada and the UK' (2007) 36 ILJ 51.

[187] *Johnson*, above n 180, [3]–[29].

[188] ibid [19].

term and the express terms of the contract because the implied term should be seen as an overarching standard of behaviour that governs the way in which the employer exercises the powers given to it in the contract, including the power of termination.[189] And third, the existence of the statutory law of unfair dismissal should not be taken to preclude the 'principled development' of the common law of wrongful dismissal.[190] This would not open the floodgates to a large volume of claims because the rules on causation and remoteness of damage would serve to limit the number of claims that could be brought.

Leaving these criticisms aside, a particular difficulty arising from the decision in *Johnson* is to determine its scope, given that the House of Lords did not overrule its own earlier decision in the *Malik* case. If an employee can recover for breaches of the implied term of mutual trust and confidence during the employment relationship, but not at the time of dismissal, where should the line between the two be drawn? Where does the *Malik* ruling stop and the '*Johnson* exclusion area' (as it has come to be known) begin?

This question arose for decision in the *Eastwood* litigation.[191] Here, employees claimed for breaches of the implied term of mutual trust and confidence which had arisen during disciplinary proceedings which eventually led to their dismissal. The litigation involved a number of joined cases with different facts but it was common to all of them that the employer had behaved appallingly, either by seeking to dismiss the employee based on trumped-up charges, or by failing to investigate serious accusations against him or her. As a result, the employees had suffered serious psychological injury with the effect that they were unfit for work. Their claims were for lost earnings. In *Eastwood*, the House of Lords confined the *Johnson* decision to the dismissal itself. If the employee's claim arose during the period leading up to the dismissal, it was not precluded by the fact that the employee was eventually dismissed. The cause of action for breach of contract survived the dismissal. But if the employee's psychological injuries or other losses resulted from the fact of dismissal, a claim would be precluded by *Johnson*.

The difficulty of drawing a line around the '*Johnson* exclusion area' is, arguably, compounded by the decision in *Edwards*.[192] In that case, Mr Edwards argued that his employer had failed to comply with a disciplinary procedure contained in his contract of employment. We will discuss the case in detail below. For present purposes, what is interesting is that the majority rejected any suggestion that failings in the disciplinary process leading up to Mr Edwards' dismissal could give rise to a claim in damages. As Lord Mance put it, 'any breach of disciplinary procedure did not cause of itself identifiably separate loss or illness' from the dismissal itself.[193] Arguably, this broadens the scope of the '*Johnson* exclusion area' to include dismissal procedures, narrowing the effect of the *Eastwood* decision, even though the majority distinguished rather than doubted that ruling.

On a practical level, this decision has, if anything, compounded the criticisms of *Johnson* because it is now very unclear where the boundaries of the '*Johnson* exclusion area' lie. On a conceptual level, the combined effect of these various decisions is to

---

[189] ibid [24].
[190] ibid [22]–[23], [27].
[191] *Eastwood v Magnox Electric Plc* [2004] UKHL 35, [2005] 1 AC 503.
[192] *Edwards v Chesterfield Royal Hospital NHS Foundation Trust* [2011] UKSC 58, [2012] 2 AC 22.
[193] ibid [99].

create a strange ordering of priorities in which the most significant decision by the employer – the dismissal – is not governed by the implied term of mutual trust and confidence, whereas arguably less significant decisions during the life of the contract are. And in relation to disciplinary proceedings leading to dismissal, the position is, at best, unclear.

9.5.3 Contractual disciplinary procedures

So far, we have been focusing on the situation in which the employee's contract is silent on the subject of discipline and dismissal, apart from a notice clause (which may be express or implied) and the implied term of mutual trust and confidence (which, as we have seen, is only partially helpful in this area). Nowadays, in order to satisfy the requirements of procedural fairness in unfair dismissal law, more and more employers are setting out formal disciplinary and dismissal procedures for their staff. These may well be incorporated into the contracts of employment of individual employees. If that is the case, but the employer fails to follow the agreed procedure, can the employee turn to the law of contract for a remedy? We will examine two possibilities in this section: obtaining an injunction to force the employer to comply with the procedure, or seeking contract damages (perhaps in excess of the maximum available for unfair dismissal) in respect of the employer's breach of the procedures.

Injunctions

Faced with the threat that the employer might not go through the contractual disciplinary procedure or might not follow it properly, an attractive option for the employee is to seek an injunction from the court forcing the employer to comply. This gives the employee a chance to speak in his or her defence and may even enable him or her to persuade the employer to change its mind. It is possible to obtain an injunction provided that certain conditions are met.

The first is that the employee must not accept the employer's repudiatory breach of contract. The injunction will not be granted if the relationship between the parties has already come to an end, because there is nothing for the court to uphold or enforce. So, when the employer threatens not to go through with the procedure, it is important that the employee (counter-intuitively, perhaps) does not storm out and treat the relationship as being at an end.

Some judges have suggested that the elective theory of termination – in which the party who is the victim of a repudiatory breach may choose whether to treat the contract as terminated or not – should not be applied to the contract of employment.[194] They have suggested instead an automatic theory of termination, in which the employer's repudiatory breach brings the contract to an end without the need for any action on the part of the employee. It is sometimes argued that this is preferable because otherwise the employee might simply refuse to accept the repudiatory breach and seek to keep the contract alive indefinitely. However, the recent decision of the Supreme Court in the *Geys* case has confirmed that the elective theory is applicable in employment cases.[195]

---

[194] For example, *Sanders v Ernest A Neale Ltd* [1974] ICR 565.
[195] *Geys v Société Générale* [2012] UKSC 63, [2013] 1 AC 523.

Assuming that the individual does not accept the employer's repudiatory breach, two conditions must be met for the employee to obtain the injunction. First, because employment is a personal relationship, there must still be mutual trust and confidence between the parties. And second, the employee must show that damages would not be a sufficient remedy. We will examine each in turn.

It might sound as if mutual trust and confidence would be difficult to demonstrate in the situation in which the employer is seeking to dismiss the employee. However, the courts have been quite creative in their approach to this question. Sometimes, the breakdown in relationships may not be between the employee and the employer as such. For example, in *Hill*, the employer was satisfied with the employee's work but came under pressure from a trade union to dismiss the employee (who refused to join the union in a closed shop situation[196]), and in *Irani*, there had been a breakdown in the relationship between the employee and his immediate boss.[197] In these cases, the court was prepared to grant the injunction on the basis that mutual trust and confidence still existed as between employee and employer.

More recent cases have adopted an objective approach. In the *Jones* case, the employer had brought disciplinary proceedings against the employee and had sought to dismiss her even though she had been vindicated.[198] The court granted an injunction to prevent Ms Jones's dismissal, despite the employer's claim that it no longer had trust and confidence in her. The court held that, objectively, there was no basis for the employer's view so mutual trust and confidence still subsisted in the relationship. Although the matter was not discussed, this also seems to be the approach of the Supreme Court in the *Chhabra* case.[199] In that case, the employer had failed to follow its own disciplinary procedures correctly and the Supreme Court granted an injunction to prevent it from accusing the employee of gross misconduct, because her wrongdoing was insufficiently serious, and to require it to conduct a full investigation before re-starting the disciplinary process. Indeed, it would be harsh to deny the employee a remedy based on mere assertions by the employer when it is the party in the wrong.

The question of the adequacy of damages as a remedy is somewhat easier to deal with. The employee can argue that the disciplinary process may enable him or her to keep the job, which is clearly better than any remedy in damages. It may be important both for the employee's reputation and his or her mental state to be able to make representations during the disciplinary process. Most importantly, the claim that damages will be inadequate has been significantly strengthened by recent case-law limiting the availability of damages for breaches of contractual disciplinary procedures.[200]

Damages

The alternative route for the aggrieved employee is to accept that the contract has come to an end and to seek damages for breach of the term entitling him or her to a disciplinary procedure. It is to this claim that we will now turn.

---

[196] See Chapter 11. *Hill v CA Parsons & Co* [1972] Ch 305 (CA).
[197] *Irani v Southampton and South West Hampshire Health Authority* [1985] ICR 590.
[198] *Jones v Gwent County Council* [1992] IRLR 521.
[199] *Chhabra v West London Mental Health NHS Trust* [2013] UKSC 80, [2014] ICR 194.
[200] ibid [39].

In the *Gunton* case, the employer dismissed the employee on disciplinary grounds without going through the disciplinary procedure laid down in his contract of employment.[201] The court accepted that the disciplinary procedure bound the employer and was not displaced by the employer's power to dismiss the employee with notice. The court then held that the appropriate measure of damages was the pay the employee could have expected to receive for the time it would have taken to conduct the disciplinary process and to dismiss him with notice.[202] In effect, the contractual disciplinary procedure served to lengthen the employee's notice period.

One of the criticisms of *Gunton* is that this measure of damages assumes that the employee would have been dismissed. It is arguable that this undervalues the role of the disciplinary process, because if the employer had given the employee a hearing, it might have emerged that the accusations against the employee were false. On this view, it might also be appropriate to award the employee additional compensation to reflect this.

In the more recent *Edwards* case, the claimant sought to go beyond the *Gunton* approach and to seek damages for loss of earnings brought about by his employer's failure to follow his contractual disciplinary procedure.[203] Edwards was a consultant surgeon who was accused of inappropriate conduct towards a patient. It was alleged that his employer failed to follow his contractual disciplinary procedure in full when making the decision to dismiss him. The case was heard with *Botham*, in which a youth worker had been accused of inappropriate behaviour towards young people in his care and had been dismissed, again without full compliance with a contractual disciplinary process. In both cases, the dismissals had devastating effects on the individuals' future employment prospects: in *Edwards*, because, after a finding of gross misconduct, the claimant would find it difficult to get another job in the NHS, and in *Botham*, because the claimant had been placed on the government's list of people deemed unsuitable to work with children (although his name was later removed). In both cases, the claimants alleged that, had the disciplinary procedures been followed properly, they would not have suffered damage to their reputations and to their ability to obtain another job.

The cases were heard by a seven-member Supreme Court which split four to three on the result. The reasoning is difficult to untangle because, in the majority, Lord Dyson gave a speech with which Lord Walker agreed, Lord Mance agreed with Lord Dyson but added some observations of his own, and Lord Phillips concurred in the result but differed as to the reasoning. Even the dissenting judges could not agree: Lord Kerr gave a dissenting speech with which Lord Wilson agreed, but Baroness Hale added a dissenting opinion of her own which was in many respects more radical than theirs.

The majority held that the claimants were precluded from recovering substantial damages because of the decision in *Johnson v Unisys*.[204] This is a puzzling outcome because, as we saw above, *Johnson* dealt with the implied term of mutual trust and confidence, whereas *Edwards* was concerned with contractually agreed disciplinary procedures. In other words, the claimant in *Johnson* was seeking to benefit from

---

[201] *Gunton v Richmond-upon-Thames London Borough Council* [1981] Ch 448 (CA).

[202] ibid 470 (Buckley LJ).

[203] *Edwards v Chesterfield Royal Hospital NHS Foundation Trust; Botham v Ministry of Defence* [2011] UKSC 58, [2012] 2 AC 22.

[204] *Johnson*, above n 180.

behavioural norms imposed by the courts, whereas the claimants in *Edwards* were seeking to enforce the terms of their contracts. In theory at least, this seems much less intrusive because it is based on what the parties have agreed.

The approach adopted by Lords Dyson, Walker and Mance developed the link to *Johnson* by arguing that there was a close connection between the statutory action for unfair dismissal and the inclusion of disciplinary procedures in contracts of employment.[205] They noted that unfair dismissal included a consideration of whether the employer had followed a fair procedure in dismissing the employee, and took from this the view that it was the intention of Parliament that employers should develop disciplinary procedures for their employees. Moreover, they suggested that these procedures would, for the most part, be contractual, because there is an obligation under s. 3(1) ERA 1996 to include them in the written statement of employment particulars to be provided to the employee under s. 1 of that Act. This is problematic given the clear conceptual distinction between the contract and the statutory written statement.[206] Against this background, they asked themselves how such procedures were intended to be enforced, and concluded that Parliament intended them to be addressed through the statutory claim for unfair dismissal. As Lord Dyson put it, 'It is necessarily to be inferred from this statutory background that, unless they otherwise expressly agree, the parties to an employment contract do not intend that a failure to comply with contractually binding disciplinary procedures will give rise to a common law claim for damages.'[207] Thus, the *Johnson* 'exclusion area' applied to claims for damages arising out of breaches of contractual disciplinary procedures as well as to claims based on the implied term of mutual trust and confidence. In relation to the facts of the case, it was held that the claims of Mr Edwards and Mr Botham both fell within the *Johnson* exclusion area and therefore failed.[208]

Lord Phillips reached the same result, but by a different route. He took the view that the focus on parliamentary intention in the other majority judgments was problematic because the attribution of intention to Parliament by judges is an artificial exercise.[209] He preferred to develop a common law approach, starting from the decision in *Addis* and treating the issues as ones of remoteness or causation.[210] He noted that this decision ruled out what he termed 'stigma damages' for wrongful dismissal. Both *Johnson* and *Eastwood* had been decided on the basis that *Addis* was still good law. The *Malik* case was distinguishable because 'the stigma damages recognised [in that case] were not caused by wrongful dismissal'.[211] He summed up his conclusion as follows:

> The chain of causation linking a failure to follow a disciplinary procedure with stigma is more tenuous than the chain of causation linking wrongful dismissal with stigma. If the law does not permit recovery of stigma damages in the latter case, it makes no sense to permit it in the former.[212]

[205] *Edwards*, above n 203, [39]–[49] Lord Dyson, [94] Lord Mance.
[206] See Chapter 5, and Alan Bogg, 'Express Disciplinary Procedures in the Contract of Employment: Parliamentary Intention and the Supreme Court' (2015) 131 LQR 15..
[207] *Edwards*, above n 203, [39].
[208] ibid [59] and [56]–[57] respectively (Lord Dyson).
[209] ibid [79].
[210] There is some confusion here. Lord Phillips states early on that he is developing a principle of remoteness, but uses causation terminology later on. Lord Mance took the view that Lord Phillips was focusing on causation.
[211] ibid [84].
[212] ibid [87].

On this view, then, it is the ruling in *Addis* (upheld by *Johnson*) which precluded the claims in *Edwards*.

The decision of the majority leaves us with two obvious questions about the cases we discussed above: what about injunctions, and what about *Gunton*? The injunction cases permit the employee to use a contractual mechanism – the injunction – to force the employer to carry out its obligations under the contract. Since the ruling in *Edwards* is that contractual disciplinary procedures are intended to be enforced through claims for unfair dismissal, and not through contractual mechanisms, the use of an injunction may now seem to be problematic. However, Lord Dyson indicated that the injunction cases were unaffected by the *Edwards* ruling.[213] This was said to be because the statutory regime for unfair dismissal does not offer any equivalent to the injunction as a means of forcing the employer to follow an agreed procedure. Instead, the employee must accept the employer's failure and seek damages (which may be increased to reflect procedural breaches). So the development of a common law remedy in this context does not 'cut across' the statutory scheme and is therefore permitted.

The status of *Gunton* is less certain. Mr Edwards was awarded damages in accordance with *Gunton* at first instance, and his employer chose not to appeal against that decision.[214] Lords Dyson and Walker stated that *Gunton* was not inconsistent with *Johnson*, which presumably means that they regarded the case as good law.[215] They treated it as a straightforward claim for wrongful dismissal in the sense of a breach of the notice rule. The employer's purported notice was invalid because it took place prior to the disciplinary process set out in the contract. Lord Phillips stated that *Gunton* was consistent with *Addis* but added the rider 'if [*Gunton*] was rightly decided',[216] which suggests a degree of doubt. Lord Mance pointed out that *Gunton* appeared to be inconsistent with Lord Hoffmann's statement in *Johnson* that contractual disciplinary procedures could not be treated as limiting the employer's power to dismiss with notice, but he made clear that his comments were obiter.[217] It is possible that *Gunton* damages may be a topic of future litigation, though since the sums involved are likely to be insignificant for many people, the point may not be pursued.

The *Edwards* case evidently divided the Supreme Court and has attracted considerable criticism.[218] Let us examine two of the main concerns: the majority's assumptions about parliamentary intention, and the role of contract law in the employment field.

The majority ruled that Parliament intended contractual disciplinary procedures to be enforceable through unfair dismissal claims and not at common law. Of course, as Lord Phillips pointed out, Parliament's intention is not 'real': it is attributed to Parliament by the judges. In other words, Lords Dyson, Walker and Mance were making a policy choice that wrongful dismissal law should not be developed in ways which 'got around' the limits on unfair dismissal claims. On one view, this is an

---

[213] ibid [44].
[214] ibid [107].
[215] ibid [48].
[216] ibid [87].
[217] ibid [108].
[218] Hugh Collins, 'Compensation for Dismissal: In Search of Principle' (2012) 41 ILJ 208; Lizzie Barmes, 'Judicial Influence and *Edwards v Chesterfield Royal Hospital NHS Foundation Trust* and *Botham v Ministry of Defence*' (2013) 42 ILJ 192.

entirely defensible approach. It can be argued that, in developing the statutory law on unfair dismissal, Parliament sought to strike a balance between the interests of employees in having some protection against arbitrary dismissal, and the interests of employers in knowing that if they do dismiss someone unfairly, there is a limit on their liability to pay compensation (unless they have discriminated). The courts should not disrupt this delicate balance by developing a large and unpredictable common law liability alongside it. On another view, it is a normal feature of the common law that it should continue to develop in an incremental way. Unless Parliament abolishes a particular action, it is hard to see why that common law development should be regarded as improper. If there is an economic or other objection to the courts' decisions, it is always open to Parliament to reverse them through legislation.

Another set of criticisms of the decision in *Edwards* relates to its treatment of the law of contract and its application in the employment context. As we have seen, this is a constant source of difficulty in the field of dismissal and in employment law more generally. In many instances, the courts are criticised for applying doctrines drawn from the law of contract in ways which defeat the worker-protective purpose of legislation. In relation to *Edwards*, the opposite criticism can be made. Normally, the courts construe contracts by focusing on the words used by the parties in order to determine their intentions. Applying this approach, it would seem that the parties intended that Mr Edwards should have the protection of disciplinary procedures and that these should be enforceable through the usual contractual remedies. However, the majority ruled that the contractual disciplinary procedures were included not because of the will of the parties but because of the need to comply with unfair dismissal law. This appears to disregard the clear language of the contract. Indeed, the majority held that if the parties wanted a failure to comply with disciplinary procedures to attract a remedy in damages, they would have to say so very clearly in their contract.[219] The criticism of the courts' treatment of the parties' 'intentions' is somewhat reinforced by the inconsistency resulting from *Edwards* as between the damages remedy and the injunction. As we saw above, the majority ruled that injunctions were still available to enforce contractual disciplinary procedures even though damages were not, because injunctions, unlike damages, did not interfere with the statutory law of unfair dismissal. But this is difficult to reconcile with the view that the parties included the procedures because of unfair dismissal law rather than because they wanted to include them and wanted them to be enforced by the law of contract. In other words, the Supreme Court seems to attribute a rather selective set of intentions to the parties.

9.5.4 Wrongful dismissal – the future

As a result of the rulings in *Johnson* and *Edwards*, it seems unlikely that the law of contract will offer claimants an opportunity to recover substantial damages for dismissal, either in respect of breaches of the implied term of mutual trust and confidence, or in respect of breaches of contractual disciplinary procedures. In some cases, it may still be worthwhile for a claimant to pursue the opportunity of obtaining damages on the *Gunton* basis for the time it would have taken to complete a disciplinary procedure plus the notice period. And there may be some scope for

---

[219] *Edwards,* above n 203, [39].

actions based on the *Malik* and *Eastwood* rulings for damages for breach of the implied term of mutual trust and confidence outside the (albeit now quite broad) '*Johnson* exclusion area'.

Perhaps the most significant role for this body of law now is as a route to obtain an injunction. As we have seen, this does not fall foul of judicial concerns about parliamentary intention because there are no equivalent powers for tribunals under the unfair dismissal legislation. In the recent *Chhabra* case, the Supreme Court recognised that this would now be claimants' primary option:

> As a general rule it is not appropriate for the courts to intervene to remedy minor irregularities in the course of disciplinary proceedings between employer and employee – its role is not the "micro-management" of such proceedings . . . But in this case the irregularities . . . are of a more serious nature. I also bear in mind that any common law damages which [the claimant] might obtain if she were to succeed in a claim based on those irregularities after her employment were terminated might be very limited: *Edwards* v *Chesterfield Royal Hospital NHS Foundation Trust* . . . [220]

It remains to be seen how this case-law will develop.

POINTS TO TAKE AWAY

Job security

- Job security is a contested idea and there are many different policy options open to the legislature.

- These range from an employment at will regime with no job security law at all, to a set of procedural and substantive controls on employers' decision-making.

- To assess the level of job security in a legal system, it is important to consider what remedies are available and how easy they are to obtain, as well as procedural and substantive controls.

Unfair dismissal

- An unfair dismissal claim is normally available to an 'employee' who has been 'dismissed' by the employer. Unless the claim relates to an 'automatically unfair' reason, the employee must normally have worked for the employer for at least two years to be able to claim.

- There are some reasons that cannot be used to justify a dismissal – the 'automatically unfair' reasons – such as pregnancy, trade union membership, claiming the minimum wage or acting as an employee representative.

- Reasons such as conduct, capability or redundancy are 'potentially fair': the employer can dismiss someone on these grounds if it acts reasonably.

- The reasonableness test as interpreted in *Iceland* asks whether the employer's decision was within a 'band of reasonable responses' and whether the employer followed a fair procedure when taking the dismissal decision; tribunals are reluctant to question employers' substantive decisions and tend to focus more on procedural fairness.

[220] *Chhabra*, above n 199, [39].

- Although it is possible to obtain reinstatement or re-engagement, the remedy for most claimants is an award of compensation, made up of a basic award to reflect length of service and a compensatory award to cover other losses, both of which are subject to maximum limits.

Wrongful dismissal

- A 'wrongful dismissal' is a dismissal in breach of the contract of employment.

- Employees have a contractual right to notice of dismissal, so a dismissal without notice will normally be in breach of contract. The employee can claim lost wages for the notice period, subject to the normal contractual rules on mitigation.

- The courts are reluctant to allow employees to use common law claims to obtain damages for dismissal in excess of the statutory cap on damages for unfair dismissal.

- A claim for damages for economic losses flowing from a breach by the employer of the implied term of mutual trust and confidence can be brought in respect of the employer's actions during the contract, but is precluded by *Johnson* if it relates to dismissal.

- An injunction may be available to enforce contractual disciplinary procedures, but a claim for damages for economic losses flowing from a failure to follow contractual disciplinary procedures is precluded by *Edwards*.

Further reading

To get a range of different perspectives on job security, you should read **Wanjiru Njoya, *Property in Work: The Employment Relationship in the Anglo-American Firm* (Ashgate 2007), chapter 1**; Hugh Collins, *Justice in Dismissal* (Clarendon Press 1992), especially chapter 2; and **RA Epstein, 'In Defence of the Contract at Will' (1984) 51 University of Chicago Law Review 947**.

For some people at least, there is a tension between job security and the emergence of 'flexible' labour markets in which workers are employed where they are most needed. On this view, job security laws encourage workers to stay in one job, instead of moving on, and contribute to the 'two-tier' labour market in which some people have a steady job and others have a series of non-standard jobs. This tension is captured in discussions at EU level about 'flexicurity': see **Commission, *Towards Common Principles of Flexicurity: More and Better Jobs through Flexibility and Security* (COM(2007) 359 final, 2007)**. It is worth thinking about how unfair dismissal law (only available to employees with, for the most part, two years' service) fits with the emergence of the different types of contract we discussed in Chapter 4.

In relation to unfair dismissal law, a key area of interest has been in what administrative lawyers call the 'standard of review' of the employer's decision-making. This is discussed by **David Cabrelli, 'The Hierarchy of Differing Behavioural Standards of Review in Labour Law' (2011) 40 ILJ 146; and ACL Davies, 'Judicial Self-restraint in Labour Law' (2009) 38 ILJ 278**. On the potential impact of human rights law, see **Hugh Collins and Virginia Mantouvalou, '*Redfearn* v *UK*: Political Association and Dismissal' (2013) 76 MLR 909**.

→

There is a large critical literature on *Johnson* and *Edwards:* **Lizzie Barmes, 'Common Law Implied Terms and Behavioural Standards at Work' (2007) 36 ILJ 35; 'Judicial Influence and *Edwards* v *Chesterfield Royal Hospital NHS Foundation Trust and Botham* v *Ministry of Defence*' (2013) 42 ILJ 192; Douglas Brodie, 'Legal Coherence and the Employment Revolution' (2001) 117 LQR 604; 'Mutual Trust and Confidence: Catalysts, Constraints and Commonality' (2008) 37 ILJ 329; Hugh Collins, 'Compensation for Dismissal: In Search of Principle' (2012) 41 ILJ 208; and Judy Fudge, 'The Spectre of *Addis* in Contracts of Employment in Canada and the UK' (2007) 36 ILJ 51.**

10 Business reorganisations

Learning outcomes

This chapter will enable readers to:

- understand and critically evaluate the law on redundancy payments, dismissals by reason of redundancy and consultation on 'collective' redundancies
- understand and critically evaluate the rules protecting workers in the event of a change in the identity of their employer, under the Acquired Rights Directive (ARD) and Transfer of Undertakings (Protection of Employment) Regulations (TUPE)
- explain the situations in which the state may be obliged to make payments to employees in the event of their employer's insolvency

10.1 INTRODUCTION

This chapter brings together the law on what we might loosely term 'business reorganisations'. This non-technical label is intended to capture three situations: where the employer's business is doing badly so the employer needs to reduce the size of its workforce; where the employer's business or a part of it is sold to a new owner; and where the employer's business becomes insolvent. These situations have two features in common. First, there are usually strong economic imperatives driving the employer's decision-making. For example, the employer may decide to make people redundant for fear of becoming insolvent, or it may decide to shed an unprofitable part of the business by selling it to someone else. Second, these situations can have substantial impacts on the affected employees, who are not normally in any way responsible for what is happening. In any of these situations, jobs may be affected. This is obviously true of redundancy. It may also be an issue when a new owner takes over (because it may want to make changes) and in an insolvency situation where the employer ceases to trade. Moreover, where the employer is insolvent, the employees may be owed their wages and other payments. As section 10.2 will explain, the law in this area attempts to balance the need to protect vulnerable employees against freedom for employers to respond to economic imperatives.

The material in this chapter has strong links with other topics. Since redundancy is one of the 'potentially fair' reasons for dismissal, the fairness or otherwise of a dismissal on this ground is determined in the same way as other unfair dismissal claims, though an important body of jurisprudence has built up around the fairness of redundancies.[1] And one of the ways in which employees are protected in redundancy situations and changes of business ownership is through duties on the

---

[1] See Chapter 9.

employer to inform and consult, duties which arise more generally under the Information and Consultation Directive.[2] However, it is illuminating to think about all the material on business reorganisations together for two reasons. First, this is how employees and employers experience it: where the business is changing hands, for example, the employees will encounter both consultation processes and the transfer itself, and the employer will have to comply with its obligations under both parts of the law. Second, seeing both the 'job security' and 'consultation' elements of the law together helps to develop a deeper and more nuanced understanding of how the law balances the competing concerns of employers and employees during business reorganisations.

10.2 THEORETICAL FRAMEWORK

The topic of business reorganisations is one in which the interests of employers and the rights of employees come into the sharpest conflict. Since wage costs are a major expenditure for most firms, dismissing employees is an obvious strategy for dealing with a downturn or a potential insolvency situation. But this is tough on the employees, who face losing their jobs through no fault of their own. The law in this area tries to strike a balance between flexibility for employers and protection for the employees. Importantly, though, this protection does not generally take the form of enabling them to keep their jobs.

Only one international human rights instrument, the ESC 1996, provides a detailed right relating to dismissal. Article 24 provides:

> With a view to ensuring the effective exercise of the right of workers to protection in cases of termination of employment, the Parties undertake to recognise:
>
> (a) the right of all workers not to have their employment terminated without valid reasons for such termination connected with their capacity or conduct or based on the operational requirements of the undertaking, establishment or service;
>
> (b) the right of workers whose employment is terminated without a valid reason to adequate compensation or other appropriate relief.
>
> To this end the Parties undertake to ensure that a worker who considers that his employment has been terminated without a valid reason shall have the right to appeal to an impartial body.

This provision does not appear in the ESC 1961 and has not therefore been ratified by the UK. The EU Charter, Article 30, also grants a right to protection against 'unjustified' dismissal 'in accordance with Community law and national laws and practices'. Importantly for our purposes, the 'operational requirements' of the firm is a potentially legitimate reason for dismissal. This is also recognised in the relevant ILO Convention.[3] Thus, there is no general right for employees to keep their jobs if the employer has an economic need to dismiss them.

Nevertheless, as we shall see, English law provides employees with a payment, even if they are fairly dismissed by the employer on grounds of redundancy. One way of

---

[2] Directive 2002/14/EC of the European Parliament and of the Council of 11 March 2002 establishing a general framework for informing and consulting employees. See Chapter 14.

[3] ILO, Termination of Employment Convention 1982 (No 158) (adopted 22 June 1982, entered into force 23 November 1985), art 4. The UK has not ratified this Convention.

viewing this is that it is an indirect means of protecting their job security: the need to make a payment will force the employer to think twice before dismissing them.[4] Another possibility is that it is a recognition of the employees' dignity: an acknowledgment of the fact that they are being dismissed despite not being at fault. But not everyone agrees with the idea of redundancy payments: Collins, for example, argues that they are not necessary to protect employees' dignity since this is not infringed by an economic dismissal, and suggests that the need to make payments may cause problems for employers, a point we will return to below.[5]

Another way of protecting workers without guaranteeing their job security is to give them information and consultation rights. The ILO Convention requires this for economic dismissals, though it allows signatories to limit the rights to large-scale dismissals, and of course many instruments contain information and consultation rights of a more general kind that might be invoked during economic changes in the workplace.[6] Information and consultation rights serve a number of different purposes. They are an important part of respecting employees' dignity – acknowledging that they rely on their jobs and should be told about impending changes – and they allow employees to prepare, for example, by looking for alternative employment. They may also give employees an opportunity to challenge the employer's decisions, though employees' ability to persuade the employer to change its mind may sometimes be rather limited in business reorganisation situations.

From the employer perspective, it can be argued that consultation requirements, redundancy payments and so on make a bad situation worse by requiring the employer to spend more money during a downturn in the business. However, there are ways of arguing that rules of this kind offer benefits to employers. When the EU agreed directives on redundancy consultation, changes in business ownership and insolvency in the 1970s, Europe was suffering a significant economic downturn as traditional industries such as coal and steel fell into decline and new forms of employment in service industries began to emerge.[7] It is often suggested that the underlying reason for this group of directives was that – by offering information and other modest protections – they would reduce employees' resistance to change. A similar argument is commonly made about the introduction of the redundancy payments legislation in the 1960s in the UK.[8] Rather than trying to prevent or deter redundancies, Parliament's aim was to compensate employees so that there would be fewer strikes in response to proposed redundancies. Although these arguments may seem rather cynical, there is some force in the idea that a successful economy requires workers to move from failing industries to growing ones.

Nowadays, a discussion about the protection of employees in times of change may seem rather old-fashioned, since it does not take into account the position of non-standard workers. The rights to be considered in this chapter generally apply only to 'employees', though some of the rights when a business changes hands are also for 'workers'. An employee who works continuously for a firm for two years or more will receive a payment if he or she is dismissed for redundancy, whereas a person

---

[4] For a critical discussion, see Robert H Fryer, 'The Myths of the Redundancy Payments Act' (1973) 2 ILJ 1.

[5] Hugh Collins, *Justice in Dismissal* (Clarendon Press 1992) chapter 5.

[6] ILO Convention (No 158) (n 3), art 13.

[7] See Jeff Kenner, *EU Employment Law* (Hart 2003) chapter 2.

[8] Paul Davies and Mark Freedland, *Labour Legislation and Public Policy* (Clarendon Press 1993) 152–159.

hired on a 'casual as required' basis might work regularly for two years or more for the same firm but receive nothing if he or she is told that there is no more work on offer during a downturn (unless a creative argument can be made that he or she is, in reality, an employee). Employers can reduce their costs by using non-standard workers instead of employees with statutory rights. Freedland and Kountouris have described this as a process of 'demutualisation', in which the risk of an economic downturn, which used to be borne largely by the employer, is gradually being transferred to the workforce through the increasing use of non-standard working.[9] It might be tempting to think that employees somehow 'deserve' more rights because they are dependent on the firm, but this is usually a mistake: non-standard workers may be just as dependent in practice, and most people do not have the option of bargaining with the employer about their contract type.

This presents something of a policy dilemma. On the one hand, it might be argued that protections for employees are too extensive and that the solution to the 'two-tier workforce' is to reduce the protections afforded to the privileged tier. Indeed, it is often suggested that the growth in non-standard working arrangements is driven, in part at least, by the cost of employing 'typical' employees. On the other hand, it might be argued that employers should not be allowed to engage in extensive demutualisation. On this view, either the courts should be more generous in their interpretation of the employee concept, or Parliament should extend 'employee' protections to some or all non-standard workers.

10.3 REDUNDANCY

The law on redundancy has two key components: individual and collective. The individual element gives an employee who is made redundant a right to a redundancy payment (to reflect the fact that he or she is not to blame for the dismissal) and a right to a fair procedure for selecting people for redundancy. The individual element is domestic in origin and has close links to the law of unfair dismissal in terms of its structure. The collective element seeks to ensure that the employer notifies the government and consults representatives of the workforce when it is considering making a large number of people redundant. Although the consultation process is supposed to consider ways of avoiding the redundancies, in practice it is more likely to play a role in informing the workforce of the employer's proposals and providing an opportunity for discussion of the numbers of redundancies and the terms of any financial package to be offered beyond the statutory minimum.

10.3.1 Individual redundancies

Where an employer dismisses an employee for economic reasons, it is necessary to:

- determine whether he or she is 'redundant' and therefore entitled to a redundancy payment under s. 135 ERA;

- determine whether the redundancy was also unfair, in which case the employee is entitled to claim unfair dismissal compensation in addition to the redundancy payment.

[9] Mark Freedland and Nicola Kountouris, *The Legal Construction of Personal Work Relations* (OUP 2011) 433–446.

An individual is only eligible to claim a redundancy payment or to argue that his or her redundancy also constituted an unfair dismissal if he or she is an employee[10] and has worked for the employer continuously for two years.[11]

Dismissal and re-employment

To claim a redundancy payment on dismissal, the employee must be 'dismissed', defined in s. 136 in broadly similar terms as those for unfair dismissal. There are some rather complex rules designed to deal with the situation in which the employer either re-employs the employee on the same basis as before (in effect, changing its mind about the redundancy) or offers the employee alternative employment.

Under s. 138 ERA, if the employer offers the employee a new contract before the old one ends, to start within four weeks, there is no 'dismissal' for the purposes of redundancy. This prevents the employee from claiming a redundancy payment when he or she is immediately re-employed. Under s. 138(2), if the new contract differs from the old one, the employee is entitled to a 'trial period' of four weeks, during which he or she can terminate the new contract and, in effect, turn the clock back to the original termination and regard him- or herself as having been made redundant at that point.[12] However, there is a very significant limitation on the right to a redundancy payment in this situation. By virtue of s. 141(4), the employee loses the right to a redundancy payment if:

(c) the employment is suitable in relation to him, and

(d) during the trial period he unreasonably terminates the contract, or unreasonably gives notice to terminate it and it is in consequence terminated.

This means that it is for the tribunal to determine the key questions of the 'suitability' of the work and the 'reasonableness' of the employee's decision.

Similar issues arise under the remainder of s. 141, which deals with the situation in which the employer offers the employee a new contract but the employee refuses. The employee is not entitled to a redundancy payment if he or she 'unreasonably' refuses the offer and either the new job is the same as the old one, or the new job, though different, is 'suitable'.

The question of 'suitability' is to be assessed objectively by the tribunal, considering the nature of the job relative to the employee's qualifications and experience.[13] The reasonableness test in this context is not the 'band of reasonable responses' found elsewhere in dismissal law.[14] Instead, it is a subjective test, focusing on the particular employee and the facts as they appeared to him or her at the time. For example, in *Everest*, the employee refused an offer of alternative employment with the employer in a redundancy situation because she thought she was about to be offered a job with another firm.[15] It was held that she had acted reasonably even though the other firm had not made a formal offer. The two elements of the test are related, in the sense

---

[10] ERA 1996, s 135(1). See Chapter 4.
[11] ibid s 155.
[12] *Optical Express Ltd* v *Williams* [2008] ICR 1 (EAT).
[13] *Commission for Healthcare Audit & Inspection* v *Ward* (2008) UKEAT/0579/07/JOJ.
[14] *Readman* v *Devon Primary Care Trust* [2013] EWCA Civ 1110, [2013] IRLR 878.
[15] *Executors of JF Everest* v *Cox* [1980] ICR 415 (EAT).

that if the job is only 'marginally' suitable, it may be easier to find that the employee has acted reasonably in refusing it.[16]

The statutory objective here is clear: it is to encourage employers to find ways of re-deploying potentially redundant employees. This helps to protect jobs and is to be welcomed. However, it does mean that employees may have to put up with offers of re-deployment that they are not particularly happy with, because if they refuse an offer or terminate a trial period, they are at risk of losing their right to a redundancy payment if a tribunal rules that their refusal was unreasonable.

The definition of redundancy

The concept of redundancy is defined in s. 139:

(1) For the purposes of this Act an employee who is dismissed shall be taken to be dismissed by reason of redundancy if the dismissal is wholly or mainly attributable to–

(a) the fact that his employer has ceased or intends to cease–

(i) to carry on the business for the purposes of which the employee was employed by him, or

(ii) to carry on that business in the place where the employee was so employed, or

(b) the fact that the requirements of that business–

(i) for employees to carry out work of a particular kind, or

(ii) for employees to carry out work of a particular kind in the place where the employee was employed by the employer, have ceased or diminished or are expected to cease or diminish.

(2) For the purposes of subsection (1) the business of the employer together with the business or businesses of his associated employers shall be treated as one (unless either of the conditions specified in paragraphs (a) and (b) of that subsection would be satisfied without so treating them) . . .

(6) (6) In subsection (1) "cease" and "diminish" mean cease and diminish either permanently or temporarily and for whatever reason.

This definition is quite complex, in contrast to the EU definition we will examine below. This has led to some difficulties of application. In some cases, the employer will want to argue that the individual is not redundant in order to avoid having to make a redundancy payment. The employer will therefore suggest that the individual has been dismissed, fairly, for 'some other substantial reason'. Some judges have found these arguments persuasive on the ground that the requirement to make redundancy payments might deter an employer from undertaking necessary business reorganisations. In other cases, employees have sought to challenge the idea that they are redundant, either as a means of trying to get their jobs back or in order to show that their dismissal was unfair.

The statute envisages four broad redundancy scenarios:

• the employer's business (or the part for which the employee worked) shuts down altogether;

• the employer closes the workplace at which the employee worked;

---

[16] *Commission for Healthcare Audit & Inspection*, above n 13.

- the employer does not need so many (or any) people to do the work the employee is doing;

- the employer does not need so many (or any) people to do the work the employee is doing in the workplace at which the employee works.

Importantly, the employer's need of employees may already have reduced, or the employer may make people redundant in anticipation of a change in its requirements.

Some of the cases have been concerned with identifying the employee's workplace, for the purposes of the second or fourth scenario. In most cases, it is quite obvious where someone works. However, problems can arise where the employee's contract contains a 'mobility clause' entitling the employer to move him or her to a different workplace.[17] On one view, which we might call the 'factual' view, the employee is redundant if the employer's requirements have reduced at the place he or she normally works. On the alternative, 'contractual' view, the employee is not redundant where the employer's other workplaces – at which he or she could be required to work under the contract – remain open. In the leading case of *High Table* v *Horst*, the employees were employed by a firm which provided catering services at various different sites.[18] They normally worked at a particular site. When the employer's catering contract at that site was cut back, they were made redundant. They argued that they were not redundant because they could have been redeployed to another site in accordance with the contractual mobility clause. Peter Gibson LJ preferred the 'factual' approach:

> It would be unfortunate if the law were to encourage the inclusion of mobility clauses in contracts of employment to defeat genuine redundancy claims. Parliament has recognised the importance of the employee's right to a redundancy payment. If the work of the employee for his employer has involved a change of location, as would be the case where the nature of the work required the employee to go from place to place, then the contract of employment may be helpful to determine the extent of the place where the employee was employed. But it cannot be right to let the contract be the sole determinant, regardless of where the employee actually worked for the employer. The question of what the place of employment was is one that can safely be left to the good sense of the Industrial Tribunal.[19]

Although the factual approach was not the one contended for by the employees in that case, it can work in their favour. For example, in *Bass Leisure*, the claimant worked at a depot near her home.[20] The employer closed the depot and sought to relocate the claimant to another depot 20 miles away. The claimant did not want to relocate because the longer travel time to work would interfere with her child-care arrangements. The EAT upheld her claim that she was redundant, rejecting the employer's argument that her 'place of work' was anywhere she could be required under her contract to work.

A similar set of issues arises in relation to the concept of 'work of a particular kind'. What happens if the employer no longer needs so many (or any) employees to

---

[17] For discussion, see Steven Anderman, 'The Interpretation of Protective Employment Statutes and Contracts of Employment' (2000) 29 ILJ 223.

[18] [1998] ICR 409 (CA).

[19] ibid 419–420.

[20] *Bass Leisure Ltd* v *Thomas* [1994] IRLR 104 (EAT).

do X, the work normally done by the employees, but still needs employees to do Y, a type of work the employees could be obliged under their contract to undertake? The leading case on this question is the decision of the House of Lords in *Murray* v *Foyle Meats*.[21] In that case, the employers ran a slaughterhouse. The employees worked in the slaughter hall but could be required to do other kinds of work and occasionally did so. Due to a downturn in business, the employer sought to reduce the number of people employed in the slaughter hall and made the claimants redundant. They argued that they did not work specifically in the slaughter hall (since they could be required to do other work). Lord Irvine said:

> My Lords, the language . . . is in my view simplicity itself. It asks two questions of fact. The first is whether one or other of various states of economic affairs exists. In this case, the relevant one is whether the requirements of the business for employees to carry out work of a particular kind have diminished. The second question is whether the dismissal is attributable, wholly or mainly, to that state of affairs. This is a question of causation. In the present case, the tribunal found as a fact that the requirements of the business for employees to work in the slaughter hall had diminished. Secondly, they found that that state of affairs had led to the applicants being dismissed. That, in my opinion, is the end of the matter.[22]

The judges rejected both the 'factual test' and the 'contract test', holding that tribunals should focus instead on causation: did the employer's reduced requirement for employees *cause* the individual's dismissal? However, as Barnard points out, this effectively ignores the 'work of a particular kind' element altogether.[23] Later cases – like the recent decision in *Servisair* – have summed this up by focusing on whether there is a 'reduced headcount'.[24] Switching some employees from full-time to part-time contracts has also been held to constitute a 'reduced headcount' (even though the number of employees may remain the same).[25]

However, the notion of 'work of a particular kind' does occasionally play a role, particularly where the employer wants to reorganise or restructure the business or to introduce new working methods. For example, in *Shawkat*, the claimant was a thoracic surgeon who was required to do more cardiac surgery as part of a hospital reorganisation.[26] He did not want to change his job and argued that he was redundant. However, this aspect of his claim was rejected. The hospital's requirement for thoracic surgery had not diminished overall – just its requirement for the claimant to perform this type of surgery – so the facts did not disclose a redundancy situation. This was so even though the claimant's replacement did in practice carry out less thoracic surgery. Similarly, in *North Riding Garages* v *Butterwick*, the claimant was not redundant where the employer required him to do more administrative work (which he was not so good at) and less practical repair work (which he was good at) than the previous owner.[27] The employer's overall needs had not changed, and the employee was expected to adapt to the employer's requirements.

[21] [2000] 1 AC 51 (HL).
[22] ibid 56.
[23] Catherine Barnard, 'Redundant Approaches to Redundancy' (2000) 59 CLJ 36.
[24] *Servisair UK Ltd v O'Hare* (2013) UKEAT/0118/13.
[25] *Packman (t/a Packman Lucas Associates) v Fauchon* [2012] ICR 1362.
[26] *Shawkat v Nottingham City Hospital NHS Trust* [2001] EWCA Civ 954, [2002] ICR 7.
[27] [1967] 2 QB 56.

The upshot of all of this is that the statutory definition of redundancy is quite technical. In general terms, the courts regard redundancy as a situation in which the 'headcount' – the number of employees needed by the employer – is reduced. If the reduced headcount causes a particular individual's dismissal, he or she is redundant. The courts have resisted arguments that contractual 'mobility clauses' can defeat a redundancy claim, with a view to protecting employees (though the argument can sometimes work against them). And they have generally resisted arguments that business reorganisations or changes in working methods give rise to redundancy situations unless the 'reduced headcount' test is met.

There are two ways of looking at this. On the one hand, the relatively strict construction gives employers a degree of flexibility to engage in restructuring without necessarily having to make redundancy payments to people who do not like the new arrangements or are unwilling to adapt. On the other hand, if the aim of redundancy payments is to reduce employees' resistance to change, or to compensate them for dismissals that are not their fault, it might be thought that a more generous construction would be more likely to fulfil the statutory purpose.

The redundancy payment

Whether the redundancy is fair or unfair, the employee is entitled to a redundancy payment. This is calculated using the same formula used to work out the 'basic award' in an unfair dismissal claim.[28] The formula in s. 162(2) is:

(a) one and a half weeks' pay for a year of employment in which the employee was not below the age of forty-one,

(b) one week's pay for a year of employment (not within paragraph (a)) in which he was not below the age of twenty-two, and

(c) half a week's pay for each year of employment not within paragraph (a) or (b).

For these purposes, the tribunal may not take into account employment for more than 20 years.[29] A 'week's pay' is calculated in accordance with ss. 220–229, and is subject to a maximum in s. 227, currently set at £464. The maximum available is £13,920, based on the (probably unlikely) scenario of someone working 20 years for the same employer from the age of 41 onwards. An employer may agree higher redundancy payments with the employee either as part of his or her contract of employment, or when the redundancy situation arises.

Overall, then, the level of redundancy payments is quite low. Most people nowadays do not work for long periods for the same employer, thus reducing their entitlement, and the cap on the week's pay means that well-paid employees will get disproportionately low payments relative to their earnings. Those who regard redundancy payments as rather anomalous see this as a good thing. There is certainty for employers about how much they will have to pay, and there is no real risk that having to make redundancy payments will deter an employer from a necessary reorganisation of its workforce. Moreover, many employers choose to offer a better redundancy package to employees who choose to take so-called 'voluntary redundancy'. An announcement by an employer that redundancies are in prospect generally damages morale at the workplace, because people are worried

[28] See Chapter 9.
[29] ERA 1996, s 162(3).

about their jobs and wonder who will be selected. By, in effect, 'bribing' people to leave (perhaps those who were unhappy anyway, or contemplating a career change or retirement) the employer can avoid having to dismiss so many people, with a beneficial effect on the atmosphere at work. Higher statutory redundancy payments would make this harder to do. However, those who think that redundancy law should be more clearly focused on job security would no doubt argue that the payments should be higher, to force employers to think of more creative ways of dealing with a downturn, without dismissing employees.

Time off rights

An employee who is given notice of redundancy is entitled to take reasonable time off to look for work or to attend training courses under s. 52 ERA. This time off is to be paid at the employee's normal rate.[30] The employee may complain to the employment tribunal if the employer refuses to allow the time off or to pay him or her during that time.[31]

Obviously, the policy here is to ensure that employees facing redundancy have the chance of securing fresh employment without having to endure a period of unemployment, by enabling them to start their job search or to retrain before the old job comes to an end.

Is the redundancy also an unfair dismissal?

We have seen so far that an employee who is made redundant is entitled to a redundancy payment. But it is important to remember that redundancy is only a 'potentially fair' reason for dismissal under the law of unfair dismissal.[32] This means that an employee who is made redundant may also be able to argue that he or she has been unfairly dismissed. This involves showing that, in dismissing the employee for redundancy, the employer acted outside the 'band of reasonable responses'.[33]

Tribunals are not generally willing to engage in scrutiny of the employer's substantive decision to make people redundant. For example, in *James W Cook & Co (Wivenhoe) Ltd v Tipper*, the employer closed its business with the inevitable result that its employees were made redundant.[34] Neill LJ stated that:

> In my judgment it is not open to the court to investigate the commercial and economic reasons which prompted the closure.[35]

Thus, even if it is clear that the employer's irresponsible management of the business led to the redundancy situation, this is not relevant to the fairness or otherwise of the employees' dismissals.

In practice, attention focuses most closely on the employer's selection criteria to decide who to dismiss, and the procedure followed by the employer. We will examine each in turn.

[30] ibid s 53.
[31] ibid s 54.
[32] ibid s 98.
[33] *Iceland Frozen Foods v Jones* [1983] ICR 17 (EAT).
[34] [1990] ICR 716 (CA). See also *St John of God (Care Services) Ltd v Brooks* [1992] ICR 715.
[35] ibid 729.

The leading case on selection criteria is *Williams v Compair Maxam*.[36] In that case, the employer directed the managers of its various departments to draw up lists of people to be made redundant, retaining those who would be, in their view, of the greatest long-term value to the company. The EAT held that this was unfair because the choice of employees to be made redundant was left to the managers' discretion. The employer should have put in place transparent and objective selection criteria.

The reasons that make a dismissal 'automatically unfair' are generally also automatically unfair if they are used as redundancy selection criteria.[37] Thus, for example, if an employer used a redundancy situation as an excuse to get rid of trade union representatives, their redundancies would be unfair if they could prove that the employer had selected them because of their representative role.[38] This is the effect of s. 105(1) ERA 1996:

> An employee who is dismissed shall be regarded for the purposes of this Part as unfairly dismissed if–
>
> (a) the reason (or, if more than one, the principal reason) for the dismissal is that the employee was redundant,
>
> (b) it is shown that the circumstances constituting the redundancy applied equally to one or more other employees in the same undertaking who held positions similar to that held by the employee and who have not been dismissed by the employer, and
>
> (c) it is shown that any of subsections (2A) to (7N) applies.

The subsections mentioned in subsection (1)(c) list the various automatically unfair reasons to which this rule applies.

Another factor to consider is whether the redundancy selection criteria might be discriminatory, in breach of the Equality Act 2010.[39] At one time, it was common for firms to make part-timers redundant before full-timers, on the basis that the full-timers were thought to be more economically dependent on their wages. However, in *Clarke v Eley (IMI) Kynoch*, it was ruled that this constituted indirect sex discrimination because the majority of part-time workers are women.[40] More recently, in the *Rolls-Royce* case, the Court of Appeal considered a length of service criterion for redundancy in the light of the law on age discrimination.[41] It held that although the criterion discriminated against younger workers (who would not have accumulated as much service as older workers), on the facts, it was a 'proportionate means of achieving a legitimate aim':

> . . . The legitimate aim is the reward of loyalty, and the overall desirability of achieving a stable workforce in the context of a fair process of redundancy selection. The proportionate means is in my judgment amply demonstrated by the fact that the length of service criterion is only one of a substantial number of criteria for measuring employee suitability for redundancy, and that it is by no means determinative.[42]

---

[36] [1982] ICR 156 (EAT). See also *Swinburne and Jackson LLP v Simpson* (2013) UKEAT/0551/12/LA.
[37] See Chapter 9.
[38] TULRCA 1992, s 153.
[39] EA 2010, s 39.
[40] [1983] ICR 165 (EAT).
[41] *Rolls-Royce Plc v Unite the Union* [2009] EWCA Civ 387, [2010] ICR 1.
[42] ibid [100].

This does not mean that it is always fair to use length of service as a criterion, though. As the Court of Appeal made clear, the limited weight given to the criterion was important in its finding that the employer had satisfied the proportionality test. Moreover, length of service should also be examined closely from a sex discrimination perspective since women are more likely to take breaks and thus find it harder to accrue long service.[43]

Finally, it is important that the employer applies the objective selection criteria fairly. This should normally include giving the employee information about the criteria and an opportunity to challenge the way in which they have been applied to him or her. However, there are limits to the role of tribunals here and it is not regarded as part of the tribunal's role to review the scores given to a particular employee, provided that the overall process is within the band of reasonable responses.[44] Nor will redundant employees generally be allowed to see the scores given to other employees who were not selected for redundancy, even though this might help to reveal unfairness in the application of the criteria.[45]

The courts also consider the employer's redundancy procedure more generally when determining whether a redundancy is fair. They examine the consultation process leading up to the redundancies, the employer's choice of the pool of employees from which to select for redundancy, and the possibility of offering alternative employment.

As we shall see, EU law imposes obligations on employers to consult the workforce about impending redundancies where larger numbers of people are to be made redundant. However, there is also a purely domestic obligation to consult as a result, again, of the decision in *Williams* v *Compair Maxam*.[46] In that case, the employer simply announced redundancies without any prior notification or consultation with the claimants' union. The EAT held that, for a redundancy to be fair, the employer should give as much warning as possible and should consult with the union representing the workforce. Although the EAT did not address the situation of non-unionised workplaces, because it was not relevant to the decision in the case, the obligation to consult may involve talking to other suitable representatives or to the employees themselves.[47]

A second issue is the choice of the 'pool' of employees from which to select for redundancy. When an employer decides to go ahead with redundancies, it often identifies a group of people – referred to as the 'pool' – who are at risk of dismissal, and then makes a selection from within that group. The choice of pool may determine who is to be made redundant, so employees often argue that the employer should have looked at a broader range of people and that its failure to do so makes their redundancies unfair.[48] Tribunals are entitled to consider whether the employer's choice of pool is reasonable but may not substitute their judgment for that of the employer on this matter.[49] Importantly, although pools are common in practice, there is no reason why an employer may not simply make one person redundant without setting up any kind of pool.[50]

---

[43] See (in the context of pay) Case C-17/05 *Cadman* v *Health and Safety Executive* [2006] ECR I-9583.
[44] *Nicholls* v *Rockwell Automation Ltd* (2012) UKEAT/0540/11/SM.
[45] *British Aerospace plc* v *Green* [1995] ICR 1006 (CA).
[46] *Williams* (n 36).
[47] *Rowell* v *Hubbard Group Services Ltd* [1995] IRLR 195 (EAT).
[48] As we saw above, they may also use this to argue that they are not redundant at all.
[49] *Kvaerner* v *Parker* (2003) UKEAT/0444/03/RN.
[50] *Wrexham Golf Co Ltd* v *Ingham* (2012) UKEAT/0190/12/RN.

Finally, tribunals consider whether the employer thought about offering the employees to be made redundant a different job within the employing firm. The *Williams* case is authority for the proposition that the employer must take reasonable steps to consider whether alternative employment can be offered.[51] Again, though, it is not generally permissible for a tribunal to challenge an employer's claim that no vacancies exist.[52]

To sum up, as in many areas of unfair dismissal law, an important body of jurisprudence has built up around what makes a redundancy fair, focusing on the selection criteria and the procedure followed by the employer. However, it is always necessary to go back to the underlying statutory obligation on the employer, which is to act reasonably (or within the 'band of reasonable responses' as interpreted in the *Iceland* case).[53] As a result, it is wrong to treat the various elements of a fair procedure identified in the case-law as a binding 'code' for employers to follow.

Claiming the redundancy payment

Under s. 164, if the employer does not make the redundancy payment voluntarily, the employee must take steps to claim it within six months of the date of termination, by giving notice in writing to the employer or issuing proceedings in the employment tribunal. A tribunal may award a redundancy payment even if the employee does not claim in time if it considers it 'just and equitable' to do so.[54] When the employer makes the payment, it must give the employee a written statement explaining how the redundancy payment has been calculated.[55] Failure to do so is, unusually, a criminal offence under s. 165.

If the employee is unable to obtain the payment to which he or she is entitled from the employer, it may be possible to get the money from the government under s. 166(1):

> Where an employee claims that his employer is liable to pay to him an employer's payment and either–
>
> (a) that the employee has taken all reasonable steps, other than legal proceedings, to recover the payment from the employer and the employer has refused or failed to pay it, or has paid part of it and has refused or failed to pay the balance, or
>
> (b) that the employer is insolvent and the whole or part of the payment remains unpaid,
>
> the employee may apply to the Secretary of State for a payment under this section.

Payments are made by the Redundancy Payments Service, part of the Insolvency Service, from the National Insurance fund. The government acquires the right to pursue the employer for payment if it makes a payment to the employee.[56] We will examine employees' other rights if their employer becomes insolvent below.

---

[51] *Williams* (n 36), 162, 166–167.
[52] For discussion of the proper approach to alternative employment, see *Virgin Media Ltd v Seddington* (2009) UKEAT/0539/08/DM.
[53] *Iceland* (n 33).
[54] ERA 1996, s 164(2).
[55] ibid s 165(1).
[56] ibid s 167.

Redundancy in lay-off or short time cases

The vast majority of claims for redundancy payments nowadays arise in dismissal situations. However, the statute also makes provision for redundancy payments in cases of lay-off or short time: in effect, when the employee remains employed but there is no work, or less work than usual, for him or her to do. Many employers now deal with fluctuating demand by using agency workers or casual workers on an 'as required' basis. Since people doing these types of work are unlikely to be the employer's employees in law, they do not benefit from this set of statutory provisions. Although they may seem old-fashioned and irrelevant, it is worth knowing a bit about them because they show what a more worker-protective regime can look like.

The concepts of lay-off and short time are defined in s. 147 ERA 1996 as follows:

(1) For the purposes of this Part an employee shall be taken to be laid off for a week if–

    (a) he is employed under a contract on terms and conditions such that his remuneration under the contract depends on his being provided by the employer with work of the kind which he is employed to do, but

    (b) he is not entitled to any remuneration under the contract in respect of the week because the employer does not provide such work for him.

(2) For the purposes of this Part an employee shall be taken to be kept on short-time for a week if by reason of a diminution in the work provided for the employee by his employer (being work of a kind which under his contract the employee is employed to do) the employee's remuneration for the week is less than half a week's pay.

The employee must resign his or her job, and claim the payment within four weeks of qualifying for it.[57] The employee qualifies by being laid off or kept on short time for four consecutive weeks or for six weeks (of which no more than three may be consecutive) within a period of 13 weeks.[58] If the employer contests the claim, the employee must take his or her case to the employment tribunal.[59] The employee is not entitled to claim if it was 'reasonably to be expected' that he or she would cease to be laid off or kept on short time within four weeks of the claim, provided that the work would last for at least 13 weeks.[60]

These provisions are rather complex. In particular, the fact that the employee may not claim if there is a prospect of the short time or lay-off situation coming to an end is difficult because it requires the tribunal to predict an uncertain future. They are also not particularly worker-protective in the sense that the employee must resign in order to claim. However, the rules do prevent avoidance of the redundancy payments rules by employers, who might otherwise try to drive people out by keeping them on short time instead of dismissing them and making redundancy payments. They also allow enterprising employees at a failing firm to get a job elsewhere without forfeiting their redundancy payments.

---

[57] ERA 1996, s 150.
[58] ibid s 148(2).
[59] ibid s 149.
[60] ibid s 152(1).

10.3.2 Collective redundancies

So far, we have focused on the domestic law relating to individual redundancies, and on the individual's right to claim a redundancy payment and to challenge the fairness of his or her redundancy. This law includes some obligation on the employer to consult employees and their union or other representatives about the impending redundancies, derived from the case-law and based on the general requirement on the employer to act reasonably. EU law also imposes obligations on employers to engage in redundancy consultation but only in the event of redundancies on a relatively large scale. We will consider the relevant Directive and its implementation in this section.

The duty to consult on collective redundancies originates from Directive 75/129/EEC and is currently found in Directive 98/59/EC. The original directive was enacted at a time of significant economic change in the EU, as traditional manufacturing industries began to decline and new employment opportunities gradually took their place. The directive was part of a package of measures designed to smooth the transition by reducing workers' resistance to change.[61] The directive is purely procedural in nature. Although the consultation process might result in a decision by the employer to reduce the number of redundancies (or even to avoid them altogether), the directive itself is satisfied simply by consulting with worker representatives. The directive is currently implemented in English law by ss. 188–198B TULRCA 1992.

The Directive defines 'redundancies' ('dismissals effected by an employer for one or more reasons not related to the individual workers concerned')[62] but leaves the definition of 'collective' to the discretion of the Member States. The number may be:

    (i) either, over a period of 30 days:

        – at least 10 in establishments normally employing more than 20 and less than 100 workers,

        – at least 10% of the number of workers in establishments normally employing at least 100 but less than 300 workers,

        – at least 30 in establishments normally employing 300 workers or more,

    (ii) or, over a period of 90 days, at least 20, whatever the number of workers normally employed in the establishments in question.[63]

The UK has chosen the second of these options: at least 20 redundancies over a 90-day period.[64]

However, s. 188(1) uses the phrase 'at one establishment'. In the *Ethel Austin* case, a chain of clothes shops became insolvent and it was held that the employer had failed to consult on the impending redundancies.[65] Some of the shops had more than 20 employees; others did not. In the employment tribunal, only the employees in the shops with more than 20 employees were held to be entitled to compensation in respect of the failure to consult. The EAT held that this did not give effect to the Directive and that a purposive construction should be adopted in which the employer's entire retail business could be regarded as one 'establishment'.[66] In order to prevent

---

[61] Kenner, above n 7.
[62] Council Directive 98/59/EC of 20 July 1998 on the approximation of the laws of the Member States relating to collective redundancies, [1998] OJ L225/16, art 1(1).
[63] ibid art 1(1)(a).
[64] TULRCA, s 188(1).
[65] *USDAW v Ethel Austin Ltd* [2013] ICR 1300 (EAT).
[66] ibid [49]–[56].

problems in future cases, the EAT also held that the words 'at one establishment' should be, in effect, deleted from s. 188. At the time of writing, the Court of Appeal has referred the matter to the Court of Justice of the European Union (CJEU) for decision.[67]

The identity of the representatives with whom the employer must consult is a matter for the Member States, though their discretion in this regard is not wholly unfettered. Initially, the UK government required consultation with representatives of recognised trade unions, these being the only type of representative known to the law in the 1970s. However, in an important ruling, the Court of Justice held that the UK had failed to implement the directive in respect of the many workplaces in which there was no recognised trade union.[68] As a result, the UK government was forced to amend the law to make provision for consultation with non-union representatives in workplaces with no union. This was the beginning of the shift away from the UK's 'single-channel' tradition of representation.[69] For a time, the law offered employers a choice between consulting union and non-union representatives, a highly controversial move which threatened to undermine unions by enabling employers to consult with (potentially less powerful) non-union representatives in redundancy situations. Nowadays, the law gives unions priority under s. 188(1B):

> For the purposes of this section the appropriate representatives of any affected employees are–
>
> (a) if the employees are of a description in respect of which an independent trade union is recognised by their employer, representatives of the trade union, or
>
> (b) in any other case, whichever of the following employee representatives the employer chooses:–
>
>   (i) employee representatives appointed or elected by the affected employees otherwise than for the purposes of this section, who (having regard to the purposes for and the method by which they were appointed or elected) have authority from those employees to receive information and to be consulted about the proposed dismissals on their behalf;
>
>   (ii) employee representatives elected by the affected employees, for the purposes of this section, in an election satisfying the requirements of section 188A(1).

This achieves a better 'fit' between the requirement to consult on redundancies and the established role of trade unions in some workplaces. However, there remains a problem with sub-paragraph (b), which allows the employer to undermine well-established consultation mechanisms (such as a works council) by getting the affected employees to elect ad hoc representatives instead. The requirements for election in s. 188A are relatively minimal. The election can be run by the employer without independent supervision, and matters such as the number of representatives are for the employer to determine.

A matter of particular difficulty in both EU and domestic law has been the timing of the consultation process. The earlier it takes place, the greater the impact the representatives are likely to have on the decision. Once the employer's mind is made up, the consultation process may just be a formality. However, employers are unlikely

[67] [2014] EWCA Civ 142, [2014] 2 CMLR 45.
[68] Case C-383/92 *Commission v UK* [1994] ECR 1-2479 (collective redundancies).
[69] Paul Davies and Claire Kilpatrick, 'UK Worker Representation after Single Channel' (2004) 33 ILJ 121.

to want to raise the question of redundancies – which can impact badly on morale – unless they are fairly sure that they will go ahead. Under Article 2(1) of the Directive:

> Where an employer is *contemplating* collective redundancies, he shall begin consultations with the workers' representatives *in good time* with a view to reaching an agreement.[70]

In many cases, the employer's decision is a commercial one – to close a factory, for example – which then triggers a need to make people redundant. In the *AEK* case, the Court of Justice held that:

> [t]he consultation procedure must be started by the employer once a strategic or commercial decision compelling him to contemplate or plan for collective redundancies has been taken.[71]

In other words, there is no need to begin redundancy consultation when contemplating a factory closure, even if redundancies are an inevitable consequence of that decision. This is quite problematic because the opportunity to change the employer's mind may already have passed when consultation starts. However, the Court was concerned not to impose consultation obligations on employers at too early a stage before they had considered the workforce implications.[72]

The timing problem is exacerbated in English law by the language used in implementing the directive. TULRCA s. 188 uses the phrase '[w]here an employer is *proposing* to dismiss as redundant' (emphasis added), which many people believe implies that consultation should begin at a later stage in the employer's thought process than when redundancies are 'contemplated' as stated in the Directive.[73] The English courts have accepted that s. 188 fails to implement the Directive in this regard, but have held that it is impossible, without distortion, to construe 'proposing' to mean 'contemplating'.[74] Because directives do not have horizontal direct effect, they cannot be relied upon by employees against (private sector) employers. The EAT in the recent case of *Kelly* v *Hesley* suggested that the effect of *AEK* might be to reduce the distinction between 'proposing' and 'contemplating', though this is not the only possible reading of *AEK*.[75] Although the issue was referred to the Court of Justice by the Court of Appeal in *USA* v *Nolan*, the issue remains unresolved because the Court refused to hear the case for unrelated technical reasons.[76]

TULRCA s. 188 now provides, in subsection (1A):

> The consultation shall begin in good time and in any event–
>
> (a) where the employer is proposing to dismiss 100 or more employees as mentioned in subsection (1), at least 45 days, and
>
> (b) otherwise, at least 30 days,

before the first of the dismissals takes effect.

---

[70] Emphasis added.
[71] Case C-44/08 *Akavan Erityisalojen Keskusliitto AEK ry* v *Fujitsu Siemens Computors Oy* [2009] ECR I-8163 [48]. See also *UK Coal Mining Ltd* v *National Union of Mineworkers (Northumberland Area)* [2008] ICR 163 (EAT).
[72] ibid [37]–[47].
[73] Directive 98/59/EC, art 2(1).
[74] *MSF* v *Refuge Assurance Plc* [2002] ICR 1365 (EAT).
[75] [2013] IRLR 514 [18].
[76] Case C-583/10 [2013] ICR 193. For the latest development in the case at the time of writing, see *United States of America* v *Nolan* [2014] EWCA Civ 71, [2014] ICR 685.

The law was changed in 2013 to provide for a 45-day consultation period for large-scale redundancies instead of the previous 90-day period.[77] The government resisted calls from businesses to reduce the time period to 30 days across the board.[78] However, it did accept the argument that 90 days was too long, leading to uncertainty and reduced morale, and adopted 45 days as the compromise. The Directive simply requires consultation to begin 'in good time',[79] so there may be some room for argument as to whether the government's decision to specify time periods is a legitimate exercise of its discretion to implement the Directive.

Reflecting the language of the Directive,[80] s. 188(2) provides that:

> The consultation shall include consultation about ways of–
>
> (a) avoiding the dismissals,
> (b) reducing the numbers of employees to be dismissed, and
> (c) mitigating the consequences of the dismissals,
>
> and shall be undertaken by the employer with a view to reaching agreement with the appropriate representatives.

It is important that the employer consults on all three elements. In *Middlesbrough BC v TGWU*, the employer was found to be in breach of its duty because it had already made up its mind that redundancies were necessary and had only consulted on the practicalities.[81] Nonetheless, this may be difficult to reconcile in practice with the issue discussed above about the timing of consultation: the later the process begins, the harder it is likely to be to persuade the employer that redundancies are unnecessary. The provision adopts – in accordance with the Directive – a 'strong' definition of consultation, 'with a view to reaching agreement', but this does not require the employer to succeed in reaching an agreement with the representatives.[82] Under s. 188(4), and in accordance with the Directive, the employer is obliged to provide quite a detailed list of information to the representatives in writing. The employer need not comply with the full consultation requirements where there are 'special circumstances', but in the *Clarks of Hove* case the Court of Appeal construed this restrictively, holding that it referred to something 'out of the ordinary'.[83] The employer's insolvency after last-ditch attempts to save it did not count as 'special circumstances'.

The duty to consult under s. 188 is enforced by means of proceedings in the employment tribunal. The appropriate claimant depends on the nature of the employer's alleged breach, under s. 189(1):

> Where an employer has failed to comply with a requirement of section 188 or section 188A, a complaint may be presented to an employment tribunal on that ground–
>
> (a) in the case of a failure relating to the election of employee representatives, by any of the affected employees or by any of the employees who have been dismissed as redundant;

---

[77] Words substituted by TULRCA 1992 (Amendment) Order 2013, SI 2013/763, art 3(2).
[78] DBIS, *Collective Redundancies: Government Response to Consultation on Changes to the Rules* (December 2012) (BIS/12/1352).
[79] Directive 98/59/EC, art 2(2).
[80] ibid art 2(1).
[81] [2002] IRLR 332 (EAT).
[82] TULRCA 1992, s 188(2).
[83] *Clarks of Hove Ltd v Bakers Union* [1978] ICR 1076.

(b) in the case of any other failure relating to employee representatives, by any of the employee representatives to whom the failure related,

(c) in the case of failure relating to representatives of a trade union, by the trade union, and

(d) in any other case, by any of the affected employees or by any of the employees who have been dismissed as redundant.

The remedy is a declaration and also a 'protective award' of up to 90 days' pay for the employees who were made redundant or whose redundancy was proposed.[84] The courts have held that where the employer fails to consult altogether, the starting-point is the maximum award of 90 days' pay, unless the employer can make a plausible argument that the sum should be reduced.[85] Critics point out that – despite the courts' strict approach – some employers might prefer simply to pay the money rather than to engage in meaningful consultation. A more demanding strategy would be to bar employers from making people redundant until they had completed the consultation process but, not surprisingly, this idea has met with strong resistance from employers.[86]

10.4 CHANGES OF OWNERSHIP

In this section, we will consider what happens when a business changes hands. This is generally a worrying time for the workforce, because the new owner's policies are unknown and because their jobs may be at risk. The Acquired Rights Directive (ARD),[87] implemented by the Transfer of Undertakings (Protection of Employment) Regulations (TUPE),[88] pursues three main goals. First, it seeks to preserve people's jobs by enabling them to transfer from the old employer to the new one (if they want to), subject to an exception for the employer where there is a legitimate business reason for dismissals. Second, it seeks to preserve existing terms and conditions of employment, and collective bargaining arrangements, for the transferred workforce. And third, it tries to ensure that the workforces of both the old and new employer are consulted about the proposed transfer.

As with the other EU directives we are considering in this chapter, job security is probably not the primary aim of the ARD.[89] It was enacted during a significant economic downturn in the European economy. At such times, changes of business ownership become common as firms seek to acquire unsuccessful competitors, or to shed unprofitable elements of their own business. Rather like the Collective Redundancies Directive, the ARD can be seen as a means of reducing workforce resistance to change, in particular, through its emphasis on keeping people informed. However, there is some evidence of job security as a subsidiary aim. The ARD does

---

[84] TULRCA 1992, s 189(3)–(4).

[85] *Susie Radin Ltd* v *GMB* [2004] EWCA Civ 180, [2004] ICR 893.

[86] Brian Bercusson, *European Labour Law* (2nd edn, CUP 2009) 492.

[87] Council Directive 2001/23/EC of 12 March 2001 on the approximation of the laws of Member States relating to the safeguarding of employees' rights in the event of transfers of undertakings, businesses or parts of undertakings or businesses [2001] OJ L82/16.

[88] TUPE 2006, SI 2006/246, as amended. See, generally, John McMullen, 'An Analysis of the Transfer of Undertakings (Protection of Employment) Regulations 2006' (2006) 35 ILJ 113; 'TUPE: Ringing the (Wrong) Changes. The Collective Redundancies and Transfer of Undertakings (Protection of Employment) (Amendment) Regulations 2014' (2014) 43 ILJ 149.

[89] Kenner, above n 7.

prohibit the use of the transfer itself as an excuse to dismiss people, but at the same time it allows the old and new employers to dismiss people where there are economic reasons for doing so. This balance between preserving jobs and facilitating transfers is quite a delicate one, so the Directive attracts criticism from both sides: for not protecting job security strongly enough, and for putting obstacles in the way of economically valuable transfers.

A second important point to bear in mind before we look at the Directive in detail is that its drafting is relatively vague (though it has become somewhat more precise over time), thus leaving quite a lot of scope for the CJEU to interpret its content. Important concepts, including the concept of a transfer itself, have been developed (more or less successfully) by the Court.

Finally, it is important to be aware of the Directive's impact in the UK. Many UK businesses change hands by sale of shares. This means that the legal identity of the employer company remains the same, but the underlying ownership changes because the old owners sell their shares to the new owners. Of course, the new owners may have different ideas about employment practices, but the ARD and TUPE do not apply. The ARD and TUPE regime is only applicable where a business or part of a business is sold to a new owner which becomes the employer, so that the legal identity of the employer changes. This limits the Directive's impact. However, the Directive also has an important role to play in 'contracting out' situations. Contracting out is a popular policy in the UK public sector: local councils use private firms to collect the rubbish, for example, or the NHS uses private firms to do catering or cleaning in hospitals. In a series of important decisions, the CJEU has held that the ARD applies to various different types of contracting-out situations. Thus, although the Directive has had a limited (but not wholly insignificant) effect on private sector transactions, it is quite important when private firms get involved in the delivery of public services.

10.4.1 The common law position

At common law, if the employer sells the business without first taking steps to dismiss the employees, the sale itself will constitute a repudiatory breach of the contract of employment, giving rise to an action for wrongful dismissal.[90] This is because a contract of employment is personal on both sides: just as an employee cannot send someone else to do his or her work, an employer cannot substitute another employer for itself (even though nowadays, in practice, most people are employed by legal persons such as companies rather than individual human beings, making this analysis rather artificial). Whether the termination of the contract is also actionable as an unfair dismissal would depend on the circumstances.

The termination of the contract does mean that the employees are free to take up employment with the new owner of the business. However, whether to hire them is entirely a decision for the new owner and would involve the offer of a new contract of employment, potentially on entirely different terms and conditions.

---

[90] *Litster v Forth Dry Dock & Engineering Co Ltd* [1990] 1 AC 546 (HL) 568 (Lord Oliver).

10.4.2 When does the ARD/TUPE apply?

We will begin by considering the scope of application of the ARD and TUPE. We will consider the personal scope of the rules – the people who are protected by them – before examining the meaning of a 'transfer of the undertaking'. We will also examine how the rules apply in insolvency situations.

Personal scope

As with most Directives, the ARD leaves to the national authorities the definition of who is protected.[91] In TUPE, the term used is 'employee' and the definition is:

> "employee" means any individual who works for another person whether under a contract of service or apprenticeship or otherwise but does not include anyone who provides services under a contract for services and references to a person's employer shall be construed accordingly . . . [92]

This is an interesting definition. It excludes the self-employed (because of the reference to contracts for services) but is clearly broader than the classical 'employee' definition because of the inclusion of the phrase 'or otherwise'.[93] This suggests that some people who would fall under the 'worker' definition would be protected by TUPE, though this depends on whether a worker's contract is properly regarded as a contract for services or not, a matter which is currently far from clear. In any event, the unfair dismissal elements of TUPE can only apply to employees by virtue of reg. 7(6), which makes it clear that the only possible claimants are those who would be eligible under 'normal' unfair dismissal law.

Transfer of an undertaking

TUPE applies to 'a transfer of an undertaking, business or part of an undertaking or business situated immediately before the transfer in the United Kingdom'.[94]

The simplest form of transfer is where the new owner (the transferee) buys a business or part of a business from the old owner (the transferor). For example, company A might sell its unsuccessful manufacturing division to company B, or it might contract out its office cleaning to company B, or it might decide to bring the office cleaning back in-house from company B. All of these are relatively straightforward transfer situations. However, in some important rulings, the Court has expanded the concept of a transfer in various ways. First, the Court has held that there need not be any direct contractual relationship between the transferor and the transferee.[95] So, if company A contracts out its office cleaning to company B, then later invites other firms to bid for the contract and replaces company B with company C, there is a transfer situation between B and C even though there is no direct relationship between them.

---

[91] Directive 2001/23/EC, art 2(1)(d).
[92] TUPE 2006, reg 2.
[93] See Chapter 4.
[94] TUPE 2006, reg 3(1)(a).
[95] Case C-171/94 *Merckx* v *Ford Motors Co Belgium SA* [1996] ECR I-1253.

The rules are limited in their application to the public sector because of the exclusion, in Article 1(1)(c) ARD and reg. 3(5) TUPE, of an 'administrative reorganisation of public administrative authorities or the transfer of administrative functions between public administrative authorities'. However, this only excludes purely public situations: where the government abolishes a public body and transfers its activities to another public body. For example, in *Henke*, a group of municipal authorities pooled their administrative functions, so that some of their staff were transferred from their employment to a collective body.[96] The CJEU held that the Directive did not apply to this situation. In the UK, the government tends to apply equivalent protections even where the situation falls outside the ARD. There is a Cabinet Office code of practice on the matter[97] and under the Employment Relations Act 1999, s. 38, the Secretary of State has the power to make regulations to extend TUPE protections to otherwise excluded situations.

Under reg. 3(4)(a), the Regulations apply to 'public and private undertakings engaged in economic activities whether or not they are operating for gain'. This is taken from Article 1(1)(c) of the Directive. This means that transfers – even between public bodies – are caught where the activity in question does not relate to the exercise of public powers and might be in competition between private firms. So, for example, if public authority A contracts out its school catering contract to private company B, this situation constitutes a transfer covered by the rules.[98] Indeed, the CJEU has gone further, holding that legislative or administrative acts of public authorities, not just contracts placed by them, may give rise to transfer situations. For example, a transfer may take place when a public service is privatised[99] or where a public authority awards a grant to charity B instead of charity A.[100]

Transferor and transferee

The transferor is the person (natural or legal) who 'ceases to be the employer'[101] and the transferee is the person (natural or legal) who 'becomes the employer'.[102]

However, it is worth noting that the CJEU has adopted a broad and purposive understanding of the 'transferor' concept. In the *Albron* case, the employees worked for a group of companies.[103] They were all employed by one company within the group (the 'contractual employer') and assigned by that company to work at other companies in the group (referred to in the case as the 'non-contractual employer'). The claimant was then transferred by the 'non-contractual employer' to another company outside the group. He argued that the ARD should apply. The Court held that the 'non-contractual employer' could be regarded as the transferor for the purposes of the Directive. The Court reasoned that the Directive only requires the transferor to be in an 'employment relationship' with the employees, and thus does not assume that the transferor is their contractual employer. This helps to ensure the effective application of the Directive in complex corporate structures.

---

[96] Case C-298/94 *Henke v Gemeinde Schierke* [1996] ECR I-4989.
[97] Cabinet Office, *Staff Transfers in the Public Sector: Statement of Practice* (December 2013).
[98] Case C-108/10 *Scattolon v Ministero dell'Istruzione, dell'Università e della Ricerca* [2011] ECR I-7491.
[99] Case C-4/01 *Martin v South Bank University* [2003] ECR I-12859.
[100] Case C-29/91 *Dr Sophie Redmond Stichting v Bartol* [1992] ECR I-3189.
[101] Directive 2001/23/EC, art 2(1)(a); TUPE 2006, reg 2.
[102] ibid art 2(1)(b); TUPE 2006, reg 2.
[103] Case C-242/09 *Albron Catering BV v FNV Bondgenoten* [2011] ICR 373.

Entity

We have seen that the concepts of undertaking, transfer and transferor are defined in broad terms in EU law. We are now in a position to consider the object of the transfer: the 'economic entity'. The CJEU's approach to this concept has been the subject of much criticism. English law tries to avoid some of the problems associated with the case-law through the concept of 'service provision change' in TUPE, which we will examine in the next section.

A good starting-point is Article 1(1)(b) ARD:

> [T]here is a transfer within the meaning of this Directive where there is a transfer of an economic entity which retains its identity, meaning an organised grouping of resources which has the objective of pursuing an economic activity, whether or not that activity is central or ancillary . . . [104]

This definition codifies the Court's decision in the *Süzen* case.[105] The claimant in the case was a school cleaner who lost her job when the school terminated the cleaning contract with the company employing her and awarded it to another company. As we saw above, there is a transfer in this situation, but the Court also insisted that there must be a transfer of an identifiable 'entity'.

To decide that question, the Court drew a distinction between 'asset-intensive' and 'labour-intensive' businesses.[106] If the business is 'asset-intensive', the 'entity' consists of the assets of the business and a relevant transfer only takes place if the new owner takes on the assets. If the business is 'labour-intensive', the 'entity' consists of the workforce, and a relevant transfer only takes place if the new owner takes on the workforce. In *Süzen* itself, the cleaning contract was classified as labour-intensive, and since the transferee had not hired the claimant, she could not bring a claim *in respect of losing her job*. This is a ridiculous position for the law to adopt, for three reasons.[107]

First, the Court's approach offers transferees a simple route to avoiding the application of the rules: if a transferee is buying a labour-intensive business, but does not want to be bound by the ARD, it can simply refuse to take the workforce on, and if a transferee is buying an asset-intensive business, but does not want to be bound by the ARD, it can simply refuse to buy the transferor's assets. Of course, this may not work in all cases – the transferee may not be able to predict how the Court would classify the entity, or the transferee may not be able to run the contract without taking on some of the workers or assets. Nevertheless, it is a significant risk at least some of the time. Second, even if the transferee is not seeking to avoid the rules, the workers may lose their protection for reasons that are hard to justify. For example, in *Oy Liikenne*, a city decided to award a contract for bus services to a new operator.[108] The new operator chose to buy new buses instead of taking on the previous contractor's old ones. The business was classified as asset-intensive, with the effect that the transferee's decision to buy new buses meant that the rules did not apply and the workforce lost its protection. The decision to buy new buses may have been made for a variety of reasons and it seems unfair to make the workers' rights

---

[104] Replicated in TUPE 2006, reg 3.
[105] Case C-13/95 *Süzen v Zehnacker Gebäudereinigung GmbH Krankenhausservice* [1997] ECR I-1259.
[106] ibid [14], [18], [21].
[107] Paul Davies, 'Taken to the Cleaners? Contracting Out of Services Yet Again' (1997) 26 ILJ 193.
[108] Case C-172/99 *Oy Liikenne AB v Liskojarvi* [2001] ECR I-745.

depend on that decision. Third, the distinction between labour- and asset-intensive activities is not always easy to apply. In *Abler*, a case involving the termination and re-tendering of a hospital catering contract, the new contractor took over the hospital kitchen but not the staff.[109] It argued that there was no transfer because catering is labour-intensive, but the Court disagreed, finding that catering was asset-intensive. This means that, even where the transferee is trying to do the right thing, it may not be easy to work out what the law requires.

So far, we have focused on the case-law determining whether an 'entity' has been transferred. But the 'entity' must also 'retain its identity'.[110] The Court has focused on this latter requirement in some of the recent cases involving labour-intensive transfers. Often, the transferee will want to integrate the newly acquired workers into its existing business structures. Importantly, the Court has held that this does not preclude a finding that the rules apply (because, again, this would offer an easy route to avoidance). However, under the ruling in *Klarenberg*, there must be a 'functional link between the various elements transferred' and they must be used by the transferee 'to pursue an identical or analogous economic activity'.[111] This raises the prospect that the rules may not apply if the transferee uses the newly acquired workforce to do different tasks.

Service provision change

Initially, TUPE simply contained the same definition of a transfer as that found in the Directive. The English courts struggled to apply the *Süzen* test to labour-intensive businesses, and sometimes fell back on the older EU case-law.[112] This generated considerable uncertainty. In an important amendment in 2006, the government added the concept of a 'service provision change' (SPC) to the existing definition.[113] This goes beyond what is strictly required by EU law and was designed to offer greater protection to employees and greater certainty for employers.[114] However, critics argue that it is unnecessary 'gold-plating' and inhibits legitimate commercial activity.

It is worth setting out the SPC definition in full, in the context of the 'classic' definition of a transfer.

(1) These Regulations apply to–

    (a) a transfer of an undertaking, business or part of an undertaking or business situated immediately before the transfer in the United Kingdom to another person where there is a transfer of an economic entity which retains its identity;

    (b) a service provision change, that is a situation in which–

        (i) activities cease to be carried out by a person ("a client") on his own behalf and are carried out instead by another person on the client's behalf ("a contractor");

---

[109] Case C-340/01 *Alber v Sodexho MM Catering GmbH* [2003] ECR I-14023.

[110] ARD, art 1(1)(b); TUPE 2006, reg 3.

[111] Case C-466/07 *Klarenberg v Ferrotron Technologies GmbH* [2009] ECR I-803.

[112] *ECM (Vehicle Delivery) Ltd v Cox* [1999] ICR 1162 (CA); *RCO Support Services Ltd v Unison* [2002] EWCA Civ 464, [2002] ICR 751.

[113] TUPE 2006, reg 2(1). For discussion see, generally, Charles Wynn-Evans, 'In Defence of Service Provision Changes?' (2013) 42 ILJ 152.

[114] This is permitted by the directive: Case C-458/12 *Amatori v Telecom Italia SpA* [2014] IRLR 400.

(ii) activities cease to be carried out by a contractor on a client's behalf (whether or not those activities had previously been carried out by the client on his own behalf) and are carried out instead by another person ("a subsequent contractor") on the client's behalf; or

(iii) activities cease to be carried out by a contractor or a subsequent contractor on a client's behalf (whether or not those activities had previously been carried out by the client on his own behalf) and are carried out instead by the client on his own behalf,

and in which the conditions set out in paragraph (3) are satisfied.

(2) In this regulation "economic entity" means an organised grouping of resources which has the objective of pursuing an economic activity, whether or not that activity is central or ancillary.

(2A) References in paragraph (1)(b) to activities being carried out instead by another person (including the client) are to activities which are fundamentally the same as the activities carried out by the person who has ceased to carry them out.

(3) The conditions referred to in paragraph (1)(b) are that–

(a) immediately before the service provision change–

(i) there is an organised grouping of employees situated in Great Britain which has as its principal purpose the carrying out of the activities concerned on behalf of the client;

(ii) the client intends that the activities will, following the service provision change, be carried out by the transferee other than in connection with a single specific event or task of short-term duration; and

(b) the activities concerned do not consist wholly or mainly of the supply of goods for the client's use.[115]

Because the SPC is a domestic concept, there is – in theory at least – no need to interpret it purposively in order to achieve the purposes of the ARD. This was confirmed by Elias LJ in *McCarrick v Hunter*:

> There are no underlying EU provisions against which the statute has to be measured. The concept of a change of service provision is not complex and there is no reason to think that the language does not accurately define the range of situations which the draftsman intended to fall within the scope of this purely domestic protection.[116]

Thus, when the courts are interpreting the 'classic' definition of a transfer, they must do so with reference to the ARD, whereas the interpretation of the SPC is a straightforward matter of statutory construction. A particular fact situation may give rise either to a classic transfer, or an SPC, or both.

The SPC covers the three main types of outsourcing activity: contracting out (reg. 3(1)(b)(i)); change of contractor (reg. 3(1)(b)(ii)); and contracting in (reg. 3(1)(b)(iii)). The definition uses the term 'client' to describe the person who is receiving the services. This person may be the transferor (in contracting out) or the transferee (in contracting in) or neither (in a change of contractor situation). The SPC concept only

---

[115] ibid reg 3.
[116] [2012] EWCA Civ 1399, [2013] ICR 235 [22]. For discussion, see John McMullen, 'Service Provision Change Under TUPE: Not Quite What We Thought' (2012) 41 ILJ 471.

applies where the client remains the same throughout.[117] There are four further conditions that must be met:

- there must be 'an organised grouping of employees situated in Great Britain which has as its principal purpose the carrying out of the activities concerned on behalf of the client' (reg. 3(3)(a)(i))

- the client and the transferee are entering into a long-term arrangement (reg. 3(3)(a)(ii))

- the activities in question must be the provision of services rather than the supply of goods (reg. 3(3)(b))

- the activities before and after the transfer must be 'fundamentally the same' (new reg. 3(2A), introduced in 2014)

The second and third requirements are quite straightforward. There is no SPC where the client engages a firm for a short-term project (catering or security for an event, for example) or buys goods. The first and fourth requirements warrant some discussion. The first requirement is that there must be an 'organised grouping of employees'. This involves showing that the employees engaged in providing the service to the client are clearly and formally identifiable as such. For example, in *Eddie Stobart Ltd v Moreman*, the EAT found no SPC: the employees regularly worked to fulfil a particular client's requirements but this was largely due to the coincidence of their shift patterns.[118] The fourth requirement is that the activities must be 'fundamentally the same' before and after the alleged transfer. This was introduced in 2014 and codifies the decision in *Metropolitan Resources*.[119] Whether this requirement is met is a question of fact for the tribunal, which may disregard trivial changes. For example, in *OCS Group UK Ltd v Jones*, it was held that there was no SPC when a contract to provide catering to factory workers was awarded to a new bidder which stopped providing hot food in a restaurant and sold sandwiches from kiosks instead.[120]

As Wynn-Evans explains, the SPC concept is not as different to the classic definition of a transfer as is sometimes imagined.[121] The ARD refers to an 'entity' which 'retains its identity' and defines this as an 'organised grouping of resources'. The SPC concept refers to an 'organised grouping of employees'. Many SPC cases could equally be argued on the basis of the classic transfer definition. However, it is far from pointless. Under EU law, where the business is labour-intensive, the transferee can avoid the application of the ARD if it does not take on the employees, as we saw in *Süzen*.[122] Under the SPC concept, where the employees constitute an 'organised grouping' and the other conditions are met, a transfer takes place, and the employees would be able to challenge their dismissals.

---

[117] ibid.
[118] [2012] ICR 919 (EAT).
[119] *Metropolitan Resources Ltd v Churchill Dulwich Ltd* [2009] ICR 1380 (EAT).
[120] (2009) UKEAT/0038/09/CEA.
[121] Wynn-Evans, above n 113, 176–179.
[122] *Süzen* (n 105).

Conclusion

To sum up, then, TUPE applies where there is either:

(a) a transfer of an undertaking or part of an undertaking; or
(b) a service provision change.

Option (a) is based on the ARD as interpreted by the CJEU. There must be an 'entity', in the sense of an 'organised grouping of resources' (assets or employees), which 'retains its identity', and is transferred from the transferor to the transferee. Option (b) is a domestic concept but reflects some of the CJEU case-law on the classic transfer definition. There is an SPC in outsourcing situations where there is an 'organised grouping of employees' carrying out 'fundamentally the same' activities for the same client.

It is easy to conclude from all of this that the scope of application of TUPE is highly uncertain and thus problematic. However, it is important that a balance is struck between protecting employees' rights and giving firms a degree of flexibility in their commercial arrangements. Let us consider a common 'change of contractor' situation: a hospital terminates its catering contract with company A and awards it to company B instead. The ARD/TUPE regime makes life difficult for company B: it cannot just promise to cut the employees' wages in order to make a cheaper bid for the contract. But this is the social purpose of the regime in action: it protects the employees by taking their terms and conditions, and their jobs, out of competition. If the hospital wants to adopt a new catering regime – replacing sandwiches with freshly cooked hot meals, for example – company B will need different equipment and employees with different skills. In this situation, it is unlikely that a transfer has taken place (either a classic transfer or an SPC) because of the change of assets and employees, or the change in the nature of the activities. This allows company B a degree of commercial flexibility.

Of course, all of this assumes that the rights granted by the ARD/TUPE are expressed in relatively stringent terms. In fact, they also offer transferors and transferees some flexibility. We will now examine them in detail, starting with the transfer itself and the preservation of terms and conditions of employment before turning to job security, and rights to be informed and consulted about the transfer.

10.4.3 The right to transfer

We saw above that, at common law, the sale of the business would normally terminate the employees' contracts of employment. The ARD/TUPE regime provides instead that the employees should transfer to the transferee, who becomes their employer and takes on the rights and liabilities of the transferor.

The basis for this is ARD Article 3(1):

The transferor's rights and obligations arising from a contract of employment or from an employment relationship existing on the date of a transfer shall, by reason of such transfer, be transferred to the transferee.

This is given effect in English law by TUPE, reg. 4(1):

a relevant transfer shall not operate so as to terminate the contract of employment of any person employed by the transferor and assigned to the organised grouping of resources or employees that is subject to the relevant transfer, which would otherwise be terminated by the transfer, but any such contract shall have effect after the transfer as if originally made between the person so employed and the transferee.

Under reg. 4(3), this applies to 'a person so employed immediately before the transfer, or who would have been so employed if he had not been dismissed in the circumstances described in regulation 7(1)'. The latter phrase addresses the situation (exemplified by the *Litster* case)[123] in which the transferor, under pressure from the transferee, dismisses the employees shortly before the transfer because the transferee does not want to take them on. At first sight, reg. 4(3) appears to operate so that employees dismissed immediately before the transfer would still transfer to the transferee, rendering their dismissals of no effect. Arguably, the CJEU's ruling in *Bork* supports the view that this is what the ARD requires:

> . . . the employees of the undertaking whose contract of employment or employment relationship was terminated with effect from a date prior to that of the transfer, contrary to Article 4(1) of the directive, must be regarded as still in the employ of the undertaking on the date of the transfer, with the result, in particular, that the employer's obligations towards them are automatically transferred from the transferor to the transferee in accordance with Article 3(1) of the directive.[124]

However, government guidance refutes the idea that the transferee must take on dismissed employees,[125] and existing domestic case-law only goes so far as to allow the employees' unfair dismissal claims under reg. 7(1) to be brought against the transferee.[126] The problem is that English law does not have an obvious mechanism for making a dismissal ineffective so the only 'employer's obligations' in existence at the time of the transfer are those arising in the law of unfair dismissal. The law in this area is very unclear.

Of course, not all employees may want to transfer to the transferee. In *Katsikas*, the CJEU confirmed that an employee cannot be transferred without his or her consent.[127] However, the effect of a refusal to transfer is for each Member State to determine. In English law, the right to refuse to transfer is clearly stated in reg. 4(7) TUPE. But under reg. 4(8), the employee's refusal terminates his or her contract of employment with the transferor and does not count as a dismissal. Thus, there is nothing to be gained by refusing to transfer.

10.4.4 Terms and conditions of employment

A second key element of the protection afforded by the ARD and TUPE is that the transferred employees should continue to enjoy the same terms and conditions of employment that they had with the transferor (with the important exception of those relating to company pensions)[128] once they start working for the transferee. We will begin by examining individual contracts of employment before turning to the position

---

[123] Above n 90.
[124] Case C-101/87 *P Bork International A/S v Foreningen af Arbejdsledere I Danmark* [1988] ECR 3057 [18].
[125] DBIS, *Employment Rights on the Transfer of an Undertaking* (January 2014) 15.
[126] *Litster*, n 90.
[127] Case C-132/91 *Katsikas v Konstantinidis* [1992] ECR I-6577. For discussion, see John McMullen, 'The "Right" to Object to Transfer of Employment under TUPE' (2008) 37 ILJ 169.
[128] TUPE 2006, reg 10.

governing collective agreements and collective bargaining arrangements, which are an important source of terms and conditions for some employees.

The preservation of individuals' terms and conditions is required by Article 3(1) ARD, quoted above. Under reg. 4(4) TUPE, any purported variation of an employee's contract is void if the 'sole or principal reason' is the transfer. This applies to variations by the transferor in anticipation of the transfer and to variations by the transferee once the transfer has taken place. A transferee acquiring a new business will often want to 'integrate' the transferring employees by getting them to work the same hours as its existing employees or by putting them onto the same pay and grading structure. However, the courts have generally regarded moves of this kind as directly attributable to the transfer and therefore void.[129]

A question worth considering is whether, after a sufficient amount of time has elapsed since the transfer, it becomes acceptable for the transferee to vary the employees' terms and conditions in order to integrate them into the business without it being arguable that the change is attributable to the transfer. According to the Court of Justice's ruling in *Daddy's Dance Hall*, while the transferee is free to vary contracts in accordance with national law, the transfer itself 'may *never* constitute the reason for that amendment',[130] though in the *St Helen's* case Lord Slynn suggested that the link with the transfer might eventually be broken.[131]

Under reg. 4(5), there are two exceptions to the general rule that the transferred employees' contracts cannot be varied:

> Paragraph (4) does not prevent a variation of the contract of employment if–
>
> (a) the sole or principal reason for the variation is an economic, technical, or organisational reason entailing changes in the workforce, provided that the employer and employee agree that variation; or
>
> (b) the terms of that contract permit the employer to make such a variation.

First, the contract may be varied for what is often known in practice as an ETO reason. There is very little analysis of the difference between 'economic, technical or organisational' reasons in the case-law, but this is not surprising since the phrase is broad and there is nothing to be gained by drawing sharp distinctions between the different components. The ETO reason must be the 'sole or principal' reason for the variation, and it must entail 'changes in the workforce'. If the transferor or transferee is motivated by an ETO reason but this does not entail 'changes in the workforce', the ETO provisions do not apply. Thus, if the transferee wants to harmonise terms and conditions of the transferring employees, for example, it cannot invoke ETO if it is not making any changes to the number of employees it employs, the functions they perform, or (by virtue of a recent amendment) their place of work.[132] This is the effect of the long-standing decision in *Berriman v Delabole Slate*.[133] Importantly, the employer and employee must agree the variation. However, this offers less of a

---

[129] *Manchester College v Hazel* [2014] EWCA Civ 72, [2014] ICR 989.

[130] Case 324/86 *Foreningen af Arbejdsledere I Danmark v Daddy's Dance Hall* [1988] ECR 739 [17], emphasis added.

[131] *Wilson v St Helen's Borough Council* [1999] 2 AC 52, 89. For discussion of recent EAT rulings on this matter, see John McMullen, 'Re-structuring and TUPE' (2012) 41 ILJ 358.

[132] TUPE 2006, reg 4(5A).

[133] [1985] ICR 546 (CA).

safeguard than might at first appear because of the employee's limited bargaining power and the possibility that an employee who refuses to agree to the variation might be dismissed.

Second, the contract may be varied by the employer if its terms so permit. As the *Bateman* case demonstrates, some employers reserve a right unilaterally to vary the contract of employment.[134] Where the transferee acquires a contract with a right of this kind, it may take advantage. Of course, the employees in this situation lose the preservation of their terms and conditions, though these are never set in stone in a contract of this type.

So far, we have focused on individual contracts of employment. The ARD also addresses collective agreements, in Article 3(3):

> Following the transfer, the transferee shall continue to observe the terms and conditions agreed in any collective agreement on the same terms applicable to the transferor under that agreement, until the date of termination or expiry of the collective agreement or the entry into force or application of another collective agreement.
>
> Member States may limit the period for observing such terms and conditions with the proviso that it shall not be less than one year.

The implementation of this provision in English law is quite complicated, for two reasons. First, collective agreements are presumed not to be legally binding. Second, (in contrast to other Member States) the incorporation of collectively agreed terms into individual employees' contracts of employment is not automatic, but depends instead on the terms of those contracts of employment.[135]

The position regarding the collective agreement itself is dealt with in reg. 5 TUPE by stating that it 'shall . . . have effect' as if made between the union and the transferee. This is of limited value given that the vast majority of collective agreements are binding in honour only. However, where the individual employee benefits from collectively agreed terms and conditions, these will transfer under reg. 4 as part of the individual's contract of employment. The 'bridging term', which enables the individual's terms and conditions to be set by the collective agreement, will also become binding on the transferee. This is subject to an important limitation in new reg. 4A, introduced to implement the controversial decision of the CJEU in the *Alemo-Herron* case:[136]

(1) Where a contract of employment, which is transferred by regulation 4(1), incorporates provisions of collective agreements as may be agreed from time to time, regulation 4(2) does not transfer any rights, powers, duties and liabilities in relation to any provision of a collective agreement if the following conditions are met–

    (a) the provision of the collective agreement is agreed after the date of the transfer; and

    (b) the transferee is not a participant in the collective bargaining for that provision.

(2) For the purposes of regulation 4(1), the contract of employment has effect after the transfer as if it does not incorporate provisions of a collective agreement which meet the conditions in paragraph (1).

---

[134] *Bateman* v *Asda Stores* [2010] IRLR 370 (EAT).
[135] See Chapter 5.
[136] Case C-426/11 *Alemo-Herron* v *Parkwood Leisure* [2014] 1 CMLR 21, noted by Jeremias Prassl, 'Freedom of Contract as a General Principle of EU Law? Transfers of Undertakings and the Protection of Employer Rights in EU Labour Law: Case C-426/11 *Alemo-Herron and others* v *Parkwood Leisure Ltd*' (2013) 42 ILJ 434.

In *Alemo-Herron*, a local authority contracted out its leisure services to a private firm. The employees' contracts of employment contained a clause to the effect that their pay would be set from time to time by the local government collective bargaining machinery. After the transfer, this clause became binding on the transferee. The transferee could not participate in the local government collective bargaining process because it was a private firm. It argued that it should not be bound by the clause. The CJEU agreed, holding that (following the *Werhof* decision)[137] the ARD only required the transferee to be bound by the collective agreement in existence at the date of the transfer, and that although the UK could adopt more worker-protective measures, it was in breach of the transferee's right to conduct a business, protected by Article 16 of the EU Charter of Fundamental Rights, in doing so. New reg. 4A ensures that the transferee is not bound to give effect in individual contracts to the provisions of a collective agreement reached after the date of the transfer where it has not participated in the collective bargaining process. This significantly reduces the potential for public sector employees (who tend to benefit from collective bargaining and better pay) to retain these advantages when they transfer to the private sector.

Although *Alemo-Herron* is an example of a case in which the transferee could not participate in the collective bargaining process previously applicable to the employees, the ARD and TUPE also provide that (if certain conditions are met) the transferee may be treated as having recognised a union previously recognised by the transferor. The ARD expresses this broadly, given the variety of different representation arrangements in force in the Member States. Article 6(1) provides that:

> If the undertaking, business or part of an undertaking or business preserves its autonomy, the status and function of the representatives or of the representation of the employees affected by the transfer shall be preserved on the same terms and subject to the same conditions as existed before the date of the transfer by virtue of law, regulation, administrative provision or agreement, provided that the conditions necessary for the constitution of the employee's representation are fulfilled.

This is given effect in English law by TUPE, reg. 6:

(1) This regulation applies where after a relevant transfer the transferred organised grouping of resources or employees maintains an identity distinct from the remainder of the transferee's undertaking.

(2) Where before such a transfer an independent trade union is recognised to any extent by the transferor in respect of employees of any description who in consequence of the transfer become employees of the transferee, then, after the transfer–

   (a) the trade union shall be deemed to have been recognised by the transferee to the same extent in respect of employees of that description so employed; and

   (b) any agreement for recognition may be varied or rescinded accordingly.

There are two key points to note about these provisions. First, they only apply where the transferred entity 'preserves its autonomy' (ARD)[138] or 'maintains an identity distinct from the remainder of the transferee's undertaking' (TUPE). Thus, trade union recognition will not be carried over to the transferee if the transferred

---

[137] Case C-499/04 *Werhof* v *Freeway Traffic Systems GmbH & Co KG* [2006] ECR 1-2397.
[138] Case C-151/09 *Federacion de Servicios Publicos de la UGT (UGT-FSP)* v *Ayuntamiento de la Linea de la Concepcion* [2010] ECR I-7591 indicates that this is not the same as an entity retaining its identity.

workers are simply absorbed into the transferee's business. Second, the significance of deeming the transferee to have recognised the union is quite limited in English law. Where the transferor recognised the union voluntarily, the transferee may simply derecognise the union immediately, provided that it can withstand any industrial action organised by the affected employees. Where the transferor was obliged to recognise the union under the Schedule A1 recognition procedure, any derecognition by the transferee would have to comply with the derecognition rules laid down in Schedule A1, so there is slightly more protection for the employees in this situation.[139]

10.4.5 Dismissal

We have seen so far that the ARD and TUPE seek to ensure that the affected employees transfer to the transferee with their terms and conditions of employment intact. This objective could not be realised if it was open to either the transferor or the transferee simply to dismiss the affected employees. However, employers are generally free to dismiss employees on economic grounds, as we saw in the discussion of redundancy, above. The ARD/TUPE regime balances these competing claims by providing that employees may not be dismissed because of the transfer, but that they may be dismissed for 'economic, technical or other' (ETO) reasons. Not surprisingly, this distinction can be quite difficult to apply in practice.

The ARD deals with dismissal in Article 4:

(1) The transfer of the undertaking, business or part of the undertaking or business shall not in itself constitute grounds for dismissal by the transferor or the transferee. This provision shall not stand in the way of dismissals that may take place for economic, technical or organisational reasons entailing changes in the workforce.

Member States may provide that the first subparagraph shall not apply to certain specific categories of employees who are not covered by the laws or practice of the Member States in respect of protection against dismissal.

(2) If the contract of employment or the employment relationship is terminated because the transfer involves a substantial change in working conditions to the detriment of the employee, the employer shall be regarded as having been responsible for termination of the contract of employment or of the employment relationship.

Article 4(1) draws the distinction between dismissals attributable to the transfer (by either the transferor or the transferee), and dismissals for ETO reasons. Article 4(2) provides for what we regard in English law as 'constructive dismissal', in which a person may resign in response to a repudiatory breach of contract by the employer and treat that as a dismissal.

The distinction between dismissals attributable to the transfer, and ETO dismissals, is captured in TUPE, reg. 7:

(1) Where either before or after a relevant transfer, any employee of the transferor or transferee is dismissed, that employee is to be treated for the purposes of Part X of the 1996 Act (unfair dismissal) as unfairly dismissed if the sole or principal reason for the dismissal is the transfer.

---

[139] See Chapter 12.

(2) This paragraph applies where the sole or principal reason for the dismissal is an economic, technical or organisational reason entailing changes in the workforce of either the transferor or the transferee before or after a relevant transfer.

(3) Where paragraph (2) applies–

    (a) paragraph (1) does not apply . . .

Thus, it is 'automatically unfair' for the transferor or transferee to dismiss an employee if the 'sole or principal reason is the transfer'. The phrase 'sole or principal reason' was introduced when TUPE was amended in 2014, and may make it more difficult to show that a dismissal is because of the transfer where the employer can argue that it has multiple motives.[140]

If the dismissal is found to be for an ETO reason, the dismissal is potentially fair either as a redundancy (where the usual definition is satisfied) or as a dismissal for 'some other substantial reason' (SOSR):

(b) without prejudice to the application of section 98(4) of the 1996 Act (test of fair dismissal), for the purposes of sections 98(1) and 135 of that Act (reason for dismissal)–

    (i) the dismissal is regarded as having been for redundancy where section 98(2)(c) of that Act applies; or

    (ii) in any other case, the dismissal is regarded as having been for a substantial reason of a kind such as to justify the dismissal of an employee holding the position which that employee held.[141]

If the dismissal is found to be a redundancy, the employee will be entitled to a redundancy payment on the usual basis. Whether the dismissal is for redundancy or SOSR, it remains open to the tribunal to find that it is unfair (so that the employee might be entitled to compensation), for example, where an unfair procedure has been followed.

Given the consequences, it is important to be able to distinguish a dismissal because of the transfer (automatically unfair) from a dismissal for an ETO reason (potentially fair). This requires a detailed assessment of the facts of the case and the timing of the dismissal, as the CJEU explained in the *Bork* case:

In order to determine whether the employees were dismissed solely as a result of the transfer, contrary to Article 4(1), it is necessary to take into consideration the objective circumstances in which the dismissal took place and, in particular, in a case such as this, the fact that it took effect on a date close to that of the transfer . . . [142]

It also requires a careful consideration of the ETO definition. The phrase in full is 'an economic, technical or organisational reason entailing changes in the workforce of either the transferor or the transferee before or after a relevant transfer',[143] and for the ETO provisions to apply, this must be the 'sole or principal' reason for the dismissal. As we saw above in relation to contract variations, if the transferor or transferee is motivated by an ETO reason but this does not entail 'changes in the workforce', the ETO provisions do not apply.[144] Thus, ETO can

---

[140] Collective Redundancies and Transfer of Undertakings (Protection of Employment) (Amendment) Regulations 2014, SI 2014/16.
[141] TUPE 2006, reg 7(3)(b).
[142] *P Bork International* (n 124) [18].
[143] TUPE 2006, reg 7(2).
[144] *Berriman,* above n 133; *Hazel,* above n 129.

only be invoked if the employer is changing the number of employees it employs, the functions they perform, or (by virtue of a recent amendment to TUPE itself) their place of work.[145]

The case-law has generated some fine distinctions. One common fact scenario is that the transferor dismisses some of the employees who might otherwise transfer, perhaps as a means of making the business more attractive to potential buyers. In the *Spaceright* case, the administrators of a company dismissed the chief executive in order to make the company more attractive to potential buyers (who would want to install their own chief executive).[146] The Court of Appeal upheld the employment tribunal's decision that the dismissal was automatically unfair because making the business more attractive to potential buyers was 'connected with' (under the law as it then stood) the transfer. It did not entail 'changes in the workforce' because a chief executive was still required. However, in *Kavanagh*, the administrator of a football club dismissed non-playing staff during the summer to cut costs and avoid liquidation with a view to an eventual sale.[147] The Court of Appeal in that case held that the tribunal was right to conclude that these were ETO dismissals because the reason was to reduce staffing levels (thus entailing 'changes in the workforce') and to cut costs, with any increase in the club's appeal to potential buyers as a side-effect. Wynn-Evans has criticised the *Kavanagh* decision on the grounds that the judges appeared to have been influenced by the administrator's desire to 'rescue' the club at the expense of protection for the employees.[148]

Another common fact scenario is that after the transfer, the transferee seeks to vary the transferred employees' terms and conditions, either because it has miscalculated the economic benefits of the transfer, or simply to harmonise terms and conditions with those of its existing employees for administrative convenience. The employee refuses to accept the variation and resigns, claiming constructive dismissal.[149] This was the scenario in the recent case of *Hazel v Manchester College*.[150] The employer offered the claimants new contracts with substantially reduced pay as part of a post-transfer restructuring designed to cut costs and harmonise terms and conditions. It was held that ETO was not available to the employer because the reason for the dismissals did not entail 'changes in the workforce'. The employees were not dismissed to reduce workforce numbers but because of their refusal to agree to the changes. Thus, their dismissals were automatically unfair under reg. 7(1).

Finally, it is important to remember that an unfair dismissal claim in TUPE only lies when the normal conditions for such a claim are met. This is the effect of reg. 7(6). It means that individuals who are protected by TUPE but do not meet the strict 'employee' definition used in unfair dismissal law are unable to claim (a situation permitted by Article 4(1) ARD, which allows the scope of dismissal protection to be the same as that normally applicable in domestic law). It also means that anyone without two years' qualifying service will be unable to claim.

---

[145] TUPE 2006, reg 7(3A).
[146] *Spaceright Europe Ltd v Baillavoine* [2011] EWCA Civ 1565, [2012] ICR 520.
[147] *Kavanagh v Crystal Palace FC 2000 Ltd* [2013] EWCA Civ 1410, [2014] ICR 251.
[148] Charles Wynn-Evans, 'TUPE and Mothballs: *Crystal Palace FC Limited and Another v Kavanagh and Others*' (2014) 43 ILJ 185, 191–192.
[149] TUPE 2006, reg 4(9).
[150] [2014] EWCA Civ 72, [2014] IRLR 392. For discussion, see John McMullen, 'TUPE, Variation of Employment Terms, and the ETO Reason' (2014) 43 ILJ 364.

10.4.6 Consultation

A third limb of protection under the ARD/TUPE regime is a requirement on *both* the transferor and the transferee to inform and consult affected employees. Of course, the transfer will have a much greater impact on the employees being transferred, but the law also acknowledges that it may be a worrying time for the transferee's employees too.

The obligation to inform is set out in Article 7(1) of the Directive and implemented in reg. 13(2) TUPE:

> Long enough before a relevant transfer to enable the employer of any affected employees to consult the appropriate representatives of any affected employees, the employer shall inform those representatives of–
>
> (a) the fact that the transfer is to take place, the date or proposed date of the transfer and the reasons for it;
> (b) the legal, economic and social implications of the transfer for any affected employees;
> (c) the measures which he envisages he will, in connection with the transfer, take in relation to any affected employees or, if he envisages that no measures will be so taken, that fact; and
> (d) if the employer is the transferor, the measures, in connection with the transfer, which he envisages the transferee will take in relation to any affected employees who will become employees of the transferee after the transfer by virtue of regulation 4 or, if he envisages that no measures will be so taken, that fact.[151]

The 'appropriate representatives' are trade union representatives, where a union is recognised in respect of the affected employees, or the employer's choice of pre-existing employee representatives or representatives elected especially for the purpose.[152] A recent amendment allows a firm with fewer than 10 employees to inform and consult them individually.[153]

Article 7(2) of the Directive imposes an obligation to consult appropriate representatives where it is envisaged that 'measures' will be taken in respect of an affected employee. This is implemented in reg. 13(6) and (7), as follows:

> (6) An employer of an affected employee who envisages that he will take measures in relation to an affected employee, in connection with the relevant transfer, shall consult the appropriate representatives of that employee with a view to seeking their agreement to the intended measures.
>
> (7) In the course of those consultations the employer shall–
>
> (a) consider any representations made by the appropriate representatives; and
> (b) reply to those representations and, if he rejects any of those representations, state his reasons.

This is quite a strong implementation of the reference in the Directive to consultation 'with a view to reaching an agreement'. It is not entirely clear what constitutes a 'measure' in relation to an employee, though presumably the transfer of an employee will always amount to a 'measure'.

---

[151] Under reg 13(4), the transferee must give the transferor information for this purpose.
[152] TUPE 2006, reg 13(3).
[153] ibid reg 13A, based on art 7(5) of the Directive.

10.4.7 TUPE in insolvency situations

It is quite common in practice for a business to be sold when it has become, or is about to become, insolvent. This gives rise to a particularly acute tension between the rights of workers and the need for flexibility for the transferee. If the business is sold, the employees have a better chance of keeping their jobs. But if the ARD/TUPE regime applies, there is a risk that the employees' acquired rights may deter potential buyers or make it difficult for them to rescue the firm.

Insolvency regimes are a matter for national law and vary substantially across the different Member States. The original ARD did not mention insolvency at all. In the case of *Abels*, the Court of Justice held that the Directive did not apply where the business was in liquidation (though a Member State was free to apply the rules if it wanted to), but would normally apply where the business was subject to other types of insolvency proceedings aimed at rescuing the business as a going concern.[154] The Court was concerned to ensure that the Directive did not interfere with national insolvency law by giving employees priority over other creditors. The current version, in Article 5, confirms that the Directive only applies to liquidations at the Member State's discretion, and gives the Member State greater flexibility to modify some of the Directive's requirements when applying it to liquidations or to other insolvency situations.

In revising TUPE, the government took full advantage of the flexibility offered by the Directive. First, where insolvency proceedings 'have been instituted with a view to the liquidation of the assets of the transferor', the employees do not transfer to the transferee and have no unfair dismissal claim against the transferee.[155] Only the duties to inform and consult the employees continue to apply. Second, where insolvency proceedings 'have been opened in relation to the transferor not with a view to the liquidation of the assets of the transferor', any unfair dismissal or redundancy liability towards the employees remains with the transferor and does not transfer to the transferee.[156] Since the transferor is insolvent, this means that the cost will be met by the state under the insolvency regime (discussed below). Moreover, under reg. 9, the transferor, transferee or insolvency practitioner may agree contract variations with employee representatives. These may be attributable to the transfer provided that they are 'designed to safeguard employment opportunities by ensuring the survival of the undertaking'.[157] The thinking behind this approach is that the transferee is more likely to buy the business if it does not have to take on unfair dismissal or redundancy liabilities, and if it can vary the terms and conditions of employment of any employees who transfer. This may save some people's jobs.

One of the difficulties with the insolvency provisions in TUPE is that they were drafted with reference to the terminology used in the Directive, not English insolvency law terminology, making it difficult to determine their exact scope of application. For example, while administration is normally designed to rescue the business as a going concern, some administrations end in liquidation in practice. This left the courts with a choice between treating administration as a process 'not with a view

---

[154] Case 135/83 *Abels v Administrative Board of the Bedrijfsvereniging Voor de Metaal-Industie en de Electrotechnische Industrie* [1985] ECR 469.
[155] TUPE 2006, reg 8(7).
[156] ibid reg 8(6).
[157] ibid reg 9(7)(b).

to . . . liquidation' in all cases, since this is the legal objective of administration, or to adopt a context-sensitive approach in which the TUPE treatment of administration would depend on the facts of the case. In the *Key2Law* case, the Court of Appeal adopted the former approach to administration, on the basis that a 'bright line' rule would promote legal certainty.[158]

We saw above that another common feature of impending insolvency is that the transferor might dismiss employees with a view to attracting a buyer for the business. If this is the 'sole or principal' reason for the dismissal it is likely to be attributed to the transfer and thus be automatically unfair, though the case-law in this area is quite complex and prone to subtle distinctions.

10.5 INSOLVENCY

An insolvency situation arises where the employer (whether it is an individual or a company) is no longer able to pay its debts. In relation to an individual, this usually means that he or she has either entered into a voluntary arrangement with creditors or has been declared bankrupt.[159] In relation to a company, it may have entered into a voluntary arrangement with creditors, been put into administration (where the insolvency practitioner tries to rescue it), been put into receivership (where its assets are sold to pay a secured creditor, like a bank) or been put into liquidation (where it is closed down).

It will often be the case that the insolvent employer will owe money to its employees. Most obviously, the employer may not have paid their wages, though other debts are possible too: if the employment is terminated, which will normally be the case, the employees may be entitled to redundancy payments and payments in lieu of notice. The employees have an action against the employer[160] but this may not be of any value because there may not be enough money to go around. The EU Insolvency Directive requires the state to make payments to employees to cover certain employer liabilities in this situation.[161]

10.5.1 Claims against the employer

Insolvency law works by ranking the claims of the various creditors of the insolvent company: determining who gets the first claim over the remaining assets. This is important because those with lower priority may find that there is no money left to satisfy their claim.

Money owed to employees is a 'preferential debt' under s. 386 Insolvency Act 1986. The types of employee claim that fall within the 'preferential' category are defined in Schedule 6, Category 5, of the Act. Unpaid wages for four months up to the date of the insolvency are covered,[162] but this is subject to a limit of £800.[163]

---

[158] *Key2Law (Surrey) LLP* v *De'Antiquis* [2011] EWCA Civ 1567, [2012] ICR 881.
[159] For ease of explanation, the discussion from now on will refer only to companies.
[160] Where a company is put into administration, there may also be a claim against the administrator in some circumstances.
[161] Council Directive 2008/94/EC of 22 October 2008 on the protection of employees in the event of the insolvency of their employer [200] OJ L283/36, art 3.
[162] Insolvency Act 1986, sch 6, para 9.
[163] Insolvency Proceedings (Monetary Limits) Order 1986, SI 1986/1996, reg 4.

Accrued holiday pay is covered if the employment is terminated,[164] and payments to pension schemes,[165] together with the following miscellaneous group of payments:

> An amount falls within this sub-paragraph if it is–
>
> (a) a guarantee payment under Part III of the Employment Rights Act 1996 (employee without work to do);
> (b) any payment for time off under section 53 (time off to look for work or arrange training) or section 56 (time off for ante-natal care) of that Act or under section 169 of the Trade Union and Labour Relations (Consolidation) Act 1992 (time off for carrying out trade union duties etc.);
> (c) remuneration on suspension on medical grounds, or on maternity grounds, under Part VII of the Employment Rights Act 1996; or
> (d) remuneration under a protective award under section 189 of the Trade Union and Labour Relations (Consolidation) Act 1992 (redundancy dismissal with compensation).[166]

'Preferential' creditor status puts employees above 'unsecured' creditors (such as suppliers or customers) and, in the case of a company, its shareholders, in the ranking. However, there are two reasons why these provisions are less protective of employees than they might seem. First, employees rank behind 'secured' creditors. These are people with a charge over a particular asset of the company, such as a bank with a charge over the company's premises. Once the secured creditors have been paid, there may not be much money left for preferential creditors. Second, the preferential creditors rank equally with each other so any remaining money will be divided between them. Any other debts owed to employees that do not come within the categories described above are treated as unsecured debts, so they stand even less chance of being recovered.

10.5.2 Claims against the state

The state's duty to step in and pay the employees where the insolvent employer cannot do so is laid down by Directive 80/987/EEC as amended by Directive 2002/74/EC and now codified in Directive 2008/94/EC. The Directive requires the state to set up a 'guarantee institution' to meet the employer's liabilities. In the UK, this is the Insolvency Service, with the money being paid by the National Insurance fund. The relevant provisions are in ss. 182–190 ERA 1996, and apply when the employer is insolvent[167] and the employee's employment has been terminated.[168]

Under Article 3 of the Directive:

> Member States shall take the measures necessary to ensure that guarantee institutions guarantee, subject to Article 4, payment of employees' outstanding claims resulting from contracts of employment or employment relationships, including, where provided for by national law, severance pay on termination of employment relationships.

---

[164] Insolvency Act 1986, sch 6, para 10.
[165] ibid sch 6, para 8.
[166] ibid sch 6, para 13(2).
[167] Insolvency is defined for these purposes in art 2 of the Directive and ERA 1996, s 183.
[168] ERA 1996, s 182.

The Directive leaves it to Member States to define 'employee' for these purposes (though the Member States may not exclude part-time, fixed-term or temporary agency employees).[169] In the UK, the standard 'employee' definition is used.[170] Where the insolvent employer operates in more than one Member State, the guarantee institution liable to meet the employees' claims is that of the state in which they 'habitually work'.[171] In *Holmqvist*, the CJEU held that the claimant lorry driver habitually worked in Sweden, where he was based, rather than in Italy, the country to which he normally drove.[172] In most cases, it is likely to be easier for claimants to apply for reimbursement in the place in which they have been working.

The Directive does not define the 'outstanding claims' to which it applies, but ERA 1996, s. 184(1), provides a list (which is similar to but not quite the same as the list of 'preferential debts' considered above):

This Part applies to the following debts–

(a) any arrears of pay in respect of one or more (but not more than eight) weeks,

(b) any amount which the employer is liable to pay the employee for the period of notice required by section 86(1) or (2) or for any failure of the employer to give the period of notice required by section 86(1),

(c) any holiday pay–

    (i) in respect of a period or periods of holiday not exceeding six weeks in all, and

    (ii) to which the employee became entitled during the twelve months ending with the appropriate date,

(d) any basic award of compensation for unfair dismissal or so much of an award under a designated dismissal procedures agreement as does not exceed any basic award of compensation for unfair dismissal to which the employee would be entitled but for the agreement . . . [173]

Thus, the main debts covered are arrears of pay, pay for the notice period, holiday pay and the basic (but not compensatory) award for unfair dismissal.[174] We saw above that ERA 1996, s. 166, enables an employee to claim a redundancy payment from the state where it is not paid by the employer.

The Directive allows the Member State to limit its liability under Article 4. ERA applies two limits: arrears of pay can only be claimed for eight weeks, under s. 184(1)(a), and a week's pay for these purposes is capped at £464 under s. 186. Article 4(2)'s starting-point is that the Member State can limit its liability to the last three months of the employment relationship. However, the provision goes on to say that:

Member States having a reference period of not less than 18 months may limit the period for which outstanding claims are met by the guarantee institution to eight weeks . . .

---

[169] Directive 2008/94/EC, art 2(2).

[170] ERA 1996, s 203(1).

[171] Directive 2008/94/EC, art 9(1).

[172] Case C-310/07 *Svenska staten* v *Holmqvist* [2008] ECR I-7871.

[173] ERA 1996, s 184(2) includes some other miscellaneous payments.

[174] The directive also deals with social security and occupational pensions but we will not consider these matters in detail here: Directive 2008/94/EC, arts 6–8.

Since ERA does not use a reference period at all, the UK is able to limit its liability to eight weeks. This is relatively short compared to most other Member States.[175] Under Article 4(3):

> Member States may set ceilings on the payments made by the guarantee institution. These ceilings must not fall below a level which is socially compatible with the social objective of this Directive.

The Commission appears to take the view that the level is sufficient provided that it exceeds the NMW, a requirement currently satisfied by the UK.[176]

ERA makes provision for the government to obtain information from the insolvency practitioner about any payments made out of the employer's assets to the employees, in order to ensure that the debts have not already been settled.[177] The government acquires the right to pursue the employer for any money it has paid out under the insolvency provisions.[178]

POINTS TO TAKE AWAY

- If an employee is 'redundant', he or she is entitled to a redundancy payment. A redundancy arises where the employer's business closes altogether, where the employee's workplace closes, or where the employer no longer needs so many people to do the job the employee was doing.

- A dismissal by reason of redundancy is 'potentially fair' in the law of unfair dismissal. It will be unfair, entitling the employee to a compensatory award, where the employer acts outside the 'band of reasonable responses', for example, by failing to use objective selection criteria or failing to follow a fair procedure.

- Where the employer 'proposes' to dismiss at least 20 people for economic reasons at one establishment over a 90-day period, it must consult union representatives or workforce representatives about ways of avoiding or reducing the number of dismissals. This obligation flows from the Collective Redundancies Directive and it is arguable that there are some flaws in English law's implementation of the Directive.

- Where a business changes hands – where there is a 'transfer of an economic entity which retains its identity' or a service provision change – the affected employees become employees of the transferee. Their terms and conditions of employment are preserved and they may not be dismissed because of the transfer, though if certain conditions are met their terms and conditions may be changed or they may be dismissed for an 'economic, technical or organisational' reason. The transferor and transferee must inform and consult the workforce.

---

[175] Commission, *Report on the Implementation and Application of Certain Provisions of Directive 2008/94/EC on the Protection of Employees in the Event of the Insolvency of their Employer* (COM(2011) 84 final, 2011), para 3.
[176] ibid.
[177] ERA 1996, s 187(1).
[178] ibid s 189.

- If an employer becomes insolvent, employees who are owed certain debts (for example, wage arrears) have priority over unsecured creditors and shareholders in the insolvency. Where there are insufficient funds to cover these debts, the employees may recover them from the state.

Further reading

There is an important theoretical debate about the purposes of the law on individual redundancies and, in particular, its relationship (if any) to job security. For discussion, see **Hugh Collins, *Justice in Dismissal* (Clarendon Press 1992), chapter 5, and Robert H Fryer, 'The Myths of the Redundancy Payments Act' (1973) 2 ILJ 1**.

On the historical development of the directives on collective redundancies, transfers and insolvency see **Jeff Kenner, *EU Employment Law* (Hart 2003), chapters 2 and 7**. For more detail on the directives themselves and the associated case-law, see **Catherine Barnard, *EU Employment Law* (4th edn, OUP 2012), chapters 13 and 14**. TUPE in particular is the subject of a substantial body of case-law and a considerable practitioner literature. For more detail, see **Charles Wynn-Evans, *The Law of TUPE Transfers* (OUP 2013)**.

The law on collective redundancies seeks to protect employees by creating a process for consultation with their representatives. This is also one of the elements of protection in the ARD/TUPE regime. Issues surrounding workplace consultation are addressed in more detail in Chapter 14 of this book.

11 Trade unions and their members

Learning outcomes

This chapter will enable readers to:

- understand the functions of trade unions
- evaluate the justifications for, and criticisms of, trade unions in the political process and in the labour market
- understand and critically analyse the legal regulation of: trade unions' internal affairs; trade unions' rules on the exclusion, discipline and expulsion of members; and the 'closed shop'

11.1 INTRODUCTION

The statutory definition of a 'trade union' is given in s. 1 Trade Union and Labour Relations (Consolidation) Act 1992 (TULRCA 1992):

> In this Act a "trade union" means an organisation (whether temporary or permanent)—
> (a) which consists wholly or mainly of workers of one or more descriptions and whose principal purposes include the regulation of relations between workers of that description or those descriptions and employers or employers' associations . . .

A trade union, then, is a workers' organisation. But importantly, it is not just inward-looking: one of the core functions of a trade union is to regulate relations between workers and employers. Thus, unions are key players in a system of *collective bargaining*: a mechanism in which employers and unions negotiate together to determine workers' terms and conditions of employment.

Of course, negotiations between workers and employers could (and often do) occur on an individual basis: when a worker gets a new job, he or she might be able to negotiate with the employer on pay, for example. But for most workers, the scope for meaningful negotiation is limited because their bargaining power is much less strong than that of the employer. If the worker demands a high wage, in most cases the employer will be able to find someone else to do the job. The point of organising groups of workers into trade unions, then, is to increase their bargaining power against that of the employer. It is much harder to ignore the demands of the whole workforce, or a significant section of the workforce, than it is to ignore the demands of one individual. This is especially so if the workforce is able to make a credible threat of strike action. Thus, unions are one of the ways of fulfilling what is often regarded as the central purpose of employment law: to combat inequality of bargaining power between a worker and his or her employer.[1] We will examine the law relating to collective bargaining and strikes in the next two chapters.

Around 6.5 million employees – 25.6% of the workforce – were trade union members in 2013.[2] There is an important public/private divide in trade union activity: 14.4% of private sector employees are trade union members, whereas in the public sector the proportion is 55.4%. Around 19% of the workforce is employed in the public sector. It is important to be aware that employers generally apply a collective agreement to all relevant employees – not just to those who are members of the trade union that negotiated it – so more people have their terms and conditions of employment determined by collective agreement than are members of trade unions. The figures for 2013 show that 29.5% of the workforce is covered by a collective agreement, split into 16.6% in the private sector and 63.8% in the public sector.[3]

Given that trade union membership has fallen considerably from its peak of 13 million in 1979, students often wonder why it is necessary to study trade unions at all. Trade unionism might seem like an old-fashioned idea, no longer relevant to the modern workplace. Nevertheless, there are some very good reasons to study trade unions and their activities. First, in purely practical terms, collective bargaining is still relevant for 29% of the workforce, which is by no means insignificant. Second, although trade union membership has been in decline since 1979, the statistics seem to suggest that the decline has tailed off a little.[4] Third, from a historical perspective, it is difficult to understand the development of employment law in the UK without any awareness of the trade union movement. Statutory rights for workers have been overlaid onto a well-established system of collective bargaining.[5] And fourth, learning about trade unions can help in understanding employment law in other legal systems, particularly in Europe, and certain features of EU law. For example, the social dialogue procedure for agreeing EU employment laws depends on there being a functioning system of trade unions in the Member States.[6]

We will begin by considering the role of trade unions, the justifications for having them and the various critiques commonly offered of their role in politics and in the labour market (section 11.2). We will consider how the controversial nature of unions has affected the regulatory regime to which they are subject. We will then examine that regulatory regime in detail, looking first at unions' internal affairs (such as their finances) (section 11.3) before turning to their membership rules in section 11.4 and the law on the 'closed shop' in section 11.5.

11.2 THEORETICAL FRAMEWORK

We saw above that the statutory definition of a trade union focuses on collective bargaining as unions' main role. However, trade unions are engaged in a broader range of activities than the definition might imply. In this section, we will examine

---

[1] Otto Kahn-Freund, 'Legal Framework', in Allan Flanders and Hugh A Clegg (eds), *The System of Industrial Relations in Great Britain: Its History, Law and Institutions* (Blackwell 1954).
[2] Department for Business, Innovation and Skills, *Trade Union Membership 2013* (2014) 5. The Certification Officer puts the figure slightly higher, at just over 7 million: ibid 21.
[3] ibid 31.
[4] ibid 5.
[5] See Chapter 1.
[6] See Chapter 2.

these activities and consider the debate about the position of trade unions in industrial relations and society today.

11.2.1 Functions

In a helpful analysis Ewing has identified five functions of trade unions: service provision, workplace representation, regulation, government and public administration.[7]

The 'service provision' function refers to the role of unions in providing services to their members.[8] Historically, unions often functioned rather like friendly societies, helping union members financially when they were unable to work through illness, for example. Nowadays, unions often secure discounts for their members on goods and services, and offer legal advice to members who encounter problems at work.

The 'workplace representation' function refers to two possibilities: representing an individual who has a grievance (which overlaps with the service function just discussed) or representing the workforce collectively in negotiations with the employer.[9] The latter might take the form of 'collective bargaining', in which the union and the employer negotiate with the aim of reaching a 'collective agreement' to govern the terms and conditions of employment of the relevant workers, or it might be a more ad hoc process in which the union and the employer have discussions on issues of concern to the workers. When an employer agrees to treat a union as the representative of the workers for the purposes of collective bargaining, we say that the union is 'recognised'.[10] Ewing stresses that what he calls the 'workplace representation' function is directed at the particular employing enterprise and does not have implications beyond it.[11] Most collective bargaining in the UK now takes place at this level.

This brings about a contrast with the 'regulatory' function of trade unions.[12] This is used by Ewing to cover the situation in which unions bargain on a larger scale – with an employers' association representing a whole sector of activity, for example – and thus set terms and conditions not just for one workplace but for several. For example, a union representing people working in car manufacturing might negotiate with the car manufacturers' employers' association to reach an agreement governing the pay and basic conditions of different grades of worker across the industry. Historically, this form of collective bargaining was common in the UK, but declined from the 1970s onwards so that it is rare in the private sector today. However, it remains important in the public sector in the UK (for hospital consultants or teachers, for example) and in other European countries such as Germany and Sweden. The aim was to take wages and other terms of employment 'out of competition': so firms could get on with other tasks such as designing new products and improving productivity. Ewing suggests that another way in which unions might perform a 'regulatory' function is indirectly, by persuading the government to legislate to protect working people.[13]

---

[7] KD Ewing, 'The Function of Trade Unions' (2005) 34 ILJ 1.
[8] ibid 5.
[9] ibid 8.
[10] See Chapter 12.
[11] Ewing, above n 7, 4.
[12] ibid 13.
[13] ibid 15.

This leads us neatly to the 'governmental' and 'public administration' functions. When trade unions perform the 'governmental' function, they act as the political representatives of working people.[14] In the UK, the union movement has had a long association with the Labour party, which was founded in part by trade unionists. Some of the larger unions are 'affiliated' with the Labour party, which means that they help to fund it and have a significant say in its activities.[15] At the time of writing, these arrangements are under review by the Labour party itself.[16] Ewing notes that the 'governmental' function overlaps with the 'regulatory' function – in the sense that unions' political activities may enable them to secure regulatory legislation to protect working people – but argues that unions' political campaigns may, and often do, extend beyond employment laws to other issues such as housing or social security benefits. The 'public administration' function refers to the role of unions in delivering governmental objectives.[17] For example, in the 1970s, the government tried to persuade unions to limit their wage demands in order to control inflation.[18] In more recent times, the government has encouraged the union movement to negotiate with employers' organisations about the implementation of EU directives, notably on agency work.[19]

Although it is possible to find examples of all five functions in the UK industrial relations context, there has been a general trend since the 1970s towards the narrowing of unions' sphere of influence. The Donovan Commission, reporting in 1968, found that the system of collective bargaining had become chaotic because although unions and employers negotiated sectoral collective agreements, they tended to vary or supplement them with company-level agreements.[20] Thus, it recommended that collective bargaining should take place at company or workplace level. While this addressed the immediate problem, it reduced unions' 'regulatory' function so that nowadays, this is largely confined to persuading government to enact favourable employment laws. Similarly, while unions still play a 'governmental' role on occasion – as the example of agency work shows – this is much-reduced from the close interactions between government and unions in the 1970s.

11.2.2 Justifications

As we shall see later in this chapter, the right to form and join a trade union (an aspect of freedom of association) is a fundamental human right in various instruments to which the UK is a party, including the ECHR.[21] So on one level, it might be thought to be unnecessary to examine the justifications for having trade unions. However, since trade unions are often the subject of political debate, it is worth thinking about why they exist and why the drafters of human rights instruments might have included them.

---

[14] ibid 15.
[15] http://www.unionstogether.org.uk/pages/about_us (last visited 12 September 2014).
[16] 'Labour backs extensive reforms over links with trade unions', *The Guardian*, 1 March 2014.
[17] Ewing, above n 7, 17.
[18] Paul Davies and Mark Freedland, *Labour Legislation and Public Policy* (Clarendon Press 1994) chapter 8.
[19] *Agency Workers: Joint Declaration by Government, the CBI and the TUC*, 20 May 2008.
[20] Royal Commission on Trade Unions and Employers' Associations, 1965–1968 (Chairman: The Rt. Hon. Lord Donovan) (Cmnd. 3623, HMSO 1968).
[21] ECHR, art 11.

A good starting-point is to consider why individuals want to form organisations or join organisations that already exist. In the political context, it is usually because they want to gather together with like-minded people, and to influence public policy by campaigning for particular objectives.[22] If everyone who stood for election to Parliament stood as an independent, it would be difficult for voters to figure out for whom to vote, and once elected, it would be hard for individual politicians to achieve anything without complex negotiations with others. Political parties help to structure the democratic process by grouping people together according to a shared set of opinions. Voters can choose between parties, and parties can more easily run campaigns and form governments. In a healthy democracy, though, political organisations should be many and varied and not just confined to political parties. For example, what are often referred to as 'pressure groups' exist to campaign on particular issues, such as conservation, animal rights or equality. And interest groups exist to represent people who may share a common set of interests across a range of issues: farmers, footballers, employers, workers and so on. These different groups help to ensure that the public debate is diverse and well-informed (that the government must consider alternative views) and that power does not become too concentrated in one place. Undemocratic governments tend to ban or repress political parties or other groups that might oppose their point of view, whereas we expect democratic governments to explain and justify their approach and to engage in debate with their opponents.

Some of these arguments apply to trade unions because, as we saw above, they have both political and industrial roles. As political actors, they campaign on behalf of the interests of working people in much the same way that employers' associations might campaign on behalf of business interests. Moreover, one of the advantages often claimed for trade unions in particular is that they offer a route through which ordinary people can get involved in politics. A dispute at work might prompt an individual to join a union, but in turn this might lead him or her to get more involved in the union's wider campaigns and to take an interest in national politics. This might help to combat problems like low voter turnout at elections.

Of course, as we saw above, trade unions are workplace actors as well as political actors. In the workplace, their main role is to represent workers in their dealings with employers, particularly though not exclusively through collective bargaining. The aim of collective bargaining is that the union and the employer (or group of employers) should reach a collective agreement to govern the terms and conditions of employment of a particular group of workers. But why is collective bargaining regarded as a good thing? From the workers' perspective, its main advantage is that it helps to address the inequality of bargaining power between workers and employers.[23] If one worker goes to the employer and asks for a pay rise, it is easy for the employer to say no: the worker usually needs his or her job more than the employer needs him or her, unless he or she has very special skills. But if workers approach the employer as a group, then the employer has more reason to listen and negotiate. It is harder to manage without a group of workers than it is to manage without one worker. This is especially the case if the workers can back up their request with a credible threat of strike action.

[22] Bernadette Rainey et al., *Jacobs, White and Ovey: the European Convention on Human Rights* (6th edn, OUP 2014) chapter 19.
[23] P Davies and M Freedland, *Kahn-Freund's Labour and the Law* (Stevens and Sons 1983) chapter 1.

But what are the advantages of collective bargaining from the perspective of employers, and indeed wider society? One argument commonly made in favour of collective bargaining is the 'voice' argument developed by Freeman and Medoff, among others.[24] They argue that workers who have some say in what is happening in their workplace are happier than those who do not, and are thus more likely to stay loyal to the firm. This means that the firm will be more productive because it has long-serving, enthusiastic workers and does not need to deal with the recruitment and training costs that come with a high turnover of staff. Better channels of communication between workers and bosses should also mean that the firm is able to harness its workers' ideas on how to improve production processes, customer service and so on. Another argument often made in favour of collective bargaining, perhaps more from the state's perspective, is that it provides a way of resolving conflict in society at minimal cost. On this view, workers and employers are bound to have different opinions about matters such as wages, working time and so on. The state could step in to regulate these issues, but this is costly and risks imposing 'one size fits all' solutions on different businesses and different sectors. If the state instead allows the interested parties to work out their own solutions through collective bargaining, employers and workers will come up with approaches that suit their particular needs. Importantly, this does not mean that the state can step back completely: legal intervention may be needed to permit, support and facilitate collective bargaining. But this type of law – in the old parlance, 'negative' law, and in modern parlance, 'reflexive' law – can be kept at a much higher level of generality.[25]

11.2.3 The critique of trade unions

Of course, not everyone thinks that trade unions are a good thing, either at the political level or at the workplace level. In the UK in particular, the close relationship between the trade union movement and the Labour party has the inevitable consequence that unions themselves are politically controversial. In this section, we will consider some common criticisms, focusing first on trade unions as political actors, and then on trade unions as workplace actors.

On the political level, the charge laid at the union movement is that it has a distorting effect on politics. Politicians on the right of the political spectrum tend to argue that unions exercise undue influence over the Labour party, because of the party's reliance on the unions for funding, and that union leaders are more radical than their members, so that the views being put forward by the union movement do not reflect the views of ordinary working people.[26] At the time of writing, the links between the union movement and the Labour party are under review, in part because the union movement no longer feels that the Labour party reflects its opinions, and in part because the party itself is concerned about the ongoing criticism.[27] We saw above that union advocates argue that unions offer a form of grassroots political participation. And in the UK in particular, as this chapter will demonstrate, union

---

[24] Richard B Freeman and James L Medoff, *What Do Unions Do?* (Basic Books 1984) chapter 6.

[25] Kahn-Freund, above n 1, 44; Ralf Rogowski, *Reflexive Labour Law in the World Society* (Edward Elgar 2013) chapter 2.

[26] For discussion in relation to the Trade Union Act 1984, see Davies and Freedland, above n 18, 436–441.

[27] Above n 16.

leaders can point to a high level of legal intervention designed to ensure that unions are democratically run. Nevertheless, the criticism has a high degree of persistence.

At the workplace level, there are at least three common criticisms levelled at unions and at the system of collective bargaining. First, from an economics perspective, it is argued that unions are bad for the economy and for the workers they purport to help.[28] By persuading employers to pay higher wages, they extract what economists call 'rents': payments that are beyond the market rate for the job. This means that a unionised firm must pay more for labour than a non-unionised firm, making it harder for that firm to compete with its rivals. Moreover, if the firm is forced to pay higher wages, it will cut costs by employing fewer people. Thus, it is argued, unions help workers to make gains in the short term but this comes at a high price: the firm becomes uncompetitive, which may harm the workers in the long term if it cannot stay in business, and fewer people are employed. There are two responses to these criticisms: improving workers' pay may simply involve cutting the owner's or shareholders' profits, rather than threatening the firm's competitiveness, and a union which demanded pay rises that might put the firm out of business would not be pursuing a sensible negotiating strategy.

The 'rents' criticism leads to a second criticism, about protectionism. This is the idea that unions protect their members' interests at the expense of the interests of non-members, thus contributing to the emergence of a two-tier labour market.[29] For example, a union with a good level of membership among the employer's permanent workers might campaign for temporary or casual workers to get the same rates of pay. This might seem to be a benefit for the casual workers, but another way of looking at the situation is that it protects the permanent workers' jobs by ensuring that they are not 'undercut' by the casuals. It reduces the attractiveness to the employer of hiring casuals and takes away an opportunity for them to find work. Trade unionists might well respond to this by pointing out that the objective of collective bargaining is to insulate wages – to some extent at least – against market forces. This might indeed create situations in which there are winners and losers and union members are among the winners, but this is not necessarily unfair if – as is the case in the UK at present – it is open to anyone to protect themselves by joining a union.

A third criticism of trade unions' workplace activities is that they reflect an adversarial understanding of industrial relations in which the interests of the union and the employer are opposed.[30] It is argued that this is an old-fashioned, 'left versus right' view of the world and that we should think instead of what workers and their employers have in common. Both groups are interested in creating successful firms (workers to secure their jobs and employers to make a profit) so it is more appropriate to think in terms of a partnership between them. Of course, in practice, much depends on how unions choose to negotiate. They may adopt a combination of partnership and adversarial approaches depending on the issue at hand. The 'voice' argument explored above suggests that opportunities to challenge the employer can make workers happier.

---

[28] See FA Hayek, *The Constitution of Liberty* (University of Chicago Press 1960) chapter 18; RA Posner, *Economic Analysis of Law* (8th edn, Wolters Kluwer 2011) chapter 11.

[29] ACL Davies, 'One Step Forward, Two Steps Back? The *Viking* and *Laval* Cases in the ECJ' (2008) 37 ILJ 126, 148.

[30] Department of Trade and Industry, Fairness at Work (Cm 3968, 1998) chapter 4. For empirical analysis and critique of 'partnership' ideas, see Martin Upchurch *et al.*, *The Realities of Partnership at Work* (Palgrave Macmillan 2008).

11.2.4 Regulatory implications

The debate about the place of trade unions in politics and industrial relations has had important implications for legal regulation, because some governments have been positively encouraging of the trade union movement, others openly hostile, and others indifferent. Much of the legislation enacted by a hostile government remains in place today, even though the recent political environment has been rather more indifferent towards trade unions.

Early attempts to form trade unions and to bargain collectively with employers were met with criminal sanctions both in statute and at common law.[31] Trade unions were treated as criminal conspiracies and as being 'in restraint of trade', what we would nowadays regard as in breach of competition law. These obstacles to unionisation were removed by the Trade Union Act 1871. However, it remained difficult for trade unionists to engage in meaningful collective bargaining because industrial action generally gave rise to criminal liability. For example, it was a criminal offence for an individual to breach his or her contract of employment.[32] It was not until the Employers and Workmen Act 1875 and the Conspiracy and Protection of Property Act 1875 that the criminal law was largely withdrawn from the field of industrial action, though some criminal liability did remain in respect of violent acts.[33] The courts (generally regarded as hostile to trade unions and their activities) then set about controlling industrial action through the development of tort liability at common law, for example, for inducing breach of contract.[34] This meant that while unions and their members were no longer exposed to criminal liability, they were exposed to tort liability with potentially serious consequences for unions' funds. The Trade Disputes Act 1906 gave unions a blanket immunity against tort liability and a more limited immunity to strike organisers provided certain conditions were met.

This regime remained in place – apart from changes during wartime – well into the twentieth century. It led Kahn-Freund to develop his theory of 'collective laissez-faire' to describe the UK's approach towards industrial relations.[35] This was the idea that unions and employers should be allowed to determine working conditions for themselves through the process of collective bargaining. The role of the legislature was confined largely to creating the conditions for successful collective bargaining rather than legislating to set terms and conditions of employment. In the 1960s and 1970s, the legislature's role came back into focus. With relatively high levels of strike action, the judges began to develop new torts, so the immunities had to be updated to keep pace.[36] At the same time, the political controversy surrounding unions grew more acute. The Conservative government tried to enact wholesale reforms in 1971, but the Act failed because it was boycotted by the unions,[37] and subsequent Labour governments enacted legislation designed to protect and promote trade unionism, such as the statutory recognition procedure.[38]

[31] See, generally, Douglas Brodie, *A History of British Labour Law 1867–1945* (Hart 2003).
[32] Master and Servant Act 1867.
[33] For example, the Combination Act 1825 created vague offences of molestation, obstruction and intimidation.
[34] *Taff Vale Rly v ASRS* [1901] AC 426.
[35] Above n 1.
[36] The Trade Disputes Act 1965 was introduced to extend the immunity to the tort of 'intimidation' in light of *Rookes v Barnard* [1964] AC 1129.
[37] Industrial Relations Act 1971.
[38] Employment Protection Act 1975.

Most of the modern law on trade unions and their members was enacted during the period of Conservative governments between 1979 and 1997.[39] A significant period of strike action, known as the 'winter of discontent', took place before the 1979 general election, and the Conservatives came to power partly on the basis of a promise to limit the power of the trade unions. Rather than attempting to enact a comprehensive reform, as their predecessors had tried to do in 1971, they enacted a series of smaller reforms, with a new Act roughly every two years tackling some aspect of industrial relations. The 1992 Act consolidated these various reforms into a single statute. In broad terms, we can characterise the reforms as designed to limit the power and influence of trade unions. Within this broad aim, three sub-themes can be identified.

First, the reforms sought to promote democracy within trade unions and choice for trade union members. Unions were required to ballot their members on various issues[40] and union members were given rights to question or challenge the running of the union.[41] Individuals were given a choice whether to join a union at all, and if so which one, and (once they had joined) whether to join in with any of its activities, such as strikes.[42] Some aspects of these reforms are (relatively) uncontroversial. As we shall see, the idea that trade union membership might be compulsory in a particular workplace no longer accords with the ECtHR jurisprudence, so statutory protection for the right not to join a union is consistent with that.[43] However, critics argue that because the motivation underlying these reforms was to challenge the power of the trade union movement, they went beyond what was necessary to promote democracy and protect choice. For example, it is questionable whether, once someone has joined an organisation voluntarily, he or she should have the option of disregarding its rules.

Second, the reforms sought to discourage solidarity between unions and between workers at different workplaces. For example, as we shall see in later chapters, 'secondary' strike action, in which workers at firm A (who are not in dispute) strike to support workers at firm B, who are in dispute, was rendered unlawful.[44] Similarly, unions were effectively prevented from maintaining a system – known as the 'Bridlington principles' – under which they undertook not to poach members from other unions.[45] This was achieved by making it unlawful for a union to exclude or expel someone on the grounds that he or she had previously been a member of another union.[46] Critics saw these changes as a way of promoting a climate of individualism, which might ultimately lead people to reject the whole concept of collective activity through trade unions.

Third, attempts were made to discourage unions from engaging in political activities, and to narrow their focus to the industrial relations functions outlined above. Unions were not allowed to take into account an individual's membership of

---

[39] For an overview, see Davies and Freedland, above n 18, chapter 9.

[40] See now, for example, TULRCA, s 226.

[41] See now, for example, ibid s 230.

[42] See now ibid s 65(2)(a).

[43] *Sorenson v Denmark* (2008) 46 EHRR 29.

[44] See now TULRCA, s 244(1).

[45] For discussion, see Jane Elgar and Bob Simpson, 'A Final Appraisal of "Bridlington"? An Evaluation of TUC Disputes Committee Decisions 1974–1991' (1994) 32 BJIR 47; Bob Simpson, 'Bridlington "2"' (1994) 23 ILJ 170.

[46] See now TULRCA, s 174(2).

a political party when making membership decisions, with the effect that they could not exclude people from hostile parties (who might be joining for subversive reasons) or require people to join pro-union parties, such as Labour.[47] And if they wanted to engage in political campaigns, they had to maintain a separate fund for this purpose and ballot the membership every 10 years on the continuation of the fund.[48] The government believed that ordinary trade union members were less politically engaged than their leaders and would vote against political funds, but in practice this turned out not to be the case.[49]

Some changes were introduced by the Labour governments between 1997 and 2010, but most of the 1980s legislation remains in force today. The atmosphere, however, is very different. As we noted in the introduction, trade union membership has been declining and the trade union movement is no longer able to cause the level of disruption that occurred in, say, 1979. There is quite a debate about why this change has come about. Some commentators attribute the decline in trade unionism largely to the legislation. Others point to important economic and social changes during the same period: for example, industries in which unions were very strong (coal, steel, car manufacturing and so on) fell into decline and a greater proportion of people began working in the harder-to-organise service sector.[50] Whatever the reason, the need to keep the trade union movement under control is no longer a pressing policy concern. This has given rise to a situation in which it is unlikely that the government will initiate an overhaul of the law of its own motion, even though the law does not fit very well with modern conditions.

Recent developments in trade union law have come instead from an unlikely source: the ECtHR. Freedom of association, which includes the right to form and join trade unions, is protected under Article 11. There is a growing body of jurisprudence on Article 11 in which the Court has done two important things: it has adopted an understanding of freedom of association which is both 'collective' and 'dynamic'. It is collective in that it recognises that freedom of association is not just a right for individuals who want to join (or who want not to join) a union, but is also a collective right for unions themselves to make decisions about membership and to take action on behalf of their members.[51] It is dynamic in the sense that it recognises that union membership is not just about joining an organisation but also about engaging in activities – collective bargaining, strikes and so on – as part of that organisation.[52] Although there is not very much case-law, we shall see that its overall tone is in marked contrast to the UK approach as laid down in the 1992 Act, and on occasion the government has been forced to introduce amendments to reflect ECtHR rulings.[53] This opens up the possibility that further changes could be brought about through judicial interpretation under the HRA, though given the courts' traditional

---

[47] However, see now the changes introduced by TULRCA, ss 174(4A)–(4H).

[48] See now ibid ss 71(1)(b)(i) and 73(3).

[49] Davies and Freedland, above n 18.

[50] For discussion, see Jeremy Waddington, 'Trade Union Membership in Britain, 1980–1987: Unemployment and Reconstructing' (1992) 30 BJIR 287.

[51] See, for example, *ASLEF v UK* (2007) 45 EHRR 34.

[52] See, for example, *Wilson v UK* (2002) 35 EHRR 20; *Demir and Baykara v Turkey* (2009) 48 EHRR 54.

[53] For example, TULRCA, ss 145A and 145B were introduced by the Employment Relations Act 2004, following the ECtHR ruling in *Wilson v UK* (above n 52).

hostility towards trade unions, there is some reason to be sceptical on this score. Finally, it is worth bearing in mind that the UK government has ratified the core ILO conventions on freedom of association.[54] Even though successive governments have shown themselves willing to disregard criticism from the ILO, these conventions offer a detailed benchmark against which to assess the law and may also have some indirect influence because ILO materials are sometimes cited by the ECtHR.[55]

11.3 THE REGULATION OF TRADE UNIONS' INTERNAL AFFAIRS

We will begin by considering how the law regulates trade unions' internal affairs, such as their finances and governance mechanisms, before turning in the next section to questions about membership. These two topics are interrelated in the sense that unions' 'internal' duties are owed to their members, but it helps to split them up for explanatory purposes.

11.3.1 ECHR and ILO norms

The ECHR protects freedom of association, including the right to form and join trade unions, under Article 11. Any interference with freedom of association must be prescribed by law and must be a proportionate means of achieving a legitimate aim within Article 11(2). Most of the Court's decided cases on state interference with associations have quite extreme facts – usually, that the state has banned or refused to 'register' the association – though, as we shall see in the next section, there have been cases on trade unions' membership decisions. Thus, it is difficult to extract precise guidance from the Convention jurisprudence on state regulation of trade unions of less extreme kinds. However, the general principles are clear: unions have the right to 'administer their own affairs',[56] and any state interference is subject to assessment under Article 11(2). This suggests strong protection for unions' autonomy.

The ILO regards freedom of association as a fundamental right guaranteed under its constitution and other instruments such as the Declaration of Fundamental Principles and Rights at Work 1998. For detail, though, we need to look at Convention 87, which deals with the state's obligations towards unions and employers' associations.[57] Convention 87 requires signatory states to enable unions and employers' associations (and federations of unions or employers' associations) to operate with a high degree of autonomy. Article 3 emphasises the right of unions and employers' associations to regulate their own affairs:

(1) Workers' and employers' organisations shall have the right to draw up their constitutions and rules, to elect their representatives in full freedom, to organise their administration and activities and to formulate their programmes.

(2) The public authorities shall refrain from any interference which would restrict this right or impede the lawful exercise thereof.

---

[54] ILO, Convention on the Freedom of Association and Protection of the Right to Organise Convention (No 87, 1948); Convention on the Right to Organise and Collective Bargaining (No 98, 1949).
[55] For discussion of the 'integrated' approach to interpretation, see Virginia Mantouvalou, 'Labour Rights in the European Convention in Human Rights: an Intellectual Justification' (2013) 13 HRL Rev 529.
[56] *ASLEF*, above n 51, [38].
[57] This Convention has been ratified by 152 states (out of a possible 185) including the UK.

However, this is subject to Article 8, which states that such organisations, 'like other persons or organised collectivities, shall respect the law of the land'. This means that while unions and employers' associations should not be singled out for special treatment by the law, they can be subject to the rules that are more generally applicable. Thus, there is no objection to requiring trade unions to comply with equality law.

The Digest of Decisions of the Committee on Freedom of Association (CFA) and the various comments of the Committee of Experts on the Application of Recommendations and Regulations (CEACR) are useful sources of additional guidance on the interpretation of these provisions. In general terms, the CFA has accepted that a system of registration of trade unions is acceptable – since official recognition of the existence of a trade union may help it to function more effectively – provided that the requirements for registration are minimal and the registration process is not used as a means of inhibiting freedom of association.[58] Similarly, some legal regulation to ensure that trade unions are run democratically and that their finances are properly managed is acceptable, provided that it is genuinely intended to safeguard the interests of trade union members.[59] Although the CFA usually emphasises that the primary role of trade unions is to advance the interests of their members in the workplace, it rejects any restriction on the political activities of trade unions, noting that the line between political and industrial activities is very difficult to draw, so any such restriction might impair freedom of association.[60] The CFA has indicated a preference for legislation and judicial control, rather than administrative discretion, as a means of regulating trade unions, because of the risk that public officials might use their discretion to hinder legitimate trade union activities.[61] Moreover, any such legislation should be kept as general as possible: in an observation adopted in 1995, the Committee of Experts noted (in relation to the UK) that 'the continuing regulation of the smallest details of the internal functioning of workers' organizations may reach a point where the cumulative effect of such regulation, by virtue of its detail, complexity and extent . . . constitutes an interference in the rights of such organizations under Article 3 of the Convention'.[62]

11.3.2 The legal status of trade unions

Before delving into the detail, it is important to know something about the basic legal underpinnings of a trade union. Trade unions are unincorporated associations, but statute gives them many of the attributes of a corporation, such as the power to make contracts and the capacity to sue and be sued in their own name.[63] Technically, and somewhat artificially, a member joins a trade union (like any other unincorporated association) by entering into a contract with the other members.[64] This is so even though in practice the new member will probably only have communicated with the union's membership department or with a local branch official. A union will usually have a

---

[58] ILO, *Digest of Decisions of the Committee on Freedom of Association* (5th edn, 2006) [294]–[308].
[59] ibid [369].
[60] ibid [497]–[507].
[61] For example, ibid [699].
[62] CEACR, *Observation adopted 1995, published 82nd ILC session (1995) on the Freedom of Association and Protection of the Right to Organise Convention, 1948 (No 87) – United Kingdom (Ratification 1949)*, para 5.
[63] TULRCA, s 10.
[64] See, for example, *Faramus v Film Artistes' Association* [1964] AC 925.

constitution or rule-book of some kind. This derives its authority from the members' contracts: in other words, the members are bound by it because they have agreed to be bound. But the trade union's capacity to set its own rules by this mechanism is limited by the need to comply with the various statutory requirements we are about to consider.

11.3.3 Listing and independence

A public official known as the Certification Officer maintains a publicly available list of trade unions.[65] Inclusion on the list simply means that the organisation in question meets the statutory definition of a trade union in s. 1 TULRCA. A union may choose not to be listed, though it must still comply with the law on trade unions whether it is listed or not. Listing confers a few advantages on a trade union, most of which are fairly technical in nature,[66] though a couple are potentially significant. One is that listing is evidence that the organisation is a trade union.[67] Another is that it affords some protection to the union's name, because the Certification Officer may not list another union with the same or a similar name if it might lead to confusion.[68]

Once listed,[69] a union may apply to the Certification Officer for a certificate of independence.[70] This is an important step because many of the statutory rights afforded to trade unions are confined to 'independent' trade unions. These include rights relating to collective bargaining.[71] The definition of an 'independent trade union' is found in s. 5 TULRCA:

> In this Act an "independent trade union" means a trade union which–
>
> (a) is not under the domination or control of an employer or group of employers or of one or more employers' associations, and
>
> (b) is not liable to interference by an employer or any such group or association (arising out of the provision of financial or material support or by any other means whatsoever) tending towards such control;
>
> and references to "independence", in relation to a trade union, shall be construed accordingly.

This definition seeks to distinguish 'genuine' trade unions from 'staff associations' set up by the employer, and to ensure that rights intended for trade unions are not extended to such associations.

Under s. 9 TULRCA, an appeal lies to the EAT against a decision of the Certification Officer on listing or independence.

11.3.4 The register of members

Under s. 24 TULRCA, the union is under a duty to keep a register of the names and addresses of its members, and must 'secure, so far as is reasonably practicable, that the entries in the register are accurate and are kept up-to-date'. The union must

---

[65] See http://www.certoffice.org (last visited 12 September 2014); TULRCA, s 2(1).
[66] For example, TULRCA, s 13.
[67] TULRCA, s 2(4).
[68] ibid s 3(4).
[69] ibid s 5(3).
[70] ibid s 6(1).
[71] See Chapter 12.

supply a member with a copy of the entry relating to him or her if asked to do so. Any breach of the s. 24 duty is challengeable by way of complaint to the Certification Officer under s. 25 or to the court under s. 26.

The Transparency of Lobbying, Non-Party Campaigning and Trade Union Administration Act 2014 (which has not, at the time of writing, been brought fully into force) will introduce an additional requirement in TULRCA, s. 24ZA for unions to certify to the Certification Officer that they are in compliance with s. 24. Smaller unions may simply provide a certificate signed by an official, but for unions with more than 10,000 members, an independent 'assurer' must be used.[72] Under s. 24ZD(3), the assurer's certificate must state whether 'the trade union's system for compiling and maintaining the register of the names and addresses of its members was satisfactory'. The Certification Officer has power to investigate if 'it appears to the Officer that there are circumstances suggesting that the union has failed to comply with a requirement of section 24(1), 24ZA or 24ZB',[73] and to issue an enforcement order.[74] Unions have criticised the bureaucratic nature of these requirements and the risk that having to disclose their membership lists will result in members being identified and discriminated against, though the Act now contains confidentiality requirements to tackle this.[75]

The requirement to maintain an accurate register may seem trivial – after all, any membership organisation is likely to want to maintain a list of its members for the purposes of communicating with them and collecting their subscriptions – but as we shall see below,[76] the accuracy of the membership register is in fact a critical issue for trade unions. They are required to ballot their members on various issues, including a decision to take industrial action, and can face serious consequences if they do not send a ballot paper to everyone who is entitled to vote. This means that it is very important to keep the register up-to-date if members change their job or address, for example, regardless of the provisions just considered.

11.3.5 Democracy

Trade unions have long been seen as a vehicle for 'grass roots' democracy, so we might well expect them to be run democratically as a matter of course, regardless of statutory regulation. In practice, though, unions are required by law to observe democratic principles in certain circumstances.

Under s. 46(2) TULRCA, unions are obliged to ensure that elections are held at five-yearly intervals for the positions of president, general secretary and members of the executive. The union may not 'unreasonably' exclude anyone from standing for election to one of these positions, nor may it require candidates to be members of a political party.[77] The conduct of the election must be managed by an independent scrutineer.[78] All members of the union must be afforded the entitlement to vote (though there are some exceptions to this, for example, for those who are in arrears

---

[72] TULRCA, s 24ZB.
[73] ibid s 24ZI.
[74] ibid s 24B.
[75] ibid s 24ZG.
[76] See also Chapter 13.
[77] TULRCA, ss 47(1) and (2).
[78] ibid s 49(1).

with their subscriptions).[79] The election must be conducted by postal vote, and the union is obliged to include with the ballot paper election addresses from all the candidates.[80] If the union fails to comply with any of the requirements, a member or a candidate may apply either to the Certification Officer or to the court for a declaration to that effect.[81] If the application is successful, the union will normally be required to hold another election in accordance with the rules or take some other steps to rectify the problem.[82]

As the number of trade union members has declined, so the number of unions has declined, because it is difficult for smaller organisations to remain financially viable or to campaign or bargain effectively. Under TULRCA, unions may merge in one of two ways: by transfer or by amalgamation.[83] Where a transfer takes place, the members of union A are transferred into union B, which retains its identity. Where an amalgamation takes place, the members of unions A and B become members of new union C. In both situations, the unions involved must draft terms of agreement and a notice to members, and secure the Certification Officer's approval of these documents.[84] Then they must conduct a postal ballot supervised by an independent scrutineer.[85] In the case of a transfer, only the members of union A must be balloted, whereas in the case of an amalgamation, the members of both union A and union B must be balloted.[86] The unions in question may not make a recommendation to their members as to how to vote in the ballot.[87] The Certification Officer may hear complaints about the conduct of these procedures.[88]

Unions are also required by statute to ballot their members on two other important issues: whether to take industrial action[89] and whether to maintain a special fund, called the 'political fund', which can be used for political campaigns.[90] We will consider these elsewhere.[91]

11.3.6 Financial matters

Trade unions' property is held in trust for them.[92]

Under s. 28 TULRCA, a trade union is obliged to keep accounts.[93] These must be audited, and made available to a member of the union on request. Under s. 32, the union must make an 'annual return' to the Certification Officer. This must include the union's accounts, a statement from the auditor, details of the salaries paid to union leaders, and a copy of the union's rules, among other things. Under s. 32A, the

---

[79] ibid s 50(1).
[80] ibid s 51(4).
[81] ibid ss 55(1) and 56(1).
[82] ibid ss 55(5A) and 56(4).
[83] ibid ss 97(1) and (2).
[84] ibid ss 98(1) and 99(1).
[85] ibid s 100A(1).
[86] ibid s 97.
[87] ibid s 99(3A).
[88] ibid s 103(1).
[89] ibid s 226.
[90] ibid s 71.
[91] See Chapter 13 on industrial action, and the discussion of unions' finances below.
[92] TULRCA, s 12.
[93] There is special treatment of unions' provident funds: see, for example, TULRCA, s 19.

union must make a statement to its members, in effect summarising the key points from the annual return, and telling them – in terms set out in the statute – how to take forward any concerns they may have about irregularities in the union's financial dealings. The Certification Officer has extensive powers to investigate unions' financial affairs where he or she suspects fraud or where any of the rules laid down in TULRCA have not been followed.[94]

We saw above that one of the functions commonly performed by trade unions is to engage in political campaigning. In the 1980s, the Conservative government introduced a special regulatory regime for trade unions' political activities, claiming that ordinary trade union members were less politically engaged or radical than their leaders and would reject unions' political role if given the opportunity to do so.[95] This turned out not to be the case, though the regulatory regime has introduced some extra costs for trade unions.

Under s. 71 TULRCA, a union may not use its funds for political campaigning unless its members approve of this by resolution. This resolution must be renewed every 10 years.[96] If a political resolution is in place, the union must maintain a political fund separate from its other resources to pay for its campaigning, and must ensure that any member who objects to making contributions to the political fund is exempt from doing so.[97] If a union applies its general funds for political purposes, a member may make a complaint to the Certification Officer (or potentially the court).[98]

Political 'objects' are defined in s. 72(1) as follows:

The political objects to which this Chapter applies are the expenditure of money–

(a) on any contribution to the funds of, or on the payment of expenses incurred directly or indirectly by, a political party;

(b) on the provision of any service or property for use by or on behalf of any political party;

(c) in connection with the registration of electors, the candidature of any person, the selection of any candidate or the holding of any ballot by the union in connection with any election to a political office;

(d) on the maintenance of any holder of a political office;

(e) on the holding of any conference or meeting by or on behalf of a political party or of any other meeting the main purpose of which is the transaction of business in connection with a political party;

(f) on the production, publication or distribution of any literature, document, film, sound recording or advertisement the main purpose of which is to persuade people to vote for a political party or candidate or to persuade them not to vote for a political party or candidate.

The union's rules on the conduct of the ballot for the political resolution must be approved by the Certification Officer and must comply with various requirements similar to those discussed above in relation to elections for important trade union

---

[94] ibid s 37B.
[95] Davies and Freedland, above n 18.
[96] TULRCA, s 73.
[97] ibid s 71(1)(b).
[98] ibid s 72A.

offices.[99] The ballot must be fully postal and must be run by an independent scrutineer.[100] Every member of the union must be afforded entitlement to vote.[101] A member who is dissatisfied with the conduct of the process may complain to the Certification Officer or to the court.[102]

Once the political fund is in place, the union must inform its members of their right to be exempt from contributing to it if they so choose.[103] The union may not require members to contribute to the political fund as a condition of being a member, nor may it disadvantage anyone who chooses not to contribute.[104] Where the member pays his or her union subscription by 'check off' (where the employer deducts it from his or her wages and passes it on to the union), he or she may seek a remedy at the Employment Tribunal if the employer wrongly deducts a political fund contribution when an exemption notice is in force.[105]

According to the Certification Officer's annual report, 25 unions had political funds in 2013.[106] This represents around a quarter of the trade unions with certificates of independence. However, it is important to bear in mind that political funds are concentrated among the big unions, so some 4.8 million trade union members (a majority) contribute to a political fund. A further 848,000 members of unions with political funds have opted out. The sums involved are substantial: trade union political funds had a total income of £24 million in 2013. These statistics seem to contradict the government's claim that trade union members would not want their unions to spend money on political campaigns (though it is worth noting that the number of people opting out is not insignificant). Indeed, the fact that political funds are democratically authorised may have served to increase their legitimacy.

It is worth noting that unions are also subject to the rules applicable to 'non-party campaigners' under electoral law. This means that, for example, in the run-up to a general election, the union must comply with expenditure limits and report its activities to the Electoral Commission if its political campaigns are intended to persuade people to vote for a particular political party or for candidates who support particular policies. Recent reforms in the Transparency of Lobbying, Non Party Campaigning and Trade Union Administration Act 2014 have made these rules more stringent, for example, by extending the range of campaign activities covered by the spending limits.

11.3.7 Complaints and enforcement

We saw above that a union member has a contractual relationship with his or her union. If the union breaches its own rules, a member could seek a remedy for breach of contract through the courts.[107] Indeed, a union may not deny a member access to the courts by providing in its rules that certain disputes can only be

---

[99] ibid s 74(1).
[100] ibid ss 75(1) and 77(4).
[101] ibid s 76.
[102] ibid ss 80(1) and 81(1).
[103] ibid s 82(1)(b).
[104] ibid ss 82(1)(c) and 82(1)(d).
[105] ibid s 87(1).
[106] Certification Officer, *Annual Report of the Certification Officer 2013–2014* (2014) chapter 7.
[107] For example, *Lee v Showmen's Guild of Great Britain* [1952] 2 QB 329; *Esterman v NALGO* [1974] ICR 625.

decided under the union's own procedures.[108] However, litigation is an expensive option for the average trade union member. For a time, there existed a public official known as the Commissioner for the Rights of Trade Union Members whose role it was to assist union members in bringing legal proceedings against their unions, but very few people approached the Commissioner and the office was abolished in 1999.[109]

Since 1999, the Certification Officer has played a more general role in helping union members to ensure that their union complies with its rules.[110] Under s. 108A TULRCA, a union member may apply to the Certification Officer in respect of a 'breach or threatened breach' of union rules in relation to:

(a) the appointment or election of a person to, or the removal of a person from, any office;
(b) disciplinary proceedings by the union (including expulsion);
(c) the balloting of members on any issue other than industrial action;
(d) the constitution or proceedings of any executive committee or of any decision-making meeting;
(e) such other matters as may be specified in an order made by the Secretary of State.[111]

This is in addition to the various possibilities of seeking help from the Certification Officer in relation to specific rules discussed above, such as the rules on political funds. The member must choose between approaching the Certification Officer and going to court, though this does not preclude a legal challenge to the Certification Officer's decision on the complaint (which lies to the EAT under s. 108C). The Certification Officer has power to investigate the complaint, to make a declaration, and to make an enforcement order requiring the union to take steps to remedy the problem.[112] The Certification Officer deals with a small number of complaints each year (17 new complaints in 2013–14).[113]

11.3.8 Conclusion

We saw above that both the ILO and the ECtHR have emphasised the status of trade unions as autonomous organisations with the freedom to draw up their own rules without interference from the authorities. However, this is qualified in various ways, so it may be acceptable to impose some requirements on unions, for example, to guard against the misuse of union funds. It is quite difficult to assess English law against these standards: English law does not inhibit unions in obvious ways, and the regulatory objectives it pursues are generally legitimate. Nevertheless, there is room for debate about whether the level of detail in the 1992 Act goes beyond what is truly necessary to protect union members. This issue arises in more acute form when we consider how the law regulates trade unions' decisions on the exclusion, expulsion and disciplining of their members, to which we will now turn.

---

[108] TULRCA, s 63.
[109] By the Employment Relations Act 1999. For discussion, see KD Ewing, 'Freedom of Association and the Employment Relations Act 1999' (1999) 28 ILJ 283, 296–298.
[110] The union is under a duty to supply anyone who makes a request with a copy of its rules under s 27 TULRCA.
[111] TULRCA, s 108A(2).
[112] ibid s 108B.
[113] Certification Officer, *Annual Report 2013–2014* (2014) chapter 9.

11.4 TRADE UNIONS AND THEIR MEMBERS

In this section, we will consider three key issues relating to trade union membership:

- a union's refusal to allow an individual to join ('exclusion');
- disciplinary measures taken by a union against a member;
- a union's decision to terminate an individual's membership ('expulsion').

English law engages in extensive regulation of trade unions' membership decisions, both at common law and in statute.[114] The courts' intervention in this area was driven by the emergence of the 'closed shop', an arrangement in which a union and an employer would reach an agreement that everyone employed in the particular workplace would have to join the union. Where a closed shop was in operation, an individual who was expelled from the union also stood to lose his or her job. Thus, the courts intervened on the basis that they were protecting vulnerable individuals from potential abuses of unions' dominant position. Now that the closed shop is unenforceable (as s. 5 below will explain) the status of this case-law is uncertain.

In any event, the common law rules have been largely superseded by a very extensive statutory regime which controls unions' decisions on exclusion, expulsion and discipline. These controls were introduced in the 1980s, and were justified in broad terms as a means of promoting individual choice both about and within trade unions.[115] So, for example, the legislation sought to ensure that individuals could choose whether to join a union at all, which union to join if they did opt to join, and to what extent they wished to take part in union activities having joined. In particular, the government sought to ensure that going on strike was a matter of individual choice, by barring unions from disciplining or expelling those who chose to continue working. Critics argued that this undermined the idea of solidarity between workers that underpins the very concept of trade unionism. Detailed regulation of unions' membership decisions may also conflict with freedom of association as understood by the ILO and the ECtHR.

11.4.1 ILO and ECHR

Both the ILO and the ECtHR emphasise that unions should have autonomy to run their own affairs and to set their own membership rules. There are some subtle differences in their approaches, which we will explore, but in general terms, both indicate that unions enjoy the freedom not to associate with particular individuals.

The ECtHR's reasoning under Article 11 has two strands. The first is the idea that unions enjoy the right to 'administer their own affairs' as part of the right to form a trade union under Article 11(1).[116] The second and more recent strand is that – now that the Court has held that individuals enjoy a right not to join a union under Article 11 – unions themselves have a right not to admit certain individuals to membership because freedom of association is a reciprocal idea. Both lines of thinking are subject

---

[114] It should be noted that some public sector workers are prohibited from joining unions. The international instruments are generally permissive of restrictions in 'essential services'. See, for example, TULRCA s 280 (dealing with police officers).

[115] Davies and Freedland, above n 18, chapter 9.

[116] *ASLEF*, above n 51, [38].

to the state's duty under Article 11(2) to regulate unions' activities to ensure that they do not abuse a dominant position to the detriment of the individual. The challenge, then, is to figure out when exactly the state is entitled to intervene.

The leading decision on the issue is *ASLEF v UK*.[117] In that case, the trade union ASLEF challenged UK legislation that entitled individuals who were expelled from a union because of their membership of a political party to challenge the union's decision and, potentially, claim compensation. ASLEF had fallen foul of these rules in a case in which it had expelled a member of the British National Party (BNP).[118] ASLEF argued that membership of the BNP was incompatible with its anti-racism objectives and that its freedom of association was infringed by rules which, in effect, forced it to associate with BNP supporters. The ECtHR upheld ASLEF's claim. The Court affirmed that unions had a right to decide their own membership:

> Where associations are formed by people, who, espousing particular values or ideals, intend to pursue common goals, it would run counter to the very effectiveness of the freedom at stake if they had no control over their membership.[119]

The Court then qualified this by saying that the state was under a duty to protect individuals against the abuse of a dominant position by a trade union.[120] It explained that:

> such abuse might occur, for example, where exclusion or expulsion from a trade union was not in accordance with union rules or where the rules were wholly unreasonable or arbitrary or where the consequences of exclusion or expulsion resulted in exceptional hardship . . . [121]

In relation to the case itself, the Court found that ASLEF has acted within its rules and that the BNP member's expulsion had not caused him 'exceptional hardship' because there was no closed shop and because he would still benefit from any collective agreement negotiated by ASLEF and applied at his workplace.[122] As we shall see below, the reform of English law to bring it into line with the *ASLEF* ruling has proved controversial.

The ILO also offers strong protection to the union's right to refuse membership to a particular individual, though the basis for doing so is slightly different to that adopted by the ECtHR. The ILO does not have a clear position on the closed shop, leaving this to the discretion of states, so it cannot base the union's freedom to refuse someone membership on the individual's freedom not to join. Instead, the ILO's approach derives from a more general requirement of autonomy for trade unions in formulating their own rules laid down in Article 3 of Convention 87. It is most apparent from Article 2 of the Convention:

> Workers and employers, without distinction whatsoever, shall have the right to establish and, *subject only to the rules of the organisation concerned*, to join organisations of their own choosing without previous authorisation.[123]

---

[117] Above n 51. See Keith Ewing, 'The Implications of the *ASLEF* Case' (2007) 36 ILJ 425.
[118] *ASLEF v Lee* (EAT 24 February 2004). See John Hendy and KD Ewing, 'Trade Unions, Human Rights and the BNP' (2005) 34 ILJ 197.
[119] *ASLEF* (n 51) [39].
[120] ibid [40].
[121] ibid [43].
[122] ibid [50].
[123] Emphasis added.

This is subject to Article 8, the requirement that unions should respect the law of the land. Thus, we can infer that – provided that unions refrain from unlawful discrimination, for example – they should be permitted to draw up and enforce their own rules on membership.

The CEACR has repeatedly condemned English law's restrictive approach to trade unions' rules on membership.[124] It has argued in particular that unions should be free to decide for themselves whether or not to expel or otherwise discipline individuals who refuse to take part in strike action. It has also been critical of English law on the exclusion and expulsion of members on the grounds of their political views both prior to the *ASLEF* decision in the ECtHR, and in the light of the statutory changes introduced with a view to bringing the law into line with *ASLEF*.[125]

In the remainder of this section, we will examine the details of English law with Article 11 and Convention 87 in mind. While the UK government seems happy to ignore the ILO's criticisms, Article 11 has direct consequences in English law because the courts are obliged to take into account ECtHR decisions (which may refer to ILO materials) under s. 2 HRA, to develop the common law consistently with the Convention under s. 6, and to interpret statute law to bring it into line with Convention rights under s. 3 (or, if that is not possible, to issue a declaration of incompatibility under s. 4). However, as we have already seen, there are reasons for being sceptical about the capacity of the HRA to bring about radical reform in this area. The courts nowadays have a tendency to see matters of employment law as more appropriately determined by the government and Parliament because of their economic implications. Moreover, it is the overall complexity of trade union legislation in the UK, as much as any particular rule taken by itself, that casts doubt on the effective realisation of freedom of association. Because courts are only called upon to decide particular cases, it is difficult for them to address broader concerns of this kind.

11.4.2 Exclusion, discipline and expulsion at common law

We noted above that the common law on unions' membership decisions may have been overtaken by events: now that there is detailed statutory regulation, individuals are more likely to rely on that than on the common law, and now that there are no closed shops, a key intellectual justification for the judges' strict approach is no longer applicable. As a result, no-one has brought a case at common law in this area recently, and if someone did, it is not clear how it would be decided. Nevertheless, it is worth knowing a bit about the cases, for two reasons. First, if the statutory regime was abolished (as the ILO would advocate), it is important to remember that the courts would still be able to regulate unions' relationships with their members by interpreting the contract of membership. The level of autonomy unions would enjoy would depend on how the courts went about this task. Second, the cases help to explain many labour lawyers' critical attitudes towards the courts in this area.

---

[124] See, for example, CEACR, *Observation – adopted 2004, published 93rd ILC session (2005) Freedom of Association and Protection of the Right to Organise Convention, 1948 (No. 87) – United Kingdom (Ratification: 1949).*

[125] CEACR, *Observation – adopted 2012, published 102nd ILC session (2013) Freedom of Association and Protection of the Right to Organise Convention, 1948 (No. 87) – United Kingdom (Ratification: 1949).*

We will begin by considering exclusion before turning to discipline and expulsion. Under the statute, all three are dealt with in similar ways, but at common law, there are important differences between exclusion on the one hand, and discipline and expulsion on the other.

Exclusion

We saw above that the relationship between a trade union and its members is based on the law of contract. One of the central principles of the law of contract is freedom of contract: the idea that people can make whatever contracts they like with whoever they like. Applying this principle, a trade union would in theory be free to refuse to enter into a membership contract with any potential member for any reason, good or bad. This approach is borne out by the *Faramus* case.[126] The rules of the union in that case stated that anyone with a criminal conviction could not be a member. The claimant had some convictions in his youth (some in Jersey under Nazi occupation) but did not declare them when he joined. The union later found out about the convictions and told him that he was ineligible for membership. The court expressed sympathy with the claimant but held that he had never validly been a member of the union. Attempts to argue that the rule was somehow unreasonable or contrary to public policy failed. This was so even though the union operated a closed shop, so that the claimant would find it difficult to get work without union membership.

Just occasionally, the courts made an exception to this. In *Nagle* v *Feilden*, a woman was refused a racehorse trainer's licence by the Jockey Club, apparently because of her gender.[127] The Court of Appeal held that because the Jockey Club had a monopoly over horse-racing it was arguable that the ban on granting licences to women was contrary to public policy and therefore void because it infringed her 'right to work'. This was so even though there could be no contractual remedy in the case. Although this case concerned a monopolistic regulator, rather than a trade union operating a closed shop, it is often cited as potentially relevant to unions too.

Outside the extreme case of *Nagle* – which would be dealt with under statute nowadays anyway – it seems unlikely that an individual who was refused membership of a union would be able to get a remedy at common law. This is reinforced by the fact that closed shops are no longer in operation so the case for bending the common law rules to provide some kind of remedy to an excluded individual is much weaker. Thus, in this area, the common law rules appear to safeguard the idea of trade union autonomy.

Expulsion

The picture is rather different when we turn to the question of discipline and expulsion. Once an individual has joined the union, his or her relationship with the union is governed by the contract of membership. This means that there is scope for the individual to complain to the Certification Officer or bring proceedings for breach of contract if, for example, the union has not complied with its own rules in taking a disciplinary decision. The courts traditionally adopted a highly interventionist stance

[126] *Faramus v Film Artistes' Association* [1964] AC 925.
[127] *Nagle v Feilden* [1966] 2 QB 633.

when construing the contract of membership, but the value of the older precedents today remains unclear.

One common theme in the closed-shop era case-law was to require unions to observe the rules of natural justice in their dealings with individuals, particularly where their jobs were at stake. Thus, in *Edwards* v *SOGAT*, the individual's union membership terminated automatically because his subscriptions had not been paid.[128] It emerged that the non-payment of his subscriptions was due to a clerical error on the part of a union official of which the individual was not aware. A majority in the Court of Appeal found that the automatic termination rule was contrary to public policy and therefore void, because it did not provide for a hearing of any kind. In *Lawlor* v *Union of Post Office Workers*, some trade union activists were expelled by the union for proposing industrial action contrary to the policy of the union's executive.[129] The judge held that the principles of natural justice should be implied into the union's power to expel members and that the principles had been breached in the case because the individuals had not been given a hearing. In general terms, a requirement to observe natural justice is not objectionable, particularly when an individual's job is at stake, as it was in *Edwards*. However, critics have noted that the courts have been much quicker to imply natural justice into union membership contracts than into contracts of employment, even though the same reasoning clearly applies.[130]

Another of the courts' concerns was that unions should not be able to oust the courts' jurisdiction. Again, the basic principle is not in doubt: access to the courts is a fundamental right, and in the case of trade union members, it is now specifically protected by statute.[131] However, the courts went further, in two respects. First, they held that, in some situations at least, they might be willing to hear an individual who had come to court without exhausting internal avenues of appeal within the union, even if this involved disregarding an express requirement to that effect in the union's rules.[132] Second, in the *Esterman* case, the court went so far as to grant an injunction precluding the union from hearing a case concerning whether the claimant was 'unfit' to retain her membership of the union, on the basis that no reasonable tribunal could find that she should be expelled.[133] In both instances, critics expressed concern that the courts were anticipating wrongdoing on the part of unions instead of allowing them to complete their procedures.

The more recent decision in *McVitae* may indicate a softening of attitudes within the courts now that there is extensive regulation of unions' activities and no closed shop.[134] In that case, a number of unions merged to form Unison without making provision for disciplinary action that was underway in the predecessor unions. The court was willing to imply a power for Unison to continue the disciplinary proceedings, provided that the offence of which the members were accused was contrary to the rules of both the predecessor union and Unison. This suggests a more facilitative

---

[128] *Edwards* v *SOGAT* [1971] Ch 354.
[129] *Lawlor* v *Union of Post Office Workers* [1965] Ch 712.
[130] Patrick Elias and KD Ewing, *Trade Union Democracy, Members' Rights, and the Law* (Mansell 1987) chapter 2.
[131] TULRCA, s 63.
[132] *Leigh* v *NUR* [1970] Ch 326.
[133] *Esterman* v *NALGO* [1974] ICR 625.
[134] *McVitae* v *UNISON* [1996] IRLR 33.

attitude. However, the facts of the case were rather unusual, and since all the other recent cases have arisen under the statutory regime, it is difficult to draw general conclusions.

In terms of the human rights implications of the common law approach, the picture is mixed. On the one hand, the ILO accepts that unions should comply with their own rules and that remedies should be available in the event that they do not, preferably before courts rather than administrative authorities.[135] The ECtHR has emphasised in the context of Article 11 that the state should intervene to ensure that unions do not abuse a dominant position (as might occur where, for example, the individual stands to lose his or her job as a result of union exclusion or expulsion).[136] On the other hand, the principle of autonomy enshrined in both regimes suggests a high degree of freedom for unions to make their own internal decisions, and this casts doubt on the legitimacy of the courts' decisions to intervene before unions have completed their internal procedures.

11.4.3 Exclusion, discipline and expulsion under statute

TULRCA contains two main groups of provisions on exclusion, discipline and expulsion. Sections 64 and 65 deal with 'unjustifiable' discipline: in effect, a list of prohibited grounds for disciplining trade union members. Section 174 and related sections deal with exclusion and expulsion, by providing that a union may only exclude or expel someone where the statute permits. The two groups of provisions are connected in that anything that would fall foul of ss. 64–65 cannot be used to exclude or expel someone under s. 174. It is also possible for an individual to seek a remedy for discrimination by a union under the Equality Act 2010. We will examine these various provisions in this section.

Equality law

Under s. 57 Equality Act 2010, it is unlawful for a 'trade organisation' – which includes a trade union under s. 57(7) – to discriminate on grounds of any of the characteristics protected under the Act. The provision is comprehensive, and covers refusing to admit someone as a member, denying him or her access to facilities or services, detriment and expulsion. Thus, it is not lawful to have a 'men-only' trade union, for example, or to deny a member access to certain facilities because of his or her disability.

TULRCA (1) – Exclusion and expulsion

TULRCA s. 174 lays down a comprehensive regulatory scheme for trade unions' membership decisions. It applies to both exclusion and expulsion. It operates by setting out four situations in which the union is *permitted* to exclude or expel someone. Thus, the union may not exclude or expel a person unless he or she fits into one of the four categories. We will examine each in turn.

---

[135] Above n 61.
[136] *ASLEF* (n 51), [43].

Under s. 174(2)(a), exclusion or expulsion is permitted if the individual 'does not satisfy, or no longer satisfies, an enforceable membership requirement contained in the rules of the union'. The concept of an enforceable membership requirement is defined in s. 174(3) to cover employment in a particular 'trade, industry or profession', job category or qualifications. In simple terms, this provision allows unions to specialise in representing particular kinds of worker and to exclude or expel people accordingly (so a union could specialise in representing train drivers and could refuse to admit nurses to membership).

Under s. 174(2)(b), exclusion or expulsion is permitted if the individual 'does not qualify, or no longer qualifies, for membership of the union by reason of the union operating only in a particular part or particular parts of Great Britain'. So the 'train drivers union of Scotland' could confine its membership to people who worked in Scotland, for example.

Under s. 174(2)(c), exclusion or expulsion is permitted 'in the case of a union whose purpose is the regulation of relations between its members and one particular employer or a number of particular employers who are associated' where the individual 'is not, or is no longer, employed by that employer or one of those employers'. This is self-explanatory.

The most complicated provision is s. 174(2)(d): 'the exclusion or expulsion is entirely attributable to conduct of his (other than excluded conduct) and the conduct to which it is wholly or mainly attributable is not protected conduct'. This mysterious piece of legislative drafting achieves four things:

- it bars a union from excluding or expelling someone because of certain types of behaviour that fall within the definition of 'excluded conduct';

- it allows a union to exclude or expel someone because of his or her behaviour where this falls outside the definition of 'excluded conduct';

- it allows a union to exclude or expel someone because of his or her activities undertaken as a member of a political party;

- it may allow a union to exclude or expel someone because of his or her membership, non-membership or past membership of a political party provided certain conditions are met.

We will examine these four possibilities in turn.

Under s. 174(4), 'excluded conduct' is defined as follows:

(a) conduct which consists in his being or ceasing to be, or having been or ceased to be, a member of another trade union,
(b) conduct which consists in his being or ceasing to be, or having been or ceased to be, employed by a particular employer or at a particular place, or
(c) conduct to which section 65 (conduct for which an individual may not be disciplined by a union) applies or would apply if the references in that section to the trade union which is relevant for the purposes of that section were references to any trade union.

The effect of s. 174(4)(a) is to give individuals a choice amongst different unions. Before the provision was enacted, unions affiliated to the TUC operated a system (known as the Bridlington Principles) in which they agreed not to poach each other's members.[137] The idea was that if union A had decided to organise a particular

---

[137] Above n 45.

workplace and seek recognition there, union B should not come along and disrupt its efforts by poaching some of its members. If some members of union A sought to join union B, union B was supposed to turn them away. Because of s. 174(4)(a), union B can no longer exclude or expel someone for having been a member of union A.[138] In effect, then, there is a 'marketplace' of unions for potential members to choose from, though in practice, there is now much less inter-union competition in a time of declining membership.

Under s. 174(4)(c), unions are prohibited from excluding or expelling people on grounds that would not be permitted when unions are disciplining people. We will discuss s. 65 in detail below, but for present purposes the two main things it covers are refusing to take part in or support a strike, and asserting rights against the union.[139] Thus, a union cannot exclude or expel from membership someone who is an opponent of strike action, or someone it might perceive as a 'trouble-maker'. The second of these seems quite straightforward: if the law grants someone a set of rights, we do not normally see it as acceptable for that person to suffer harm if he or she asserts those rights. But the first is more difficult, because it requires trade unions to allow people to join and remain in membership even if they do not support one of the key features of trade union activity: industrial action. We will discuss this issue in more detail below.

Outside these limitations, unions are free to exclude or expel people because of their conduct. So, for example, if a particular individual falls behind with the payment of his or her subscriptions, he or she could legitimately be expelled.[140] And under s. 174(4B), activities undertaken by the individual as a member of a political party may be a ground for exclusion. Of course, many trade unionists are politically active, and their union is unlikely to want to exclude them if they are, for example, handing out Labour party leaflets in their spare time. But this provision could be relevant if an activist from a far-right (or possibly far-left) party wanted to join the union for subversive reasons.

This leads us neatly to the issue of political party membership (as opposed to activities undertaken as a member). The union can treat this as a reason for excluding an applicant for membership or expelling a member, but only if membership of the political party is contrary to the union's rules or objectives and certain procedural requirements are observed.[141] The history of this set of provisions is interesting. They were introduced with a view to bringing English law into line with the ECtHR's decision in *ASLEF*, discussed above.[142] The government initially proposed removing all references to political party membership from the legislation, thus leaving unions to make their own decisions on the matter.[143] But during the passage of the legislation through Parliament, the Joint Committee on Human Rights expressed concern that this approach would not strike a proper balance between a union's freedom of association (as outlined in *ASLEF*) and individuals' expression and association rights

---

[138] Bob Simpson, 'Individualism versus Collectivism: an Evaluation of section 14 of the Trade Union Reform and Employment Rights Act 1993' (1993) 22 ILJ 181.

[139] For example, TULRCA, s 65(2)(a) and (c).

[140] Perhaps subject to natural justice at common law: above n 128.

[141] See, generally, KD Ewing, 'Employment Act 2008: Implementing the *ASLEF* Decision – a Victory for the BNP?' (2009) 38 ILJ 50.

[142] Above n 51.

[143] BERR, *ECHR Judgment in ASLEF v UK Case – Implications for Trade Union Law: Government response to Public Consultation* (November 2007).

in relation to political parties.[144] Thus, a number of amendments were introduced during the passage of the legislation with a view to offering individuals greater protection. We will examine the detailed law first, and consider the policy issues below.

Assume that the union wants to exclude or expel someone because he or she is or has been a member of a political party to which the union has strong objections. This will only be lawful if the following conditions are met:

(1) Membership of the political party in question is contrary to a rule or an objective of the union (s. 174(4C)). The union cannot rely on an 'objective' to exclude someone if it was not 'reasonably practicable for the objective to be ascertained by a person working in the same trade, industry or profession as the individual'. The union cannot rely on an 'objective' to expel someone if it was not 'reasonably practicable for the objective to be ascertained by a member of the union'. The inclusion of objectives gives unions greater freedom because they do not have to amend their rules to mention specific political parties and can rely instead on a more general 'lack of fit' between, say, membership of a political party with racist policies and the union's objective of securing racial equality. However, there is obviously more scope for litigation on whether there is a clash of objectives and on whether the union's objectives are sufficiently well-known, though in relation to members this requirement is rather odd given their right of access to the union's rule-book.[145]

(2) The union must act in accordance with its own rules (s. 174(4G)(a)).

(3) The union must act in a way that is procedurally fair as laid down in s. 174(4H). The individual must be given notice of, and reasons for, the decision to exclude or expel him or her, and an opportunity to make representations, and the representations must be considered fairly. It is worth noting that the same procedural requirements apply to exclusion and expulsion here, even though at common law procedural requirements would only apply to expulsion.[146]

(4) The individual must not 'lose his livelihood or suffer other exceptional hardship' by virtue of not being allowed to join the union or ceasing to be a member (s. 174(4G)(c)). As we saw above, now that closed shops are unlawful, the first of these is not an issue and the latter seems difficult to envisage.[147]

Thus, it is possible for, say, a union with clear anti-racist objectives to exclude or expel members of far right parties, but they must proceed with caution when doing so. A key question to think about in considering these provisions is whether they do, in fact, comply with the *ASLEF* ruling. In their defence, it can be said that they address the precise points raised by the ruling and they try to strike a balance between the individual's Article 10 rights and the union's Article 11 rights. However, as critics (and the ILO) have pointed out, the provisions are unnecessarily complex and, as a result, may still err too much on the side of protecting the individual.[148] The ECtHR's comments were intended to explain the Court's reasoning rather than to offer a model for domestic legislation. So, for example, since we can say with some certainty that

---

[144] JCHR, Seventeenth Report, Session 2007–2008, HL 95/HC 501, 28 April 2008.
[145] Above n 110.
[146] Ewing, above n 141, 54.
[147] ibid 55.
[148] ILO, above n 125; Ewing, above n 141.

an individual is unlikely to lose his or her livelihood as a result of being expelled from a union, there was no need to include an express reference to this in the legislation.

If an individual believes that he or she has been wrongly excluded or expelled from a union, he or she may bring a claim to the employment tribunal.[149] If the claim is well-founded, the tribunal may make a declaration to that effect.[150] The claimant may then apply for compensation. This is such compensation as is 'just and equitable' with an upper limit which consists of 30 times the statutory maximum week's pay (currently £464 per week[151]), giving a figure of £13,920, plus the maximum compensatory award for unfair dismissal (52 times the person's actual weekly pay (not subject to the maximum of £464) or £76,574, whichever is the lower).[152] This complex set of calculations has the potential to generate quite a high maximum award, though it is not clear in practice that tribunals would be willing to award very substantial sums here. If, at the time the individual applies for compensation, he or she has not been admitted or re-admitted to the union, the tribunal is required to award at least £8669.[153] However, this minimum award does not apply where the tribunal makes additional declarations to the effect that the exclusion or expulsion was mainly attributable to protected conduct but partially attributable to conduct contrary to the union's rules or objectives.[154]

TULRCA (2) – Disciplinary action

When someone joins a union, he or she agrees to be bound by its rules. If he or she breaks the rules, the union might want to take some kind of action – known as 'disciplinary action' against him or her. Of course, expulsion is the most extreme sanction but there are other, lesser, possibilities too, such as requiring the person to pay a fine or depriving him or her of access to union benefits or services for a period of time.

Under s. 64(1) TULRCA, union members have a right not to be 'unjustifiably disciplined' by their unions. This concept is defined in s. 65(2) as follows:

(a) failing to participate in or support a strike or other industrial action (whether by members of the union or by others), or indicating opposition to or a lack of support for such action;

(b) failing to contravene, for a purpose connected with such a strike or other industrial action, a requirement imposed on him by or under a contract of employment;

(c) asserting (whether by bringing proceedings or otherwise) that the union, any official or representative of it or a trustee of its property has contravened, or is proposing to contravene, a requirement which is, or is thought to be, imposed by or under the rules of the union or any other agreement or by or under any enactment (whenever passed) or any rule of law;

(d) encouraging or assisting a person–

(i) to perform an obligation imposed on him by a contract of employment, or

(ii) to make or attempt to vindicate any such assertion as is mentioned in paragraph (c);

---

[149] TULRCA, s 174(5).
[150] ibid s 176(1).
[151] ERA 1996, s 227.
[152] TULRCA, s 176(2)–(6).
[153] ibid s 176(6A).
[154] ibid ss 176(1B) and 176(6B).

(e) contravening a requirement imposed by or in consequence of a determination which infringes the individual's or another individual's right not to be unjustifiably disciplined,

(f) failing to agree, or withdrawing agreement, to the making from his wages (in accordance with arrangements between his employer and the union) of deductions representing payments to the union in respect of his membership,

(g) resigning or proposing to resign from the union or from another union, becoming or proposing to become a member of another union, refusing to become a member of another union, or being a member of another union,

(h) working with, or proposing to work with, individuals who are not members of the union or who are or are not members of another union,

(i) working for, or proposing to work for, an employer who employs or who has employed individuals who are not members of the union or who are or are not members of another union, or

(j) requiring the union to do an act which the union is, by any provision of this Act, required to do on the requisition of a member.

This long list of acts for which individuals cannot be disciplined can be divided into two main groups. First, some of the provisions (paragraphs (c) and (j), for example) are designed to protect individuals who assert their statutory rights against the union (unless they do so in bad faith). This seems relatively uncontroversial in the sense that we provide similar protection to individuals in relation to their employers through the provisions on victimisation. There is no point giving individuals a right to ask for the rule book or to see the accounts if they can be disciplined for doing so. In *Unison* v *Kelly*, the EAT held that there was no conflict between s. 65(2)(c) and Article 11 ECHR, though the judgment does hint that other aspects of s. 65(2) on strike action may be open to question.[155] Second, most of the other provisions are designed to preserve the individual's choice as to whether or not to take part in particular union activities, most notably, industrial action. The government's justification for introducing these provisions was that when people take industrial action, they generally breach their contracts of employment, which has various legal and practical consequences: they may be liable to be dismissed and they will not be paid for the duration of the strike.[156] Thus, the government argued, the decision to go on strike should be a matter of choice for the individual, who should not be subject to pressure from the union in the form of possible disciplinary action. Critics offered two main responses to these claims. One was to point out that the draconian consequences of strike action for the individual in English law are, in themselves, problematic.[157] In many other countries, the contract of employment is suspended for the duration of the strike, and the ILO has been critical of English law's treatment of individual strikers. The other was to note the contrast between the government's individualistic approach and the notion of solidarity with other workers that is an important part of the trade union tradition.[158] To take a simple example, if all the workers in a particular workgroup take part in a strike, there is protection against harsh treatment because it is hard for the employer to victimise everyone without making the situation worse, whereas if some people take part and others do not, that protection is lost. Moreover, while deciding not to take part may help an individual in the short term,

---

[155] [2012] IRLR 442.
[156] Department of Employment, *Trade Unions and their Members* (Cm 95, 1987) [2.22].
[157] See Chapter 13.
[158] Ewan McKendrick, 'The Rights of Trade Union Members – Part I of the Employment Act 1988' (1988) 17 ILJ 141.

a strike that is not well-supported is less effective, thus weakening the trade union and making it harder for it to achieve better terms and conditions for the workgroup in the long term.

11.4.4 ILO and ECHR revisited

We saw above that both the ILO and the ECtHR have, in their different ways, emphasised the autonomy of trade unions to choose their members and to draw up their membership rules. The difficulty with English law is that it starts from the opposite point of view: unions may only exclude, discipline or expel people if certain conditions are met as laid down in statute. Thus, its very conceptualisation is at odds with international standards. This makes it very difficult for the English courts – even if they could be persuaded to do so – to bring the law into line with Article 11, because a human rights challenge is likely to focus on a few provisions and is not a suitable mechanism for unravelling the whole statutory scheme.

More generally, the provisions are based very clearly on the policy of promoting 'choice' for individuals which we identified above as a central element of the Conservative government's attack on the trade union movement in the 1980s and early 1990s. Thus, individuals are (in effect) presented with a marketplace of unions among which to choose, and once they have joined, they are free to choose their level of engagement with the union's activities. It is difficult to be against choice, and indeed many would argue that some aspects of the reforms (such as the ending of the closed shop, to be discussed next) were beneficial. But critics argue that the choice agenda went too far, discouraging union members from pursuing collective objectives and weakening unions in the process.

11.5 THE 'CLOSED SHOP'

The concept of a 'closed shop' refers to a situation in which it is compulsory for everyone in a particular workplace to be a member of a trade union. Nowadays, closed shops are regarded as an infringement of freedom of association – because they take away the individual's right to choose not to join a union – and are unenforceable in law. But it is worth understanding something about them as a background to the rules on trade union membership today.

Closed shops were an established feature of the landscape in the heyday of trade unionism, in the 1950s, 1960s and 1970s. They could take one of two forms: pre-entry, where the individual had to be a member of the relevant trade union before he or she could be considered for a job at a particular workplace, or post-entry, in which an individual would have to join the relevant union soon after getting a job in the relevant workplace or face dismissal. From the perspective of unions, it is obvious why closed shops were beneficial: they put the union in a strong bargaining position against the employer, and avoided the problem of 'free riders' (people who take the benefit of the union's collective bargaining activities but without contributing either through subscriptions to the union or by taking part in any industrial action). Unions argued that although individuals might be reluctant to join a union initially, they would benefit in the long term from collective bargaining. But closed shops were surprisingly popular with employers too. One of the key reasons for this was that they could play a valuable role in simplifying industrial relations. If the employer was confronted with two unions fighting with each other to organise the workplace – hard to imagine now, but commonplace in a time of strong trade unionism – it might be less disruptive to reach a closed shop agreement with one of them to the exclusion of the other. This might reduce the level of strike action and lead to improvements in productivity.

The system of closed shops was dismantled gradually during the 1980s, as the government placed increasingly onerous rules on unions seeking to enforce them.[159] We will examine the ILO and ECHR perspectives on these issues first, before examining why closed shops are now unenforceable.

11.5.1 ILO

ILO Convention No. 87 is silent on the question of the closed shop.[160] This has been interpreted to mean that states have a discretion to prohibit or permit the closed shop as they choose.[161] The ILO Committee of Experts has stated that 'systems which prohibit union security practices in order to guarantee the right not to join an organisation, as well as systems which authorise such practices, are compatible with the Convention'.[162] The main qualification to this is that a closed shop will only be permitted where it results from a voluntary agreement between unions and employers. States are not allowed to impose closed shops through legislation.[163]

11.5.2 ECHR

Article 11 ECHR is a right to 'form and join' trade unions for the protection of the individual's interests. Article 20(2) of the UDHR expressly states that 'no-one may be compelled to belong to an association', but the ECHR contains no equivalent provision. The *travaux préparatoires* reveal that this was a deliberate decision by the drafters because of the prevalence of closed shop arrangements in some European countries when the Convention was being drawn up.[164] However, the Court's case-law on the point has evolved over time.

In *Young, James and Webster* v *UK*, the applicants worked for British Rail.[165] A closed shop was agreed between the employer and three unions at a later date. The applicants objected to trade union membership, largely on political grounds, and were eventually dismissed for refusing to join any of the unions. The ECtHR expressly declined to rule on the compatibility of the closed shop system as a whole with Article 11. However, it found that Article 11 had been infringed in all three cases because the applicants were required to join particular unions (not the union of their choice), because the trade union membership requirement had been imposed after they had worked for the employer for some time, and because they lost their jobs as a result of refusing to join.

---

[159] Davies and Freedland, above n 18.

[160] ILO (1948), Freedom of Association and Protection of the Right to Organise Convention (Convention No. 87).

[161] CEACR, *International Labour Conference, 43rd Session, Report of the Committee of Experts, Report III (Part IV)* (1959), [36].

[162] ILO (1994), *General Survey on Freedom of Association and Collective Bargaining*, [100].

[163] ibid [102]–[103].

[164] European Commission on Human Rights, *Preparatory Work on Article 11* (DH (56) 16, 1956).

[165] (1982) 4 EHRR 38.

The *Young* case left open the possibility that it might not be a breach of Article 11 to require someone to join a union as a condition of getting a job, since this would not involve a dismissal as such. However, in *Sigurjonsson*, the applicant applied for a taxi licence and was compelled by law to join an association as a condition of obtaining the licence.[166] The Court held that this was a breach of Article 11. The Court also developed its jurisprudence beyond the decision in the *Young* case, holding that there was a right not to join a union under Article 11, though it did not decide whether that right was on an 'equal footing' with the right to join.[167]

An important feature of *Sigurjonsson* was that the compulsion to join an association was imposed by law (rather than by agreement between a union and an employer, for example). As we saw above, this is a breach of ILO norms.[168] So the case once again left open a possibility: that a requirement to join a union at the same time as getting a job might not breach Article 11 if the closed shop resulted from an agreement rather than from the law. This was put to the test in *Sorensen and Rasmussen v Denmark*.[169] Here, the claimants were required to join a particular union when they got their respective jobs. The closed shops in both cases resulted from an agreement between the union and the employer. The Court held that Article 11 had been violated in both cases because the individuals were forced to join organisations they did not support. It rejected the distinction between pre- and post-entry closed shops, holding that an individual's economic circumstances might leave him or her with no real choice but to take a job with a union membership requirement to which he or she objected. And it held that the Danish state had failed to justify the system of closed shops, not least because most international instruments and most signatory states no longer regarded them as necessary to a functioning system of industrial relations. Once again, the Court left a degree of ambiguity in its ruling:

> The Court does not in principle exclude that the negative and the positive aspects of the Art. 11 right should be afforded the same level of protection in the area under consideration. However, it is difficult to decide this issue in the abstract since it is a matter that can only be properly addressed in the circumstances of a given case.[170]

But it is now very difficult to envisage how a state might justify a requirement to join a union in the light of the Court's ruling.

11.5.3 English law

The closed shop has been unenforceable in the UK since 1990.[171] We will examine the provisions protecting workers against compulsory trade union membership in this section. It is important to bear in mind that although the gradual dismantling of the closed shop in the 1980s fitted in well with the ECtHR's decision in *Young*, it would be wrong to treat it as a reaction to that decision: the government of the time was opposed to the closed shop and would have sought to abolish it anyway.

The law against the closed shop takes two main forms: provisions directed at employers and provisions directed at unions. We will consider each in turn. At first

---

[166] *Sigurjonsson v Iceland* (1993) 16 EHRR 462.
[167] ibid [35].
[168] Above n 163.
[169] (2008) 46 EHRR 29.
[170] ibid [56].
[171] For the history of its gradual abolition, see Davies and Freedland, above n 18.

sight, it may seem odd that the most important protections against the closed shop are directed at employers rather than unions. However, the closed shop was always enforced primarily by employers, because it depended on dismissing – or not hiring – those who refused to join a union. These decisions are obviously taken by employers. The provisions directed at unions address some of the ways in which unions might pressurise employers into agreeing to maintain a closed shop.

Under s. 137 TULRCA, it is unlawful for an employer to refuse someone employment because they are not a member of a trade union or are unwilling to join:[172]

(1) It is unlawful to refuse a person employment–

    (a) because he is, or is not, a member of a trade union, or

    (b) because he is unwilling to accept a requirement–

        (i) to take steps to become or cease to be, or to remain or not to become, a member of a trade union, or

        (ii) to make payments or suffer deductions in the event of his not being a member of a trade union.

(2) A person who is thus unlawfully refused employment has a right of complaint to an employment tribunal.

(3) Where an advertisement is published which indicates, or might reasonably be understood as indicating—

    (a) that employment to which the advertisement relates is open only to a person who is, or is not, a member of a trade union, or

    (b) that any such requirement as is mentioned in subsection (1)(b) will be imposed in relation to employment to which the advertisement relates, a person who does not satisfy that condition or, as the case may be, is unwilling to accept that requirement, and who seeks and is refused employment to which the advertisement relates, shall be conclusively presumed to have been refused employment for that reason.

(4) Where there is an arrangement or practice under which employment is offered only to persons put forward or approved by a trade union, and the trade union puts forward or approves only persons who are members of the union, a person who is not a member of the union and who is refused employment in pursuance of the arrangement or practice shall be taken to have been refused employment because he is not a member of the trade union.

(5) A person shall be taken to be refused employment if he seeks employment of any description with a person and that person–

    (a) refuses or deliberately omits to entertain and process his application or enquiry, or

    (b) causes him to withdraw or cease to pursue his application or enquiry, or

    (c) refuses or deliberately omits to offer him employment of that description, or

    (d) makes him an offer of such employment the terms of which are such as no reasonable employer who wished to fill the post would offer and which is not accepted, or

    (e) makes him an offer of such employment but withdraws it or causes him not to accept it.

---

[172] Note that this provision also protects union members against discrimination. We will examine this in detail in the next chapter.

(6) Where a person is offered employment on terms which include a requirement that he is, or is not, a member of a trade union, or any such requirement as is mentioned in subsection (1)(b), and he does not accept the offer because he does not satisfy or, as the case may be, is unwilling to accept that requirement, he shall be treated as having been refused employment for that reason . . .

This provision is broadly framed, so that it includes, for example, cases in which the individual is offered the job by the employer but declines to accept it because of the union membership requirement. The only significant limitation is that it applies to offers of employment under a contract of employment only, and thus does not protect people who might be hired under a worker's contract.

Under s. 152(1), it is automatically unfair[173] for an employer to dismiss an employee on grounds of non-membership:

(1) For purposes of Part X of the Employment Rights Act 1996 (unfair dismissal) the dismissal of an employee shall be regarded as unfair if the reason for it (or, if more than one, the principal reason) was that the employee–

. . . (c) was not a member of any trade union, or of a particular trade union, or of one of a number of particular trade unions, or had refused, or proposed to refuse, to become or remain a member.[174]

A dismissal on this ground attracts a minimum basic award under s. 156, and a tougher approach to re-employment than is the case for 'normal' unfair dismissal claims under ss. 163–164. Where the individual is dismissed after pressure from a trade union, under s. 160 the union may be made a party to the proceedings and may be required to pay some or all of any compensation awarded by the tribunal. As with almost all provisions on unfair dismissal, s. 152 applies only to employees, though a worker who was refused assignments on the grounds of non-membership of a trade union would probably be able to invoke the protection against detrimental treatment, the 'sole or main purpose' of which is to compel someone to join a union, in s. 146 TULRCA.

In the heyday of the closed shop, one of the techniques used by unions to extend union influence was to put pressure on the employer to refuse to deal with other firms that did not recognise unions or maintain closed shops. The law now restricts this technique by making it unlawful for a person to refuse to deal with a supplier because the work in question might be done by people who are not union members (s. 145) or because the supplier does not recognise a union (s. 187). Moreover, any term in a contract is void if it purports to require the relevant work to be done by union members (s. 144) or if it purports to require the other party to consult with or recognise a trade union (s. 186). This means that the employer is at risk of legal action if it caves in to pressure from the union.

Let us now turn to the measures directed at unions themselves. The main technique through which unions put pressure on employers to act in certain ways is industrial action. However, unions are only able to take industrial action without incurring legal liability (to have 'immunity') if they meet some stringent conditions.[175] Industrial

---

[173] See Chapter 9.
[174] TULRCA, s 153 offers equivalent protection in the event that the individual is selected for redundancy.
[175] See Chapter 13.

action designed to enforce a closed shop at the workplace is not immune by virtue of s. 222 TULRCA. Similarly, action aimed at persuading the employer to act in ways that would contravene ss. 144 or 145, and ss. 186 or 187, loses its immunity by virtue of ss. 222 and 225 respectively.

11.5.4 Conclusion

The position in relation to the closed shop is straightforward: English law makes it impossible for unions and employers lawfully to enforce a closed shop, and this is consistent with international norms. One point that it does reinforce, however, is that the decision to join a union – even if there is an active union at the workplace – is a free one for the individual. This tends to suggest, as we noted above, that there is no particular hardship in requiring someone who has chosen to join a union and can choose to resign from it, to comply with its rules while he or she remains a member. But English law provides the individual with a choice here too.

POINTS TO TAKE AWAY

- Unions perform a variety of functions (Ewing) but the most important nowadays are providing services to their members, representing members individually or collectively at work, and campaigning in the political sphere on labour law and other matters.

- The right to form and join trade unions is a fundamental human right. Unions give ordinary workers the opportunity to bargain with their employer about terms and conditions of employment and to have a say at work and in the political sphere. Critics claim that they distort the labour market and the political process.

- English law regulates unions' internal affairs, such as finances, in some detail.

- English law controls the circumstances in which an individual can be excluded from membership of a union, disciplined by a union or expelled from membership. It is argued that these controls are necessary to protect individuals against unfair treatment and to preserve their freedom of choice, though international standards and human rights instruments suggest that unions should have a degree of autonomy to set their own membership rules.

- The 'closed shop' – in which union membership is a condition of having a job at a particular workplace – is unlawful in English law because it discriminates against those who are not union members. The ECtHR has been generally supportive of individuals who do not want to join a union in a closed shop situation.

Further reading

On the role of trade unions generally, see **KD Ewing, 'The Function of Trade Unions' (2005) 34 ILJ 1.** We will discuss trade unions' workplace functions, especially collective bargaining, in Chapter 12.

The common law rules on the contract of membership between a trade union and its members are clearly explained by **Patrick Elias and KD Ewing, _Trade Union Democracy,_**

→

Members' Rights, and the Law (Mansell 1987), especially chapter 2. To understand the historical development of statutory regulation of members' rights against their unions and the gradual dismantling of the closed shop, the best source is **Paul Davies and Mark Freedland,** *Labour Legislation and Public Policy* (Clarendon Press 1994), chapter 9.

On freedom of association in the ECHR, see, generally, **Bernadette Rainey** *et al.*, *Jacobs, White and Ovey: the European Convention on Human Rights* (6th edn, OUP 2014), **chapter 19.** For a detailed discussion of the *ASLEF* litigation and the legislative response, see **John Hendy and KD Ewing,** 'Trade Unions, Human Rights and the BNP' (2005) 34 ILJ 197; Keith Ewing, 'The Implications of the *ASLEF* Case' (2007) 36 ILJ 425; and **KD Ewing, 'Employment Act 2008: Implementing the *ASLEF* Decision – a Victory for the BNP?' (2009) 38 ILJ 50.**

12 Trade union representation at work and collective bargaining

Learning outcomes

This chapter will enable readers to:

- understand and critically evaluate the law on discrimination against trade union members by employers, and trade union members' rights to use their union's services in the workplace

- understand the concepts of trade union recognition and collective bargaining, and critically analyse the statutory recognition procedure and the law applicable to recognised trade unions

12.1 INTRODUCTION

This chapter deals with the law on trade unions and their members with a particular focus on how they relate to employers. Trade unions differ from other kinds of membership organisations because one of their main functions is to represent workers in their dealings with employers. Although some employers welcome a trade union presence in the workplace, many do not, so the law supports the collective bargaining process by protecting individual trade union members against discrimination at work and by promoting employer engagement with trade unions. Whether the law supports collective activities to a sufficient extent is a central question in this chapter.

Section 12.2 considers the right of trade union members not to be discriminated against by employers because of their trade union membership at all stages of the employment relationship: at the hiring stage, during the relationship and when it is terminated. Although the law here has been changed in response to the decision of the ECtHR in the *Wilson* case,[1] commentators have mounted a sustained attack on the extent of the protection afforded to trade union members in this area.

Section 12.3 focuses on the relationship between trade unions and employers. Trade unions obtain the right to bargain with employers on behalf of their members through recognition, which may be voluntary or statutory. We will outline the statutory recognition procedure and the various legal rights afforded to trade unions when they are recognised. We will conclude with an analysis of the process of derecognising a trade union.

---

[1] *Wilson v United Kingdom* (2002) 35 EHRR 20. For discussion, see KD Ewing, 'The Implications of *Wilson* and *Palmer*' (2003) 32 ILJ 1.

12.2 TRADE UNION MEMBERS AT WORK

One of the core functions of trade unions is to negotiate with employers on behalf of their members.[2] Thus, joining a trade union (unlike joining some other organisation in order to take part in a hobby outside work) is an action that may have consequences at work. Since not all employers are keen on dealing with trade unions, those who are members (and more particularly, active members) may experience discrimination when they are looking for work, or encounter hostility at the workplace. If employers were free to refuse to hire trade union members, or to pay trade union members less than non-members, for example, many people would feel compelled to give up their trade union membership and freedom of association would not be effectively protected. English law affords rights to trade union members not to be discriminated against at the hiring stage, during the employment relationship and at dismissal. These rights correspond to those afforded to people who are *not* members of trade unions in order to prevent employers from enforcing the closed shop.[3] In relation to the protection of trade union members, critics argue that there are various gaps in the way the provisions are formulated, thus giving employers opportunities to discriminate. We will consider the human rights position first, before examining the law in detail.

12.2.1 The ECHR and the ILO

Both the ECHR and the ILO prohibit acts of discrimination by employers against union members.

Perhaps the most helpful starting-point is ILO Convention 98 on collective bargaining (1949), which the UK has ratified. Article 1 states that:

(1) Workers shall enjoy adequate protection against acts of anti-union discrimination in respect of their employment.

(2) Such protection shall apply more particularly in respect of acts calculated to–

  (a) make the employment of a worker subject to the condition that he shall not join a union or shall relinquish trade union membership;

  (b) cause the dismissal of or otherwise prejudice a worker by reason of union membership or because of participation in union activities outside working hours or, with the consent of the employer, within working hours.

There are two important things to note about this provision. First, it applies at all stages of the employment relationship. Sub-paragraph 2(a) deals with hiring and sub-paragraph 2(b) deals with discrimination during the employment relationship ('otherwise prejudice') and dismissal. Second, it covers union membership and participation in union activities. This is important because for most people, the point of joining a union is not simply to have the membership card in their purse or wallet, but to get help from the union in bargaining with the employer. And inevitably, participation in union activities is more likely to attract a hostile reaction from the employer than mere membership of a union. As we shall see, English law has tended to be better at protecting membership than activities, and continues to attract criticism from the ILO supervisory bodies on various points of detail.

[2] See Chapter 11.
[3] See Chapter 11.

Under the ECHR, the state's responsibility to ensure that employers do not discriminate against trade unionists (for example, by dismissing them) is an inherent element of the effective protection of freedom of association under Article 11.[4] The Court has not been called upon to decide any straightforward cases of, for example, dismissal for trade union membership, but it is clear from the Court's decisions in more complex cases such as *Palomo Sanchez* and *Wilson* that the state's failure to address this situation would constitute a violation of Article 11.[5] We will discuss the *Wilson* decision in more detail below, in the section on collective bargaining, but for now it is worth noting that the Court's interpretation of trade union membership is a 'dynamic' one, like that of the ILO, incorporating activities as well as mere membership. Mr Wilson was a trade union member who was offered a pay rise if he signed a new contract of employment that did not refer to terms and conditions bargained collectively by his trade union with the employer. In other words, the employer was offering him extra money as an incentive to give up collective bargaining. The Court held that English law's failure to protect Mr Wilson and his union in this situation was a breach of the state's positive obligations under Article 11. It had this to say about trade union membership:

> . . . it is of the essence of the right to join a trade union for the protection of their interests that employees should be free to instruct or permit the union to make representations to their employer or to take action in support of their interests on their behalf. If workers are prevented from so doing, their freedom to belong to a trade union, for the protection of their interests, becomes illusory. It is the role of the State to ensure that trade union members are not prevented or restrained from using their union to represent them in attempts to regulate their relations with their employers.[6]

Thus, it is important that statutory protection goes beyond mere membership and also protects trade union members when they seek help from their union in dealing with their employer.

12.2.2 The hiring stage

The ECHR and ILO materials just considered would suggest that English law should provide job applicants with protection against being refused a job because of their trade union membership, or trade union activities in a previous job. In this section, we will see that English law tackles this issue in a variety of ways but nevertheless does not quite succeed in providing comprehensive protection.

The basic non-discrimination right at the hiring stage is contained in TULRCA, s. 137(1):

> It is unlawful to refuse a person employment–
>
> (a) because he is . . . a member of a trade union, or
> (b) because he is unwilling to accept a requirement–
>
>> (i) to take steps to . . . cease to be, or . . . not to become, a member of a trade union . . .

An individual who believes that he or she has been refused employment because of trade union membership may take a case to an employment tribunal. Under s. 137(5),

---

[4] *Palomo Sanchez v Spain* (2012) 54 EHRR 24.
[5] ibid; *Wilson*, above n 1.
[6] Above n 1, [46].

a broad definition is given of what it means to refuse someone employment, so for example refusing to process a person's enquiry or offering the job on unreasonable terms are included.[7] Section 137 also protects non-members in closed shop situations, so the detailed and comprehensive nature of the provision is as much (if not more) designed to address that situation as it is to protect trade union members.[8]

There are two noticeable gaps in the protection afforded by s. 137. First, under s. 143, 'employment' means employment under a contract of employment. This has the consequence that people applying for 'worker' jobs are not covered. They must rely instead on the provision against detriment in s. 146 (discussed below), relying on the fact that 'worker' is defined in s. 151 (by reference to s. 296) to include a person who 'seeks to work' under a worker's contract. This seems unnecessarily complicated.

Second, and more importantly, s. 137 does not make any mention of the individual's participation in trade union activities. This is not an accidental oversight: when these provisions were introduced, the then government argued that employers should be able to exclude 'known troublemakers' from the workplace.[9] However, in the *Harrison* case, the EAT held that it was open to tribunals to conclude that a refusal of employment on grounds of trade union activities also amounted to a refusal of employment on grounds of trade union membership and thus fell foul of s. 137.[10] In so holding, the EAT took the view that it was not possible to draw a sharp distinction between trade union membership and activities, and noted that since active members were more likely to encounter discrimination, a purposive approach to the section should be adopted.[11] Nowadays, this conclusion would be reinforced by the need to give effect to Article 11 ECHR, and to the purposive understanding of trade union membership adopted in the *Wilson* case.[12]

The potential for discrimination at the hiring stage – as opposed to during employment, when the employer probably knows a lot more about the worker – turns on the ability of employers to discover that particular applicants are trade union members or activists. A rather sinister way of doing this is to use a 'blacklist'. Blacklists are lists of union members or activists compiled by employers or groups of employers or even by people hoping to sell them to employers. In the 1990s, the ILO's Committee on Freedom of Association heard a complaint from the TUC about blacklisting by an organisation called the Economic League, and was critical of the then government's position that the right not to be discriminated against on grounds of trade union membership (then in the Employment Act 1990) was sufficient to deal with the problem.[13] The Labour government elected in 1997 took a power to make regulations on blacklisting in the Employment Relations Act 1999, s. 3. However, it argued that – by that time – there was no evidence of widespread blacklisting and therefore no obligation to bring the regulations into force.[14] The situation changed in 2008, when the Information Commissioner's Office (ICO) closed down a list that

---

[7] Refusal by an employment agency to offer its services is addressed by TULRCA, s 138.

[8] See Chapter 11.

[9] Patrick Nicholls, Parliamentary Under-Secretary of State for Employment, House of Commons, Official Report of Standing Committee D, col 27, 8 February 1990.

[10] *Harrison* v *Kent County Council* [1995] ICR 434.

[11] ibid 443.

[12] Above n 1.

[13] ILO Committee on Freedom of Association, Case No. 1618, Report No 283 (1992) and Report No 287 (1993).

[14] DTI, *Draft Regulations to Prohibit the Blacklisting of Trade Unionists – A Consultation Document* (URN 03/648, February 2003).

was in use in the construction industry.[15] This contained the names of over 3000 workers, most of whom had no idea that their names were on the list. Many of them had found it difficult to obtain work in the industry over a number of years. This prompted the government to bring regulations on blacklisting into force.[16] But before we examine them in detail, it is worth exploring the position under the Data Protection Act 1998, since this offers an alternative means of dealing with blacklisting.

The Data Protection Act 1998 imposes certain key obligations on anyone (referred to as a 'data controller') who processes individuals' personal data.[17] A data controller must register with the ICO and observe eight data protection principles, which include having legitimate reasons for collecting the data, and allowing individuals to access, correct and object to the use of data held about them.[18] Anyone maintaining a blacklist is likely to breach several of these principles. For example, blacklists tend to be compiled without the knowledge or consent of the individuals listed, and they are used for the illegitimate purpose of discriminating against trade unionists. In the case of the construction industry blacklist, the person who operated the list was prosecuted and fined for failing to register with the ICO, and firms using the list were ordered to stop by means of enforcement notices.[19] It is also possible for an individual to sue the data controller for compensation for damage suffered as a result of a breach of the Act.[20]

The example of the construction industry blacklist prompted the government to enact more targeted measures in the form of the Employment Relations Act 1999 (Blacklists) Regulations 2010.[21] Under reg. 3(2), a blacklist is defined as a list that:

(a) contains details of persons who are or have been members of trade unions or persons who are taking part or have taken part in the activities of trade unions, and

(b) is compiled with a view to being used by employers or employment agencies for the purposes of discrimination in relation to recruitment or in relation to the treatment of workers.

It is unlawful to 'compile, use, sell or supply a prohibited list' unless one of the exceptions in reg. 4 is applicable.[22] In its observations to the ILO Committee of Experts, the TUC has pointed out that there is no definition of 'trade union activities' for this purpose.[23] This gives rise to a risk that the courts might interpret the phrase narrowly. One potential problem relates to industrial action. In other areas of trade union law, the phrase 'trade union activities' is often used with the phrase 'at an appropriate time', and thus refers to activities outside working hours, or during working hours with the employer's permission.[24] As a result, it excludes taking part in industrial action. The blacklisting provisions would be significantly weakened if they did not cover lists of participants in past industrial action.[25] It is not clear

---

[15] See Keith Ewing, *Ruined Lives: Blacklisting in the UK Construction Industry* (Institute of Employment Rights 2009).

[16] Employment Relations Act 1999 (Blacklists) Regulations 2010, SI 2010/493.

[17] Data Protection Act 1998, s 1.

[18] ibid, sch 1, Part 1.

[19] http://ico.org.uk/for_the_public/topic_specific_guides/construction_blacklist (last visited 15 September 2014).

[20] Data Protection Act 1998, s 13.

[21] SI 2010/493. For discussion, see Charles Barrow, 'The Employment Relations Act 1999 (Blacklists) Regulations 2010: SI 2010 No 493' (2010) 39 ILJ 300.

[22] ERABR, reg 3(1).

[23] CEACR, Direct Request – adopted 2012, published 102nd ILC session (2013) Right to Organise and Collective Bargaining Convention, 1949 (No. 98) – United Kingdom (Ratification: 1950).

[24] See, for example, TULRCA 1992, s 146(1)(ba) and s 146(2).

[25] Barrow, above n 21, 304–305.

whether the omission of the phrase 'at an appropriate time' is sufficient to guarantee an interpretation of the provision that covers industrial action. Another potential problem pointed out by the TUC is that the construction industry blacklist included names of people who had raised health and safety concerns, not necessarily as part of their trade union activities.[26] However, this reflects a more general problem that English law does not require employers to make 'fair' hiring decisions, only ones that do not discriminate on specific grounds laid down in statute.

An action for breach of statutory duty may be brought against a person who infringes reg. 3, and the court may issue an injunction to restrain further breaches and award compensation.[27] Importantly, this action may be brought by a trade union so does not depend on the ability or willingness of individuals to bring proceedings, though the union may only claim compensation for its own losses, not those of its members.

Under reg. 5, an individual who is refused employment because of a blacklist may bring proceedings in the employment tribunal.[28] Under reg. 5(3), the burden of proof is reversed, so that if the facts point towards a blacklist having been used, the tribunal must find that a blacklist was used unless the defendant can prove otherwise. This is very important because it is of the essence of blacklisting that it takes place in secret, making evidence-gathering very difficult. The main remedy is an award of compensation, subject to a minimum of £5000 (though this may be subject to certain deductions)[29] and a maximum of £65,300.[30] The tribunal may also make 'a recommendation that the respondent take within a specified period action appearing to the tribunal to be practicable for the purpose of obviating or reducing the adverse effect on the complainant of any conduct to which the complaint relates'.[31] Although the normal three-month time limit applies, there is a discretion to hear a case out of time if the tribunal considers it just and equitable to do so.[32] This could prove to be important because (as the construction work example shows) job applicants may not discover straight away that they were refused employment because of a blacklist.

Although blacklisting is likely to be used by employers primarily as a means of avoiding hiring trade unionists, the regulations also include protection against detriment (reg. 9) and dismissal of an employee (reg. 12). We will consider these provisions further below.

We began this discussion with the example of the construction industry blacklist. At the time of writing, the ICO is working with trade unions to identify and make contact with people who were on the list so that they can find out what information was held about them.[33] The affected individuals do not have any remedies under the 1999 Regulations because the blacklisting to which they were subject occurred before the Regulations came into force, but they are pursuing legal action on a range of other grounds.

Looking to the future, it remains to be seen whether the combination of s. 137 (coupled with a generous interpretation by the courts) and the 1999 Regulations will prove to be an effective package of measures to combat discrimination against trade union members and activists when seeking work. A key difficulty here – as with other

[26] Above n 23.
[27] ERABR, reg 13(3).
[28] ibid reg 6 addresses an employment agency's refusal to provide services.
[29] ibid reg 8(3).
[30] ibid reg 8(7).
[31] ibid reg 8(1)(b).
[32] ibid reg 7(2).
[33] Above n 19.

forms of discrimination – is that most employers who engage in discriminatory practices will not admit it. Thus, despite measures such as the reversed burden of proof, individuals may find it difficult to succeed in litigation. For example, in the recent *Miller* case, the claimant trade union officials ('shop stewards') argued that they had been refused employment because of their trade union membership, but the tribunal accepted the employer's argument that the manager in charge of hiring did not select them because he resented the trade union's pressure to employ a shop steward on every project undertaken by the firm.[34] In upholding the tribunal's decision, the EAT said:

> It is not in every case that an employer who refuses to engage a potential shop steward suggested to him by a recognised trade union will be able to persuade a tribunal that his reasons had nothing to do with the candidate's trade union activities; and indeed we would expect any such explanation to be scrutinised narrowly.[35]

This demonstrates the fine factual distinctions tribunals may be called upon to make in this area.

12.2.3 During employment

In this section, we will examine the protections afforded to trade union members during employment, focusing on two main provisions: s. 145A TULRCA relating to inducements to give up trade union membership, and s. 146 dealing with detrimental treatment in relation to trade union membership. The statute deals separately with attempts by an employer to persuade an individual to accept a so-called 'personal contract' in which his or her terms and conditions of employment are not determined by collective bargaining, so we will examine this below as part of a discussion about the derecognition of trade unions.

The protection against detriment in s. 146(1) is as follows:

> A worker has the right not to be subjected to any detriment as an individual by any act, or any deliberate failure to act, by his employer if the act or failure takes place for the sole or main purpose of–
>
> (a) preventing or deterring him from being or seeking to become a member of an independent trade union, or penalising him for doing so,
>
> (b) preventing or deterring him from taking part in the activities of an independent trade union at an appropriate time, or penalising him for doing so,
>
> (c) preventing or deterring him from making use of trade union services at an appropriate time, or penalising him for doing so . . .

In s. 145A, the same formulation is used but the right is 'not to have an offer made to him by his employer' (a pay rise, for example) for these purposes. Under s. 146(2C), the worker is protected against detrimental treatment for refusing to accept an offer made in contravention of s. 145A, and under s. 146(2D), failure to confer on a worker a benefit that he or she would have received had she accepted such an offer is also a detriment for the purposes of s. 146. Thus, to put it simply, the worker is protected against detriment because of trade unionism, inducements

---

[34] *Miller v Interserve Industrial Services Ltd* [2013] ICR 445.
[35] ibid [20].

to give up trade unionism, detriment for not accepting an inducement, and being denied an inducement that should not have been offered in the first place. It might be asked why people need to be protected against being offered inducements, but from a trade union perspective this represents a big threat to their capacity to organise a workplace. It may be difficult to persuade people of the long-term benefits of trade unionism when they are faced with an immediate offer of cash. However, the effectiveness of these provisions is somewhat undermined by the fact that they depend on the affected individuals being willing to bring proceedings, and do not give unions themselves any right to challenge the employer's actions, as we shall see below.

There are several points to note about ss. 146 and 145A.[36] The use of the term 'worker' ensures that the protection is broadly framed in terms of personal scope. Under ss. 151(1B) and 145F(3) respectively, 'worker' is defined in accordance with s. 296(1). This is similar to the definition used in areas such as working time, but broadened out to include a person who 'normally works or seeks to work' under this type of contract, with an exception for professionals with clients but not businesses with customers.

Both provisions require that the employer's anti-union purpose be its 'sole or main purpose'. Of course, since the protection is against anti-union discrimination, it is important to establish the reason for the employer's action. For example, the employer might make deductions from an individual's pay (one possible type of detriment) or offer a pay rise (which might be construed as an inducement) for legitimate business reasons related to the individual's performance at work. It is for the employer to prove the reason for which it acted.[37] However, if the employer asserts a legitimate business purpose, it may be very difficult in practice for an individual who suspects that this is not the employer's true motivation to prove this to the satisfaction of a tribunal.

We saw above that s. 137 (protection at the hiring stage) is framed only in terms of trade union membership, though it may apply more broadly in practice. Sections 146 and 145A expressly includes taking part in trade union activities and making use of trade union services. It is worth thinking about what these mean. Both are limited by the expression 'at an appropriate time'. This is defined in ss. 146(2) and 145A(2) respectively to mean outside the individual's working hours, or within working hours with the employer's permission. One important consequence of this is that taking part in a strike is not protected because this occurs during working hours without the employer's permission.[38] But it also means that if, for example, an individual wants to consult with his or her union representative, he or she is not protected if he or she does this during working hours when this is not permitted by the rules of the workplace.

The concept of 'making use of union services' is further defined in s. 146(2A) (and s. 145A(4)):

In this section–

(a) "trade union services" means services made available to the worker by an independent trade union by virtue of his membership of the union, and
(b) references to a worker's "making use" of trade union services include his consenting to the raising of a matter on his behalf by an independent trade union of which he is a member.

[36] See, generally, Alan L Bogg, 'Employment Relations Act 2004: Another False Dawn for Collectivism?' (2005) 34 ILJ 72.
[37] TULRCA, s 145D(1) for s 145A; s 148(1) for s 146.
[38] See Chapter 13.

The inclusion of union services was added as part of the government's response to the *Wilson* v *UK* decision in which the ECtHR adopted a dynamic interpretation of trade union membership, as discussed above.[39] However, the above definition is, as Bogg has pointed out, highly individualistic.[40] It protects an individual who asks the union to make representations on his or her behalf (for example, about his or her working hours) or to accompany him or her to a disciplinary hearing (discussed further below). But, because of s. 145B(4), it does not protect individuals where they want the union to engage in collective bargaining on their behalf. This does not matter so much in relation to the inducements provision, s. 145A, because another section, s. 145B, tackles inducements designed to encourage an individual to give up a contract covered by collective bargaining. However, there is no equivalent of s. 146 in relation to collective bargaining, which means that an employer wishing to stop collective bargaining in the workplace is legally free to subject its workers to detrimental treatment in order to get them to agree. This is hard to justify and will be examined further below. It is another example of the phenomenon of government policy confining unions to 'service provision' rather than collective bargaining functions.[41]

Both provisions are enforceable in the employment tribunal, with the burden of proof on the employer to show what its 'sole or main purpose' was.[42] The remedies on offer are different for each section. In the case of s. 146 (detriment), the position is governed by s. 149:

> (2) The amount of the compensation awarded shall be such as the tribunal considers just and equitable in all the circumstances having regard to the infringement complained of and to any loss sustained by the complainant which is attributable to the act or failure which infringed his right.
>
> (3) The loss shall be taken to include–
>
>> (a) any expenses reasonably incurred by the complainant in consequence of the act or failure complained of, and
>>
>> (b) loss of any benefit which he might reasonably be expected to have had but for that act or failure . . .

This is subject to the duty to mitigate at common law. Thus, for example, if the employer refused to offer a worker any further engagements on trade union grounds, the court would take into account whether the worker did – or could have – found alternative work when assessing compensation. In the case of s. 145A (inducements), the compensation on offer under s. 145E(3) is £3715. However, under s. 145E(4), the worker is allowed to keep any sums of money he or she has already received by way of inducements from the employer.[43]

Perhaps the biggest flaw in ss. 146 and 145A is that the remedies are for individuals. Of course, it is true that detriments or inducements are given to individuals and, in some cases, perhaps only one person might be affected. But these kinds of tactics are

---

[39] Above n 1.
[40] Above n 36, 75.
[41] See Chapter 11.
[42] TULRCA, s 145D(1) places the burden on the employer for s 145A; s 148(1) places the burden on the employer for s 146.
[43] If the worker has agreed to vary his or her contract at some future time, this is unenforceable, but variations that have already taken place still stand under this provision.

a common response to a campaign by a union to organise a particular workplace and perhaps seek recognition for collective bargaining. In these situations, many people are affected and the employer's action is designed to harm the union's campaign by attacking individuals who get involved. There are several problems with individual remedies in these circumstances.[44] First, some people may be too afraid to litigate, or unable to afford it. Indeed, the employer may take advantage of this, targeting more vulnerable individuals until the union's support has been whittled away. Of course, the union can help individuals behind the scenes, but this may not always be sufficient. Second, in the *Wilson* case, the ECtHR made clear that the union had Article 11 rights which were infringed when Mr Wilson was offered a pay rise to give up collective bargaining.[45] Thus, although the government denies this, it is arguable that the law is not compliant with Article 11 because there is no remedy for the union.[46] Of course, such a remedy would not be easy to design, but that is no reason not to consider it.

12.2.4 Dismissal

Finally, we will turn to what happens when the individual suspects that his or her employment has been terminated on trade union grounds. Here, we need to distinguish between people who are 'workers' and people who are 'employees'.

Under s. 146(5A), the protection against detriment does not apply where the individual is an employee and the detriment in question is a dismissal. This is because the protection against unfair dismissal on this ground, contained in s. 152(1), applies instead:

> For purposes of Part X of the Employment Rights Act 1996 (unfair dismissal) the dismissal of an employee shall be regarded as unfair if the reason for it (or, if more than one, the principal reason) was that the employee–
>
> (a) was, or proposed to become, a member of an independent trade union,
> (b) had taken part, or proposed to take part, in the activities of an independent trade union at an appropriate time,
> (c) had made use, or proposed to make use, of trade union services at an appropriate time,
> (d) had failed to accept an offer made in contravention of section 145A or 145B . . .

Under s. 153, protection extends to selection for redundancy on trade union grounds. There are a number of points to note about these provisions. First, they use the phrase 'principal reason' rather than 'sole or main purpose', which may be somewhat less stringent as a standard. Second, a dismissal or redundancy selection on trade union grounds is automatically unfair. This means that there is no scope for argument that the dismissal was reasonable.[47] Third, as is generally the case with automatically unfair reasons for dismissal, there is no qualifying period, so if the employer hires someone, discovers his or her trade union activities and dismisses him or her straight away, a claim for unfair dismissal can still be brought.[48] Fourth, the remedies are

---

[44] Bogg, above n 36.
[45] Above n 1, [48].
[46] See Joint Committee on Human Rights Thirteenth Report (Session 2003-4), Scrutiny of Bills: Sixth Progress Report (HL 102/HC 640), paras 2.18–2.19.
[47] See Chapter 9.
[48] TULRCA, s 154.

enhanced, with a minimum basic award of £5676.[49] Fifth, there is a possibility of seeking interim relief under s. 161. This means that there should be a prompt hearing before a tribunal at which, if the tribunal thinks that it is likely to find that the dismissal is unfair under s. 152, it may invite the employer to reinstate the employee in the same job or re-engage him or her in another job. If the employer does not appear, or does not agree to reinstatement or re-engagement, or if the individual reasonably refuses an offer of re-engagement (for example, because the job has much worse terms and conditions), the tribunal may order the continuation of the individual's contract of employment. This means that the individual will continue to be paid until the final decision in the case. If the employer agrees to reinstatement or re-engagement and then fails to comply, additional compensation may be awarded.[50] These provisions are quite important, at least in theory, because they increase the chances that an individual dismissed on trade union grounds will be able to get his or her job back. This is supposed to be an aim of unfair dismissal law more generally but it is rarely realised in practice.[51] However, in more general terms, it may be questioned whether – even with these extra protections – the law is sufficiently strong to deter an employer from dismissing someone on trade union grounds.

Workers must rely on the detriment provision in s. 146 in order to challenge the termination of their employment, because the law on unfair dismissal does not apply to them.[52] It is clearly a 'detriment' if the employer brings a worker's contract to an end or refuses to offer new assignments. As we saw above, compensation is at the tribunal's discretion but is subject to the duty to mitigate.[53]

12.2.5 Right to be accompanied

So far, we have focused on workers' rights to be protected against various forms of discrimination by their employers on grounds of their union membership (all of which are important if trade unions are to be an effective presence in workplaces even where the employer is hostile). In this sub-section, we turn to a positive right to make use of trade union assistance at work: the right to be accompanied at a disciplinary or grievance hearing.

This right is set out in the Employment Relations Act 1999 (ERelA), s. 10.[54] It applies to disciplinary and grievance hearings, defined in s. 13 as follows:

(4) For the purposes of section 10 a disciplinary hearing is a hearing which could result in–

    (a) the administration of a formal warning to a worker by his employer,

    (b) the taking of some other action in respect of a worker by his employer, or

    (c) the confirmation of a warning issued or some other action taken.

(5) For the purposes of section 10 a grievance hearing is a hearing which concerns the performance of a duty by an employer in relation to a worker.[55]

---

[49] ibid s 156(1).
[50] ibid s 166(1).
[51] See Chapter 9.
[52] See Chapter 9.
[53] TULRCA, s 149(4).
[54] It applies to workers broadly defined: ERelA, s 13.
[55] For interpretation, see *London Underground Ltd v Ferenc-Batchelor* [2003] ICR 656.

The right only applies where the worker 'reasonably requests' to be accompanied at such a hearing, though it is not clear in what circumstances an employer would be entitled to conclude that the worker's request was not reasonable.

The worker may choose to be accompanied by any of the following:

(a) [a person] employed by a trade union of which he is an official within the meaning of sections 1 and 119 of the Trade Union and Labour Relations (Consolidation) Act 1992,

(b) an official of a trade union (within that meaning) whom the union has reasonably certified in writing as having experience of, or as having received training in, acting as a worker's companion at disciplinary or grievance hearings, or

(c) another of the employer's workers.[56]

Paragraph (a) refers to an official employed by the union,[57] whereas paragraph (b) allows workplace union officials to act as representatives provided that the union certifies that they have experience in, or training for, the role. For our purposes, the key point is that this right provides workers with access to trade union representation at a time of particular vulnerability. Importantly, it is not necessary for the union to be recognised by the employer in order for a union official to be a permitted representative. This is significant because it offers non-recognised unions a way of demonstrating to workers one of the benefits of a union presence at the workplace.[58] Nor is the right limited to trade union members. Of course, some unions might take the view that they are only willing to expend resources on representing members, but in some situations a more generous approach might help a union to build support and organise a workplace. However, in cases where there is no union presence at all in a workplace, it is unlikely that workers will feel able to approach a union, in which case paragraph (c) offers the possibility of being accompanied by a work colleague of the worker's choosing.[59]

12.3 RECOGNITION AND COLLECTIVE BARGAINING

A key aim of trade unions is to engage in collective bargaining: to negotiate terms and conditions of employment with an employer or group of employers on behalf of workers.[60] In this section, we will consider the law relating to that process, in three stages. First, we will examine the process of securing 'recognition': in other words, an agreement from the employer that it will engage in collective bargaining with the union. Then, we will examine the consequences of recognition: the rights this secures for union members and representatives, and the process of collective bargaining and its output, the collective agreement. Finally, we will examine 'derecognition', focusing in particular on what strategies the employer can and cannot use when it no longer wants to engage in collective bargaining with a trade union. But before we delve into the legal detail, we will examine some of the international materials on collective bargaining and some contextual detail on the prevalence of collective bargaining in the UK today.

---

[56] ERelA 1999, s 10(3).
[57] The union need not have a certificate of independence for these purposes.
[58] Paul Davies and Claire Kilpatrick, 'UK Worker Representation after Single Channel' (2004) 33 ILJ 121, 138–9.
[59] *Roberts* v *GB Oils Ltd* [2014] ICR 462.
[60] See Chapter 11.

12.3.1 International norms and human rights perspectives

In this section, we will examine the positions of the ILO and the two European human rights institutions, the ECHR and the ESC, on collective bargaining. A key point to get clear at the outset is that collective bargaining is a *procedure* through which employers (or employers' associations) and trade unions seek to negotiate collective agreements. This has consequences from the perspective of legal regulation. First, the state's role is to facilitate and encourage the process of collective bargaining, not to guarantee particular outcomes. Indeed, an important value in this area is the autonomy of the social partners to manage their own relationships. Too much state interference can be a bad thing. Second, there is a contradiction inherent in the idea of compulsory negotiation: if one party does not want to participate and is unwilling to make any concessions or alter its position, it is very difficult to force it to do so. Thus, there may be limits to what legal regulation can achieve in this area. However, in the case of the UK, the state is some way from a position of strong encouragement of collective bargaining so these problems are not particularly acute.

The key ILO instruments on collective bargaining are Convention 98, the Right to Organise and Collective Bargaining Convention (1949), and Convention 135, the Workers' Representatives Convention (1971), both of which have been ratified by the UK, and Convention 154, the Collective Bargaining Convention (1981), which has not been ratified by the UK. There are also some relevant recommendations, including Recommendation 91, the Collective Agreements Recommendation (1951), and Recommendation 92, the Voluntary Conciliation and Arbitration Recommendation (1951). From these various instruments, we will draw out two main issues for discussion: the state's duty to promote collective bargaining (which includes matters such as the provision of bargaining machinery, mechanisms for the extension of collective agreements, and the creation of conciliation and arbitration services) and protection for union representatives. Of course, other issues, such as the protection of individual trade union members at work and the provision of an effective right to strike, are also relevant, but these are discussed elsewhere.

The state's duty to promote collective bargaining is set out clearly in Article 4 of Convention 98:

> Measures appropriate to national conditions shall be taken, where necessary, to encourage and promote the full development and utilisation of machinery for voluntary negotiation between employers or employers' organisations and workers' organisations, with a view to the regulation of terms and conditions of employment by means of collective agreements.

This is fleshed out somewhat more fully in Convention 154. Under Article 5:

(1) Measures adapted to national conditions shall be taken to promote collective bargaining.

(2) The aims of the measures referred to in paragraph 1 of this Article shall be the following:

    (a) collective bargaining should be made possible for all employers and all groups of workers in the branches of activity covered by this Convention;

    (b) collective bargaining should be progressively extended to [determining workers' terms and conditions, regulating relations between employers and workers, and regulating relations between employers or their organisations and a workers' organisation or workers' organisations]

    (c) the establishment of rules of procedure agreed between employers' and workers' organisations should be encouraged;

(d) collective bargaining should not be hampered by the absence of rules governing the procedure to be used or by the inadequacy or inappropriateness of such rules;

(e) bodies and procedures for the settlement of labour disputes should be so conceived as to contribute to the promotion of collective bargaining.

Under Article 7, the state is obliged to consult employers' and workers' organisations and preferably to obtain their agreement before taking steps under Article 5. And Article 8 makes clear that the mechanisms put in place should not impair the 'freedom' of collective bargaining.

The first thing to note about these provisions is that they do not seek to provide a 'model' of how states should promote collective bargaining. Instead, they offer some general standards against which to judge a state's policy. This means that each state has a degree of discretion to design its own industrial relations system. The Digest of CFA decisions offers some useful pointers.[61] In general terms, the state should refrain from prohibiting particular groups from engaging in collective bargaining (with some permitted exceptions, such as the armed forces)[62] and should not seek to control the topics on which bargaining can take place (for example, by requiring the parties to exercise wage restraint in a time of high inflation).[63] A particular difficulty arises where an employer refuses to participate in collective bargaining. Steps to compel the employer to bargain may interfere with the principle of voluntariness in bargaining; nevertheless it may be open to the state to create bargaining procedures and to encourage the social partners to participate in good faith negotiations for a period of time.[64] ILO norms also require the state to ensure that collective agreements, once reached, are binding, and cannot be ignored unilaterally by employers.[65]

The choice of unions for collective bargaining purposes and the scope of application of collective agreements have given rise to particular concern. Some systems provide for the most representative union to negotiate on behalf of all the workers in a particular bargaining unit, whereas others allow both majority and minority unions to negotiate with the employer. Both systems are compatible with ILO norms, though in the former system there must be safeguards to ensure that the preferred union is truly representative.[66]

Recommendation 92 encourages states to provide mechanisms for conciliation and arbitration in industrial disputes, but these should be for the parties to invoke voluntarily.[67] They may not be compelled to use them unless, for example, essential public services are affected.

Finally, Convention 135 sets out two important provisions regarding worker representatives (whether trade union representatives or other types of elected representative in the workplace).[68] Under Article 1:

Workers' representatives in the undertaking shall enjoy effective protection against any act prejudicial to them, including dismissal, based on their status or activities as a workers'

---

[61] ILO, *Freedom of Association: Digest of Decisions and Principles of the Freedom of Association Committee of the Governing Body of the ILO* (5th edn, 2006), ch 15.
[62] ibid [885]–[911].
[63] ibid [912].
[64] ibid [925]–[931].
[65] ibid [939].
[66] ibid [949], [969].
[67] ILO Voluntary Conciliation and Arbitration Recommendation, 1951 (No. 92), para 1.
[68] See also Chapter 14.

representative or on union membership or participation in union activities, in so far as they act in conformity with existing laws or collective agreements or other jointly agreed arrangements.

And under Article 2:

(1) Such facilities in the undertaking shall be afforded to workers' representatives as may be appropriate in order to enable them to carry out their functions promptly and efficiently.

(2) In this connection account shall be taken of the characteristics of the industrial relations system of the country and the needs, size and capabilities of the undertaking concerned.

(3) The granting of such facilities shall not impair the efficient operation of the undertaking concerned.

Worker representatives are particularly vulnerable to acts of discrimination and dismissal, so the requirement that they be protected is important. Although the provision of facilities may appear to be a burden on firms, Article 2 seeks to ensure that the obligation is not unduly onerous. Moreover, it is arguable that the employer ultimately benefits from dealing with representatives who are well-prepared for negotiations.

The ESC protects the right to bargain collectively in Article 6:

With a view to ensuring the effective exercise of the right to bargain collectively, the Contracting Parties undertake:

(1) to promote joint consultation between workers and employers;

(2) to promote, where necessary and appropriate, machinery for voluntary negotiations between employers or employers' organisations and workers' organisations, with a view to the regulation of terms and conditions of employment by means of collective agreements;

(3) to promote the establishment and use of appropriate machinery for conciliation and voluntary arbitration for the settlement of labour disputes . . .

The case-law digest of the European Committee on Social Rights indicates that this provision is interpreted in very similar ways to the ILO norms, discussed above.[69] In particular, while the state is obliged to encourage collective bargaining, it must do so in a way that ensures its 'voluntary' character.

The UK government is often content to ignore adverse conclusions of the ILO supervisory regime and the ESC in formulating labour law.[70] Of particular interest, then, is the position of the ECHR on collective bargaining, because (particularly since the enactment of the HRA) the ECtHR's rulings (which may cite other international sources) are much more likely to have an impact on domestic law, either through legislative reforms or court decisions. There have been some interesting and potentially significant developments in this regard. Article 11 contains a right to form and join trade unions, but with the crucial additional phrase 'for the protection of [members'] interests'. This has long been thought to add a 'dynamic' element to the right, protecting unions' ability to engage in activities of various kinds, such as collective bargaining and industrial action.[71] However, in its early decisions, the ECtHR was

---

[69] Council of Europe, *Digest of the Case Law of the European Committee of Social Rights* (2008) 49–58.
[70] See Chapter 2.
[71] See *National Union of Belgian Police* v *Belgium* (1979–80) 1 EHRR 578.

cautious, holding that states enjoyed a wide margin of appreciation to decide how to fulfil the dynamic element, and that there was no right to collective bargaining within Article 11.[72] The ECtHR then revised its approach in the *Demir* case, holding that the right to engage in collective bargaining should, in the light of other international instruments including the ESC and relevant ILO norms, be held to be an essential part of Article 11.[73] Thus, Turkey had breached Article 11 because its legislation did not allow for civil servants to form and join trade unions or to negotiate collective agreements.

We shall see below that the ILO supervisory bodies, the European Committee on Social Rights and the ECtHR have been critical of certain aspects of English law on collective bargaining. All three have expressed concerns about the tactics employers are allowed to use when trying to persuade workers to give up collective bargaining and thus to derecognise a trade union. The ILO has also been critical of the details of the statutory trade union recognition procedure, which is designed to help unions to achieve recognition when they are met with resistance by employers. However, despite these various developments, it remains difficult to say with any certainty whether a particular state can be said to be in compliance with the very general standards laid down in this area.

12.3.2 Statistics

Before we examine the law in detail, it is worth being aware of the prevalence of collective bargaining in the UK today. In 2013, the official statistics on collective bargaining coverage (defined as the proportion of employees whose pay and conditions are governed by a collective agreement) were 17% in the private sector and 64% in the public sector.[74] This significant divergence reflects the much greater levels of union membership in the public sector. There is also a clear link between collective bargaining coverage and workplace size. Thus, collective bargaining coverage is 41% of employees working in workplaces with 50 or more employees, whereas it is 16% for workplaces with fewer than 50 employees.[75] This probably reflects the greater 'return' unions can secure by organising larger workplaces. The general trend is for collective bargaining coverage to decline in both sectors, despite the introduction in 2000 of a statutory procedure for trade unions to secure recognition.

Importantly, union 'presence' – the mere existence of a union at the workplace even if it is not recognised for collective bargaining – is much more prevalent. Thus, 29% of private sector employees and 85% of public sector employees have a trade union presence in the workplace.[76] This means that almost a third of private sector employees and the vast majority of public sector employees have some experience of trade unionism. Although this might suggest that there are significant opportunities for trade unions to secure recognition for collective bargaining in a greater proportion of workplaces, the statistics do not reveal how much support there is when a union is merely 'present', so it may not be realistic to imagine that unions could significantly increase the level of recognition.

---

[72] *Swedish Engine Drivers Union v Sweden* (1979–80) 1 EHRR 617; *Wilson*, above n 1, [44].
[73] *Demir v Turkey* (2009) 48 EHRR 54 [153]–[154].
[74] Department for Business, Innovation and Skills, *Trade Union Membership 2013* (2014) 43.
[75] ibid.
[76] ibid.

Finally, it is worth noting that there are still measurable financial benefits associated with collective bargaining. On average, trade union members earned £14.45 per hour in 2013, compared with £12.41 for non-members.[77] This gives a union wage premium of 16.4%. However, this again masks significant divergence between public and private sectors, with the premium at 7% in the private sector but 19.8% in the public sector.[78] Neo-classical economists tend to be critical of the 'union wage effect', arguing that it makes unionised firms uncompetitive and stifles job creation, by giving union members more pay than the market would indicate.[79] But of course, from the union perspective, collective bargaining is about securing advantages for workers (and not just union members, since in most cases collective agreements apply to the whole bargaining unit). These advantages may come at the expense of the employer's profits rather than the firm's competitiveness, and may have positive economic effects such as making workers more loyal and productive.[80]

12.3.3 Seeking recognition

We will now turn to the process of securing recognition. This may take one of two forms: voluntary or statutory. Voluntary recognition occurs when the union persuades the employer to recognise it for the purposes of collective bargaining, perhaps by organising or threatening to organise industrial action. Statutory recognition occurs when the union (having failed to secure voluntary recognition) invokes the procedure in Schedule A1 TULRCA. If certain conditions are met, this may lead to a legally enforceable order requiring the employer to meet with union representatives once a year to discuss pay, hours and holidays. Importantly, the two types of recognition are not unconnected. The very existence of the statutory procedure may encourage (and, initially at least, did encourage) firms to recognise unions voluntarily.[81] And during the statutory procedure, there are multiple opportunities for the employer to abandon its opposition to recognising the union and to opt to do so voluntarily without waiting for the procedure to take its course. There is also a possibility of recognition under TUPE which we will consider at the end of this section.

Voluntary recognition

It is difficult to generalise about the process of seeking voluntary recognition because – as a voluntary process – it is a matter for the parties involved and may vary considerably from workplace to workplace. However, in simple terms, a union wishing to secure voluntary recognition must persuade workers to join so that it can demonstrate to the employer that it has a good level of support in the workplace. It may also need to be able to engage in strike action – or at least threaten to do so – in order to persuade a reluctant employer to recognise it. Thus, although voluntary recognition is not a legal process as such, it depends on two main forms of 'negative'

[77] ibid 29.
[78] ibid.
[79] Richard A Posner, *Economic Analysis of Law* (8th edn, Wolters Kluwer 2011) chapter 11.
[80] Richard B Freeman and James L Medoff, *What Do Unions Do?* (Basic Books 1984).
[81] Gregor Gall, 'Union Recognition in Britain: the End of Legally Induced Voluntarism' (2012) 41 ILJ 407.

law:[82] protections for trade union members and activists against employer discrimination (discussed above) and the right to strike.[83] Since there are difficulties with both areas of law, it is not surprising that unions nowadays find it difficult to secure recognition by this route.

If a union does succeed in securing recognition, this will usually result in a recognition agreement or a procedure agreement identifying the workers covered by collective bargaining, the topics on which the union is entitled to bargain, and the process for negotiations. This agreement is, in itself, a collective agreement under s. 178 TULRCA. This has the consequence that it will not be legally enforceable unless it is in writing and contains a clear statement to the effect that it is intended to be legally enforceable.[84] This may sound surprising, since it does not give the union the security of being able to go to court and seek a remedy if the employer breaches the agreement. However, historically, unions have preferred not to involve the courts because of a perception that they are hostile towards the union movement and because collective agreements are unlikely to be drafted like contracts anyway.

As we shall see below, it is important to know whether or not a union is 'recognised' because additional statutory rights are afforded to recognised unions and their members and officials. Under s. 178(3), recognition means 'recognition . . . to any extent, for the purpose of collective bargaining' and collective bargaining means 'negotiations relating to or connected with one or more of' the following:

(a) terms and conditions of employment, or the physical conditions in which any workers are required to work;
(b) engagement or non-engagement, or termination or suspension of employment or the duties of employment, of one or more workers;
(c) allocation of work or the duties of employment between workers or groups of workers;
(d) matters of discipline;
(e) a worker's membership or non-membership of a trade union;
(f) facilities for officials of trade unions; and
(g) machinery for negotiation or consultation, and other procedures, relating to any of the above matters, including the recognition by employers or employers' associations of the right of a trade union to represent workers in such negotiation or consultation or in the carrying out of such procedures.

Thus, although we normally think of collective bargaining as being concerned primarily with matters such as pay, it is possible for a union to be recognised for the purposes of s. 178 without an agreement to negotiate on pay. As we shall see, this has advantages and disadvantages. On the positive side, it means that the rights associated with recognised union status are afforded quite widely. On the negative side, it means that an attempt to secure statutory recognition (which would involve bargaining about pay) can be defeated by the presence of a prior agreement to recognise another union for the purposes of bargaining about other matters.[85] We will consider this problem further below.

---

[82] The term 'negative law' is from Otto Kahn-Freund, 'Legal Framework', in Allan Flanders and Hugh A Clegg (eds), *The System of Industrial Relations in Great Britain: Its History, Law and Institutions* (Blackwell 1954).
[83] See Chapter 13.
[84] TULRCA, s 179.
[85] *R (Boots Management Services Ltd) v Central Arbitration Committee* [2014] EWHC 2930 (Admin) [2014] IRLR 887.

Statutory recognition

The statutory recognition procedure is contained in Schedule A1 to TULRCA and was inserted in 2000.[86] In simple terms, the procedure is designed to offer assistance to a union where it has a high level of support and is seeking recognition but the employer refuses to engage voluntarily in collective bargaining. It continues to prioritise voluntary collective bargaining by providing several opportunities for the parties to 'exit' the procedure and reach a voluntary agreement, though if the employer resists throughout, the union can achieve a legally enforceable procedure agreement for bargaining on pay, hours and holidays. Many employers recognised unions in the run-up to the introduction of the new procedure, but in more recent times the effectiveness of statutory recognition has declined, largely because unions have used up their supply of firms with high levels of union membership.[87] The procedure has been criticised in several ways: it is complex, it does not offer sufficient protection where the employer is hostile, the threshold for achieving recognition is unduly high, and the eventual outcome is disappointing.[88]

The procedure is quite complicated so, for ease of explanation, it will be outlined here in six steps.

1. Preliminary requirements

- The statutory recognition procedure may only be invoked by an independent union (discussed above)[89] against an employer that employs more than 21 workers.[90]

- The union must make a request to the employer.[91]

At this point the parties may reach a recognition agreement.[92] If they cannot agree, or the employer refuses to negotiate or does not respond to the request, the union may proceed to step 2.[93]

2. Union application to the CAC

The CAC may only accept the union's application if:

- There is no union already recognised in respect of the workers in the bargaining unit.[94]

---

[86] By ERelA 1999, implementing proposals in Department of Trade and Industry, *Fairness at Work* (Cm 3968 1998).

[87] Gall, above n 81.

[88] See, for example, Alan L Bogg, 'The Political Theory of Trade Union Recognition Campaigns: Legislating for Democratic Competitiveness' (2001) 64 MLR 875; Alan L Bogg, 'Employment Relations Act 2004: Another False Dawn for Collectivism?' (2005) 34 ILJ 72; Alan Bogg, *The Democratic Aspects of Trade Union Recognition* (Hart 2009); Ruth Dukes, 'The Statutory Recognition Procedure 1999: no Bias in Favour of Recognition?' (2008) 37 ILJ 236; Bob Simpson, 'Trade Union Recognition and the Law, a New Approach – Parts I and II of Schedule A1 to the Trade Union and Labour Relations (Consolidation) Act 1992' (2000) 29 ILJ 193.

[89] TULRCA, sch A1, para 6.

[90] ibid para 7.

[91] ibid para 4. The conditions for validity are set out in para 8.

[92] ibid para 10.

[93] ibid paras 11–12.

[94] ibid para 35. Part VI sets out a derecognition procedure where the employer has an agreement with a non-independent union.

- At least 10% of the workers in the bargaining unit are members of the union.[95]
- The CAC considers it likely that a majority of workers in the bargaining unit will support recognition.[96]

3. The CAC's roles

The CAC has two roles:

- To decide whether the bargaining unit is appropriate (unless the employer and union have already reached an agreement on this).[97]
- To decide whether the union should be recognised:
  - where the CAC is satisfied that more than 50% of workers in the bargaining unit are members of the union, the CAC may declare the union to be recognised;[98]
  - where this is not the case (or where the CAC thinks that good industrial relations so require)[99] the CAC arranges a ballot.[100]

4. The ballot

The union will be recognised if a majority of those voting and at least 40% of the workers in the bargaining unit vote in favour of recognition.[101]

Once the ballot has been ordered, the employer must:

- co-operate with the union and with the independent organiser of the ballot;[102]
- give the union access to the workforce;[103]
- give the CAC the names and addresses of the workers in the bargaining unit (to enable the union to distribute campaign literature via the independent ballot organiser, as well as facilitating the conduct of the ballot);[104]
- refrain from 'unfair practices' such as inducements or threats to workers to persuade them not to vote for recognition.[105]

5. If the vote is for recognition

The union and the employer are encouraged to negotiate on how they will conduct collective bargaining.[106]

If negotiations fail, the CAC may specify a 'method' for them.[107]

---

[95] ibid para 36(1)(a).
[96] ibid para 36(1)(b).
[97] ibid para 18.
[98] ibid para 22.
[99] ibid para 22(3) and (4).
[100] ibid para 23.
[101] ibid para 29.
[102] ibid para 26(2).
[103] ibid para 26(3).
[104] ibid para 26(4).
[105] ibid para 26(4A)–(4B).
[106] ibid para 30(2).
[107] ibid para 31(3).

6. The 'method'

The 'method' sets out a process whereby the union makes proposals to the employer and the employer responds to them, culminating in an annual meeting.[108]

It is enforceable by an order for specific performance.[109]

But:

- it only applies to pay, hours and holidays;[110]

- there is no express obligation to bargain in good faith or 'with a view to reaching an agreement'.[111]

Assessment Now that we have outlined the Schedule A1 procedure, we are in a position to examine some of the main criticisms that have been made of it. We will explore five main problem areas before looking at the research on how the procedure has worked in practice.

First, it is arguable that there are too many obstacles in the way of unions seeking to invoke the procedure. One is the limitation to employers employing at least 21 workers. The government itself admitted that this would exclude some 30% of the workforce from access to the procedure.[112] Given that the government emphasised workers' right to choose their preferred form of representation, it is not obvious why this choice should be confined to people in larger workplaces. The government suggested that collective bargaining might not work very well in small businesses, where it may be possible for workers to have a personal relationship with the boss, but there is no guarantee that this is always the case or that workers are always happy with this approach. Another problem is that, under para. 35 of Schedule A1, a union cannot invoke the recognition procedure where a union is already recognised in respect of the bargaining unit. This provision exists to protect the recognition procedure from becoming embroiled in inter-union disputes, in which one union seeks to displace another union from a particular workplace. However, it opens up the possibility that an employer may recognise a favourable or 'sweetheart' union or recognise a union for limited bargaining (given the broad definition in s. 178) with the effect that a genuinely representative union cannot secure recognition for bargaining on the key issues of pay, hours and holidays. In the *Boots* case, the CAC found that the provision infringed Article 11 ECHR and held that it should be interpreted to avoid this result.[113] This decision was the subject of an application for judicial review.[114] The judge in the Administrative Court agreed with the CAC that collective bargaining without negotiation over pay, hours and holidays was 'meaningless'.[115] However, he held that the CAC was wrong to read additional words into para. 35 because this involved a direct contradiction of the wording of the Schedule. Since the High Court (unlike the CAC) may make a declaration of incompatibility under s. 4 HRA, the judge invited the parties to pursue that option.

---

[108] Trade Union Recognition (Method of Collective Bargaining) Order 2000, SI 2000/1300.

[109] sch A1, para 31(6).

[110] ibid para 3.

[111] Above n 108, para 29, requires that: 'The employer and the union shall take all reasonable steps to ensure that this method to conduct collective bargaining is applied efficiently and effectively.'

[112] Bob Simpson, 'Trade Union Recognition and the Law, a New Approach – Parts I and II of Schedule A1 to the Trade Union and Labour Relations (Consolidation) Act 1992' (2000) 29 ILJ 193, 195–196.

[113] *The Pharmacists' Defence Association Union (PDAU) and Boots Management Services Ltd* (CAC TUR1/823/2012, 29 January 2013).

[114] *R (Boots Management Services Ltd) v Central Arbitration Committee* [2014] EWHC 65 (Admin), [2014] IRLR 278.

[115] ibid [26].

When the case returned to the High Court, a different approach was adopted.[116] The judge held that the union seeking recognition could use Part VI of Schedule A1 to get the incumbent union derecognised, because the definition of collective bargaining for those purposes should be treated as 'negotiations over any matters which the parties have agreed should be the subject of collective bargaining'.[117] Once this procedure had been completed, the union seeking recognition would not be hindered by para. 35. This meant that there was no need to invoke the HRA or to adopt a broad construction of para. 35. While this does solve the problem, it means that a trade union seeking recognition faces an extra hurdle where there is an incumbent union: it must persuade a worker to apply to the CAC for that union to be derecognised. It cannot take the necessary steps itself. Both limitations of the Schedule A1 procedure have been the subject of critical comment by the ILO Committee of Experts.[118]

Second, Simpson has argued that the recognition procedure is too complex, seeking as it does to anticipate every possible scenario rather than giving the CAC discretion to decide how to proceed.[119] For example, when a trade union applies to the CAC, the CAC must assess whether or not the application is admissible by reference to the bargaining unit proposed by the union. However, at this stage, the bargaining unit may not be accepted by the employer, so there are further procedural steps during which the union and the employer may either agree the bargaining unit or the CAC may determine it. The bargaining unit in respect of which the union finally seeks recognition may thus be different to the one originally proposed. The CAC must then conduct an examination of the 'validity' of the union's application examining the same set of issues (pre-existing recognition, 10% membership and so on) which were examined at the 'admissibility' stage.[120] This seems unnecessarily complicated.

Third, as Bogg has argued, the recognition procedure may not offer sufficient protection where the employer is hostile.[121] Schedule A1 as initially enacted simply provided individual workers with protection against detrimental treatment and dismissal in relation to certain aspects of the union's recognition campaign.[122] This suffered from two weaknesses: it did not apply to employer activities that targeted the workforce as a whole, rather than the individual (like threatening to close down the workplace), and it relied on individuals to enforce their rights by going to the tribunal and claiming compensation (which was unlikely to happen and did nothing to help the union to secure recognition). After considerable pressure from the TUC and commentators, the government amended Schedule A1 in the Employment Relations Act 2004 to introduce the 'unfair practice' provision. This applies symmetrically to employers and unions. Importantly, it does not give rights to individuals (though they may have rights under other provisions which are unaffected) but instead gives unions (or employers) a right to complain to the CAC.[123] The CAC must make a declaration to the effect that unfair practices have been committed and may order the offending party to take steps to mitigate the problem. If this fails, it is possible in some circumstances for the CAC simply to order that the union is recognised (or not, where the union is to blame).[124] Thus, the provision is designed to overcome some of the problems with the individual rights approach.

[116] *R (Boots Management Services Ltd)* v *Central Arbitration Committee* [2014] EWHC 2930 (Admin).
[117] ibid [19].
[118] ILO Committee of Experts, *Observations on Convention No. 98* (2006).
[119] Above n 112, 217.
[120] ibid 205–208.
[121] Alan Bogg, 'The Mouse that Never Roared: Unfair Practices and Union Recognition' (2009) 38 ILJ 390.
[122] TULRCA, sch A1, paras 156–165. See Bogg, above n 36.
[123] ibid 27A(4).
[124] ibid para 27D.

The detail is set out in para 27A(2):

A party uses an unfair practice if, with a view to influencing the result of the ballot, the party–

    (a) offers to pay money or give money's worth to a worker entitled to vote in the ballot in return for the worker's agreement to vote in a particular way or to abstain from voting,

    (b) makes an outcome-specific offer to a worker entitled to vote in the ballot,

    (c) coerces or attempts to coerce a worker entitled to vote in the ballot to disclose–

        (i) whether he intends to vote or to abstain from voting in the ballot, or

        (ii) how he intends to vote, or how he has voted, in the ballot,

    (d) dismisses or threatens to dismiss a worker,

    (e) takes or threatens to take disciplinary action against a worker,

    (f) subjects or threatens to subject a worker to any other detriment, or

    (g) uses or attempts to use undue influence on a worker entitled to vote in the ballot.

As this quotation shows, the provision is comprehensive and seeks to cover all the possible strategies an employer might use in order to persuade workers not to vote for recognition. In particular, as Bogg points out, the 'undue influence' provision is expressed in very general terms and is apt to cover situations in which the employer threatens the workforce more generally (for example, with closing the workplace) rather than as individuals.[125] However, three problems remain. First, the protection only applies once the CAC has ordered a ballot. This means that an employer may be able to use unfair tactics to discourage workers from supporting the union's initial approach. This may mean that, for example, the union cannot achieve 10% membership in the bargaining unit or a likelihood of majority support for recognition. The ILO has been critical of this aspect of the procedure.[126] Second, under para 27B(4):

A complaint is well-founded if–

    (a) the CAC finds that the party complained against used an unfair practice, and

    (b) the CAC is satisfied that the use of that practice changed or was likely to change, in the case of a worker entitled to vote in the ballot–

        (i)   his intention to vote or to abstain from voting,

        (ii) his intention to vote in a particular way, or

        (iii) how he voted.

As Bogg points out, this requires the CAC to consider the impact of the employer's tactics on the worker's voting intentions.[127] This may be difficult to determine and puts an additional hurdle in the union's way when bringing an unfair practices complaint. Third, the CAC has been cautious in its interpretation of the unfair practices provisions with the effect that few complaints have been successful.[128]

---

[125] Bogg, above n 121, 392.

[126] CEACR, *Observation – adopted 2008, published 98th ILC session (2009) Right to Organise and Collective Bargaining Convention, 1949 (No. 98) – United Kingdom (Ratification: 1950)*.

[127] Bogg, above n 121, 398.

[128] Bogg, above n 121.

Fourth, the threshold for achieving recognition is often thought to be unduly high. The government argued that employers should not be required to engage with a union unless there was clear support for this in the workplace.[129] A simple majority requirement would allow a few union activists to impose recognition on an otherwise apathetic workforce. However, it can be difficult for unions to persuade people to join when they are unrecognised, because those with no previous experience of unions cannot see the benefits.[130] Support for unions often goes up once recognition has been achieved. On this view, the requirement of a majority and 40% of the workers in the bargaining unit is unrealistically high and will stop unions with good but not outstanding levels of support from achieving recognition. Although the ILO has criticised the 40% requirement for preventing unions with lower levels of support from securing recognition,[131] the government has countered by pointing out that there is no obstacle to voluntary recognition in these circumstances, just no access to the statutory procedure.[132]

Fifth, the eventual outcome of the procedure is disappointing. As noted in the outline, if the union is unable to reach a voluntary agreement with the employer, the CAC will impose a 'method' on the parties. However, this does not include any obligation on the employer to negotiate in good faith or 'with a view to reaching an agreement', a formula used elsewhere (for example, in the law on consultation).[133] As a result, as Simpson points out, the employer's duty is simply to 'meet and talk', a duty which can be met quite easily without making any meaningful effort to engage in bargaining with the union.[134] Moreover, the scope of collective bargaining under the procedure – confined as it is to pay, hours and holidays – is quite limited compared to the more general understanding of collective bargaining in s. 178 TULRCA. Earlier incarnations of the recognition procedure provided for binding arbitration in the event that the parties could not achieve a collective agreement.[135] Arguably, this is more effective than the Schedule A1 mechanism of specific performance of the method, because it gives the employer an incentive to reach an agreement with the union in order to avoid an arbitration award. Specific performance of the method just obliges the employer to 'meet and talk' and does not do very much to increase the likelihood that meeting and talking will generate any measurable results for the affected workers.

As Gall has demonstrated, the Schedule A1 procedure generated a significant 'shadow' effect, encouraging employers to recognise unions before it came into force in 2000, and some early gains for unions, with relatively high levels of new recognition agreements in 2001 and 2002.[136] However, since then, use of the procedure has tailed off considerably. More recently, the number of new recognition agreements has dropped to below the level before Schedule A1 was contemplated. Overall levels of collective agreement coverage in the private sector have continued to decline over time. Perhaps most worryingly, Gall points out that the recognition procedure

[129] Department of Trade and Industry, above n 86, [4.17].
[130] See Dukes, above n 88, and Bogg, *Democratic Aspects*, above n 88 for a critique of the 'neutrality' of the provisions.
[131] CEACR, *Observation – adopted 2006, published 96th ILC session (2007) Right to Organise and Collective Bargaining Convention, 1949 (No. 98) – United Kingdom (Ratification: 1950)*.
[132] CEACR, *Observation – adopted 2010, published 100th ILC session (2011) Right to Organise and Collective Bargaining Convention, 1949 (No. 98) – United Kingdom (Ratification: 1950)*.
[133] See Chapter 14.
[134] Above n 112, 215.
[135] Paul Davies and Mark Freedland, *Labour Legislation and Public Policy* (Clarendon Press 1994) 392–393.
[136] Gall, above n 81, 415.

– rather than being a floor on which unions could build voluntary recognition – has become a ceiling, with unions now finding it difficult to secure recognition outside the statutory procedure or on a broader range of issues than pay, hours and holidays.[137] As Gall suggests, a key problem with the procedure is that it is only of use to a union where it already enjoys a significant level of support in the workplace.[138] Unions 'used up' their easy targets in the early years. Now they are faced with the much more challenging prospect of organising workplaces with little or no union membership. But the recognition procedure cannot help with this because, among other things, the unfair practices jurisdiction does not apply until a ballot has been ordered. This means that when a union first approaches a workplace, it can easily be pushed away by a hostile employer, with no means of redress.

Overall, as several commentators have concluded, the biggest problem with the recognition procedure is its neutrality.[139] It does not treat trade union recognition as a good outcome to be promoted in the face of employer opposition. Instead, reflecting the *Fairness at Work* White Paper, trade union recognition is seen as one way of conducting workplace relations but only where there is a high level of support for it among the workforce.[140] This ignores the fact that, as trade unionism has declined, the balance of power has shifted towards employers and unions may need more help and support than the recognition procedure offers. Indeed, it is hard to see how the recognition procedure can transform the industrial relations landscape given the many other problems with trade union law considered in this chapter and elsewhere.

Recognition under TUPE

The purpose of the Acquired Rights Directive (ARD),[141] implemented by the Transfer of Undertakings (Protection of Employment) Regulations (TUPE),[142] is to protect employees' job security and terms and conditions of employment in the event that there is a change of ownership of the firm for which they are working.[143] The application of TUPE in the UK is much more important in the public sector, in contracting-out situations, than it is in the private sector, where businesses often change hands by sale of shares rather than by changes in the identity of the legal owner. In relation to trade union recognition, TUPE seeks to ensure that, if certain conditions are met, the transferee can be deemed to have recognised a union in respect of the transferred workers if the transferor did so. The relevant provision is reg. 6:

(1) This regulation applies where after a relevant transfer the transferred organised grouping of resources or employees maintains an identity distinct from the remainder of the transferee's undertaking.

(2) Where before such a transfer an independent trade union is recognised to any extent by the transferor in respect of employees of any description who in consequence of the transfer become employees of the transferee, then, after the transfer–

---

[137] ibid 419.
[138] ibid 422.
[139] See, especially, above n 130.
[140] Above n 86.
[141] Directive 2001/23/EC on the safeguarding of employees rights in the event of transfers of undertakings, businesses or parts of undertakings or businesses.
[142] Transfer of Undertakings (Protection of Employment) Regulations 2006, SI 2006/246.
[143] See Chapter 10.

(a) the trade union shall be deemed to have been recognised by the transferee to the same extent in respect of employees of that description so employed; and

(b) any agreement for recognition may be varied or rescinded accordingly.

However, there are at least two significant limitations on the impact of this provision in English law. First, the requirement in reg. 6(1) that the transferred employees retain a distinct identity within the transferee undertaking may not be satisfied if the transferee integrates its new acquisition into the firm. Second, as reg. 6(2)(b) confirms, the transferee may derecognise the union. Where the original recognition by the transferor was voluntary, there is no particular obstacle to this (other than resistance on the part of the affected employees); where the original recognition was statutory, the transferee may be subject to the three-year waiting period, discussed below. A further complication arises because TUPE only protects the rights of employees, whereas the statutory recognition procedure includes workers too, with the effect that the transferor may be able to escape the three-year waiting period for derecognition by arguing that the bargaining unit has changed.

12.3.4 Collective agreements

Once a union has been recognised by an employer for the purposes of collective bargaining, whether by the voluntary or statutory route, its aim will be to reach a collective agreement with the employer. Where recognition has been achieved voluntarily, or where the CAC has declared the union recognised and the parties have reached a voluntary procedure agreement, the parties themselves are free to determine both the procedure for bargaining and the subject-matter of the bargaining (though as we have seen, there is a growing tendency for voluntary collective bargaining to focus predominantly on pay, hours and holidays).[144] Where the CAC has imposed a method under the statutory recognition procedure, we saw above that this sets out a structure within which the parties must meet and talk about pay, hours and holidays.[145] In either case, one of the key factors determining the union's ability to persuade the employer to make concessions is its capacity to make credible threats of industrial action if its demands are not met.[146] In this section, we will explore some issues about the nature and status of collective agreements themselves.

A collective agreement is defined in TULRCA as an agreement between a union or unions and one or more employers or employers' associations relating to one or more of the matters specified in s. 178(2). As we saw above, these matters are wide-ranging and include, but extend far beyond, pay, hours and holidays. Under s. 179 TULRCA, a collective agreement is not legally binding unless it is in writing and contains a provision to the effect that the parties intend it to be legally binding. At first sight, this may seem somewhat surprising since it means that (unless the presumption is rebutted) collective agreements do not have contractual effect and cannot therefore be enforced in court. However, traditionally, both employers and unions have been keen to keep their collective agreements out of court and it is very rare to come across an agreement in which the presumption has been rebutted. There are several reasons for this. First, unions tend to be suspicious of courts and to fear that the judges

---

[144] Above n 81.
[145] TULRCA, sch A1, para 31(3).
[146] See Chapter 13.

will interpret agreements in the employer's favour. Second, the costs associated with drafting an agreement in contractual language and enforcing it in court would be quite substantial. And third, both sides value the flexibility of agreements 'binding in honour only'. Any 'enforcement' of collective agreements thus tends to take place through the parties' industrial weapons so, for example, a union might call a strike if the employer disregarded the provisions of the agreement.

In English law, the question whether the provisions of a collective agreement have been incorporated into the contracts of employment of individual workers is not automatic and depends upon a close examination of the individuals' contracts and the collective agreement itself.[147] If the employer chose to disregard a provision of a collective agreement that had been incorporated into individuals' contracts, the affected individuals would be entitled to invoke the normal remedies for breach of contract.

We saw above that TUPE may operate so that, where the transferor had recognised a union in respect of the transferring employees, the transferee would also be obliged to recognise the union.[148] TUPE also applies where there is a collective agreement in force in respect of the transferring employees, by virtue of reg. 5:

> Where at the time of a relevant transfer there exists a collective agreement made by or on behalf of the transferor with a trade union recognised by the transferor in respect of any employee whose contract of employment is preserved by regulation 4(1) above, then–
>
> (a) without prejudice to sections 179 and 180 of the 1992 Act (collective agreements presumed to be unenforceable in specified circumstances) that agreement, in its application in relation to the employee, shall, after the transfer, have effect as if made by or on behalf of the transferee with that trade union, and accordingly anything done under or in connection with it, in its application in relation to the employee, by or in relation to the transferor before the transfer, shall, after the transfer, be deemed to have been done by or in relation to the transferee; and
> (b) any order made in respect of that agreement, in its application in relation to the employee, shall, after the transfer, have effect as if the transferee were a party to the agreement.

Of course, collective agreements are not normally legally binding in English law, so the curious effect of this provision is to render the transferee bound 'in honour' just like the transferor. In practice, it is more significant that the transferee is bound by provisions in collective agreements via individual employees' contracts of employment,[149] though recent amendments to TUPE have sought to limit transferees' obligations in this regard.[150]

12.3.5 Other consequences of recognition

Obviously, the main purpose of recognition for a trade union is to engage in collective bargaining with the employer. However, certain rights also attach to a union (and its members and officials) once it is recognised. We will consider these in this section. A key question to think about is whether it is justified to confine some of these rights

---

[147] See Chapter 5.
[148] TUPE, reg 6(2)(a).
[149] TUPE, reg 4.
[150] See Chapter 10 for a full discussion.

to recognised trade unions. Successive governments have tended to take the view that employers should only be obliged to accommodate trade unions once they have agreed to bargain with them, but from a trade union perspective it may be difficult to secure recognition without having effective officials in place with good access to the workforce.

Information

In order to engage in effective collective bargaining, it is important for union representatives to be well-informed about the workplace. Most obviously, union representatives need to know about the current terms and conditions of workers in the bargaining unit, in order to engage in a meaningful conversation with the employer about improving those terms and conditions. It might also be argued that union representatives would be assisted by other types of information, such as the terms and conditions of other workers in the firm (to make comparisons) or the state of the business more generally (to assess whether claims for pay rises are realistic, or whether redundancies are likely). A recognised union has a statutory right to seek certain information, laid down in s. 181 TULRCA:

(1) An employer who recognises an independent trade union shall, for the purposes of all stages of collective bargaining about matters, and in relation to descriptions of workers, in respect of which the union is recognised by him, disclose to representatives of the union, on request, the information required by this section.

In this section and sections 182 to 185 "representative", in relation to a trade union, means an official or other person authorised by the union to carry on such collective bargaining.

(2) The information to be disclosed is all information relating to the employer's undertaking (including information relating to use of agency workers in that undertaking) which is in his possession, or that of an associated employer, and is information–

    (a) without which the trade union representatives would be to a material extent impeded in carrying on collective bargaining with him, and

    (b) which it would be in accordance with good industrial relations practice that he should disclose to them for the purposes of collective bargaining.

Importantly, the right to seek disclosure is confined to recognised unions for collective bargaining, so it applies only to matters on which the union is recognised and it applies only to information needed for collective bargaining. Thus, a union recognised for pay bargaining cannot use the provisions to obtain information about, for example, disciplinary policy, nor can a union use the provisions to obtain information for its other activities, such as dealing with individual grievances.[151]

Moreover, the exact nature of the information to be disclosed is rather unclear, governed as it is by the vague concepts of 'materially impeding' collective bargaining, and 'good industrial relations practice'. Some assistance is derived from the ACAS

---

[151] R v *Central Arbitration Committee, ex p BTP Tioxide* [1981] ICR 843.

Code of Practice to which regard must be had when interpreting s. 181(2)(b).[152] The Code suggests the following:

(i) Pay and benefits: principles and structure of payment systems; job evaluation systems and grading criteria; earnings and hours analysed according to work-group, grade, plant, sex, out-workers and homeworkers, department or division, giving, where appropriate, distributions and make-up of pay showing any additions to basic rate or salary; total pay bill; details of fringe benefits and non-wage labour costs.

(ii) Conditions of service: policies on recruitment, redeployment, redundancy, training, equal opportunity, and promotion; appraisal systems; health, welfare and safety matters.

(iii) Manpower: numbers employed analysed according to grade, department, location, age and sex; labour turnover; absenteeism; overtime and short-time; manning standards; planned changes in work methods, materials, equipment or organisation; available manpower plans; investment plans.

(iv) Performance: productivity and efficiency data; savings from increased productivity and output, return on capital invested; sales and state of order book.

(v) Financial: cost structures; gross and net profits; sources of earnings; assets; liabilities; allocation of profits; details of government financial assistance; transfer prices; loans to parent or subsidiary companies and interest charged.[153]

However, the Code is very clear that this list is simply meant to be indicative of the types of information that might be relevant, and should not be treated as a checklist.[154] In particular, the exact nature of the information to be disclosed depends on the nature of the bargaining process: the topics it covers and the level at which it takes place.

Importantly, s. 182 lays down some limits on the employer's duty of disclosure. So, for example, the employer need not disclose confidential information, or information relating to an individual unless he or she has consented.[155] Nor is the employer obliged to disclose information where assembling it for the purposes of disclosure would involve disproportionate effort relative to its importance to the bargaining process.[156]

Under s. 183, the trade union may complain to the CAC if the employer fails to provide it with the information it requests. The CAC may, in the first instance, refer the matter to ACAS for conciliation.[157] If the attempt at conciliation fails (or if the CAC decides that it is not worth pursuing) the CAC may determine the union's complaint.[158] If the complaint is well-founded, the CAC may make a declaration to that effect and may order the employer to disclose the information by a set deadline.[159] If the employer does not comply, the union may apply to the CAC for a further

---

[152] ACAS, *Code of Practice 2: Disclosure of Information to Trade Unions for Collective Bargaining Purposes* (2003).
[153] ibid [11].
[154] ibid [12].
[155] TULRCA 1992, ss 182(1)(c) and (d).
[156] ibid s 182(2)(b).
[157] ibid s 183(2).
[158] ibid s 183(3).
[159] ibid s 183(5).

determination under s. 184. At the same time, the union may apply to the CAC for an 'award': a declaration that the employer is required to observe certain terms and conditions of employment in respect of the employees for whom the union is recognised.[160] Since most employers would not want to have terms and conditions imposed on them by the CAC, this remedy is intended to act as a strong encouragement to the employer to disclose information to the union. It is noticeable that more recent interventions in collective bargaining, such as the Schedule A1 procedure, do not provide for this tough option in relation to recalcitrant employers.

Section 181 is not much used by trade unions, though there have been fluctuations over time.[161] To some extent, the purpose of s. 181 (rather like Schedule A1) is to encourage voluntary compliance by employers, so the fact that there are few cases should not necessarily lead us to the conclusion that the provision is wholly ineffective. It may have a significant indirect effect. And of course, the more general decline in collective bargaining is bound to lead to some decline in the use of supporting legal provisions. The real problem with s. 181 is its narrow scope. It only applies to information for the purposes of collective bargaining and thus does not contribute to transparency in the workplace more generally. For example, it does not apply to unrecognised unions, nor does it enable recognised unions to acquire information unrelated to collective bargaining. These objectives may be better pursued through the EU directives on workplace consultation, though these are not without their problems.[162]

Time off and facilities for trade union representatives

Another important right that flows from recognition is a right for employees who are also trade union officials to take paid time off in connection with their duties.[163] This right is set out in s. 168:

(1) An employer shall permit an employee of his who is an official of an independent trade union recognised by the employer to take time off during his working hours for the purpose of carrying out any duties of his, as such an official, concerned with–

(a) negotiations with the employer related to or connected with matters falling within section 178(2) (collective bargaining) in relation to which the trade union is recognised by the employer, or

(b) the performance on behalf of employees of the employer of functions related to or connected with matters falling within that provision which the employer has agreed may be so performed by the trade union . . .

(2) He shall also permit such an employee to take time off during his working hours for the purpose of undergoing training in aspects of industrial relations–

(a) relevant to the carrying out of such duties as are mentioned in subsection (1), and

(b) approved by the Trades Union Congress or by the independent trade union of which he is an official.

---

[160] ibid s 185.
[161] Howard Gospel and Graeme Lockwood, 'Disclosure of Information for Collective Bargaining: the CAC Approach Revisited' (1999) 28 ILJ 233. For more recent data, see CAC, *Annual Report 2013/2014* (2014) 12–13, revealing that the CAC dealt with 11 new complaints in that reporting year.
[162] See Chapter 14.
[163] Time off rights in other situations are examined in Chapter 14.

(3) The amount of time off which an employee is to be permitted to take under this section and the purposes for which, the occasions on which and any conditions subject to which time off may be so taken are those that are reasonable in all the circumstances having regard to any relevant provisions of a Code of Practice issued by ACAS.

Thus, the ACAS Code suggests that employees who are union officials are entitled to time off for activities such as preparing for and attending meetings with the employer to negotiate about terms and conditions of employment, and informing other employees about the outcome.[164] They are also entitled to time off to attend training courses run by the union or the TUC to help them perform their duties more effectively, such as training on negotiation skills or changes in the law.[165] The time off must be paid at the employee's usual rate.[166] If the employer does not comply with the provision, the employee official has a right to complain to the Employment Tribunal and to seek compensation.[167] The *Skiggs* case established the important principle that compensation is available even if the employee official has not suffered any quantifiable loss because, even though the aim of the award is compensatory not punitive, there is a loss associated with being prevented from carrying out trade union duties.[168]

There are two limitations on s. 168. First, the right is to 'reasonable' time off.[169] This is inevitable, given the many different circumstances that might arise, but it has the result that (despite the existence of the ACAS Code) disputes could very easily arise between employers and employee officials about what counts as 'reasonable'. A complaint to the Employment Tribunal is the only way to obtain an authoritative determination of this. Second, the right is to have the employer's permission to take time off.[170] This means that if the employer unreasonably withholds permission, the employee official would not be well-advised simply to take the time off anyway, since being absent without permission is likely to be a disciplinary offence even if a tribunal subsequently supports the employee's claim. The problem is that by the time the tribunal has heard the claim, the employee official's need for time off may long since have disappeared.

Another important practical issue for trade union representatives is the provision of facilities in order to carry out their duties at work. This might be something as simple as a notice board, or use of a room in which to hold meetings with fellow workers, or perhaps a dedicated office. The ACAS Code offers some guidance on these matters although there are no underlying legal rights.[171]

Time off for trade union members

Under s. 170, there is a right for employees who are members of a recognised trade union to take time off for trade union activities:

(1) An employer shall permit an employee of his who is a member of an independent trade union recognised by the employer in respect of that description of employee to take time off during his working hours for the purpose of taking part in–

---

[164] ACAS, *Code of Practice – Time Off for Trade Union Duties and Activities* (2010) [12]–[15].
[165] ibid [21]–[35].
[166] TULRCA, s 169.
[167] ibid ss 171–172.
[168] *Skiggs* v *South West Trains Ltd* [2005] IRLR 459.
[169] TULRCA, s 168(3).
[170] This is made clear in *Ryford Ltd* v *Drinkwater* [1996] IRLR 16.
[171] ACAS, above n 164, [46]. There are legal rights to facilities for representatives in relation to collective redundancy and TUPE consultation (discussed in Chapter 14): see, for example, TULRCA, s 188(5A).

(a) any activities of the union, and

(b) any activities in relation to which the employee is acting as a representative of the union.

(2) The right conferred by subsection (1) does not extend to activities which themselves consist of industrial action, whether or not in contemplation or furtherance of a trade dispute . . .

(3) The amount of time off which an employee is to be permitted to take under this section and the purposes for which, the occasions on which and any conditions subject to which time off may be so taken are those that are reasonable in all the circumstances having regard to any relevant provisions of a Code of Practice issued by ACAS.

The ACAS Code indicates that this right covers things like attending trade union meetings or voting in elections, and for employees who are representatives, attending branch or national meetings of the union.[172] Importantly, unlike s. 168, this right is not a right to paid time off, though the ACAS Code suggests that it might be good practice for employers to offer payment in some circumstances. As subsection 2 makes clear, the right does not extend to industrial action, which English law treats as a breach of contract by individual strikers.[173]

Conclusion

There are two ways of viewing the rights consequent on recognition that we have considered in this section. One is as an onerous set of additional requirements on employers in addition to the obligation to engage in collective bargaining, with the potential to distract employees from their core tasks by allowing them to take time off either as union members or as officials. The other is as a way of ensuring that – if there is to be collective bargaining – it takes place in the most efficient way possible, with well-informed and well-prepared union representatives who are able to liaise effectively between the employer and the workforce. More radically, it may be questioned whether these rights should be confined to *recognised* unions, given how difficult it is to secure recognition. For example, the time off rights would be equally valuable to unrecognised unions in helping them to make contact with potential members and build support in the workplace.

12.3.6 Derecognition

In a time of declining trade union membership and collective bargaining coverage, derecognition is obviously an issue of some topical relevance. There are two main issues to consider. The first is how the employer goes about derecognising the union. This varies according to whether the initial recognition was voluntary or statutory. The second is how the employer persuades the workforce to accept this, particularly where they have a contractual entitlement to collective bargaining and would thus be expected to accept a variation in their contracts.

---

[172] Above n 164, [36]–[41].
[173] See Chapter 13.

As against the union

Where a union has been recognised voluntarily, it is open to the employer unilaterally to withdraw recognition at any time. Of course, the union may organise industrial action to protest at this, so it is up to the employer to gauge how well-supported that action might be and whether it can withstand it.

Where the union has been recognised under the Schedule A1 procedure, there are some restrictions on derecognition. These are designed to ensure that a reluctant employer cannot begin the process of seeking derecognition as soon as the union wins recognition. There are two situations to distinguish. First, if the union was recognised by the employer voluntarily but after a request to the CAC, the employer cannot unilaterally derecognise the union until three years have elapsed since recognition (unless the parties themselves have agreed a shorter time-limit).[174] Second, if the union was recognised after an order by the CAC, there is a derecognition process that must be followed.[175] Again, the process cannot be started until a period of three years has elapsed.[176] Where the initial recognition was automatic, based on 50% trade union membership in the bargaining unit, the employer may apply to the CAC for derecognition.[177] The CAC can only accept the application for derecognition where membership has dropped below this level.[178] Where the recognition was based on a ballot, either a worker or the employer may apply.[179] The CAC can only accept the application if at least 10% of the bargaining unit support derecognition.[180] In either case, the CAC must organise a derecognition ballot which works in the same way as a recognition ballot, requiring a majority and 40% of those voting to vote in favour of derecognition.[181]

As against individuals

In relation to individual trade unionists, the employer faces two issues. First, individuals may oppose derecognition, so that when the employer attempts to secure derecognition they may participate in industrial action or vote to maintain recognition in a ballot, if applicable. And second, where individuals' contracts incorporate collectively bargained terms, they may refuse to sign new contracts (sometimes referred to as 'personal contracts') that contain no link with collective bargaining. The question for discussion in this section is what measures the law permits the employer to take in order to persuade its workers to give up collective bargaining. Again, there is a distinction to be drawn between voluntary and statutory derecognition.

It is worth reminding ourselves that the incorporation of collectively bargained terms into individual contracts of employment is not a straightforward matter and depends on the construction of the particular contract in question.[182] Assuming there

---

[174] TULRCA, sch A1, para 56.
[175] ibid para 96; paras 122–124.
[176] ibid para 97; para 125.
[177] ibid paras 122–133.
[178] ibid para 131.
[179] ibid paras 104–111 (employer request); paras 112–116 (worker request).
[180] ibid para 110.
[181] ibid paras 117–121; para 133.
[182] See Chapter 5.

is a 'bridging term', which succeeds in incorporating collectively agreed terms, the employer's refusal to continue with collective bargaining would not affect that term, which would remain in force until the affected workers agreed to vary their contracts. Thus, in the *Robertson* case, the employees were able to sue for unpaid wages when the employer stopped paying them in accordance with a collectively bargained bonus scheme without securing their consent to vary their contracts.[183] However, this is subject to the possibility of the employer dismissing the workers and re-engaging them on new terms and conditions.[184] Whether such a dismissal is fair or unfair would depend on a tribunal's assessment of the circumstances, and of course the very possibility of bringing an unfair dismissal claim is only available to employees with qualifying service.

Of course, most employers would prefer to avoid confrontation with their workforce where possible. One strategy for doing this is to offer 'inducements', such as a pay rise, to individuals who sign up to personal contracts. In the well-known *Wilson* v *UK* case, the claimant trade unionists were denied a pay rise when they refused to accept personal contracts as part of the employer's derecognition campaign.[185] They succeeded at the ECtHR in claims that the government had not done enough to protect their Article 11 rights, because the employer's actions did not constitute actionable discrimination against trade unionists under the law as it stood at that time. TULRCA s. 145B now purports to address the *Wilson* scenario:

(1) A worker who is a member of an independent trade union which is recognised, or seeking to be recognised, by his employer has the right not to have an offer made to him by his employer if–

    (a) acceptance of the offer, together with other workers' acceptance of offers which the employer also makes to them, would have the prohibited result, and

    (b) the employer's sole or main purpose in making the offers is to achieve that result.

(2) The prohibited result is that the workers' terms of employment, or any of those terms, will not (or will no longer) be determined by collective agreement negotiated by or on behalf of the union.

(3) It is immaterial for the purposes of subsection (1) whether the offers are made to the workers simultaneously . . .

(4) A worker or former worker may present a complaint to an employment tribunal on the ground that his employer has made him an offer in contravention of this section.

We saw above in our discussion of s. 145A that there are a number of drafting problems with these provisions. First, there is no right of action for the trade union – just for the affected individuals, many of whom may not bother to sue for the limited remedies on offer (£3715 in compensation).[186] Second, the union must be 'recognised or seeking to be recognised' which may be difficult to demonstrate in a derecognition situation, unless a court is prepared to assume that a union which has been derecognised against its wishes is inherently 'seeking recognition'.[187] Third, the 'sole or main purpose' test may make it possible for an employer to create doubt in

---

[183] *Robertson* v *British Gas Corp* [1983] ICR 351.
[184] See Chapter 5.
[185] Above n 1.
[186] TULRCA, s 145E.
[187] ibid s 145B(1). See Bogg, above n 36, 72–75.

the minds of tribunal members as to whether derecognition was the driving force behind its actions.[188] Fourth, although the worker's agreement to vary his or her contract in future is unenforceable under the provisions, any variation that has already taken effect remains enforceable even if a tribunal finds that it was brought about by an unlawful inducement.[189] Thus, although the existence of s. 145B may deter some employers from offering inducements, a well-advised employer could still make successful use of this strategy, relying the low chance of litigation and the low compensatory award if anyone does sue.

Another much more worrying possibility is that an employer might threaten workers in order to persuade them to sign new contracts. So for example they might be threatened with deductions from pay or demotions or the loss of other privileges at work. The law specifically excludes this situation from protection. Under s. 145B(4):

> Having terms of employment determined by collective agreement shall not be regarded for the purposes of section 145A (or section 146 or 152) as making use of a trade union service.

The effect of this is that the detriment (s. 146) and dismissal (s. 152) protections for trade unionists do not help when collective bargaining is the issue at stake. The government might argue that the exclusion of s. 152 protection in these circumstances simply places reliance on the ordinary law of unfair dismissal to determine whether or not a contract variation dismissal is fair or unfair. But the exclusion of s. 146 removes all protection from workers (who cannot claim unfair dismissal) and leaves employees exposed to many kinds of hostile tactics short of dismissal to persuade them to give up their collectively bargained contracts.

Where a statutory derecognition situation arises, workers have additional protection under Schedule A1. Thus, as we saw above, there are individual rights not to be subjected to detriment or dismissal on various grounds relating to the recognition or derecognition procedure.[190] There is also a more general duty on the employer (or union) to refrain from unfair practices, breach of which can be the subject of a complaint by the union (or employer) to the CAC.[191] The comments made above about the effectiveness of these protections are also relevant here.

POINTS TO TAKE AWAY

- English law prohibits blacklisting of trade unionists, discrimination against trade union members during the hiring process, detrimental treatment of trade union members during employment, and dismissal on the grounds of trade union membership. Critics argue that the statutory provisions in this area have fundamental flaws.

- A union is 'recognised' when an employer agrees to engage in collective bargaining with it. The employer may recognise the union voluntarily, but if it does not, the union may invoke the statutory recognition procedure under Schedule A1 TULRCA. This procedure has had limited impact.

---

[188] Despite TULRCA, s 145D placing the burden on the employer.
[189] TULRCA, s 145E(4).
[190] Above n 122.
[191] TULRCA, sch A1, paras 119A–I.

- The parties to a collective bargaining process may reach a 'collective agreement'. In English law, collective agreements are presumed not to be legally binding.

- Recognised trade unions have rights to information for the purposes of collective bargaining. Officials of recognised trade unions are entitled to paid time off to perform their duties.

- The process of derecognising a union is not legally regulated where the initial recognition took place voluntarily, but there is a procedure to follow for derecognition under Schedule A1. The law controls the tactics employers may use to persuade individual workers to give up collective bargaining through a provision against 'inducements', but this has been heavily criticised by commentators.

Further reading

We saw at the outset that levels of trade union membership and collective bargaining coverage have declined over time. This means that a significant proportion of workers are 'never-members': people who have never joined a trade union. The data on this are analysed by **Alex Bryson and Rafael Gomez, 'Why Have Workers Stopped Joining Unions? The Rise in Never-Membership in Britain' (2005) 43 BJIR 67**. One of the points they highlight is the centrality of recognition to membership: people are more likely to join a union if they can see that it will bring benefits at work.

This links to an important theme in the labour law literature: the 'neutrality' of the recognition procedure. This is the idea that the recognition procedure does not *favour* recognition. For discussion, see **Alan Bogg, *The Democratic Aspects of Trade Union Recognition* (Hart 2009)**; and **Ruth Dukes, 'The Statutory Recognition Procedure 1999: no Bias in Favour of Recognition?' (2008) 37 ILJ 236**. The concern expressed by these and other authors is that unions do not start from a position of strength, so a neutral recognition procedure, requiring them to show high levels of support in the workplace, in fact disadvantages them.

There is lots of empirical evidence about the operation of the recognition procedure. See, for example, **Gregor Gall, 'Union Recognition in Britain: the End of Legally Induced Voluntarism' (2012) 41 ILJ 407**; and **Sian Moore, Sonia McKay and Sarah Veale, *Statutory Regulation and Employment Relations: The Impact of Statutory Trade Union Recognition* (Palgrave Macmillan 2013)**. The Central Arbitration Committee's annual reports are a good source of up-to-date facts and figures about the usage of the procedure.

The ILO has consistently criticised the English industrial relations landscape for its 'all or nothing' approach. Recognised unions get various rights and privileges, but *unrecognised* unions get nothing. This makes it difficult for unrecognised unions to get a foothold in the workplace and to expand their membership. For an interesting discussion, linking this chapter to Chapter 14, see **Paul Davies and Claire Kilpatrick, 'UK Worker Representation after Single Channel' (2004) 33 ILJ 121**.

The *Wilson* case is one of a group of important ECtHR rulings on collective labour law, illustrating the advantages and disadvantages of pursuing workers' claims by this means. For discussion of the ECtHR ruling, see **KD Ewing, 'The Implications of *Wilson* and *Palmer*' (2003) 32 ILJ 1**, and for discussion of the legislative response, see **Alan L Bogg, 'Employment Relations Act 2004: Another False Dawn for Collectivism?' (2005) 34 ILJ 72**.

13 Industrial action

Learning outcomes

This chapter will enable readers to:

- understand the law applicable to those who organise industrial action, whether individuals or trade unions
- understand the legal position of workers who take part in industrial action and picketing
- analyse the status of the right to strike in international and European instruments and critically evaluate English law against that right

13.1 INTRODUCTION

In this chapter, we will consider the law on industrial action. The most obvious form of industrial action is the strike, in which workers withdraw their labour completely until the dispute with the employer is resolved. The aim is to cause disruption to the employer until the employer calculates that its interests are best served by making concessions. Although it is more unusual in practice, employers also have an equivalent weapon, the 'lock-out'. In this situation, the employer refuses to allow the workers to work until they accept the employer's terms. On the surface, it may seem odd that the law should permit employers and workers to engage in these kinds of behaviour, since they disrupt productivity and cause inconvenience to the firm's customers. But industrial action has long been regarded as an essential part of the system of collective bargaining, and (on some theories at least) as an important form of protest in the workplace.

Since workers do not get paid when they are on strike, they have tended to seek ways of disrupting the employer's business without engaging in a strike for an indefinite period of time. One possibility is 'action short of a strike', in which workers continue to work but refuse to co-operate fully with the employer (for example, by working to rule (following instructions to the letter in order to cause disruption), going slow (continuing to work, but not at normal speed) or refusing to perform certain parts of the job. However, as we shall see, the courts have tended to hold that the legal consequences of these types of action are the same as for a full withdrawal of labour, with the effect that the employer may still refuse to pay the workers. Nowadays, a common strategy is the 'one-day' strike, in which workers withdraw their labour for a day at a time (one day per week, for example) until the dispute is resolved. The term 'industrial action' is used as the title for this chapter in order to make clear that we will be considering not just strikes, but other types of action too.

In general terms, industrial action is becoming less common in the UK. For the 20-year period between 1973 and 1992, an average of 7.8 million working days per year were lost through strikes, compared to a mere 615,000 days in the following 20-year period, 1993–2012.[1] However, there are substantial fluctuations from year to year depending on whether any large-scale disputes arise. The most recent figures, for 2013, are 443,600 working days lost from 114 stoppages of work, of which 50 were in the public sector and 64 in the private sector.[2] This reflects the stronger trade union presence in the public sector. Some 94% of the working days lost were due to one-day stoppages, confirming the point made above that this is now the most popular type of strike action.[3] The vast majority of strikes relate to pay (broadly defined, to include pay cuts, possible pay rises, and pensions) or proposed redundancies.[4] Predictably, workers take the serious step of going on strike only in relation to the issues that really matter to them.

The law on industrial action covers three main topics: the legal position of those who organise strikes (which includes both individual organisers and trade unions) (section 13.3), the legal position of individual workers who take part in a strike (section 13.4), and the law governing picketing (when workers protest outside the workplace during industrial action) (section 13.5). But before we explore the legal details, we will examine the theoretical underpinnings of industrial action and its treatment in international human rights instruments.

13.2 THEORETICAL FRAMEWORK

The right to strike occupies a complex position in international human rights instruments. It features expressly in economic and social rights instruments, but may also be implied into civil and political rights instruments as an aspect of freedom of association. The relevant International Labour Organization (ILO) materials also treat the right to strike as an extension of freedom of association. Before we examine these provisions, it is worth pausing to think about the theoretical basis for the right to strike. After all, strikes disrupt the employer's business and may inconvenience people who are not connected to the dispute. So why should the right to strike be regarded as a right at all?

13.2.1 Justifications

Various different theories have been advanced to support a right for workers to withdraw their labour. Probably the most popular theory links the right to strike to the right to engage in collective bargaining, so we will consider that first, before examining other possibilities.[5]

Collective bargaining is a mechanism for workers (via their unions) and employers or employers' associations to reach collective agreements governing workers' terms

---

[1] Office of National Statistics, *Labour Disputes – Annual Article, 2013* (July 2014) 3. The statistics do not cover action short of a strike.

[2] ibid 1.

[3] ibid 14.

[4] ibid 12–14.

[5] For an excellent overview, see Tonia Novitz, *International and European Protection of the Right to Strike* (OUP 2003) Part I.

and conditions of employment, after a period of negotiation.[6] A key problem faced by workers when seeking to negotiate with an employer is inequality of bargaining power.[7] The employer has things that the workers want – jobs and pay – but the employer is not normally quite so reliant upon the workers. Of course, the employer needs workers to run its business, but if one group of workers refuses to work for a particular wage, for example, the employer will often be able to find other workers to take their jobs instead, unless there is a labour shortage or the workers have special skills. Put simply, it is easier for the employer to find new workers than it is for the workers to find new jobs. Part of the solution to this inequality of bargaining power is for workers to group together in trade unions: it is harder for the employer to ignore the collective demands of its workforce than it is to ignore the demands of one individual. But this may not be enough. If the union goes to the employer and asks for a pay rise for the workers, the employer may still refuse to accede to its demands. At this point, the role of the strike becomes apparent. If the workers refuse to continue working until their demands are met, they show that they are serious about the claims they are making, and they cause disruption to the employer's business. The employer must then recalculate the balance of advantages and disadvantages in making concessions to the union. If it wants to get the workers back to work, it will have to go back to the negotiating table. Similarly, if the union makes unreasonable demands, the employer may decide to lock the workers out – preventing them from working and earning money – until they moderate their claims. Of course, in many cases, the strike or lock-out does not happen: merely being able to make a credible threat is sufficient to tip the balance in the bargaining process. Either way, the possibility of taking industrial action is central to collective bargaining.

Of course, while this approach justifies causing harm to the other party to the bargaining process – in order to bring about a change of heart – it may be less easy to see why it justifies disrupting customers and the public at large. Here, it is important to distinguish quite carefully between inconvenience and actual harm.[8] In some occupations – the police, for example – many countries have a total ban on strike action because of the potential harm to public safety and security if it were known that the police were not at work. In other occupations where strikes are permitted but essential services may be affected, it is common either for the law or for collective agreements to provide that some minimum level of service must be maintained during the strike. For example, if members of the fire service were on strike, it would be appropriate for a skeleton staff to be obliged to provide cover in the event of a serious fire in which lives were at risk. Thus, firefighters would be withdrawing their labour in relation to less essential work such as providing advice on fire safety or attending minor incidents. In other cases – public transport, for example – there is disruption and inconvenience but no direct threat to life or limb. This is more difficult to deal with. On the one hand, it is clear that disruption does justify some regulation of the right to strike, to ensure that (for example) a strong union with a radical membership does not use the strike weapon in a frivolous way. On the other hand, if we regard striking as a right at all, we should be willing to put up with some consequences when people exercise their right. Moreover, these consequences are likely to be limited by

---

[6] See Chapter 12.
[7] Novitz, above n 5, 49–56.
[8] ibid chapter 4.

practical considerations: striking workers will not want to be on strike for too long if they are not being paid and if they risk losing public support for their cause.

Importantly, some theorists justify the right to strike in ways other than through the link to collective bargaining. One possibility is that the right to strike is an aspect of the freedom from forced labour.[9] This right has particular importance because it guarantees freedom from slavery and other types of 'unfree' work, such as debt bondage. The underlying idea is that work should be voluntary. However, while a strike involves a withdrawal of labour, it is designed to prompt the employer to make changes with a view to the workers returning to work on better terms and conditions. Thus, while it is an expression of the voluntariness of labour, that is not its primary purpose. Another justificatory possibility is that the right to strike is an aspect of freedom of expression.[10] Although we tend to think of expression as speech, it can involve many other methods of putting views across. For workers, the strike is an obvious means of conveying unhappiness at terms and conditions of work, or broader matters such as labour legislation, minimum wage levels or government policy more generally. The key attraction of freedom of expression as a basis for industrial action law is that it would potentially justify a much broader subject-matter for legitimate industrial action. Whereas a right to strike based on collective bargaining must pertain to matters within the scope of collective bargaining, freedom of expression is not so limited and would allow workers to use the strike weapon as a more general form of protest. However, freedom of expression is not an unlimited right, and the downside of using it as the basis for the right to strike is that striking is one of the more disruptive forms of expression to the rights and freedoms of others. So, for example, it might be difficult to overcome a requirement to show that a strike was the 'least restrictive' method of putting across workers' views on, say, the level of the minimum wage. Thus, the broader basis might bring with it greater scope for justified restrictions.

13.2.2 Human rights instruments

The next step in our analysis is to consider the treatment of the right to strike in international human rights instruments. Here, an important distinction arises between those instruments that recognise the right to strike explicitly, and those that have recognised it through their interpretive mechanisms as an aspect of some other right, usually freedom of association. With the possible exception of the EU Charter, those instruments with indirect recognition of the right to strike are the ones more likely to have an impact in the UK.

Express rights to strike

Predictably, express rights to strike tend to be found in economic and social rights instruments. Thus, Article 8(1) International Covenant on Economic, Social and Cultural Rights (ICESCR) provides:

> The States Parties to the present Covenant undertake to ensure . . .

> (d) The right to strike, provided that it is exercised in conformity with the laws of the particular country.

[9] Ruth Ben Israel, *International Labour Standards: The Case of Freedom to Strike* (Kluwer 1988) 24–25.
[10] See, for example, Seth Kupferberg, 'Political Strikes, Labor Law and Democratic Rights' (1985) 71 Virginia Law Review 685.

This right allows scope to the state to limit the right to strike through legislation, though any such legislation should not be such as to preclude the effective exercise of the right to strike itself.

The European Social Charter (ESC) also recognises the right to strike in Article 6. This is unchanged as between the 1961 and 1996 versions of the Charter, and has been accepted by the UK:

> With a view to ensuring the effective exercise of the right to bargain collectively, the Contracting Parties . . . recognise:
>
> > the right of workers and employers to collective action in cases of conflicts of interest, including the right to strike, subject to obligations that might arise out of collective agreements previously entered into.

This formulation of the right links it closely with collective bargaining, and allows for a common phenomenon in some other European legal systems, the 'peace obligation'.[11] In some systems, collective agreements have a definite end-date. During the currency of the collective agreement, unions are only allowed to organise a strike if the employer is not complying with the agreement. But once the agreement has come to an end and a new agreement is being negotiated, a strike may be used to secure a better deal. Undertakings not to strike are much less common in collective agreements in the UK.

The right to strike is also explicitly guaranteed in Article 28 of the EU Charter:

> Workers and employers, or their respective organisations, have, in accordance with Community law and national laws and practices, the right to negotiate and conclude collective agreements at the appropriate levels and, in cases of conflicts of interest, to take collective action to defend their interests, including strike action.

Like the ICESCR right, this right is limited by reference to national laws and practices. Moreover, the EU Charter is itself confined to acts of the EU institutions and the Member States only when they are implementing EU law.[12] Nevertheless, the UK government (together with the Polish government) was hostile to the inclusion of legally enforceable 'solidarity' rights in the Charter and negotiated a protocol containing the following provisions:

Article 1

(1) The Charter does not extend the ability of the Court of Justice of the European Union, or any court or tribunal of Poland or of the United Kingdom, to find that the laws, regulations or administrative provisions, practices or action of Poland or of the United Kingdom are inconsistent with the fundamental rights, freedoms and principles that it reaffirms.

(2) In particular, and for the avoidance of doubt, nothing in Title IV of the Charter creates justiciable rights applicable to Poland or the United Kingdom except in so far as Poland or the United Kingdom has provided for such rights in its national law.

---

[11] Antoine TJM Jacobs, 'The Law of Strikes and Lockouts', in Roger Blanpain (ed), *Comparative Labour Law and Industrial Relations in Industrialized Market Economies* (11th edn, Kluwer 2014).
[12] See Chapter 2.

Article 2

To the extent that a provision of the Charter refers to national laws and practices, it shall only apply to Poland or the United Kingdom to the extent that the rights or principles that it contains are recognised in the law or practices of Poland or of the United Kingdom.[13]

The exact effect of these provisions is unclear. The government was keen to ensure that it could claim that the Charter did not create a justiciable right to strike in English law. Arguably, the protocol confirms this because there is no express right to strike in English law so Article 28 is excluded by Article 1(2). However, the Charter does not give rise to free-standing justiciable rights anyway, because of its more general limitations, so it is not clear that the protocol makes any difference. The position is further complicated by the existence of Article 12 in the Charter. As we shall see in the next section, this provision, on freedom of association, mirrors Article 11 ECHR and, to the extent that Article 11 gives rise to a right to strike, Article 12 may do so too.

Overall, while the express rights to strike do not give much detail on the scope of the right or permissible limitations, they do perform the important function of confirming that (despite the concerns noted above about disruption to employers and others) engaging in industrial action can be regarded as a *right* for workers.

Implied rights to strike

Perhaps surprisingly, the ILO instruments do not contain an express right to strike. This is the effect of the ILO's tripartite structure. The employers' group has always been reluctant to concede the existence of a right to strike, and this has prevented the ILO from securing agreement to a convention on the topic. However, the ILO's key committees, the Committee on Freedom of Association (CFA) and the Committee of Experts on the Application of Conventions and Recommendations (CEACR), have both accepted that the right to strike is inherent in freedom of association and should therefore be protected by states signed up to Convention 87.[14] The CFA first recognised the right to strike in 1952,[15] and the CEACR in 1959.[16] Both regard it as flowing from the right of unions to organise their own programmes of activity in Convention 87.[17] Both link the right to strike quite closely with collective bargaining and have rejected the idea of 'purely political' strikes, but do accept that in some situations it might be appropriate to allow workers to use a strike to protest at economic and social conditions.[18] They recognise that the right to strike is not unlimited but have been concerned to ensure that any limitations, such as balloting or notice requirements, are not designed so as to impede the exercise of the right to strike.[19] So, for example, a requirement to secure anything more than a simple majority in favour of a strike is an infringement of the right.[20] Many of the CFA's

---

[13] Protocol on the Application of the Charter of Fundamental Rights of the European Union to Poland and to the United Kingdom, C 306/156 EN Official Journal of the European Union 17.12.2007.

[14] ILO, Convention 87 on Freedom of Association and Protection of the Right to Organise (1948).

[15] CFA, *Digest of decisions and principles of the Freedom of Association Committee of the Governing Body of the ILO* (5th edn 2006), chapter 10.

[16] CEACR, *General Survey on the Fundamental Conventions Concerning Rights at Work in Light of the ILO Declaration on Social Justice for a Fair Globalization, 2008* (2012), 46–65.

[17] Above n 14, art 3.

[18] Above n 15, [526]– 528]; above n 16, [124].

[19] Above n 15, [547].

[20] Above n 15, [556].

cases have concerned restrictions on strikes in essential services.[21] While these are acceptable in principle, the CFA has been concerned to ensure that states do not define essential services in an unnecessarily broad way.

At the time of writing, the employers' group within the ILO is contesting the committees' recognition of the right to strike.[22] The employers argue that the right to strike is not explicit in Convention 87 and thus it was an illegitimate use of the powers of the CFA and CEACR to interpret ILO norms to develop a right to strike. The CEACR has mounted a robust defence of its position, pointing out that the employers have accepted the right to strike for many years, that interpretation is a legitimate part of its mandate, that many states recognise the right to strike and that its interpretations are, in any event, not binding.[23] The matter has been referred to the ILO's Governing Body for discussion in November 2014.

The ECHR, as a civil and political rights instrument, does not contain an express right to strike. However, it has long recognised that Article 11, on freedom of association, has a 'dynamic' or purposive aspect: it protects unions' ability to strive for the protection of their members' interests. Initially, the Court allowed signatory states a wide margin of appreciation in respect of the possibilities they should afford unions for this purpose.[24] Over time, the Court has become more rigorous. In *Unison v UK*, the government argued that it provided unions with a right to strike to protect their members' interests, and for the first time, the Court scrutinised restrictions on the right to strike in order to determine whether they were proportionate.[25] But in *Enerji Yapi-Yol Sen v Turkey*, the Court went further, condemning Turkey's ban on strikes in the public sector.[26] The Court recognised that the right to strike was not absolute and could be restricted for state officials, but held that the category should be defined as narrowly as possible. Although the brief judgment is not particularly clear on the point, it would appear that the right to strike was regarded by the Court as an aspect of the state's positive obligation to fulfil Article 11, following on from the judgment in *Demir* in which collective bargaining was given that status.[27]

In the subsequent *RMT* decision, the Court has elaborated its position somewhat.[28] We will consider the facts – which concerned English law – in greater detail below. For now, there are two key points to note. First, the Court accepted that strike action was 'clearly protected by Article 11' as a result of *Enerji* and other decisions.[29] However, it went on to say this:

> The Court therefore does not discern any need in the present case to determine whether the taking of industrial action should now be accorded the status of an essential element of the Article 11 guarantee.[30]

---

[21] Above n 15, [573].
[22] Claire La Hovary, 'Showdown at the ILO? A Historical Perspective on the Employers' Group's 2012 Challenge to the Right to Strike' (2013) 42 ILJ 338.
[23] CEACR, General Report: Application of International Labour Standards 2014 (2014) [14]–[31].
[24] *Schmidt and Dahlströhm v Sweden* (1979–80) 1 EHRR 687.
[25] *UNISON v United Kingdom* [2002] IRLR 497.
[26] *Enerji Yapi-Yol Sen v Turkey* (2009) (unreported).
[27] *Demir v Turkey* (2009) 48 EHRR 54.
[28] *National Union of Rail, Maritime and Transport Workers v United Kingdom* (2015) 60 EHRR 10. For discussion, see Alan Bogg and KD Ewing, 'The Implications of the *RMT* Case' (2014) 43 ILJ 221.
[29] ibid [84].
[30] ibid.

Thus, the status of the right to strike within Article 11 remains uncertain. Second, the Court drew a distinction between 'core' and 'accessory' aspects of trade union activity:

> If a legislative restriction strikes at the core of trade union activity, a lesser margin of appreciation is to be recognised to the national legislature and more is required to justify the proportionality of the resultant interference, in the general interest, with the exercise of trade union freedom. Conversely, if it is not the core but a secondary or accessory aspect of trade union activity that is affected, the margin is wider and the interference is, by its nature, more likely to be proportionate as far as its consequences for the exercise of trade union freedom are concerned.[31]

It remains to be seen how this distinction (which does not seem to have any theoretical basis)[32] will be drawn in future cases. The risk is that Article 11 will only prove to be useful in extreme situations – like the Turkish ban on public sector industrial action – and of no assistance in tackling restrictions on strikes in states like the UK where the right to strike is heavily regulated but not entirely outlawed.[33] This is because it is likely to prove relatively easy for the state to argue that restrictions on the right to strike are a proportionate means of achieving a legitimate aim, especially when the state is given a wide margin of appreciation within which to pursue its policy choices. In *RMT* itself, the UK's ban on secondary industrial action (in which workers not involved in a dispute strike to support fellow-workers who are) was found to be proportionate because of the potential disruption to the economy if secondary action were to be permitted in the UK. This was despite the fact that the ILO supports secondary action as a legitimate exercise of the right to strike.[34]

The recognition of a right to strike at some level within Article 11 raises an interesting question for the status of the right to strike within the EU Charter. Although, as we saw above, Article 28 protects the right to strike, Article 12 protects freedom of association and is the equivalent of Article 11 ECHR. According to Article 52(3), where the EU Charter has an equivalent ECHR provision, it should be interpreted in the same way as that provision (unless EU law offers better protection), a point reinforced by the EU's imminent accession to the ECHR. This would suggest that to the extent that there is a right to strike in Article 11 ECHR, there is a right to strike in Article 12 EU Charter. If this is so, Articles 1(2) and 2 of the protocol on the application of the Charter to the UK are not relevant to this 'version' of the right to strike.

Conclusion

In general terms, then, the UK is a signatory to a number of instruments which recognise the right to strike, whether expressly, or indirectly through interpretation. Importantly, though, they all recognise that the right to strike is not an absolute right and may be limited by signatory states in various ways. The most detailed source of information on possible limitations is the ILO, through the cases of the CFA and the

---

[31] ibid [87].
[32] Bogg and Ewing, above n 28.
[33] A more interesting avenue may be offered by the requirement that restrictions be 'clear and foreseeable' in *Tymoshenko v Ukraine*, (2014) 58 EHRR 3, though this is a brief judgment in a different context.
[34] Above n 15, [534].

interpretations of the CEACR, even though, as we saw above, the ILO's recognition of the right to strike is rather controversial at present. During the discussion of English law, below, we will see how it measures up to these standards.

13.3 THE LAW GOVERNING STRIKE ORGANISERS AND TRADE UNIONS

We will now turn to the first part of our discussion of English law, focusing on those who organise strikes. The provisions we are about to discuss apply to anyone who organises a strike, whether he or she is a trade union official or not. Where a trade union is responsible for the strike organiser – in accordance with a set of legal rules on trade union responsibility – additional duties apply to the trade union. Probably the most obvious feature of this body of statute law is that it does not grant an express 'right' to strike. Instead, the organisation of a strike generally gives rise to liability for one or more of the economic torts, but – if certain conditions are met – strike organisers and trade unions may be able to claim a statutory 'immunity' against tort liability. Nowadays, this is overlaid by the possibility that a right to strike might be recognised under the ECHR or in EU law, so that the courts might have to interpret the statute to give effect to that right. It is arguable that English law might still be able to offer a right to strike *in practice* (if not in form) by the immunity method. But this depends on how the conditions for obtaining the immunity are designed in the legislation and interpreted by the courts. We will explore these crucial questions in this section.

The discussion will proceed in four main parts. We will begin by considering sectors in which strike action is prohibited. We will then turn to a brief examination of the economic torts, in order to demonstrate some of the ways in which the activities of a strike organiser might incur liability in tort. In the third part of the discussion, we will examine the statutory immunity and the various requirements for acquiring and retaining it, including the definition of a 'trade dispute' and the balloting and notice requirements for trade unions. Finally, we will consider the remedies for unlawful industrial action with a particular emphasis on injunctions.

13.3.1 Excluded sectors

Most international instruments accept that the right to strike can be excluded in certain sectors, often referred to as 'essential services', where there would be a serious threat to public safety or security if a strike took place. In these situations, the ILO supervisory bodies indicate that the state should adopt other means of protecting workers' interests.[35]

In English law, there is no clear concept of 'essential services' and there are no strike 'bans' as such. Instead, there are specific pieces of legislation directed at people who attempt to organise strikes in certain sectors.[36] Thus, anyone who seeks to induce a police officer[37] or a member of the armed forces[38] not to perform his or her

---

[35] Above n 15, [572]–[603].

[36] TULRCA, s 240 does contain a general offence of 'wilfully and maliciously' breaking a contract knowing that it will endanger life, or cause serious injury to people or property.

[37] Police Act 1996, s 91.

[38] Incitement to Disaffection Act 1934, s 1.

duties commits a criminal offence. Anyone who seeks to induce a prison officer[39] or an officer of the National Crime Agency[40] to strike commits a breach of statutory duty and can be the subject of action by the Secretary of State. Particular controversy has arisen surrounding the position of prison officers. Nowadays, many prisons are run on behalf of the government by private firms. The strike ban applies to both private and public sector prison officers. For those in the public sector, special negotiation arrangements protect their pay and other terms and conditions of employment (though their effectiveness is open to question),[41] but for those in the private sector, no such arrangements exist.[42] Thus, their terms and conditions of employment are at the mercy of their employer with no prospect of industrial action. This has been the subject of a long-running complaint by the Prison Officers Association to the ILO, which is continuing to press the government to address the problem.[43]

In other key public services, such as the fire and ambulance services, there are no restrictions on industrial action other than those in the ordinary law applicable to all workers. However, it would clearly be quite problematic if no arrangements were made during strikes in these areas. One option is for unions and employers to agree to provide a minimum level of cover during the strike, for example, if there is a risk to life. The other, more controversial, option is for the government to deploy troops or use emergency powers to provide cover. This is controversial because the impact of a strike is greatly reduced if substitute workers are found and there is thus no real stoppage. The ILO bodies generally regard it as a breach of the right to strike if the employer is allowed to 'break' the strike by hiring substitute workers, unless there is a genuine emergency.[44] If an agreement on cover cannot be reached, the government may have no alternative but to intervene. Although there is no limit on the government's capacity to deploy troops, the Civil Contingencies Act 2004 does at least contain one limitation, which is that it may not be used to deny someone the right to strike.[45] In other words, the government cannot use emergency powers to order strikers back to work. But the provision does not preclude the use of emergency powers in a way that would undermine a strike.

13.3.2 Liability of strike organisers in tort

Outside the special cases considered in the previous section, the starting-point for determining the legal situation of a strike organiser is the law of tort. The 1992 Act offers immunity to those who commit torts in the context of organising industrial action provided that certain conditions are met. In order to understand how the immunity works, it is helpful to have some background on the scope and nature of the underlying torts.[46] Perhaps the most important problem to note here is that the boundaries of the torts are uncertain, since they are created and developed by the

---

[39] Criminal Justice and Public Order Act 1994, s 127. This can be suspended under s 127A.

[40] Crime and Courts Act 2013, s 13.

[41] The Prison Service Pay Review Body makes non-binding recommendations to the Secretary of State: *Ministry of Justice v Prison Officers Association* [2008] EWHC 239, [2008] ICR 702.

[42] Gillian S Morris, 'The New Legal Regime for Prison Officers' (1994) 23 ILJ 326.

[43] CFA, Case No 2383 (United Kingdom) – The Prison Officers Association (2004).

[44] ILO, above n 15, [632] and [636].

[45] Civil Contingencies Act 2004, s 23(3)(b).

[46] For a more detailed account, see Hazel Carty, *An Analysis of the Economic Torts* (2nd edn, OUP 2010).

judges, but Parliament has chosen to provide immunity in respect of specific named torts. Thus, judicial creativity in the law of tort could serve to weaken the immunities unless Parliament is willing to 'catch up' by amending them.

The most basic of the economic torts is 'inducing breach of contract'. This originates from the famous case of *Lumley* v *Gye*, in which a singer who was under contract to perform at a theatre was persuaded to breach her contract and perform instead at the defendant's theatre.[47] The elements of the tort were clarified by the House of Lords in the important *OBG* decision.[48] First, there must be a *breach* of contract, because the defendant's liability is as an accessory to the contracting party's wrong. Thus, for example, the tort is not committed where the contracting party is protected against liability for breach of contract by a term of the contract.[49] Second, the defendant must either *know* that he or she is procuring a breach of contract, or have decided deliberately not to enquire into the matter. Third, the defendant must *intend* to procure a breach of the contract. Mere foreseeability that a breach will occur is not sufficient. However, it is not a requirement that the defendant should intend to harm the other party to the contract, so it is no defence to argue, for example, that the other party would be better off in the event of a breach.[50]

In the industrial action context, these requirements are easily fulfilled. As we shall see below, most industrial action is a breach of contract because the striking worker is refusing to perform his or her contractual duties (or refusing to do so to the full extent required by the employer). In most cases, the strike organiser will have a good knowledge of the terms of the contract: the core duties (such as turning up for work) are obvious and the strike organiser may well be familiar with the contract from the collective bargaining process anyway. Calling someone out on strike is likely to be a clear manifestation of intention.

Another key economic tort is 'causing loss by unlawful means'. For some years, this tort was treated as an extension of the tort we have just examined, inducing breach of contract. However, in *OBG*, the House of Lords held that decisions to this effect were incorrect and that the two torts should be regarded as conceptually distinct.[51] Whereas liability for inducing breach of contract is a form of accessory liability (to the actions of the contract-breaker), liability for causing loss by unlawful means is a primary wrong. Cases that were decided under an expanded version of inducing breach of contract in the 1970s and 1980s now fall to be reconsidered under this heading. Lord Nicholls drew the same distinction but labelled the tort more precisely as 'interfering with the claimant's business by unlawful means'.[52]

Lord Hoffmann explained the key elements as follows:

> The essence of the tort therefore appears to be (a) a wrongful interference with the actions of a third party in which the claimant has an economic interest and (b) an intention thereby to cause loss to the claimant.[53]

---

[47] *Lumley* v *Gye* (1853) 118 ER 749.
[48] *OBG Ltd* v *Allan* [2007] UKHL 21, [2008] 1 AC 1 [39]–[44] (Lord Hoffmann).
[49] This effectively overrules the line of case-law beginning with *Torquay Hotel Co Ltd* v *Cousins* [1969] 2 Ch 106(CA).
[50] *South Wales Miners' Federation* v *Glamorgan Coal Co Ltd* [1905] AC 239 (HL).
[51] *OBG*, above n 48, [38].
[52] ibid [141].
[53] ibid [47].

The 'wrongfulness' or unlawful means element of the tort requires that the defendant's actions were unlawful as regards the third party and were thus actionable by him (or would have been actionable had the third party in fact suffered any loss).[54] The unlawful acts must interfere with the third party's ability to deal freely with the claimant. The defendant must have intended to cause the claimant loss. According to Lord Hoffmann, this does not extend to cases in which the loss was a foreseeable consequence of the defendant's actions. Thus, the case of *Barretts & Baird*, in which the owner of an abattoir who was unable to obtain various permissions during a civil service strike failed in his claim against the strike organisers, was held to be rightly decided because the civil servants' intention was to put pressure on the government.[55]

A simple example of the tort outside the industrial action context would be where a firm threatened the customers of a rival firm in order to secure their custom and drive the rival out of business. In the industrial action context, there are various ways of committing this broadly framed tort but a central example is afforded by the case of *Stratford v Lindley*, originally decided under the broad interpretation of inducing breach of contract mentioned above.[56] There, the union was in dispute with company A and instructed its members (who were employed under the Dock Labour Scheme by various employers, not company A) to refuse to have any dealings with company B, which was owned by the same individual as company A. Thus, the union's action in inducing the workers to breach their contracts of employment as against their employers was a tortious act which was intended to cause loss to company A.

Historically, the tort of intimidation has been treated as separate. It was elaborated most clearly in *Rookes v Barnard*.[57] In that case, the union and the employer had agreed to operate a closed shop in the workplace. Rookes resigned from the union because he was unhappy with its decisions. The union officials then threatened to organise a strike (with the result that they would breach their contracts and induce other workers to do the same) if the employer did not dismiss Rookes. The employer dismissed Rookes (lawfully, with proper notice)[58] and Rookes brought proceedings in tort against the union organisers. The House of Lords held that the union officials had committed the tort of intimidation because they had threatened to do something they had no right to do (breach their contracts and induce others to breach theirs) in a way that they knew would cause the claimant loss. Thus, this tort requires a threat to use unlawful means knowing that this will cause loss to the claimant. Importantly, the tort applied even though the employer was entitled (under the law as it then stood) to dismiss Rookes, so that the act the employer was persuaded to do was a lawful one. In *OBG*, Lord Hoffmann treated intimidation as a species of causing loss by unlawful means: the threat to induce breaches of contract by calling a strike constituted the unlawful means, and it was intended to cause loss to the claimant by prompting the employer to terminate his employment.[59]

The *Rookes* case is an example of three-party intimidation: the union threatens the employer, the employer is induced to dismiss the claimant who suffers loss. It has occasionally been suggested that there is an actionable tort of two-party intimidation

---

[54] ibid [45]–[64].
[55] ibid [64]; *Barretts & Baird (Wholesale) Ltd v Institution of Professional Civil Servants* [1987] IRLR 3 (QBD).
[56] *JT Stratford & Son Ltd v Lindley* [1969] 1 WLR 1547 (CA).
[57] *Rookes v Barnard* [1964] AC 1129 (HL).
[58] The case pre-dates unfair dismissal law.
[59] *OBG*, above n 48, [7].

in which the claimant is induced by intimidation to act to his or her own detriment.[60] This might have arisen if, for example, in a *Rookes*-type situation, the employer suffered loss by dismissing the employee (for example, because the employee had special skills or because the employer acted unlawfully and had to pay the employee damages). Lord Hoffmann in *OBG* pointed out that this tort could not be regarded as a species of causing loss by unlawful means (which is a three-party tort) and thus did not comment on it.[61] Cases of this type of intimidation appear to be quite rare.

Finally, there is a tort of conspiracy. This exists in two versions: 'simple' and 'unlawful means'. Both are relevant to industrial disputes because they can be used in any case where there is an agreement involving more than one strike organiser. Simple conspiracy involves an agreement to do acts which result in damage to the claimant even if the acts themselves are entirely lawful.[62] Simple conspiracy is particularly controversial because it renders tortious acts that would be lawful if done by one person acting alone, even if they resulted in damage to the claimant. However, its scope of application was much-reduced by the decision in the *Crofter* case, in which it was held that trade unionists who were seeking to promote their own interests by lawful means did not have the necessary intention to harm the claimant and did not therefore commit the tort.[63] Unlawful means conspiracy involves an agreement to use unlawful means with the intention of causing damage to the claimant. We saw above that in the tort of causing loss by unlawful means, the unlawful means must be actionable by the victim, but in the *Total Network SL* case, it was held that this limitation did not apply to unlawful means conspiracy.[64] This means that, for example, the commission of a criminal offence could constitute the unlawful means for this tort.

Using the economic torts as the starting-point for industrial action law can be quite problematic. Since they are developed by the courts at common law, they are the subject of a gradual process of evolution through the case-law. This means that their boundaries are uncertain. Strike organisers may not be able to predict their own liability with any certainty, and are always vulnerable to the decisions of a creative judge who is determined to stop their action. Moreover, although in the past many economic tort cases were concerned with industrial action, the economic torts have a much broader range of application, tackling other problems such as unfair competition between rival firms. As a result, the law may evolve to tackle unfair competitive practices (for example) with unintended consequences for industrial action.

There are many twentieth-century examples of the judges developing the economic torts in order to 'catch' industrial action cases. *Rookes* itself is notorious because the House of Lords identified the tort of intimidation and then went on to hold that it was not protected by the statutory immunity as drafted at that time.[65] Parliament was forced to change the law as a result. However, it is possible that judges today would be more circumspect. In *OBG*, Lord Hoffmann noted the role of statute in regulating industrial action (though of course the statutory regime does not address

---

[60] *Godwin v Uzoigwe* [1993] Fam Law 65 (CA).
[61] *OBG*, above n 48, [61].
[62] *Quinn v Leathem* [1901] AC 495 (HL).
[63] *Crofter Hand Woven Harris Tweed Co Ltd v Veitch* [1942] AC 435 (HL).
[64] *Customs and Excise Commissioners v Total Network SL* [2008] UKHL 19, [2008] 1 AC 1174.
[65] Above n 57.

liability for industrial action, leaving this to the common law) and warned that the courts should be slow to interfere.[66] His emphasis on keeping the torts within boundaries – insisting on intention rather than foreseeability, for example – may also help to limit any expansion. But some uncertainty is bound to remain. For example, those organising strikes in the public sector may be faced with actions for inducing breach of statutory duty (rather than contract) which is not covered by the immunity, at least where the breach of statutory duty is itself actionable.[67]

13.3.3 Immunity

The statutory immunity against tort liability for strike organisers is set out in TULRCA 1992, s. 219:

(1) An act done by a person in contemplation or furtherance of a trade dispute is not actionable in tort on the ground only–

    (a) that it induces another person to break a contract or interferes or induces another person to interfere with its performance, or

    (b) that it consists in his threatening that a contract (whether one to which he is a party or not) will be broken or its performance interfered with, or that he will induce another person to break a contract or interfere with its performance.

(2) An agreement or combination by two or more persons to do or procure the doing of an act in contemplation or furtherance of a trade dispute is not actionable in tort if the act is one which if done without any such agreement or combination would not be actionable in tort.

There are three important elements to discuss in relation to this provision: the torts it covers, and the two elements of the so-called 'golden formula', 'contemplation or furtherance' and 'trade dispute'. We will examine each in turn.

In terms of the torts covered, it is relatively easy to identify inducing breach of contract (subsection (1)(a)), intimidation (subsection (1)(b)) and simple conspiracy (subsection (2)) in s. 219. If Lord Hoffmann is right in *OBG* that intimidation is just a subset of causing loss by unlawful means, its separate inclusion here is unnecessary, though as Simpson points out, the change in the common law should not serve to reduce the protection Parliament clearly intended to provide.[68] Moreover, two-party intimidation is left untouched by *OBG*. As we saw above, the decision in *Crofter* probably renders subsection (2) unnecessary though it does offer an important reinforcement of the decision in that case. The tort of causing loss (or interfering with the claimant's business) by unlawful means is not expressly listed so the availability of immunity for this tort is less certain. Subsection (1)(a) does refer to interfering with the performance of a contract (or inducing others to do so) but, as Simpson points out, it is not entirely clear whether this would capture all possible examples of the tort.

However, these concerns are mitigated to some extent by the decision in *Hadmor Productions* v *Hamilton*,[69] in which it was confirmed that once a particular tort was

---

[66] *OBG*, above n 48, [56].

[67] For an (unsuccessful) attempt to develop this, see *Associated British Ports* v *Transport and General Workers Union* [1989] ICR 557 (HL).

[68] Bob Simpson, 'Economic Tort Liability in Labour Disputes: the Potential Impact of the House of Lords' Decision in *OBG v Allan*' (2007) 36 ILJ 468, 476–479.

[69] *Hadmor Productions* v *Hamilton* [1983] 1 AC 191 (HL).

covered by the immunity, this applied whether the tort in question was relied upon in itself or as the unlawful means element of another tort. Thus, Hadmor's argument that the union had interfered with its business by means of unlawful intimidation failed in part because of the clear immunity attaching to intimidation.

Assuming that the torts committed by the strike organiser are covered by s. 219, the next step is to determine whether he or she acted 'in contemplation or furtherance' of a trade dispute. In the 1970s, the Court of Appeal in a series of cases interpreted this aspect objectively.[70] In other words, the judges reserved for themselves a right to determine whether the strike organiser's actions would in fact advance the dispute. The House of Lords, albeit with some reluctance, overturned this line of case-law and reinstated a subjective interpretation.[71] Thus, a strike organiser is protected if he or she believes that the action in question will advance his or her cause. This is quite important because it reduces the need for the courts to get drawn into a discussion of the merits of the dispute, which could lead them into risky political territory.

Attention then shifts to the definition of a trade dispute. This is set out in s. 244(1) TULRCA:

> In this Part a "trade dispute" means a dispute between workers and their employer which relates wholly or mainly to one or more of the following–
>
> (a) terms and conditions of employment, or the physical conditions in which any workers are required to work;
>
> (b) engagement or non-engagement, or termination or suspension of employment or the duties of employment, of one or more workers;
>
> (c) allocation of work or the duties of employment between workers or groups of workers;
>
> (d) matters of discipline;
>
> (e) a worker's membership or non-membership of a trade union;
>
> (f) facilities for officials of trade unions; and
>
> (g) machinery for negotiation or consultation, and other procedures, relating to any of the above matters, including the recognition by employers or employers' associations of the right of a trade union to represent workers in such negotiation or consultation or in the carrying out of such procedures.

There are three important points to note about this provision. First, the dispute must be between 'workers and their employer'. Although the statute also contains specific provision on the matter, this serves to exclude 'secondary action' from the scope of protection. Secondary action occurs where workers who are not in dispute with their own employer go on strike in support of other workers who are engaged in a dispute. We will discuss secondary action in detail below.

Second, the dispute must relate 'wholly or mainly' to the listed matters. This means that unions must formulate the aims of a strike carefully to ensure that any 'unprotected' issues of concern to the workforce are not presented as aims of the strike.

---

[70] See, for example, *Beaverbrook Newspapers Ltd* v *Keys* [1978] ICR 582; *Express Newspapers* v *McShane* [1979] ICR 210 (CA); *Duport Steels Ltd* v *Sirs* [1980] ICR 161 (CA).

[71] *Express Newspapers Ltd* v *McShane* [1980] AC 672 (HL); *Duport Steels Ltd* v *Sirs* [1980] ICR 161 (HL).

Third, the listed matters themselves are closely linked to collective bargaining, thus demonstrating that English law – to the extent that it permits strike action – does so because of its relationship to collective bargaining. Broader objectives – such as an increase in the minimum wage or a change in government policy – are not permitted objectives for a strike. This is contrary to the interpretations put forward by the relevant ILO bodies.[72] Although the ILO does not support strikes as a general form of protest, it encourages states to permit strikes when they are intended to further the economic and social interests of union members, even if this might involve attacks on government policy.

The exclusion of strikes with political purposes and the 'wholly or mainly' requirement taken together can pose difficulties for public sector unions. For example, as the *Mercury* case illustrates, a union campaign against privatisation of a public service might be formulated in different ways, some of which would be protected and some not.[73] A general campaign against privatisation is not a legitimate subject for a strike, whereas worker concerns about impending job losses clearly are. Strike organisers must be careful not to lose the immunity by adopting too broad a formulation of their objectives, even though it is often tempting to do so when trying to whip up worker support for the action.

Ways to lose the immunity

So far, we have established that trade unions and strike organisers are protected by the immunity provided that the tort they have committed is included in the statute and provided that they act 'in contemplation or furtherance of a trade dispute'. However, the story does not end there. There are three main ways in which the immunity might be 'lost'. First, the statute identifies four types of action for which the immunity is not available. Second, where the strike is organised by a trade union (a matter itself determined by statutory provisions) the immunity can be lost if the union does not comply with a complex set of balloting and notice requirements. And third, where the action has cross-border implications, the domestic framework for regulating strike action may be displaced entirely by directly effective provisions of EU law. We will consider each of these possibilities in turn.

1. Action not covered by the immunity

Sections 222–225 TULRCA identify four scenarios in which the immunity is not available. These provisions are quite significant because they highlight some key policy objectives of the government's regulation of industrial action. First, s. 222 ensures that a strike loses its immunity if its purpose is to enforce a closed shop, whether this is at the workplace in dispute (s. 222(1) and (2)) or at a third party (s. 222(3)). It is worth noting that s. 222(1) is particularly broad, applying to action which has enforcing a closed shop as 'one of' its purposes, not necessarily a main purpose. Second, s. 223 ensures that a strike is unprotected if 'one of' the reasons for it is to protest at the dismissal of strikers who have engaged in unofficial industrial action. We will examine the provisions on dismissal of individual strikers in greater detail below, but for now it is sufficient to observe that this is designed to ensure that,

---

[72] Above n 18.
[73] *Mercury Communications Ltd v Scott-Garner* [1984] Ch 37 (CA).

where there is a union presence, strikers follow the union's instructions and do not organise industrial action on their own.

Third, the remaining two provisions, ss. 224 and 225, are designed to combat secondary action even though, as we saw above, the definition of a trade dispute already precludes some forms of secondary action. Under s. 224, immunity is lost:

> when, and only when, a person–
>
> (a) induces another to break a contract of employment or interferes or induces another to interfere with its performance, or
> (b) threatens that a contract of employment under which he or another is employed will be broken or its performance interfered with, or that he will induce another to break a contract of employment or to interfere with its performance,
>
> and the employer under the contract of employment is not the employer party to the dispute.

Under s. 225(1), the immunity is lost where workers pressure their employer to refuse to deal with a supplier because it does not recognise a union or to include in contracts with suppliers requirements to recognise unions. And under s. 225(2), immunity is lost where a strike by the employer's workers interferes with the supply of goods or services from a third party supplier on the grounds that the supplier does not recognise or consult with a union.

The UK's ban on secondary action has been criticised by the ILO supervisory bodies, but the government has not acted upon their criticisms.[74] The law on secondary action was also challenged before the ECtHR in the *RMT* case.[75] The facts of the case help to explain why secondary action might sometimes be a useful tool for a union. Some 20 members of the union were transferred from firm A with a strong union presence to firm B which was not unionised. B proposed a pay cut for the 20 employees to align their terms and conditions with those of its existing employees. The employees took strike action but this had little impact on B. The union argued that it could have mobilised workers at A to support the striking members at B had it been lawful in English law to do so, and that this would have materially increased the impact of the strike. It therefore argued that the ban on secondary action infringed its Article 11 rights. The Court rejected the claim, noting that the union had been able to organise a strike, albeit not a particularly effective one. It further held that the government enjoyed a wide margin of appreciation in respect of secondary action because it was not a core part of the right to strike, and that the government had pursued a legitimate aim of preventing disruption to the economy and harm to third parties by instituting a ban. Anything less than a ban would lead to litigation and uncertainty, so the ban was found to be proportionate. Thus, there is no real prospect of using a human rights argument to overturn the ban on secondary action in English law.

2. Trade union liability, ballots and notice

The law we have considered so far is applicable to anyone who organises a strike. In practice, though, most strikes are organised by trade union officials in their capacity as such. The law attaches additional requirements where a strike is authorised or

---

[74] For example, CEACR, *Individual Observation concerning Convention No. 87, Freedom of Association and Protection of the Right to Organise, 1948* (United Kingdom 2003) para 2.

[75] Above n 28. For critique, see Bogg and Ewing, above n 28.

endorsed by a trade union. The union must conduct a ballot of those members who are to be called upon to take part, and must give various notices to the employer about the ballot and the strike itself. If the union fails to comply with these requirements, any immunity otherwise attaching to the action will be lost. Because so much turns on whether or not the union is responsible for the strike, the law determines this matter in some detail too.

(a) Trade union liability TULRCA s. 20 determines under what circumstances a union is to be regarded as liable for any of the torts covered by the statutory immunity.[76] The core of the provision is s. 20(2):

> An act shall be taken to have been authorised or endorsed by a trade union if it was done, or was authorised or endorsed–
>
> (a) by any person empowered by the rules to do, authorise or endorse acts of the kind in question, or
> (b) by the principal executive committee or the president or general secretary, or
> (c) by any other committee of the union or any other official of the union (whether employed by it or not).

Thus, a union may be liable for a strike even where, for example, a lowly shop steward (an official under (c)) organises a walkout without consulting the union hierarchy, or where a group of members take action without consulting the union hierarchy and the president (an honorary position in many unions, but included in (b)) makes a speech praising their decision. Under s. 20(4), the rules in s. 20(2) apply regardless of the union's own rules. Thus, the union cannot avoid liability by providing in its rules that only certain officials (those who know and understand the legal requirements, for example) are empowered to call a strike.

Where the union finds itself liable for action by virtue of s. 20(2)(c) (action organised by a committee or official), it has the option of repudiating the action under s. 21. This is a double-edged sword for unions. On the one hand, it enables the union to deny responsibility for the action, so that if the action does not qualify for immunity (for example, because the balloting requirements were not followed) the union will be able to avoid liability in tort. On the other hand, repudiation of the action by the union will render it 'unofficial' in law. This means that those taking part in the action may be dismissed by their employer and will have no redress in unfair dismissal law. Thus, the union is forced to choose between safeguarding its own funds, and protecting its members' jobs.

If the union does choose to repudiate, the requirements of s. 21 are quite strict. The act must be 'repudiated by the executive, president or general secretary as soon as reasonably practicable after coming to the knowledge of any of them'. The repudiation must be in writing to the relevant committee or official, and the union must also write to the employer and to individuals it believes may be taking part. The statute specifies a form of words to be used in the notice to the members, warning them of the possibility of dismissal. The repudiation is ineffective if the executive, president or general secretary subsequently acts inconsistently with it, for example, by indicating support for the strikers.

---

[76] The union's liability does not mean that others may not also be liable (e.g. the strike organisers in their own names) by virtue of s. 20(5), though in general terms employers prefer to proceed against a union rather than making 'martyrs' out of individual activists.

The aim of these two sections is to impose on unions a requirement to keep their members on a tight leash, and to combat the problem prevalent in the 1960s and 1970s of sudden small-scale 'wildcat' strikes. Although they promote compliance with the statutory requirements for lawful industrial action (by channelling responsibility for organising action to knowledgeable union officials) they do so at the expense of a substantial interference with unions' ability to determine their own internal governance arrangements.

(b) The courts' approach to the balloting and notice provisions The remainder of this section will examine the balloting and notice provisions in some detail. But before we do so, it is worth saying something about the courts' general approach to these provisions. As we shall see below, if an employer can persuade a judge that a proposed strike is not covered by the immunity, it will generally be able to obtain an injunction to stop the strike from going ahead. Because the balloting and notice provisions are highly complex, they are a fertile hunting-ground for employers looking for possible infringements by unions. Thus, they constitute one of the commonest reasons for industrial action to be stopped by the courts. This means that it is particularly important to consider how the courts think about the law in this area.

In the 1970s and early 1980s, there was a tendency among some judges to regard the immunities with some hostility.[77] This probably reflected a degree of political opposition to trade unionism among the traditionally rather conservative and individualistic judiciary, coupled with a sense that the term 'immunity' implied special privileges against legal liability and should therefore be interpreted restrictively. We saw above that, for example, there was some judicial reluctance to construe the phrase 'acting in contemplation or furtherance of a trade dispute' subjectively, with some decisions seeking to include an objective element.[78] This would have allowed the courts to rule that industrial action was unlawful if it did not advance the trade dispute to a measurable extent. In relation to the balloting and notice requirements, some decisions have – arguably – adopted quite strict constructions of the relevant provisions. For example, in *Metrobus*, it was held that a union had failed to notify the employer of the ballot result 'as soon as reasonably practicable' when the ballot result had been known on the afternoon of 1 September but not notified to the employer until the morning of 3 September.[79] The delay was caused in part by a fax going astray, and in part by the union's own procedures, which required the local official to wait for authorisation from the general secretary before acting on the ballot result. The court thought that it was not acceptable for the union to have such a procedure given the need to comply with the statutory duty to notify the employer. Thus, although there was a clear ballot in favour of strike action, an injunction was granted to stop it from going ahead because of this error and some other failings.

Since the HRA has come into force, and particularly since the decision in *Enerji*, it has been possible to argue that the courts should interpret the statutory requirements in a way that protects the right to strike as recognised in that decision.[80] In *Metrobus*, the court was sceptical about this argument, holding that *Enerji* – as a relatively brief

---

[77] Lord Diplock famously described them as 'intrinsically repugnant' in *Duport Steels*, above n 71, 177.
[78] Above n 70.
[79] *Metrobus Ltd* v *Unite the Union* [2009] EWCA Civ 829, [2010] ICR 173.
[80] Above n 26.

judgment of a chamber of the ECtHR rather than the Grand Chamber – was not sufficient authority for the proposition that a right to strike was recognised under Article 11.[81] However, more recently, in the *Serco* case, Elias LJ recognised the existence of a right to strike as an element of Article 11, albeit one that could be restricted under Article 11(2).[82] Because of the authority of *Metrobus*, it was not open to the court in *Serco* to revisit the question of the compatibility of the balloting and notice provisions in TULRCA in the light of the right to strike under Article 11. Nevertheless, Elias LJ did suggest that there was a role for the right to strike in determining how the legislation should be construed. He rejected the traditional approach of construing the immunities strictly against the union, and held instead that a neutral construction should be adopted:

> It is for Parliament to determine how the conflicting interests of employers and unions should be reconciled in the field of industrial relations. But if one starts from the premise that the legislation should be strictly construed against those seeking the benefit of the immunities, the effect is the same as it would be if there were a presumption that Parliament intends that the interests of the employers should hold sway unless the legislation clearly dictates otherwise. I do not think this is now a legitimate approach, if it ever was. In my judgment the legislation should simply be construed in the normal way, without presumptions one way or the other.[83]

This approach resulted in a less rigorous construction of the TULRCA requirements. In particular, Elias LJ was willing to invoke the *de minimis* principle as a means of disregarding small errors even though there is an exception in the Act for 'small accidental failures' which does not apply in respect of all provisions.[84]

It remains to be seen what impact the *RMT* decision in the ECtHR will have on the approach of the English courts.[85] *RMT* holds that the right to strike is recognised under Article 11, which confirms that Elias LJ was right to decide this in *Serco*. But the ruling in *RMT* distinguishes between 'core' and 'accessory' aspects of trade union activity, suggesting that regulation of the latter will attract a wide margin of appreciation. The Court said that the dissolution of a trade union in *Demir* struck at the 'core' of trade union activity, but that its ruling in that case was 'not to be understood as narrowing decisively and definitively the domestic authorities' margin of appreciation in relation to regulating, through normal democratic processes, the exercise of trade union freedom within the social and economic framework of the country concerned'.[86] It is far from clear how the distinction between 'core' and 'accessory' elements will be applied in practice, particularly in the context of the right to strike. Most labour lawyers would argue that the right to strike is a core aspect of trade union activity, but it is not clear what view the Court would take given its ambivalence about the right to strike within Article 11.

More specifically, the union's challenge to the strike notice provisions in *RMT* was ruled inadmissible, because the union had eventually been able to organise a strike. This highlights the problem that courts can only consider the provisions that

---

[81] *Metrobus*, above n 79, [35].
[82] *Serco Ltd v National Union of Rail, Maritime & Transport Workers* [2011] EWCA Civ 226, [2011] ICR 848.
[83] ibid [9].
[84] ibid [87].
[85] Above n 28.
[86] ibid [86].

are before them in any given case. They cannot consider the legal regime as a whole. This limits the potential impact of human rights scrutiny in the context of balloting and notice provisions because, often, it is the cumulative effect of the law that is problematic, not necessarily particular provisions taken by themselves.

All of this would seem to suggest that judicial scrutiny of restrictions on the right to strike post-*RMT* is likely to be quite 'light touch' in nature. Nevertheless, *RMT* does not offer any justification for going back on the neutral construction advocated by Elias LJ in *Serco*. In what follows, we will examine the balloting and notice provisions in detail, considering as we go along whether anything is to be gained from adopting a neutral construction (as suggested in *Serco*) or from an argument that the provision is disproportionate.

(c) **Balloting** TULRCA requires a union to obtain a simple majority in favour of strike action in a properly conducted ballot in order to retain the immunity against tort liability.

There are a number of reasons why it might be in a union's interests to ballot its members on strike action. First, the union's strike call will only be effective if the workers support it, so it would seem sensible to gauge their opinion before making threats to the employer that cannot be carried out. This is particularly true in English law given that, as we shall see below, unions have no possibility of disciplining members who refuse to take part in a strike, other than by applying peer pressure. Second, as democratic organisations, it might be expected that union leaders would consult their members on major decisions. A strike is an important step in the bargaining process and imposes considerable costs on those who take part, since they do not get paid during the strike.

However, we need to think a bit more carefully about why it might be appropriate for the state to *require* unions to ballot their members on strike action. One argument made by the government when it introduced the measures is that union leaders may be more radical than their members, so the strike ballot provides a way for moderate voices to make themselves heard.[87] This argument is somewhat undermined by the point made above, that if union members do not support the strike they may simply choose not to take part. Perhaps a more plausible argument is that strikes impose costs on employers and, often, on third parties, such as consumers, so it is appropriate to make sure that they only take place where they have the strong support of the workforce. This may also help to explain why the employer is given the opportunity to seek an injunction to stop a strike that does not have the support of a properly conducted ballot. If the balloting requirement is simply about democracy within unions, it might be thought that it should be for the members to enforce. But if the requirement is designed to offer some protection to employers, it is easier to see why it may be appropriate for them to have the option of enforcing it (and, of course, they have a strong interest in doing so).

The ILO materials, discussed above, treat ballot requirements as legitimate provided that they do not impede the fundamental freedom to strike.[88] TULRCA's critics argue that the complex, detailed balloting requirements go beyond what is necessary to ensure that a strike has democratic support within the union, and instead

---

[87] Paul Davies and Mark Freedland, *Labour Legislation and Public Policy* (Clarendon Press 1994) chapter 9.
[88] ILO Digest, above n 15, para 559.

constitute a serious restriction on unions' capacity to organise lawful strikes, even if they are trying to comply with the law.[89] We will consider this point of view in what follows.

The requirement to conduct a ballot is laid down in s. 226. Unless the ballot involves fewer than 50 people,[90] the union must appoint an independent scrutineer to run the process.[91] Under s. 228, the union is supposed to hold a separate ballot for each workplace involved in the dispute, but this is subject to some broadly framed exceptions under s. 228A, with the effect that, in practice, most ballots take the form of a single aggregate ballot even where multiple workplaces are involved. So, for example, an aggregate ballot is permitted if the union ballots all of its members employed by a particular employer.[92]

The ballot must be conducted by post. Ballot papers must normally be sent to the voters' home addresses,[93] and they must normally be able to return them at no cost to themselves, in 'freepost' envelopes.[94] This (coupled with the need to pay the scrutineer) makes the conduct of a ballot quite an expensive business for the union. Voters must 'be allowed to vote without interference from, or constraint imposed by, the union or any of its members, officials or employees'[95] and the ballot must be conducted so that 'so far as is reasonably practicable, those voting do so in secret'.[96] Where ballot papers are sent to people's homes, it seems unlikely that either of these issues would arise, though it might be more of a problem if members opted to give the workplace as their address for use by the union. Although it is not objectionable in principle to require that voters should vote in secret and without interference, this requirement has changed the dynamics of trade unionism in significant ways. Under the old system of workplace meetings with voting by a show of hands, workers taking part in a strike had a much greater sense of solidarity with their colleagues, and those who were doubtful about supporting a strike might be encouraged by the votes of others. But this could also be viewed as a form of intimidation, in which people who did not want to strike were inhibited from expressing their moderate views by peer pressure from more radical colleagues.

The prescribed content of the ballot paper is set out in some detail in s. 229. One of the more controversial aspects of this is s. 229(4):

> The following statement must (without being qualified or commented upon by anything else on the voting paper) appear on every voting paper–
>
> > 'If you take part in a strike or other industrial action, you may be in breach of your contract of employment. However, if you are dismissed for taking part in strike or other industrial action which is called officially and is otherwise lawful, the dismissal will be unfair if it takes place fewer than twelve weeks after you started taking part in the action, and depending on the circumstances may be unfair if it takes place later.'

---

[89] See, for example, the sustained critique by Bob Simpson: 'Trade Disputes and Industrial Action Ballots in the Twenty-First Century' (2002) 31 ILJ 270; 'Strike Ballots and the Law: Round Six' (2005) 34 ILJ 331; 'The Labour Injunction and Industrial Action Ballots' (2013) 42 ILJ 54.
[90] TULRCA, s 226C.
[91] ibid s 226B.
[92] ibid s 228A(4).
[93] ibid s 230(2).
[94] ibid s 230(1)(b).
[95] ibid s 230(1)(a).
[96] ibid s 230(4)(a).

When this provision was first introduced, there was no unfair dismissal protection, so the statement simply contained the first sentence. It was amended by the Employment Relations Act 1999 to reflect the introduction of unfair dismissal protection.[97] The stated justification for the provision was that it would enable trade union members to make a more informed decision when voting. However, critics argue that the provision is intended to intimidate union members into voting against a strike, or will at least have that effect in some cases. The mere statement that someone is in breach of their contract of employment is not particularly informative. Although a breach of contract does have serious consequences – such as not getting paid – some union members might imagine all kinds of things.

One of the provisions that has given rise to the most litigation and controversy is the seemingly straightforward s. 227(1):

> Entitlement to vote in the ballot must be accorded equally to all the members of the trade union who it is reasonable at the time of the ballot for the union to believe will be induced by the union to take part or, as the case may be, to continue to take part in the industrial action in question, and to no others.

This provision has the obvious objective of ensuring that all those likely to be involved in the strike have the entitlement to vote, and that the result is not skewed by including the votes of people who are not likely to be involved. It is related to, but distinct from, s. 230(2)(b), which requires that 'every person who is entitled to vote in the ballot must . . . be given a convenient opportunity to vote by post'. Although this does not include the converse proposition – that those who are not entitled to vote should not be given the opportunity – Elias LJ in the *Serco* case held that this should be implied into the provision.[98] The difference between them is that s. 227 is concerned with 'entitlement' whereas s. 230 is concerned with 'opportunity'. So if a union mistakenly fails to send a ballot paper to a member who is entitled to vote (for example, because it is not aware that the member has recently taken a job at the workplace where the dispute is taking place) but would do so if the member contacted the union to complain, the failure is one of 'opportunity' rather than 'entitlement'. Section 230(2)(b) applies 'so far as is reasonably practicable', which may afford the union a defence. Section 227(1) does not have this qualification. However, the distinction between the two provisions may not be critical because both are covered by s. 232B, which allows a failure which is 'accidental and on a scale which is unlikely to affect the result of the ballot' to be disregarded in determining whether the union has complied with the law.

In practice, then, much turns on the availability of s. 232B. In *British Airways Plc v Unite the Union*, the union was unable to invoke s. 232B.[99] In that case, the union balloted 10,286 members, of whom 9,514 voted in favour of a strike. However, the employer had set up a voluntary redundancy scheme which meant that around 1000 employees would in fact have left by the time the strike took place. These employees should have been excluded from the ballot. Although their inclusion did not affect the ballot result, it was held that the union could not rely on s. 232B because it did not have a 'reasonable' belief within s. 227 (the provision held to be applicable to the case) that it was balloting the correct constituency. It knew about the voluntary

---

[97] The Employment Relations Act 2004 increased the protected period from eight to 12 weeks.
[98] *Serco*, above n 82, [53].
[99] [2009] EWHC 3541, [2010] IRLR 423.

redundancy scheme but had not done enough to exclude the ineligible employees from the ballot. However, in *Serco*, the union's errors were saved by s. 232B.[100] In that case, the union had sent ballot papers to two members who were not involved in the dispute, one because he worked for a different employer, and the other because he had been promoted. The Court of Appeal held that this was a breach of s. 230(2) (in that they were wrongly given an opportunity to vote when they were not entitled) but that it was saved by s. 232B: the union believed that it was balloting the correct people but failed to do so because of human error.

The ballot result is to be determined by the independent scrutineer. At present, a simple majority of those voting is required, though there have been some suggestions that a turnout requirement ought also to be imposed (for example, that the union should secure a 40% turnout and a majority of those voting).[101] This would make it more difficult for unions to secure authorisation for a strike. Under s. 230(4), accidental errors in counting the votes which do not affect the outcome may be disregarded. The ballot result must be reported to those who voted:

> As soon as is reasonably practicable after the holding of the ballot, the trade union shall take such steps as are reasonably necessary to ensure that all persons entitled to vote in the ballot are informed of the number of–
>
> (a) votes cast in the ballot,
> (b) individuals answering "Yes" to the question, or as the case may be, to each question,
> (c) individuals answering "No" to the question, or, as the case may be, to each question, and
> (d) spoiled voting papers.[102]

In the *British Airways* case, it was held by a majority that there was no need for the union to communicate the result individually to each voter: posting the result on the union's website was sufficient to fulfil this requirement.[103] The scrutineer must prepare a report on the conduct of the ballot under s. 231B, which must be made available to voters upon request within six months of the date of the ballot.

Assuming that there is a majority in favour of taking industrial action, the next step is to act on the ballot result by calling the strike or other action. Under s. 233, the union loses its immunity if it calls the strike before the date of the ballot. The strike must be called by a person specified on the ballot paper. The ballot is 'valid' for four weeks, so the strike must be called within that time period. However, the union may agree with the employer to extend that period to up to eight weeks, for example, if negotiations to settle the dispute are ongoing.[104] If the union is prevented from calling the strike by a court order during the validity period of the ballot, it may apply to the court for an extension of that period.[105] But this may not extend the total time beyond 12 weeks from the date of the ballot, and the court may refuse to grant an extension if it takes the view that the ballot no longer reflects the members' views.[106] While it is clearly important from a democratic perspective that the union

---

[100] *Serco*, above n 82, [56].
[101] Nigel Morris, 'NUT strike: David Cameron announces crackdown on strike action ahead of mass industrial action', *The Independent*, 9 July 2014.
[102] TULRCA, s 231.
[103] *British Airways*, above n 99, [55].
[104] TULRCA, s 234(1).
[105] ibid s 234(2).
[106] ibid s 234(4) and (6).

acts promptly on the result of the ballot, and should not be able to keep the result 'up its sleeve' for later, these provisions can put unions to considerable trouble and expense. For example, if the employer obtains an injunction to stop the strike, the union may well find that, even if the injunction is discharged, the limited nature of the extension provisions means that it is forced to start the balloting process (with all the attendant costs) all over again.

A key provision in relation to the strike call is s. 232A:

> Industrial action shall not be regarded as having the support of a ballot if the following conditions apply in the case of any person–
>
> (a) he was a member of the trade union at the time when the ballot was held,
> (b) it was reasonable at that time for the trade union to believe he would be induced to take part or, as the case may be, to continue to take part in the industrial action,
> (c) he was not accorded entitlement to vote in the ballot, and
> (d) he was induced by the trade union to take part or, as the case may be, to continue to take part in the industrial action.

This provision obviously has links to s. 227 (entitlement to vote) and s. 230 (opportunity to vote) but focuses instead on a later stage in the process: on who is called upon by the union to take part in the strike. Like those provisions, it is subject to s. 232B (the exception for small, accidental failures). It was at issue in *P v NASUWT*, in which the union called a strike among teachers at a school who wished to protest at being required to teach a disruptive and violent pupil.[107] Two of the teachers who were called upon to take part in the action had been members of the union at the time of the ballot, but were not sent ballot papers because they had only recently moved to the school and the union's records did not reflect this. The union was found not to be in breach of s. 232A because its failure to send out two ballot papers (and consequent breaches of either s. 227 or s. 230) was saved by s. 232B.

In fact, some people think that s. 232A is not about reinforcing the sections on balloting but instead was intended to address a different problem suggested in some older case-law: what happens if the union calls people out on strike who did not vote in the ballot either because they were not members of the union at the time, or because they were members of the union but not employed by the employer?[108] On this view, s. 232A implicitly confirms the logical position that the union should only lose its immunity if it fails to ballot people it could reasonably have balloted at the relevant time. It seems likely that – if there is a serious dispute in the workplace – the union may well attract some new members, and it would be quite problematic in practical terms for the union to exclude them from the strike.

These various requirements are enforceable at the suit of an individual union member who has been or is likely to be induced to take part in the action by virtue of s. 62, or at the suit of the affected employer. It is much more common for employers than union members to challenge the conduct of a ballot. Although damages are a possible remedy in respect of unlawful industrial action, employers usually seek an injunction to stop the action going ahead. We will consider this further below.

---

[107] *P v National Association of School Masters Union of Women Teachers (NASUWT)* [2003] UKHL 8, [2003] 2 AC 663.

[108] *Post Office v Union of Communication Workers* [1990] 1 WLR 981, 990 (Lord Donaldson MR), disapproved in *London Underground Ltd v National Union of Railwaymen, Maritime and Transport Staff* [1996] ICR 170.

(d) Notices At various points during the balloting process, the union must give notice to the employer of those voting in the ballot. The notice provisions serve two main functions. First, they enable the employer to prepare for the industrial action by providing information about who will be on strike and when the strike will take place. Of course, from a union perspective, the disadvantage of this is that it enables the employer to minimise the effects of the action, but given that industrial action harms the employer some form of notice may well be justified. Second, they enable the employer to identify possible infringements of the balloting provisions just considered by providing it with information about how the ballot is being conducted. As we saw above, the idea that the employer should be able to enforce compliance with the balloting requirements is, itself, controversial. A particular difficulty with the notice requirements is that they are, in themselves, highly complicated, so they offer another hurdle for unions to overcome if they are to organise a lawful strike and, inevitably, another set of opportunities for employers to seek an injunction to stop the action going ahead.

(i) Notice of the ballot Under s. 226A, the union must give the employer notice of the ballot. This is a much-litigated provision because the union must include in the notice information about who is entitled to vote in the ballot. From the employer perspective, this is crucial information because it helps the employer to plan for a potential strike, and to check whether the union has complied with the requirements (discussed above) to ballot the correct group of members. However, from the union perspective, the fear is that employers will use the information inappropriately to intimidate members so that they do not vote for the strike. For this reason, the union is not required to disclose the individuals' names. But inaccuracies in what the union is required to disclose have proved to be a fertile hunting-ground for employers seeking injunctions.

The requirement to provide a ballot notice is couched in 'reasonableness' language:

> The trade union must take such steps as are reasonably necessary to ensure that–
>
> (a) not later than the seventh day before the opening day of the ballot, the notice specified in subsection (2) . . .
>   is received by every person who it is reasonable for the union to believe (at the latest time when steps could be taken to comply with paragraph (a)) will be the employer of persons who will be entitled to vote in the ballot.[109]

The details of the notice to be provided are set out in subsections (2) to (2G). These are quite complex so they are worth quoting in full:

> (2) The notice referred to in paragraph (a) of subsection (1) is a notice in writing–
>
> (a) stating that the union intends to hold the ballot,
> (b) specifying the date which the union reasonably believes will be the opening day of the ballot, and
> (c) containing–
>
> (i) the lists mentioned in subsection (2A) and the figures mentioned in subsection (2B), together with an explanation of how those figures were arrived at, or

---

[109] TULRCA, s 226A(1).

(ii) where some or all of the employees concerned are employees from whose wages the employer makes deductions representing payments to the union, either those lists and figures and that explanation or the information mentioned in subsection (2C).

(2A) The lists are–

(a) a list of the categories of employee to which the employees concerned belong, and

(b) a list of the workplaces at which the employees concerned work.

(2B) The figures are–

(a) the total number of employees concerned,

(b) the number of the employees concerned in each of the categories in the list mentioned in subsection (2A)(a), and

(c) the number of the employees concerned who work at each workplace in the list mentioned in subsection (2A)(b).

(2C) The information referred to in subsection (2)(c)(ii) is such information as will enable the employer readily to deduce–

(a) the total number of employees concerned,

(b) the categories of employee to which the employees concerned belong and the number of the employees concerned in each of those categories, and

(c) the workplaces at which the employees concerned work and the number of them who work at each of those workplaces.

(2D) The lists and figures supplied under this section, or the information mentioned in subsection (2C) that is so supplied, must be as accurate as is reasonably practicable in the light of the information in the possession of the union at the time when it complies with subsection (1)(a).

(2E) For the purposes of subsection (2D) information is in the possession of the union if it is held, for union purposes–

(a) in a document, whether in electronic form or any other form, and

(b) in the possession or under the control of an officer or employee of the union . . .

(2G) Nothing in this section requires a union to supply an employer with the names of the employees concerned.

The requirements imposed by s. 226A were considered by the Court of Appeal in the *Serco* case.[110] This suggested a somewhat less strict application of the section than has hitherto been the case. In *Serco*, there were some inaccuracies in the lists and figures sent by the union to the employer because its records were not entirely up to date. At first instance, the judge granted an injunction to stop the strike on the basis that the union could have provided accurate lists and figures had it had better record-keeping systems in place. However, the Court of Appeal placed reliance on the phrase in subsection (2D): that the lists and figures 'must be as accurate as is reasonably practicable in the light of the information in the possession of the union at the time when it complies' with the requirement. On this view, the union was simply required to disclose the information it had, rather than actively to seek out additional information. Counsel for the employer objected that this would create a perverse

---

[110] *Serco*, above n 82, [70]–[77].

incentive for unions not to seek out accurate information, but Elias LJ rejected this concern on the ground that most unions would want to maintain records for their own internal purposes so that this would not be a problem in practice.[111]

Moreover, in *Serco*, the Court of Appeal also stated, obiter, that the *de minimis* principle might be applied in relation to breaches of s. 226A.[112] This section is not subject to the s. 232B defence, but it was suggested that this did not preclude the application of the more general legal principle that trivial errors could be disregarded. In *Serco* itself, there were two inaccuracies in a ballot of around 600 people, so had subsection (2D) not saved the union, the *de minimis* principle could have been invoked. This is a potentially important recognition of the fact that it may be quite difficult in practice for unions to maintain accurate records when members move regularly between jobs and do not always appreciate the importance of telling their union.

Finally, the Court of Appeal considered the nature of the explanation the union was required to provide within subsection (2)(c)(i). Here, it was held that the union should simply comply with the statutory code of practice,[113] which requires the union to state the source of its information and to identify any known inaccuracies in that information.[114] The union was not required to give more detail, such as when the figures had last been updated. Although Elias LJ noted that the explanation might be formulaic and uninformative from the employer's perspective, he held that the judge at first instance in *Serco* (and in the joined *RMT* case) had been wrong to require a more elaborate explanation.[115]

Although the *Serco* case clearly adopted a much more flexible construction of the relevant provisions, unions must still approach them with caution. This is demonstrated by the *Metroline* case.[116] In that case, the union was seeking a bonus payment for bus drivers who were required to do extra work during the London Olympics. The employer bus companies provided both public and private bus services. Only the public bus services were affected by the dispute. However, the union's notice stating that it intended to ballot all those members who worked on public bus services was held to be insufficient because it was too vague and did not enable the employer to identify the ballot constituency in accordance with subsection 2C.

An attempt to challenge the provisions before the ECtHR in the *RMT* case was declared inadmissible.[117] RMT notified an employer that it was balloting 'technicians' at particular workplaces. The employer secured an injunction on the basis that it did not use the category 'technicians' and so could not identify which workers were involved in the action.[118] RMT was subsequently able to proceed with the strike after obtaining better information about the workers' job titles. The Court rejected the

---

[111] ibid [72].
[112] ibid [87].
[113] Department of Trade and Industry, *Code of Practice: Industrial Action Ballots and Notice to Employers* (2005) [16].
[114] *Serco*, above n 82, [94].
[115] ibid [97]–[99].
[116] *Metroline Travel Ltd* v *Unite the Union* [2012] EWHC 1778, [2012] IRLR 749.
[117] Above n 28.
[118] *EDF Energy Powerlink Ltd* v *National Union of Rail, Maritime and Transport Workers* [2009] EWHC 2852, [2010] IRLR 114.

claim because the strike had eventually been able to go ahead so it did not regard this as a violation of RMT's Article 11 rights. As Bogg and Ewing argue, this adopts a tough test for finding an 'interference' with a right – since the litigation was costly and delayed the union's action – which is not found elsewhere in the Convention case-law.[119]

(ii) Sample voting paper Section 226A TULRCA also requires the employer to send a sample ballot paper to the employer. This is laid down in subsection (1), as follows:

> The trade union must take such steps as are reasonably necessary to ensure that . . .
>
> (b) not later than the third day before the opening day of the ballot, the sample voting paper specified in subsection (2F),
>
> is received by every person who it is reasonable for the union to believe (at the latest time when steps could be taken to comply with paragraph (a)) will be the employer of persons who will be entitled to vote in the ballot.

This must be a sample of the voting paper or papers to be used in the ballot. Presumably, the objective is to enable the employer to identify any errors in the preparation of the ballot paper, given that the statute is quite specific about what it may and may not contain.

(iii) Notice of the ballot result Under s. 231A, '[a]s soon as reasonably practicable after the holding of the ballot, the trade union shall take such steps as are reasonably necessary to ensure that every relevant employer is informed of the matters mentioned in section 231'. These are the number of votes cast, the number of 'yes' votes, the number of 'no' votes, and the number of spoiled ballot papers. This serves the obvious purpose of ensuring that the employer knows the outcome of the ballot. The level of detail required may also be useful since it enables the employer to discern the strength of feeling in the workforce. For example, if there is a high turnout and a considerable majority in favour of the strike, the employer may decide to make further concessions.

The timing of this notice was the subject of discussion in the *Metrobus* case.[120] In that case, the fax sent by the independent scrutineer containing the ballot result had gone astray, then the local union official had waited for authorisation from the general secretary (in accordance with the union's rules) before giving the notice to the employer. This led to a delay of about 48 hours in notifying the employer of the ballot result. The Court of Appeal held that this breached the requirement to notify the employer as 'soon as reasonably practicable'.

At any time up to six months from the date of the ballot, the employer may request a copy of the independent scrutineer's report on the conduct of the ballot.[121]

(iv) The strike notice Finally, the union must give notice to the employer under s. 234A about the strike itself. This is regarded as particularly important by employers in terms of enabling them to determine how badly the strike will disrupt their business

---

[119] Bogg and Ewing, above n 28, 231–235.
[120] *Metrobus,* above n 79.
[121] TULRCA, s 231B.

and to take steps to minimise the disruption, though from the union point of view this may reduce the impact of the strike.

The notice must be in writing and must contain the lists and figures of affected employees in a similar way to the ballot notice discussed above.[122] The main difference between them is that the ballot notice relates to the people entitled to vote in the ballot, whereas the strike notice relates to the people who will be induced to take part in the strike. Most importantly, s. 234A(3)(b) requires detail to be provided about the strike itself. The notice must:

[state] whether industrial action is intended to be continuous or discontinuous and [specify]–

  (i) where it is to be continuous, the intended date for any of the affected employees to begin to take part in the action,

  (ii) where it is to be discontinuous, the intended dates for any of the affected employees to take part in the action.

The union must take 'such steps as are reasonably necessary to ensure that the employer receives' the notice, which must be given seven days before the strike is due to start.[123]

(e) Conclusion This section has examined the law governing trade unions when they are liable for a strike. Unions are required to ballot those who will be called upon to strike and to give a set of notices to the employer. The requirement to hold a ballot is a safeguard for democracy within unions, and the requirement to give notice to the employer can be justified as a means of enabling the employer to plan for the disruption. On a basic level, then, both policies can be regarded as legitimate. However, as the ILO materials consistently make clear, it is important that regulation of the right to strike does not 'impair' the right itself. As the ILO supervisory bodies have found, some aspects of the rules just considered are so complex and demanding that they fall foul of that principle, particularly in relation to voting entitlement and the ballot notice. The only chance of persuading the English courts to adopt a more generous construction is through the HRA, as *Serco* illustrates, but this strategy may be more difficult to pursue after the *RMT* decision.

3. Strike action in EU law

It might be supposed that this very elaborate set of domestic law rules on industrial action would be sufficient in order to determine whether or not a strike is lawful. However, this is not the case. If the industrial action has some kind of cross-border dimension to it, EU law may be engaged. Where this is the case, additional requirements – in the shape of a proportionality test – must be satisfied if the strike is to be lawful. The CJEU's intervention in these issues was unexpected and has attracted a great deal of criticism from labour lawyers, and also from the ILO.[124]

---

[122] ibid s 234A(3)(a).
[123] ibid ss 234A(1) and (4).
[124] CEACR, *Observation – adopted 2009, published 99th ILC session (2010) Freedom of Association and Protection of the Right to Organise Convention, 1948 (No. 87) – United Kingdom (Ratification: 1949).*

The EU has no legislative competence over the right to strike, by virtue of Article 153(5) TFEU.[125] However, in a series of important cases, the CJEU has held that industrial action may infringe on an employer's economic freedoms in the internal market. So, for example, if an employer established in the UK wanted to change its place of establishment to a (cheaper) location in another Member State, but a union organised a strike to try to stop it from doing so, the union's action would fall to be scrutinised under EU law because of its impact on the employer's economic freedom of establishment under Article 49 TFEU. Similarly, if an employer wanted to use 'posted workers' (workers sent to the UK temporarily from another Member State to perform a specific task) and a union in the UK blockaded the workplace to protest at this (for example, because this might undercut local terms and conditions or reduce job opportunities for local workers), the industrial action would engage EU law. This is because the employer's entitlement to use 'posted workers' stems from the Article 56 TFEU freedom to provide services in other Member States.

The CJEU's approach to cases of this kind was laid down in two key decisions, *Viking* and *Laval*. In *Viking*, the union organised a very effective boycott of a shipping company when it proposed to 'reflag' a ship from Finland to Estonia.[126] Reflagging a ship is an exercise of freedom of establishment under EU law. Companies often 'reflag' to states with lower labour standards as a means of saving money, though the employer in this case denied that this was its objective.[127] In *Laval*, the employer was a Latvian firm that won a contract to build a school in Sweden.[128] It sought to bring its own workforce as 'posted workers', exercising its cross-border freedom to provide services. The Swedish trade union blockaded the building site in order to persuade the Latvian firm to sign up to the local collective agreement. The firm refused to sign the collective agreement and was unable to build the school.

In both *Viking* and *Laval*, the CJEU recognised that the unions were exercising the right to strike, a right recognised in the constitutions of many Member States and in various international instruments.[129] However, the CJEU gave primacy to the employers' economic freedoms. It held that the industrial action in both cases was deterring the employers from exercising their freedom of establishment or freedom to provide services. Thus, the industrial action should be examined to see whether it was a *proportionate restriction* on those economic freedoms.[130] This involved considering what aim the union was pursuing – for example, to protect its members' jobs or terms and conditions – and whether it could have adopted a means that was less restrictive of the employer's economic freedoms. Although the application of the proportionality test to the facts of the cases is a matter for the national courts, the CJEU's guidance on the matter suggested that it would be rather difficult for the unions in both cases to persuade a court that their action was proportionate.

---

[125] For a more general discussion of this, see ACL Davies, 'Should the EU Have the Power to Set Minimum Standards for Collective Labour Rights in the Member States?', in Philip Alston (ed), *Labour Rights as Human Rights* (OUP 2005).

[126] Case C-438/05 *International Transport Workers Federation* v *Viking Line ABP* [2007] ECR I-10779.

[127] See Tonia Novitz, 'Resistance to Re-flagging: a Restricted Right to Strike' [2008] LMCLQ 266, 272.

[128] Case C-341/05 *Laval un Partneri Ltd* v *Svenska Byggnadsarbetareförbundet* [2007] ECR I-11767.

[129] For example, *Viking*, above n 126, [43]–[44].

[130] ibid [86]–[87].

There are many problems with the Court's reasoning in these cases, but we will focus on two issues here.[131] First, although the Court recognised that the unions were exercising a right to strike, they did not begin their analysis with the right. Instead, the unions were only permitted to exercise their right to the extent that it constituted a proportionate interference with the employers' free movement interests. This is not the normal way to reason when rights are involved. It is usual to begin with the right and consider whether any restrictions placed upon the right (for example, by the state) are proportionate. This aspect of the decisions has been strongly criticised by the ILO, though EU lawyers tend to point out that the Court could hardly have decided otherwise given the centrality of the free movement provisions to the EU's internal market.[132] Second, the application of the proportionality test to industrial action is, itself, quite problematic. Industrial action is, as we have seen, designed to cause harm to the employer and thus to redress the imbalance in bargaining power between the workers (and their unions) and the employer. Judging whether the union's objectives justify the level of harm the strike is imposing on the employer requires quite a difficult value judgement about the merits of the strike. The more effective the union's action, the harder it will be to justify under the Court's approach, because of the harm it causes to the employer. Although some countries do use a proportionality test to judge industrial action, English law avoids embroiling the courts in the merits of the dispute by regulating the purpose of and procedures for industrial action instead. The risk is that, in the hands of an unsympathetic or inexpert court, the proportionality test could make it very difficult to justify industrial action, particularly where that action is effective.

Since the decisions in *Viking* and *Laval*, there have been some interesting developments. The Commission proposed the so-called 'Monti II' Regulation, which would have required the Court to apply a 'double proportionality' analysis, in which it would balance the employer's free movement interests against the right to strike.[133] However, this Regulation was rejected by national parliaments in the first use of the 'yellow card' procedure.[134] Meanwhile, the ECtHR has recognised the right to strike, subject to the various caveats we considered above.[135] The EU is currently negotiating to accede to the ECHR, as required by the Lisbon Treaty.[136] Some commentators have argued that there is (or is likely to be) a conflict between the two courts, in the sense that the ECtHR's recognition of the right to strike would not give way to the economic freedoms in the way that the CJEU's has done.[137] If they are correct, the CJEU would have to modify its approach in order to bring it into line with that required by the

---

[131] There is a large critical literature. See, for example, ACL Davies, 'One Step Forward, Two Steps Back? The *Viking* and *Laval* Cases in the ECJ' (2008) 37 ILJ 126; Phil Syrpis and Tonia Novitz, 'A Proportionate Response to Proportionality in the Field of Collective Action' (2012) 37 EL Rev 117.

[132] For example, Alicia Hinarejos, '*Laval* and *Viking*: the Right to Collective Action Versus EU Fundamental Freedoms' (2008) 8 HRL Rev 714, 728.

[133] Proposal for a Council Regulation on the exercise of the right to take collective action within the context of the freedom of establishment and the freedom to provide services, COM(2012) 130.

[134] For discussion, see Marco Goldoni, 'The Early Warning System and the Monti II Regulation: The Case for a Political Interpretation' (2014) 10 European Constitutional Law Review 90.

[135] Above nn 26 and 28.

[136] Article 6(2) TEU. For the latest on the negotiations, see http://www.coe.int/t/dghl/standardsetting/hrpolicy/Accession/default_en.asp (last visited 18 September 2014).

[137] KD Ewing and John Hendy, 'The Dramatic Implications of *Demir* and *Baykara*' (2010) 39 ILJ 2, 38–47.

Convention.[138] But for now, unions engaged in industrial disputes with a cross-border dimension need to be very careful of the *Viking* and *Laval* line of case-law.

Remedies

In this section, we will turn to the remedies that are available in the event of unlawful industrial action. As we saw at the beginning of the chapter, those who organise industrial action (whether individuals or trade unions) usually commit one or more of the economic torts. Thus, if they fail to comply with the statutory conditions for securing immunity (which are more onerous for trade unions than for individuals because of the balloting and notice provisions) they are liable to the employer in tort. Thus, tort damages are one form of remedy in respect of unlawful industrial action. However, in many instances, the employer's objective will be to stop the strike from going ahead rather than seeking compensation afterwards. This is done by asking the court for an injunction. This remedy is also available to trade union members and to consumers affected by the strike if certain conditions are met.

In terms of the protection of the right to strike, it is quite important to consider what happens if a strike is – or might be – unlawful. Large awards of damages might put a union out of business altogether. And readily available injunctions, even when it is only the case that a strike *might* be unlawful, make it more difficult for unions to organise effective industrial action. Even if the injunction is later discharged, so that the strike can go ahead, the union may find that its members have lost enthusiasm for the idea or that enough time has passed that a new ballot is needed. Of course, against these considerations we must set the argument from employers that strikes are costly, and that if the union or strike organiser does not follow the rules, either the strike should not be allowed to happen at all, or the employer should be compensated for its losses.

Damages In general terms, the purpose of bringing a claim for damages in tort is to compensate the employer for the foreseeable losses it has suffered as a result of the economic torts committed by the strike organiser or the union. This is likely to include the loss of business consequent on the strike, so could involve quite large sums of money.

Although individual strike organisers are potentially liable to the employer in tort, actions against them are, in practice, rare. First, the requirements for securing immunity are more straightforward for individuals, since they focus primarily on the nature of the dispute (s. 219 and related provisions). Individual strike organisers are not subject to the balloting and notice requirements. Second, the employer is unlikely to be able to recover substantial sums from individuals (unless the union indemnifies them) and may make itself unpopular if it makes individuals 'martyrs' for their cause.[139]

In practice, it is more likely that the employer would want to sue the union. It is easier for the union to lose its immunity by making errors in balloting or notice, and

---

[138] For a possible way forward, see Catherine Barnard, 'A Proportionate Response to Proportionality in the Field of Collective Action' (2012) 37 EL Rev 117.

[139] Under s. 15 TULRCA, the union cannot indemnify an individual against a criminal penalty or a fine for contempt of court.

it is likely to have more resources to pay compensation. However, in s. 22 TULRCA, Parliament has limited unions' liability in tort by providing for maximum levels of compensation linked to membership levels:

> In any proceedings in tort to which this section applies the amount which may awarded against the union by way of damages shall not exceed the following limit–

Number of members of union	*Maximum award of damages*
Less than 5,000	£10,000
5,000 or more but less than 25,000	£50,000
25,000 or more but less than 100,000	£125,000
100,000 or more	£250,000[140]

This reduces employers' incentive to sue in damages and offers another reason for seeking an injunction to prevent the industrial action from going ahead.

One area of considerable uncertainty is whether the limits laid down in s. 22 apply where the union is engaged in a cross-border dispute and is thus being held liable for infringing the employer's economic freedoms under the TFEU.[141] First, it is not clear whether a union's liability in EU law would constitute 'proceedings in tort' within s. 22, though it might be argued that it is tortious by analogy with state liability in EU law.[142] Second, even if the union's liability is treated as tortious, Apps points out that an employer might try to challenge the cap on damages on the basis that it does not fulfil EU law's requirement for an effective remedy.[143] But it would also be open to the union to counter this by arguing that the aim of s. 22 is to uphold the right to strike by preventing the 'chilling effect' that would arise if unions faced unlimited damages liability for taking strike action.

These issues arose in the British Airline Pilots Association (BALPA) dispute. In that case, a union representing airline pilots was in dispute with British Airways (BA) over the setting up of a subsidiary company in another Member State. BA argued that the strike would be in breach of its economic freedoms in EU law and that its losses would be £100 million per day. BALPA abandoned the action, arguing that a claim for damages at that level would have led to its bankruptcy. The ILO supported BALPA's complaint that it was denied the practical exercise of the right to strike by the fear of unlimited liability.[144] The UK government rejected the criticism, arguing (among other things) that it was not clear that the s. 22 limit on damages would be disregarded in such a claim. This leaves unions facing a real difficulty: it may turn out that s. 22 does offer protection, but engaging in a dispute (and consequent litigation) that would test this could turn out to be a very risky strategy indeed.

A final question to consider before we leave the issue of damages is whether consumers who are affected by the strike might be able to seek compensation from the union. This issue arose in the County Court case of *Falconer* v *ASLEF*.[145] It was

---

[140] TULRCA 1992, s 22(2). Some types of tort claim are excluded by s 22(1).
[141] Katherine Apps, 'Damages Claims against Trade Unions after *Viking* and *Laval*' (2009) 34 EL Rev 141.
[142] *R* v *Secretary of State for Transport, ex p Factortame Ltd (No. 6)* [2001] 1 WLR 942.
[143] Above n 141, 152–154.
[144] CEACR, Report of the Committee of Experts, International Labour Conference, 99th Session, 2010; *Observation – adopted 2009, published 99th ILC session (2010), Freedom of Association and Protection of the Right to Organise Convention, 1948 (No. 87) – United Kingdom (Ratification: 1949)*.
[145] [1986] IRLR 331.

held that the claimant, whose business trip to London was disrupted by a train strike, could obtain damages in tort from the union which had failed to ballot its members before calling a strike. The union's liability in tort was held to be based on the 'three-party' version of interference with business set out in *Thomson v Deakin*.[146] In other words, the union unlawfully induced its members to breach their contracts with the train operator, and thus interfered with the train operator's ability to perform its contract to provide travel for the claimant. However, it seems unlikely that such a claim would succeed today, because in *OBG*, Lord Hoffmann stated that *intention to cause loss* to the claimant – not just foreseeability that loss might be caused – is required.[147] A further source of uncertainty is the position in EU law if the strike organised by the union might infringe the economic freedoms under the Treaty. As Apps explains, since we know very little about liability in this context, we cannot be sure that employers are the only possible claimants: consumers affected by the dispute might also be able to sue in respect of their losses.[148]

Injunctions In this section, we will consider ways of stopping the strike by obtaining an injunction. The usual applicant in these cases is the employer, but union members and consumers may also seek court orders to stop unlawful strikes. The controversy in this area stems from the fact that most of the cases involve applications for interim injunctions. These are meant to be temporary, pending a full trial of the action, but in practice, they tend to be determinative of the dispute. The problem is that the requirements for obtaining an interim injunction are not onerous. Critics argue that – coupled with the complexity of the balloting and notice provisions – the low threshold for obtaining an interim injunction makes it too easy for employers to put a stop to potentially legitimate strikes.

The test for obtaining an interim injunction is set out in the well-known *American Cyanamid* case.[149] The applicant must show that there is a 'serious issue to be tried', that damages would not be an adequate remedy for the loss it would suffer if the injunction was not granted, and that the 'balance of convenience' favours the granting of the injunction.[150] However, in the context of industrial action, TULRCA, s. 221 attempts to make some adjustments to protect unions:

(1) Where–

(a) an application for an injunction . . . is made to a court in the absence of the party against whom it is sought or any representative of his, and

(b) he claims, or in the opinion of the court would be likely to claim, that he acted in contemplation or furtherance of a trade dispute,

the court shall not grant the injunction . . . unless satisfied that all steps which in the circumstances were reasonable have been taken with a view to securing that notice of the application and an opportunity of being heard with respect to the application have been given to him.

---

[146] [1952] Ch 646.
[147] *OBG*, above n 48, [62]. See also *Barretts & Baird*, above n 55.
[148] Apps, above n 141, 151.
[149] *American Cyanamid v Ethicon* [1975] AC 396.
[150] ibid 406–409 (Lord Diplock).

(2) Where–

(a) an application for an interlocutory injunction is made to a court pending the trial of an action, and

(b) the party against whom it is sought claims that he acted in contemplation or furtherance of a trade dispute,

the court shall, in exercising its discretion whether or not to grant the injunction, have regard to the likelihood of that party's succeeding at the trial of the action in establishing any matter which would afford a defence to the action under section 219 (protection from certain tort liabilities) . . .

There are two key elements to this provision. First, although it is normally possible to obtain an injunction 'ex parte', in the absence of the defendant, in the trade union context 'reasonable' steps must be taken to contact the union or strike organiser so that a defence can be presented. Second, the court considering the grant of the injunction must consider the likelihood that the action might attract the immunity. In the *Balfour Beatty* case, the judge explained this by saying that it would not be sufficient for the employer to satisfy the *American Cyanamid* test.[151] It would also have to address its arguments to the likelihood or otherwise of the immunity being established. However, in some respects this does not help very much: given the complexity of the provisions, it is not difficult for the employer to make plausible allegations that the union has failed to comply. This helps to explain why the relative strictness of the courts' interpretations – discussed above – is such a crucial issue in determining the extent of any right to strike in English law.

Under s. 62 TULRCA, a union member who believes that he or she is being called upon to take part in a strike that does not have the support of a ballot may apply to the court for an order to stop the strike. In practice, it is far more likely that the employer will challenge the action, but in the absence of this right it would be hard for the government to claim that the balloting provisions were concerned with democracy in trade unions. For a time, there was a Commissioner in place to support union members in bringing these claims, but even with help no serious claims emerged, and the role was eventually abolished.[152]

Under s. 235A TULRCA, there is a possibility for a consumer to obtain a court order to stop unlawful industrial action:

(1) Where an individual claims that–

(a) any trade union or other person has done, or is likely to do, an unlawful act to induce any person to take part, or to continue to take part, in industrial action, and

(b) an effect, or a likely effect, of the industrial action is or will be to–

(i) prevent or delay the supply of goods or services, or

(ii) reduce the quality of goods or services supplied,

to the individual making the claim,

he may apply to the High Court . . . for an order under this section.

---

[151] *Balfour Beatty Engineering Services Ltd* v *Unite the Union* [2012] EWHC 267, [2012] ICR 822.

[152] It was created by the Trade Union Reform and Employment Rights Act 1993 and repealed by the Employment Relations Act 1999.

(2) For the purposes of this section an act to induce any person to take part, or to continue to take part, in industrial action is unlawful–

(a) if it is actionable in tort by any one or more persons, or

(b) (where it is or would be the act of a trade union) if it could form the basis of an application by a member under section 62.

(3) In determining whether an individual may make an application under this section it is immaterial whether or not the individual is entitled to be supplied with the goods or services in question.

This provision applies against unions or strike organisers where the industrial action is actionable in tort because it is not protected by the immunity (or does not have the support of a ballot and could be stopped under s. 62, though this does not add anything). It is very broadly framed indeed, extending beyond anything that might conceivably be arguable in tort. For example, it does not require that the individual had a contractual right to the goods or services, or that the union intended to interfere with the individual's right. Although (as for trade union members) the government for a time provided a Commissioner to support the bringing of these claims, the provision has rarely been invoked and the Commissioner role has been abolished.[153] The only well-known example is *P v NASUWT*, a claim brought by a school pupil in respect of industrial action by teachers who refused to teach him because they argued that he was disruptive.[154] The House of Lords refused to grant the injunction on the grounds that the industrial action was protected by the immunity. Presumably, few individuals have the resources to bring claims under s. 235A, not least because the remedy is an injunction rather than damages.

A final point to note before we leave the topic of injunctions is that the penalties for breaching a court order are severe because it constitutes a contempt of court.[155] Fines for contempt are not subject to the limits in s. 22, nor can the union indemnify individual strike organisers against them.[156] Individuals can be imprisoned, or a union's assets seized. Thus, once an injunction has been granted it is crucial that union leaders and their members observe it.

13.4 THE LAW GOVERNING INDIVIDUAL STRIKERS

We saw at the outset that when a working person engages in industrial action, he or she usually breaches his or her contract of employment. This is one of the key elements in establishing that those who organise industrial action commit economic torts (such as inducing breach of contract). At common law, this has serious consequences: the working person is not entitled to be paid, and may be dismissed by his or her employer. In some other legal systems, these consequences are avoided by treating the contract of employment as 'suspended' during the strike.[157]

---

[153] It was created by the Trade Union Reform and Employment Rights Act 1993 and repealed by the Employment Relations Act 1999.

[154] Above n 107.

[155] For discussion, see Richard Kidner, 'Sanctions for Contempt by a Trade Union' (1986) 6 LS 18; Catherine O'Regan, 'Contempt of Court and the Enforcement of Labour Injunctions' (1991) 54 MLR 385.

[156] Above n 139.

[157] Jacobs, above n 11.

However, following the traditional pattern of English law, Parliament has intervened to offer some statutory protection to strikers against dismissal (if certain conditions are met) whilst leaving the underlying common law position untouched. We will examine three issues in turn: the breach itself, the effect it has on pay and the rules governing dismissal.

13.4.1 Industrial action as a breach of the contract of employment

In considering the effect of industrial action on the contract of employment, we need to distinguish strikes (in the sense of a total stoppage of work) from various forms of action short of a strike.

In relation to strikes, the orthodox position is stated by the EAT (Phillips J) in *Simmons v Hoover*:

> [H]ere there was a settled, confirmed and continued intention on the part of the employee not to do any of the work which under his contract he had engaged to do; which was the whole purpose of the contract. Judged by the usual standards, such conduct by the employee appears to us to be repudiatory of the contract of employment. We should not be taken to be saying that all strikes are necessarily repudiatory, though usually they will be. For example, it could hardly be said that a strike of employees in opposition to demands by an employer in breach of contract by him would be repudiatory. But what may be called a "real" strike in our judgment always will be.[158]

This confirms that a long-term work stoppage is a *repudiatory* breach of contract, which has (as we shall see) significant consequences in terms of dismissal. Nowadays, many strikes take place over shorter periods of time – a series of one-day stoppages, for example – but again, it seems likely that the courts would treat such strikes as a repudiatory breach.

Action short of a strike is designed to disrupt the employer's operations without a complete stoppage of work. It might involve a 'work to rule' or a 'go slow', in which workers deliberately disrupt operations by obeying the employer's instructions to the letter, or by working at a slower pace, or it might involve a refusal to perform selected aspects of the job (chosen either because they are the subject of the dispute, or because of their capacity to irritate the employer). In general terms, the courts have treated these kinds of action as breaches of the contract of employment, though whether they are regarded as repudiatory or not depends on the facts of the case. In some cases, the workers' action may be in breach of an express term of the contract. Where this is not the case, the courts have tended to treat the action as a breach of an implied term. So, for example, in *ASLEF* it was held that the implied duty of co-operation was breached by working to rule.[159]

The only type of action short of a strike that clearly does not constitute a breach of the contract of employment is a refusal to perform extra tasks that workers normally perform but that are not duties under their contracts at all.[160] However, it is difficult to rely on this principle in practice because of the vagueness of the implied terms in the contract of employment. This is illustrated by *Sim*, in which a group of

---

[158] [1977] QB 284, 299. Although Lord Denning attempted to develop a 'suspension' doctrine in *Morgan v Fry* [1968] 2 QB 710, this approach did not attract wider support.
[159] *Secretary of State for Employment* v *ASLEF (No 2)* [1972] 2 QB 455.
[160] *Stevedoring Services Ltd* v *Burgess* [2002] UKPC 39, [2002] 1 WLR 2838.

teachers refused to provide cover for absent colleagues as part of an industrial dispute.[161] They argued that nothing in their contracts of employment obliged them to do this particular task. But the court held that they were in breach of their contracts because they were under a duty to obey the head teacher's reasonable instructions about the running of the school.

13.4.2 Pay

A worker who is on strike is refusing to perform his or her side of the bargain and is thus not entitled to be paid by the employer. Indeed, it would be possible for the employer to seek damages from the worker in respect of any losses caused to the business by the strike. However, this is unlikely in practice because the costs of suing the workers would usually outweigh what the employer could expect to recover. Most workers would not have the resources to pay compensation, and in any event each worker would only be liable for the loss he or she had caused, which would be difficult to quantify.

Matters are more complicated when we turn to action short of a strike. Here, it is clear that the employer can make deductions from the workers' wages in respect of work not performed. So, for example, in *Miles* v *Wakefield*, the worker in question was a registrar who worked a 37-hour week including Saturday mornings.[162] As part of an industrial dispute, he refused to carry out wedding ceremonies on Saturday mornings, presumably a particularly popular time for such ceremonies, though he attended work and carried out other tasks. His employer withheld three hours' pay in respect of Saturday mornings. The House of Lords held that he was only entitled to be paid if he was willing to do the work he was employed to do, so the employer was entitled to make the deduction.

Where the employer makes a deduction from wages, the question arises of how that deduction should be calculated. Does it represent what the employee would have been paid during the relevant time, or does it represent the loss suffered by the employer? This question reveals some ambiguity between the decisions in *Sim* and in *Miles*. In *Sim*, the court appeared to conceptualise the case as the use by the employer of the 'self-help' remedy of making a deduction from pay rather than suing the employees for damages (the 'employer loss' approach).[163] In *Miles*, the action was a claim for unpaid wages brought by the worker against the employer, so the court focused on what the worker had precluded himself from claiming by going on strike (the 'pay' approach).[164] This issue was addressed in *Cooper* v *Isle of Wight College*.[165] In that case, Blake J followed *Miles* and distinguished *Sim*, on the basis that the workers in *Cooper* were suing for unpaid wages. This meant that the employer could only deduct the amount of money that the workers would have earned had they not been on strike. On the facts of the case, the 'pay' approach led to a lower deduction than would have been the case under the 'employer loss' approach.

---

[161] *Sim* v *Rotherham Metropolitan Borough Council* [1987] Ch 216.
[162] [1987] AC 539 (HL).
[163] *Sim*, above n 161, 255.
[164] *Miles* above n 162, 561.
[165] [2007] EWHC 2831, [2008] IRLR 124. For detail on the calculation of the deduction, see *Amey* v *Peter Symonds College* [2013] EWHC 2788, [2014] IRLR 206.

More controversially, it was held in *Wiluszynski* that the employer could refuse to pay workers engaged in action short of a strike *at all*, even if they performed the bulk of their contractual duties.[166] The claimant in that case was a council worker who refused to answer councillors' queries over a five-week period. This represented two to three hours' work, though it obviously had considerable 'irritation value' for the councillors. The council wrote to the claimant stating that he would not be paid unless he resumed normal working, but did not take any steps to exclude him from the workplace or to prevent him from continuing to work. The Court of Appeal held that the council was entitled to refuse to pay him and had not acted inconsistently with its stated intention by allowing him to continue working. There was no obligation on an employer to institute a 'lock out' in order to be entitled to refuse to pay for partial performance.

The *Wiluszynski* decision has been the subject of considerable criticism. It seems to allow the employer to 'have its cake and eat it', in the sense that it gains the benefit of the worker's performance without having to pay anything for that performance, provided that the employer makes its position clear.[167] However, the same point could also be made about workers in the converse situation: carefully designed action short of a strike, if it attracted partial pay, could enable the workers to earn most of their normal pay (which would make it possible for the action to go on for a long time) whilst causing considerable irritation to the employer. In terms of public policy, it might be thought that the government would want to encourage workers to take less extreme forms of action, not least because this would reduce the disruption strikes often cause. In that sense, *Wilusyznski* generates the wrong incentive: a worker might decide that if he or she is not going to be paid anyway, it is better to stop work completely.

More generally, while it is difficult to argue that an employer should be forced to pay striking workers for work they are not doing, the absence of pay during a strike (and potentially also during action short of a strike) creates a natural brake on industrial action. This is because most workers cannot afford to manage for very long without their pay. Moreover, striking workers cannot claim social security benefits.[168] The only possible source of help is 'strike pay' from the union's own resources, which may not be very extensive. This may help to explain the popularity in recent years of intermittent one-day strikes as a common form of industrial action. Although each one-day strike is likely to result in the loss of a day's pay, this is easier to manage than a longer stoppage, and less complicated legally than a refusal to perform certain duties over a longer period of time.

13.4.3 Dismissal

The most extreme response to industrial action is for the employer to dismiss the striking workers and hire replacements. This will not always be workable in practice. For example, if a large proportion of the workforce is on strike, the employer may not have the administrative resources to recruit and train a sufficient number of new workers. Nonetheless, the ILO regards it as an important requirement of respect for

---

[166] *Wiluszynski v London Borough of Tower Hamlets* [1989] ICR 493.
[167] For discussion, see Geoffrey H Mead, 'Employer's Right to Withhold Wages' (1990) 106 LQR 192.
[168] Jobseekers Act 1995, s 14.

the right to strike that it is not lawful for the employer to dismiss striking workers.[169] English law on the topic is quite complex. The basic starting-point is that the jurisdiction of the Employment Tribunal to hear an unfair dismissal claim is excluded if the employee is participating in a strike or other industrial action.[170] However, the law carves out a patchwork of exceptions to this which apply if certain (quite complex) conditions are met.

The employee/worker distinction

Unfair dismissal law only applies to employees. This means that such protections as are available to strikers are only available to employees. The position of workers is determined in accordance with the common law. Since a long-term strike is regarded as a repudiatory breach of contract, strikers can be dismissed without notice. Action short of a strike may or may not be a repudiatory breach depending on the circumstances. If it is not a repudiatory breach, the employer may still dismiss the worker but must give notice. However, in most cases workers will not be entitled to particularly lengthy notice periods. Indeed, someone with a casual work arrangement would probably find that he or she would be removed from the employer's list of potential workers if he or she took part in industrial action. Of course, people without employee status are in a precarious position at work anyway, so in a sense the law in this area does not make them worse off, but it does mean that using industrial action as a means of protest at poor terms and conditions is not a viable option for them, unless they are confident that their union's 'industrial muscle' will be enough to keep them in work.

Unofficial industrial action

In general terms, an employee who is taking part in 'unofficial' industrial action has no right to complain of unfair dismissal.[171] We will examine the meaning of 'unofficial' before noting the exceptions to this basic rule.

The definition of 'unofficial' action is given in s. 237(2):

A strike or other industrial action is unofficial in relation to an employee unless–

(a) he is a member of a trade union and the action is authorised or endorsed by that union, or

(b) he is not a member of a trade union but there are among those taking part in the industrial action members of a trade union by which the action has been authorised or endorsed.

Provided that, a strike or other industrial action shall not be regarded as unofficial if none of those taking part in it are members of a trade union.

This provision is quite complex. The first thing to note is that it only makes action unofficial if there is some union involvement. Action in a non-unionised workplace does not count as unofficial. Where there is union involvement, s. 237 needs to be

---

[169] ILO, *Digest of Decisions*, above n 15, [661].
[170] TULRCA, s 238(2).
[171] TULRCA, s 237.

read in conjunction with s. 20 (discussed above), which determines when a union has 'authorised or endorsed' industrial action. The effect of s. 20 is to make it quite difficult for a union *not* to have 'authorised or endorsed' industrial action, because it deems this to have occurred whenever the action has been called by a union official or committee. However, under s. 21, the union can repudiate the action. A union facing legal action by the employer in tort (for example, because the action was organised by low-level officials without following proper procedures) might protect itself by repudiating, though of course this has the significant disadvantage of removing the striking employees' unfair dismissal protection.

Under s. 237(1A), the exclusion of the tribunal's jurisdiction for unofficial strikers does not apply where it can be shown that one of a list of automatically unfair reasons for dismissal applies, such as pregnancy or acting as a worker representative. Thus, even unofficial strikers retain some protection, though it may be difficult in practice to prove that one of these reasons was the true reason for the dismissal.

Automatically unfair dismissal of striking employees

At the opposite end of the spectrum of protection, it is possible to argue that the dismissal of an employee *because* he or she is taking part in a strike is automatically unfair by virtue of s. 238A. However, there are conditions attached to this protection and, in general terms, it only lasts for 12 weeks.

It is automatically unfair to dismiss an employee if the reason for the dismissal is that he or she is taking part in 'protected' industrial action, defined in s. 238A(1) in the following terms:

> For the purposes of this section an employee takes protected industrial action if he commits an act which, or a series of acts each of which, he is induced to commit by an act which by virtue of section 219 is not actionable in tort.

This means that the employee's dismissal protection turns on the conduct of the strike organiser or trade union, which must have satisfied the conditions for immunity in s. 219. Importantly, this does not just mean that the action is 'in contemplation or furtherance of a trade dispute': by virtue of s. 219(4), the provisions on excluded action, ballots and notice must also be fulfilled.

If the employee is taking part in a strike that fulfils the conditions for immunity, attention then shifts to the timing of the dismissal. The simplest form of protection is for 12 weeks (plus any time during that period for which the employer institutes a lock-out) from the date on which the employee first takes part in the action.[172] Although this has not been tested in court, it appears to be the case that the clock ticks continuously from the first day of action, so that someone taking part in a series of weekly one-day strikes would only be protected for 12 such strikes.

There are two further options. First, the employee is also protected if he or she stops taking part in the action during the 12-week period (plus any extension) but is dismissed after it has ended.[173] This enhances the 12-week protection by discouraging employers from simply waiting until the end of that time and dismissing people for taking part in the strike even though they have returned to work. Second, the

---

[172] TULRCA, s 238A(3).
[173] ibid s 238A(4).

employee is protected if he or she continues striking beyond 12 weeks if 'the employer had not taken such procedural steps as would have been reasonable for the purposes of resolving the dispute to which the protected industrial action relates'.[174] The statute sets out in some detail what might constitute reasonable 'procedural steps' (offering to re-open negotiations or to use conciliation or mediation and behaviour during the latter two processes)[175] but they must be considered in relation to the union as well as the employer. Although tribunals are directed not to have regard to the merits of the dispute,[176] these provisions do, in effect, require them to think about the closely related question of who is 'to blame' for the dispute not having been settled. It is only if the employer is 'to blame' that the protection can be extended beyond 12 weeks.

The ILO has criticised the provisions on automatically unfair dismissal because of the 12-week limit, arguing that this does not reflect its position that there is never any justification for dismissing striking workers.[177] The government, by contrast, argues that dismissal should be possible as a last resort and that most industrial action is resolved long before the 12 weeks are up, making the protection highly effective in practice. Perhaps more importantly, striking employees are highly dependent on the strike organiser or union to ensure that the action is immune if they are to secure their dismissal protection. Of course, no government is likely to want to protect people taking part in an unlawful strike, but given the uncertainties surrounding s. 219 and related provisions, the effectiveness of s. 238A is much reduced, and through no fault of those participating in the strike.

'Selective dismissal' protection

The final element of protection to consider is the protection against selective dismissals in s. 238. This is less effective than s. 238A, because it simply gives the tribunal jurisdiction to hear an unfair dismissal claim, rather than making the individual's dismissal automatically unfair. However, it applies more broadly, because it depends on the action being 'not unofficial' within the meaning of s. 237 and not on it being immune.

Section 238 applies where at the time of dismissal, the employer was conducting a lock-out or the employee was participating in a strike. Under s. 238(2):

> In such a case an employment tribunal shall not determine whether the dismissal was fair or unfair unless it is shown–
>
> (a) that one or more relevant employees of the same employer have not been dismissed, or
> (b) that a relevant employee has before the expiry of the period of three months beginning with the date of his dismissal been offered re-engagement and that the complainant has not been offered re-engagement.

Re-engagement means 'in the job which he held immediately before the date of dismissal or in a different job which would be reasonably suitable in his case'.[178]

---

[174] ibid s 238A(5).
[175] ibid s 238B.
[176] ibid s 238A(7).
[177] Above n 15.
[178] TULRCA, s 238(4).

In effect, s. 238 forces the employer to dismiss all of the striking employees and not to re-engage any of them within a three-month period. Otherwise it may face unfair dismissal claims. The advantage of the provision is that, particularly where a large group of employees are on strike, the employer may not be readily able to replace all of them, making this a strong form of protection. However, its effectiveness is diminished where the employees are easily replaceable (for example, because they are few in number or do not have special skills). Moreover, the provision only serves to give the employment tribunal jurisdiction to hear the case. Thus, it is possible that the tribunal might find that the employee's dismissal was fair, for example, if the employer decided to restructure the workplace during the strike and so dismissed certain employees on 'SOSR' grounds.

Section 238 applies where ss. 237 and 238A are not applicable. Thus, an employee who took part in a strike protected by s. 238A, but who continued to strike beyond the protected period, would have the benefit of s. 238. Section 237 removes any protection from what it defines as 'unofficial' action. This means that it must be authorised or endorsed, and not repudiated, by a trade union (or that there must be no trade union members involved in the strike). As a result, s. 238 protects 'not unofficial' (but not necessarily immune) action. It is therefore potentially useful in two situations: a non-union strike, and a union strike that is not immune. However, in the latter situation – a union strike that is not immune – there is always the possibility that the union will seek to avoid tort liability by repudiating the strike. If this happens, the employees must return to work promptly or face a fair dismissal under s. 237.

13.5 PICKETING AND PROTEST

Picketing occurs where a group of union members congregate outside the workplace during a strike. Picketing has traditionally played an important role in strikes, for three main reasons. First, it provides a way for trade unions and their members to publicise their grievances against the employer and attract wider support for their cause. Second, it reinforces the effectiveness of the strike within the workplace. Anyone who wishes to continue working must 'cross the picket line' and is likely to face hostility from their fellow-workers. This may deter them from choosing not to strike. Third, it may reinforce the effectiveness of the strike as a means of disrupting the employer's business more generally, since customers and suppliers (delivery drivers, for example) may also refuse to cross the picket line.

However, picketing can be quite controversial, for much the same reasons. One problem is that a picket line can be quite intimidating for those who wish to continue working or for others doing business with the employer.[179] For example, while the law does not allow unions to discipline members who refuse to go on strike,[180] an effective picket line may achieve much the same effect, either by making non-striking workers too scared to go to work, or by allowing strikers to identify them and ostracise them once the dispute is over. Another problem is that, as with any other gathering

---

[179] A recent inquiry into alleged intimidation during industrial action did not produce any recommendations: Bruce Carr, *The Carr Report: The Report of the Independent Review of the Law Governing Industrial Disputes* (October 2014).

[180] See Chapter 11.

of protesters, a picket line may generate public order problems if violence erupts. Thus, there is a need to ensure that any assembly (which is a right protected by Article 11 ECHR) is peaceful and does not infringe the rights and freedoms of others.

The legal regime for picketing follows a similar pattern to that we have already encountered – tort liability plus immunity if certain conditions are met – though it is also possible for pickets to incur criminal liability. We will examine each in turn. An important caveat in the following discussion is that many of the cases on picketing were decided prior to the HRA and may require reconsideration in the light of Article 11, so the exact state of the current law is a matter of some speculation.

13.5.1 Tort liability and immunity

In this section, we will note some of the torts that might be committed during picketing, and examine the operation of the immunities in this context.

In general terms, pickets might commit many of the same torts as we encountered above in relation to strikes. For example, if a picket persuades a fellow-worker not to go to work, he or she induces that worker to breach his or her contract and thus commits a tort. Similarly, if a picket persuades a delivery driver not to deliver to the workplace in breach of the driver's contract of employment with his or her employer, the picket may well commit the tort of causing loss by unlawful means as regards the picket's own employer. But tort liability in respect of picketing may extend beyond the economic torts to include, among other things, private nuisance (unlawful interference with a person's use of land or rights over it)[181] or harassment under the Protection from Harassment Act 1997.

There are two routes to securing immunity for picketing. First, in respect of the economic torts, s. 219 is potentially applicable. However, this is only available where the conditions for immunity are met (which would include balloting if the action is organised by a trade union) and where the requirements of s. 220 (which governs lawful picketing) are met.[182] Second, s. 220 affords a more general immunity (not confined to the economic torts) specifically directed at picketing. Thus, for either route, it is necessary to have a detailed appreciation of the requirements of s. 220. According to s. 220(1):

> It is lawful for a person in contemplation or furtherance of a trade dispute to attend–
>
> (a) at or near his own place of work, or
>
> (b) if he is an official of a trade union, at or near the place of work of a member of the union whom he is accompanying and whom he represents,
>
> for the purpose only of peacefully obtaining or communicating information, or peacefully persuading any person to work or abstain from working.

There are three things to note about this provision. First, there must be a trade dispute, defined in the usual way, and the pickets must act 'in contemplation or furtherance' of it. One of the common features of picketing is that it may involve an element of secondary action – for example, persuading people who work for another employer not to cross the picket line, as in our delivery driver example – but if the picket is lawful under s. 220, it benefits from an exception to the general prohibition on secondary action in s. 224 and the immunity is *not* lost.[183]

---

[181] *Hunter* v *Canary Wharf Ltd* [1997] AC 655.
[182] TULRCA, s 219(3).
[183] TULRCA, s 224(1).

Second, the pickets must act 'peacefully' for the listed purposes. This means that the immunity may be lost if the pickets go beyond 'communicating' or 'persuading', for example, by physically preventing people from crossing the picket line or attempting to force people to listen to what they have to say. In construing this aspect of the provision, the courts have been influenced by the government Code of Practice on Picketing, which they are required by statute to take into account in legal proceedings.[184] Paragraph 51 of the Code is as follows:

Large numbers on a picket line are also likely to give rise to fear and resentment amongst those seeking to cross that picket line, even where no criminal offence is committed. They exacerbate disputes and sour relations not only between management and employees but between the pickets and their fellow employees. Accordingly pickets and their organisers should ensure that in general the number of pickets does not exceed six at any entrance to, or exit from, a workplace; frequently a smaller number will be appropriate.

In *Thomas* v *NUM*, in which 50–70 strikers were on the picket line, the judge held that their purpose could not be 'peaceful communication' with those who were continuing to work because it was not practical for so many people to engage in communication.[185] More recently, in *Gate Gourmet* v *TGWU*, the judge noted the relevance of the right to peaceful assembly and stated that a limit on numbers would mean that 'many who have not in any way breached the law will be denied an opportunity to express their point of view and concerns in this public way'.[186] Although he granted an injunction that would limit the number of pickets, he did so only in respect of one of the two picket lines in the case. This case shows the potential for Article 11 to make a difference in this area.

Third, the location of the picket 'at or near' the individual's place of work is very important. In *Rayware*, the workplace was situated on a privately owned industrial estate.[187] The picket was set up at the entrance to the industrial estate, which was as close as the workers could get to the workplace without trespassing on private property. The Court of Appeal adopted a common-sense approach to the provision, holding that this should be regarded as 'near' to the workplace. Workers with no fixed place of work (travelling salespersons, for example) or whose place of work is not a practicable location for a picket (the classic example is an oil rig) are allowed by virtue of s. 220(2) to picket 'any premises of his employer from which he works or from which his work is administered'. A worker who has been dismissed because of a trade dispute, or whose dismissal gave rise to a trade dispute, and who is not in work, may picket his or her former place of work in accordance with s. 220(3). Despite these various extensions and the Court of Appeal's purposive approach in *Rayware*, it is worth noting an important limitation: pickets cannot choose the *most effective* location for their protest if they want to rely on s. 220. Thus, for example, if the strikers want to change the minds of company bosses, they might want to picket head office, but this is not covered by s. 220 unless that is where the strikers work.

---

[184] TULRCA, s 207.
[185] *Thomas* v *National Union of Mineworkers (South Wales Area)* [1986] Ch 20.
[186] *Gate Gourmet London Limited* v *Transport and General Workers Union* [2005] EWHC 1889, [2005] IRLR 881 [26].
[187] *Rayware* v *Transport and General Workers Union* [1989] ICR 457 (CA).

Where picketing is not immune under s. 219 or s. 220, those taking part are liable in tort. As with strikes more generally, the employer may prefer to seek an injunction to stop further picketing rather than suing for damages.

13.5.2 Criminal law

In addition to the possibility of tort liability, those involved in picketing may commit criminal offences. For example, where pickets refuse to co-operate with the police, they may commit the offence of obstructing a constable in the execution of his or her duty,[188] and where pickets protest on public roads, they may commit the offence of obstructing the highway.[189] If violence breaks out on a picket line, criminal offences such as assault would be relevant.

TULRCA s. 241 sets out a specific criminal offence of intimidation:

(1) A person commits an offence who, with a view to compelling another person to abstain from doing or to do any act which that person has a legal right to do or abstain from doing, wrongfully and without legal authority–

　　(a) uses violence to or intimidates that person or his spouse or civil partner or children, or injures his property,

　　(b) persistently follows that person about from place to place,

　　(c) hides any tools, clothes or other property owned or used by that person, or deprives him of or hinders him in the use thereof,

　　(d) watches or besets the house or other place where that person resides, works, carries on business or happens to be, or the approach to any such house or place, or

　　(e) follows that person with two or more other persons in a disorderly manner in or through any street or road.

(2) A person guilty of an offence under this section is liable on summary conviction to imprisonment for a term not exceeding six months or a fine not exceeding level 5 on the standard scale, or both.

This broadly framed provision is not confined to industrial action.[190] In applying it, the key elements are 'compelling', which suggests particularly strong pressure, and 'wrongfully and without legal authority'. This latter phrase has been held by the courts to require that conduct must be tortious before it can give rise to criminal liability under s. 241.[191] This is important because s. 241(1)(d) could be read to apply to peaceful picketing, but if the picketing is lawful by virtue of s. 220, it is arguable that it should not be an offence under s. 241.

Finally, it is worth noting that under s. 15 TULRCA, a union may not indemnify an individual against criminal penalties so anyone who commits an offence during picketing may not have his or her fine paid by the union.

---

[188] Police Act 1996, s 89(2).
[189] Highways Act 1980, s 137.
[190] *DPP v Todd* [1996] Crim LR 344.
[191] *Thomas*, above n 185.

POINTS TO TAKE AWAY

- The right to strike is generally regarded as a central aspect of the right to form and join trade unions, because it is an important means by which unions can protect their members' interests. It is particularly essential to support the collective bargaining process.

- The right to strike is protected expressly in some international instruments and by extension of freedom of association in others. Its position is somewhat precarious, given employer opposition at the ILO and the cautiously evolving jurisprudence of the ECtHR.

- Anyone who organises a strike is likely to be liable for one or more of the economic torts. But he or she may be protected by statutory immunity if he or she acts 'in contemplation or furtherance of a trade dispute'. The immunity is prone to being overtaken by judicial developments in the law of tort.

- Where a union organises a strike, it must secure majority support for the strike in a ballot of the affected members, and it must provide a series of notices to the employer. These provisions are highly complex and the employer may be able to obtain an injunction to stop the strike if it can make a *prima facie* case that they have been breached.

- Individual strikers are in breach of their contract of employment and are not entitled to be paid. The employer may be able to refuse to pay them if they take action short of a strike, too.

- It is automatically unfair to dismiss individual strikers taking part in lawful industrial action organised by a trade union during the first 12 weeks of the action. Strikers taking part in an unofficial strike have no recourse if they are dismissed.

- Strikers who take part in a picket outside the workplace may be liable in tort but benefit from a statutory immunity if the picket is peaceful and in 'contemplation or furtherance' of a trade dispute. The criminal law may also be relevant to picketing.

Further reading

For a more detailed account of the various possible justifications for the right to strike, and potential restrictions of the right, see **Tonia Novitz, *International and European Protection of the Right to Strike* (OUP 2003), Part I.** To see how the right is regulated in other countries, a good starting-point is **Antoine TJM Jacobs, 'The Law of Strikes and Lockouts', in Roger Blanpain (ed), *Comparative Labour Law and Industrial Relations in Industrialized Market Economies* (11th edn, Kluwer 2014).**

The right to strike is of considerable international interest at the moment. It has been recognised, but heavily constrained, by EU law; it has been recognised, but with limitations, by the ECtHR; and its long-standing acceptance at the ILO is subject to challenge by the employer group. On EU developments, see **Catherine Barnard, 'A Proportionate Response to Proportionality in the Field of Collective Action' (2012) 37 EL Rev 117; ACL Davies,**

→

'One Step Forward, Two Steps Back? The *Viking* and *Laval* Cases in the ECJ' (2008) 37 ILJ 126; and **Phil Syrpis and Tonia Novitz, 'A Proportionate Response to Proportionality in the Field of Collective Action' (2012) 37 EL Rev 117.** On ECtHR developments, see **Alan Bogg and KD Ewing, 'The Implications of the *RMT* Case' (2014) 43 ILJ 221.** On the ILO, see **Keith D Ewing, 'Myth and Reality of the Right to Strike as a "Fundamental Labour Right"' (2013) 29 International Journal of Comparative Labour Law and Industrial Relations 145; and Claire La Hovary, 'Showdown at the ILO? A Historical Perspective on the Employers' Group's 2012 Challenge to the Right to Strike' (2013) 42 ILJ 338.**

14 Worker information, consultation and participation

Learning outcomes

This chapter will enable readers to:

- understand the various levels of worker information, consultation and participation in the workplace, critically evaluate the possible justifications for these rights, and understand their relationship with collective bargaining
- understand the possibilities for, and limitations of, worker participation in corporate governance, through board-level representation and share ownership
- analyse the European Works Councils Directive and the Information and Consultation Directive, and critically evaluate their implementation in English law
- understand other statutory regimes for the information, consultation and participation of workers on specific workplace issues, like collective redundancies and working time arrangements
- understand the statutory rights of workplace representatives

14.1 INTRODUCTION

In this chapter, we will consider the law on worker involvement in the employer's decision-making processes. Worker involvement can take many different forms, from the simple provision of information to workers about what is going on in the firm, to joint decision-making between worker representatives and the employer. And workers might be involved in different types of decision: decisions about the future strategic direction of the business, for example, or just those affecting them directly, like decisions about redundancies.

Worker involvement in decision-making might be seen as a controversial idea. The employer risks its capital (or the shareholders in the employer firm risk their capital) in order to set up the business, so on one view, any decisions should be taken by the employer whose money is at stake. Managerial prerogative should always prevail. However, in line with the view that labour is not a commodity – workers cannot supply their labour without supplying themselves – there are various different ways of justifying worker involvement. These range from arguments that workers are 'stakeholders' in the firm, or that the workplace should be run along democratic lines, to the argument that the firm will be more productive if it harnesses workers' views. Depending on the argument one adopts, different degrees of encroachment into managerial prerogative might be justified.

In the UK, most worker involvement traditionally took place, and still does take place, through trade unions and collective bargaining. Most of the law on other types of worker involvement comes from EU directives. It might be thought that, with the decline in trade union membership, other forms of worker involvement might prove popular as an alternative, with workers seizing the chance to gain some of the benefits of involvement without the need to join a trade union. However, this has not turned out to be the case, probably because it would require quite a big culture change to get workers familiar with the idea of involvement other than through collective bargaining.

An important theme running through this chapter is the 'limits of law'. This is the idea that there is only so much that the law can do to promote worker involvement. It can create mechanisms, but employers and workers have to operate them. If the employer is hostile, it might be difficult to achieve anything. Equally, if the employer is keen on worker involvement, it might set up mechanisms that are not required by law at all, and these might prove to be highly successful. For this reason, we will consider some mechanisms for worker participation that English law does not currently require, so that you can see the whole package an enthusiastic employer might be able to put in place.

Once we have explored some of the theories about worker involvement (section 14.2), we will examine worker involvement in corporate governance (section 14.3) before turning to the two main EU directives on information and consultation, the Information and Consultation Directive (which applies to large national firms) and what is often referred to as the European Works Councils Directive (which applies to large pan-European firms) (section 14.4). In section 14.5, we will give a brief overview of other situations in which an employer might be obliged to – or encouraged to – consult the workforce, most of which are dealt with in detail in other chapters of this book, before explaining the protections the law affords to worker representatives (section 14.6).

14.2 THEORETICAL FRAMEWORK

Since 'worker involvement' may mean different things to different people, we will begin this section by discussing its meaning. We will then turn to justifications for worker involvement, drawing on rights arguments and claims about productivity from the labour law tradition, and 'stakeholder' theories from the corporate governance tradition. We will conclude with an examination of the relationship between consultation and collective bargaining, and a brief discussion of the role of law in this area.

14.2.1 Mechanisms and levels of involvement

Worker involvement does not admit of a simple definition. Instead, it is an umbrella term for a range of different mechanisms. It may be easiest to begin with a list of some of the most obvious possibilities:

- providing workers with information about what is going on in the business;

- creating ad hoc forums for discussion when particular issues arise, usually involving elected representatives of the workforce;

- creating a regular forum for discussion such as a works council or a consultative committee, usually involving elected representatives of the workforce;

- giving workers a voice as shareholders in the company;

- engaging in collective bargaining with a trade union representing the workers;

- structuring the business as a co-operative;

- having worker representatives as directors on the company board.

From this list, we can see that these various mechanisms involve different degrees of *influence* over the employer, or different degrees of encroachment on managerial prerogative. Simply providing the workers with information does not limit management freedom at all, whereas having worker representatives on the board of directors would entitle those representatives to take part in the firm's strategic decisions together with the other directors.

Moreover, different degrees of influence may be possible within each mechanism depending on how it is designed and implemented. As we shall see, the law offers different definitions of 'consultation' depending on the circumstances, so that consultation might involve the 'exchange of views and establishment of a dialogue',[1] or 'consultation with a view to reaching an agreement'.[2] The latter comes closer to a joint decision-making process between management and worker representatives, whereas the former just requires a discussion and leaves managerial prerogative largely intact.

A further factor to consider is the *subject-matter* of the worker involvement. The law sometimes requires the employer to set up a consultation process to deal with a particular problem, such as impending redundancies.[3] Here, whatever influence the workers have is limited to that problem. Other mechanisms might deal with worker concerns more generally – collective bargaining usually covers pay, hours and holidays and may extend to other topics too[4] – giving the workers a voice in decisions about terms and conditions of employment that affect their immediate interests. Yet other mechanisms might require the employer to include workers in discussions about the state of the business or its strategic direction more generally.

Both these variables – how much of a say the workers get, and on what topics – are important when we come to consider how worker involvement can be justified. Different types of justifications might be required for different forms and levels of worker involvement.

14.2.2 Justifications

Justifications for worker involvement come from two broad traditions in the scholarship: corporate governance and labour law. Scholars in the corporate governance tradition are interested in the way that firms are run. They are critical of the usual approach of directors being accountable to shareholders, and argue instead that directors should be accountable to a broader range of 'stakeholders' affected by their decisions, including workers. Scholars in the labour law tradition tend to focus

---

[1] Information and Consultation of Employees Regulations 2004, SI 2004/3426, reg 2 (ICER).
[2] TULRCA, s 188(2).
[3] TULRCA, s 188, discussed in more detail below.
[4] See Chapter 12.

on the need to respect workers' dignity by enabling them to participate in decisions affecting their daily working lives. We will examine each in turn, but before we do so, we will take a brief look at the employing enterprise itself.

Managerial prerogative

Most (though not all) discussions about worker involvement take as their starting-point the idea that the firm should be run by its owners or by managers on behalf of the owners. They do not challenge the basic concept of managerial prerogative. It may be worth pausing to explain why this is the case.

There is a long tradition in labour law scholarship of referring to the employer as 'he', as if 'he' were a real person.[5] Some small businesses do indeed operate as sole traders. In this situation, the employer is a real person who has chosen to run a business without setting up a separate legal entity. He or she is the employer and is personally liable for any debts incurred by the business.[6]

In this book, we have used 'it' to refer to the employer, reflecting the fact that most people do not work for a particular human being (who would not necessarily be male anyway). Instead, they work for a legal entity such as a company.[7] One of the key reasons for setting up a company is to limit the liability of the company's owners for its debts.[8] Most companies are limited by shares. Those who own the company are only liable for the amount they have invested in the company by buying shares. Anyone may buy shares in a public limited company (a plc). Shares in a private limited company (which must have Ltd after its name) cannot be offered for general sale. The ownership of private limited companies generally depends on the rules of the company. The sale of shares also provides a way for the company to raise money to finance its activities, making it easier to enlarge the business.

In the standard analysis, company directors (who run the company on a day-to-day basis) owe various legal duties to the company itself, but are accountable to the shareholders.[9] At the company's annual meeting, the shareholders may propose and vote on resolutions or even remove directors. In practice, these powers can be quite difficult to use, but the fact of their existence tends to motivate the directors to achieve good returns for shareholders as a means of avoiding controversy.

From an employment perspective, the key point is that the company's workers have contractual relationships with the company and not with its ultimate owners, who are not liable, for example, for unpaid wages if the company becomes insolvent. In practice, companies often exist in complex corporate groups, so that the employing company may be controlled by a 'parent' company. The doctrine of the 'corporate veil' means that the courts rarely look beyond the formal legal structures.[10] They will treat an employee of company A as an employee of company A even if it is clear that company A is controlled by company B.

---

[5] For discussion, see Jeremias Prassl, 'The Notion of the Employer' (2013) 129 LQR 380.
[6] See, for example, ERA, s 133 dealing with death of the employer (or employee) in the dismissal context.
[7] Or a partnership, which we cannot discuss here for reasons of space.
[8] See, generally, Paul Davies and Sarah Worthington, *Gower & Davies: Principles of Modern Company Law* (9th edn, Sweet & Maxwell 2012) chapter 1.
[9] ibid chapter 16.
[10] See, for example, *Duport Steels Ltd v Sirs* [1980] ICR 161 (HL).

Whether a business is run by a sole trader or as a company, classical economic theory would regard the individual business owner, or the shareholders, as having risked their capital in order to set up the business. This is what gives them an entitlement to decide how the business should be run: to exercise managerial prerogative, or to delegate it to directors and managers. Of course, not all businesses are run like this. One alternative is to set up a worker co-operative.[11] In this form, the workers are themselves shareholders in the business (sometimes along with other types of shareholder, like consumers). In this situation, there is no external 'owner' of the business because the people who work for the business are also its owners, and therefore have the opportunity through voting to determine how the business should be run. However, co-operatives are relatively unusual, so in most work situations, there is a business owner who is 'in charge'. This basic capitalist set-up explains why we need to justify worker involvement.

Labour law arguments – rights

Justifications for worker involvement from the labour law tradition often start from the International Labour Organization's (ILO's) famous statement that 'labour is not a commodity'.[12] When a person supplies his or her labour, he or she has no alternative but to supply him- or herself as well. As a result, it is important that the workplace is an environment in which workers' dignity is respected.

Probably because of the long-standing emphasis on freedom of association and collective bargaining, rights for workers to be consulted are only found in more recent instruments. The revised European Social Charter of 1996 (to which the UK is not a party) contains three rights relating to consultation, and a supplementary right protecting worker representatives.[13] The most general is Article 21:

> With a view to ensuring the effective exercise of the right of workers to be informed and consulted within the undertaking, the Parties undertake to adopt or encourage measures enabling workers or their representatives, in accordance with national legislation and practice:
>
> (a) to be informed regularly or at the appropriate time and in a comprehensible way about the economic and financial situation of the undertaking employing them, on the understanding that the disclosure of certain information which could be prejudicial to the undertaking may be refused or subject to confidentiality; and
>
> (b) to be consulted in good time on proposed decisions which could substantially affect the interests of workers, particularly on those decisions which could have an important impact on the employment situation in the undertaking.

There are two points to note about this provision. First, it makes reference to 'national legislation and practice' as the source of detailed guidance on how information and consultation rights should be implemented. Second, it draws a distinction (in fact mirrored in EU and English law, as we shall see) between 'information' about the general state of the business, and 'consultation' about issues affecting workers. This reflects a commonly-held view that workers might be entitled to more than one

---

[11] For discussion in relation to employee involvement, see Ian Snaith, 'Employee Involvement in the European Cooperative Society: a Range of Stakeholders?' (2006) 22 IJCLLIR 213.

[12] ILO, *Declaration of Philadelphia* (1944).

[13] ESC 1996, art 28, discussed below.

position on the spectrum of involvement we noted at the start, depending on what is at stake for them. The greater the relevance of the issue to workers' interests, the stronger their involvement should be.

Article 22 addresses working conditions and the working environment:

> With a view to ensuring the effective exercise of the right of workers to take part in the determination and improvement of the working conditions and working environment in the undertaking, the Parties undertake to adopt or encourage measures enabling workers or their representatives, in accordance with national legislation and practice, to contribute:
>
>> to the determination and the improvement of the working conditions, work organisation and working environment;
>>
>> to the protection of health and safety within the undertaking;
>>
>> to the organisation of social and socio-cultural services and facilities within the undertaking;
>>
>> to the supervision of the observance of regulations on these matters.

While this right is more specific in terms of the topics it covers, it is vaguer than Article 21 in its reference to 'enabling workers . . . to contribute' to the listed matters. Finally, Article 29 deals with the particular situation of collective redundancies:

> With a view to ensuring the effective exercise of the right of workers to be informed and consulted in situations of collective redundancies, the Parties undertake to ensure that employers shall inform and consult workers' representatives, in good time prior to such collective redundancies, on ways and means of avoiding collective redundancies or limiting their occurrence and mitigating their consequences, for example by recourse to accompanying social measures aimed, in particular, at aid for the redeployment or retraining of the workers concerned.

Although this right does not define collective redundancies, the European Committee on Social Rights (ECSR) has indicated that it applies to economic dismissals which are no fault of the workers concerned, where several workers are to be dismissed within a period of time set by national law.[14] The right is quite specific in terms of the topics for consultation and, as we shall see, mirrors EU obligations in this regard.

Of course, since the UK is not a party to the revised European Social Charter, these rights are of limited value in English law unless they are referred to by some other institution, such as the ECtHR. Of greater relevance, perhaps, is the EU Charter, which provides a right to consultation in Article 27:

> Workers or their representatives must, at the appropriate levels, be guaranteed information and consultation in good time in the cases and under the conditions provided for by Community law and national laws and practices.

This right is of limited value in the sense that it refers to EU and national law as the source of detail about information and consultation.[15] In *AMS* the Court of Justice of the European Union (CJEU) held that Article 27 could not be invoked in a case between private parties in order to disapply national law which did not properly implement EU law on information and consultation.[16] This was because it required

---

[14] European Committee on Social Rights, *Conclusions 2003*, 92.

[15] Article 27 is also subject to the general limitation on Charter rights, that they do not create new powers or competences for the EU: Charter of Fundamental Rights of the European Union, article 51(2).

[16] Case C-176/12 *Association de médiation sociale* v *Union locale des syndicats* [2014] IRLR 310.

further action by the EU or the Member States, and thus could not be treated as giving rise to rights for individuals to rely on in court.[17] However, the Court did regard Article 27 as a 'fundamental right' and this may influence the way it construes the relevant directives in future.[18]

Given that the inclusion of worker involvement in human rights instruments is relatively recent, and is based heavily on existing EU and national law, it is helpful to think a bit more deeply about why respect for workers' dignity might require that they have a right to involvement in workplace decisions. One way of justifying this is by using a democratic analogy.[19] As citizens, our lives are governed by a vast body of legislation. We accept that this is legitimate because we have a say in how it is formulated. We vote for our representatives and we can participate in other ways, through consultation exercises or campaigns directed at securing, or preventing, the enactment of legislation on a particular topic. At work, our lives are governed by detailed rules laid down by management. Some of these are contractual; others are laid down in workplace handbooks or by managerial direction. The democratic analogy would suggest that management's power to govern would be more legitimate if we had the chance to comment on, or take part in the formulation of, the rules we are expected to obey. The natural time at which to do this is when the employment relationship begins, because there may be an opportunity to negotiate about terms and conditions of employment before the contract is formed. However, in practice, individual negotiations are unrealistic for many people, and even more so at later stages in the work relationship when the employer might decide to change the rules.

Of course, the democratic analogy is imperfect. In the citizenship context, we elect the people who have the power to govern. In the workplace, we do not (though we do have the 'option' of working elsewhere, if another job is available). But perhaps this is part of its strength: it explains why workers should have some possibility of participation in decision-making (because work rules govern people's daily lives) but also why management should have the ultimate power to decide (because the workplace is not normally a true democracy run on behalf of the workers). This might also suggest that workers' participation should focus primarily on the issues most closely affecting them, and less so on broader matters of company policy.

Labour law arguments – reflexivity and productivity

Worker involvement has been a key area in which writers in the labour law tradition have sought to develop the argument that legal regulation can bring positive benefits for firms and should not always be regarded negatively as a source of extra costs. We will examine two such arguments here: reflexivity and productivity.

The idea of 'reflexive law' is particularly associated with the work of Teubner,[20] and in labour law, with Rogowski.[21] Advocates of reflexive law express the concern that traditional 'command and control' legal regulation – which tells employers and workers what to do – is often ineffective or counter-productive because it does not

---

[17] ibid [45].
[18] ibid [42].
[19] See, for example, Hugh Collins, 'Against Abstentionism in Labour Law', in John Eekelaar and John Bell (eds), *Oxford Essays in Jurisprudence* (Clarendon Press 1987).
[20] Gunther Teubner, 'Substantive and Reflexive Elements in Modern Law' (1983) 17 Law & Soc Rev 239.
[21] Ralf Rogowski, *Reflexive Labour Law in the World Society* (Edward Elgar 2013) chapter 2.

acknowledge the importance of their preferences. They argue that the law should focus instead on encouraging employers and workers to regulate their own affairs by providing them with the tools for self-regulation. Of course, this idea is by no means novel in labour law, since the system of collective bargaining operated precisely in this way.[22] The law supported the process indirectly (for example, by ensuring that trade unions were lawful and could (to some extent at least) take industrial action) but left the parties to set terms and conditions of employment for themselves. Reflexive law, then, is a rediscovery of these ideas and a reinvention of them for modern conditions. For example, it might be argued that, in a time of declining trade union membership, it is important to provide alternative ways for workers to participate with their employers in the process of regulating the employment relationship. This is precisely what information and consultation mechanisms might be able to offer.

The productivity justification for worker participation rests on the simple claim that workers who are given a say at work will feel happier and work harder. The Workplace Employment Relations Survey (WERS) 2011 found some association between employee involvement and loyalty: '91% of those who were satisfied with their involvement felt loyal to their organisation, compared with 49% among those who were not satisfied'.[23] This sense of loyalty may have a number of practical benefits: workers may 'go the extra mile' for the firm or its customers, they may stay longer with the firm (thus repaying any investment the firm makes in training them), and they may make helpful suggestions about how the business might be run more efficiently.

Corporate governance perspectives

So far, we have employed the neoclassical view of the company in which the shareholders are treated as the owners. They invest (and risk) their capital, and for this reason the company is accountable to them. However, there is an alternative 'stakeholder' model of the company which challenges these assumptions. Although this model does not focus solely on improving the lot of workers, they are one constituency that might benefit from the 'stakeholder' view.

Critics argue that the shareholder view is flawed. One problem is that nowadays, shareholders are often relatively passive investors and do not take an active interest in the performance of the company's management.[24] Nor does company law require the directors to maximise shareholder profits as their sole concern. In practice, various different groups 'invest' in the company in different ways: shareholders, workers, customers, suppliers, creditors and so on.[25] These groups can be seen as 'stakeholders' and their existence challenges the idea that the interests of shareholders should be treated as having primacy. English law imposes much more complex duties on company directors to strike a balance between the interests of different stakeholders.[26]

---

[22] See Chapter 12.
[23] Brigid van Wanrooy et al., The 2011 Workplace Employment Relations Study: First Findings, 19.
[24] Adolf A Berle and Gardiner C Means, The Modern Corporation and Private Property (Macmillan 1932).
[25] Margaret M Blair and Lynn A Stout, 'A Team Production Theory of Corporate Law' (1999) 85 Va Law Rev 247.
[26] Companies Act 2006, s 172, and see Gower and Davies, above n 8, chapter 16.

The 'stakeholder' theory itself has attracted criticism from writers in the neoclassical tradition. One claim is that company law has pursued the shareholder model over time because it is the most efficient structure.[27] These critics point to, for example, the rarity of worker-owned firms such as co-operatives and suggest that if these were efficient and profitable corporate structures they would be more prevalent. However, as Njoya has argued, it may not be appropriate to apply scientific ideas like evolution or natural selection to corporate forms, given that they are dictated by the surrounding economic and legal environment which is ultimately the product of choices made by governments and market actors.[28] The other claim is that the stakeholder theory is vague as to who counts as a stakeholder.[29] For example, while it is clear that consumers have an interest of some kind in the firm (such as obtaining the goods they have ordered on time) this is very different in nature from the 'investment' made by a shareholder or a creditor (investing money in, or lending money to, the firm). However, this point is less pressing for our purposes because it is relatively easy to conceptualise the investment made by workers. Workers 'invest' in firms by acquiring firm-specific skills.[30] These skills are only of value to the worker if he or she can continue to be employed at the firm, because they are not useful for getting a job elsewhere in the labour market. The worker's investment is 'human capital' in contrast to the financial capital invested by shareholders.

The stakeholder model might be used to justify worker involvement in two different ways. One route is to argue that traditional forms of shareholder involvement should also be applied to workers. The most obvious way of doing this is to turn workers into shareholders, for example, by giving them share options as part of their pay package. However, while this would give workers the opportunity to have input into the general running of the business (to the extent that shareholders exercise any control at all), it would not give them close involvement in worker-specific issues. The other route is to use the idea of workers as stakeholders to justify other forms of worker involvement. On this line of reasoning, we recognise that there are differences between different stakeholders in the firm and adjust their rights and entitlements accordingly. Thus, we might argue that a works council – in which both the general state of the business and worker-related issues can be discussed – is the best way of reflecting workers' investment in acquiring firm-specific human capital.

14.2.3 Worker involvement and collective bargaining

In the UK context, it is particularly important to think about the relationship between collective bargaining and other forms of worker involvement. Traditionally, most worker involvement in the UK took place through collective bargaining. This is sometimes referred to as a 'single-channel' system.[31] Of course, this was supplemented by other possibilities – some firms used employee share options or had consultative

---

[27] Henry Hansmann and Reinier Kraakman, 'The End of History for Corporate Law' (2001) 89 Geo L 439.
[28] Wanjiru Njoya, 'Employee Ownership and Efficiency: an Evolutionary Perspective' (2004) 33 ILJ 211.
[29] Samuel F Mansell, *Capitalism, Corporations and the Social Contract: A Critique of Stakeholder Theory* (CUP 2013).
[30] Margaret M Blair, 'Firm-Specific Human Capital and Theories of the Firm' in Margaret M Blair and Mark J Roe (eds), *Employees and Corporate Governance* (Brookings Institution Press 1999).
[31] Paul Davies and Claire Kilpatrick, 'UK Worker Representation After Single Channel' (2004) 33 ILJ 121.

committees – but these activities were not required or supported by law and were relatively unusual. EU membership has required the UK to adopt a 'dual channel' model because the EU has enacted a number of directives on 'information and consultation', an approach which is much more common in other Member States.[32]

A first point to consider is how collective bargaining differs from other forms of worker involvement. Collective bargaining has four important features in this regard.[33] First, collective bargaining is inherently *collective* in nature, as the name suggests. It involves workers grouping together to negotiate with the employer, usually through representatives. This may strengthen workers' claims and encourage them to show solidarity with each other. Worker involvement mechanisms may share this characteristic, but some of them do not: giving employees information or making them shareholders tend to be ways of involving them as individuals without the added benefit of collective strength. Second, because it generally takes place through trade unions, it is only effective where workers are willing to join a trade union and take part in its activities. Although worker involvement mechanisms may be able to accommodate the presence of an outside organisation, they do not usually require it. Advocates of worker involvement may see this as an advantage, in that it can spread involvement more widely even where union membership rates are low, whereas critics tend to see it as reflecting the 'passive' and thus ineffective nature of worker involvement compared to collective bargaining. Third, collective bargaining generally requires the employer to reach an agreement with trade union representatives – a collective agreement – with the threat of strike action or a lock-out if no agreement can be reached. While some forms of worker involvement may take a similar approach, such as consultation 'with a view to reaching an agreement',[34] worker involvement tends to leave the final decision in the hands of the employer. It intrudes less far into managerial prerogative. Again, this might be seen as an advantage or a disadvantage depending on one's perspective. Fourth, collective bargaining tends to focus on issues immediately affecting workers such as pay and other terms and conditions of employment. Thus, it gives workers a potentially high level of influence (because of the expectation of reaching an agreement) over a small (but important) number of topics. Worker involvement is often less influential but it can range more widely over general business decisions. Views are likely to differ on the value of this broader involvement. In general, then, collective bargaining can be seen as a distinctive form of worker involvement, albeit one that shares some characteristics with other mechanisms.

This leads to a broader issue: what should be the relationship between collective bargaining and other forms of worker involvement? The traditional collective laissez-faire answer might have been to say that other forms of worker involvement would harm collective bargaining by reducing the incentive for workers to join trade unions. However, even if we take this pro-single-channel approach, there is no prospect of implementing it while the UK remains a member of the EU. At the opposite extreme, it might be argued that other forms of worker involvement should

---

[32] See Case C-382/92 *Commission v UK* [1994] ECR 1-2435 (transfers); Case C-383/92 *Commission v UK* [1994] ECR 1-2479 (collective redundancies). For discussion see Paul Davies, 'A Challenge to Single Channel' (1994) 23 ILJ 272.

[33] See Chapter 12.

[34] Above n 2.

be seen as preferable to collective bargaining and should be given priority in public policy. Trade union membership continues to decline a little each year, suggesting that many workers no longer regard collective bargaining as a useful means of protection. While there are many possible reasons for this, one might be that workers regard the adversarial nature of trade unionism as inappropriate and prefer to see their interests and those of their employer as more closely aligned. On this view, other less adversarial mechanisms of worker involvement, like works councils, might be more attractive, giving workers the chance to have their say but without the accompanying threat of industrial action. But given that freedom of association is a fundamental right protected by English law, there is equally no prospect of banning trade unionism and moving to a consultation-only model.

A more realistic option is to embrace the 'dual channel' approach, recognising that collective bargaining and other forms of worker involvement now co-exist in English law, and thinking instead about how to build a coherent system out of the various legal regimes. Davies and Kilpatrick argue that the government's piecemeal implementation of the EU directives on consultation has led to a fragmented system that does not fit particularly well with the UK's collective bargaining tradition.[35] They argue for an approach in which unions are encouraged to make use of consultation mechanisms as a way of gaining a foothold in non-unionised workplaces, building support and eventually pursuing recognition for the purposes of collective bargaining. In our discussion of the law, we will consider possible roles for unions in each of the worker involvement mechanisms we examine.

14.2.4 Limits of law

A final point to note before we examine the law in detail is that a fully effective system of worker involvement requires a degree of enthusiasm on the part of the employer and the workers. There is only so much that the law can do to bring this about. It can require employers to set up procedures for talking to workers, but it cannot force them to take an active interest in sharing information and responding to workers' comments. The most we can hope for is that some employers will embrace worker involvement, and that others will be 'won round' over time.[36]

Critics of consultation might point out that this is one of its inherent weaknesses relative to collective bargaining. Collective bargaining also requires a degree of enthusiasm on the part of workers for joining a trade union and taking part in its activities, but once they have done so, they have a certain amount of leverage, through threats of industrial action, to bring the employer to the negotiating table. The logic of collective bargaining is that it seeks to redress the inequality of bargaining power between workers and their employer: it is a process driven as much by economics as by law. However, two points might be made in response. First, collective bargaining is itself increasingly reliant on the law, particularly in workplaces where unions cannot secure recognition without using the statutory recognition procedure.[37] On this view, the 'limits of law' problem is common to worker involvement and collective bargaining.

---

[35] Above n 31.

[36] For a discussion of the role of law in shaping workers' preferences, see Alan Bogg, *The Democratic Aspects of Trade Union Recognition* (Hart 2009) chapter 6.

[37] See Chapter 12.

Second, for some at least, the point of worker involvement is that it does not intrude very much into managerial prerogative. The fact that workers have limited means of getting the employer to take notice might be seen as a strength rather than a weakness of worker involvement mechanisms.

14.3 WORKER PARTICIPATION IN CORPORATE GOVERNANCE

In this section, we will consider two main forms of worker participation in corporate governance: worker representatives on company boards, and employee shareholder schemes. Neither of these forms of involvement is required by English law, though neither is forbidden and the second is quite common in some sectors. They provide an important backdrop to our consideration of the law on worker involvement in the remaining two sections. Of course, as we noted above, the most radical form of worker participation in corporate governance is the worker-owned co-operative. But here we will concentrate on ways of involving workers in the typical corporate form: the company limited by shares.

14.3.1 Board-level representation

The UK is relatively unusual among EU countries in not providing for worker representation on company boards. Here, we will offer a brief examination of the practices adopted by other countries in this regard, before considering how these practices have affected developments in EU company law. By virtue of the EU provisions, some companies registered in the UK may in fact be legally obliged to have worker representatives on their boards.

The idea of worker representatives on company boards is commonly associated with Germany.[38] German company law adopts a two-tier board structure, in which the day-to-day running of the company is entrusted to a management board, the activities of which are monitored by the supervisory board. Firms with 500–2000 employees are required to give one-third of the seats on the supervisory board to worker representatives, and firms with more than 2000 employees are required to give half the seats on the supervisory board to worker representatives.[39] The worker representatives are elected by the employees of the company. In general, the representatives must be employees of the company themselves, though it is also possible to elect an external trade union representative in some circumstances. Critics of worker representation often suggest that it is a uniquely German cultural phenomenon, closely linked to the two-tier board structure.[40] In English company law, the board of directors is unitary – consisting of executive directors with day-to-day responsibility for running the company, and non-executive directors with a supervisory role – so it is often argued that worker representation would not work in this context.[41]

---

[38] Aline Conchon, *Workers' Voice in Corporate Governance: A European Perspective* (TUC 2013) 7.

[39] ibid 18. Special rules (not discussed here) apply to the coal and steel industries.

[40] For discussion of its possible transplantation to the UK, see Paul Davies, 'Efficiency Arguments for the Collective Representation of Workers: A Sketch', in Alan Bogg *et al.* (eds), *The Autonomy of Labour Law* (Hart 2015).

[41] Though the difference between two-tier and unitary board structures may not be as significant as it seems: see Markus Roth, 'Corporate Boards in Germany' in Paul Davies *et al.* (eds), *Corporate Boards in Law and Practice* (OUP 2013).

However, a wider examination of the other EU Member States reveals that Germany is one of 13 Member States with this form of worker participation in both public and private sectors.[42] A further six EU Member States provide for worker participation in certain types of firm, such as state-owned or privatised industries.[43] Thus, board-level participation is by no means a uniquely German phenomenon, nor is it linked to the presence of a two-tier board structure. Some countries with a requirement to have worker representatives on company boards have unitary boards (Sweden, for example) or allow companies to choose (the Netherlands, for example).[44]

Within the 13 Member States with board-level participation, there are some important differences in what the law requires. First, there are differences in the size of companies to which the rules apply. In Austria, board-level representation is only required for limited companies with more than 300 employees, whereas in Denmark, a union or the employees may request representation in a company with more than 35 employees.[45] Second, there are differences in the number or proportion of worker representatives the company may be required to have. As we have seen, large German companies can be required to have 'parity codetermination', with worker representatives making up half the supervisory board, whereas in Croatia, the entitlement is simply to one worker representative on the board.[46] Third, there are differences in how the representatives are nominated and appointed or elected to the board. Nomination may be by a certain percentage of employees themselves, by the works council or by a trade union.[47] While most countries provide for the representatives to be elected by the employees of the company, there are exceptions: in Austria, for example, the worker representatives are appointed by the works council.[48]

The effectiveness of board-level participation is, of course, a matter of debate. One common argument is that Germany's economic success relative to other Member States might, in part at least, be attributed to its more enlightened corporate governance mechanisms, though this argument is somewhat undermined once we appreciate the broader use of worker involvement around the EU. The empirical evidence is inconclusive.[49] Nevertheless, proponents claim that board-level representation creates a greater sense of 'ownership' of the employing enterprise among workers, and enables a wider range of interests to be taken into account when setting the direction of the company. The criticisms of board-level representation are many and varied. One claim is that worker representatives make boards inefficient – they pressure boards into focusing more on labour issues rather than on holding the directors to account for the company's performance more generally.[50] Another, rather

[42] Conchon, above n 38, 13.
[43] ibid.
[44] ibid 19 and 22.
[45] ibid 16.
[46] ibid.
[47] ibid 16–22.
[48] ibid 16.
[49] For discussion, see Bernd Frick and Erik Lehman, 'Corporate Governance in Germany: Ownership, Codetermination and Firm Performance in a Stakeholder Economy' in Howard Gospel and Andrew Pendleton (eds), *Corporate Governance and Labour Management* (OUP 2006).
[50] Jean J Du Plessis and Otto Sandrock, 'The Rise and Fall of Supervisory Codetermination in Germany?' (2005) 16 ICCLR 67; Katharina Pistor, 'Codetermination: A Sociopolitical Model with Governance Externalities', in Margaret M Blair and Mark J Roe (eds), *Employees and Corporate Governance* (Brookings Institution 1999).

different, criticism is that members of the board may come to identify more with each other than with the constituency they are supposed to represent, so that worker representatives cease to argue strongly for workers' interests. Clearly, factors such as the proportion of worker representatives on the board and the way in which the board is chaired will play a part here, making it difficult to generalise.

The prevalence of worker representatives on company boards has had important implications for company law at the EU level. The Commission has been keen to simplify the position of companies in the internal market by creating European company forms and by facilitating mergers taking place across national borders.[51] The Court of Justice has also encouraged the movement of companies between Member States through its freedom of establishment case-law.[52] However, states with worker representation rights have tended to oppose these developments on the ground that they might enable companies established under their national law to 'escape' those rights. And states with no worker representation rights have been reluctant to agree to the development of such rights at EU level. The result has been a compromise between these two positions which is designed to ensure that companies cannot use EU measures to avoid pre-existing obligations to workers under national law. However, the effectiveness of these measures has been questioned.

The European Company Statute provides for a new company form, the Societas Europaea (SE).[53] This was initially envisaged as a means of giving a company a European identity by providing an alternative to establishing under a particular national law, though in practice, the SE regime requires the SE to register in a particular Member State and thus to comply with various rules in that Member State's national law. The SE can only be formed from existing companies, by transformation, merger, formation of a holding company or formation of a subsidiary.[54] The European Company Statute was accompanied by a directive on worker involvement.[55] This requires management to initiate discussions with worker representatives about information, consultation and participation arrangements in the SE by setting up a Special Negotiating Body (SNB).[56] The express reference to participation means that it would, in theory at least, be possible to agree that the SE should have worker representatives on its supervisory board even if none of the companies forming the SE had this beforehand. However, more significantly in practice, the Directive seeks to ensure that where board-level representation was in place beforehand, it should be preserved. First, when a company with board-level worker representatives simply transforms into an SE, it must continue to have

---

[51] Gower and Davies, above n 8, 137–158.

[52] Such countries also face deregulatory pressure from the CJEU's freedom of establishment case-law: Case C-212/97 *Centros Ltd v Erhvervs- og Selskabsstyrelsen* [1999] ECR I-1459. For the relationship between this case-law and the SE, see WG Ringe, 'The European Company Statute in the Context of Freedom of Establishment' (2007) 7 Journal of Corporate Law Studies 185.

[53] Regulation (EC) 2157/2001 of 8 October 2001 on the Statute for a European Company (SE) [2001] OJ L294/1, implemented in English law by the European Public Limited-Liability Company Regulations 2004, SI 2004/2326.

[54] ibid art 2; SI 2004/2326 regs 5–10.

[55] Directive 2001/86/EC of 8 October 2001 supplementing the Statute for a European Company with regard to the involvement of employees [2001] OJ L294/22, implemented in English law by the European Public Limited-Liability Company (Employee Involvement) (Great Britain) Regulations 2009, SI 2009/2401.

[56] ibid art 3(2); SI 2009/2401, regs 7–9.

board-level worker representatives under Article 4(4).[57] Second, where the company is formed by merger or by the creation of a holding company or subsidiary, and participation arrangements are already in place covering a certain proportion of the employees, participation can only be reduced if a two-thirds majority of the SNB agrees to the change.[58] And third, where the SNB and management cannot reach agreement on worker information, consultation and participation arrangements, the default provisions that then take effect provide for board-level representation where it was already in place for a certain proportion of the employees prior to the creation of the SE.[59]

In practice, the SE has only proved popular where it can be used (paradoxically) to escape codetermination.[60] In company law terms, the SE is not particularly attractive because of its ongoing dependence on national law. Thus, it does not offer companies any obvious advantages over registration under the national law of a Member State. But despite the complex rules aimed at protecting existing worker participation mechanisms, such mechanisms are relatively easy to evade. For example, one obvious option is to set up a shelf SE with no employees, so that there is no prior worker participation to preserve, and then transfer the employees to the SE at a later date.[61]

The Directive on Cross-Border Mergers aims to solve the co-ordination problems arising where companies from different Member States seek to merge.[62] It enables the companies to draw up draft terms for the merger and then to comply with their own national rules on mergers (subject to minimum requirements set out in the Directive). The resulting company may be established in any Member State.[63] Although the SE was envisaged as a means of facilitating mergers, the Directive has proved more effective because it tackles the lack of co-ordination between national rules on mergers in a straightforward fashion.

In terms of worker participation, the new company resulting from a cross-border merger is subject to the rules in its state of registration.[64] However, as with the SE arrangements, the Directive seeks to prevent the use of mergers as a means of 'escaping' pre-existing worker participation arrangements. Article 16(2) explains when the anti-avoidance rules apply:

> However, the rules in force concerning employee participation, if any, in the Member State where the company resulting from the cross-border merger has its registered office shall not apply, where at least one of the merging companies has, in the six months before the publication of the draft terms of the cross-border merger as referred to in Article 6, an average number of employees that exceeds 500 and is operating under an employee

---

[57] SI 2009/2401, reg 15(4).

[58] Directive 2001/86, art 3(4); SI 2009/2401, reg 16(3).

[59] ibid art 7(2); reg 19.

[60] See Horst Eidenmüller *et al.*, 'Incorporating under European Law: The Societas Europaea as a Vehicle for Legal Arbitrage' (2009) 10 European Business Organization Law Review 1.

[61] For discussion, see Wanjiru Njoya, 'Employee Ownership in the European Company: Reflexive Law, Reincorporation and Escaping Co-Determination' (2011) 11 JCLS 267.

[62] Directive 2005/56/EC of 26 October 2005 on cross-border mergers of limited liability companies [2005] OJ L310/1, implemented in English law by the Companies (Cross-Border Mergers) Regulations 2007, SI 2007/2974.

[63] Gower and Davies, above n 8, 1119–1120.

[64] Above n 62, art 16(1); SI 2007/2974, reg 22.

participation system . . . , or where the national law applicable to the company resulting from the cross-border merger does not

(a) provide for at least the same level of employee participation as operated in the relevant merging companies, measured by reference to the proportion of employee representatives amongst the members of the administrative or supervisory organ or their committees or of the management group which covers the profit units of the company, subject to employee representation, or

(b) provide for employees of establishments of the company resulting from the cross-border merger that are situated in other Member States the same entitlement to exercise participation rights as is enjoyed by those employees employed in the Member State where the company resulting from the cross-border merger has its registered office.

If any of these exceptions applies, the merged company must have worker participation even if that is not normally required in the state of registration. There are three possible routes. First, the new company may opt to apply the default worker participation rules immediately, without any negotiation with worker representatives.[65] Second, the new company may set up a SNB and negotiate with worker representatives.[66] The SNB may agree to reduced participation rights but only by a two-thirds majority. Third, if the company and the SNB cannot agree, the default rules again apply,[67] but in this situation the new company may limit worker representatives to one-third of the seats on the board, even if some of the merging companies had more extensive worker representation.[68] This 'cap' is one of the biggest differences between this directive and the SE regime.

The Directive on Cross-Border Mergers is less worker-protective than the equivalent arrangements for SEs. The option of immediately invoking the default rules reduces the scope for worker involvement while the merger is taking place, and there are various ways in which the level of worker participation in the resulting company may be reduced when compared with the companies from which it is formed (for example, via the one-third cap). More generally, Member States are only obliged to preserve the worker involvement arrangements for three years, so there is the possibility that (for example) if the resulting company was registered in the UK, it could merge with another UK company after three years and escape worker involvement at that point.[69]

There are three broader points to take away from this discussion. First, it is possible that a company registered in the UK might be obliged by EU law to have worker representatives on its board, despite the absence of any general requirement of this kind in English law. Second, although the UK is one of several EU Member States without worker participation requirements, such requirements are by no means uncommon and are not confined to countries with particular traditions such as two-tier board structures. Third (and relatedly), the EU position is potentially quite unstable. Given the diverging traditions of the Member States, EU-wide harmonisation of the law on worker participation at board level is highly unlikely to occur. There are enough Member States with no experience of worker participation

---

[65] ibid art 16(4)(a); reg 36.

[66] ibid art 16(4)(b); regs 25 and 30.

[67] This is subject to a requirement that one-third of the employees in the merging companies were previously covered by worker participation, a tougher requirement than the 25% in the SE regime.

[68] Above n 62, art 16(4)(c); regs 36–40.

[69] Above n 62, reg 40.

to be able to block any initiatives in that direction. Those Member States with rights for workers to be represented on company boards remain vulnerable to attempts at evasion (despite the directives we have examined) and to any broader attempts by the Court of Justice to enable companies to move more freely between the Member States.

14.3.2 Employees as shareholders

We saw above that in the classical economic theory of the firm, the shareholders are treated as the firm's owners. Although in English law directors' duties are complex and do not simply require directors to maximise value for shareholders, in practice directors have considerable incentives to do so.[70] One way of improving worker involvement, then, is for workers to hold shares in the company. This will give them the same set of rights, interests and benefits as other kinds of shareholder. We will begin by examining the rights of shareholders before considering ways in which workers might acquire shares in their employing company.

Most corporate decision-making takes place within the board of directors, described by Gower and Davies as the 'black box' of company law.[71] However, the shareholders are not without power, in two main respects. First, the law requires shareholder approval for certain decisions, such as changes to the company's articles of association.[72] Second, under s. 168 Companies Act 2006, the shareholders may by ordinary resolution (which requires a simple majority) at a meeting remove a director from office. This power is highly significant. Ordinary resolutions passed by shareholders requiring the directors to follow or to refrain from following certain courses of action are not normally binding on the directors. However, if the board chooses to ignore the shareholders, the directors may find that their jobs are at risk. The s. 168 power means that shareholders have a method – albeit quite a drastic one – of getting the board to do what they want. There is one important qualification to make to this picture: not all shareholders in a particular company may be entitled to vote. Although the law sets out a 'one share, one vote' default position, the company's articles of association may make alternative provision so that certain classes of shareholder have additional votes or no votes at all.[73]

More generally, some commentators argue that the role of shareholders nowadays is quite limited. In a famous article, Berle and Means claimed that shareholders in large publicly quoted companies would not normally find it worthwhile to play an active role in corporate governance.[74] The costs of proposing resolutions and voting at meetings would not be outweighed by the benefits in terms of increased share value. However, others have challenged this view, pointing to the role of large institutional investors such as pension funds and hedge funds in using the corporate governance tools available to them in order to improve firms' performance.[75] For our purposes, the key point to take away from this debate is that (as in any 'democratic'

---

[70] Above n 26.
[71] Gower and Davies, above n 8, 432.
[72] ibid 77–78.
[73] ibid chapter 23.
[74] Adolf Berle and Gardiner Means, *The Modern Corporation and Private Property* (New York: Macmillan 1932).
[75] For example, Bernard S Black, 'Shareholder Passivity Re-examined' (1990) 89 Michigan Law Review 520, but cf Roberta Romano, 'Public Pension Fund Activism in Corporate Governance Reconsidered' (1993) 93 Columbia Law Review 795.

forum) it is generally easier for large voting 'blocs' to exercise real influence than it is for a diffuse body of shareholders each with a small stake in the company.

There are three main ways in which workers might acquire shares in the company that employs them. First, where a company is publicly traded, it would be open to a worker simply to buy shares in the same way as any other investor. Second, the company might include options to buy shares in the worker's remuneration package. The government encourages this type of share ownership through tax breaks.[76] From the worker's perspective, the advantage of this over the first method is that the employer generally offers the shares at a reduced price, thereby giving the worker a financial benefit, though it is often the case that the worker forfeits the shares if his or her employment is terminated.[77] Third, the new 'employee shareholder' status allows employers to offer shares to employees in exchange for reduced entitlement to employment rights.[78] This has the advantage that the employer must give the worker at least £2000-worth of shares at no cost to the worker, and again, there are tax breaks. However, as commentators have pointed out, there are complex questions about valuation of the shares in companies that are not publicly traded, and £2000 may not be a sufficient compensation for the ensuing loss of employment rights.[79] Moreover, it may be difficult for employee shareholders to realise any financial benefits from the shares since the shares need not carry an entitlement to receive dividends and there may be restrictions on their sale or transfer.

Employee share ownership is generally promoted in the UK as a motivational tool. As the government guidance on employee shareholder status puts it:

> An employee shareholder would have a stake in the company. This may lead to that individual feeling greater responsibility towards the company, improving their productivity, and going the extra mile to ensure it does well.[80]

This type of justification assumes that employees will be motivated by share ownership because, in their capacity as shareholders, they will benefit from any improvements in the profitability of the firm. As we have seen, however, there may be a gap between the justification and the reality, particularly where there are restrictions on employees' entitlement to trade their shares or to receive dividends. For present purposes, what is more important is that the government does not present share ownership as a route to greater employee involvement in corporate governance. In general terms, a company's articles of association may restrict the voting rights of certain classes of shareholder. People with 'employee shareholder' status need not be given any voting rights with their shares. Even if workers who own shares do have voting rights, it may be difficult for them to make any impact on corporate governance, since they may have relatively small shareholdings and may find it difficult to co-ordinate their activities with like-minded shareholders. Nor is it likely that proposals favoured by workers – for improved terms and conditions, for example – would find favour with other investors.

---

[76] There are four approved schemes: Share Incentive Plans, Save As You Earn, Company Share Option Plans, and Enterprise Management Incentives. See https://www.gov.uk/tax-employee-share-schemes/overview (last visited 20 September 2014).

[77] See Chapter 5.

[78] Growth and Infrastructure Act 2013, s 31. For further detail, see Chapter 4.

[79] Jeremias Prassl, 'Employee Shareholder "Status": Dismantling the Contract of Employment' (2013) 42 ILJ 307.

[80] https://www.gov.uk/employee-shareholders (last visited 20 September 2014).

14.4 INFORMATION AND CONSULTATION

In this section, we will examine two EU directives that were designed to bring about the development of mechanisms for workers to be informed and consulted on a regular basis, and their implementation in English law. We will consider the law in detail before assessing their (very limited) impact in UK firms.

One of the directives is the European Works Councils (EWC) Directive,[81] which applies to large pan-European firms, and is implemented by the Transnational Information and Consultation of Employees Regulations (TICER).[82] The EWC Directive was first agreed in 1994, under the Agreement on Social Policy adopted at Maastricht.[83] Because of the UK's 'opt-out' from the Agreement, the Directive did not apply in the UK until the 'opt-out' was reversed in 1997. One of the driving forces behind the Directive was a concern that firms with operations in different Member States were encouraging competition between those operations, particularly if there might be a need for redundancies or closures. The EWC was seen as a way of giving workers an opportunity to co-ordinate across national borders in their dealings with the firm. The Directive was revised in 2009, largely with a view to improving the co-ordination between EWCs and national information and consultation mechanisms.

The other measure to be considered here is the Directive on Informing and Consulting Employees (I&C),[84] which applies to large national firms, implemented by the Information and Consultation of Employees Regulations (ICER).[85] This Directive was highly controversial. Whereas the justification for regulating consultation in pan-European firms at EU level was self-evident, the I&C Directive was perceived as much more intrusive into national systems, particularly those (like the UK) with no real tradition of consultation.[86] Two main arguments were made for the Directive.[87] First, as we shall see below, the EU had already legislated to require consultation on certain specific issues such as large-scale redundancies. It was argued that these provisions did not work well in countries with no other form of consultation. Second, Member States with consultation mechanisms argued that their firms were at a competitive disadvantage when compared with firms from other Member States with no such obligations.

Although the two directives are fairly similar in objectives and content, the EWC Directive is somewhat more prescriptive than the I&C Directive. This reflects its Europe-wide nature. There is a greater need to ensure common treatment of workers

---

[81] Council Directive 2009/38/EC of 6 May 2009 on the establishment of a European Works Council or a procedure in Community-scale undertakings and Community-scale groups of undertakings for the purposes of informing and consulting employees (recast) [2009] OJ L122/28.

[82] The Transnational Information and Consultation of Employees Regulations 1999, SI 1999/3323. For discussion, see Mark Carley and Mark Hall, 'The Implementation of the European Works Councils Directive' (2000) 29 ILJ 103.

[83] Council Directive 94/45/EC of 22 September 1994 on the establishment of a European Works Council or a procedure in Community-scale undertakings and Community-scale groups of undertakings for the purposes of informing and consulting employees [1994] OJ L254/64.

[84] Council Directive 2002/14/EC of 11 March 2002 establishing a general framework for informing and consulting employees in the European Community [2002] OJ L80/29.

[85] The Information and Consultation of Employees Regulations 2004, SI 2004/3426. For discussion, see KD Ewing and GM Truter, 'The Information and Consultation of Employees Regulations: Voluntarism's Bitter Legacy' (2005) 68 MLR 626; Mark Hall, 'Assessing the Information and Consultation of Employees Regulations' (2005) 34 ILJ 103.

[86] For discussion of the development of the Directive, see Brian Bercusson, 'The European Social Model Comes to Britain' (2002) 31 ILJ 209.

[87] Commission, *Communication on Worker Information and Consultation* COM(95) 547 final (1995).

in different Member States, and while some pan-European firms may already have consultation mechanisms of some kind, there is no pre-existing law on the subject to be taken into account.

14.4.1 Scope of application

Both Directives apply to larger firms, but the obvious distinction between them is that the EWC Directive applies only to firms with a presence in more than one Member State.

The EWC Directive applies to 'Community-scale undertakings' and groups of undertakings.[88] The former is defined in Article 2(1)(a) as: 'any undertaking with at least 1000 employees within the Member States and at least 150 employees in each of at least two Member States'. The latter is defined in Article 2(1)(c) as:

> . . . a group of undertakings with the following characteristics:
> – at least 1000 employees within the Member States,
> – at least two group undertakings in different Member States,

and

> – at least one group undertaking with at least 150 employees in one Member State and at least one other group undertaking with at least 150 employees in another Member State. . .

These definitions are replicated in TICER, reg. 2. In accordance with Article 11(1) of the Directive, the obligation to set up a works council under the UK implementing provisions only arises where the central management is situated in the UK.[89] The task of calculating how many employees a firm has must be performed by looking at the average over the past two years, including part-time workers, under Article 2(2).[90] The details are left to national law with the odd result that in the UK, management may count each part-time worker as half a person in accordance with reg. 6(3).

The I&C Directive offers Member States a degree of discretion in relation to firm size:

> This Directive shall apply, according to the choice made by Member States, to:
>
> (a) undertakings employing at least 50 employees in any one Member State, or
> (b) establishments employing at least 20 employees in any one Member State.
>
> Member States shall determine the method for calculating the thresholds of employees employed.[91]

After a transitional period in which the UK was allowed to use higher thresholds because it had no tradition of consultation, ICER applies to undertakings with at least 50 employees.[92] Again, part-timers may be counted as half people for this purpose.

---

[88] EWC, art 1(1).
[89] TICER, reg 5(1).
[90] TICER, reg 6.
[91] I&C, art 3(1).
[92] ICER, reg 3(1).

Both TICER and ICER use the 'employee' definition when determining firm size, not the (potentially broader) 'worker' concept.[93] Thus, a firm with 60 staff, of whom only 30 had contracts of employment, would not be subject to ICER. This has the potential to generate unnecessary technical disputes about people's employment status and to reduce the scope of application of the information and consultation provisions.

14.4.2 Triggers

Both TICER and ICER contain 'trigger' provisions. This means that there is no automatic obligation on management to initiate information and consultation discussions (though management may opt to do so if it so chooses). The obligation to initiate discussions only arises if a certain proportion of the workforce requests it. On the one hand, this can be seen as a sensible reflection of the practical realities of the situation. If the workers are not interested in information and consultation, then there is no point in forcing management to expend time and effort on the process. On the other hand, it might be argued that if workers do not know about the possibility of information and consultation, they will not be able to 'pull the trigger' or even form a view about whether or not such a mechanism would be desirable. On this view, the implementation reduces the law's potential to educate workers about their options and shape their preferences.[94]

The 'trigger' is found in Article 5 of the EWC Directive and is implemented by TICER reg. 9(2), as follows:

A valid request may consist of–

(a) a single request made by at least 100 employees, or employees' representatives who represent at least that number, in at least two undertakings or establishments in at least two different Member States; or

(b) a number of separate requests made on the same or different days by employees, or by employees' representatives, which when taken together mean that at least 100 employees, or employees' representatives who represent at least that number, in at least two undertakings or establishments in at least two different Member States have made requests.

Under the I&C Directive, the practical arrangements for information and consultation are for the Member States to determine.[95] Unlike the EWC Directive, there is no express provision for a trigger. However, the UK implementation contains one in reg. 7. This requires 10% of the employees in the undertaking to request negotiations (either in a single request or in several separate requests within six months). This is subject to minimum and maximum limits of 15 and 2500 employees, so that (for example) in a firm of 60 employees, 15 employees would have to request negotiations (rather than six, which would be 10%). It is not entirely clear whether the introduction of the trigger is a legitimate exercise of the UK's discretion to implement the Directive.

[93] ICER, reg 2; TICER reg 2.
[94] Above n 36.
[95] I&C, art 4(1).

14.4.3 The negotiation process

Once the employees have made their request (or at the initiative of management), the next step is to begin negotiations for the establishment of the EWC or an information and consultation mechanism. This illustrates the 'reflexive' nature of both pieces of legislation: rather than imposing a model on employees and firms, they create procedures through which employees and firms are meant to reach their own agreement on information and consultation. However, in both cases there are default provisions that come into effect if agreement cannot be reached. These operate as minimum standards in the sense that there is no real incentive for the employee representatives to agree to anything less effective than the default provisions (assuming that they know about them), which will take effect if they refuse to agree to the employer's proposals. Thus, the employees and management 'bargain in the shadow of the law' in this context.

Under the EWC Directive, the central management must initiate the process by setting up a SNB.[96] Under TICER, reg. 11:

> The special negotiating body shall have the task of determining, with the central management, by written agreement, the scope, composition, functions, and term of office of a European Works Council or the arrangements for implementing an information and consultation procedure.

Article 5 of the Directive provides that there should be one seat on the SNB for every 10% (or smaller percentage) of the employees in the pan-European firm, arranged by Member State. So if 20% of the employees are in Germany, they should have two representatives, but if 8% of the employees are in the UK, they should have one representative. This may have some distorting effects but it is difficult to see how it could be otherwise, since national constituencies are the obvious way to organise the representatives.

The precise method of selecting the representatives in each Member State is for national law to determine. Regulation 13 TICER provides for the representatives to be elected by a secret ballot among the firm's UK employees, supervised by an independent person. However, where the firm has a consultative committee, it may nominate the members of the SNB.[97] This may be a useful mechanism for ensuring that the EWC 'meshes' with pre-existing consultation arrangements in a particular firm, though in the UK context (with no tradition of consultation) it gives rise to a concern that management might use it to subvert the balloting process. The main safeguard against this lies in the definition of a 'consultative committee', which is in fact quite strict:

> In this regulation, "a consultative committee" means a body of persons–
>
> (a) whose normal functions include or comprise the carrying out of an information and consultation function;
> (b) which is able to carry out its information and consultation function without interference from the UK management, or from the central management (where it is not also the UK management);
> (c) which, in carrying out its information and consultation function, represents all the UK employees; and

---

[96] EWC, art 5(2).
[97] TICER, reg 15(1).

(d) which consists wholly of persons who were elected by a ballot (which may have consisted of a number of separate ballots) in which all the employees who, at the time, were UK employees were entitled to vote.[98]

The I&C Directive is even less prescriptive about the negotiating process, leaving this entirely to the discretion of the Member States.[99] The UK implementation is not particularly detailed. Under reg. 14 ICER, the employer must make arrangements for the employees to elect or appoint representatives. The only requirements for this are set out in reg. 14(2):

(a) the election or appointment of the representatives must be arranged in such a way that, following their election or appointment, all employees of the undertaking are represented by one or more representatives; and
(b) all employees of the undertaking must be entitled to take part in the election or appointment of the representatives and, where there is an election, all employees of the undertaking on the day on which the votes may be cast in the ballot, or if the votes may be cast on more than one day, on the first day of those days, must be given an entitlement to vote in the ballot.

There are a number of difficulties with these provisions. First, they do not guarantee that the representatives will be elected, nor do they specify how any democratic element might be injected into an appointment process. This is in marked contrast to TICER. Second, they allow any ballot to be run by the employer rather than by an independent person, again in contrast to TICER. Third, they do not offer employers any guidance as to how many representatives should be elected or how constituencies should be determined. This may leave employers feeling vulnerable to challenge.

A further point worth noting about the negotiating process under ICER is that it makes special provision for pre-existing agreements (sometimes known as PEAs). These are agreements which:

(a) are in writing;
(b) cover all the employees of the undertaking;
(c) have been approved by the employees; and
(d) set out how the employer is to give information to the employees or their representatives and seek their views on such information.[100]

If the employees make a request to initiate negotiations when a PEA is already in force, the 'trigger' threshold is much higher. The employer is only required to start negotiating if the request is supported by more than 40% of the employees.[101] If the request has a lower level of support, the employer may choose to hold a ballot. The employer is then only required to start negotiating if at least 40% of those eligible to vote and a majority of those voting in the ballot endorse the request.[102] Critics have argued that this opens up the possibility that a firm might impose a PEA on unwitting employees as a means of foreclosing a subsequent request for negotiations under ICER.[103] Although there are some requirements for PEAs, these are

---

[98] ibid reg 15(4).
[99] I&C, art 4.
[100] ICER, reg 8(1).
[101] ibid.
[102] ibid reg 8(6).
[103] Ruth Dukes, 'The ICE Regulations: Pre-Existing Agreements and Standard Provisions: a Warning to Employers' (2007) 36 ILJ 329.

fairly minimal: for example, although the employees must 'approve' the PEA, this need not be done by ballot.[104] However, the PEA provisions are designed to ensure that ICER does not disrupt existing arrangements in the workplace. The case of *Stewart v Moray Council,* in which a collective agreement was argued to be a PEA, is a good illustration of the courts using the PEA provisions to ensure that existing consultation with trade unions was not undermined by the preference of a minority of employees for non-union representation.[105]

Once the SNB (under TICER) or the representatives (under ICER) are in place, the negotiating process can begin. The law gives the parties a limited time for negotiations before the default provisions come into effect. This prevents the employer from delaying the process indefinitely.

Under the EWC Directive and TICER, the central management must convene a meeting with the SNB.[106] Provision is made for the SNB to have a meeting beforehand without management representatives, presumably in order to determine its negotiating strategy.[107] The SNB may have access to experts (who may be trade union representatives) though management is only obliged to pay the expenses of one expert.[108] Under TICER, reg. 17(1):

> The central management and the special negotiating body are under a duty to negotiate in a spirit of cooperation with a view to reaching a written agreement on the detailed arrangements for the information and consultation of employees in a Community-scale undertaking or Community-scale group of undertakings.[109]

The agreement must be in writing and must set out in some detail the basic arrangements for establishing an EWC.[110] However, there is no obligation to set up an EWC and the parties may agree to establish some other form of information and consultation procedure instead.[111] The SNB is to take decisions by simple majority, except where it decides to terminate negotiations, in which case a two-thirds majority is required.[112] This is important because if negotiations are actively terminated by the SNB, the default provisions do not come into effect, and the workforce cannot trigger another negotiating process until a two-year period has elapsed.[113]

Although the aim is to encourage the parties to negotiate, the law offers some guidance and imposes some obligations on the parties. For example, it is worth noting that consultation is defined as: 'the exchange of views and establishment of dialogue' between employee representatives and central management (whether in an EWC or not).[114] Management is obliged to provide information in good time to enable the representatives to prepare for consultation and to support the members of the EWC in fulfilling their duties.[115] And the parties must negotiate in a 'spirit of co-operation'.[116]

---

[104] *Stewart v Moray Council* [2006] ICR 1253(EAT) [35]–[38] (Elias J).
[105] ibid.
[106] EWC, art 5(4); TICER, reg 16.
[107] ibid.
[108] ibid.
[109] EWC, art 6.
[110] EWC art 6(2); TICER reg 17.
[111] ibid art 6(3); reg 17(3).
[112] ibid art 6(5), 5(5); reg 16(2) and (3).
[113] ibid art 5(5); reg 16(4).
[114] ibid art 2(1)(g); reg 2(1).
[115] ibid art 4; reg 18A and reg 19A.
[116] ibid art 6(1); reg 19.

However, the EWC or other procedure is confined to the consideration of 'transnational' questions, a restriction introduced when the Directive was revised in 2009, with a view to achieving a better fit with national mechanisms.[117] Transnational is defined as affecting the pan-European firm as a whole, or at least two undertakings or establishments in different Member States.[118] This may give rise to some difficulties of application in practice.

Under the I&C Directive, it is for the Member States to determine the details of the negotiating process.[119] ICER, reg. 16(1), sets out what the negotiations are meant to achieve:

> A negotiated agreement must cover all employees of the undertaking and may consist either of a single agreement or of different parts . . . which, taken together, cover all the employees of the undertaking. The single agreement or each part must–
>
> (a) set out the circumstances in which the employer must inform and consult the employees to which it relates;
>
> (b) be in writing;
>
> (c) be dated;
>
> (d) be approved in accordance with paragraphs (3) to (5);
>
> (e) be signed by or on behalf of the employer;
>
> (f) either–
>
> > (i) provide for the appointment or election of information and consultation representatives to whom the employer must provide the information and whom the employer must consult in the circumstances referred to in sub-paragraph (a); or
> >
> > (ii) provide that the employer must provide information directly to the employees to which it relates and consult those employees directly in the circumstances referred to in sub-paragraph (a) . . .

For these purposes consultation means 'the exchange of views and establishment of a dialogue' and information means 'data transmitted by the employer . . . in order to enable . . . representatives or . . . employees to examine and to acquaint themselves with the subject matter of the data'.[120] One of the most controversial aspects of the UK's implementation is sub-paragraph (ii), which permits the negotiated agreement to provide for information and consultation to take place on an individual level. Critics argue that this is not what the Directive intended, because it bypasses employee representatives and does not provide for any collective input into the employer's decision-making.[121] They suggest that individual consultation is unlikely to be effective because it does not make use of the employees' strength in numbers. It is arguable that the implementation is in breach of the Directive, which refers throughout to consultation 'with representatives', but the matter remains unclear because Article 5 allows for agreements between management and employees to derogate from its basic understanding of information and consultation as laid down in Article 4.

---

[117] ibid art 1(3); reg 18A(7).
[118] ibid art 1(4); reg 2(4A).
[119] I&C, art 4.
[120] ICER, reg 2.
[121] See, for example, Mark Hall, 'Assessing the Information and Consultation of Employees Regulations' (2005) 34 ILJ 103.

Any 'negotiated agreement' (or set of agreements) reached by the employee representatives and management must be 'approved'.[122] This can be done in one of two ways. The simplest is that the agreement is regarded as approved if it was signed unanimously by all the employee representatives.[123] If only a majority of representatives sign the agreement, further steps are necessary, so that the agreement is either:

(i) approved in writing by at least 50% of employees employed in the undertaking, or

(ii) approved by a ballot of those employees. . . in which at least 50% of the employees voting, voted in favour of approval.[124]

These requirements seem unnecessarily complicated.

If the SNB (under TICER) or the employee representatives (under ICER) fail to reach an agreement with the employer, the default provisions apply.[125] A key issue is how much time the parties are allowed for negotiation. Under TICER, the default provisions are applicable either if management fails to commence negotiations within six months of receiving a valid request, or if the parties cannot agree within a three-year period from the start of negotiations.[126] Under ICER, the default provisions are applicable either if management fails to commence negotiations within six months of receiving a valid request, or if the parties cannot agree within a six-month period of commencing negotiations.[127] Thus, the time limit under ICER is much shorter, though it can be extended if the employer and a majority of the representatives agree to this.[128] There is no ICER equivalent of the TICER provision allowing the representatives to terminate the negotiations (without triggering the default provisions) by a two-thirds majority.[129]

14.4.4 Default provisions

The default provisions serve two functions. First, they ensure that some kind of information and consultation mechanism will come into effect even if the parties cannot reach an agreement. They prevent management from simply stalling the process indefinitely. Second, they act as a baseline for the negotiations. In theory at least, there is no reason for the employee representatives to agree to less effective arrangements, because by refusing to accept management's proposals, they can simply bring the default provisions into effect once the relevant deadline has passed. However, as we have seen, there is no bar on the representatives agreeing to less effective arrangements so this may not always work in practice, either because management offers some benefit in return, or because the representatives do not know about the default provisions.

Under the EWC Directive, the default provisions are quite detailed, again because of the need to ensure uniformity across the Member States. They are referred to as 'subsidiary requirements' and appear in Annex I of the Directive and Schedule 1 of the implementing regulations. The seats on the default EWC are to be allocated

---

[122] ICER, reg 16(1)(d).
[123] ibid reg 16(3).
[124] ibid.
[125] TICER, reg 18; ICER, reg 18(1).
[126] TICER, reg 18.
[127] ICER, reg 18(1).
[128] ibid reg 14(5).
[129] TICER, reg 16(3).

in the same way as those on the SNB: one for every 10% (or smaller percentage) of employees in each Member State. The UK members of the default EWC may be appointed or elected, as follows:

(1) The UK members of the European Works Council must be UK employees and–

    (a) in a case where all of those employees are represented by UK employees' representatives, shall be elected or appointed by such employees' representatives;

    (b) in a case where not all of those employees are represented by UK employees' representatives, shall be elected by ballot.

(2) For the purposes of this paragraph all of the UK employees are represented by UK employees' representatives if each of the employees referred to in sub-paragraph (1) is a UK employee–

    (a) in respect of which an independent trade union is recognised by his employer for the purpose of collective bargaining; or

    (b) who has elected or appointed an employees' representative for the purpose of receiving, on the employee's behalf, information–

        (i) which is relevant to the employee's terms and conditions of employment; or

        (ii) about the activities of the undertaking which may significantly affect the employee's interests

        but excluding representatives who are expected to receive information relevant only to a specific aspect of the terms and conditions or interests of the employee, such as health and safety or collective redundancies.[130]

This provision is quite controversial. It does not provide for the UK employees to elect their representatives unless not all of them are covered by representative arrangements. Where there are representatives in place – whether because there is collective bargaining with an independent trade union, or an existing representative structure – those representatives are responsible for selecting the members of the EWC. On the one hand, this enables the EWC to 'fit' better with existing representative arrangements. For example, members of the UK consultative committee in a particular firm might nominate some of their own number to join the EWC, so that they bring a detailed knowledge of the firm's UK operations and can co-ordinate negotiations where both national and pan-European interests are affected. The provisions also prioritise trade union representatives, thereby bringing about greater co-ordination between EU consultation provisions and the UK's collective bargaining tradition. On the other hand, the provision removes an opportunity for workplace democracy and may prove damaging where the national-level consultation mechanism is ineffective, so that its members cannot make a positive contribution to the EWC.

The EWC is confined to the consideration of transnational questions, as discussed above. Perhaps one of the most disappointing features of the Directive and the implementing Regulations is that the basic obligation on management is to hold an annual meeting with the EWC. The details are set out in para 7 of the Schedule, reflecting the language of the Directive:[131]

---

[130] TICER, sch 1, para 3.
[131] EWC, Annex 1, paras 1–2.

(1) Subject to paragraph 8, the European Works Council shall have the right to meet with the central management once a year in an information and consultation meeting, to be informed and consulted, on the basis of a report drawn up by the central management, on the progress of the business of the Community-scale undertaking or Community-scale group of undertakings and its prospects.

(2) The central management shall inform the local managements accordingly.

(3) The information provided to the European Works Council shall relate in particular to the structure, economic and financial situation, the probable development of the business and of production and sales of the Community-scale undertaking or Community-scale group of undertakings.

(4) The information and consultation meeting shall relate in particular to the situation and probable trend of employment, investments, and substantial changes concerning organisation, introduction of new working methods or production processes, transfers of production, mergers, cut-backs or closures of undertakings, establishments or important parts of such undertakings or establishments, and collective redundancies.

This provision draws a distinction between the requirement simply to provide information (which applies to the state of the business as a whole) and the requirement to consult the representatives (which applies to matters relating more closely to employees and their interests). However, as we have seen, consultation in this context is confined to 'the exchange of views and establishment of dialogue', so there is little, if any, obligation on management to take account of the representatives' views.[132]

The obligation to hold an annual meeting is subject to the provision in para 8 for 'exceptional' meetings.[133] This provides as follows:

> Where there are exceptional circumstances affecting the employees' interests to a considerable extent, particularly in the event of relocations, the closure of establishments or undertakings or collective redundancies . . . the European Works Council shall have the right to be informed. It shall have the right to meet in an exceptional information and consultation meeting, at its request, the central management, or any other more appropriate level of management within the Community-scale undertaking or group of undertakings having its own powers of decision, so as to be informed and consulted.

This reflects one of the driving forces behind the EWC Directive: the concern that firms were treating their operations in different Member States as being in competition with each other, and were initiating closures without proper consultation in some cases. However, dealing with this situation presents practical challenges for EWCs. Even if the firm does not adopt a 'divide and conquer' strategy, representatives from the Member State in which the firm might close its operations may not get much support from representatives from another Member State to which some of the work might be transferred, thereby safeguarding or even creating jobs.

The default provisions also govern some of the practical details of the operation of the EWC. For example, its members are entitled to meet before the annual meeting with management.[134] The EWC may be assisted by experts, though management is only obliged to pay the expenses of one expert.[135] The management is obliged to fund

---

[132] Above n 114.
[133] EWC, Annex 1, para 3.
[134] EWC, Annex 1, para 4; TICER, sch 1, para 9(1).
[135] ibid Annex 1, para 6; sch 1, para 9(5).

the EWC.[136] Finally, after four years, the EWC must consider whether to continue operating under the default provisions or whether to initiate negotiations with a view to concluding an agreement with management.[137]

The I&C Directive is somewhat less specific about the default arrangements, leaving more discretion to the Member States.[138] The UK implementation requires the employer to start the process by holding a ballot for the employees to elect their representatives.[139] There must be one representative for every 50 employees, subject to a minimum of two and a maximum of 25.[140] It then largely copies out the provisions of the Directive, without offering much guidance to employers as to what is expected of them. Under reg. 20(1):

> Where the standard information and consultation provisions apply pursuant to regulation 18, the employer must provide the information and consultation representatives with information on–
>
> (a) the recent and probable development of the undertaking's activities and economic situation;
> (b) the situation, structure and probable development of employment within the undertaking . . . and on any anticipatory measures envisaged, in particular, where there is a threat to employment within the undertaking; and
> (c) subject to paragraph (5), decisions likely to lead to substantial changes in work organisation or in contractual relations, including those referred to in–
>> (i) sections 188 to 192 of the Trade Union and Labour Relations (Consolidation) Act 1992; and
>> (ii) regulations 13 to 16 of the Transfer of Undertakings (Protection of Employment) Regulations 2006.

Again, there are three 'layers' to the provision: the general state of the business, general employment issues and particular problems such as proposed redundancies. The representatives are entitled to information on the first layer (the general state of the business), to be consulted on the second layer (general employment issues) and to be consulted 'with a view to reaching an agreement' on the third layer (particular employment problems). There is some overlap between the third layer and existing legal obligations to consult on collective redundancies and changes in the ownership of the business (which we will discuss in more detail below). Under reg. 20(5), the employer may opt to comply with this legislation instead of consulting the representatives under ICER. This provision is worrying because it might enable the employer to bypass well-established information and consultation arrangements in favour of (less effective) ad hoc ones, though where a union is recognised in respect of the affected employees the employer choosing not to proceed under ICER would be obliged to consult the union representatives. More generally, the employer must provide information in good time to enable the representatives to study it and prepare for consultation where appropriate.[141] The consultation elements (layers two and three) must be conducted 'in such a way as to enable the information and

---

[136] ibid Annex 1, para 6; sch 1, para 9(6).
[137] ibid Annex 1, para 1; sch 1, para 10(1).
[138] I&C, art 4.
[139] ICER, reg 19(1).
[140] ibid reg 19(3).
[141] ibid reg 20(2).

consultation representatives to meet the employer at the relevant level of management depending on the subject under discussion and to obtain a reasoned response from the employer to any . . . opinion' put forward by the representatives.[142] Reflecting the case-law of the Court of Justice, 'a failure on the part of a person who controls the employer (either directly or indirectly) to provide information to the employer shall not constitute a valid reason for the employer failing to inform and consult'.[143]

14.4.5 Enforcement

Enforcement is a matter for the Member States, subject to the usual general requirements in EU law to provide methods that are effective and equivalent to those applicable in similar areas of national law. In the UK, the main focus is on resolution of complaints by the Central Arbitration Committee (CAC), the body responsible for supervising the trade union recognition procedure.

Under TICER, complaints about failures to comply with the Regulations (for example, about a failure to establish or operate the EWC as agreed, or to supply information to it) must be presented to the CAC in the first instance.[144] There are quite complex provisions about who has standing to present a complaint depending on the nature of the alleged failure. So, for example, a complaint about a failure to set up a SNB can be presented by an employee,[145] whereas a complaint about a failure to provide timely information to the EWC can only be presented by the EWC itself.[146] Where the complaint is well-founded, the CAC must make an order setting out what steps the party in default must take to come into compliance with the Regulations.[147] One of the more cumbersome features of the Regulations is that it is also possible to apply to the EAT for a penalty notice against management where the CAC upholds the complaint.[148] The EAT may order management to pay a penalty of up to £100,000 to the Secretary of State.[149] However, there is little incentive for applicants to pursue this option, given that it requires them to pursue two separate sets of proceedings (before the CAC and then the EAT) and that any penalty is paid to the Secretary of State and not the affected employees.

Under ICER, very similar arrangements apply. Complaints may be presented to the CAC, which – if they are well-founded – makes orders detailing what steps are necessary to achieve compliance with the Regulations.[150] Standing to present a complaint to the CAC varies, so that if the complaint is that the employer has failed to comply with the terms of a negotiated agreement or with the default provisions, the complaint must be presented by an employee representative where they have been elected or appointed, or by an employee where no representatives have been elected

---

[142] ibid reg 20(4)(c).
[143] ibid reg 20(6). See, for example, Case C-449/93 *Rockfon* v *Specialarbejderforbundet i Danmark* [1995] ECR I-4291.
[144] TICER, reg 20 and reg 21.
[145] ibid reg 20(3)
[146] ibid reg 21(3).
[147] ibid reg 20(4) and reg 21(4).
[148] ibid reg 22.
[149] ibid reg 22(2).
[150] ICER, reg 22(1).

or appointed.[151] Again, there is a possibility of applying to the EAT for a penalty of up to £75,000 if the CAC upholds the complaint, but this suffers from the problems just considered.[152]

The CAC's annual report for 2013–14 reveals that two new complaints were received under ICER, one of which was withdrawn and the other decided by the CAC, and two complaints were received under TICER, both of which were resolved by CAC decisions.[153] Since the enactment of ICER, there have been three reported cases in which the employer was required by the EAT to pay a penalty.[154] There have been no reported penalty cases under TICER. Of course, this information could indicate that the two sets of Regulations are working well with little need for intervention by the CAC or the EAT. Employers and employees are 'bargaining in the shadow of the law' without the need for recourse to enforcement mechanisms. However, it seems more likely that the low numbers indicate limited usage of ICER and TICER in practice.

14.4.6 Usage

This brings us neatly to the final part of our discussion, on usage. What does the empirical evidence tell us about the extent to which ICER and TICER are used in practice?

Since EWCs are a Europe-wide measure rather than a UK one, the Europe-wide data is of interest. According to the European Commission, there are some 820 EWCs in operation, covering about 36% of eligible firms.[155] According to the WERS, 16% of UK workplaces that formed part of a pan-European firm were covered by an EWC.[156] This suggests relatively low take-up of the legislation. Because the detailed arrangements for EWCs are a matter for negotiation, it is not surprising to find that their roles can vary considerably in practice. One important area to consider is the impact of EWCs on company restructuring, the issue that prompted the development of the legislation in the first place. A comprehensive study of this topic by Carley and Hall found that substantial involvement by the EWC in negotiating aspects of the restructuring process with management was rare.[157] In many cases, the EWC was informed about the proposed restructuring at the same time as the company made a public announcement, leaving no room for meaningful discussions. Of course, one response to this might be to say that EWCs should not be judged as if they were collective bargaining processes, since their design (as evidenced by the definition of consultation as 'exchange of views and establishment of dialogue') implies a much lower level of influence. Nonetheless, the exclusion of EWCs from issues such as restructuring is a cause for concern.

---

[151] ibid reg 22(3).
[152] ibid reg 23.
[153] Central Arbitration Committee, *Annual Report 2013–2014* (2014) 13–14.
[154] *Amicus v MacMillan Publishers Ltd* [2007] IRLR 885; *Darnton v Bournemouth University* (2010) UKEAT/0391/09/RN; *Brown v G4 Security (Cheltenham)* (2010) UKEAT/0526/09/RN.
[155] Commission, *Proposal for a Directive on the establishment of a European Works Council or a procedure in Community-scale undertakings and Community-scale groups of undertakings for the purposes of informing and consulting employees (Recast)* (COM(2008) 419, 2008), para 3. There is a database of EWC agreements at http://www.ewcdb.eu/ (last visited 22 September 2014).
[156] Brigid van Wanrooy *et al.*, *The 2011 Workplace Employment Relations Study First Findings* (DBIS 2013) 15.
[157] Mark Carley and Mark Hall, *European Works Councils and Transnational Restructuring* (Eurofound 2007).

Assessing the impact of ICER is rather more difficult, not least because it is hard to separate out workplaces in which management voluntarily consults with employee representatives from workplaces in which management is obliged to consult with employee representatives because of ICER. Indeed, the introduction of a consultation arrangement just prior to the introduction of ICER could be a coincidence or a 'shadow effect' of the legislation. The WERS does not attempt to separate out different types of consultation. However, WERS 2011 indicates that some 8% of workplaces had a 'joint consultative committee', a figure that is largely unchanged since WERS 2004.[158] This suggests a limited impact for ICER. The statistics are reinforced by an in-depth study of firms with consultation arrangements conducted by Hall et al.[159] The study suggested that the impact of ICER was limited to prompting some firms to introduce consultation arrangements, but their operation in practice depended primarily upon the culture within the firm and the attitudes of management.

14.5 INFORMATION AND CONSULTATION ON SPECIFIC ISSUES

In this section, we will turn our attention to legal rules that either require the employer to consult the workforce, or offer the employer the option of consulting the workforce, on a specific question or problem. Much – though not all – of the law here is derived from EU Directives. Where consultation is required, it tends to be because the employer is contemplating a decision that will have a serious effect on the immediate interests of the employees, such as large-scale redundancies. The aim is to give employees some notice of the decision and a possibility of having some input into it. Where consultation is offered as an option, the underlying policy objective is to allow employers some flexibility, provided that they agree the arrangements with worker representatives. The Working Time Directive (WTD) makes use of this approach as a means of enabling firms to adapt the Directive to their particular needs.[160] The discussion in this section is intended to complete the picture of worker involvement mechanisms in English law and to illuminate the theoretical framework presented in section 14.2.[161]

14.5.1 Duties to consult

EU law requires consultation in three main situations:

- where the employer is contemplating large-scale redundancies;[162]

- where the employer is proposing to sell the business to a new owner (a 'transfer of the undertaking');[163]

---

[158] Brigid van Wanrooy et al., *Employment Relations in the Shadow of Recession* (Palgrave Macmillan 2013) 61.

[159] Mark Hall et al., 'Promoting Effective Consultation? Assessing the Impact of the ICE Regulations' (2013) 51 BJIR 355.

[160] Council Directive 2003/88/EC of 4 November 2003 concerning certain aspects of the organisation of working time [2003] OJ L299/9.

[161] See Chapter 8 for further detail on working time and Chapter 10 for further detail on business reorganisations.

[162] Council Directive 98/59/EC of 20 July 1998 on the approximation of the laws of the Member States relating to collective redundancies [1998] OJ L225/16.

[163] Council Directive 2001/23/EC of 12 March 2001 on the approximation of the laws of the Member States relating to the safeguarding of employees' rights in the event of transfers of undertakings, businesses or parts of undertakings or businesses [2001] OJ L82/16.

- on health and safety issues.[164]

There are also two main sets of domestic duties to consult:

- on various changes to pension schemes;[165]

- on training, though this only applies in limited circumstances to trade unions recognised under Schedule A1 TULRCA.[166]

We will take collective redundancies as our case study in this section.

Collective redundancies

The duty to consult on collective redundancies originates from Directive 75/129/EEC and is currently found in Directive 98/59/EC (hereafter the CRD). The Directive is purely procedural in nature. Although the consultation process might result in a decision by the employer to reduce the number of redundancies (or even to avoid them altogether), the Directive itself is satisfied simply by consulting with worker representatives. The Directive is currently implemented in English law by ss. 188–198B TULRCA 1992. Our focus here will be on two aspects of the provisions: the identity of the representatives and the definition of consultation.

The identity of the representatives for the purposes of redundancy consultation is important for two reasons. First, it determines the relationship between the redundancy consultation provisions and other forms of worker involvement. And second, it may have some impact on the effectiveness of the redundancy consultation process itself, since this is likely to work better if the employees are represented by experienced and knowledgeable people.

Under the CRD, the identity of the representatives with whom the employer must consult is a matter for the Member States, though their discretion in this regard is not wholly unfettered. Initially, the legislation required consultation with representatives of recognised trade unions, these being the only type of representative known to the law in the 1970s under the 'single channel' system. However, in an important ruling, the Court of Justice held that the UK had failed to implement the Directive in respect of the many workplaces in which there was no recognised trade union.[167] As a result, the UK government was forced to amend the law to make provision for consultation with non-union representatives in workplaces with no union.[168] For a time, the law offered employers a choice between consulting union and non-union representatives, a highly controversial move which threatened to

---

[164] This legislation is domestic in origin (Health and Safety at Work etc. Act 1974) but has been amended in the light of EU law: Directive 89/391/EEC on measures to improve safety and health at work.

[165] Pensions Act 2004, s 260 and the Occupational and Personal Pension Schemes (Consultation by Employers and Miscellaneous Amendment) Regulations 2006, SI 2006/349 (as amended) (on changes to employer-run pension schemes); Pension Schemes Act 1993 and Pensions Act 1995 and the Occupational Pension Schemes (Contracting-out) Regulations 1996, SI 1996/1172 (on contracting out of the state earnings-related pension scheme); Public Service Pensions Act 2013, s 21 (on changes to public sector pension schemes).

[166] See Chapter 12. The provision is TULRCA, s 70B and only applies where the CAC has imposed a 'method' of collective bargaining on the union and the employer.

[167] Case C-383/92 *Commission v UK* [1994] ECR 1-2479, and see Paul Davies, 'A Challenge to Single Channel' (1994) 23 ILJ 272.

[168] Collective Redundancies and Transfer of Undertakings (Protection of Employment) (Amendment) Regulations 1995, SI 1995/2587.

undermine unions by enabling employers to consult with (potentially less powerful) non-union representatives in redundancy situations. Nowadays, the law gives unions priority under s. 188(1B):

> For the purposes of this section the appropriate representatives of any affected employees are–
>
> (a) if the employees are of a description in respect of which an independent trade union is recognised by their employer, representatives of the trade union, or
> (b) in any other case, whichever of the following employee representatives the employer chooses:–
>
> > (i) employee representatives appointed or elected by the affected employees otherwise than for the purposes of this section, who (having regard to the purposes for and the method by which they were appointed or elected) have authority from those employees to receive information and to be consulted about the proposed dismissals on their behalf;
> > (ii) employee representatives elected by the affected employees, for the purposes of this section, in an election satisfying the requirements of section 188A(1).

This achieves a better 'fit' between the requirement to consult on redundancies and the established role of trade unions in some workplaces. However, sub-paragraph (b) remains problematic. This would allow an employer to bypass a consultation mechanism established under ICER, for example, by getting the affected employees to elect ad hoc representatives instead. The requirements for election in s. 188A are relatively minimal. The election can be run by the employer without independent supervision, and matters such as the number of representatives are for the employer to determine. The ad hoc representatives may be less knowledgeable than those elected under ICER and any ICER mechanism may lose respect among the workforce if it can be ignored when redundancy situations arise.

As we have seen, consultation may be defined in various ways, giving a greater or lesser degree of involvement to the workforce. Reflecting the language of the Directive,[169] s. 188(2) provides that consultation shall be undertaken by the employer with a view to reaching agreement with the appropriate representatives. This is a 'strong' definition – the closest consultation comes to collective bargaining – but of course there is no obligation to reach an agreement. The workforce is only likely to be able to protest effectively against proposed redundancies if there is a union presence in the workplace and people are willing to take industrial action in response to the redundancy threat.

14.5.2 Options to consult

Some labour laws provide that they may be varied by agreement between the employer and representatives of the workforce. These laws are in the 'reflexive' tradition discussed in section 14.2. They allow the employer and the workforce to 'self-regulate'. This has two main advantages. First, it may enable the parties to adapt the legal provisions to their particular circumstances, rather than requiring compliance with rigid, 'one size fits all' norms. Second, it may mean that workers are able (collectively) to bargain: if the employer wants to bring about a variation, there

[169] Above n 162, art 2(2).

is an opportunity for the workers to negotiate for something in exchange (a pay rise, for example). However, there is always a concern that 'reflexive' laws may be open to abuse. For example, a well-informed employer may be able to persuade vulnerable representatives to give up significant employment rights. In theory at least, this should not happen where the law provides a 'default' rule. The representatives should just refuse to agree to anything that would be worse than the default. But this depends on the representatives knowing the default rule and knowing that they can refuse to reach an agreement with the employer.

'Reflexivity' is used to a very considerable extent in the WTD and Working Time Regulations 1998 (WTR),[170] which we will take as our case study, but there are a couple of other examples too:

- the detailed provisions on the exercise of the right to take parental leave are default provisions which only apply where there is no collective or workforce agreement on the matter applicable to the employees in question;[171]

- the provisions preventing abuse of successive fixed-term contracts may be varied by collective agreement or workforce agreement.[172]

Working time

The Working Time Directive (WTD) is an ambitious attempt to provide a single set of minimum standards on working time across the vast majority of economic sectors, with the exception of transport, where a set of sectoral directives is applicable.[173] The Directive provides various mechanisms by which the basic model it offers can be adapted. Under Article 18:

Derogations may be made . . . by means of collective agreements or agreements concluded between the two sides of industry at national or regional level or, in conformity with the rules laid down by them, by means of collective agreements or agreements concluded between the two sides of industry at a lower level . . .

The derogations . . . shall be allowed on condition that equivalent compensating rest periods are granted to the workers concerned or, in exceptional cases where it is not possible for objective reasons to grant such periods, the workers concerned are afforded appropriate protection.

Under the WTR, reg. 23(a), a collective or workforce agreement may 'modify or exclude' the following entitlements:

- the eight-hour limit on night work in reg. 6;

- the 11-hour rest period in every 24 hours in reg. 10;

- the 24-hour rest period in every seven days (or 48-hour rest period in every 14 days) under reg. 11;

- the rest break in a working day of more than six hours in reg. 12.

---

[170] Above n 160; Working Time Regulations 1998, SI 1998/1833.
[171] Maternity and Parental Leave etc. Regulations 1999, SI 1999/3312, reg 16.
[172] Fixed-term Employees (Prevention of Less Favourable Treatment) Regulations 2002, SI 2002/2034, reg 8(5).
[173] Above, n 160. See Chapter 8.

Under reg. 12(3), the rest break is set at a default 20 minutes away from the worker's workstation, but this is subject to any provisions of a collective or workforce agreement specifying the details of the break.

Under reg. 23(b), a collective or workforce agreement may 'for objective or technical reasons or reasons concerning the organization of work' substitute any period of up to 52 weeks for the default reference period of 17 weeks used to calculate a worker's weekly working hours for the purposes of the 48-hour limit under reg. 4. This is of limited significance given that many workers sign individual opt-outs from the 48-hour limit.

There are two key points to note about these provisions. First, they allow for derogations from (in the Directive) or exclusions of (in the Regulations) the relevant rights. This means that, rather than allowing collective negotiations to build upon the floor of rights offered by the regime, or perhaps to adapt it to particular circumstances, the process may be used to disapply core aspects of the protections.[174] This means that workers may lose some of their rights. Of course, the fact that the negotiations take place collectively is meant to offer protection, but it may fail to do so where the employer has superior bargaining power or where the representatives are not well-informed. Second, the requirement to provide 'compensating rest' is implemented as an obligation on the employer under reg. 24, rather than as a requirement for the collective or workforce agreement. If negotiations are to be allowed at all, it would make more sense for them to involve a process of bargaining in which the representatives negotiated for alternatives to the excluded rights.

A collective agreement for these purposes must be made with an independent trade union and is defined in the usual way under s. 178 TULRCA.[175] Of greater interest is the meaning of a workforce agreement set out in Schedule 1 WTR. A workforce agreement can only be concluded in respect of workers whose terms and conditions are not governed by a collective agreement, thereby safeguarding the priority of trade unions in this area.[176] The conditions of a valid workforce agreement are set out in para 1. The agreement must be in writing and for a duration of not more than five years, and signed by the representatives of the workforce or the relevant part of the workforce. The affected workers must be provided with 'copies of the text of the agreement and such guidance as those workers might reasonably require in order to understand it fully'. However, although a workforce agreement sounds as if it must be collective in nature – an agreement between the employer and representatives of the workforce – an employer with fewer than 20 workers may conclude the agreement by getting a majority of the workers to sign it.

The electoral process for obtaining workforce representatives is set out in para 3, as follows:

The requirements concerning elections referred to in paragraph 2 are that–

(a) the number of representatives to be elected is determined by the employer;
(b) the candidates for election as representatives of the workforce are relevant members of the workforce, and the candidates for election as representatives of a group are members of the group;

---

[174] Catherine Barnard, 'The Working Time Regulations 1998' (1999) 28 ILJ 61, 67.
[175] WTR, reg 2(1).
[176] WTR, sch 1 para 2.

(c) no worker who is eligible to be a candidate is unreasonably excluded from standing for election;

(d) all the relevant members of the workforce are entitled to vote for representatives of the workforce, and all the members of a particular group are entitled to vote for representatives of the group;

(e) the workers entitled to vote may vote for as many candidates as there are representatives to be elected;

(f) the election is conducted so as to secure that–

    (i) so far as is reasonably practicable, those voting do so in secret, and

    (ii) the votes given at the election are fairly and accurately counted.

This provision has been much criticised because it is very limited in terms of the safeguards it offers to workers, particularly when compared with the elaborate arrangements the law applies to trade union ballots.

More generally, while the WTR give a welcome priority to collective agreements, which are more likely to involve an effective bargaining process, it is a matter for concern that they have not been amended to give second place to any established consultation mechanism (under ICER) over the election of ad hoc representatives. The only real safeguard they contain is the requirement that the parties reach an agreement. They are not simply a consultation mechanism, and if the representatives refuse to sign, the employer cannot go ahead with the derogation anyway. But this is only an effective safeguard if the representatives know their rights and have the confidence to take a stand.

14.5.3 Conclusion

It is hard to avoid the conclusion that the various duties or options to consult on specific workplace issues have simply been introduced into English law by copying out the relevant directives (for the most part) without giving serious thought to how they might fit into the more general scheme of workplace participation.[177] It is now the case that recognised trade unions take priority in most of these situations, thus ensuring that the employer is not able to bypass what is likely to be the most effective mechanism of worker involvement. But it is by no means established that – where a works council or other general consultation mechanism exists – it should take priority over ad hoc representatives. This reflects a general unwillingness to embrace ICER in English law. More generally, there is a risk that ad hoc representatives – without access to independent sources of information and support – may be pressured by the employer into accepting a poor deal on behalf of the workforce.

14.6 RIGHTS FOR WORKER REPRESENTATIVES

Worker representatives are especially vulnerable to harsh treatment by the employer, particularly if they criticise its policies or (where relevant) refuse to agree to its demands. Thus, it is generally acknowledged that they are in need of special protection.

ILO Convention 135, the Workers' Representatives Convention, which the UK has ratified, provides that worker representatives should be protected against 'prejudicial'

---

[177] Davies and Kilpatrick, above n 31.

acts, including dismissal, because of their representative role.[178] They should also be provided with facilities to enable them to perform their duties.[179] The Convention applies to trade union representatives and to elected representatives of the workforce.

There are three main elements to the protection afforded to representatives in English law. First, it is usually automatically unfair to dismiss someone because he or she performs functions or activities either as a candidate for election or in his or her capacity as a representative.[180] Second, candidates and representatives are protected against detrimental treatment by the employer ('the right not to be subjected to any detriment by any act, or any deliberate failure to act')[181] because they performed functions in either of those capacities. Third, the law offers some candidates and representatives a 'reasonable' amount of time off during working hours, paid at their normal rate, in order to perform their duties as representatives. This is true of representatives under ICER[182] and TICER,[183] and for the purposes of consultation on collective redundancies and TUPE transfers.[184] It can be argued that, although this may cause some inconvenience to the employer, it is more efficient to negotiate with well-prepared representatives, who should not be forced to do their preparation in their spare time. However, the provisions are difficult to enforce against a hostile employer, because the only option if the employer 'unreasonably' refuses to allow time off is to complain to an employment tribunal. This is a cumbersome mechanism and seems to incorporate a 'double dose' of reasonableness: the right is to 'reasonable' time off but a complaint only lies if the employer 'unreasonably' refuses.

POINTS TO TAKE AWAY

- Workers may have different levels of involvement in workplace decisions: they may be informed about them, consulted on them or entitled to participate in them. Worker involvement may be justified using 'labour law' arguments about rights and dignity, arguments about productivity and 'reflexive' regulation, or arguments drawn from the 'stakeholder' theory of the firm.

- English law is unusual in not providing for worker representation at board level in companies, a feature common to many EU systems, though some companies registered in the UK may be required to provide for this under EU company law. Workers may acquire shares in the employing company but this is unlikely to offer them much input into corporate governance.

- EU directives create opportunities for information and consultation mechanisms in large pan-European firms (the EWC Directive) and in large national firms (the I&C Directive), implemented by TICER and ICER respectively. These measures create a process whereby the workforce can trigger negotiations with management about information and consultation procedures. The negotiations take place against the background of default provisions which will take effect

---

[178] ILO, Workers' Representatives Convention (Convention 135, 1971) art 1.
[179] ibid art 2.
[180] For example, ICER, reg 30; TICER, reg 28; ERA, s 103 (TUPE and collective redundancies).
[181] For example, ICER, reg 32; TICER, reg 31; ERA, s. 47 (TUPE and collective redundancies).
[182] ICER, regs 27–28.
[183] TICER, regs 25–26.
[184] ERA, s 61.

if no agreement can be reached. The take-up of these measures in the UK has been limited, and they do not integrate particularly well with the UK's tradition of collective bargaining and representation through trade unions.

- Employers are also obliged to consult workers in other situations, for example, where collective redundancies are proposed or there is a transfer of the undertaking. Employers may be able to secure exemptions from working time rules by negotiating a collective agreement or a workforce agreement. Again, there are problems about the integration of these mechanisms into a coherent system.

- Worker representatives are protected against detrimental treatment and dismissal and may have the right to take 'reasonable' paid time off during working hours to perform their roles.

Further reading

As we have seen, most of the law in this area is derived from an EU source. The EU Member States have very diverse traditions: **Marco Biagi and Michele Tiraboschi, 'Forms of Employee Representational Participation', in Roger Blanpain (ed), *Comparative Labour Law and Industrial Relations in Industrialized Market Economies* (11th edn, Kluwer 2014)**. It is therefore useful to think about what purpose EU-level regulation might serve. One of the best general discussions of this is **Simon Deakin and Frank Wilkinson, 'Rights vs Efficiency? The Economic Case for Transnational Labour Standards' (1994) 23 ILJ 289**. For an application of the idea that EU law might promote a 'race to the top' in labour standards to the employee involvement context, see **Wanjiru Njoya, 'Employee Ownership in the European Company: Reflexive Law, Reincorporation and Escaping Co-determination' (2011) 11 Journal of Corporate Law Studies 267**.

Of course, the UK's tradition is of 'single channel' collective bargaining through trade unions. The 'culture clash' is brought out nicely by **Brian Bercusson, 'The European Social Model Comes to Britain' (2002) 31 ILJ 209**. For an interesting discussion on how to integrate the various measures (with collective bargaining) into a coherent system, see **Paul Davies and Claire Kilpatrick, 'UK Worker Representation After Single Channel' (2004) 33 ILJ 121**. For an in-depth study of consultation and the problems of implementing ICER in the UK, see **Mark Hall and John Purcell, *Consultation at Work: Regulation and Practice* (OUP 2012)**.

An important theme in this area is flexibility: the UK government sought to maximise flexibility for firms when implementing ICER, for example, by allowing them to retain pre-existing arrangements. But there is always a risk that flexibility for employers will come at the expense of employees' interests. See, for example, **KD Ewing and GM Truter, 'The Information and Consultation of Employees Regulations: Voluntarism's Bitter Legacy' (2005) 68 MLR 626**; and **Aristea Koukiadaki, 'Reflexive Law and the Reformulation of EC-level Employee Consultation Norms in the British Systems of Labour Law and Industrial Relations' (2009) 5 International Journal of Law in Context 393**. More generally, there is a question about the *impact* of laws on employee involvement. For a detailed empirical analysis in the context of ICER, see **Mark Hall et al., 'Promoting Effective Consultation? Assessing the Impact of the ICE Regulations' (2013) 51 BJIR 355**, arguing that the role of the law in promoting employee involvement is marginal.

→

We saw at the start of the chapter that employee involvement might be justified from a corporate governance perspective, focusing on employees' contribution to the firm rather than on traditional 'labour law' arguments about rights and democracy. For discussion, see **Marc Moore, 'Why is Labour External to Anglo-American Corporate Governance?' (March 20, 2014),** available at SSRN: http://ssrn.com/abstract=2411980; and **Wanjiru Njoya, 'Employee Ownership and Efficiency: An Evolutionary Perspective' (2004) 33 ILJ 211.** Note that the authors differ on whether the *design* of employee involvement should be based on labour law or corporate governance approaches.

Index